Praise for *Advanced Web Metrics with Google Analytics, Third Edition*

"It would be a cliché to say Brian Clifton knows Google Analytics like the back of his hand. But he does. So if there is only one book you can buy on Google Analytics... buy this book and you'll be on your way to being an Analysis Ninja!"
—Avinash Kaushik, author of *Web Analytics 2.0* (Sybex, 2010) and Digital Marketing Evangelist, Google

"With this new edition of Advanced Web Metrics with Google Analytics, *Brian Clifton continues to raise the bar in explaining advanced web analytics— not just the mechanics but why certain things are crucial to measure, while other 'metrics' are actually red herrings and can harm rather than help your web success. A must-read if you're playing in the big leagues."*
—Chris Sherman, Executive Editor, Search Engine Land

"A great practitioner's resource that not only covers the technical details for a best practice setup, but also ties it back to the business objectives. That's quite a unique combination for this subject."
—Sara Andersson, Founder of Search Integration AB and Chairperson, Search Engine Marketing Professional Organization (SEMPO), Scandinavia

"There is no doubt web analytics is evolving quickly. Brian's third edition of the book is chock full of the latest tips and guidance to get the most out of Google Analytics. Once again, he is sharing his great knowledge and expertise so everyone can benefit. With a good mix of concepts, examples and how-tos, the book structure and writing style will please both marketers and technically inclined analysts and even help reconcile both universes. Advanced Web Metrics with Google Analytics *is a must on every analyst's bookshelf—and if you had a previous edition, don't hesitate to upgrade as this new release covers all the cool new stuff like social media, visitors, flow, multi-channel funnels, and a lot more!"*
—Stéphane Hamel, Director of Strategic Services, Cardinal Path

"Brian has proven in the previous editions of his book that he is the authority on how Google Analytics works. His latest edition continues to enhance this reputation. It includes his unique insights on the latest version of GA and includes descriptions of how to use the new features and reports. As Google Analytics itself evolves into a more powerful enterprise tool, Brian's book updates to keep up with the ever evolving feature set and long may it continue."
—Steve Jackson, Chief Analytics Officer, Kwantic

Advanced Web Metrics with Google Analytics™

Third Edition

Brian Clifton

John Wiley & Sons, Inc.

Senior Acquisitions Editor: WILLEM KNIBBE
Development Editor: DICK MARGULIS
Technical Editor: TREVOR CLAIBORNE
Production Editor: LIZ BRITTEN
Copy Editor: JUDY FLYNN
Editorial Manager: PETE GAUGHAN
Production Manager: TIM TATE
Vice President and Executive Group Publisher: RICHARD SWADLEY
Vice President and Publisher: NEIL EDDE
Book Designer: FRANZ BAUMHACKL
Compositor: MAUREEN FORYS, HAPPENSTANCE TYPE-O-RAMA
Proofreader: NANCY BELL
Indexer: TED LAUX
Project Coordinator, Cover: KATHERINE CROCKER
Cover Designer: RYAN SNEED
Cover Image: © ANDIPANTZ/ISTOCKPHOTO

Dear Reader,

Thank you for choosing *Advanced Web Metrics with Google Analytics, Third Edition*. This book is part of a family of premium-quality Sybex books, all of which are written by outstanding authors who combine practical experience with a gift for teaching.

Sybex was founded in 1976. More than 30 years later, we're still committed to producing consistently exceptional books. With each of our titles, we're working hard to set a new standard for the industry. From the paper we print on, to the authors we work with, our goal is to bring you the best books available.

I hope you see all that reflected in these pages. I'd be very interested to hear your comments and get your feedback on how we're doing. Feel free to let me know what you think about this or any other Sybex book by sending me an email at nedde@wiley.com. If you think you've found a technical error in this book, please visit http://sybex.custhelp.com. Customer feedback is critical to our efforts at Sybex.

Best regards,

Neil Edde
Vice President and Publisher
Sybex, an imprint of Wiley

"Web analytics is the study of the online visitor experience in order to improve it."
—THE AUTHOR, circa 2007

"Advanced web metrics is about doing the basics very well and applying it in a clever way."
—SARA ANDERSSON, CEO, Search Integration AB

Acknowledgments

After the first two editions of this book, writing this third edition has been both very rewarding and very hard work. Thankfully, my writing style has much improved—mainly due to the valuable feedback I have received from readers, clients, and workshop attendees alike. This has enabled me to produce this third edition not only with the latest features and updates from Google Analytics, but also in an improved pedagogical manner. I hope you consider it a worthy enhancement.

I have never considered myself a natural writer. Endlessly agonizing over every sentence, I would yearn for perfection, or at the very least adequacy. The first edition of this book, written while working 12 hours a day at Google, took me 18 months to finish (mainly written on trains and planes or in various hotel rooms across Europe or in the United States). I got myself organized and even more obsessive (if that were possible) and completed the second edition in six months. For the third edition, I am down to five months—to the relief of my much-supportive partner, Sara, and my friends and family.

Yet the process of writing remains enjoyable. In fact, I am already looking forward to my next writing project, though I am undecided as to what that should be—I said that in the last edition! However, I am not a one-man band, and many people have happily contributed their time to make this edition even better than the previous editions.

First, special thanks go to Trevor Claiborne, Brad Townsend, Alex Ortiz-Rosado, Nick Michailovski, and Tomas Remotigue, all of Google, who have significantly contributed to my knowledge and understanding of the internal workings of Google Analytics over the years. All worked in their own time to sanity-check and expand on the technical aspects of this and previous editions of this book. Trevor is my much-appreciated technical editor. His eagle eye for detail and breadth of knowledge for all things Google have enabled me to write a much more comprehensive book.

Significant feedback, help, and brainstorming were also freely provided by Shelby Thayer, a web analytics practitioner, enthusiast, advocate, and all-round nice person working for Penn State University. As with the last edition, Shelby has kindly proofread and commented on *every* page of this book, ensuring content relevance and continuity. Her informed questions and detailed feedback have been invaluable to me.

Thanks also go to Leonardo Naressi of Direct Performance for his expertise and advice with Flash event and mobile tracking; Jeremy Aube of ROI Revolution, who provided expertise and help with updating content on Google Website Optimizer and who is a great asset of the GACP community; Sara Andersson for her generous advice and strategic thinking regarding integrating offline and online marketing and for sharing her ideas on search marketing, social media engagement, and life in general; Jim Sterne for reviewing this book and for honoring me by writing the foreword; Mikael Thuneberg (automateanalytics.com), John Babb (idemension), James Bake (Hanson Inc.), Henrik Lauritzen (UserReport), and Paul Walsh (Infinity Tracking Ltd.) for providing case study content to include with Chapter 12; and all members of the Google Analytics Certified Partners (GACP) network for their stimulating discussions, experiences, and thoughts when implementing and using Google Analytics for their clients.

Last but not least, many thanks to the Wiley publishing team: Willem Knibbe, whose enthusiasm for this topic keeps me wanting to produce further editions of this book; Dick Margulis, who originally helped me with the first edition and kept the structure and cohesion going in a straight line throughout the process of writing this edition; Pete Gaughan, Liz Britten, Judy Flynn, and the many other people at Wiley who work tirelessly in the background to help create and polish what I hope you will consider is an enjoyable and informative read. Ultimately this was my mission for what potentially can be a very dry subject.

That's quite a long list, with people from all over the world (at least seven countries) helping to shape, expand, and improve the content provided. I hope I have remembered everyone.

About the Author

Brian Clifton, PhD, is an internationally recognized Google Analytics expert who consults on website performance optimization for global clients. Coming from a web development and search engine optimization (SEO) background, he has worked in these fields since 1997. His business was the first UK partner for Urchin Software Inc., the company that later became Google Analytics.

In 2005, Brian joined Google Europe. As former head of web analytics for Google Europe, Middle East, and Africa, he defined the strategy for adoption and built a team of pan-European product specialists. He is now Director of Data Insights and Analytics at Search Integration AB.

Brian received a BSc in chemistry from the University of Bristol in 1991 and a PhD in physical and theoretical chemistry in 1996. Further work as a postdoctoral researcher culminated in publishing several scientific papers in journals, including *Molecular Physics*, *Colloids and Surfaces*, and *Langmuir*. During that time, he was also an international weightlifter, representing Great Britain at world and European championships.

Studying science at university during the early nineties meant witnessing the incredible beginnings of the Web. In 1991, Tim Berners-Lee, a scientist working at the CERN laboratory in Switzerland, launched the first web browser and web server to the academic community, thereby sowing the first seeds of the World Wide Web.

Although the communication potential of the Web was immediately clear to Brian, it took a little while for ideas to formulate around business opportunities. In 1997 he left academia to found Omega Digital Media, a UK company specializing in the provision of professional services to organizations wishing to utilize the new digital medium.

Since leaving the field of chemical research (and weightlifting), Brian has continued to write—on his blog, Measuring Success (www.advanced-web-metrics.com/blog); as a guest writer on industry forums, and via white papers.

Brian holds the title of associate instructor at the University of British Columbia for his contribution to teaching modules in support of the Award of Achievement in Web Analytics. You can also hear him speak at numerous conferences around the word, where he discusses data-driven online strategies and site optimization. Brian was born in Manchester, United Kingdom, and now lives in Sweden.

Contents

Foreword

In 1990, the first web server hosted the first website at http://info .cern.ch. *Tim Berners-Lee, a physicist at the European Organization for Nuclear Research, thought it might be a good idea. Turns out he was right.*

As a transactional system, the web server was built with a logging capability that was a standard method for stockpiling details should everything go belly up.

It didn't take long for the data in these log files to attract the attention of those trying to make the systems work better. The first question, asked by webmasters like Tim, was whether the server was robust enough and the connection to the Internet was fast enough to keep up with demand. It was a technical challenge.

Eventually, the marketing department became aware that the geeks and nerds in the IT department were running the equivalent of electronic brochures on something called the World Wide Web. These marketing people were interested in system performance as well. But for them, it was not a technical matter but a question of customer experience.

Next, the marketing department wanted to know how many potential customers visited their websites every day. What did they do there? How deep did they dig? How often did they come back? How economical was the process of attracting them to the site?

As these questions became more and more complex, tool vendors bubbled up out of academia, the IT industry, and keyboards of those trying to answer their own questions using GREP and PERL.

Concurrently, a postdoctoral researcher at the University of Bristol was publishing completely unassociated papers like "Simulation of liquid benzene between two graphite surfaces," "The adsorption of tri-block copolymers at the solid-liquid and liquid-liquid interfaces," and "Calculation of Silberberg's polymer segmental adsorption energy by a free space molecular modeling technique." Brian Clifton did not know it at the time, but these papers turned out to be just the sort of education required for delving into what would be known as web analytics.

It takes the same combination of deep technical understanding and inclusive, lateral creativity to come up with different ways to look at data. It doesn't matter if you are creating "Methods for calculating solvent enthalpy of vaporization values by a molecular modeling technique" or trying to model human web surfing and buying behavior.

This mixture of left brain and right brain thinking is essential for modern marketing.

We will always need wildly imaginative, massively artistic, and enormously intuitive advertising "creatives." But the smooth, sophisticated, and slightly jaded Mad Men who have ruled on gut feeling and intuition have been joined by the geeks and nerds in the marketing analytics department. These are the people who can verify that those brilliant ideas are brilliant in the eyes of the public as well as in the eyes of the award presenters.

What's required is that magic mixture of technological smarts (where do these data come from?), psychological acumen (why do people act that way?), marketing mastery (how can we communicate our point more poignantly?), and analytics ingenuity (what if we looked at it from a different angle?).

This is where Brian Clifton stepped into the picture. He offered consulting services to companies that were struggling with the concept of online marketing. He realized that the best way to communicate with his clients was to show them the numbers. If they followed his advice, they could see an increase in brand recognition, purchase intent, prospect engagement, revenue, and customer satisfaction in black and white.

To make all of this as clear as possible, Brian became an expert with one of the best tools on the market, a web analytics tool that was so valuable, Google bought it. Recognizing that tools alone do not build empires, Google hired Brian to represent the product in Europe, the Middle East, and Asia.

In this tome, Brian does more than simply unmask the technical particulars of Google Analytics. He also stays steadfastly practical. He, yes, walks you through the nuts and bolts of Google Analytics, but always with an eye on its usefulness. He doesn't just show you how the internal combustion engine works, he explains how to drive the car and then—perhaps most important of all—how to navigate in order to get to your desired destination.

You are lucky to have this book in your hands. If you are new to the idea of online marketing metrics, there is no better way to get started. If you've been around web analytics for a long time, even if you have read Brian's previous two editions, it is worth your while to dig into this one as well.

Think of this book as a refresher course with some new surprises thrown in. Google Analytics is constantly changing, and Brian clarifies how to harness the new powers Google has incorporated into the latest versions.

I am honored to join those who have penned forewords to Brian's previous editions: Chris Sherman, executive editor at Search Engine Land, partner at Third Door Media, and search expert extraordinaire; and Avinash Kaushik, digital marketing evangelist at Google, cofounder at Market Motive, author of *Web Analytics: An Hour A Day* and *Web Analytics 2.0*, and the most fervent advocate of the marketing analytics industry.

I am pleased to add my voice to the chorus of praise for Brian Clifton, his talents in the web analytics arena, and this resulting edition of *Advanced Web Metrics with Google Analytics*.

—Jim Sterne
  Founder of the eMetrics Marketing Optimization Summit
  Chairman of the Web Analytics Association

Introduction

Although the birth of the Web took place in August 1991, it did not become commercial until around 1995. In those early days, it was kind of fun to have a spinning logo, a few pictures, and your contact details as the basis of your online presence. My first website was just that— no more than my curriculum vitae online at the University of Bristol. Then companies decided to copy (or worse, scan) their paper catalogs and brochures and simply dump these on their websites. This was a step forward in providing more content, but the user experience was poor to say the least, and no one was really measuring conversions. The most anyone kept track of was hits, which nobody ever really understood, though they were assumed (incorrectly) to be visits.

Around the year 2000, and propelled by the dot-com boom, people suddenly seemed to realize the potential of the Web as a useful medium to find information; the number of visitors using it grew rapidly. Organizations started to think about fundamental questions such as, *"What is the purpose of having a website?"* and considered how to build relevant content for their online presence. With that, user experience improved. Then, when widespread broadband adoption began, those organizations wanted to attract the huge audience that was now online, hence the reason for the rapid growth in search engine marketing that followed.

Now, with businesses accepting the growing importance of their online presence, they are prepared to invest. But how much money and what resources should an organization put into this? What are the pain points for a visitor that stop them from transitioning from an anonymous visitor to a new lead or new customer? What is the most cost-efficient way to market the site, which channels produce the most valuable leads, and can we predict the return on investment for the next campaign?

Answering such questions requires data and hence a measurement tool. Put simply, this is what web analytics tools, such as Google Analytics, allow you to do—study the online experience in order to improve it.

But what can be measured, how accurate is this, and with the plethora of data, which are the important metrics? In other words, how do you measure success? Using best practice principles I have gained as a professional practitioner, this book uses real-world examples that clearly demonstrate how to manage Google Analytics. These include not only installation and configuration guides but also how to turn data into information that enables you to understand and benchmark your website visitors' experience. With this understanding, you can then build business action items to drive improvements in visitor acquisition (both online and offline), conversion rates, repeat visit rates, customer retention, and ultimately your bottom line.

Who Should Read This Book

As a great friend and mentor to me once said, "Advanced web metrics is about doing the basics very well and applying it in a clever way." I wish I had thought of that phrase! It epitomizes everything about my approach to web analytics and this book. Thus, I have attempted to make this book's subject matter accessible to a broad spectrum of readers—essentially anyone with a business interest in making their website work better. After all, the concept of measuring success is a universal desire.

The content is not aimed at the complete web novice, nor is it aimed at engineers—I am not one myself. Installing, configuring, or using Google Analytics does not require the knowledge of an engineer! Rather, I hope that *Advanced Web Metrics with Google Analytics* will appeal to existing users of business data as well as readers new to the field of web measurement.

As the title implies, this book is intended for people who want to go beyond the basics of simply counting hits. These can be grouped into three types of users:

Marketers These are users who have experience with search engine marketing (paid and organic search), email marketing, social search, PR, and affiliate management but have not yet managed to find a unified measurement tool to compare these side by side. If you are in this group, focus your reading efforts on Chapters 1 to 5 and then Chapters 10 to 12because these are nontechnical and do not require a technical knowledge of the implementation.

Webmasters These are experienced website builders who have the skill set and authorization to modify a website. For this group of users, the book offers sections and exercises that require you to modify your web page content; after all, web analytics is all about instigating change using reliable metrics as your guide. Therefore, knowledge of HTML (the ability to read browser source code) and experience with JavaScript are required. If you fall within this group, the book's entire content for you. The technical implementation parts are contained in Chapters 6 through 9.

Senior managers These are decision makers who require guidance on preparing a data-driven strategy and action plan for their organization. I hope to supply these readers with an understanding of what can and cannot be achieved with web analytics and specifically provide information they need to plan the resources and timelines required for building an effective web measurement strategy. My aim for this group is to provide you with the information necessary to make informed managerial decisions. Focus your reading efforts on Chapters 1 to 5 in the first instance, and delve further if required.

With a better understanding of your website visitors, you will be able to tailor page content and marketing budgets with laser-like precision for a better return on investment. I also discuss advanced configurations (Chapter 9, "Google Analytics Customizations"), which provide you with an even greater understanding of your website visitors so that you can dive into the metrics that make sense for your organization. In as many areas as possible, I include real-world practical examples that are currently employed by advanced users.

You can use this book in several ways. The most straightforward (and demanding) is to start at the beginning and follow all the steps to completion, building your knowledge in a step-wise fashion. Alternatively, I have deliberately designed the book so that you can skip around and delve straight into a chapter as needed. To help with this approach, I frequently reference content within the book or other resources for further reading. However, I do recommend you put time aside to review the initial chapters (Chapters 1 through 5) because they introduce important approaches to web measurement, such as accuracy and privacy considerations, as well as the key features and components of the reporting interface. Web analytics is still a nascent industry, and I am actively blogging about Google Analytics, the book's content, and measurement issues in general at www.advanced-web-metrics.com. You can also follow my thoughts or what I am currently reading on Twitter (@brianclifton). All code examples presented can be downloaded from the site using the referenced links within each chapter.

What You Will Learn

You will learn how to implement and *use* Google Analytics in a best-practice way. I deliberately emphasize the word *use* because this is the primary purpose of this book. That is, you will learn how to leverage Google Analytics to optimize your website—and therefore your business—in terms of marketing, user experience, and ultimately conversions, all based on solid, reliable data.

What You Need

First and foremost, you need an inquisitive mind! This is not an engineering book, and you require no additional software or tools to apply the advice—just a good understanding of what your website is supposed to achieve and how your organization is marketing it and an idea of the type of metrics that would help you judge its success.

That said, a couple of chapters do require you to have a good understanding of HTML and basic JavaScript skills. If that doesn't describe you, read Chapters 1 through 5, then Chapters 10 through 12. Then pass the book to a technical colleague who can help you with Chapters 6 through 9. As you will learn, web analytics requires a multidisciplinary skill set, and collaboration is the key to success.

What Is Covered in This Book

Advanced Web Metrics with Google Analytics is organized to provide you with a clear step-wise progression of knowledge building.

Chapter 1, "Why Understanding Your Web Traffic Is Important to Your Business," introduces you to the world of web measurement, where it fits in, and what you can achieve.

Chapter 2, "Available Methodologies and Their Accuracy," provides the context of what can be measured via web analytics and its limitations.

Chapter 3, "Google Analytics Features, Benefits, and Limitations," focuses on what Google Analytics can do for you.

Chapter 4, "Using the Google Analytics Interface," walks you through the user interface, highlighting the key functionality.

Chapter 5, "Reports Explained," reviews in detail the top reports you need to understand.

Chapter 6, "Getting Started: Initial Setup," gets you quickly up and running with the basic install.

Chapter 7, "Advanced Implementation," takes you beyond the basics to give you a more complete picture of your website's activity.

Chapter 8, "Best Practices Configuration Guide," provides you with the knowledge to define success metrics (KPIs) and segment your data.

Chapter 9, "Google Analytics Customizations," gives you some lateral thinking for adding extra functionality to Google Analytics.

Chapter 10, "Focusing on Key Performance Indicators," is about how you focus on the metrics most important to you—KPIs and the process required to build them.

Chapter 11, "Real-World Tasks," jump-starts your analytical skills by showing you how to identify and optimize poor-performing pages, site search, and online and offline marketing. Website Optimizer is introduced as a method for testing a hypothesis.

Chapter 12, "Integrating Google Analytics with Third-Party Applications," shows you how to integrate data either by capturing cookies or using the new Google Analytics export API.

Appendix A, "Regular Expression Overview," gives you an introduction to understanding regular expressions.

Appendix B, "Useful Tools," describes some useful tools for helping you implement and use Google Analytics.

Appendix C, "Recommended Further Reading," gathers together books, blogs, and other web resources that can help you.

Google Analytics Individual Qualification

Democratizing web analytics data was a big part of the initial adoption strategy of Google Analytics. In 2007, while I was at Google, we really wanted to see such useful data being shared between sales, marketing, PR, senior management—anyone who had an interest in improving the company's website.

However, providing such large-scale access to data presented another problem: People didn't know how to interpret the data or what to do next. There was a serious dearth of web analytics education available to help people. I knew I could assist by writing this book, and another ambition was to establish an online learning center for Google Analytics.

It was therefore a logical step to produce an online version of our tiered internal training system so that any person, not just Googlers, could work through the online tutorials and then take the exam to demonstrate to their peers and potential employers their analytical and product-specific skills.

We started building the www.conversionuniversity.com online learning center in late 2007 and introduced the Google Analytics Individual Qualification (GA IQ) in November 2008. It was a huge achievement for the team and one that I am immensely proud of.

While there is nothing like a classroom workshop for a great learning environment—you not only learn the necessary skills, you also gain from the expertise of the trainer (as well as have time to pick their brains directly over a coffee!)—that's not always possible. Fortunately, this book, www.conversionuniversity.com, and the GA IQ help users learn Google Analytics and then have tangible proof of their proficiency. If you haven't taken the test, I encourage you to do so soon after reading this book.

How to Contact the Author

I welcome feedback from you about this book or about anything related to website measurement and optimization. You can reach me via any of the following means:

- Website: www.advanced-web-metrics.com

- LinkedIn interactive group for readers of this book: www.linkedin.com/groupInvitation?groupID=66386

- Twitter: http://twitter.com/brianclifton

- LinkedIn profile: http://uk.linkedin.com/in/brianclifton

Sybex strives to keep you supplied with the latest tools and information you need for your work. Please check its website at www.sybex.com, where we'll post additional content and updates that supplement this book if the need arises. Enter **advanced web metrics** in the Search box (or type the book's ISBN—**9781118168448**), and click Go to get to the book's update page.

Measuring
Success

Lord Kelvin is often quoted on the reason metrics are so important: "*If you cannot measure
it, you cannot improve it.*" That statement is
ultimately the rationale for web analytics. By
enabling you to identify what works and what
doesn't from a visitor's point of view, web analytics is the foundation for running a successful website. Even if you get those wrong, web
analytics provides the feedback mechanism that
enables you to identify mistakes quickly.

In Part I, you will learn the following:

Why Understanding Your Web Traffic Is Important to Your Business

1

Web analytics is a thermometer for your website, constantly checking and monitoring your online health. As a methodology, it is the study of online experience in order to improve it; without it, you are flying blind. How else would you determine whether your search engine marketing is effective, or even sufficient, for capturing your potential audience or whether your investment in creating a social media buzz has been worth it? Is the visitor experience a good one, encouraging engagement, repeat visits, and sales, or are visitors bouncing off your website after viewing only a single page?

In Chapter 1, you will learn:

The kinds of information you can obtain from analyzing traffic on your site

The kinds of decisions that web analytics can help you make

The ROI of web analytics

How web analytics helps you understand your web traffic

Where web analytics fits into your organization

Website Measurement—Why Do This?

It's an obvious question and one that has an obvious answer—as provided by the 19th century scientist Lord Kelvin and included in the introduction to Part I. The idea of applying a measurement tool to assess a website's effectiveness is an easy sell. Every business owner or executive understands the importance of measurement. But there's another question that comes up at initial meetings within an organization where website performance is being discussed: Why do we need another measurement tool in our business?

The most common fear is data overload—collecting more information, just because you can, inevitably leads to more confusion, not clarity. This is particularly the case when your website is operating as a silo, that is, not integrated with the rest of your business—a common problem if yours is a nontransactional website. Therefore, an important early step when deciding on a website measurement strategy is to define the value that web measurement can bring to your business. You can achieve this whether yours is a transactional site or not (see "Monetizing a Non-E-Commerce Website," in Chapter 11, "Real-World Tasks"), though here I illustrate value using transactional examples because these are easier to grasp in the first instance.

Figure 1.1 shows the improvement a travel website gained by optimizing its online booking process—that is, the steps a visitor takes in order to book a chosen vacation. (In Google Analytics terminology, the booking process steps are referred to as a *funnel*—directly analogous to any sales funnel in your organization.)

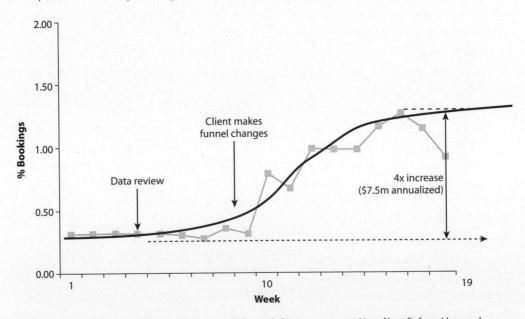

Figure 1.1 Conversion rate change of a travel website before and after improvements. Line of best fit for guidance only.

As you can see, the changes to the booking process took several weeks to implement (the client was not confident enough to take on board all the recommendations at once), but the cumulative impact was dramatic—a 383 percent increase in its booking conversion rate. Put in monetary terms, this equated to an annualized increase in revenue of $7.5 million.

The second example of the value of web measurement is shown in Figure 1.2. In this case, a measurement tool was able to quickly identify problems following the launch of a new site redesign. Essentially, server redirects were incorrectly assigned in the new site, resulting in a 48 percent loss of search engine traffic and a 21 percent loss in sales revenue. Following the identification of the problem, the client's visitor and revenue numbers were back to previous levels within four weeks.

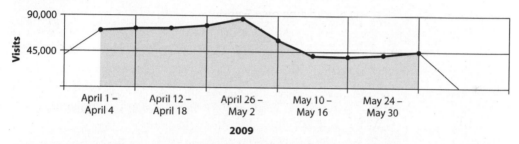

Search Engines

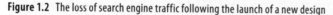

Figure 1.2 The loss of search engine traffic following the launch of a new design

If your website is an important part of your business strategy, then website measurement is also important to that strategy. The magnitudes of each are strongly correlated—that is, the more you spend (or earn) from your website, the greater the need for solid, reliable data from your web measurement tools. Such tools can be used to identify growth opportunities, measure efficiency improvements, and highlight when things go wrong.

Some people will say, "We are only interested in visitors who convert," that is, become a customer, "and not the rest of the reports," but that is misguided thinking. The conversion rate—the proportion of visitors that build a relationship with you (download a brochure or fact sheet, for example) or become a customer directly—is usually only 1 to 3 percent of your total visitor traffic (see Figure 1.4 later in this chapter). While this is clearly a valuable segment of your current business, the other 97-plus percent represents the greatest potential for future improvement.

Conversely, I also hear, "We already track brochure downloads (or e-commerce transactions) in our customer relationship management (CRM system), so we don't need that feature in our web analytics tool." But can your CRM system tell you what marketing campaigns, search engine keywords, or referral links drove visitors to your site in the first place? Perhaps there were multiple campaigns and referrals involved, including email and social links on Facebook, Twitter, and so forth. Can your CRM system tell you which customers are easier—cheaper—to acquire and rank them accordingly? Or is it able to provide information on which parts of your content are most relevant to your customers? To be honest, I have yet to discover a CRM system that comes even remotely close to closing the loop on customer acquisition, unless it is integrated with a web analytics tool.

Glossary of Terms

At this stage it would be useful for you to be familiar with some of the terminology used in Google Analytics. The following is a short summary. A more complete list can be found at the following location:

`http://support.google.com/analytics/bin/answer.py?hl=en&answer=1033060`

Bounced visitor A visitor who views only a single page on your website and has no further actions. This is generally considered a bad experience.

Campaign The name of a specific campaign, for example, book sales (for a paid search campaign), spring sale (for a banner campaign), January newsletter (for an email shot), Facebook offer (for a social media promotion).

Google Analytics Tracking Code (GATC) This snippet of code must be added to every page on your website to enable Google Analytics to collect and report on visit data. Also more generally referred to as the *page tag*.

Goal conversion Often abbreviated to just *goal* or *conversion*, this is a desired page or action on your website that is defined as being more valuable than a standard pageview. For example, a "purchase confirmation" page (visitor becomes a customer), a "thank you for registering" page (visitor becomes a prospect), a file download or "click to play video" page (visitor is engaged).

Funnel A well-defined process (most usually pages) leading to a conversion goal, such as, for example, using a check-out system.

Landing page The first page visitors arrive on when they visit your website. Also known as the *entrance page*.

Medium In the context of campaign tracking, *medium* indicates the channel by which a visitor to your site received the link to you, such as, for example, "organic" and "cost-per-click" for search engine links, "email" and "PDF" in the case of newsletters, "referral" for sites that link to you, and "direct" for a visitor who types your web address directly into their browser.

Referrer The URL of an HTML page that refers visitors to a site. That is, the external page from which visitors come to your website.

Return on investment (ROI) Calculated as (revenue − cost) / cost and displayed as a percentage.

Session Also referred to as a *visit* or *visitor session*, this is the measured period of interaction a visitor has with your website. A session starts when a visitor views the first page of your website and ends when one of the following three conditions is met as defined by Google Analytics: 30 minutes has elapsed without visitor activity; the session has reached the end of the day (for the time zone defined in Google Analytics); or the same visitor returns to the website but with new referral parameters. For example, a visitor first arrives at your website via an organic search, closes their browser, then returns (within 30 minutes) via a click on a banner link. The detection of the second visit with the new campaign parameters closes the first session and begins a new one for this visitor. The session time-out value can be adjusted (see Chapter 7, "Advanced Implementation"), though 30 minutes is the unwritten industry standard.

Site search A website's *internal* site search facility (internal search engine), mostly used on sites with large volumes of content in order to improve the user experience, that is, help the user find information faster.

Source In the context of campaign tracking, the source is the origin of a referral, for example, `google.com`, `yahoo.co.uk`, the name of a newsletter, or the name of a referring website.

URL (Uniform Resource Locator) A means of identifying an exact location on the Internet. It is how Google Analytics tracks and reports on pageview activity for your website, for example, `http://www.mysite.com/products/widget1.php`. URLs typically have four parts: protocol type (`HTTP://`), host domain name (`www.mysite.com`), directory path (`/products/`), and filename (`widget1.php`).

Information Web Analytics Can Provide

To do business effectively on the Web, you need to continually refine and optimize your online marketing strategy, social search strategy, site navigation, and page content (as well as how your offline marketing, press releases, and communications interact with your website). A low-performing website will starve your return on investment (ROI) and can damage your brand. But you need to understand what is performing poorly—the targeting of your marketing campaigns, poor reviews of your products or services on the Web, or your website's ability to convert once a visitor arrives. Web analytics provides the tools for gathering this information and enables you to benchmark the effects.

Note that I have been deliberately using the word *tools* in its plural form. This is because the term *web analytics* covers many areas that require different methodologies or data-collection techniques. For example, *offsite tools* are used to measure the size of your potential audience (opportunity), your share of voice (visibility), and the buzz (comments and sentiment) that is happening on the Internet as a whole. These are relevant metrics regardless of your website's existence. Conversely, *onsite tools* measure the visitor's onsite journey, its drivers, and your website's performance. These are directly related to your website's existence.

Figure 1.3 schematically illustrates how onsite and offsite web analytics tools fit together. From a vendor perspective, the separation of methodologies is not as mutually exclusive as Figure 1.3 suggests. For example, Hitwise, comScore, and Nielsen//NetRatings also have onsite measurement tools, while Google, Yahoo!, and Microsoft have the ability to provide offsite search query data to complement their onsite tools—see, for example, Google Insights (`www.google.com/insights/search/`).

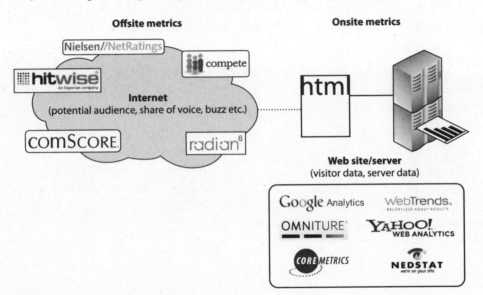

Figure 1.3 Onsite versus offsite web analytics

The differences in methodology between offsite and onsite web measurement tools are significant, and this leads to very different results. Even for basic website numbers, such as the number of visitors a website receives or the total number of pageviews, the values can vary dramatically. This is a constant and exasperating problem for site owners, media buyers, and marketers alike who attempt the futile task of reconciling the metrics. The truth is that metrics obtained with offsite methods cannot be reconciled with those from onsite tools—it's like comparing apples to oranges, and often the differences are large; for example, ±100 percent is not uncommon.

Note: The issues faced when attempting to compare different onsite tools are discussed in Chapter 2, "Available Methodologies and Their Accuracy."

Whenever I'm confronted with this problem from a client, I summarize the differences as follows: Offsite web analytics tools measure your potential website audience. They are the macro tools that allow you to see the bigger picture of how your website compares to others. Onsite web analytics tools measure the actual visitor traffic arriving on your website. They are capable of tracking the engagements and interactions your visitors have, such as, for example, whether they convert to a customer or lead, how they got to that point, or where they dropped out of the process altogether. It is not logical to use one methodology to measure the impact of another. Offsite and onsite analytics should be used to complement each other, not compete against each other.

Google Analytics is an onsite visitor-reporting tool. From here on, when I use the general term *web analytics*, I am referring to onsite measurement tools.

Where to Start

If you have already experienced looking at metrics from pay-per-click advertising campaigns, Google Analytics is simply the widening of that report view to see all referrals and behavior of visitors. If you are new to any kind of web metrics reporting, then the amount of information available can feel overwhelming at first. However, bear with me—this book is intended to guide you through the important aspects of what you need to know to be up and running with Google Analytics quickly and efficiently.

If you are implementing web analytics for the first time, then you will want to gain an insight into the initial visitor metrics to ascertain your traffic levels and visitor distribution. Here are some examples of first-level metrics:

- How many daily visitors you receive
- Your average conversion rate (sales, registration, download, and so on)
- Your top-visited pages
- The average visit time on site and how often visitors come back
- The referral source or channel that is driving the most traffic
- The geographic distribution of visitors and what language setting they are using
- How "sticky" your pages are: whether visitors stay or simply bounce off (single-page visits)

If your website has an e-commerce facility, then you will also want to know the following:

- The revenue your site is generating
- Where your customers are coming from (channel and campaigns)
- What your top-selling products are
- The average order value of your top-selling products

These metrics enable you to establish a baseline from which you can increase your knowledge. Be warned, though, Google Analytics gives you statistics so readily that you can become obsessive about checking them. Hence, as you move deeper into your analysis, you will start to ask more complicated questions of your data:

- Where do my most valuable visitors come from (referral source and geography)?
- Which of the most valuable visitors are most likely to make a purchase, and which of those visitors are most likely to make the highest value purchases?
- Which are my most valuable content pages; that is, not just popular pages, but pages that also contribute to the conversion process?
- How do existing customers (or subscribers, downloaders, or social media followers) use the site compared to new visitors?
- Am I wasting money on campaigns that bounce; that is, attracting visitors that only view a single page and then leave?
- Is my site engaging with visitors; that is, does anything on the site help build a relationship with an otherwise anonymous visitor?
- Is my internal site search helping or hindering conversions; that is, can visitors find what they are looking for once on my site?
- How many visits and how much time does it take for a visitor to become a customer (which affects promotion campaigns, email follow-ups, and affiliate relationships)?

All of these questions can be answered with Google Analytics reports.

Consider Figure 1.4, a typical model that most websites fit. It illustrates that the vast majority of websites have low (single-figure) conversion rates. In fact, according to the e-tailing group's 10th Annual Merchant Survey of 2011, the most commonly reported purchase conversion rate for US merchants is between 1.0 and 2.9 percent (see Figure 1.5). Why is that so low, and can it be improved? I can say with certainty that in my 17 years of either developing websites or simply viewing web content for business or pleasure, there has always been room for improvement from a user-experience point of view—including on my own websites. Ultimately, assuming you have a good product or service to offer, the user experience of your visitors will determine the success of your website, and web analytics tools provide the means to investigate this.

 Note: The average conversion rate reported by the e-tailing group corresponds closely with that of Forrester Research, July 2007, and the Fireclick Index (http://index.fireclick.com/fireindex.php). Amazon is often cited as the benchmark standard for optimizing the conversion of visitors to customers. Its conversion rate was reported as 17.2 percent in January 2009 (source: Nielsen Online via www.marketingcharts.com).

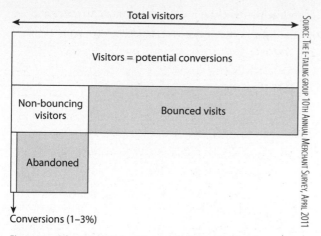

SOURCE: THE E-TAILING GROUP 10TH ANNUAL MERCHANT SURVEY, APRIL 2011

Figure 1.4 Schematic website visitor model illustrating the low conversion rates of most websites

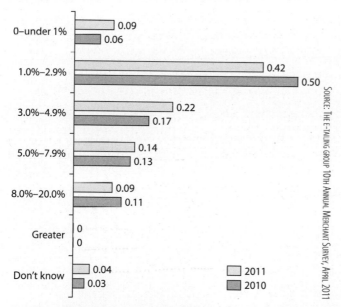

SOURCE: THE E-TAILING GROUP 10TH ANNUAL MERCHANT SURVEY, APRIL 2011

Figure 1.5 The most common US merchant conversion rates are between 1.0 and 2.9 (number of orders / number of unique visitors).

Keep in mind that web analytics are tools, not ends in themselves. They cannot tell you why visitors behave the way they do or which improvements you should make. For that you need to invest in report analysis, and that means hiring expertise, training existing staff, using the services of an external consultant, or using a combination of all of these. Often, you may need to employ multiple tools to gain an insight as to why.

These include the use of voice-of-the-customer tools (surveys, customer ratings, and feedback) as well as offsite analytics measurement (market size, social network mentions, sentiment, and so forth).

Decisions Web Analytics Can Help You Make

Knowledge without action is meaningless. The purpose of web analytics is to give you the knowledge from which you can make informed decisions about changing your online strategy—for the better. So it's important to include change—that is, changing your website or its marketing—as part of your metrics strategy. That sounds easy in theory, though often for large organizations, getting all stakeholders aligned and implementing a change is a project in and of itself. Therefore, ensure that you have that buy-in from an early stage; otherwise, you will rapidly become frustrated at your unrewarded efforts (the process is discussed in Chapter 10, "Focusing on Key Performance Indicators").

In terms of benchmarks, it is important that any organization spend time planning its *key performance indicators* (KPIs). KPIs provide a distillation of the plethora of website visitor data available to you as clear, actionable information. Simply put, KPIs represent the key factors, specific to your organization, that measure success.

Google Analytics gives you the data from which KPIs are built and in some cases can provide a KPI directly. For example, saying "We made $10,000 this week" is providing a piece of data. A KPI based on this could be "Our online revenue is up 10 percent month on month"—that is an indicator saying things are looking good. Good KPIs typically have a monetary value, though most are ratios or percentages that enable you to take action. The job of an analyst is to build KPIs specific to your organization. I discuss building KPIs in detail in Chapter 10.

Using KPIs, typical decisions you can make include those shown in Table 1.1.

▶ **Table 1.1** Typical decisions based on KPIs

Observation	Action
We have a new top-selling product that is delivering 20 percent more by revenue than any other.	Reward the web and marketing teams for a job well done!
The average visits per day from organic search has halved compared to last week.	Call the web development team. Investigate any changes in content, redirection, or site architecture.
	Call the SEO team. Investigate what changes have been implemented recently.
Our last banner campaign cost $5,000 and generated four sales worth a total of $1,000.	Drop the banner campaign ASAP! Then investigate any landing page issues and the marketing message. Perhaps an offer has expired.

Observation	Action
Online purchases increase by 50 percent if we send a follow-up email to new registered visitors within one week.	Ensure that email marketing is an integral part of your business strategy and is tracked within your web analytics tool.
Internal site search is being actively used by 70 percent of visitors. However, most search results are zero, and those that are not generate little revenue.	Call the IT/web team. Investigate changing your internal search engine to improve the user experience and boost sales.
Visits from social media sites are driving goal conversions (brochure downloads), but the paid-search visitors are driving transactions.	Call the marketing team. Acquire more social media visitors to drive branding, reach, and goal conversions. Acquire more paid-search visitors to provide further revenue growth.
	Call the content team. Investigate up-sell and cross-sell promotions for brochure downloads.

While engaging in this process to improve your website's performance, consider the changes as part of a continuous process, not a one-hit fix. That is, your website is likely to be continuously evolving with new content and products added and removed as well as new technologies deployed to show and display them. Think in terms of the AMAT acronym:

- Acquisition of visitors
- Measurement of performance
- Analysis of trends
- Testing to improve

The ROI of Web Analytics

Google Analytics is a free data collection and reporting tool. However, implementing, analyzing, interpreting, and making website changes all require a resource outlay at your end. The amount of investment you make in web analytics, therefore, depends on how significant your website is to your overall business.

How Much Should I Invest in This?

A great question often heard from Jim Sterne at his eMetrics conference series (www.emetrics.org) is, "What is the ROI of measuring your ROI?" In other words, how much time and effort should you spend on data measurement and analysis, considering that the vast majority of people performing this job role also have other responsibilities, such as webmaster, online marketer, offline marketer, content creator—even running a business. After all, you need to focus on delivering for your visitors and generating revenue or leads from your website.

I like to use the following analogy: Analyzing your web analytics reports is similar to visiting the gym. Unless you go regularly, don't waste your time there because you will only become frustrated at the little impact made from previous sessions. I recommend going to the gym (or performing your preferred form of exercise) at least three times per week. That way, your condition and health improve because of the regularity of the exertion (I have spent a lot of time in gyms). Similarly, regular website analysis is required to provide the insights needed to recommend change. Otherwise, all you have is a hit counter—you will never be able to improve your website because you don't have the insights to do so.

The key to calculating what your web analytics investment should be is understanding the value of your website in monetary terms—either directly as an e-commerce site or indirectly from lead generation or advertisement click-throughs. Marketers are smart, but they are not fortune-tellers. Purchasing clicks and doing nothing to measure their effectiveness is like scattering seeds in the air. Even highly paid experts can be wrong. Moreover, content that works today can become stale tomorrow. Using web analytics, you can ascertain the impact your work has and what that is worth to your organization.

Table 1.2 demonstrates a before-and-after example of what making use of web analytics data can achieve. In this hypothetical case, the target was to grow the online conversion rate by 1 percent, using an understanding of visitor acquisition and onsite factors such as checkout funnel analysis, exit points, bounce rates, and engagement metrics. When this increase is achieved, the values of total profit, P, and ROI, R, shown in the last two rows of the table, put the analysis into context—that is, profit will rise by \$37,500 and return on investment will quadruple to 50 percent. Note that this is achieved solely by improving the conversion rate of the site—visitor acquisition costs remain the same.

▶ **Table 1.2** Economic effect of a 1 percent increase in conversion rate

		Before	After
v	Visitors	100,000	100,000
c	Cost per visit	\$1.00	\$1.00
c_T	Cost of all visits ($v \times c$)	\$100,000	\$100,000
r	Conversion rate	3%	**4%**
C	Conversions ($r \times v$)	3,000	4,000
V	Revenue per conversion	\$75	\$75
T	**Total revenue ($V \times C$)**	**\$225,000**	**\$300,000**
m	Non-marketing profit margin	50%	50%
n	Non-marketing costs ($(1-m) \times T$)	\$112,500	\$150,000
c_T	Marketing costs ($v \times c$)	\$100,000	\$100,000
P	**Total profit ($T - (n + c_T)$)**	**\$12,500**	**\$50,000**
R	**Total marketing ROI (P/c_T)**	**13%**	**50%**

How much to invest in web analytics

Putting Table 1.2 into context, an achievable target would be to increase your conversion by 1 percent by the end of 12 months. From then on, this hypothetical website would be generating an additional $37,500 per month, per quarter, or per year—depending on the time it takes for you to acquire 100,000 visitors. Therefore, invest up to $37,000 in your web analytics over the same time period to achieve this. Your investment will include the time and resources required to implement and manage your web analytics tool as well as the time and resources required to analyze its subsequent reports in order to gain insights. Assuming you will be using Google Analytics, your data acquisition costs and tool usage costs are zero.

The point is, once you have achieved your 1 percent increase, you will be making more money than your initial web measurement investment cost. Of course, the compounded impact of your work will last much longer, so the actual lifetime value of improvement is always higher than this calculation suggests. At this point, you could of course end your investment—revenue is up. However, as described in the previous section, you will want to use the AMAT approach for continuous improvement and grow to the next level.

Table 1.2 uses a transactional site as an easy-to-understand example of the power of what using a web analytics tool can deliver. However, the same approach can be applied if you have a nontransactional site. In this case, substitute the revenue per conversion value (V) with your approximate revenue per lead value. That is, the potential revenue you expect to earn from a qualified lead. This technique is discussed in Chapter 11, "Monetizing a Non-E-Commerce Website."

How Much to Spend on Web Analytics

To manage expectations, I suggest organizations allocate 5 to 10 percent of their total online marketing budget to visitor measurement and its analysis—that is, putting aside any data collection or licensing fees (if you are not a Google Analytics user). The reasoning is that investing in a good person and good setup can easily save or grow that amount back for you; often the return is much greater.

If your online marketing budget is $100,000 per year or less, you clearly cannot afford to have a dedicated in-house person, and the workload will not be sufficient to justify it. Instead, buy in professional services from an expert to support and train you on a part-time or ad hoc basis. If you have a $1 million online marketing budget per year, consider a dedicated in-house person to manage your tracking and analysis needs, and so on. I list where you can get help at the end of this chapter.

How Web Analytics Helps You Understand Your Web Traffic

As discussed earlier, viewing the 100-plus reports in Google Analytics can at first appear overwhelming—there is simply too much data to consume in one go. Of course, all of this data is relevant, but some of it will be more relevant to you, depending on your business model. Therefore, once you have visitor data coming in and populating your reports, you will likely want to view a smaller subset—the key touch points with your potential customers. To help you distill visitor information, you can configure Google Analytics to report on goal conversions, then refine these further with advanced segments.

Identifying goals is probably the single most important step of building a website—it enables you to define success. Think of goal conversions as specific, measurable actions that you want your visitors to complete before they leave your website. For example, an obvious goal for an e-commerce site is the completion of a transaction—that is, buying something. However, not all visitors will complete a transaction on their first visit, so another useful e-commerce goal is quantifying the number of people who add an item to the shopping cart, whether they complete the purchase or not—in other words, how many begin the shopping process.

Regardless of whether you have an e-commerce website or not, your website has goals. A *goal* is any action or engagement that builds a relationship with your visitors, such as the completion of a feedback form, a subscription request, leaving a comment on a blog post, downloading a PDF white paper, viewing a special offers page, or clicking a social media button, such as a Facebook Like button, Google +1 button, or Follow Us on Twitter icon. Think of a goal as something more valuable to you than a standard pageview. As you begin this exercise, you will realize that you actually have many website goals. Defining goals is discussed in Chapter 8, "Best Practices Configuration Guide."

With goals clearly defined, you simplify the viewing of your visitor data and the forming of a hypothesis. Your goal conversions become your at-a-glance key metrics. They are the focus for further analysis with advanced segmentation, for example. Knowing instantly how many, and what proportion, of your visitors convert enables you to promptly ascertain the performance of your website—whether you should do something about it or relax and let the computers continue to do the work for you.

Where Web Analytics Fits In

As you might expect, I consider web analytics to be at the center of the universe (well, the digital universe anyhow)—see Figure 1.6. The Web is both your research tool and your feedback tool. For example, what are people looking for online and what do they think of your products or services—both before and after purchase? Whether you are actively engaged in digital marketing or not, it is highly likely that potential new customers will be looking online for a company just like yours to help them. Your existing customers use the Web to find updates, your contact details, or support information or to submit valuable product suggestions. There are even job seekers and investors to consider.

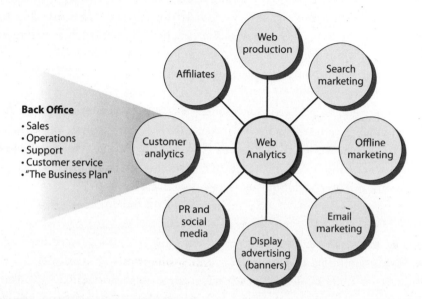

Figure 1.6 Where web analytics fits in an organization

Of course, I am preaching to the choir—why else would you be reading this book? The point I wish to make is that for a *switched-on* organization, your website touches all parts of your business. Hence, your web analytics tool is in a unique position to provide a unified measurement platform that all sides of your business can use—a common currency for measurement, so to speak.

That doesn't mean that you have to force all sides of your business to use only one measurement tool. That would be foolish to attempt. For example, customer analytics (data mining of CRM, or customer relationship management, systems) is a very different field from the almost completely anonymous world of web analytics, hence the dashed line connecting these two in Figure 1.6. Similarly, measuring the buzz and sentiment of your brand on social networks and search engines requires the use of offsite web analytics tools, which use very different techniques from onsite web analytics.

Nonetheless, it is still possible (and desirable) to have a unified web analytics tool that can support all aspects of the business to a greater or lesser extent, while more specialized tools can be used to dig into finer detail if required.

How Is Google Analytics Different?

Google Analytics was launched on November 11, 2005, and a major part of the announcement was that the product was free. This was a tipping point in the industry. Overnight, Google rewrote the entire industry business model—giving away a deep-dive web analytics tool while everyone else charged based on volume of traffic.

The impact of that decision was dramatic. An industry that once counted its customers in the tens of thousands now exploded. In fact, so dramatic was the uptake of the service that it had to close to new subscribers for 10 months while new machines were allocated to the number-crunching tasks at Google's data centers. However, once we reopened, the user base of Google Analytics rapidly expanded and went beyond 1 million in a matter of months.

There is a common, old-economy saying, "There's no such thing as a free lunch." However, providing free products has been a key driver for the growth of the Internet over the past 15 years. Pioneered in the early days by products such as Linux, Apache, and Hotmail, and further extended by Google, Mozilla (Firefox), Facebook, YouTube, Twitter, and many others (including my favorite radio station RadioParadise.com), the business ethos has been rewritten—offering items for free in order to make gains elsewhere.

For Google Analytics, the "gains elsewhere" are Google's advertising products—AdWords and AdSense. By providing a tool that helps website owners, in particular digital marketers, understand the performance of their website, Google hopes you will have the confidence to spend more money with its web advertising products. Google Analytics therefore provides transparency and accountability for these revenue-generating products (Google dominates online advertising globally with its $40-billion-a-year turnover).

Many books discuss the free and open-source business ethos of companies such as Google and its peers. I recommend those written by Chris Andersson, John Battelle, and Seth Godin as great examples.

Is Google Analytics Really Free?

Although the data collection and reporting from Google are free, an investment is required from your organization in order to have Google Analytics implemented correctly, staff trained, and insights gleaned. However, the use of Google Analytics remains free, whether you are an advertiser or not. The only caveat is that if you receive more than 10 million data hits per month—that is, a combined traffic volume from pageviews, events, and transactions—you need to either sample your data collection so that it falls below this threshold, or upgrade to the Premium, paid-for, product. Google Analytics Premium is discussed in Chapter 3.

Targeting Digital Marketers Rather Than IT Departments

Historically, and still to a great extent today, web analytics vendors target IT departments to sell their products. Hence the focus is on features, technology, complexity, and the big budgets required to utilize these. Google's approach to analytics is the opposite of the industry trend (key reason I joined the company!). Targeting marketing departments by simplifying the implementation, minimizing complexity, and removing the barrier to adoption, that is, providing the product for free, has proved to be an extraordinary success.

The Google Analytics philosophy, therefore, is for you to focus your budget on insights rather than data collection and reporting. That way, you are much more likely to invest online with products such as AdWords and AdSense.

> **Tip:** For more on the approach and vision of Google Analytics, read Occam's Razor (kaushik.net/avinash), the popular blog from Avinash Kaushik, official Google Analytics evangelist, author, and all-around nice guy.

Where to Get Help

Apart from reading this book to expand your knowledge, you can tap into Google itself for a number of self-help resources. There are also numerous self-help groups, forums, and enthusiasts and a global network of official Google Analytics Certified Partners.

Resources Provided by Google (Free)

Google has the largest free resource of web analytics information available in the world. In addition to being regularly updated (by Patricia Boswell and her team at Google), it is also available in all the Google Analytics supported languages—currently numbering 31 languages.

- Google Analytics Help—an online searchable manual and reference guide: www.google.com/support/googleanalytics.

- Google Conversion University—structured learning enabling you to become qualified in Google Analytics. The Google Analytics Individual Qualification (IQ) is proof of implementation proficiency. A step-by-step curriculum is provided via YouTube video walk-throughs to help you prepare for the test: www.conversionuniversity.com.

- YouTube official Google Analytics channel—clear and concise video walk-throughs of features and real-world usage: www.youtube.com/googleanalytics.

- Official Google Analytics blog—news blog of the latest product announcements, what's new, events, Conversion University, Help Center, and more: http://analytics.blogspot.com.

Non-Google Resources (Free)

With the huge adoption of Google Analytics (now millions of accounts), there are a large number of independent blogs and user forums that you can turn to for advice and help.

- Measuring Success—the official blog and companion site for this book: www.advanced-web-metrics.com.

- Google Analytics Help Forum—a threaded message-board system. Members are any Google Analytics users (and potential new users). Google Analytics Certified Partners regularly participate as well as the occasional Google support staff: http://groups.google.com/group/analytics-help.

- Numerous other helpful blogs and forums are listed in Appendix C.

Official Google Analytics Certified Partners (Paid)

The Google business model gives you a free product with the option to purchase a tailored professional services package directly from an authorized consultant in your region. If you are investing in web analytics yet cannot afford full-time resources in-house, a global network of third-party Google Analytics Certified Partners (GACP) is available.

GACPs are independent of Google, are often experts with multiple vendor tools, have a proven track record in their field, and provide paid-for professional services such as strategic planning, custom installation, onsite or remote training, data analysis, and consultation. The full list of GACPs can be found at www.google.com/analytics/partners.html.

Summary

In Chapter 1, you have learned the following:

The opportunities and benefits web analytics can bring your organization These include growing your business, improving efficiency, and reducing costs.

The kinds of information you can obtain from analyzing traffic on your site This includes visitor and page value, traffic volumes, top referrers, time on site and depth on site to conversion rates, page stickiness, visitor latency, frequency, revenue, and geographic distribution, to name a few.

The kinds of decisions that web analytics can help you with For example, web analytics can help you determine whether visitors from social media sites such as Facebook, Twitter, and LinkedIn have a positive impact on your website's reach and conversions; which visitor acquisition channels work best and to what extent these should be increased or decreased; whether site search is worth the investment; and whether overseas visitors would be better served with more localized content.

The ROI of web analytics Knowing how much time and effort to invest in web analytics, without losing site of your objectives, will keep you focused on improving your organization's bottom line.

How web analytics helps you understand your web traffic By focusing metrics on goal-driven web design, you concentrate not only your own efforts but also those of your visitors on clear calls to action. This simplifies the process of forming a hypothesis from observed visitor patterns.

Where web analytics fits in Integrating web analytics into your entire organization helps keep everyone on the same page when it comes to measuring performance.

Where to get help The growth of web analytics adoption over recent years has led to a plethora of resources to turn to, should you wish to explore beyond this book.

Available Methodologies and Their Accuracy

Web analytics can be incredibly powerful and insightful. An astonishing amount of information is available when compared to any other forms of traditional marketing. The danger, however, is taking web analytics reports at face value, and this raises the issue of accuracy.

The key to successfully utilizing the volume of information collected is to get comfortable with your data—what it can tell you, what it can't, and the limitations therein. This requires an understanding of the data-collection methodologies. Essentially, there are two common techniques: page tags and server logfiles. Google Analytics uses a page tag technique.

In Chapter 2, you will learn:

How web visitor data is collected

The relative advantages of page tags and logfiles

The role of cookies in web analytics

The accuracy limitations of web traffic information

How to think about web analytics in relation to user privacy concerns

Page Tags and Logfiles

Page tags collect data via the visitor's web browser and send information to remote data-collection servers. The analytics user views reports from the remote server (see Figure 2.1). This information is usually captured by JavaScript code (known as *tags* or *beacons*) placed on each page of your site. Some vendors also add multiple custom tags to collect additional data. This technique is known as *client-side data collection* and is used mostly by outsourced, Software as a Service (SaaS) vendor solutions.

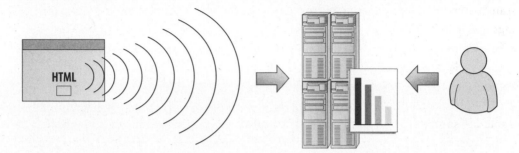

Figure 2.1 Schematic page tag methodology: Page tags broadcast information to remote data-collection servers, thus enabling the analytics customer to view reports.

Note: Google Analytics is a Software as a Service (SaaS) page tag service.

Logfiles contain data collected by your web server and are independent of a visitor's browser: A web server logs its activity to a text file that is usually local. That is, on the same network or even the same machine as your web server. The analytics user views reports from the local server, as shown in Figure 2.2. This technique, known as *server-side data collection*, captures all requests made to your web server, including pages, images, and PDFs, and is most frequently used by stand-alone licensed software vendors.

Figure 2.2 Schematic logfile methodology: The web server logs its activity to a text file locally, thereby enabling the analytics customer to view the reports on the local server.

In the past, the easy availability of web server logfiles made this technique the one most frequently adopted for understanding the behavior of visitors to your site. In fact, most Internet service providers (ISPs) supply a freeware log analyzer with their web-hosting accounts (Analog, Webalizer, and AWStats are some examples). Although this is probably the most common way people first come in contact with web analytics, such freeware tools are too basic when it comes to measuring visitor behavior and are not considered further in this book.

In recent years, page tags have become more popular and are now the de facto standard method for collecting visitor data. Not only is the implementation of page tags easier from a technical point of view, but data-management requirements are significantly reduced because the data is collected and processed by external SaaS servers (your vendor), saving website owners the expense and maintenance of running licensed software to capture, store, and archive information.

Note that both techniques, when considered in isolation, have their limitations. Table 2.1 summarizes the differences. A common myth is that page tags are technically superior to other methods, but as Table 2.1 shows, that depends on what you are looking at. By combining both techniques, however, the advantages of one counter the disadvantages of the other. This is known as a *hybrid* method and some vendors can provide this.

Note: Google Analytics can be configured as a hybrid data collector—see "Backup: Keeping a Local Copy of Your Data," in Chapter 6, "Getting Started: Initial Setup."

▶ **Table 2.1** Page tag versus logfile data collection

Methodology	Advantages	Disadvantages
Page tags	• Breaks through proxy and caching servers—provides more accurate session tracking.	• Web pages require modification. You have to make changes to your website pages (add tags) in order to collect data.
	• Tracks client-side events—e.g., JavaScript, Flash, Web 2.0 (Ajax).	• Setup errors lead to data loss. If you make a mistake with your tags, data is lost and you cannot go back and reanalyze.
	• Captures client-side e-commerce data. Server-side access can be problematic.	• Firewalls can mangle or restrict tags.
	• Collects and processes visitor data in nearly real time.	• Cannot track bandwidth or completed downloads. Tags are set when the page or file is requested, not when the download is complete.
	• Allows the vendor to perform program updates for you.	• Cannot track search engine spiders. Robots ignore page tags.
	• Allows the vendor to perform data storage and archiving for you.	

Methodology	Advantages	Disadvantages
Logfile analysis software	• Automatic data collection. Does not require any changes to your web pages. • Historical data can be reprocessed easily. • No firewall issues to worry about. • Can track bandwidth and completed downloads, and can differentiate between completed and partial downloads. • Tracks search engine spiders and robots by default. • Tracks legacy mobile visitors by default.	• Proxy and caching inaccuracies. If a page is cached, no record is logged on your web server. • No event tracking—e.g., no JavaScript, Flash, Web 2.0 tracking (Ajax). • Requires your own team to perform program updates. • Requires your own team to perform data storage and archiving. • Robots inflate visit counts and this can be significant.

Other Data-Collection Methods

Although logfile analysis and page tagging are by far the most widely used methods for collecting web visitor data, they are not the only methods. Network data-collection devices (packet sniffers) gather web traffic data from routers into black-box appliances. Another technique is to use a web server application programming interface (API) or loadable module (also known as a plug-in, though this is not strictly correct terminology). These are programs that extend the capabilities of the web server—for example, enhancing or extending the fields that are logged. Typically, the collected data is then streamed to a reporting server in real time.

As you can see, the advantages of one data-collection method cancel out the disadvantages of the other. However, freeware tools aside, the SaaS page tagging technique is by far the most widely adopted method because of its ease of implementation and low IT overhead and support cost.

Cookies in Web Analytics

Page tag solutions track visitors by using cookies. *Cookies* are small text files that a web server transmits to a web browser so that it can keep track of the user's activity on a specific website. The visitor's browser stores the cookie information on the local hard drive as name/value pairs. *Persistent cookies* are those that are still available when the browser is closed and later reopened. *Session cookies* last only for the duration of a visitor's session (visit) on your site.

For web analytics, the main purpose of cookies is to identify users for later use—most often with an anonymous visitor ID. Among many things, cookies can be used to determine how many first-time or repeat visitors a site has received, how many times a visitor returns each period, and how much time passes between visits. Web analytics aside, web servers can also use cookie information to present personalized web pages. A returning customer might see a different page than the one a first-time visitor would view, such as a "welcome back" message to give them a more individual experience or an auto-login for a returning subscriber.

The following are some cookie facts:

- Cookies are small text files (no larger than 4 KB), stored locally, that are associated with visited website domains.
- Cookie information can be viewed by users of your computer, either within the browser settings themselves or using a text editor application.
- There are two types of cookies: first party and third party.
  - A first-party cookie is one created by the website domain. A visitor requests it directly by typing the URL into their browser or by following a link.
  - A third-party cookie is one that operates in the background and is usually associated with advertisements or embedded content that is delivered by a third-party domain not directly requested by the visitor.
- For first-party cookies, only the website domain setting the cookie information can retrieve the data. This is a security feature built into all web browsers.
- For third-party cookies, the website domain setting the cookie can also list other domains allowed to view this information. The user is not involved in the transfer of third-party cookie information and is usually not even aware that this is happening.
- Cookies are not malicious and can't harm your computer. They can be deleted by the user at any time.
- A maximum of 50 cookies are allowed per domain for the latest versions of Internet Explorer and Firefox. Other browsers may vary (Opera 10 currently has a limit of 30; Safari and Google Chrome have no limit on the number of cookies per domain).

> **Note:** From a visitors' privacy viewpoint, using first-party cookies is best practice. Google Analytics uses first-party cookies only.

Understanding Web Analytics Data Accuracy

When it comes to benchmarking the performance of your website, web analytics is critical. However, this information is accurate only if you avoid common errors associated with collecting the data—especially comparing numbers from different sources.

Unfortunately, too many businesses take web analytics reports at face value. After all, it isn't difficult to get the numbers. The harsh truth is that web analytics data can never be 100 percent accurate, and even measuring the error bars can be difficult. So what's the point?

Despite the pitfalls, error bars remain relatively constant on a weekly, or even a monthly, basis. Even comparing year-by-year behavior can be safe as long as there are no dramatic changes in technology or end-user behavior. As long as you use the same yardstick, visitor number trends will be accurate. For example, web analytics data may reveal patterns like the following:

- Thirty percent of site traffic came from search engines.

- Fifteen percent of site revenue was generated by product page x.html.

- We increased subscription conversions from our email campaigns by 20 percent last week.

- Bounce rate decreased 10 percent for our category pages during March.

With these types of metrics, marketers and webmasters can determine the direct impact of specific marketing campaigns. The level of detail is critical. For example, you can determine if an increase in pay-per-click advertising spending—for a set of keywords on a single search engine—increased the return on investment during that time period. As long as you can minimize inaccuracies, web analytics tools are effective for measuring visitor traffic to your online business.

Conflicting Data Points Are Common

A UK survey of 800 organizations revealed that almost two-thirds (63 percent) of respondents say they experience conflicting information from different sources of online measurement data (*Online Measurement and Strategy Report 2009*, Econsultancy.com, June 2009).

Next, I'll discuss in detail why such inaccuracies arise, so you can put this information into perspective. The aim is for you to arrive at an acceptable level of accuracy with respect to your analytics data. Recall from Table 2.1 that there are two main methods for collecting web visitor data—logfiles and page tags—and both have limitations.

Issues Affecting Visitor Data Accuracy for Logfiles

Logfile tracking is usually set up by default on web servers. Perhaps because of this, system administrators rarely consider any further implications when it comes to tracking.

Dynamically Assigned IP Addresses

Generally, a logfile solution tracks visitor sessions by attributing all hits from the same IP address and web browser signature to one person. This becomes a problem when ISPs assign different IP addresses throughout the session. A US-based comScore study showed that a typical home PC averages 10.5 different IP addresses per month.

> www.comscore.com/Press_Events/Presentations_Whitepapers/2007/
> Cookie_Deletion_Whitepaper

Those visits will be counted as 10 unique visitors by a logfile analyzer. This issue is becoming more severe because it is now much easier for users to have the latest updates of their browser, making differentiation by browser signature much harder. As a result, visitor numbers are often vastly overcounted. This limitation is overcome with the use of cookies.

Client-Side Cached Pages

Client-side caching means a previously visited page is stored on a visitor's computer. In this case, visiting the same page again results in that page being served locally from the visitor's computer, and therefore the visit is not recorded at the web server.

Server-side caching can come from any web accelerator technology that caches a copy of a website and serves it from their servers to speed up delivery. This means that all subsequent site requests come from the cache and not from the site itself, leading to a loss in tracking. Today, most of the Web is in some way cached to improve performance. For example, see Wikipedia's cache description at http://en.wikipedia.org/wiki/Cache.

Counting Robots

Robots, also known as spiders or web crawlers, are most often used by search engines to fetch and index pages. However, other robots exist that check server performance—uptime, download speed, and so on—as well as those used for page scraping, including price comparison, email harvesting, competitive research, and so on. These affect web analytics because a logfile solution will also show all data for robot activity on your website, even though robots are not real visitors.

When you are counting visitor numbers, robots can make up a significant proportion of your pageview traffic. Unfortunately, these are difficult to filter out completely because thousands of homegrown and unnamed robots exist. For this reason, a logfile analyzer solution is likely to overcount visitor numbers, and in most cases this overcounting can be dramatic.

Issues Affecting Visitor Data from Page Tags

Deploying a page tag on every single page is a process that can be automated in many cases. However, for larger sites, 100 percent correct deployment is rarely achieved.

Perhaps it is because the page tag is hidden from the human eye or there is so much other data available that those errors often go unnoticed for long periods. Having a full deployment is crucial to the accuracy and validity of data collected by this method.

Setup Errors Causing Missed Tags

The most frequent error by far observed for page tagging solutions comes from their setup. Unlike web servers, which are configured to log everything delivered by default, a page tag solution requires the webmaster to add the tracking code to each page. Even with an automated content management system, pages can and do get missed.

In fact, evidence from analysts at MAXAMINE (www.maxamine.com)—now part of Accenture Marketing Sciences—who used their automatic page auditing tool has shown that with some sites claiming that all pages are tagged, as many as 20 percent of pages are actually missing the page tag—something the webmaster was completely unaware of. In one case, a corporate business-to-business site was found to have 70 percent of its pages missing tags. Missing tags equals no data for those pageviews.

JavaScript Errors Halting Page Loading

Page tags work well, provided that JavaScript is enabled on the visitor's browser. Fortunately, only a small proportion of Internet users have disabled JavaScript on their browsers, as shown in Figure 2.3. However, the inconsistent use of JavaScript code on web pages can cause a bigger problem: Any errors in other JavaScript on the page will immediately halt the browser scripting engine at that point, so a page tag may not execute.

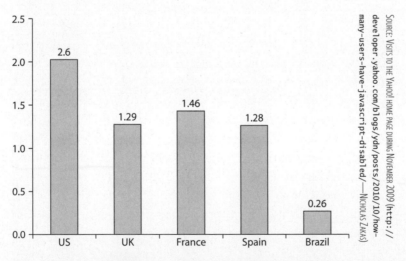

SOURCE: VISITS TO THE YAHOO! HOME PAGE DURING NOVEMBER 2009 (http://developer.yahoo.com/blogs/ydn/posts/2010/10/how-many-users-have-javascript-disabled/—NICHOLAS ZAKAS)

Figure 2.3 Percentage of Internet users with JavaScript-disabled browsers

Firewalls Blocking Page Tags

Corporate and personal firewalls can prevent page tag solutions from sending data to collecting servers. In addition, firewalls can be set up to reject or delete cookies automatically. Once again, the effect on visitor data can be significant. Some web analytics vendors can revert to using the visitor's IP address for tracking in these instances, but mixing methods is not recommended. As discussed previously in "Issues Affecting Visitor Data Accuracy for Logfiles" (comScore report), using visitor IP addresses is far less accurate than simply not counting such visitors. It is therefore better to be consistent with the processing of data.

Page Tag Implementation Study

The following data is from over 10,000 websites whose page tags were validated. The page tags checked are from a variety of web analytics vendors. (Thanks to Stephen Kirby of MAXAMINE for this information.)

Summary

The more frequently a website's content changes, the more prone the site is to missing page tags. In the following image, website content was updated on January 14; by mistake, the updated pages did not include page tags.

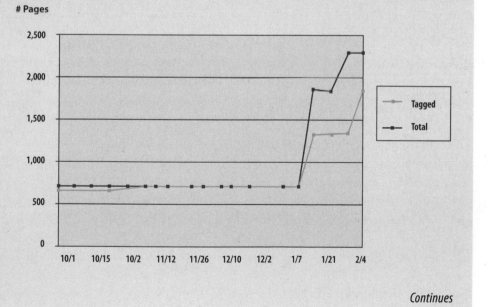

Continues

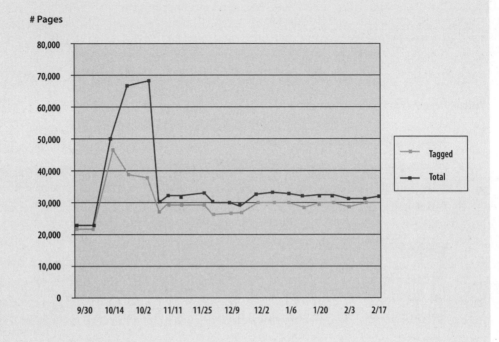

Page Tag Implementation Study (*Continued*)

Large websites very rarely achieve 100 percent tagging accuracy, as shown in the following chart.

Tracking Legacy Mobile Visitors

A mobile web audience study by comScore back in January 2007 showed that in the United States, 30 million (or 19 percent) of Internet users accessed the Internet from a mobile device.

    www.comscore.com/press/release.asp?press=1432

At that time, the vast majority of mobile phones did not understand JavaScript or cookies, and hence only logfile tools were able to track visitors who browsed using their mobile phones. By December 2010, this had grown to 109 million users accessing the Internet from a mobile device (comScore: The 2010 Mobile Year in Review), thanks mainly to the phenomenal success of smartphones such as the iPhone.

A key driver for Internet access from mobile visitors is the processing power that smartphones have brought to the device market—creating a user experience that is very similar to (though obviously smaller than) desktop usage. A consequence of this is mobile browser software that is comparable to that found on regular laptops and PCs, that is, where both JavaScript and cookies are used. Hence, visitors to your website from smartphone mobile devices can be tracked with page tag web analytics in the same way as other visitors.

If tracking legacy (feature-phone) mobile visitors is important to you, see "Tracking Mobile Visitors" in Chapter 6, "Getting Started: Initial Setup."

Issues Affecting Visitor Data When Using Cookies

Using cookies is a simple, well-established way of tracking visitors. However, their simplicity and transparency (any user can remove them) present issues in and of themselves. The debate of using cookies or not remains a hot topic of conversation in web analytics circles.

Visitors Rejecting or Deleting Cookies

Cookie information is vital for web analytics because it identifies visitors and their referring source and provides subsequent pageview data. The current best practice is for vendors to process first-party cookies only. This is because visitors often view third-party cookies as infringing on their privacy, opaquely transferring their information to third parties without explicit consent. Therefore, many antispyware programs and firewalls exist to block third-party cookies automatically. It is also easy to do this within the browser itself. By contrast, anecdotal evidence shows that first-party cookies are accepted by more than 95 percent of visitors.

Visitors are also becoming savvier and often delete cookies. Recent research published by comScore shows that for Latin America during February 2011, France during August 2010, and Australia during April 2010, the percent of Internet users who clear their first-party cookies in a month is 33, 28, and 28 percent respectively. This follows independent surveys conducted by Belden Associates (2004), JupiterResearch (2005), Nielsen (2005), and comScore (2007) that concluded that cookies are deleted by at least 30 percent of Internet users in a month.

Users Owning and Sharing Multiple Computers

User behavior has a dramatic effect on the accuracy of information gathered through cookies. Consider the following scenarios:

Same user, multiple computers Today, people access the Internet in any number of ways—from work, home, mobile, tablets, or public places such as Internet cafes. One person working from three different machines still results in three cookie settings, and all current web analytics solutions will count each of these user sessions as unique.

Different users, same computer People share their computers all the time, particularly with their families, which means that cookies are shared too (unless you log off or switch off your computer each time it is used by a different person). In some instances, cookies are deleted deliberately. For example, reputable Internet cafes are set up to do this automatically at the end of each session, so even if a visitor uses that cafe regularly and works from the same machine, the web analytics solution will consider that visitor a different and new visitor every time.

Correcting Data for Cookie Deletion and Rejection

Calculating a correction factor to account for your visitors either deleting or rejecting your web analytics cookies is quite straightforward. All you need is a website that requires a user login. That way you can count the number of unique login IDs and divide it by the number of unique users your web analytics tool reports. The result is a correction factor that can be applied to subsequent data (number of unique visitors, number of new visitors, or number of returning visitors).

Having a website that requires a user login is, thankfully in my view, quite rare because people wish to access information freely and as easily as possible. So, although the correction-factor calculation is straightforward, you most probably don't have any login data to process. Fortunately, a small number of websites can calculate a correction factor to shed light on this issue. These include online banks and popular brands such as Amazon, FedEx, and social network sites, where there is a real user benefit to both having an account and (most important) using it when visiting the site.

A specific example is Sun Microsystems Forums (`http://forums.sun.com`), a global community of developers with nearly 1 million contributors. A 2009 study by Paul Strupp and Garrett Clark, published at `http://blogs.sun.com/pstrupp/`, reveals some interesting data.

When using third-party cookies:

- The correction factor is 78 percent for monthly unique users.
- Twenty percent of users delete (more correctly defined as *lose*) their measurement cookie at least once per month.
- Five percent of users block the third-party measurement cookie.

When using first-party cookies:

- The correction factor improves to 83 percent.
- Percentage of users who delete their measurement cookie at least once per month decreases to 14 percent.
- Percentage of users who block the first-party measurement cookie drops to less than 1 percent.

Note that this is a tech-savvy audience—those who can delete or block an individual cookie without a second thought.

An interesting observation from the study that Paul himself highlights is the relatively small value of the correction factor. That is, when using a first-party cookie, a more precise unique visitor count is 0.83 multiplied by the reported value. Putting this into context, as part of the analysis, 30 percent of users who used more than one computer in a month to visit the forum were removed from the data prior to analysis. This indicates that multiple-device access happens more frequently than cookie deletion.

It is tempting to think that this data can be used to correct your own unique visitor counts. However, the correction factor is a complicated function of cookie deletion, multiple computer use, and visitor return frequency. These factors will almost certainly be different for your specific website. Nonetheless, it is a useful rule-of-thumb guide.

Latency Leaving Room for Inaccuracy

The time it takes for a visitor to be converted into a customer (latency) can have a significant effect on accuracy. For example, most low-value items are either instant purchases or are purchased within seven days of the initial website visit. With such a short time period between visitor arrival and purchase, your web analytics solution has the best possible chance of capturing all the visitor pageview and behavior information and therefore reporting more accurate results.

Higher-value items usually mean a longer consideration time before the visitor commits to becoming a customer. For example, in the travel and finance industries, the consideration time between the initial visit and the purchase can be as long as 90 days. During this time, there's an increased risk of the user deleting cookies, reinstalling the browser, upgrading the operating system, buying a new computer, or dealing with a system crash. Any of these occurrences will result in users being seen as new visitors when they finally make their purchase. Offsite factors such as seasonality, adverse publicity, offline promotions, or published blog articles or comments can also affect latency.

Offline Visits Skewing Data Collection

Some problems are unrelated to the method used to measure visitor behavior but still pose a threat to data accuracy. High-value purchases such as cars, loans, and mortgages are often first researched online and then purchased offline. Connecting offline purchases with online visitor behavior is a long-standing enigma for web analytics tools. Currently, the best-practice way to overcome this limitation is to use online voucher schemes that visitors can print and take with them to claim a free gift, upgrade, or discount at your store. If you would prefer to receive your orders online, consider providing similar incentives, such as web-only pricing, free delivery if ordered online, and the like.

Another issue to consider is how your offline marketing is tracked. Without taking this into account, visitors who result from your offline campaign efforts will be incorrectly assigned or grouped with other referral sources and will therefore skew your data. How to measure offline marketing is discussed in detail in Chapter 11, "Real-World Tasks."

Comparing Data from Different Vendors

As shown earlier, it is virtually impossible to compare the results of one data-collection method with another. The association simply isn't valid. However, given two comparable data-collection methods—both page tags—can you achieve consistency? Unfortunately, even comparing vendors that employ page tags has its difficulties.

Factors that lead to differing vendor metrics are described in the following sections.

First-Party versus Third-Party Cookies

There is little correlation between the two because of the higher blocking rates of third-party cookies by users, firewalls, and antispyware software. For example, the latest versions of Microsoft Internet Explorer block third-party cookies by default if a site doesn't have a compact privacy policy (see http://www.w3.org/P3P).

Page Tags: Placement Considerations

JavaScript, as with other web code, loads in *series* within a web browser; that is, coming one after another with the other page content, such as text, style sheets, and images. Because of this, page tag vendors recommend that their page tags be placed just above the </body> tag of your HTML page (at the bottom of the page) to ensure that the visual content of the page loads first. This means that any delays from the vendor's servers will not interfere with your page loading. The potential problem here is that repeat visitors, those more familiar with your website navigation, may navigate quickly, clicking onto another page before the page tag has loaded to collect data. The more content you have on your pages, the slower they will load and the more likely visitors will click away before the tracking code has executed.

The alternative is to place page tags at the tops of your pages so they load before any page content. However, the risk is that the vendor may have a delay, outage, or blip that stops your pages from loading. Neither situation is ideal, though clearly, delaying content to your visitors is the worse scenario. Hence, placement at the bottom of pages has become the de facto standard.

Tag placement was investigated in a 2009 white paper by TagMan.com. Their study of latency effects revealed that approximately 10 percent of reported traffic is lost for every extra second a page takes to load. So heavy page content results in an undercounting of traffic. Moving the Google Analytics page tag from the bottom of a page to the top increased the reported traffic by 20 percent.

In addition, nonrelated JavaScript placed at the top of the page can interfere with JavaScript page tags that have been placed lower. Most vendor page tags work independently of other JavaScript and can sit comfortably alongside other vendor page tags. However, JavaScript errors on the same page will cause the browser scripting engine to stop at that point and prevent any JavaScript below it, including your page tag, from executing.

Note: Google Analytics uses *asynchronous* JavaScript page tags. This avoids the issues of tag placement and is discussed later in this chapter, in the section "Improving the Accuracy of Web Analytics Data."

Did You Tag Everything?

Many analytics tools require links to files—such as PDFs, Word documents, or executable downloads—or outbound links to other websites to be modified in order to be tracked. This may be a manual process whereby the link to the file needs to be modified. The modification represents an event or action when it is clicked, which sometimes is referred to as a *virtual pageview*. Comparing different vendors requires this action to be carried out several times with their specific codes (usually with JavaScript). Take into consideration that whenever pages have to be coded, syntax errors are a possibility. If page updates occur frequently, consider regular website audits to validate your page tags.

Pageviews: A Visit or a Visitor?

Pageviews are quick and easy to track, and because they require only a call from the page to the tracking server, they are very similar among vendors. The challenge is differentiating a visit from a visitor; because every vendor uses a different algorithm, no two algorithms result in the same value.

Cookie Time-Outs

The allowed duration of time-outs—how long a web page is left inactive by a visitor—varies among vendors. Most page tag vendors use a visitor-session cookie time-out of 30 minutes. This means that continuing to browse the same website after 30 minutes of inactivity is considered to be a new visit. However, some vendors offer the option to change this setting. Doing so will alter any data alignment and therefore affect the analysis of reported visitors. Other cookies, such as the ones that store referrer details, will have different time-out values. For example, Google Analytics referrer cookies last six months. Differences in these time-outs between different web analytics vendors will obviously be reflected in the reported visitor numbers.

Page Tag Code Hijacking

Depending on your vendor, your page tag code could be hijacked, copied, and executed on a different or unrelated website. This contamination results in a false pageview within your reports. By using filters, you can ensure that only data from your domains are reported. To do this, see Chapter 8, "Best Practices Configuration Guide."

Data Sampling

This is the practice of selecting a subset of data from your website traffic. Sampling is widely used in statistical analysis because analyzing a subset of data gives very similar results to analyzing all of the data yet can provide significant speed benefits when processing large volumes of information. Different vendors may use different sampling techniques and criteria, resulting in data misalignment. Data sampling considerations for Google Analytics are discussed in "Understanding Data Sampling" in Chapter 5, "Reports Explained."

PDF Files: A Special Consideration

For page tag solutions, it is not the completed PDF download that is reported but the fact that a visitor has clicked a PDF file link. This is an important distinction because information on whether or not the visitor completes the download—for example a 50-page PDF file—is not available. Therefore, a click on a PDF link is reported as a single event or pageview.

Note: The situation is different for logfile solutions. When you view a PDF file within your web browser, Adobe Reader can download the file one page at a time as opposed to a full download. This results in a slightly different entry in your web server logfile, showing an HTTP status code 206 (partial file download). Logfile solutions can treat each of the 206 status code entries as individual pageviews. When all the pages of a PDF file are downloaded, a completed download is registered in your logfile with a final HTTP status code of 200 (download completed). Therefore, a logfile solution can report a completed 50-page PDF file as one download and 50 pageviews. A number of factors will determine this, however—the visitor's browser, the browser plug-in, and whether the visitor left-clicked (viewed in browser) or right-clicked (downloaded for viewing outside the browser).

E-commerce: Negative Transactions

All e-commerce organizations have to deal with product returns at some point, whether because of damaged or faulty goods, order mistakes, or other reasons. Accounting for these returns is often forgotten within web analytics reports. For some vendors, it requires the manual entry of an equivalent negative purchase transaction. Others require the reprocessing of e-commerce data files. Whichever method is required, aligning web visitor data with internal systems is never bulletproof. For example, the removal or crediting of a transaction usually takes place well after the original purchase and therefore in a different reporting period.

Filters and Settings: Potential Obstacles

Data can vary when a filter is set up in one vendor's solution but not in another. Some tools can't set up the exact same filter as another tool, or they apply filters in a different way or at a different point during data processing.

Consider, for example, a page-level filter to exclude all error pages from your reports. Visit metrics such as time on site and page depth may or may not be adjusted for the filter depending on the vendor. This is because some vendors treat page-level metrics separately from visitor-level metrics.

Time Differences

A predicament for any vendor when it comes to calculating the time on site or time on page for a visitor's session involves how to calculate for the last page viewed. For example, time spent on page A is calculated by taking the difference between the visitor's time stamp for page A and the subsequent time stamp for page B and so on. But what if there is no page C; how can the time on page be calculated for page B if there is no following time stamp?

Different vendors handle this in different ways. Some ignore the final pageview in the calculation; others use an onUnload event to add a time stamp should the visitor close their browser or go to a different website. Both are valid methods, although not every vendor uses the onUnload method. The reason some vendors prefer to ignore the last page is that it is considered the most inaccurate from a time point of view—perhaps the visitor was interrupted to run an errand or left their browser in its current state while working on something else. Many users behave in this way; that is, they complete their browsing task and simply leave their browser open on the last page while working in another application. A small number of pageviews of this type will disproportionately skew the time-on-site and time-on-page calculations; hence, most vendors avoid this issue.

Note: Google Analytics ignores the last pageview of a visitor's session when calculating the time-on-site and time-on-page metrics.

Process Frequency

The frequency of processing is best illustrated by example: Google Analytics docs its number crunching to produce reports hourly. However, because it takes time to collate all the logfiles from all of the data-collecting servers around the world, reports can be three to four hours behind the current time. In most cases, it is usually a smooth process, but sometimes things go wrong. For example, if a logfile transfer is interrupted, then only a partial logfile is processed. Because of this, Google Analytics collects and reprocesses all data for a 24-hour period at the day's end. Other vendors may do the same, so it is important not to focus on discrepancies that arise on the current day.

Note: You should not panic if you observe "missing" data from your reports—for example, no data showing for today during the period 10 a.m. to 11 a.m. This information should be picked up during the data reprocessing that takes place at the end of the day (around midnight, Pacific Standard Time). If you have waited more than 24 hours and the data is still missing, contact the Google Analytics support team at www.google.com/support/googleanalytics/bin/request.py.

Goal Conversion versus Pageviews: Establishing Consistency

Using Figure 2.4 as an example, assume that five pages are part of your defined funnel (click-stream path), with the last step (page 5) being the goal conversion (purchase).

During checkout, a visitor goes back up a page to check a delivery charge (step A) and then continues through to complete payment. The visitor is so happy with the simplicity of the entire process that she then purchases a second item using exactly the same path during the same visitor session (step B).

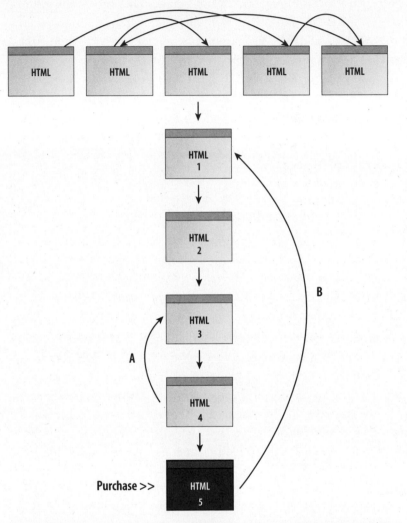

Figure 2.4 A visitor traversing a website, entering a five-page funnel and making two transactions

Depending on the vendor you use, this process can be counted in various ways, as follows:

- Twelve funnel page views, two conversions, two transactions
- Ten funnel page views (ignoring step A), two conversions, two transactions
- Five funnel page views, two conversions, two transactions
- Five funnel page views, one conversion (ignoring step B), two transactions

Most vendors, but not all, apply the last rationale to their reports. That is, the visitor has become a purchaser (one conversion), and this can happen only once in the session, so additional conversions (assuming the same goal) are ignored. For this to be valid, the same rationale must be applied to the funnel pages. In this way, the data becomes more visitor-centric. Google Analytics behaves in this way.

Note: In the example of Figure 2.4, the total number of pageviews equals 12 and would be reported as such in all pageview reports. It is the funnel and goal-conversion reports that will be different.

Why PPC Vendor Numbers Do Not Match Web Analytics Reports

If you are using pay-per-click (PPC) networks, you will typically have access to the click-through reports provided by each network. Quite often, these numbers don't exactly align with those reported in your web analytics reports. This can happen for the reasons described in the following sections.

Missing Landing Page Tracking URLs

Tracking URLs are required in your PPC account setup in order to differentiate between a nonpaid search engine visitor click-through and a PPC click-through from the same referring domain—Google.com or Yahoo.com, for example. Tracking URLs are simple modifications to your landing page URLs within your PPC account and are of the form `http://www.mysite.com?source=adwords`. Tracking URLs forgotten during setup, or sometimes simply assigned incorrectly, can lead to such visits being incorrectly assigned to nonpaid visitors.

Slow Page Load Times

As previously discussed, the best-practice location for web analytics data-collection tags is at the bottom of your pages—just above the `</body>` HTML tag. If your PPC landing pages are slow to download for whatever reason (server delays, page bloat, and so on), it is likely that visitors will click away, navigating to another page on your site or even to a different website, before the data-collection tag has had chance to load. The chance of this happening increases the longer the page load time is. The general rule of thumb for what constitutes a long page load is only 2 seconds. See

`www.akamai.com/html/about/press/releases/2009/press_091409.html`

The impact of slow loading pages should not be underestimated. Apart from the poor user experience that has a direct impact on your bottom line, a slow-loading landing page can also damage your organic search engine rankings and your AdWords acquisition costs due to a poor AdWords Quality Score.

Note: Google Analytics uses asynchronous page tags. That means they can be placed at the top of your pages, providing greater accuracy without interfering with your page content loading. Further details are contained later in this chapter, in the section "Improving the Accuracy of Web Analytics Data."

Clicks and Visits: Understanding the Difference

PPC vendors, such as Google AdWords, measure clicks. Most web analytics tools measure visitors who can accept a cookie. Those are not always going to be the same thing when you consider the effects on your web analytics data of cookie blocking, JavaScript errors, and visitors who simply navigate away from your landing page quickly—before the page tag collects its data. Because of this, web analytics tools tend to slightly underreport visits from PPC networks.

PPC Account Adjustments

Google AdWords and other PPC vendors automatically monitor invalid and fraudulent clicks and adjust PPC metrics retroactively. For example, a visitor may click your ad several times (inadvertently or on purpose) within a short space of time. Google AdWords investigates this influx and removes the additional click-throughs and charges from your account. For Google Analytics, AdWords data is imported when you request the report, and previous data may be updated to reflect the changes from the fraud-protection algorithms. Alternative web analytics tools may use a different AdWords import frequency. From a reporting point of view, the recommendation is to not place too much emphasis on AdWords visitor numbers for the current day and use longer time frames for detailed analysis. This holds true for all web analytics solutions and all PPC advertising networks.

For further information on how Google treats invalid clicks, see

```
http://adwords.google.com/support/bin/topic.py?topic=35
```

Note: Although most of the AdWords invalid-click updates take place within 24 hours, they can take longer. For this reason, even if all other factors are eliminated, AdWords click-throughs within your PPC account and those reported in your web analytics reports may never match exactly.

Keyword Matching: Bid Term versus Search Term

The bid terms you select within your PPC account and the search terms used by visitors that result in your PPC ad being displayed can often be different: think "broad match." For example, you may have set up an ad group that targets the word *shoes* and solely relies on broad matching to match all search terms that contain the word *shoes*. This is your bid term. A visitor uses the search term *blue shoes* and clicks your ad. Web analytics vendors may report the search term, the bid term, or both. Google Analytics reports both.

Losing Data via Third-Party Redirects

Using third-party ad-tracking systems—such as Adform, Atlas Search, Blue Streak, DoubleClick, Efficient Frontier, and SEM Director—to track click-throughs to your website means your visitors are passed through redirection URLs. This results in the initial click being registered by your ad company, which then automatically redirects the visitor to your actual landing page. The purpose of this two-step hop is to allow the ad-tracking network to collect visitor statistics independently of your organization, typically for billing purposes. Because this process involves a short delay, it may prevent some visitors from landing on your page. The result can be a small loss of data and therefore failure to align data.

More important, and more common, redirection URLs may break the tracking parameters that are added onto the landing pages for your own web analytics solution. For example, using generic tracking parameters, your landing page URL may look like this:

```
http://www.mysite.com/?source=google&medium=ppc&campaign=Jan12
```

When added to a third-party tracking system for redirection, it could look like this:

```
http://www.redirect.com?http://www.mywebsite.com?source=google&medium=ppc➡
&campaign=Jan12
```

The problem occurs with the second question mark in the second link because you can't have more than one in any valid URL. Some third-party ad-tracking systems will detect this error and remove the second question mark and the following tracking parameters, leading to a loss of campaign data.

Some third-party ad-tracking systems allow you to replace the second ? with a # so the URL can be processed correctly. Essentially, the test to see if this is working correctly is straightforward—following the redirect, check that your campaign parameters remain visible on your landing page URL. If not, this will need to be corrected. If you are unsure of what to do to fix the issue, you can avoid the problem completely by using encoded landing-page URLs within your third-party ad-tracking system, as described at the following site:

```
http://www.w3schools.com/tags/ref_urlencode.asp
```

Note: From my experience, the most common reasons for discrepancies between PPC vendor reports and web analytics tools arise from the first and last issues discussed in this section; that is, missing landing page tracking URLs and the loss of tracking parameters due to third-party redirects.

Why Counting Uniques Is Meaningless

The term *uniques* is often used in web analytics as an abbreviation for unique web visitors, that is, how many unique people visited your site. The problem is that counting unique visitors is fraught with problems that are so fundamental the term *uniques* is rendered meaningless.

As discussed earlier in this chapter, cookies get lost, blocked, and deleted—nearly one-third of tracking cookies can be missing after a period of four weeks. The longer the time period, the greater the chance of this happening, which makes comparing year-on-year uniques invalid, for example. In addition, browsers make it very easy these days for cookies to be removed—see the new "incognito" features of the latest Firefox, Chrome, and Internet Explorer browsers.

However, the biggest issue for counting uniques is how many devices people use to access the Web. For example, consider the following scenario:

1. You and your spouse are considering your next vacation. Your spouse first checks out possible locations on your joint PC at home and saves a list of website links.

2. The next evening you use the same PC to review these links. Unable to decide that night, you email the list to your office, and the next day you continue your vacation checks during your lunch hour at work and also review these again on your mobile while commuting home on the train.

3. Day 3 of your search resumes at your friend's house, where you seek a second opinion. Finally, you go home and book online using your shared PC.

The above scenario is actually very common—particularly if the value of the purchase is significant, which implies a longer consideration period and the seeking of a second opinion from a spouse, friends, or work colleagues.

Simply put, there is not a web analytics solution in the world that can accurately track this scenario—that is, to tie the data together from multiple devices and where multiple people have been involved—nor is there likely to be one in the near future.

Combining these limitations leads to large error bars when it comes to tracking uniques. In fact, these errors are so large that the metric becomes meaningless and should be avoided, where possible, in favor of more accurate "visit" data. That said, if you must use unique visitors as a key metric, ensure that the emphasis is on the trend, not the absolute number.

Data Misinterpretation: Lies, Damned Lies, and Statistics

Data is not always straightforward to interpret. Take the following two examples, which are not accuracy issues:

- New visitors plus repeat visitors does not equal total visitors.

A common misconception is that the sum of new visitors and repeat visitors should equal the total number of visitors. Why isn't this the case? Consider a visitor making his first visit on a given day and then returning on the same day. He is both a new and a repeat visitor for that day. Therefore, looking at a report for the given day, two visitor types will be shown, though the total number of visitors is one.

It is therefore better to think of *visitors* in terms of *visit type*—that is, the number of first-time visits plus the number of repeat visits equals the total number of visits.

- Summing the number of unique visitors per day for a week does not equal the total number of unique visitors for that week.

Consider the scenario in which you have 1,000 unique visitors to your website blog on a Monday. These are in fact the only unique visitors you receive for the entire week, so on Tuesday the same 1,000 visitors return to consume your next blog post. This pattern continues for Wednesday through Sunday.

If you were to look at the number of unique visitors for each day of the week in your reports, you would observe 1,000 unique visitors. However, you cannot say that you received 7,000 unique visitors for the entire week. For this example, the number of unique visitors for the week remains at 1,000.

Improving the Accuracy of Web Analytics Data

Clearly, web analytics is not 100 percent accurate, and the number of possible inaccuracies can appear overwhelming at first. However, as the preceding sections demonstrated, you can get comfortable with your implementation and focus on measuring trends rather than precise numbers. For example, web analytics can help you answer the following questions:

- Are visitor numbers increasing?
- By what rate are they increasing (or decreasing)?
- Have conversion rates gone up since beginning PPC advertising?
- How has the cart-abandon rate changed since the site redesign?

If the trend shows a 10.5 percent reduction, for example, this figure should be accurate regardless of the web analytics tool that was used. These examples are all high-level metrics, though the same accuracy can also be maintained as you drill down and look at, for example, which specific referrals (search engines, affiliates, social networks), campaigns (paid search, email, banners), keywords, geographies, or devices (Windows, Mac, mobile) are used.

Because you are going to be a Google Analytics user, you should be aware that Google has made significant advances in improving the accuracy of the page-tagging data-collection technique in recent years. Since 2010, the recommended implementation of the Google Analytics page tag is *asynchronous*. This is a clever way of loading JavaScript code in *parallel* with the loading of a page, as opposed to loading in *series*, which is the traditional approach. This overcomes both limitations of tag placement—the issue of missing visitor activity because the page tag did not have a chance to load when placed at the bottom of the page and any potential interference with your page content loading due to vendor issues when the page tag is placed at the top of your pages.

When the asynchronous method is used, the tracking code is loaded in the background, that is, in parallel, as soon as the page is requested. Any tracking requests made prior to the code loading fully are stored in a queue and executed when the code is available. The result is greater tracking accuracy (as the page tag is at the top of the page), without any possible interference with your page content that is normally associated with page tag placement.

When all the possibilities of inaccuracy that affect web analytics solutions are considered, it is apparent that it is ineffective to focus on absolute values or to merge numbers from different sources. If all web visitors were to have a login account in order to view your website, this issue could be overcome. In the real world, however, the vast majority of Internet users wish to remain anonymous, so this is not a viable solution.

As long as you use the same measurement for comparing data ranges, your results will be accurate. This is the universal truth of all web analytics.

Here are 11 recommendations for enhancing your web analytics accuracy:

1. Be sure to select a tool that uses page tagging and first-party cookies for data collection. Google Analytics is a page tag tool that sets only first-party cookies.

2. Use asynchronous page tagging with the code located in the head section of your pages. This is the default for Google Analytics.

3. Don't confuse visitor identifiers. For example, if first-party cookies are deleted, do not resort to using IP address information. It is better simply to ignore that visitor's activity. Google Analytics does this.

4. Remove or report separately all nonhuman activity from your data reports, such as robots and server-performance monitors. Google Analytics ignores robots that do not execute JavaScript (I have yet to come across any robot that does this).

5. Track everything. Don't limit tracking to landing pages, or even just pages. Track your entire website's activity, including file downloads, internal search terms, transactions, sales funnel click-throughs, clicks on so-called love buttons (Facebook Likes, Twitter Follows, and so forth), error pages, and outbound links. Apart from pageviews, Google Analytics will not track the others by

default—you have to configure these for yourself. See Chapter 7, Chapter 8, and Chapter 9.

6. Regularly audit your website for page tag completeness (at least monthly for large websites). Sometimes site content changes result in tags being corrupted, deleted, or forgotten. Tools to help you do this are listed in Appendix B, "Useful Tools."

7. Display a clear and easy-to-read privacy policy (required by law in the European Union). This establishes trust with your visitors because they better understand how they're being tracked and are less likely to delete cookies. A best-practice example of a privacy statement for use with Google Analytics is shown in Chapter 3, "Google Analytics Features, Benefits, and Limitations."

8. Avoid making judgments on data that is less than 24 hours old because it's often the most inaccurate. When you log into Google Analytics, the current day is omitted from the data window by default, though it can be manually included.

9. Test redirection URLs to guarantee that they maintain tracking parameters. If your landing page URL does not maintain your tracking parameters, they have been lost and this will need to be corrected.

10. Ensure that all paid online campaigns use tracking URLs to differentiate from nonpaid sources. Google Analytics does this automatically for AdWords.

11. Use *visit* metrics in preference to *unique visitor* metrics because the latter are highly inaccurate. Most Google Analytics reports show visit data for precisely this reason.

These suggestions will help you appreciate the errors often made when collecting web analytics data. Understanding what these errors are, how they happen, and how to avoid them will enable you to benchmark the performance of your website better.

Privacy Considerations for the Web Analytics Industry

With the huge proliferation of Web use, people are now much more aware of privacy issues, concerns, and obligations. In my opinion, this is a step forward—the industry needs an informed debate about online privacy. Although privacy has been bubbling under the radar of the general public for many years, there was a huge uptick in discussion when the new European Union (EU) privacy law came into effect on May 26, 2011.

Before discussing the impact of this specific new law, it is worth looking at what privacy issues web users and website owners should be aware of. This will help the reader understand why this new law came about (and will no doubt eventually be emulated in laws in other parts of the world) and why it is a good thing for the web measurement industry as a whole.

Types of Private Information

There are two types of private information:

Non–personally identifiable information (non-PII) This is anonymous aggregate data that cannot be used to identify or deduce demographic information, such as your name or address. It is best illustrated by example. Suppose you wish to monitor vehicle traffic close to a school so that you can predict and improve the safety and efficiency of the surrounding road structure. You might stand on a street corner counting the number of vehicles, their type (car, van, truck, bus, and so on), time of day, and how long it takes for them to pass the school gates. This is an example of nonpersonal information—there is nothing in this aggregate data that identifies the individual driver or owner of each vehicle. Incidentally, you also cannot identify whether the same vehicle is repeatedly driving around the school in a circle, but that is an unlikely scenario that is not considered further.

As you can see, this is a great way to collect data to improve things for all people involved (pupils, residents, shop owners, and drivers) without any interference of privacy. This example is directly analogous to using the Web. By far, the vast majority of Web users who are surveyed claim they are happy for their nonpersonal information to be collected and used to improve a website's effectiveness and ultimately their user experience.

Personally identifiable information (PII) Taking the previous non-PII example further, suppose the next day you started to collect vehicle license plate details, or stopped drivers to question them on their driving habits, or followed them home to determine whether they were local residents. These are all examples of collecting personal data—both asked-for data, such as their name, age, and address, and non-volunteered information that can be discovered, such as gender and license plate details.

Collecting personally identifiable information clearly has huge privacy implications and is regulated by law in most democratic countries. Collecting data in this way would mean that all drivers would need to be explicitly informed that data collection was occurring and offered the choice of not driving down the street. They could then make an informed decision as to whether they wish to take part in the study or not. Again, this is analogous to using the Web—asking the visitor to opt in to sharing their personal information.

The issue with regard to web privacy is that many users are confused as to what form of tracking, if any, is taking place when they visit a website. Very few people read privacy statements, and even when viewing them, the public is cynical. Often, these statements tend to be written in a legal language that is difficult to understand, they change without notice, and they primarily appear to be there to protect the website owner rather than the privacy of the visitor.

Regardless of the public's confusion, apathy, or anger about website privacy, it is your responsibility as a website owner to inform visitors about what data-collection practices are occurring when a visitor views your website. In fact, within the European Union, law requires it. View the section "Common Privacy Questions" in Chapter 3 for a best-practice example of a clear privacy statement when using Google Analytics.

The EU Privacy Law

Put into effect in 2011, this law is applicable to all websites and businesses operating within any of the 27 member countries of the European Union. The rationale for the law was the failure of the web analytics industry to self-regulate privacy policy properly. The EU lawmakers targeted the surreptitious tracking of individuals that has been going on for many years:

- Sharing cookie information collected on one website with another website via third-party cookies
- Identifying anonymous visitors—either by using data from a third-party cookie where personal information was entered or back-filling previous visit data when a visitor later creates an account or makes a purchase
- Tracking visitors even though they have set their browser privacy settings to block tracking cookies (used by Flash Shared Objects)

I use the word *cookies* because this is the current technology used for tracking visitors. However, the law is technology agnostic and therefore applies regardless of what actual data-collection technology is employed. Essentially, if you are using third-party cookies, or Flash Shared Objects, or any other similar nontransparent tracking technology, this law is very much targeting you.

To continue doing so under this law, you have to request *explicit* consent from your visitors. The purpose is to ensure transparency with your visitors. The hope is that website owners will evaluate their tracking requirements, realize that such invasive tracking is bad for business, and stop the practice—or comply with the law by placing pop-up notifications, or similar, on their pages to gain visitor consent. Pop-up alerts are disruptive and are known to be bad for business (there is a whole industry built around blocking pop-up advertisements), so the resulting poor user experience should also drive website owners to reconsider.

As a Google Analytics user, you are not doing any of the above. However, at the time of writing, the EU privacy law says that unless strictly necessary, you cannot track visitors to your website without explicit permission from each of them.

UK Guidelines Document

The Independent Commissioner's Office (ICO) is the UK independent authority to protect personal information—for all types of collected data, including online. It has published a PDF guideline document on the new EU privacy law available at

`www.ico.gov.uk/~/media/documents/library/Privacy_and_electronic/Practical_`
`application/advice_on_the_new_cookies_regulations.ashx`

The guidelines are similar for all other EU member countries, though you should check with your specific country's privacy office to understand how the law is to be applied in your country. The ICO is a Google Analytics user.

As a result of this, many people are interpreting the law as saying that web tracking is illegal because it is not "strictly necessary" when delivering a web page to the visitor—unless you ask your visitor's consent to do so at the start of their visit. However, as I am sure will be shown, this is not the intent of the lawmakers.

For me it's an obvious argument and one that is easy to justify: As a commercial part of your business, tracking the performance of your website *is* strictly necessary, in the same way that tracking other parts of your organization is strictly necessary— such as your sales performance, staff performance, marketing activities, operational processes, costs, and so forth. Measurement is a critical part of business in the 21st century; this even applies to governments and institutions that need to be accountable to taxpayers.

 Tip: The EU privacy law is still very fluid while the 27 EU member countries figure out how to interpret and implement it. You can follow the discussion on the book blog site:

`www.advanced-web-metrics.com/blog/category/privacy-accuracy/`

The Impact of Requiring Explicit Consent

The main impact of this law is to stop the surreptitious collection of personal information by making it transparent to the visitor what is being tracked and allowing them to make an informed decision as to whether they wish to share such information with the website owner. Even without visitors saying no en masse, it forces website owners to prioritize visitor privacy. That's a good thing for the Web as a whole and will hopefully spread beyond the borders of the EU.

The controversy expressed (and rightly feared) so far by website managers is that sites collecting benign non-PII data may also have to display an obtrusive and brand damaging pop-up message requesting tracking consent (to comply with "strictly necessary"). As an example of how damaging this can be to a business, consider Figure 2.5. This shows the before and after effects of requesting visitor consent even though the data collected was completely benign. The data loss is 90 percent for a best-practice implementation of Google Analytics!

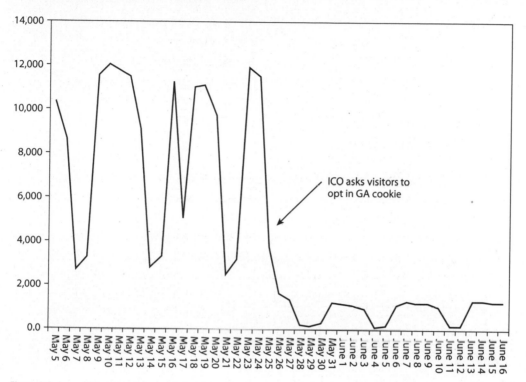

Figure 2.5 Loss of data when visitors are asked for explicit consent to be tracked benignly

There can be many reasons for the sharp drop in collected data shown in Figure 2.5. The wording of the consent message to the visitor and its design and placement are obviously critical. There is also the fear of the unknown; that is, when they first visit a website, the visitor is not interested in reading or has no time to read boring privacy text to find out what its implications may be. Therefore, they simply opt for the safe "no" option. In this example, there is no benefit for the visitor motivating them to opt in. Perhaps a retail site would fare better with a sweetener of a better deal or better shopping experience. However, my instinct tells me the drop will still be significant.

The bottom line is that at present the term "strictly necessary" is ambiguous and needs to be clarified by lawmakers.

Note: Ironically, the data shown in Figure 2.5 comes from the ICO website (www.ico.gov.uk), the organization responsible for implementing the new EU privacy law in the UK. Data was obtained as a freedom of information request to the ICO. With thanks to Vicky Brock (@brockvicky).

Requirements for Google Analytics Users

The key is to respect your visitor's privacy. That means no PII without explicit consent and all other data remaining anonymous and benign. Google Analytics fits this category and has deliberately done so since its launch. That does not mean you can ignore this law. For example, it is possible to configure Google Analytics to collect PII and therefore break the law—I have seen this happen inadvertently. Therefore, follow these four important guidelines:

- Audit and document your website tracking capabilities, such as cookie collection, and adjust your site accordingly. That can mean changing what information is collected, how it is collected, and how the practice is communicated to the visitor.
- Ensure that your privacy statement is up-to-date and accurate. Keep it simple, not full of legal jargon. An example privacy statement is shown in Chapter 3.
- If you wish to perform behavioral targeting or collect personal information, ask for explicit consent from your visitors first.
- Do not collect any PII data using Google Analytics. Even if you have tracking permission for this from your visitor, it is against the Google Analytics terms of service to collect such information using Google Analytics. That means no email addresses, usernames, or address details collected from, for example, submitted forms or logins.

Summary

In Chapter 2, you have learned the following:

The difference between page tags and logfiles I discussed how web visitor data is collected, the relative advantages of page tags and logfile tools, and why page tagging has become the de facto standard.

The perils of cookies You learned about the role of cookies in web analytics, what they contain, and why they exist, including the differences between first-party and third-party cookies.

Difficulties of interpreting traffic data We explored the accuracy limitations of web traffic information in terms of collecting web visitor data, interpreting it, and comparing numbers from different vendors.

How to improve the accuracy of your data I discussed how you can mitigate error bars and improve tracking accuracy so that you become comfortable and confident with your data.

Visitors' privacy issues You learned how to think about web analytics in relation to end-user privacy concerns and your responsibilities as a website owner to respect your visitors' privacy.

Google Analytics Features, Benefits, and Limitations

Understanding how Google Analytics data collection works is a great way to recognize what you can achieve with web analytics reporting. Don't worry—this is not an engineering book, so technicalities are kept to a minimum. However, it is important to know what can and cannot be accomplished because this knowledge will help you spot erroneous data that may show up in your reports.

As well as a discussion of the key features and capabilities of Google Analytics, included in this chapter is a description of Google Analytics Premium, the new paid-for version of Google Analytics, and Urchin software, a separate web analytics tool from Google.

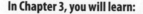

In Chapter 3, you will learn:

The key features and capabilities of Google Analytics

How Google Analytics works

What is tracked by default and what requires special consideration

What Google Analytics cannot do

The Google Analytics approach to user privacy

What Google Analytics Premium is

What Urchin software is

Key Features and Capabilities of Google Analytics

I started my career running my own business of web professionals, so I understand the analytic needs of a small company. Now, having worked at Google for a number of years, I am familiar with the other end of the spectrum—working with some of the largest organizations in the world. What still amazes me is just how similar both large and small companies are in their analytics requirements—from understanding what is happening on their website and how to interpret the data to what action to take to improve matters, small and large organizations face the same challenges.

Both types of users express an understanding of the need for measurement, yet they also fear data overload when combined with other aspects of the business and their job. Both also expect the collection and reporting of data to be at the smaller end of their investment budget, with professional services the key to unlocking their online business potential.

This list of features is not intended to be exhaustive, though it does highlight the more interesting and important ones you can find in Google Analytics. I group them into two categories, standard and advanced features.

Standard Features

I describe standard features as those that you would expect to find in any commercial-strength web analytics tool in 2012. These are the "must-have" basic metrics you need in order to get an initial understanding of your website performance. However, they are not basic reports. You can quickly extract rich detail with a couple of mouse clicks. You can, for example, cross-reference e-commerce revenue by referral source or search engine keyword. Screen shots of most of these features in use are shown in Chapter 4, "Using the Google Analytics Interface." and Chapter 5, "Reports Explained."

Full Campaign Reporting—Not Just AdWords

Google Analytics enables you to track and compare all your visitors—from nonpaid organic search, paid ads (pay per click, banners), social media, referrals, email newsletters, affiliate campaigns, links from within digital documents such as PDF files, and any other search engine or medium that forwards a visitor to your website. You can even get a handle on your offline marketing campaigns, discussed in Chapter 11, "Real-World Tasks."

Advertising ROI—Integration with AdWords and AdSense

If you manage a pay-per-click campaign, you know what a chore tagging your landing page URLs can be. Each one has to have at least one campaign variable appended to differentiate visitors who click through from nonpaid search results. In addition, you will want to import your AdWords cost and impression data. As you might expect,

Google has simplified the integration process as much as possible, in fact to just two check boxes. As a result, all your AdWords landing page URLs are tagged, and cost data is imported automatically each day.

Similarly for publishers who display AdWords on their site—that is, use AdSense—the integration is straightforward. The result is reports showing you which content drives the most revenue alongside the import of AdSense page impressions and the number of AdSense ads clicked on.

Social Media Love Buttons

Social media love buttons are the small icons you can place on your pages to encourage visitors to share your information, such as Google's +1, Facebook's Like, Twitter's Follow me, and LinkedIn's Share buttons. These represent a special type of visitor engagement, and Google Analytics therefore has a section of reports just for analyzing them.

E-commerce Reporting

You can trace transactions to campaigns and keywords, get loyalty and latency metrics, and identify your revenue sources. Similarly, you can drill down to this information on a per-product or per-category basis.

Goal Conversions (Key Performance Indicators)

A *goal conversion* is a key pageview or key event (visitor action) that brings you closer to your otherwise anonymous visitors. Think of these as your more valuable pageviews. An obvious goal conversion is an e-commerce purchase-confirmation page. However, other nontransactional goals exist, such as, for example, completing a registration or feedback form, downloading a file, watching a movie (how-to guides, product demonstrations), commenting on blogs, submitting surveys, and clicking an outbound link.

In addition to defining goal conversions as a pageview or an event, you can set thresholds. For example, time on site greater than 30 seconds or pages per visit greater than 7.5. In total, you can define up to 20 separate goals, which can be grouped into four categories (termed *goal types*).

Each goal can be monetized by assigning a monetary value once the goal is achieved.

Funnel Visualization

Funnels are set paths visitors take before achieving a goal conversion. An obvious funnel is an e-commerce checkout process. However, just as for goal conversions, other nontransactional funnels exist—for example, a multiform subscription process where each completed form is a funnel step. It is also possible to define funnel steps as the completion of individual form fields, such as name or product selection, so that partial form completion can be visualized.

By visualizing the visitor path (the funnel), you can discover which pages result in lost conversions and where your would-be customers go. Each funnel can contain up to 10 steps.

Customized Dashboards

The dashboard is a selection of abridged reports from the main sections of Google Analytics. Here you place and organize your key data selections for an at-a-glance comparison. Up to 12 reports can be added, changed, and reordered within the dashboard at any time. Dashboards are created on a per-user basis; that is, different user logins have different dashboards.

In-Page Analytics Report

In-Page Analytics provides a graphical way of looking at the popularity of links on your pages. You view your key metrics overlaid on your web page links. It's an easy-to-view snapshot of which links are working for you.

Geomap Overlay Reports

Map overlay is a graphical way of presenting data that reflects where visitors are connecting from around the world when viewing your website. Based on IP address location databases, they show your key metrics overlaid on a world, continent/subcontinent, country, or state/regional map, depending on your zoom level. This provides a clear representation of which parts of the world visitors are connecting from, down to city level. In my view, this report sets the industry standard for visualizing where visitors come from to your site.

Geo-IP information has improved dramatically in recent years, mainly driven by the security industry, that is, improvements in online credit card fraud detection. The database used in Google Analytics is the same as that used for geotargeting ads in your AdWords campaigns. Data can be as accurate as a 25-mile (40 km) radius. However, sometimes location details are not available, and this is shown as "(not set)" in your reports.

Map Overlay Accuracy

MaxMind is one company that provides geo-IP database information to third parties such as banks and web analytics vendors, though not Google Analytics. The MaxMind accuracy table presented at www.maxmind.com/app/city_accuracy is typical for this industry. As an example, for the United States, the databases are 99.8 percent accurate on a country level, 90 percent accurate on a state level, and 83 percent accurate at city level within a 25-mile (40 km) radius.

Advanced Segmentation

Advanced segmentation allows you to isolate and analyze subsets of visitor traffic side by side with other segments. For example, you can view "Paid Traffic" visits alongside "Visits with Conversions" or view "Visits lasting longer than 1 minute" next to "Visits between 10 and 60 seconds." There are predefined segments as well as a custom segment builder. Custom segments are built on a per-user basis and can be shared with other users, both within your organization and externally if you wish. There are numerous segmentation options, and cross-segmentation is available within nearly every Google Analytics report. It's a powerful feature that allows you to isolate particular visit patterns.

Closely related to advanced segmentation is *advanced table filtering*. While you're within a specific report, advanced filtering enables you to isolate specific table rows. This can be via a simple text match or more sophisticated regular expressions.

Data Export and Scheduling

Report data can be manually exported in a variety of formats, including CSV (best for Excel), TSV, and PDF (best for printing). You can also schedule any report to be emailed to you and your colleagues automatically. For example, you may want to email your e-commerce manager the list of top-selling products each week, your marketing manager a breakdown of campaign performance, or your web designer the list of error pages generated.

The key to remember with exporting is What-You-See-Is-What-You-Get (WYSIWYG). That means by default Google Analytics displays 10 rows of data, and so an export of a default report view will be for those 10 rows. If you want a greater sample size, you must expand the report view to, say, 100 rows and then export. Similarly, you can cross segment and drill into report data and then export that specific view.

> **Tip:** If you have more than 10 people who would like an email copy of a report, you can create a mailing list on your server—for example, marketing@mysite.com—and use it for your Google Analytics export list. That way, you can independently manage your mailing list members.

Internal Site Search Reporting

For complex websites (those with a large number of pages), internal site search is an important part of the site-navigation system and in many cases is critical for providing a positive user experience. A dedicated report section enables you to assess the value of your internal site search engine, comparing it with those visitors who do not search. In addition, you can discover which pages result in visitors performing a search, the search phrases used, post-search destination pages, and the conversion goals or products purchased as a result of a search.

Multiple Language Interfaces and Support

Google Analytics currently can display reports in 40 languages, and this number is continually growing. Languages include Arabic, Bulgarian, Catalan, Croatian, Czech, Simplified Chinese, Danish, Dutch, English, Greek, Filipino, Finnish, French, German, Hebrew, Hindi, Hungarian, Italian, Indonesian, Japanese, Korean, Latvian, Lithuanian, Malaysian, Norwegian, Polish, Portuguese (Brazil), Portuguese (Portugal), Romanian, Russian, Serbian, Slovak, Slovenian, Spanish, Swedish, Taiwanese, Thai, Turkish, Ukrainian, and Vietnamese.

In addition to the display of reports in multiple languages, all documentation is internationalized and each language is directly supported by Google staff.

Customized Reports

You can create, save, and edit customized reports that present the information you want to see, organized in the way you want to see it. An intuitive interface lets you select the metrics you want and define multiple levels of sub-reports. Custom reports are built on a per-user basis and can be shared with other users, both within your organization and externally.

Event Tracking

Events are defined as in-page actions that do not generate a pageview. For example, if your website incorporates Flash elements, widgets, Ajax, or embedded video, you will want to see how users interact with these separately from your pageview reports, such as clicks on play, pause, or watch the video to completion. Any Flash element, Ajax content, file download, and even load times can be reported on in this way. The Event Tracking section is a dedicated collection of reports that show your events displayed separately from pageviews. Events can be grouped into categories and even monetized.

Administrator and Individual Access Controls

There are two levels of access to Google Analytics reports—administrators and report viewers. Administrators have access to all account functionality, including all data reports, creating profiles, defining filters, funnel steps, and conversion goals. They are also the gatekeepers for creating other user access. A Google Analytics report viewer has access to report data only, though each user can customize their user interface, such as their dashboard, advanced filters, custom reports, and chart annotations.

There are no limits on the number of administrators or report viewers who can be set up with access.

High Scalability

The Google Analytics target audience can be compared to that of online advertising—just about everyone with a website. Only five years ago, the number of clients using a professional web analytics tool could be counted in the tens of thousands. Now, following the launch of Google Analytics as a free service, the number of accounts is measured in the millions (free is obviously a strong incentive!). And it's a broad spectrum of organizations. Clients range from those with a few pageviews per day to some of the best-known brands and most highly trafficked sites on the Web—that is, sites receiving more than 100 million pageviews per day. For example, see

www.advanced-web-metrics.com/who-uses-google-analytics

Market Share of Google Analytics

Measuring market share of web analytics tools turns out to be quite straightforward. Page-tag tools, the ones used by the vast majority of commercial websites (estimated at over 90 percent by this author), leave their telltale "marks" on a website—either in the form of JavaScript text that can be read by viewing a page's HTML source code or as cookie name/value pairs that vendor tools set. Both of these can be detected by viewing a page in your browser (see "Tools to Help Audit Your GATC Deployment" in Appendix B). Of course, there is also good old-fashioned survey data.

A 2011 study by Stéphane Hamel at Cardinal Path revealed 64 percent of the top 500 US retail sites and 45 percent of Fortune 500 companies use Google Analytics:

www.cardinalpath.com/web-analytics-vendors-market-share

A 2011 survey of 800 businesses (66 percent of them from the UK) revealed that 86 percent are using Google for analytics compared to 66 percent just two years ago ("Online Measurement and Strategy Report 2011," Econsultancy.com).

A 2010 study by Metric Mail, who analyzed the pages of Alexa's Top 1 million domains by searching for the GATC text within pages, found Google Analytics had a 50 percent market share:

http://metricmail.tumblr.com/post/904126172/google-analytics-market-share

You can find an updated snapshot of major brands using Google Analytics at the following location:

www.advanced-web-metrics.com/who-uses-google-analytics

Advanced Features

I describe advanced features as those that are unique to Google or are for advanced users wishing for greater metrics insight, such as, for example, multi-channel funnels, flow visualization, content grouping, intelligent alert system, animated motion charts, and pivot views. In some cases when viewing your reports, you may see these labeled as beta features.

Multi-Channel Funnels

Multi-Channel Funnels (MCF) is a reporting section that helps you answer the question of how your different marketing activities interact with each other to drive conversions, or sales, on your site. For example, in building a relationship with your organization, a visitor may click on multiple referrers and campaigns to your website before converting. Consider the scenario of a visitor coming to your site three times. On their last visit they make a purchase. The first referral that drove them to your site is an organic search; their second visit is via an AdWords click-through; their third visit is via following a link in a follow-up email message from you.

MCF reports show all three of these referrers contributing to the conversion, and their referral path with associated metrics; that is, Organic > AdWords > Email. This is shown schematically in Figure 3.1.

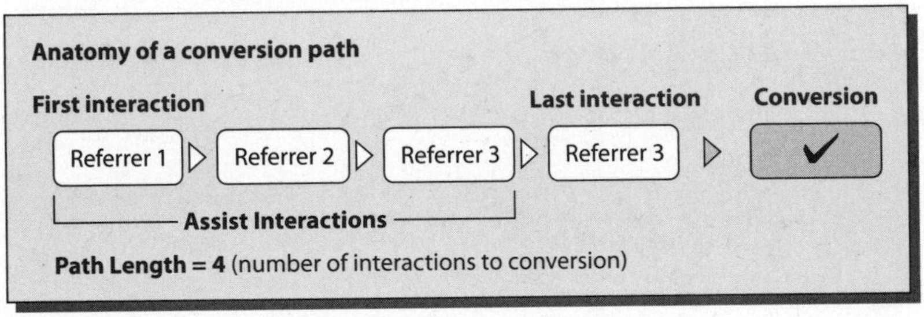

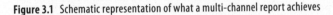

Figure 3.1 Schematic representation of what a multi-channel report achieves

MCF helps you understand how your different marketing activities work together. For example, does your branded AdWords campaign contribute to driving your generic organic traffic or to cannibalizing it? Are social networks a part of your marketing mix or a stand-alone channel for you? Note that you can view the path length for any conversion as well as for transactions. MCF reports are discussed in Chapter 5.

Flow and Goal Visualization

Think of this as visitor path analysis, but on steroids! This new feature (October 2011) is Google's attempt at redefining path analysis. The reason for it is that traditional path analysis that has been provided by other vendors has been confusing at best and irrelevant at worst. For example, often you come to the conclusion that all paths on your site are unique—there are simply too many ever so slightly different paths your visitors can take.

The Flow Visualization report overcomes this by using an intelligence algorithm that groups together the most likely visitor paths through a site. The visualization is highly interactive. You can interact with the graph to highlight different pathways, zoom in and out, and see information about specific flows. Similar to this is the Goal Visualization report, which employs the same graphical representation for how visitors flow through your defined funnel steps—and where they drop off.

Both these reports are cutting-edge, web-based data architecture and visualization aids to help you understand the movement of traffic around your site. Flow and goal visualization reports are discussed in Chapter 5.

Real-Time Reporting

A relatively new feature (October 2011), real-time reporting does exactly what you expect it to do—report your visitor data in real time. Typically, the delay between a visitor arriving on your site and showing in the real-time reports is only a couple of seconds. Not every single dimension and metric is available in the real-time reporting section. Currently the data set includes the following information:

- Locations: Visitor geolocation down to city level
- Content being viewed: Page URL
- Visitor type: New or returning
- Traffic source information: Referral source, medium, campaign name, keyword used (if via a search engine)

Real-time reports are discussed in Chapter 5.

API and Developer Platform

The Google Analytics Core Reporting application programming interface (API) allows programmers to extend Google Analytics in new and creative ways. Developers can integrate Google Analytics data into existing products or create stand-alone applications on which features can be built on (with no Google contact required). For example, users could see snapshots of their analytics data in developer-created dashboards and gadgets; have automatically updated Key Performance Indicators (KPIs) in Excel, PowerPoint, or Word documents; and view web visitor data integrated within CRM and CMS platforms.

Using the Google Analytics Core Reporting API is discussed in Chapter 12, "Integrating Google Analytics with Third-Party Applications."

Intelligence Engine and Alerts

The Google Analytics Intelligence reports provide automatic alerts for significant changes in data patterns from your website. Instead of requiring you to monitor reports and comb through data, Analytics Intelligence alerts you to the most significant information to pay attention to. In addition, you can create custom alerts and have an email sent to you when an alert is triggered. For example, Intelligence can automatically highlight a 200 percent surge in visits from Twitter last Monday or let you know that bounce rates of visitors from the United States dropped by 70 percent yesterday.

Intelligence reports are discussed in Chapter 5 and the creation of custom intelligence alerts is shown in Chapter 8, "Best Practices Configuration Guide."

Motion Charts

Motion charts are animated statistics to aid with data visualization (the result of Google's acquisition of Trendalyzer software). Motion charts add sophisticated multi-dimensional analysis to most Google Analytics reports. You can select metrics for the x-axis, y-axis, bubble size, and bubble color and view how these metrics interact over time. It's one of the first charts I look at to gain a big-picture overview of site performance prior to focusing on specific metrics. It allows you to expose data relationships that would be difficult to see in traditional static reports.

Motion charts are discussed in Chapter 5.

Page Load Time and Site Speed Reports

It has been well established by many studies that slow-to-load pages have a negative impact on the visitor experience. Reports have even monetized this for the case of an e-commerce website. Google Analytics has a dedicated report section (called Site Speed) where you can view your page download times and relate this to other metrics such as conversion rate, transaction rate, and so forth.

Page Load Time reports are discussed in Chapter 5.

Mobile Reporting

Google Analytics can track mobile visitors on smartphones and the older-generation feature phones. Smartphone users are tracked by default and do not require any modification to your tracking code or web pages. Users of feature phones (that is, those devices not able to execute JavaScript or set cookies) are tracked using a server-side code snippet on your mobile website. The Google Analytics mobile software development kit (SDK) supports PHP, Perl, JSP, and ASPX sites.

Tracking feature phone mobile visitors is discussed in the section "Tracking Mobile Visitors" in Chapter 6, "Getting Started: Initial Setup."

Pivot Views

If you are familiar with Excel, then pivot views (also known as pivot tables) will be familiar to you. Pivot views are powerful when it can be difficult to get summarized information from a flat table. Essentially, a pivot table helps you quickly gain insight, giving a table depth. Two pivot fields are available in Google Analytics reports.

Obtaining a pivot view report is shown in the section "Changing Table Views" in Chapter 4.

How Google Analytics Works

Google Analytics is both a broad brush and a scalpel when it comes to tracking and reporting on your website visitor data. In addition, because of its implementation simplicity, it is also incredibly flexible. The following sections will ensure that you understand the principles of how Google Analytics works.

The Google Analytics Tracking Code

From Chapter 2, "Available Methodologies and Their Accuracy," you gained an understanding of data-collection techniques and the role that cookies play in web analytics. Google Analytics is a page-tag solution that employs first-party cookies. By this method, all data collection, processing, maintenance, and program upgrades are managed by Google as a hosted service—also referred to as Software as a Service (SaaS). But what are the processes and data flow that make this work? These are best illustrated with the three-step schematic shown in Figure 3.2.

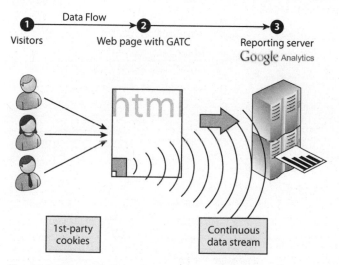

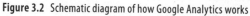

Figure 3.2 Schematic diagram of how Google Analytics works

Here are the steps:

1. Nothing happens until a visitor arrives at your website. This can be via many different routes, including search engines, social networks, email marketing, referral links, and so forth. Whatever the route, when the visitor views one of your pages with the Google Analytics Tracking Code (GATC), an automatic request is made for the file at `http://www.google-analytics.com/ga.js`. This is the Google Analytics master file—an 18 Kb JavaScript file that is downloaded only once during a visitor session. Further requests for it will be retrieved from the visitor's browser cache.

With the `ga.js` file in place, referrer information plus other visitor data (for example, page URL, time stamp, unique ID, screen resolution, color depth) are collected, and a set of first-party cookies is created to identify the visitor—or updated if the visitor is a returning one.

2. For each pageview, the GATC sends this information to Google data collection servers via a call of a transparent, 1×1-pixel GIF image (named `__utm.gif`) at `google-analytics.com`. In-page visitor actions (events) can also be tracked in this way, such as, for example, clicking to start a Flash animation. The entire transmission of data takes a fraction of a second.

3. At regular intervals, Google processes the collected data and updates your Google Analytics reports. However, because of the methodology and the huge quantity of data involved, reports are typically displayed 3 to 4 hours in arrears, and this may sometimes be longer, though it should not be more than 24 hours.

Data Processing Times and Freshness

In most cases, collating data from the multitude of data-collection servers is a smooth process, but sometimes things can go wrong. For example, a logfile transfer may be interrupted. Because of this, Google collects and reprocesses all data for a 24-hour period at the day's end. Therefore, don't panic if you have missing data for the current day. Should this persist for longer than 24 hours, contact the Google Analytics support team:

`www.google.com/support/googleanalytics/bin/request.py`

How fresh your Google Analytics data is (in other words, how up-to-date your report data is) depends on a number of factors. The most relevant is the volume of data you send to the Google Analytics collection servers. For most websites, your data is likely to be 3 to 4 hours in arrears. This may be significantly less if your site receives less than 10,000 visits per day. See the section "Google Analytics Limits" later in this chapter for further information.

By design, Google Analytics uses the same `ga.js` tracking snippet for all visitors and for all website owners. This means that it is cached by a very large proportion of web users—the advantage of having an adoption base of millions of websites including some very popular web properties. That's good news because it means that if a visitor to your website has previously visited another website that also runs Google Analytics, the `ga.js` file does not need to be downloaded at all—it will already be cached. The result is that Google Analytics has a minimal impact on your page-loading times. Typical file caching lasts for seven days, though this value can be adjusted in your browser configuration.

As you have probably realized from the description of Figure 3.2, if a visitor blocks the execution of JavaScript or blocks the setting of first-party cookies, or if you forgot to add the GATC to your page or your web server does not allow the GATC to execute (that is, it's behind a firewall), Google Analytics will not function and no data will be collected. Once data is lost, you cannot go back and reprocess it, so regular audits of your GATC deployment should be part of your implementation plan.

The GATC is discussed in greater detail in the section "Tagging Your Pages" in Chapter 6.

Do Not Use *urchin.js*

There are presently two versions of the Google Analytics Tracking Code (GATC) in existence: the original legacy code called urchin.js, which is no longer updated but still functioning, and the current ga.js code, which is what you require in order to benefit from the latest Google Analytics features, such as event tracking.

The current ga.js has been around a long time—launched at the end of 2007—and urchin .js is scheduled to be deprecated during 2012. If you are still using urchin.js, you should plan on replacing as soon as possible. To do this, log into your Google Analytics account as an administrator and click the Tracking Code link within each of your profile settings. Your new tracking code will be displayed.

Note that if you are also using urchin.js tracking code modifications (for example, capturing virtual pageviews), these will also need to be updated to the new format.

What Is Not Tracked by Default

By simply adding the GATC on your pages, you collect a wealth of information. Perhaps because there is so much data collected by default, people often assume the answer to their business question *must* be contained in the reports somewhere. However, when viewing their reports, apart from noting the overall traffic volume, they find that there are few business insights to be had. For this, you need to go beyond a basic install.

Having a complete picture of your visitor activity means tracking *all* possible visitor experience and engagement points. Once these are in place, you monetize them to obtain value. Value is the most important metric of your site—the value of a page, the value of a visitor, and the total value of your website.

Note: The last point is so important that I call it out again to double-emphasize it: Monetary value is the most important metric of your site—for both transactional and nontransactional sites. In fact, I argue that value is more important for a nontransactional site because you must first prove your return on investment if you are going to be successful in procuring the time, resources, and money to improve it. As I hope you have gathered, this book is aimed at businesses, not hobbyists!

A best practice installation of Google Analytics should include most of the following items—all of which can be achieved. However, they are not available by default in your reports. Some require a little lateral thought to set up; some require a more detailed examination of the options available to you. All are discussed in detail throughout this book:

Data structure If you own more than one website domain or subdomain—for example: mysite.com, mysite.co.uk, myproducts.com, store.mysite.com, and so on—what is the best way to structure your data so that your reports can be correlated back to the business? By default, Google Analytics collects all of your data into a single profile of reports. It cannot advise you if you should use separate profiles, separate accounts, roll-up reporting, or a combination of all three.

File downloads Files such as PDF, XLS, MP3, DOC, ZIP, and EXE are not web documents and cannot receive a GATC. Therefore, these are not tracked by default. See Chapter 7, "Advanced Implementation."

Outbound links Links that go to third-party websites, such as partners, affiliates, trade associations, and so forth, result in the visitor viewing a page that is not under your control and therefore not tracked. See Chapter 7.

In-page events In-page events that do not generate a pageview, such as clicking an Add To Cart button, are not tracked. In fact, many add-to-basket, user comments, rating systems, and fill-in forms do not generate a pageview. You therefore need to employ event tracking to capture these. See Chapter 7.

Flash animation A visitor's usage of and interaction with embedded Flash objects, such as product demos, videos, and so forth, are not tracked by default. See Chapter 7.

YouTube embedded videos A visitor's usage of and interaction with embedded YouTube videos, such as play, pause, and watch to completion, are not tracked by default. See Chapter 7.

Defining goals and monetizing them You will need to define what page URLs, events, or thresholds constitute a goal completion and assign a goal value for each of them when it is reached. Refer to Chapter 8.

E-commerce transactions Additional tracking code is required to capture e-commerce transaction and product item detail. Often a purchase will take place via a third-party payment gateway, breaking the session, yet this can be overcome. Refer to Chapter 7.

Keyword grouping Rather than look at reports on thousands of search engine keywords, you can group these along a theme, such as, for example "all branded search keywords," and so forth. Refer to "Example Custom Segments" in Chapter 8 for a method to group keywords.

Visitor types and labels Differentiate visitors who are members, subscribers, customers, almost-customers, and so forth from your anonymous and nonengaged visitors. Refer to Chapter 9.

Segmenting visitors These are groups or subsets of related data, such as, for example, only social media visits, segments by geographic location, keyword types, and so forth. Refer to Chapter 8.

Tracking error pages Often these are forgotten about for tracking purposes, or if they are tracked, they show as regular pageviews rather than error pages. Clearly tracking them is important, and Google Analytics provides the opportunity for them to be seen in content alongside other data. Once you know the answer to the question, How much do these errors cost our business? you can prioritize the fixes required. Refer to Chapter 9.

Tracking internal site-search usage This is very valuable information sent directly from your visitor's keyboard. Sometimes tracking it can be tricky if the visitor's query term is not contained in the URL. Also, tracking zero results of your site search is an important key performance indicator. Refer to Chapter 6, "Getting Started: Initial Setup," and Chapter 10, "Focusing on Key Performance Indicators," respectively.

The Default Attribution Model

By default, when you're viewing your conversion or e-commerce reports, only the last referrer is attributed the credit. For example, consider the following scenario:

- A visitor first views a banner ad on the Web and clicks through to your site. The visitor does not convert.

- Later the same day the visitor returns after performing a keyword query on a search engine. Still not convinced that they are ready to purchase (or convert into a lead), the visitor leaves your website.

- Later in the week, a friend of the visitor recommends via email a review article published on a blog. Happy with the review, the same visitor clicks the link from the blog article directly to your website. On this third visit, a purchase is made.

For this scenario, Google Analytics will show the referrer for each visit and the full referral path for this conversion—that is, banner > organic > referral (via the multichannel funnel reports mentioned earlier in this chapter and shown schematically in Figure 3.1). However, all transaction revenue, or goal revenue for a nontransactional site, is attributed to the final click-through. In this case, that's the referral blog website.

There is one exception to this rule: when the last referrer is *direct*. A direct visit means the visitor typed your website address directly into their browser or used a bookmark to arrive on your website. In that case, the penultimate referrer is given the credit. For example, using the preceding scenario, if the purchaser bookmarks your website and then later returns to make a repeat purchase by selecting the bookmark, credit for that conversion will still be given to the referring blog, the reasoning being that this was the campaign that converted your visitor into a customer and so should receive the credit. It would not make sense to attribute the credit or revenue to "direct."

As you may have guessed, a much better technique would be to attribute a share of the transaction, or goal revenue, to all of the referrers involved. After all, they all contributed to the end result. This is know as "attribution modeling" and is a Google Analytics Premium feature that is discussed later in this chapter.

 Note: The use of "direct" can be ambiguous when analyzing your referral data. Unless you have fully implemented campaign tracking, many visits can end up being classified as direct—for example, mobile app users, email marketing click-throughs, links from within documents (such as PDF, DOC, XLS, or PPT), RSS referrers, or even your email signature. Ensure that you have considered all of these possibilities for campaign tracking, as discussed in Chapter 7.

Google Analytics Limits

All software has its limits, and Google Analytics is no exception. Setting boundaries and limits prevents errors and system overload, and it ensures that other users of the service are not affected by the processing of someone else's data. For example, a website with a relatively low amount of traffic data should not have its reports delayed due to the processing of another user's data from a site that has more traffic.

Table 3.1 lists the limits set for the free version of Google Analytics to ensure that users have the best possible experience of the product. Note that most of these are advanced features that you will find described elsewhere in the book.

▶ **Table 3.1** Google Analytics limits

Limit	Value	Description	Comment
Table aggregation	50,000	The number of data rows in a table before aggregation is applied.	Once this value is reached, further data rows are aggregated into a single entry, labeled "other."
Custom variables	5		A single custom variable can have multiple values, and three scopes are available: page, visit, visitor.
Hits per session	500		A hit includes pageviews, events, transactions, or transaction items (anything that causes a __utm.gif hit to be sent). Any hits sent after this threshold are ignored.

Continues

Limit	Value	Description	Comment
Events per session	Rate limiting system	The rate limiting system starts a user with 10 tokens and awards a new token every 1 second. A maximum of 10 tokens can be accumulated.	Sending out a burst of event hits will exhaust the 10 available immediately and send out only a max of 1 hit per second until the event has slowed down long enough for the user to accumulate more than one token.
E-commerce transactions per day	50,000		This is actually the same as the table aggregation limit.
Unique dimension combinations	1,000,000	See: `http://code.google.com/apis/analytics/docs/concepts/gaConceptsSampling.html#reportSampling`	Above this limit, your report data is sampled.
Sessions for data where the report is not precalculated	500,000	See: `http://code.google.com/apis/analytics/docs/concepts/gaConceptsSampling.html#reportSampling`	Above this limit, your report data is sampled.
Goals per profile	20		Four goal sets containing up to 5 goals each.
Funnel steps per goal	10		
Number of hits per profile per day for intraday processing	1,000,000		Above this limit, data is processed only once per day (around midnight, PST).
Number of profiles per account	50		
Number of advanced segments per user login	100		
Number of characters to define a profile filter	256		
Data export limit	20,000		It is possible to manually export 20,000 rows multiple times.
`__utm.gif` request size	8,192 bytes	`http://analytics.blogspot.com/2011/04/leading-industry-with-tracking-code.html`	Requests longer than 2,048 bytes are sent via POST.
Custom variable length	128 bytes	`http://code.google.com/apis/analytics/docs/gaJS/gaJSApiBasicConfiguration.html#_gat.GA_Tracker_._setCustomVar`	Combined length cannot exceed this. Equivalent to 128 characters for single-byte character sets. The length is checked before URL encoding.

Continues

Limit	Value	Description	Comment
Rows returned by a Core Reporting API request	10,000		
Number of accounts per login	25	The number of accounts you can create from within your Google Analytics account login.	If you reach this limit, create another Google login and use this for your next 25 accounts. There is no limit to the number of accounts you can be granted access to.
Number of pageviews per month	10,000,000	As specified in the terms of service agreement.	If you exceed this limit, you will need to either sample your data collection or upgrade to Premium.
Data storage	25 months		If you require longer, consider Premium or Urchin software to archive your data.

What Google Analytics Does Not Do

As you might expect, I consider Google Analytics a great tool that has helped many organizations optimize and improve their websites. In some cases this had led to conversion improvements of tens of millions of dollars. However, the truth is that no one web analytics tool can achieve absolutely everything for an organization; there are just too many possibilities. Therefore, I'll summarize some of the things Google Analytics does not do and describe why that is and its significance.

Service-Level Agreement

Because Google Analytics is a free product, Google does not offer any guarantees or formal contract for its use. That said, many large organizations have a legal requirement for an official contract to procure products and services. If that describes you, review the Google Analytics Premium product described later in this chapter. Premium is a paid-for version of Google Analytics that includes a contract with service-levels guarantees.

Indefinite Data Retention

The current data retention policy for the free Google Analytics service is 25 months. If you require a longer period, review the Google Analytics Premium product later in this chapter. Premium is a paid-for version of Google Analytics that guarantees data for 36 months.

Provide Professional Services

The free version of Google Analytics comes with no professional services; that is, it is up to you to organize your implementation, training, analysis, and insights. To help you with this, there is a global network of third-party Google Analytics Certified Partners (GACP). The list of official GACPs is available at www.google.co.uk/analytics/partners.html.

The Google Analytics Premium product, described later in this chapter, includes professional services as part of the annual fee. You can choose to work with Google directly or with a Premium GACP.

Data Reprocessing

As shown in the schematic of Figure 3.2, the data flow of your web visitors and the processing by Google Analytics means that reports are always appending information to a previous report. So if there is an error in your implementation (for example, pages on your site missing the GATC or an incorrectly set-up filter), that error is carried through into the reports. The data will be missing or incorrect as the report timeline moves forward. Even when you correct this error, Google Analytics cannot go back in time and reprocess the data.

The reason for this is simple: The dataset of Google Analytics for all users is enormous and, prior to processing, is stored in aggregate form, that is, mixed with other Google Analytics accounts. At present it is not possible for Google to isolate and reprocess a single Google Analytics account.

Lack of data reprocessing is a genuine limitation that can be frustrating for any implementer. To mitigate this, you should always have a test profile that you can use to experiment with new filters and configuration settings before applying them to your main report profile; this is discussed in Chapter 8.

> ### The Data Mountain
>
> To give you an idea of the volume of data that Google Analytics must process each hour, 24 hours per day, consider the following:
>
> - If a typical website receives 100 visits per hour
> - And each visit generates 10 pageviews on average, or 1,000 pieces of data per hour
> - And assuming there are several million active Google Analytics accounts
>
> Google Analytics needs to process of the order of one billion lines of visit data each hour. Reprocessing a subset of this is not a simple task. However, it may be possible in the future.

Bid Management

Wouldn't it be great after viewing the performance of your AdWords visitors within your Google Analytics reports (for example, time in site, bounce rate, and e-commerce value), you could update bid strategy, pricing, and ad creatives all from within the same interface? That is not possible at present; you need to log into your AdWords account to make changes. However, I would expect Google to crack this nut in the not-too-distant future. After all, Google makes 97 percent of its $40-billion-per-year revenue from its pay-per-click advertising network.

Import Third-Party Data

At present, only cost data from AdWords and AdSense is imported, allowing ROI to be reported. That means visitor acquisition costs from, for example, other pay-per-click networks, banner advertising, email marketing, search engine optimization, and the like cannot be taken into account, and so these referrers have no associated ROI data within your reports, meaning a manual calculation for you.

Google's approach and philosophy is to provide easy access to your data—rather than becoming a data warehouse. As such, automating data access via APIs is common practice for most Google products, including Google Analytics. Therefore, if you wish to integrate your Google Analytics data with third-party information, use the Google Analytics Core Reporting API. This can be as straightforward as an import into Excel or as complicated as the building of a dedicated mash-up tool. Many developers already provide tools for doing this, and a prebuilt one may already exist. Integrating with third-party applications is discussed in Chapter 12. Third-party API tools for Google Analytics are shown in the Applications Gallery at www.google.com/analytics/apps.

Per-Visitor Tracking (against Google Policies)

In 2005, following the acquisition of the company and technology known as Urchin Software Inc., Google made the very deliberate decision not to track individuals (a feature that was in beta development at that time). That is, all website visitor data is reported within Google Analytics in an aggregate and anonymous form.

While it is attractive for advertisers to identify visitors from their previous visit behavior, from Google's point of view, it is a step too far—invading the right of the end user's privacy (that of the general public) by using Google Analytics.

Of course, if you have a special arrangement with your visitors whereby they do not mind such individual tracking, Urchin software is an alternative tool—see the last section in this chapter.

What Is Google Analytics Premium?

In September 2011, Google announced Google Analytics Premium—its paid-for version of Google Analytics. This is not a new version of Google Analytics, rather an extension of the free product to cater to the needs of enterprise clients. It's important to note that Premium does not replace the free Google Analytics product, or in any way undermine it in my opinion. In fact, it complements the free product because it specifically targets large organizations, such as, for example, Fortune 500 types that so far have had difficulty "procuring" a free product. Therefore, Google has developed the Premium version to address four enterprise needs:

- Increased processing power
- Contract and service-level agreement
- Professional services included
- Enterprise features

Note: The Google Analytics Premium website is found at: www.google.com/analytics/premium.

These are described in more detail in the following list. At present, Google Analytics Premium is billed at a flat fee of $150,000 per year.

Increased processing power The Premium product has additional processing power that can handle up to 1 billion hits per month, with a data freshness guarantee of 4 hours. There is also the option to download unsampled data. Extra processing resources are required if you have a heavily trafficked website, that is, more than 10 million data hits per months (approximately 1 million visits).

Contract and service-level agreement The guaranteed service levels are summarized as follows:

- Data collection uptime = 99.9%
- Reporting uptime = 99.0%
- Data freshness = 98.0%

In addition, the contract states explicitly that the client formally owns all collected data.

Professional services included The annual price tag of Google Analytics Premium—currently set at a flat fee of $150,000 per year—includes a comprehensive list of the following professional services:

- Implementation and setup
- Dedicated named account management
- Training and education

- Ongoing support
- 24/7 emergency escalation

These are available from Google Analytics Premium Authorized Resellers or direct from Google.

Enterprise features The approach Google adopted here is *not* to produce exclusive features for Premium but rather to include only features that are of real value to enterprise customers and of little value to smaller organizations. Hence, the criteria for a feature to be included only in the Premium product is threefold:

- The feature appeals only to a limited number of clients.
- The feature requires additional skill or service for it to be used properly. In other words, configuring the feature without fully understanding its implications could seriously damage your data insights.
- The feature would be computationally prohibitive for Google to add by default for all accounts in the free version.

Employing these criteria results in only a small number of Premium-only features. In the following paragraphs, I will present two examples of Premium-only features that are at opposite ends of the complexity spectrum.

At the simplistic level, the data retention for Premium customers is longer—set at 36 months. This compares to 25 months for the free version. This fulfills the first and second feature criteria listed for becoming a Premium-only feature. That is, it is computationally expensive to store large amounts of data for long periods of time, and the vast majority of users rarely look back at more than 12 months of data.

A Word of Caution for Attribution Modeling

Attribution modeling sounds like a panacea for a longstanding issue of deciding which of your referrers should receive credit for a conversion. The theory is, for example, that banners spark interest, organic search provides background and research material (reviews, comparisons and so forth), and paid search gives the quick purchase opportunity. With a last-click-wins approach, you would clearly overinflate the importance of paid search while undervaluing the impact of other referrers.

However, the model assumes your visitors are using the same device for each visit. With the proliferation of smartphones and tablets, along with users combining laptops and desktops—for example, checking online at home and at work—that is increasingly not the case.

At best, attribution modeling is a guide to valuing your referral marking strategy—it is not an exact science. As with all things web analytics, use relative differences and trends in your analysis and interpretation of results rather than absolute values.

> ## What Now for the Free Version?
>
> Google Analytics Premium is a relatively new offering, and the development of its enterprise features are still fluid. However, employing the listed criteria shown for features earlier results in only a small number of them made available to Premium-only customers. In fact, the vast majority of Google Analytics features are relevant to all users. The releases of real-time reporting, multi-channel funnels, and flow visualization reports are great examples of powerful features, recently announced, that are included in the free product for all users.
>
> As mention at the beginning of this chapter, both small and large organizations share the same analytics requirements. My point is that since the launch of the paid-for service, there is no sign (or intention that I am aware of) that the free version of Google Analytics is going to become a poor person's product.

A more complex Premium-only feature is attribution modeling. This fulfills the second and third selection criteria. That is, attribution modeling is only relevant to a small user base, and it requires an additional skill set to ensure that it adds value to your data rather than misleads you. Essentially, attribution modeling is an enhancement of the Multi-Channel Funnel reports mentioned earlier in this chapter in the section "Advanced Features." It enables you to attribute purchase revenue (or goal value) proportionally, back through all or some of the referrers that have contributed to the visitor becoming a customer.

For example, consider a digital campaign that is simultaneously deployed via AdWords, email, display banners, and social network engagement. Your potential customer may be exposed to many of your campaigns, possibly even all. The traditional model of web analytics, and that used in the free version, is that the last click wins. That is, the last referrer in the chain is the one that is attributed the full goal or purchase amount. The use of attribution modeling allows each referrer in the chain to be assigned a proportion of the revenue.

Comparing Google Analytics Premium versus Free

If you are happy to work with a free-of-charge product from Google without the need to sign a formal contract, then the free product is probably the best fit for you. If, however, procuring a free product is difficult for your organization, and service-level agreements are important to you, then Premium is the product to choose.

Putting your procurement process to one side, the next key factor to consider is likely to be the volume of data you need to process. If you receive less than 1 million visits per month, the free product will meet your needs. If your traffic volumes regularly exceed 1 million visits per month, then consider the Premium product. Simply put, Google Analytics Premium has greater horsepower, allowing it to not only handle the larger data volume, but also process it quicker and keep your report data fresh.

Table 3.2 compares Google Analytics Premium versus the free product in full.

▶ **Table 3.2** Comparing Google Analytics Premium versus free

	Premium	Free
Cost	$150,000 per year. Flat fee, payable monthly in arrears.	None.
Processing power	Allows for 1 billion hits per month.	Allows for 10 million hits per month. Above this and you will need to sample your data collection.
	Report freshness: Guaranteed to be no older than 4 hours, though often this is within an hour.	Report freshness: No guarantees, though for sites with between 50,000 and 1 million hits per day, freshness is typically 3–4 hours. For above 1 million hits, reports are processed once each day. Real-time reporting is not affected by this.
	Display limit: Table aggregation set at 1 million rows. After this, the remaining table data is grouped into "other."	Display limit: Table aggregation set at 50,000 rows. After this, the remaining table data is grouped into "other."
	Data is statistically sampled when a report is generated from more than 50 million visits. Unsampled report downloads available (up to 1 million rows).	Data is statistically sampled when a report is generated from more than 500,000 visits.
	Data export limit set at 1 million rows.	Data export limit set at 20,000 rows.
Features	Multi-channel attribution modeling allowing you to attribute revenue or goal value to any or all referrers that drive your conversions.	Not available.
	Number of custom variables: 50.	Number of custom variables: 5.
	Three years' data retention.	25 months' data retention.
Service-level agreement and guarantee	Yes. Data collection uptime = 99.9% Reporting uptime = 99.0% Data freshness = 98.0% Client formally owns all collected data.	No guarantees.
Professional services	Included with the annual fee: • Implementation • Training and education • Dedicated account manager • Support via telephone and email • 24/7 support emergency escalation • Professional services provided by official Google Analytics Certified Premium Partners and Google Direct	Open market. User may purchase professional services from whomever they wish. Third-party network of over 200 Google Analytics Certified Partners (GACP).

What If You Cannot Afford Premium?

There are some websites that have high traffic volumes yet cannot justify the cost of the Premium product—perhaps due to lack of internal staffing resources or the ability to make proper use of the information. If the Premium product is not within your budget, you will need to adjust your data collection strategy to mitigate the limits of the free product.

The most obvious consideration you face is the 10 million data hits per month limit—where a hit can be a pageview, an event, or a transaction item. Therefore, ensure that you are not collecting unnecessary data that is inflating your hit count. The following can help you reduce your data load and potentially avoid having to sample your data collection:

- Ensure that you exclude any session IDs or other superfluous data by using the Exclude URL Query Parameters feature in your profile settings. This is discussed in the "Initial Configuration" section of Chapter 8, "Best Practices Configuration Guide."

- Use event tracking only for events that contain useful information. For example, I have seen a Flash movie tracker triggering an event for each second of play so that the number of seconds played could be reported on. This would be better managed by bucketing the event calls into 10-second blocks, or longer, for example. However, on discussing this with the marketing team, only the fact that the movie was started and watched to completion was relevant to them. That is just two events and considerably less data sent to Google Analytics. Event tracking is discussed in Chapter 7.

- Structure your data in a way that makes sense. For example, rather than placing everything together, consider the use of spreading your data over different Google Analytics web properties and even separate Google Analytics accounts. Using extra Google Analytics accounts is discussed in "Roll-up Reporting" in Chapter 6.

If after applying some, or all, of these suggestions you still exceed the 10 million hits per month limit, you will need to sample your data collection to continue using the free product. Don't worry, this is statistically viable and will still provide good data for your reports—as long as you are not an e-commerce site. Data collection sampling is described in Chapter 7.

Google Analytics and Privacy

Those of you who have read my blog or heard me speak know that I am a strong advocate of end-user privacy, that is, the right of the end user (general public) to not be tracked in any identifiable way while using the Web.

To be clear, providing the end user with the right to not be identified does not mean giving the user the option of *opting out* of such tracking by reading verbose, jargon-filled terms and conditions (as an example, the Myspace.com privacy policy currently stands at 2,752 words and is noticeably written by a legal professional rather than from an end user's point of view). Instead, the default position should be to track visitors only in an anonymous and aggregate way, unless they give their express permission by *opting in*. That's a best practice approach and will ensure that you have the trust and loyalty of your visitors and customers—something that is always good for business.

As discussed in the previous section, all Google Analytics reports contain aggregate non–personally identifiable information. That has been a deliberate policy of Google toward its products. Speaking from my own experience, it is a vision and commitment that comes from the very top of the organization and played a key role in my decision to work for Google.

With that in mind, three parties are involved in the Google Analytics tracking scenario: Google, an independent website, and a visitor to that website. Google has designed its privacy practices to address each of these participants by requiring each website that uses Google Analytics to abide by the privacy provisions in the terms of service, specifically section 7 (see www.google.com/analytics/tos.html):

7. PRIVACY . You will not (and will not allow any third party to) use the Service to track or collect personally identifiable information of Internet users, nor will You (or will You allow any third party to) associate any data gathered from Your website(s) (or such third parties' website(s)) with any personally identifying information from any source as part of Your use (or such third parties' use) of the Service. You will have and abide by an appropriate privacy policy and will comply with all applicable laws relating to the collection of information from visitors to Your websites. You must post a privacy policy and that policy must provide notice of your use of a cookie that collects anonymous traffic data.

> **Note:** The content of section 7 of tos.html may vary depending on which country you operate in. Ensure that you view the most relevant terms of service for your country/region.

The Google Analytics cookies collect standard Internet log data and visitor behavior information in an anonymous form. They do not collect any personal information such as addresses, names, or credit card numbers. The logs include standard log information such as IP address, time and date stamp, browser type, and operating system. The behavior information includes generic surfing information such as the number of pages viewed, language setting, and screen resolution settings in the browser and can include information about whether or not a goal was completed by the visitor to the website. The website can define the goal to mean different things, such as whether a visitor downloaded a PDF file, completed an e-commerce transaction, visited more than one page, and so on. Note that Google Analytics does not track a user across multiple unrelated sites, and it uses different cookies for each website.

Google Analytics prepares anonymous and statistical reports for the websites that use it. As you will see in the next chapter, such reports include different information views and show data such as geographic location (based on generic IP-based geolocation codes), time of visit, and so on. These reports are anonymous and statistical. They do not include any information that could identify an individual visitor; for example, they do not include IP addresses.

Common Privacy Questions

The following questions are typical questions asked by potential Google Analytics clients:

- What does Google do with the data it collects?
- Who at Google sees the analytics data?
- How securely is data kept?
- As a website owner, what is my obligation to data privacy?

I answer these questions from my own perspective, having worked at Google for a number of years.

- What does Google do with the data it collects?

  Google Analytics is a tool specifically targeted at advertisers (and potential advertisers) who want to gain a better understanding of their website traffic. In fact, it is one of many tools that make up what I refer to as an advertiser's toolkit. Others include Google Trends, Google Insights, Webmaster Central, Product Search (formally Froogle), Google Maps, Website Optimizer, Google Base, and Checkout. Google Analytics provides advertisers with the transparency and accountability they need in order to have confidence in the pay-per-click, online auction model. Essentially, a happy advertiser is good for business.

  Keep in mind that the Google AdWords auction model prevents anyone from interfering with the pricing of ads. The system is completely transparent, so it would be ludicrous for Google to artificially adjust bids—destroying a business overnight. On the Web, the competition is always only one click away, and Microsoft and Yahoo! are serious competitors in this space.

Note: Google does not sell Google Analytics data to any third party. Google's general privacy policy details how it handles data of all types: www.google.com/intl/en/privacy/privacy-policy.html.

- Who at Google sees the analytics data?

  Google Analytics data, as with all data at Google, is accessed on a strict need-to-know basis; for example, it can be accessed by support staff and maintenance engineers. If, as a client, you want Google staff to look at your reports (to provide help with managing an AdWords campaign, for example), then you must request this from your Google account manager or via the Google Analytics Help Center (www.google.com/support/googleanalytics/).

  In addition, you will need to explicitly allow "support access" for your login name. You do this from your account Settings screen, as shown in Figure 3.3. Without the Support Access setting enabled, Google staff will not be able to access your report data. All internal Google access to your reports is monitored for auditing purposes.

- How securely is the analytics data kept?

  Data security and integrity are paramount for continued end-user confidence in all Google services. Therefore, Google Analytics data is subject to the same rigorous security checks and audits as all other Google products. Of course, one can never be 100 percent certain of security in any organization, but Google employs some of the best industry professionals in the world to ensure that its systems remain secure.

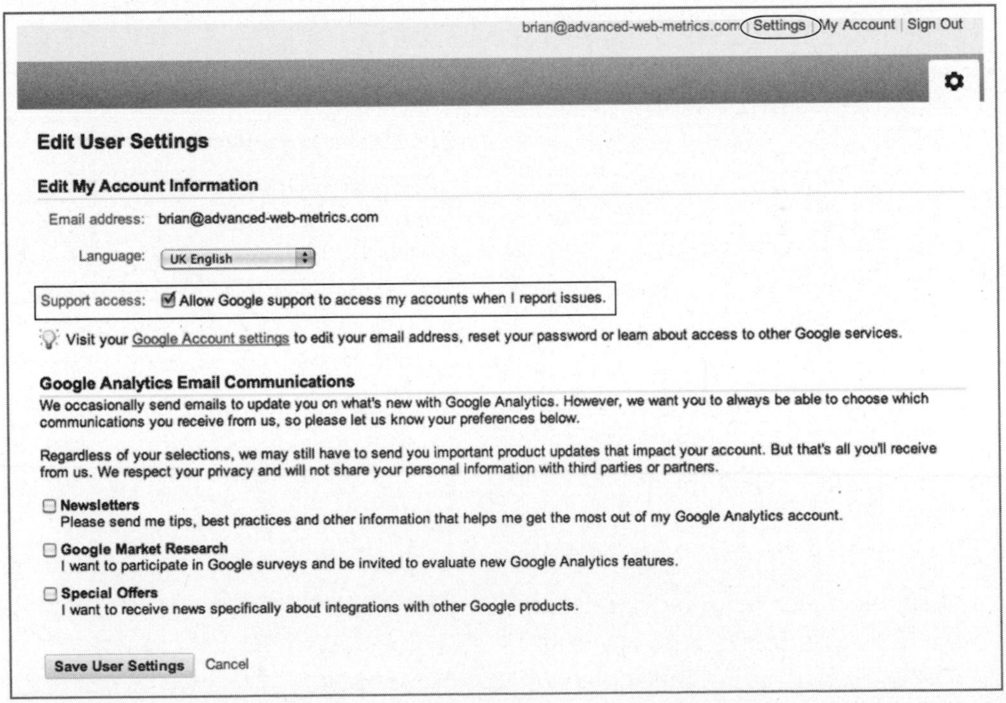

Figure 3.3 Allowing Google Analytics support staff to access your data

- As a website owner, what is my obligation to data privacy?

In addition to Google's commitment to data privacy and integrity, owners of websites that use Google Analytics also have an obligation to visitor privacy. In fact, this is true for any analytics solution. For Google Analytics, the terms of service state that you will not associate any data gathered from your website with any personally identifiable information. You will, of course, also need to comply with all applicable data protection and privacy laws relating to your use of Google Analytics and have in place (in a prominent position on your website) an appropriate privacy policy.

These are commonsense best practice approaches to owning a website and collecting visitor information about its usage. However, I recommend that you view your obligations as a website owner from the terms of service link at the bottom of any page on the Google Analytics website (www.google.com/analytics). To ensure that you read the most relevant terms for your location, select the region that most closely matches your own from the country drop-down menu at the top of the page.

Best Practice Privacy Statement When Using Google Analytics

The following is a best practice example of a clear privacy statement when using Google Analytics—modified from the Information Commissioner's Office, the UK independent authority to protect personal information (www.ico.gov.uk) and a Google Analytics user:

Our Policy for Protecting Your Online Privacy

This website uses Google Analytics to help analyze how users use the site. The tool uses "cookies," which are text files placed on your computer, to collect standard Internet log information and visitor behavior information in an anonymous form. The information generated by the cookie about your use of the website (including your IP address) is transmitted to Google. This information is then used to evaluate visitors' use of the website and to compile statistical reports on website activity for Your_Company_Name.

We will never (and will not allow any third party to) use the statistical analytics tool to track or to collect any Personally Identifiable Information of visitors to our site. Google will not associate your IP address with any other data held by Google. Neither we nor Google will link, or seek to link, an IP address with the identity of a computer user. We will not associate any data gathered from this site with any Personally Identifiable Information from any source, unless you explicitly submit that information via a fill-in form on our website.

Further Information about Cookies

The Interactive Advertising Bureau (IAB) is an industry body that develops standards and guidelines to support online business processes. It has produced a series of web pages that explain how cookies work and how they can be managed at www.allaboutcookies.org.

If you have questions concerning our privacy policy, please use our contact details to discuss them.

What Is Urchin?

Although this book's focus is Google Analytics, it is worth mentioning that Google has two web analytics products: Google Analytics and Urchin software.

Urchin Software Inc. is the company and technology that Google acquired in April 2005 that then went on to become Google Analytics—a free web analytics service that uses the resources at Google. Urchin software is a downloadable web analytics program that runs on a local server (Unix or Windows). It creates reports by processing web server logfiles and is commonly referred to as *server-side web analytics*. The server-side data collection approach is discussed in Chapter 2. Example screen shots of Urchin software (version 7) are shown in Figure 3.4 and Figure 3.5.

Urchin is essentially the same technology as Google Analytics—the difference when using Urchin is that your organization needs to provide the resources for log storage and data processing. As Table 2.1 in Chapter 2 shows, logfile tools can report on information that page-tag solutions alone cannot provide. Therefore, Urchin software provides some reports that Google Analytics currently does not (because of its methodology) and can be used to complement your Google Analytics reports. Let's look at some examples:

Per-visitor tracking Tracking individual visitors enables you to view the path a visitor takes through your website as well as their referral information. As discussed earlier in this chapter, for privacy reasons Google has deliberately made the decision not to track individuals with Google Analytics. However, with the data collection and processing under your control, you have the freedom to do this with Urchin. Each visitor is tracked anonymously.

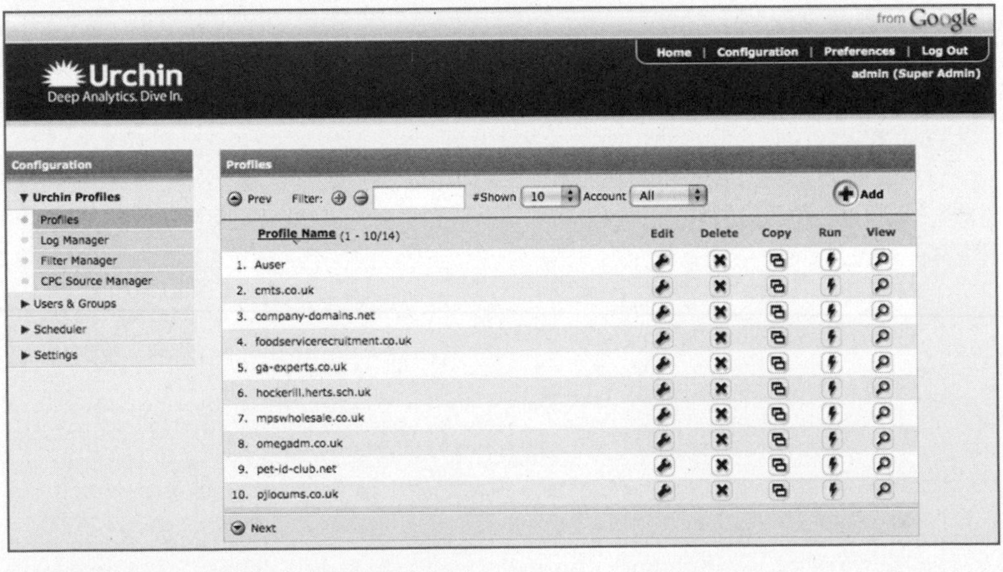

Figure 3.4 Urchin 7 administrator's configuration screen

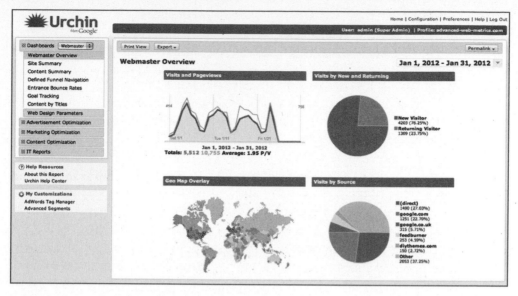

Figure 3.5 Urchin 7 visitor overview report

Not just pageviews and events More than reporting on completed page views and events that you set up (as is the case for Google Analytics), Urchin reports on all activity that your web server logs. For example, actual file downloads (not just the intent of clicking), partial downloads and any error code is reported by default in Urchin, and this is without any configuration or changes to your pages required.

Bandwidth reports Reporting on bandwidth allows you to view how "heavy" your content is and how this impacts the visitor's experience—That is, *all* content, not just pages, as is the case for Google Analytics.

Login reports If your website has a login area, you can report on this access by username. This supports standard Apache (.htaccess) or any authentication that logs usernames in the logfile.

Differences between Google Analytics and Urchin

With two analytics products from Google to choose from, how do you determine which one is right for your organization? As you may have guessed from the title of this book, Google Analytics is perfect for most organizations, for two very simple reasons:

- Google Analytics is a free service. This is generally considered a major benefit for small and medium-size organizations where budgets for analysis are tight. Urchin software is a licensed product and therefore must be purchased (currently $9,995 per installation).

- Google Analytics handles a large part of the IT overhead. That is, Google conducts the data collection, storage, program maintenance, and upgrades for you. This is generally considered a major benefit for large organizations where web analytics is a priority for the marketing department and less so for the IT department. If your organization is using Urchin software, it is responsible for the IT overhead. Hence, good interdepartmental communication (IT and marketing) is required.

The second point is not trivial. In fact, in my experience, the IT overhead of implementing tools was the main reason web analytics remained a niche industry for such a large part of its existence. Maintaining your own logfiles has an overhead, mainly because web server logfiles get very large, very quickly. As a guide, every 1,000 visits produce approximately 4 MB of log info. Therefore, 10,000 visits per month are approximately 500 MB per year. If you have 100,000 visits per month, that's 5 GB per year, and so on. Those are just estimates—for your own site, these could easily double. At the end of the day, managing large logfiles isn't something your IT department gets excited about. In fact, because it is not mission critical for running your website, it is often forgotten about—with disastrous consequences for your reporting.

Urchin also requires disk space for its processed data (stored in a proprietary database). Though this will always be a smaller size than the raw collected numbers, storing and archiving all this information is an important task because if you run out of disk space, you risk file or database corruption from disk-write errors. This kind of file corruption is almost impossible to recover from.

As an aside, if you maintain your own visitor data logfiles, the security and privacy of collected information (your visitors) also become your responsibility. The protection and privacy of online visitor data is becoming increasingly important in many countries, particularly the European Union. See the section "The EU Privacy Law" in Chapter 2 for example.

Urchin Advantages

With so many considerations and caveats, as just described, why might you consider Urchin software at all? Urchin software does have some real advantages over Google Analytics. For example, data is recorded and stored by your web server rather than streamed to Google, which means the following:

Data processing and reprocessing Urchin can process data as and when you wish, such as, for example, on the hour, every hour. You can also reprocess data—to apply a filter retroactively or to correct a filter error. Google Analytics reports are three to four hours in arrears (usually longer for high traffic websites) and cannot be reprocessed retroactively. In my opinion, the benefit of reprocessing data is the strongest advantage of Urchin.

Unlimited data storage Urchin can keep and view data for as long as you wish. Google Analytics currently commits to keeping data for a maximum of 25 months.

Third-party auditing Urchin allows your data to be audited by an independent third party. This is usually important for publishers who sell advertising space on their site, where auditing is required to verify visitor numbers and provide credibility for advertisers (trust in their rate card). Google Analytics does not pass data to third parties.

Intranets and firewalls Urchin works behind the firewall; that is, it's suitable for intranets. Google Analytics page tags cannot run behind a closed firewall.

Database access Urchin stores data locally in a proprietary database and includes tools that can be used to access the raw data outside a web browser, allowing you to run ad hoc queries. Google Analytics stores data in remote locations within Google datacenters around the world in proprietary databases and does not provide direct access to the raw data for ad hoc queries. That said, the Google Analytics Core Reporting API does allow you to query your processed data.

> **Note:** Urchin is sold and supported exclusively through a network of Urchin Software Authorized Consultants. For a full list of USACs, see www.google.com/urchin/usac.html.

Criteria for Choosing between Google Analytics and Urchin

There are a few crucial issues to consider when choosing one of the Google analytic services, detailed in the following list. Generally, in addition to intranets, Urchin is used mostly by web-hosting providers and platform or IT architecture providers, where deployment scalability for large numbers of websites is important. Google Analytics, apart from being a free service, is used by organizations that wish to have greater control of their *individual* web analytics implementation.

When Google Analytics is the best fit Select Google Analytics if you are a marketer wishing to measure the success (or not) of your website, its ability to convert, and the effectiveness of online marketing. Google Analytics is much easier to implement, has stronger AdWords integration, and by comparison is maintenance free.

When Urchin is the best fit Select Urchin if you are a developer and any of the following conditions apply:

- You have an intranet site behind a firewall that blocks Internet activity. Google Analytics is a hosted solution that needs access to the Internet in order to work.

- You are unable to add JavaScript tracking code to your pages.

- You are a hosting provider wishing to offer visitor reports to thousands of customers. Urchin has a command-line interface that can be scripted to create and modify multiple website reports at once. That is, Urchin has greater flexibility when it comes to large-scale, multiuser deployments.

When you need both Select both if you need the flexibility of maintaining your own visitor data, such as, for example, for third-party auditing purposes or long-term year-on-year analysis. Combining Google Analytics with Urchin software gives you the best of both worlds—the advanced features of Google Analytics (free) and the flexibility of Urchin (data control). The section "Back Up: Keeping a Local Copy of Your Data" in Chapter 6 discusses how you can configure your page tags to stream data to Google Analytics and Urchin simultaneously.

My personal view is to use Google Analytics wherever possible. It is easier to implement, has more advanced features, has a slicker user interface, and is primarily aimed at digital marketers. Urchin software is aimed at IT departments and should be used where there is a specific technical need that Google Analytics cannot fulfill. For example, use it for reprocessing data or retaining data for long periods of time. If you feel Urchin is a good fit for your organization, use both tools together.

Summary

In Chapter 3, you have learned the following:

Key features You explored the key features and capabilities of Google Analytics, which will enable you to ascertain what it can do for you and whether it is suitable for the analytics needs of your organization.

The principles of how it all works You learned how Google Analytics works from a nontechnical perspective so that you can understand how Google Analytics collects and processes data.

Google's position on data integrity and privacy Google Analytics takes its responsibility for visitor data seriously in terms of Google Analytics users and website visitors.

The uniqueness of the Google approach You saw how Google Analytics is different from other approaches and what drives its business model.

Considerations for server-side analytics You learned what Urchin software is, how it compares with Google Analytics, and what criteria you should consider when selecting an analytics product from Google.

Using Google Analytics Reports

Part II is intended as a familiarization jump start, aimed to get you up to speed with using the Google Analytics report interface as quickly and efficiently as possible. Consider it your user guide, walking you through the important aspects of using reports so you can understand website visitor behavior. Rather than describe every report, I've highlighted the key areas as well as how to find your way around the information presented. I've deliberately focused on the most important and interesting aspects of reports and what you need to know first to enjoy the process of discovering more of Google Analytics's capabilities and going deeper into the data in your own time.

In Part II, you will learn about the following:

II

Using the Google Analytics Interface

The Google Analytics user interface makes use of the latest developments in Web 2.0 technology to construct report data in a highly accessible, industry-leading format. For example, rather than use a side menu to navigate through different reports (though that is available), the user is encouraged to drill into the data itself.

In this chapter we review the Google Analytics interface, particularly in relation to discovering information. By understanding the report layout, you will quickly become accustomed to drilling down into the data, investigating whether a number or trend is good, bad, or indifferent for your organization.

In Chapter 4, you will learn:

Discoverability and the context of data

The difference between dimensions and metrics

How to navigate your way around the plethora of information

How to manipulate data tables and charts

How to schedule exports of data

The value of segmentation and pivot views

How to annotate charts to highlight key events

Discoverability and Initial Report Access

A common complaint from users of other web analytics tools is that the vast quantity of data generated is often overwhelming and difficult to find. The result is that report users get lost and frustrated—unable to decipher the information—and the web metrics project can stall at this point. Such feedback enabled Google to build an intuitive Google Analytics report interface focused on the user, usually a marketer, as opposed to the data. The revised user interface design (the team responsible came from MeasureMap, a Google acquisition) has proved so successful in user-experience studies that the format is being adopted throughout Google—notice the similarly styled graphs you now see in AdWords, AdSense, FeedBurner, and the geomap overlay of Google Insights, for example.

In addition to making the data very accessible, the user interface enhances *discoverability*. By this I mean how easy it is for you to ascertain whether the report you are looking at is good news, bad news, or indifferent to your organization. In other words, Google Analytics simplifies the process of turning raw data into useful information so that you can take appropriate action, such as reward your team, fix something, or change your benchmarks.

The Google Analytics drill-down interface differs from other web analytics tools that have a menu-driven style of navigation. You can select menu-driven navigation if you prefer it, but the Google Analytics interface makes it much easier to explore your data in context—that is, within the data, so that you do not waste your time navigating back and forth between reports to answer your questions. In addition, links within the reports suggest related information, and fast, interactive segmentation enables you to reorganize data on-the-fly. Short narratives, scorecards, and *sparklines* summarize your data at every level. Moreover, to help you understand, interpret, and act on data relationships, context-sensitive help articles are available in every report.

Simple and Effective Data Visualization

A sparkline is a mini-image (thumbnail) of graphical data that enables you to put numbers in a temporal context without the need to display full charts. For example, the following screen shot shows an array of numbers that on their own would be meaningless. However, the sparkline graphics show these in context by illustrating the trends over the time period selected. It's a neat and condensed way of conveying a lot of information—originally an invention of Edward Tufte, a pioneer of data visualization (http://en.wikipedia.org/wiki/Edward_Tufte).

62.43% Bounce Rate

00:02:47 Average Time on Site

74.99% Percentage New Visits

Assuming you already have a Google Analytics account (or have access to one), Figure 4.1 schematically illustrates the report-access process. As with all Google products, access to your Google Analytics account is via your *Google Login*—a Google-registered email address that can be any email address you control, such as `me@my-organization.com`. Your Google Account is your centralized access point. From it, you may have access to multiple Google Analytics accounts, each one with multiple web properties and profiles (report sets).

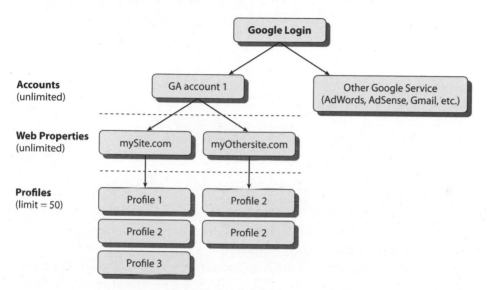

Figure 4.1 Schematic access process for Google Analytics reports

When you first log in to your Google Analytics account, you will be presented with the Account Home screen, shown in Figure 4.2. At first, this will most likely contain only a single web property and single profile, created when your Google Analytics account was initially opened. However, in an agency environment you may have access to many Google Analytics accounts and hence you will see additional accounts, web properties, and profiles. This is the case for Figure 4.2, which shows two accounts, three web properties (labeled with a P), and eight profiles. Note that if you are logging in via AdWords, the exact layout may appear slightly different.

At this stage, consider a profile to be defined as a *report set*, that is, a set of Google Analytics reports dedicated for a particular purpose, such as UK visitors only, US visitors only, and so forth. The use of profiles is discussed in the section titled "Using Accounts, Web Properties, and Profiles" in Chapter 6, "Getting Started: Initial Setup."

Tip: You can preview Google Analytics capabilities at `www.google.com/analytics/tour.html`. The walkthrough is in English, with other languages shown as subtitles.

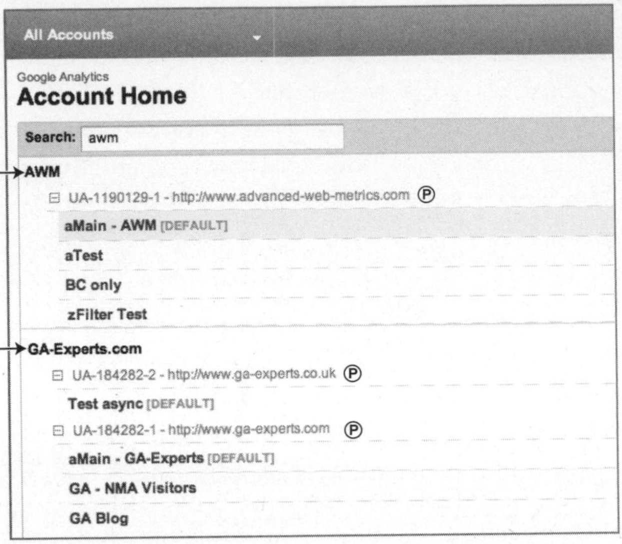

Figure 4.2 Account Home screen for two Google Analytics accounts containing three web properties and eight profiles

Navigating Your Way Around: Report Layout

As with all web-based software applications, the best way to get to know its capabilities is to see it in action. With the Google Analytics report interface, you can do this quickly, which is one of its key strengths. The report screen shots used in this chapter are taken from the Traffic Sources > Sources > All Traffic report, found by navigating through the menu shown in Figure 4.3.

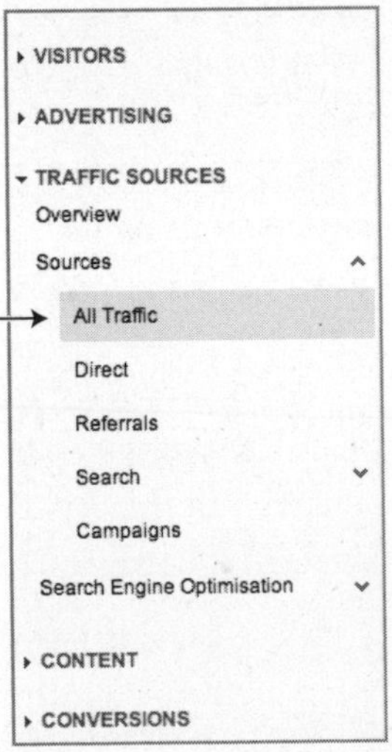

Figure 4.3 Use the All Traffic report as a starting place for learning the user interface.

An example of a typical report is shown in Figure 4.4. The key areas I describe in this chapter are labeled. I'll use this as a guide for introducing the features of the Google Analytics user interface. If you have access to a Google Analytics account, I recommend having it at hand while reading this chapter in order to become familiar with the points discussed.

> **Note:** Everything described in this chapter is part of the Standard Reporting suite in Google Analytics. This is selected by default when you view your profile reports and is highlighted in the orange menu bar at the top of Figure 4.4. Apart from Standard Reporting Suite, there are three other important menu items in the top orange bar: Home, Custom Reporting, and the Settings icon to the right—you will see the Settings icon only if you have administrative access to the profile you are viewing. The Home area contains real-time reports, your dashboards, intelligence events, and flow visualization reports. These are discussed in Chapter 5, "Reports Explained." Custom reporting is described in Chapter 9, "Google Analytics Customizations."

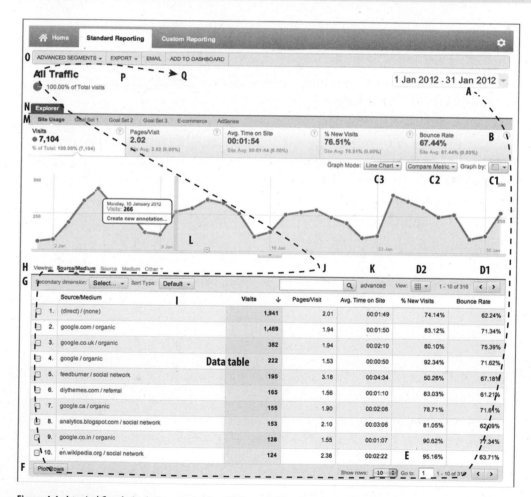

Figure 4.4 A typical Google Analytics report with guideline path (also shown in the color section)

Although Google Analytics is the industry leader for its information architecture, if you are new to web analytics, the layout of the reports can still appear daunting—there is simply a lot of information to convey and to digest. However, once you understand the basic layout, you will quickly realize just how intuitive it is to use.

The dotted path I have used in Figure 4.4 is typical for how I examine a report for the first time. Essentially, my eyes travel in a clockwise fashion—starting from the date selector at the top-right corner, down through the data table, past the footer options, around to the dimension selector and table filter, up through the data chart and the report tab menu, then across to the advanced segments, export features, and Dashboard. The path also approximately translates to the data granularity. That is, the further around you explore, the more detail is revealed.

The following sections describe each of the labels in detail. However, I first need to clarify the terminology of dimensions and metrics.

Dimensions and Metrics

Two types of data are represented in Google Analytics reports, dimensions and metrics:

- *Dimensions* are text strings that describe an item. Think of them as names, such as page URL or title, referral source, medium, keyword, campaign name, browser type, transaction ID, product name, and so on. Dimensions are the first column of data that is shown in a report—see the left side of the table in Figure 4.4.

- *Metrics* are the numbers associated with a dimension. For example, number of visitors, time on page, time on site, number of pageviews per visit, bounce rate, revenue, goal value, and so forth.

Figure 4.5 illustrates the separation of dimensions and metrics in a report table. Throughout Google Analytics you will notice that the convention is for dimensions to be color-coded green, while metrics are color-coded in blue.

Note: The labels referred to in the following sections correspond to those shown in Figure 4.4.

The Data Table

I begin the exploration of Figure 4.4 with the part highlighted as the data table. This refers to the entire table of data for a report and is the core information for your analysis. I briefly summarize the impact of changing table settings here with further details described in the sections for each label, A to R.

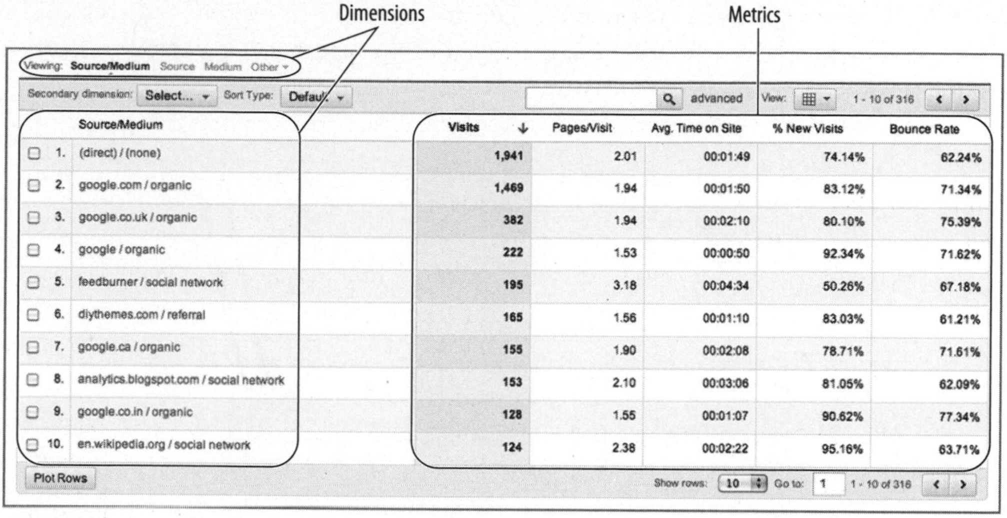

	Source/Medium	Visits	Pages/Visit	Avg. Time on Site	% New Visits	Bounce Rate
1.	(direct) / (none)	1,941	2.01	00:01:49	74.14%	62.24%
2.	google.com / organic	1,469	1.94	00:01:50	83.12%	71.34%
3.	google.co.uk / organic	382	1.94	00:02:10	80.10%	75.39%
4.	google / organic	222	1.53	00:00:50	92.34%	71.62%
5.	feedburner / social network	195	3.18	00:04:34	50.26%	67.18%
6.	diythemes.com / referral	165	1.56	00:01:10	83.03%	61.21%
7.	google.ca / organic	155	1.90	00:02:08	78.71%	71.61%
8.	analytics.blogspot.com / social network	153	2.10	00:03:06	81.05%	62.09%
9.	google.co.in / organic	128	1.55	00:01:07	90.62%	77.34%
10.	en.wikipedia.org / social network	124	2.38	00:02:22	95.16%	63.71%

Figure 4.5 The difference between dimensions and metrics: dotted lines = dimensions; solid lines = metrics (also shown in the color section)

The contents of the data table can vary greatly (see label M for changing this) and can be displayed in a variety of different ways (as explained with label D2). However, for most reports you will see the first column listing your dimension entries and the remaining five columns showing their associated metrics. A secondary dimension can also be shown (label G)

The default table view is to display the top 10 rows of data, ordered by number of visits (highest first). The order index can be changed by clicking on any of the column headings and can be set to ascending or descending. You can also apply a weighted sort algorithm for some metrics (label I). The control options displayed in the bottom footer (label E) and table header row (label D1) allow you to change how many rows and which parts of the table are shown. Individual dimensions can be plotted side by side (label F) and dimensions can be quickly searched for and filtered by (labels J and K).

For most reports, the listed dimensions are links. Clicking them allows you to drill down into that particular dimension for on-the-fly segmentation. For example, clicking on the dimension entry `google / organic` takes you to a table of the same metrics but for that dimension (segment) only. Once segmented in this way, you can then select an alternative dimension to display (label H).

Advanced segments take this a step further (label O) and you can add a "reduced view" of the table to a dashboard (label R). You can also schedule emails of your data to be sent (label Q). The maximum number of report rows that can be displayed in the user interface is 500. To view more than this you can export the data (label P).

Date Range Selector

Figure 4.4, Label A: At first glance this is very straightforward. However, there are some subtleties here that go unnoticed by many users, so I recommend getting familiar with all the date range options.

By default, when you view reports, you view the last month of activity. As discussed earlier in this chapter, for account and profile overview reports this means, assuming today is day x of the month, the default date range for reports is from day x of the previous month to day x-1 of the current month. By default, the current day is not included because this skews calculated averages.

Clicking the date area within the report allows you to make changes. This is shown in Figure 4.6. For example, perhaps you wish to focus on only a single day's activities. In that case, select only that day by clicking it on the calendar. You can also enter the date manually by using the fill-in fields provided. In this respect, the date range selector works like any other calendar tool. To select an entire calendar month, click the month name.

Figure 4.6 Selecting a date range

To compare the current date range data with any other date range, check the Compare To Past box. By default, Google Analytics will select a date range to compare. For example, if your first date range is the current day, the previous day will be automatically selected as the comparison. If your first date range is the last 30 days of data, the previous 30 days will be selected by default, and so forth. You can overwrite the second date range as required.

The result of comparing two date ranges is shown in Figure 4.7. As you can see, the two data sets are overlaid on the chart and each dimension row of the data table is now split, showing metrics for the two date ranges. The comparison data, shown as % Change, displays positive changes—that is, an increase compared with the previous period as green, whereas negative changes are shown in red. The exception to this is when viewing bounce rates. In this case, a decrease in bounce rate would be green and an increase would be red, to reflect that a decrease in bounce rate is desirable.

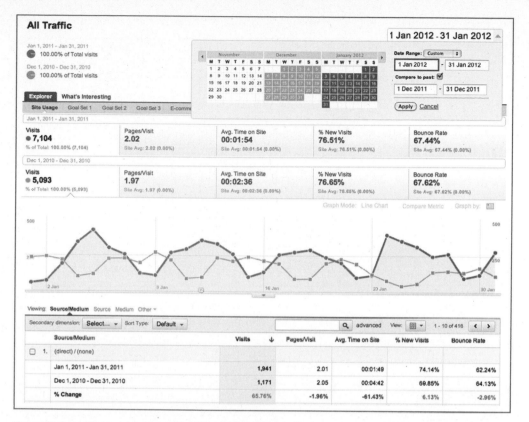

Figure 4.7 Comparing two date ranges (also shown in the color section)

> **Note:** Take care when viewing chart data for different date ranges. By default, Google Analytics will select a suitable second date range for you—the previous 30 days, for example. However, this usually does not align with the first date range—for example, Mondays may not align with Mondays. When comparing date ranges, always attempt to align days of the week. For example, compare Monday–Friday of this week with Monday–Friday of the previous week.

Aggregate Summary Metrics

Figure 4.4, Label B: Above the data-over-time graph is a summary row for the entire displayed report, as shown in the following image.

In this example, the display metrics shown are either the *sum of*, in the case of number of visitors, or *weighted average* for the other metrics, such as the weighted average for time on site, bounce rate, and so forth.

Just below these metrics is a comparison with the site as a whole. Shown in Figure 4.4 is a snapshot of all visit data. Therefore, the comparisons are the same values. If, however, you drill down into a report—for example, selecting row 2 from the table (google / organic), which reveals keyword information, the summary row shows metrics for that segment only, with comparison information to the overall site metrics. The percentage difference is also displayed in parenthesis.

A subtlety of the summary row is the small arrow pointing upward below the first column (Visits). This indicates what data is being plotted in the data-over-time graph—in Figure 4.4 this is visits over time, which is the default setting. Clicking one of the other summary columns will change this. The arrow will move to the metric being plotted.

Chart Options

There are three powerful charting options, labeled on Figure 4.4 as C1, C2, and C3. These control how much data is displayed on the chart and also provide an animation feature.

Changing Graph Intervals

Figure 4.4, Label C1: The default report graph interval is daily. That is, you see an aggregate point on the data-over-time graph for each day. That works well when viewing data from 1 to 60 days. However, for longer time periods, such as six months and further, having such a granularity will appear as noise, obscuring information contained in the signal. To improve this, and to reveal longer-term trends, change the graphing interval to weekly or monthly—using the selector shown in the following image.

Figure 4.8 shows the effect of viewing a 22-month period at different graph intervals. As you can see, for longer time periods, the higher resolution of daily data points appears as noise and is not particularly revealing. Using weekly or monthly data points is much more useful. Essentially, it's for you to decide what works best for you. I recommend weekly chart intervals for a data window of 3 to 12 months and monthly chart intervals when viewing data over more than a 12-month period.

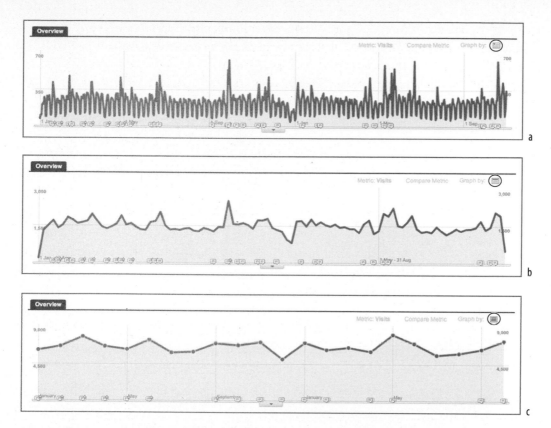

Figure 4.8 Data-over-time graph for a 22-month period showing visitors as (a) daily, (b) weekly, (c) monthly data points

Some reports also have the ability to change the graphing interval to hourly. This enables you to track at what times of the day visitor traffic arrives on your site—midnight to midnight. Knowing what times of the day are most productive for you provides powerful insight for scheduling campaigns or downtime—for example, starting and stopping ads, changing your keyword buys, viral marketing events, and the best time to perform web server maintenance. However, an important caveat to consider when interpreting the hourly reports is if you are receiving significant visitors from different time zones—for example, US versus European time zones. If this is your situation, consider segmenting your visitors using a geographical filter before interpreting these reports. See Chapter 8, "Best Practices Configuration Guide," for more information.

Plotting a Second Metric

Figure 4.4, Label C2: The default graph is always for visits, though clicking one of the other summary row metrics can change this (described for label B). By clicking the drop-down menu above the data-over-time graph (the menu is shown in the following graphic), you can add a second metric to be plotted.

Compare Metric ▾

The list of available metrics can be extensive. and the exact content will vary, depending on which report you are viewing at the time—see Figure 4.9. When comparing with a second metric, each is presented in a different color and is scaled by either the left or right y-axis. This does not affect the contents of the underlying table.

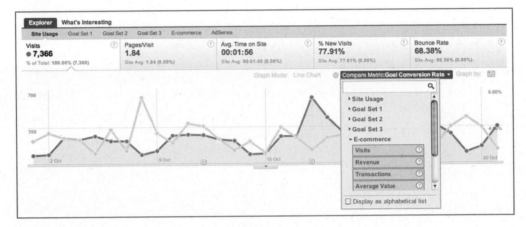

Figure 4.9 Plotting a second metric (also shown in the color section)

Graph Modes

Figure 4.4, Label C3: By default all report charts are shown as static data-over-time charts. Although important, unless you observe dramatic changes in your visitor traffic on a day-to-day basis, chances are you rarely notice anything of significance with this graphing format. An alternative is to animate your data-over-time using motion charts. Select this option from the drop-down menu, shown in the following image, to see how multiple metrics evolve over time. Motion charts are discussed in more detail in Chapter 5.

Graph Mode: Line Chart ▾

Tip: An animated chart of five dimensions is difficult to describe on paper, so I encourage you to check out the official motion charts demonstration on YouTube at www.youtube.com/watch?v=D4QePIt_TTs. If like me you become a fan of this feature, you can rate the team behind it (and their singing abilities!) at www.youtube.com/watch?v=nimrc-uG7UY.

Changing Table Views

By default, Google Analytics displays your data in a table of 10 rows, corresponding to the 10 most popular dimensions, ordered by number of visits. Clicking one of the other columns headings—for example, bounce rate—changes the ordering. Most tables contain hundreds of rows of data and often thousands, even tens of thousands for high-traffic websites. How you view the table of data clearly has an impact on your comprehension, and this is described for labels D1 and D2 of Figure 4.4.

Moving through the Table Window

Figure 4.4, Label D1: Using the arrow buttons, shown in the image below, is a very simple way of navigating through your data rows—moving forward or backward through 10 rows at a time.

You can also combine this with the option labeled E, which allows you to expand the number of rows displayed to 25, 50, 100, 250, or 500 rows at a time. Although useful, this is clearly a basic way of finding information in the table. A more advanced way is using the table search and filter options (labels J and K respectively). These are discussed later in this section.

Changing the Table Display

Figure 4.4, Label D2: If you would rather see your data in a pie chart, or bar chart, than as a flat table, the table view option available in most reports (see the following image) enables you to select a different view to display your data:

View: ▦ ▾

Data This is the default flat table showing one dimension column and five metrics columns. The default sort order is by traffic volume (visits) descending. You can change the sort order, or select a different sort criteria, by clicking the column headings.

Percentage This is a pie chart view with any of the five metrics from the summary row (label B) available to plot using the drop-down menus.

Performance This is a bar chart view and my most common selection when initially viewing a report. For me, it gives the clearest perspective of overall performance of each data row—highlighting the major influences before I investigate further.

Comparison This delta view compares the displayed metric to the site average and is my second most common table view selection. However, I find users often confuse what this report shows, so it is worth understanding how the comparison value is calculated.

I use the metrics shown in Figure 4.10 to illustrate this. The calculation is a two-step process, as follows:

$$\text{site average} = \frac{\text{total visits}}{\text{total number table rows}}$$

$$= 7{,}104 \, / \, 11$$

$$= 645.82$$

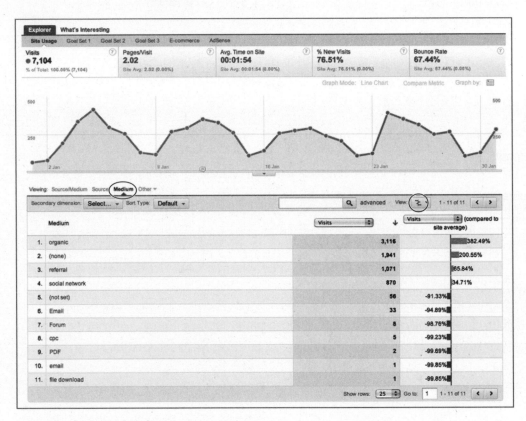

Figure 4.10 Comparison view (also shown in the color section)

The site average calculation tells me that the average traffic per medium is 645.82 visits—though this is not displayed in the report. The first medium listed (organic) actually received 3,116 visits during this time period—clearly way above the average. How much more is what the comparison metric shows. The calculation is as follows:

$$\text{Comparison}_{\text{row 1}} = (3{,}116 \, / \, 645.82) - 1$$

$$= 382.49\%$$

The comparison value is showing that organic traffic sent 382 percent more visits than might be expected from looking at the average for all mediums. Because the percentage is greater, a scaled bar is color-coded green and to the right. If it would be less than the average, the bar is color-coded red and to the left.

The comparison chart is a great way to get an at-a-glance view of what is performing well. For example, looking at the table in Figure 4.10 as a whole, the comparison column is showing that the first two mediums (organic and direct) contribute the most traffic and these are way above average. In fact, only the first four referral mediums contribute more than the average. The rest are performing below par. Without the comparison metric available, it is difficult to comprehend what a "good" value is and what is poor. Showing the comparison against the site average allows you to put this into perspective.

> **Tip:** Use the comparison view when the number of table rows is relatively few. For example, less than 50 rows. Otherwise, the metric tends to suffer from long-tail effects; that is, where you see only very large positive and large negative. Such differences are easy to spot in the default table view, therefore use the comparison option to help you find more subtle differences.

Term cloud This is a word cloud display that will be familiar if you read blog sites or conduct search engine optimization. Essentially, a word cloud is a visual depiction of the dimension column from the report table. An example for referral sites is shown in Figure 4.11.

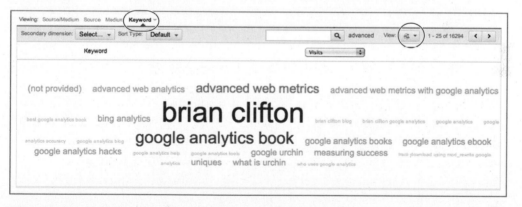

Figure 4.11 Term cloud table view for referral keywords

As you can gather from Figure 4.11, the larger the term, in this case queries used on referral search engines, the more significant it is in the report (in this case, the more visits that were received for a particular keyword). Any of the five metrics from the summary row (label B) are available to use instead from the drop-down selector menu highlighted on the right of Figure 4.11.

Tip: Term clouds are an excellent way to spot patterns in large volumes of data. Use the term cloud view when you wish to visualize data from a large data table—more than 50 rows. This avoids data blindness.

Pivot The pivot view is analogous to pivot tables in Excel. The resulting data view can appear complex at first glance, so it is worth spending some time understanding what the pivot view of Figure 4.12 is showing.

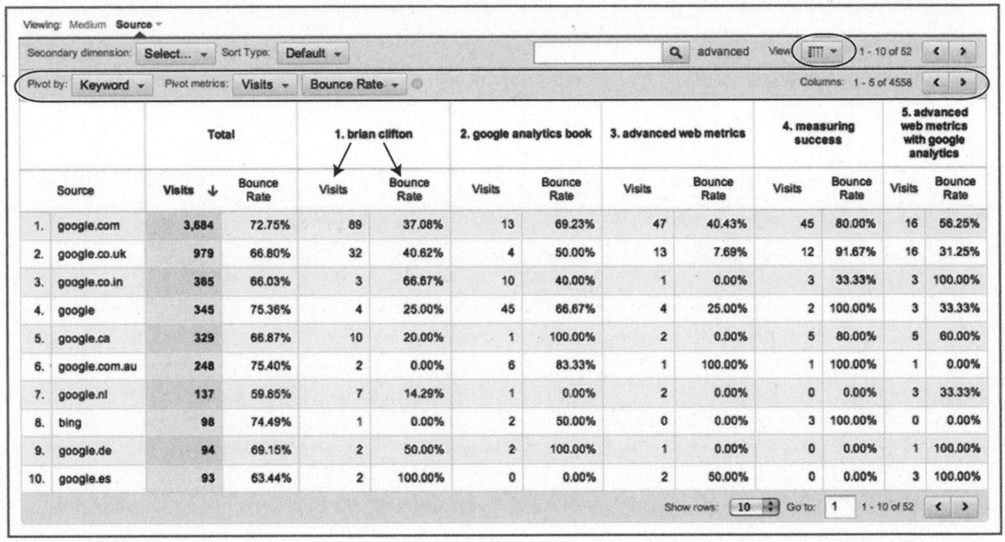

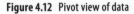

		Total		1. brian clifton		2. google analytics book		3. advanced web metrics		4. measuring success		5. advanced web metrics with google analytics	
	Source	Visits	Bounce Rate	Visits	Bounce Rate	Visits	Bounce Rate	Visits	Bounce Rate	Visits	Bounce Rate	Visits	Bounce Rate
1.	google.com	3,684	72.75%	89	37.08%	13	69.23%	47	40.43%	45	80.00%	16	56.25%
2.	google.co.uk	979	66.80%	32	40.62%	4	50.00%	13	7.69%	12	91.67%	16	31.25%
3.	google.co.in	365	66.03%	3	66.67%	10	40.00%	1	0.00%	3	33.33%	3	100.00%
4.	google	345	75.36%	4	25.00%	45	66.67%	4	25.00%	2	100.00%	3	33.33%
5.	google.ca	329	66.87%	10	20.00%	1	100.00%	2	0.00%	5	80.00%	5	60.00%
6.	google.com.au	248	75.40%	2	0.00%	6	83.33%	1	100.00%	1	100.00%	1	0.00%
7.	google.nl	137	59.85%	7	14.29%	1	0.00%	2	0.00%	0	0.00%	3	33.33%
8.	bing	98	74.49%	1	0.00%	2	50.00%	0	0.00%	3	100.00%	0	0.00%
9.	google.de	94	69.15%	2	50.00%	2	100.00%	1	0.00%	0	0.00%	1	100.00%
10.	google.es	93	63.44%	2	100.00%	0	0.00%	2	50.00%	0	0.00%	3	100.00%

Figure 4.12 Pivot view of data

To obtain the view shown in the screen shot in Figure 4.12, first select Source as the dimension for the data table; then select the pivot view. This displays the extra pivot row of options as highlighted in Figure 4.12. Choose to pivot by keyword, showing visits and bounce rate. The result is a table that lists the top five keywords along the top, each one further split to show visits and bounce rate on a per–search engine basis. The pivot table view is therefore a powerful way to view multiple data points simultaneously, without the need to navigate back and forth between different reports.

To view the next five keywords by visit volume, use the arrows on the right of the pivot row and so forth.

Tip: The pivot view places more data in one place at your fingertips. By doing this, it reduces the need to go back and forth between reports. However, don't add more data to your reports until you understand the overall trends of a particular data set first. The pivot view is for when you are ready to perform more detailed analysis and cross-referencing.

Plotting Multiple Rows

Figure 4.4, Label F: For any report containing a data table, you can plot the metrics of up to two individual dimensions by selecting the check box next to the row of interest and clicking Plot Rows, shown in the following image.

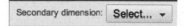

Secondary Dimensions

Figure 4.4, Label G: So far, only one primary dimension has been displayed in the example reports presented here—from Figure 4.4, this is the source / medium referral combination for a visit. You can further refine this by splitting each primary dimension with a secondary one selected from the drop-down menu at label G and shown in the following image.

Secondary dimension: Select... ▾

For example, Figure 4.13 shows each source / medium combination further split by visitor type. This of course increases the number of rows in your table as each source / medium can now have up to two entries—new and returning visitor types. Note that the sort order is maintained—by default descending by visit volume. As such, the second entry for a particular source / medium may not show next to the first. For example, most of your google / organic visits may be returning visitors. Therefore, the corresponding entry for new visitors may display much farther down in the table.

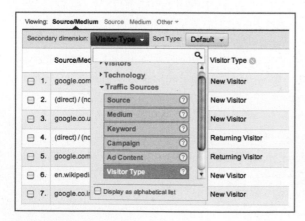

Figure 4.13 Viewing a secondary dimension (also shown in the color section)

The number of secondary dimensions available to use can vary for different reports. The example shown in Figure 4.13 allows you to ascertain, within the *same* report, which referrals are driving traffic acquisition versus which drive visitor retention. Without using the secondary dimension, you would need to view two separate reports to gather this information.

Changing the Displayed Dimension

Figure 4.4, Label H: For most reports, the listed dimensions are links. Clicking on them allows you to drill down into that particular dimension for on-the-fly segmentation. Consider the following example: Within the data table, click the dimension entry google / organic. This takes you to a table of the same metrics, but for that dimension only. Once the dimension is segmented in this way, you can then select an alternative dimension to display (as shown in the following image), such as keywords used by that segment of visits.

Viewing: **Source/Medium**   Source   Medium   Other ▾

Table Sorting

Figure 4.4, Label I: For any particular report you may be viewing, tables are initially sorted by traffic volume (visits) in descending order. To reverse the sort order, click the Visits column header entry. Alternatively, to sort on another column, click the desired column heading. However, there's an issue with this type of sorting when you are viewing large amounts of data with numerous outliers; you will see a small volume of data points with very high or very low values that are not of interest to you.

To understand the issue, let's consider a table of data sorted by bounce rate. At either ends of the spectrum you are likely to see a small volume of visits with either a 100 or 0 percent bounce rate. For example, you may see the top 10 source / medium referrers with a bounce rate of 100 percent, but each contributing only 1 visit. Clearly, this is not a helpful report. To overcome this, select Weighted from the Sort Type dropdown menu at label I, shown in the following image.

Sort Type: Default ▾

Weighted sort orders the data according to its importance and not just by its value. Essentially, it takes into account the volume of visits to weight the significance of the chosen sort metric. The final result is to give you more actionable data when you wish to sort by a ratio metric. To illustrate this, Figure 4.14 shows a data table sorted by bounce rate with and without the weight sort feature applied.

Viewing: **Source/Medium** Source Medium Other ▾

Secondary dimension: Select... ▾ Sort Type: Default ▾   🔍 advanced View: ▦ ▾ 1 - 10 of 291 ‹ ›

	Source/Medium	Visits	Pages/Visit	Avg. Time on Site	% New Visits	Bounce Rate ↓
☐ 1.	127.0.0.1 / referral	1	1.00	00:00:00	100.00%	100.00%
☐ 2.	actionable-analytics.com / referral	2	1.00	00:00:00	100.00%	100.00%
☐ 3.	alvareznavarro.es / referral	1	1.00	00:00:00	100.00%	100.00%
☐ 4.	analytics-fr.blogspot.com / social network	4	1.00	00:00:00	100.00%	100.00%
☐ 5.	analytics.blogs.pearson.com / social network	1	1.00	00:00:00	100.00%	100.00%
☐ 6.	analyticsimpact.com / referral	1	1.00	00:00:00	100.00%	100.00%
☐ 7.	antezeta.it / referral	1	1.00	00:00:00	100.00%	100.00%
☐ 8.	bimeanalytics.com / referral	1	1.00	00:00:00	100.00%	100.00%
☐ 9.	blog.romag.cz / social network	1	1.00	00:00:00	100.00%	100.00%
☐ 10.	bloggertone.com / social network	1	1.00	00:00:00	100.00%	100.00%

Plot Rows   Show rows: 10 ▾ Go to: 1 1 - 10 of 291 ‹ ›

a

Viewing: **Source/Medium** Source Medium Other ▾

Secondary dimension: Select... ▾ Sort Type: Weighted ▾   🔍 advanced View: ▦ ▾ 1 - 10 of 291 ‹ ›

	Source/Medium	Visits	Pages/Visit	Avg. Time on Site	% New Visits	Bounce Rate ↓
☐ 1.	google.com / organic	1,849	1.65	00:01:30	85.67%	73.23%
☐ 2.	t.co / referral	224	1.46	00:01:57	82.59%	81.25%
☐ 3.	(direct) / (none)	1,257	1.85	00:01:55	71.28%	70.49%
☐ 4.	feedburner / feed	379	1.50	00:01:21	78.36%	73.35%
☐ 5.	google / organic	212	1.61	00:01:17	88.68%	74.06%
☐ 6.	google.com.au / organic	106	1.47	00:01:19	85.85%	73.58%
☐ 7.	google.pl / organic	20	1.10	00:00:05	90.00%	90.00%
☐ 8.	analytics.blogspot.com / social network	181	1.57	00:01:48	81.22%	70.72%
☐ 9.	search / organic	22	1.27	00:00:16	86.36%	86.36%
☐ 10.	google.co.za / organic	21	1.33	00:01:55	71.43%	85.71%

Plot Rows   Show rows: 10 ▾ Go to: 1 1 - 10 of 291 ‹ ›

b

Figure 4.14 Report table sorted by bounce rate: (a) with default sort applied, (b) with weight sort applied

Note: In some ad reports, the weighting factor will be impressions or clicks rather than visits.

How Weighted Sort Works

Weight sort works by taking into account *importance* factors for a particular ratio metric. An obvious importance factor is traffic volume, so I use this to illustrate how the weighted sort algorithm would work if this was the only factor. Note this is not the exact approach used by Google Analytics because other factors such as impressions, click-throughs, and so forth may also be added to the calculation. However, this nicely illustrates the methodology.

Consider the bounce rates for two referral sources reported as follows:

- Source 1 Bounce Rate = 85%, receiving only 1% of the total visit traffic.
- Source 2 Bounce Rate = 55%, receiving 60% of the total visit traffic.

Using the default sort method for descending bounce rates, source 1 would appear above source 2 in the table. However, the *effective* bounce rate (used for weighted sorting) takes into account visit volume. For this calculation, I have assumed the average bounce rate for all referrers in the report is 35 percent:

$$\text{effective bounce rate}_{\text{source 1}} = (0.01 \times 85) + (0.99 \times 35)$$
$$= 35.5\%$$

$$\text{effective bounce rate}_{\text{source 2}} = (0.60 \times 55) + (0.40 \times 35)$$
$$= 47.0\%$$

As a general formula this can be written as follows:

$$\text{effective metric}_N = (\%\text{visits}_N \times \text{metric value}_N) + ((1 - \%\text{visits}_N) \times \text{average metric value}_{\text{all visits}})$$

The effective value for the bounce rate is what is used by Google Analytics when selecting a weighted sort. As you can see, source 2 now has a higher effective bounce rate than source 1 and so will show ahead of it in the table. This means the bounce rate of source 2 is considered more important to you than the bounce rate of source 1 as it received more visits.

Table Search

Figure 4.4, Label J: Websites can receive a lot of data. Even a small, moderately active blog can generate thousands of visits per month and therefore tens of thousands of data points to go with it. As shown in Figure 4.4, the total number of rows for the Source Medium report is 316—see the text next to label D1. Although expanding and changing the data window, as described for labels D1 and F, can be of help, visually browsing through each table row is clearly not going to be something you wish to do regularly (nor will it be much fun!).

To avoid such a laborious task, you can quickly search your data by using the table search box shown at label J in Figure 4.4 and in the following image.

The table search box uses a simple pattern lookup to match against in your primary dimension column. For example, if you only wanted to see Yahoo visitors in your table, you simply enter "yahoo" in the search. This is applied to all the table data, not just the visible rows. Partial matches are also allowed, so "yah" on its own will work. Likewise, to view only organic search visitors, search for "organic."

Although it's very simple and easy to use, you may quickly find yourself wanting more advanced search functions. This is available via the advanced option and is described next.

Table Filters (Advanced)

Figure 4.4, Label K: The simple table search function described for label J acts on the first dimension column only. However, what if you wish to *exclude* data from the table or use more advanced criteria, such as include data only if a metric is above a certain threshold? Using the advanced option for table filtering allows you to achieve this. An example is shown in Figure 4.15.

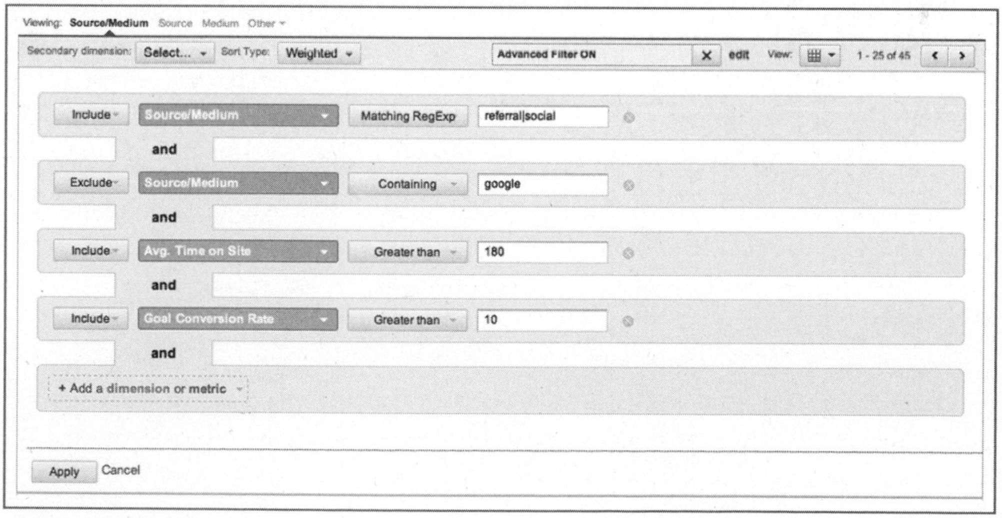

Figure 4.15 An advanced search filter for complex table filtering (also shown in the color section)

The advanced filter shown in Figure 4.15 is an example of a multiple filter that matches against two dimensions (color-coded green) and two metrics (color-coded red):

Show visits who come from a referral OR a social media website, AND

Exclude any referrals from Google (such as from my personal Google profile), AND

Have spent more than 3 minutes on the site, AND

Have achieved a goal conversion rate of greater than 10 percent.

Only data that matches all of these criteria will be shown in the resultant table. Therefore, using table filters is a powerful way of drilling down into large volumes of data by specifying either simple or complex filter criteria. Try different examples and combinations to become familiar with these.

As with the table search feature, described for Figure 4.4, label J, advanced table filters cannot be saved for later use and are only available while you're viewing a particular report. That is, if you navigate away to a different report set, your filter will be lost. If you regularly use the same filter on your table data, consider building an advanced segment instead because these are saved and can be applied to any report, profile, or Google Analytics account. Advanced segments are discussed in Chapter 8.

Note: Figure 4.15 makes use of a simple regular expression for pattern matching on the first match criteria. Appendix A contains an overview of using regular expressions. The filter criteria are not case sensitive and you can specify partial matches—for example, "social" will match both "social media" and "social networks." I have assumed you are tracking social network visitors by the method described in Chapter 7.

Chart Display and Annotation

Figure 4.4, Label L: If you mouse over any of the data points within the data-over-time graph, you will notice a pop-up bubble view that displays the data point's date and value alongside the equivalent comparison data point if Compare To Past (label A), Compare Metric (label C2), or Plot Rows (Label F) is selected. This is shown in the following image.

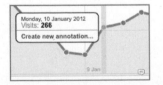

In addition, if you click on a specific chart data point, a dark vertical line highlighting the date selected is shown and the bubble view remains fixed—so that it remains in place while you mouse over other data points. For Figure 4.4, the fixed bubble view is shown for Monday, 10 January 2012 with Visits: 266.

At the bottom of the bubble view you can click to "Create new annotation." That is, you can add a note to highlight your thoughts or mark a key event relevant to your website. Consider chart annotations as your Post-it notes, allowing you to keep track of things that can help you explain data patterns. For example, perhaps you have relaunched your website with a new design, announced a new product, launched a new marketing campaign, are aware of system downtime, and so forth. All of these are important business activities that can have a dramatic impact on your website's performance. These are marked as small bubble-like icons displayed on the timeline of report charts—as shown below and to the right of label L. Click one of these icons for the detail of an existing annotation to be displayed.

Figure 4.16 is an excellent example of how useful chart annotations can be. As you can see, there was a catastrophic drop in visitor numbers on Wednesday 22 June— from an expected 10,000 plus visits down to 610 (effectively zero for this website). An investigation revealed that the Google Analytics Tracking Code (GATC) was left off by mistake during a system-wide update. At the time all those involved in the metrics team were made aware of the issue, but looking back months or even years later, the incident will be forgotten. The chart annotation ensures that the incident is labeled for all to understand what happened during that week.

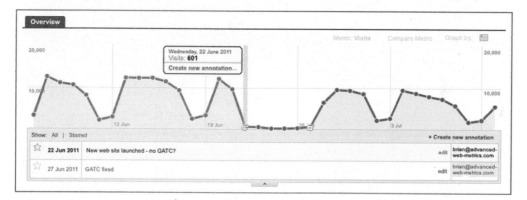

Figure 4.16 Displaying chart annotations

Annotations are applied on a per-user basis. Therefore, you can choose your notes to be private—only viewable by yourself—or public—viewable by all report users. Once set, annotations are displayed on *all* data-over-time charts within the same profile. Owners can edit or delete these at any time. The text limit is 160 characters and any day can have multiple associated annotations.

For events that are more important than others, you can highlight your annotations by adding a star (this is a highlighting technique familiar to any Gmail user). The 22 June annotation in Figure 4.16 has been highlighted in this way. Highlighted annotations are set on a per-user basis; that is, another user viewing the same profile will not see your starred annotations.

Tip: The use of chart annotations allows you to log events directly on your data charts and therefore avoid wasting time reinvestigating the issue later. Use these for whatever events you consider would significantly influence your traffic.

Report Sections

Figure 4.4, Label M: Above the summary table is a set of menu links that expand the metrics available in your reports, as shown in the following image.

Site Usage	Goal Set 1	Goal Set 2	Goal Set 3	E-commerce	AdSense

You can think of these menu links as extensions of the data table width—that is, rather than having an overly wide table containing all visit metrics, we have more manageable, shorter tables separated by type. Effectively, these menus are used to hide the extended table from view and keep the reporting interface focused.

You will notice that the Site Usage tab is always present for this report (and many others). The report provides headline metrics of Visits, Pages Per Visit, Average Time On Site, Percent New Visits, and Bounce Rate. Whether you see additional tabs will depend on your configuration. For example, if you have configured your goals (up to 20 split into five sets), use transaction tracking, or use AdWords or AdSense, then metrics for all of these configuration may be displayed in their own separate menu links. If you have not configured these configurations, the tabs will not show.

Essentially, you use menu links as if moving across a large data table. If you find an interesting data point in your Site Usage report, at the very least you will want to see if it is replicated in your goal conversion and e-commerce reports. For example, does a large influx of visitors from Twitter lead to a concomitant increase in goal conversions or revenue from that source? The menu links allow you to check for this and when clicking through you will maintain any search criteria (label J) or any advanced filters (label K) across the menu links—for the same report.

Tabbed Views

Figure 4.4, Label N: The default view for reports is the Explorer view, as shown by label N. This is the only view for standard reporting. Additional tabbed views can be added when building custom reports. Essentially, additional tabbed views allow you to extend the data table with further metrics and dimensions. Building custom reports is discussed in Chapter 9, "Google Analytics Customizations."

Advanced Segments

Figure 4.4, Label O: As you will discover from reading this book and experimenting with reports yourself, there are many ways to segment data in Google Analytics. The simplest is to drill down on a dimension within your data table. For example, clicking `google / organic` as a referral source in the screen shown in Figure 4.4 leads you to a data table for just that segment. However, the advanced segments area at label O (see the following image) provides you with much greater flexibility for visitor segmentation.

ADVANCED SEGMENTS ▾

Segmenting your data is a powerful way for you to understand your visitor personas—both geographics and demographics—and is discussed in greater detail in Chapter 8.

Export

Figure 4.4, Label P: Data export is available in three industry-standard formats: PDF, CSV, and TSV. Select Export (shown in the following image) from the top of each report to have your data exported in PDF (for printable reports), or CSV or TSV (to import into Excel or similar).

EXPORT ▾

Note: The additional CSV for Excel format is there to better handle the UTF-8 encoding used by Google Analytics reports. UTF-8 encoding is a way to ensure that non-ASCII character sets are handled correctly in web pages. Google Analytics requires this because reports need to be available in 10 plus languages. However, an import of UTF-8 encoded data into Excel does not go smoothly—hence the slightly modified format for this purpose.

The maximum number of report rows that can exported is 500 (this matches the maximum number displayed in the user interface). However, there is a workaround that allows you to export up to 20,000 rows. To do this, use the following instructions:

- In the report you want to export, set the Show Rows selector (label E) to 500.
- The report URL will update with this information at the end: `explorer-table .rowCount%3D500`, where 500 at the end of the string indicates the number of rows displayed in the report.
- Change the value of the `explorer-table.rowCount` parameter to the number of rows you want to export. For example, `explorer-table.rowCount%3D1000` sets it to 1000.
- Press the Enter key to load that URL into the browser.
- Visually confirm that the report now displays the new number of rows.
- Select the Export tab (label P). The exported data should contain all the rows you indicated in the URL.

Tip: If you require more than 20,000 rows, export the first 20,000 and then view the 20,000th line (via the control labeled E in Figure 4.4) and export again. Alternatively, update to the Premium (paid-for) version, which allows you to export up to 1 million rows. Google Analytics Premium is discussed in Chapter 3, "Google Analytics Features, Benefits, and Limitations."

Exporting data is a feature of Google Analytics that provides you with the flexibility of manipulating your web visitor data. If exporting data is a key requirement for your website analysis, consider also the automatic export options the Google Analytics export API can provide—discussed in Chapter 12, "Integrating Google Analytics with Third-Party Applications."

Email Reports

Figure 4.4, Label Q: Manually exporting data is great for manipulating it further or for creating one-off reports to present to your team. Once you have chosen which reports are important to your stakeholders, you will probably wish to have these sent to them via email—either ad hoc or scheduled on a regular basis. To do this, choose the Email link next to the Export link. You can schedule reports to be sent daily, weekly, monthly, or quarterly, as per Figure 4.17.

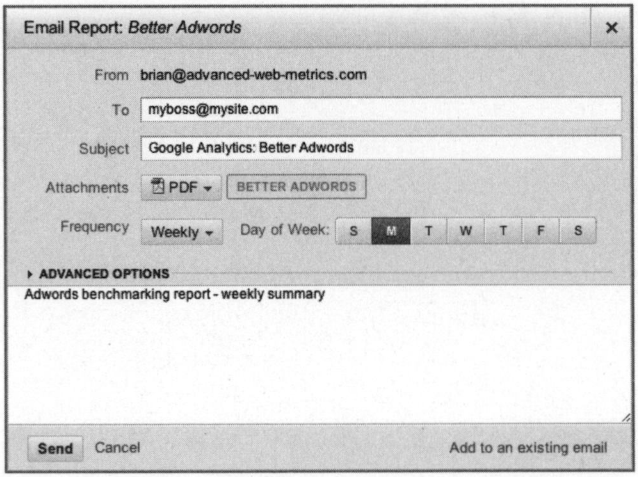

Figure 4.17 Scheduling a report for email export

If you wish to group a set of reports into an existing email schedule, use the "Add to an existing email" link, shown at the bottom of Figure 4.17. This brings up the pop-up window shown in Figure 4.18, allowing you to select which existing email to add your report to.

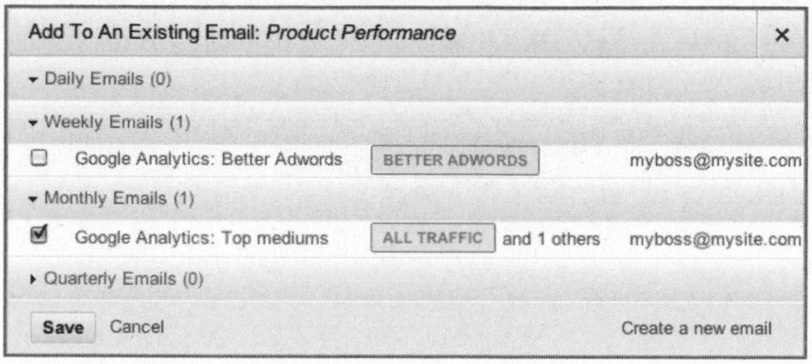

Figure 4.18 Adding a report to an existing email schedule

Settings are saved on a per-user and profile combination. Therefore, two different users viewing the same profile can set their own email schedules. When email is scheduled, all times are local to Mountain View, California (Google headquarters). Although the exact time is not specified, a daily report sent in the morning will actually be sent sometime in the afternoon for European customers.

Add to Dashboard

Figure 4.4, Label R: Almost every report in Google Analytics contains an Add To Dashboard button at the top (shown in the following image).

As the name suggests, it takes a reduced snapshot of the report you are viewing and places it in your Dashboard area—as shown in Figure 4.19. The data is *reduced* to showing up to two metrics. The reduction is applied to keep your Dashboard area concise. You can select an existing dashboard or create a new one if needed. Dashboards are discussed in further detail in Chapter 5.

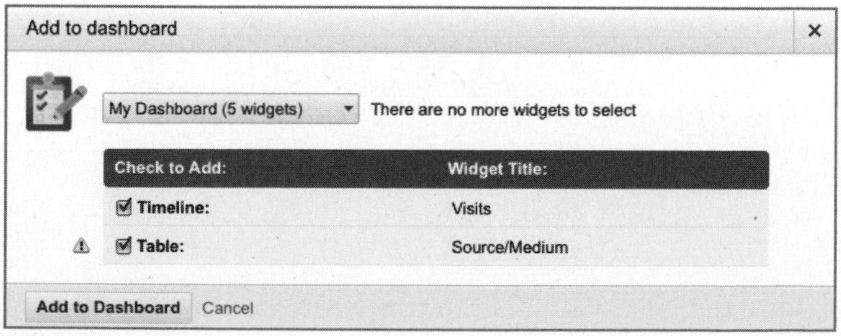

Figure 4.19 Adding a report to your dashboard area

Summary

In Chapter 4, you have learned the following:

Viewing data You now understand metrics and dimensions and the different ways you can view data with chart options, data views, and table sorting.

Navigating a report You have learned the different ways you can select and compare dimensions and secondary dimensions and how to compare date ranges or different metrics side by side.

Drilling down into data You have seen the role that search and table filters can play to refine displayed data down to a single data row or group of rows.

Looking at more than just visit numbers You know how to move between site usage reports, goal conversions, and e-commerce and AdWords reporting within the same report section.

Exporting and email scheduling You have learned how to export and schedule the emailing of reports in different file formats.

Annotating charts You now understand how to annotate charts so that important events or changes are logged for further reference.

Reports Explained

At my last count, Google Analytics had over 100 default reports—and when you take into consideration segmentation options, pivot views, intelligence alerts, flow visualization, real-time reporting, and custom reports, the number grows exponentially. Clearly, no one person is going to look at all those reports on a regular basis—nor should you try. Hence, I attempt to whet your appetite to investigate further.

In this chapter, I focus on the important reports that can give you that initial understanding or contain a great deal of insight. I strongly recommend you review Chapter 4 before reading this chapter.

Of course, my report selection may not reflect the information most important to you—every website is different. Once you understand the drivers or blocking points for your visitors, you can focus on more detail and build your own list of top reports.

In Chapter 5, you will learn:

The Home overview

The top standard reports

To understand data sampling

The Home Overview

There are three main reporting areas in Google Analytics, labeled Home, Standard Reporting, and Custom Reporting. These are available from the tabbed menu at the top of your reports—as shown in Figure 5.1. Clicking each one of the top tab menus reveals a different side menu of items. In this chapter I focus on the Home and Standard Reporting areas because this is where you will spend the vast majority of your time when viewing your data. Custom reporting is described in Chapter 9, "Google Analytics Customizations."

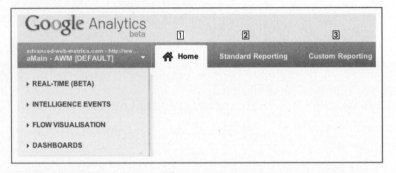

Figure 5.1 The three reporting areas of Google Analytics with the Home area selected

Real-Time Reporting

As the name suggests, this is a subset of reports that show you what's happening on your site as it happens. This can be very powerful when you launch, announce, or advertise a new product or offer and are aiming to achieve a large impact quickly. For example, you advertise via TV and radio during a particular event (halftime during a football game) and need to know the immediate impact your message has. Even if you are not performing such offline advertising, blog posts, tweets, and PR announcements also attempt to create a big time-sensitive splash in the market place.

Previously, to gain this insight you would have needed to wait until your data was processed before viewing your reports—and this can be up to 24 hours later for high-traffic sites. The real-time reports allow you to see a selection of visit data processed within only a few seconds of visitors arriving on your site. An example is shown in Figure 5.2.

The report shown in Figure 5.2 is continually updated—every second the data-over-time charts are adjusted as well as the data table below (an impressive technical achievement to provide for millions of account users). The two data-over-time charts represent the last 30 minutes and last 60 seconds of activity, with a color-coded bar chart summarizing referral sources. As with other report tables in Google Analytics, you can drill down on a particular dimension by clicking its link in the table. For example, clicking the Organic link in the table reveals the search engine name and keyword detail that visitors are using at that very moment to arrive on your site.

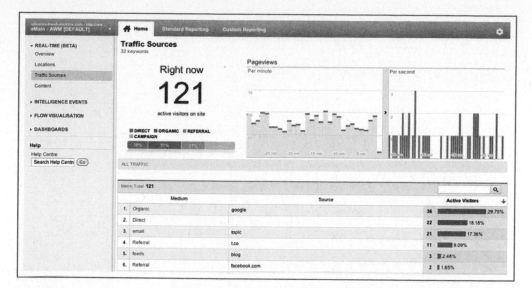

Figure 5.2 A real-time report showing up-to-the-second view of referral sources (also shown in the color section)

Other reports in this section show real-time locations of your visitors as well as how your content is performing, that is, what your top pages being viewed right now are.

> **Tip:** Another use for real-time reporting is for testing—either the testing of new content or a new marketing campaign. Quickly knowing that you can view the new data in your real-time reports ensures that updates and new campaigns launch smoothly.

Intelligence Events

The Intelligence Events report can dramatically impact your day-to-day analysis of web traffic data—for the better. It is a *key* report (deliberate emphasis) to greatly help you spot important changes in traffic patterns. This saves you the trouble of having to drill down into reports to find important changes; it actually finds the important changes for you in the first place. By that, I mean the Google Analytics intelligence engine is able to spot and highlight changes in metrics that often go unnoticed, buried beneath a plethora of other metrics—hence the name for this report set.

Intelligence works by performing statistical analysis on your previous data patterns *to predict the future!* Assuming you have reasonable levels of visits to your site each day (more than 100 visits per day) and enough historical data for the algorithms to work with (at least a month), Google Analytics will predict with reasonable accuracy what traffic levels are expected for the current day, week, and month. Comparing predicted values with the level of traffic you actually receive allows Google Analytics to highlight significant changes and optionally send you email alerts about them.

Note: Regardless of your traffic levels, Google Analytics will still generate intelligence reports for you. However, because all statistical methods require good sample sizes (at the very least hundreds of data points) to become valid, low traffic volumes can yield odd results. The larger your traffic volumes, the more accurate predicted statistics are.

Intelligence Overview

Figure 5.3 shows an example Intelligence Events Overview report. This is a summary table showing what automatic events were triggered for this particular time frame. It is broken down as follows:

Metric and Segment The particular metric that has changed significantly and the report segment from which it came.

Period The time period that the alert is applicable to. This can be daily, weekly, or monthly.

Date and Change The date range for the alert and the percentage of change observed when compared to previous time periods.

Importance The Importance bar shown for each alert row is the estimate of how real the alert is; that is, not the result of random fluctuations. The longer the histogram, the more real the result. The histogram is color-coded green for a positive change and red for a negative change.

You click the Details link to view a particular alert report.

	Intelligence Events Overview					1 Jan 2012 - 31 Jan 2012	
	Automatic Alerts Custom Alerts						
	Metric	Segment	Period	Date	Change	Importance ↓	
1.	Visits	Country/Territory: United States	Monthly	1 Jan 2012 - 31 Jan 2012	20%		Details
2.	Blog - add comment (Goal2 Value)	Source: (direct)	Monthly	1 Jan 2012 - 31 Jan 2012	212%		Details
3.	Per Visit Goal Value	All Traffic	Daily	1 Jan 2012	-100%		Details
4.	Visits	Source: (direct)	Daily	4 Jan 2012	193%		Details
5.	Goal Conversion Rate	Source: google.com	Daily	9 Jan 2012	>500%		Details
6.	Avg. Time on Site	Country/Territory: United Kingdom	Daily	26 Jan 2012	>500%		Details
7.	Avg. Time on Site	Country/Territory: United Kingdom, Region: England	Daily	26 Jan 2012	>500%		Details
8.	Visits	All Traffic	Daily	4 Jan 2012	92%		Details
9.	Visitors	All Traffic	Daily	4 Jan 2012	94%		Details
10.	Goal Conversion Rate	All Traffic	Daily	1 Jan 2012	285%		Details
				Show rows: 10	Go to: 1	1 - 10 of 199	‹ ›

Figure 5.3 The Intelligence Overview report (also shown in the color section)

In Figure 5.3, the automatic alert shown in row 1 is due to 20 percent more US visitors than expected in January, compared to previous months of activity. Row 3 shows a dramatic loss in the per-visit goal value when compared to daily trends, and row 5 shows that when compared to daily trends, conversion rates from Google on 9 January were significantly higher than expected.

For this example data, seasonality undoubtedly plays a large part in the alert triggers. However, knowing that on a particular day Google visitors convert more than six times higher than expected, for example, could be a valuable piece of information that your marketing and sales department can act on. Without the intelligence alert, this information can easily go unnoticed as just another data point hidden below a much larger total conversion rate.

What Does Alert Importance Mean?

The Importance column shown in Figure 5.3 for each alerted metric is the output of a complex calculation that determines whether the alert is real and not the result of a random fluctuation. However, in Google's traditional way, the complexity of this calculation (confidence intervals and p-values) is hidden from the user and replaced with the simple bar graphic that represents a scale of 0 to 9. The longer the bar appears, the more "real" the result. Essentially, alerts with a high Importance value should be prioritized for further investigation.

For more information on the statistics of normal distributions, see

http://en.wikipedia.org/wiki/Normal_distribution

Intelligence Detail: Daily Events

There are three levels of Intelligence Events detail: Daily, Weekly, and Monthly. The only difference between these three reports is the time period that is considered when Google Analytics calculates what the expected range is for a metric. I therefore describe only the Daily Event report here. Clicking this item from the side menu brings up a report similar to that shown in Figure 5.4.

Figure 5.4 shows the standard visits-over-time chart (that you find in most of your reports), with an alert timeline below it. Bars on the alert timeline are shown when at least one automatic or custom alert is triggered. A mouse over an alert brings up a mini data bubble showing the date and number of alerts for that period—for example, three alerts on 23 June. Clicking an alert bar reveals a table of the metrics that triggered the alert, and these are shown below the timeline. In Figure 5.4, three automatic alerts are shown that reveal significant increases in visits, visitors, and pageviews for the selected day alongside their expected values.

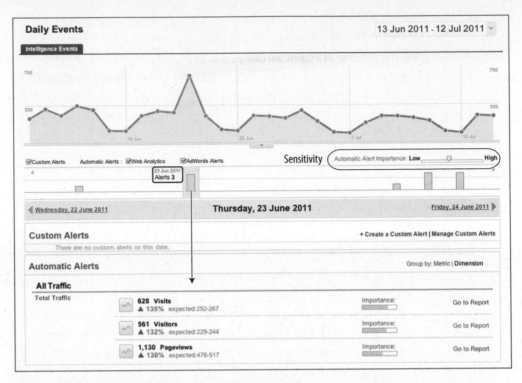

Figure 5.4 The daily intelligence report (also shown in the color section)

Tip: Once you have established the reasons for an alert, it is a good idea to add a chart annotation to your report to make it easier for others (and yourself) to remember the event.

Focusing only on the alert table of Figure 5.4, the small chart icon to the left of each alert allows you to change the standard visits-over-time chart to the alerted metric over time. Alongside each alert is an Importance bar. This is the same metric as shown in the Overview report in Figure 5.3—it is the probability that a result is not due to chance. The grayer the Importance bar appears, the more likely the result is real and not simply by coincidence. At the right side of each row is a Go To Report link that will take you to the relevant full Google Analytics report, segmented for that alert.

The Weekly Events and Monthly Events reports operate in exactly the same way as described here. The only difference is that they compare the aggregate metrics for one week (or month) against the previous weeks (or months).

What Constitutes a Significant Change for an Alert?

The Google Analytics definition of a significant change, or what triggers an alert, is when a metric varies by a magnitude of X-sigma or greater from its expected value, where X-sigma is a multiple of the metric's standard deviation. To understand this, let's look at some standard statistical theory.

A normal (Gaussian) distribution is defined by two parameters: the mean value mu (μ) and its standard deviation sigma (σ). Sigma is a measure of the average difference between a value and the mean. The universal properties of a normal distribution are such that differing from the mean by $\pm$ one standard deviation will account for 68 percent of all measured values. Differing by $\pm$ two standard deviations will account for 95 percent of all values. Differing by $\pm$ six standard deviations will represent 99.9999998 percent of all values—in other words, as close to all measured values of the distribution as possible without being pedantic.

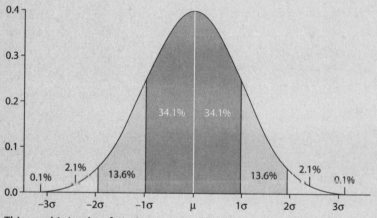

This graphic is taken from `http://en.wikipedia.org/wiki/File:Standard_deviation_diagram.svg` and is used with permission.

Alert Sensitivity

The sensitivity of an automatic alert—that is, how easy it is to trigger the alert—is determined by the Automatic Alert Importance slider bar—highlighted in Figure 5.4. Although not labeled, the slider bar scales from 7 sigma (lowest sensitivity) to 1 sigma (highest sensitivity). For example, at the highest sensitivity, if a metric is more than one standard deviation away from the predicted mean, an alert will be triggered. Conversely, at the lowest sensitivity value, a metric must be seven standard deviations away from the mean to trigger an alert. Hence, the sensitivity slider is a balance between highlighting significant changes and alert overload. My preference is to set this just to the left of halfway—approximately 3 sigma, 99.7 percent away from the mean value.

For more information on the statistics of normal distributions, see

`http://en.wikipedia.org/wiki/Normal_distribution`

Automatic Versus Custom Alerts

So far, I have discussed only automatic alerts. However as you will have noticed in Figure 5.3 and Figure 5.4, there are two types of alerts—Custom and Automatic. Automatic alerts (color-coded green) are alerts that Google Analytics has determined by its algorithmic method. That is, each day the intelligence engine checks for significant changes in the following dimensions:

- All traffic
- Visitor type (new or returning visitor)
- City
- Region
- Country/territory
- Campaign
- Keyword
- Source
- Medium
- Referral path
- Landing page
- Exit page

Note: In addition to the list shown for dimensions that are checked for automatic alerts, other dimensions may also be checked. For example, your AdWords click-through rate. However, at present there is no documentation from Google on which dimensions are used.

Any metric for these dimensions that falls outside the computed expected range is flagged as an alert. On the other hand, the creation of a custom alert gives you greater control. A custom alert allows you to set an alert criterion from *any* collected metric and apply it to *any* dimension—and even apply a custom segment. Two examples of a custom alert are shown in Figure 5.5 and Figure 5.6, created by selecting the + Create a Custom Alert link.

The custom alert setup in Figure 5.5 sends out an email to the alert creator (and optionally to other email addresses) when a new campaign actually starts to generate revenue. Often, there can be a significant time lag between when a marketing campaign is launched and when it generates new revenue. Because of this, newly generated revenue can go unnoticed—beneath all the other campaign and marketing activity the analyst needs to track. This alert takes cares of that with an email message.

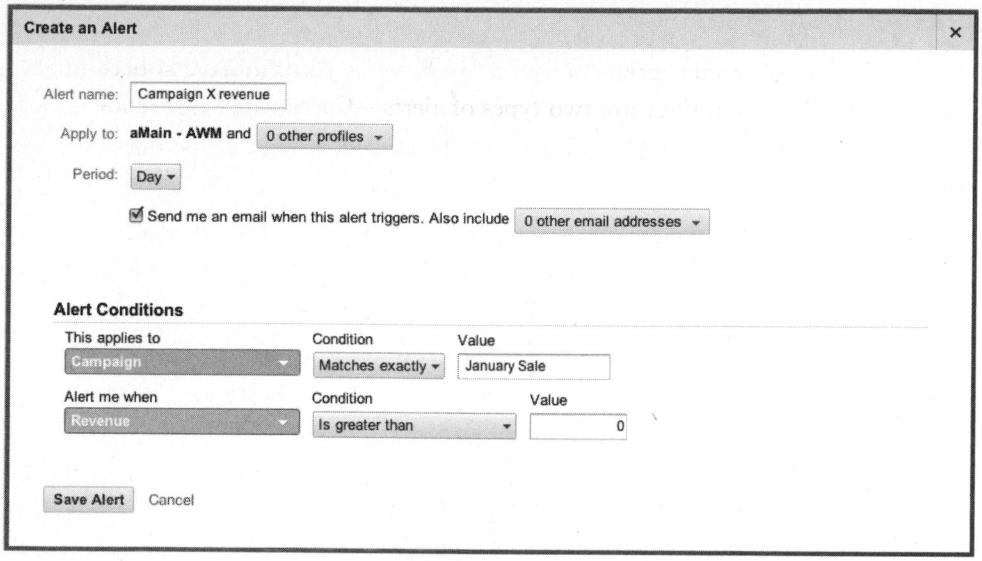

Figure 5.5 A custom alert notifying you when a new campaign generates revenue

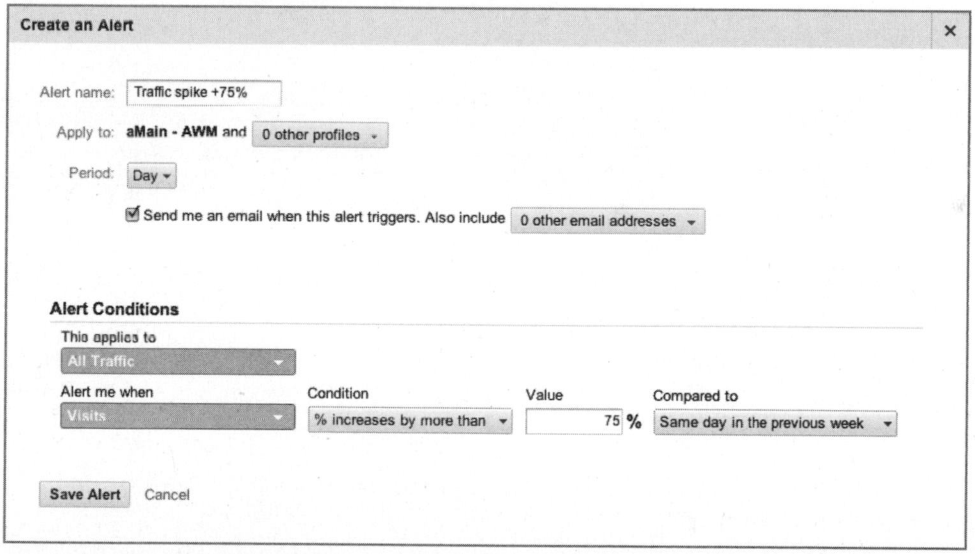

Figure 5.6 A custom alert notifying you of traffic spikes

Figure 5.6 notifies the alert owner when traffic suddenly peaks—in this case if it is more than 75 percent higher when compared to the same day the previous week. It could also be modified for traffic troughs or revenue spikes and troughs.

Note: Emailing of alerts is currently available for custom alerts only.

Flow Visualization

Flow Visualization reports present a graphical view of the paths visitors take through your website. This includes the referral source, through your various pages, and where along their paths they exited your site. An example is shown in Figure 5.7.

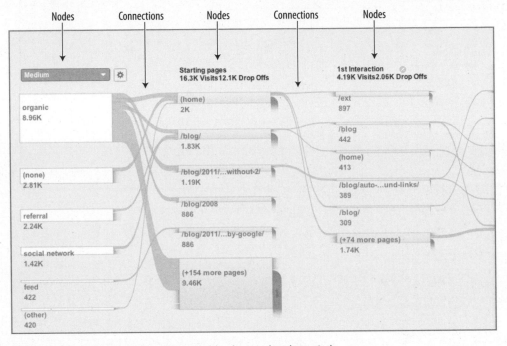

Figure 5.7 An example Flow Visualization report (also shown in the color section)

The terminology used here consists of *nodes* and *connections*. A node represents one metric of a dimension. It can be a single page or a collection of pages. For example, in Figure 5.7 the selected dimension is the referral medium and the metric is all visits. A connection represents the path from one node to another. The thickness of the connection is proportional to the volume of traffic along that path.

Note: The clever part of the Funnel Visualization report is the concept of nodes. A node can be single page from your site, but most likely it represents an auto-generated group of pages. Google Analytics automatically groups what it considers similar pages together. The result is that you view paths through similar pages rather than paths through *every* page on your site. That greatly simplifies the visualization of visitor flow and is a huge improvement over traditional path analysis reports shown by other vendor tools.

The Flow Visualization report has some powerful controls to aid your analysis—this is an industry leading report! First, any dimension can be selected as your starting node using the green drop-down item at the top left of Figure 5.7. By default, the top five matches based on traffic volume are displayed. If you wish to change this and examine a different subset of the dimension, click the gear icon next to the green dimension menu to open the Customize Dimension Items control, shown in Figure 5.8. Up to five segments can be added.

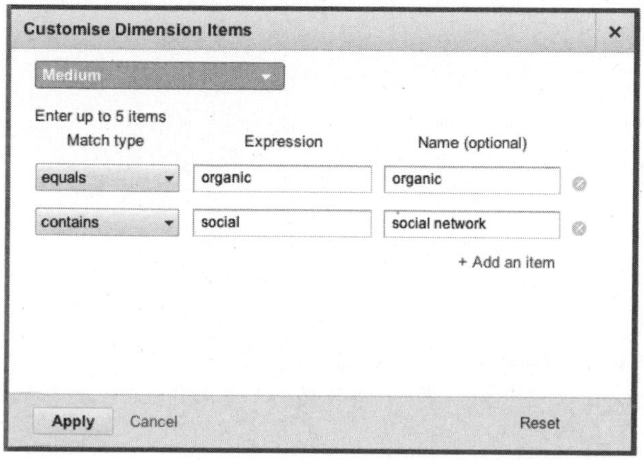

Figure 5.8 Example customized dimension for a Flow Visualization report

There is also the option to apply an advanced segment to the report using the controls placed just above the report—shown in Figure 5.9. This can be an existing default segment or a custom segment you have previously created. If no advanced segment is selected, all visitors are shown by default.

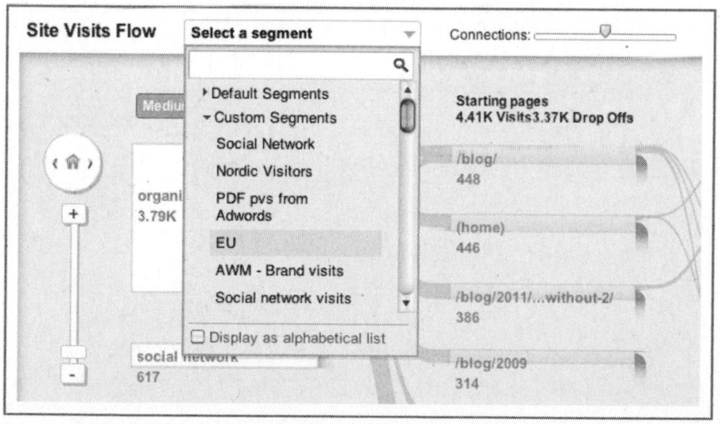

Figure 5.9 Flow Visualization controls

Next to the segment selection drop-down in Figure 5.9 is the Connections slider. Use the slider to filter the display based on connection volume. For example, moving the slider to the right increases the sensitivity of the display and will show more connections of lower visit volume. Combine this with the zoom and pan feature shown with the slider bar on the left in Figure 5.9. Note that you can also pan left and right through the visualization paths by dragging your mouse across the report.

So now you can navigate around the Flow Visualization report. However, the power of this report lies in understanding how traffic flows through your site. Hover over a connection of interest to view the flow of metrics. The connection will darken to highlight your selection and a data bubble appears showing the before and after node names and the amount of traffic that went down that particular path. Hover over an exit node to see how many visitors exited your site from that node. Click the connection to keep it permanently highlighted with a darker color, and click again to remove the highlight.

Hover over a node to view the traffic flow for that particular node—as shown in Figure 5.10. This shows not only the traffic flow through the node (defined as the path /blog), but also the number of pages this represents. In this case, Google Analytics has automatically grouped together six pages it considers similar. To view the node URLs, click the node and select Group Details from the pop-up menu.

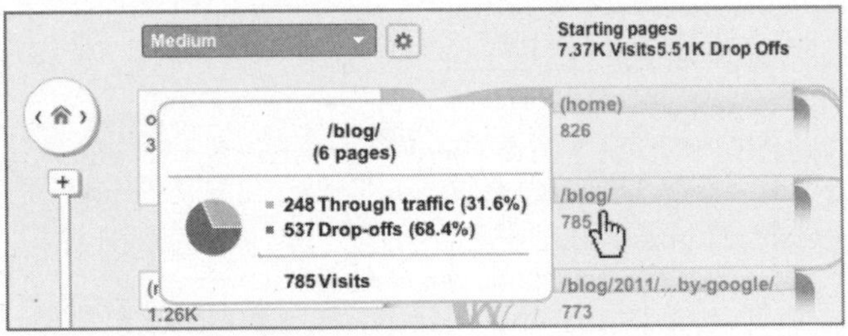

Figure 5.10 Node traffic flow

By clicking a node, you can select one of the following options:

Highlight traffic Through Here Highlights the connections for all traffic that moved through that node. To remove the highlight, click the node again, then click Clear Highlighting.

View Only This Segment Changes the visualization to show only the traffic from that dimension (segment). This option is shown for dimension nodes only.

Explore Traffic Through Here Changes the visualization to show all connections to and from the node. When used, this generates a Navigation Flow report, which is also a separate menu item in the Flow Visualization report section. This option is shown for page nodes only.

Group Details This opens a pop-up window with further options to choose from as follows:

- Top Segments (dimension nodes only): The current metric.
- Outgoing Traffic (dimension nodes only): The pages to which traffic flowed from that node.

- Top Pages: The most visited pages represented by that node. For example, if a node represents a collection of pages in the Shoes directory, then you see information about the pages in that directory that had the most traffic.
- Traffic Breakdown: The sources of traffic, based on the dimension you selected for the visualization.
- Incoming Traffic: Not available for Visitors Flow.
- Outgoing Traffic: The pages to which the node sent traffic.

Tip: Flow Visualization is a powerful way of exploring traffic patterns on your website. Google has put an enormous amount of development time into simplifying the display. However, it still remains a complex picture. Therefore, experiment with focusing on a particular segment, rather than viewing all of your traffic. Also revisit this report on many occasions as you build up your knowledge. This is certainly not a one-time view report.

Dashboards

A dashboard is an overview area where you can place a summary chart or table (known as a widget) copied from the main body of the Google Analytics reports. The idea is that a dashboard can give you an at-a-glance overview of the key metrics and trends happening on your site. From here, if you notice a significant change, you can click through to go to the detailed report section. An example dashboard is shown in Figure 5.11.

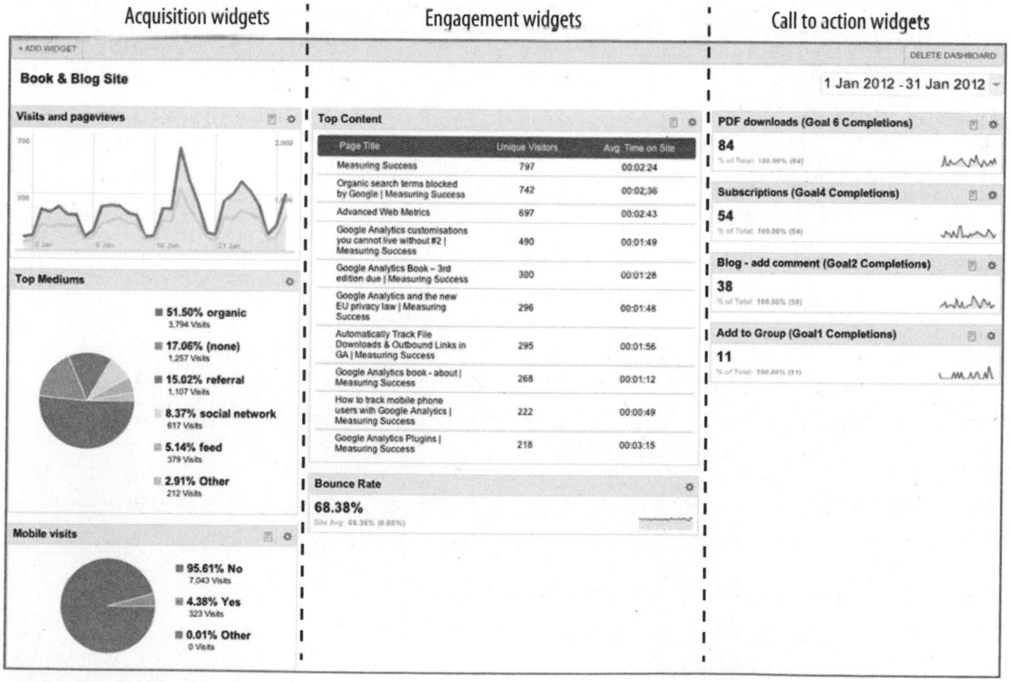

Figure 5.11 The Dashboard summary report

When viewing a dashboard, you can move a widget's placement by dragging and dropping it into another desired position. Also, you can change the selection of widgets shown at any time, with a maximum of 12 available to display per dashboard and a limit of 20 dashboards. Each dashboard has a three-column view, and you can organize it any way you wish. However, I recommend that rather than randomly displaying your widgets across a dashboard, you build your dashboards so that widgets are grouped by type—that is, traffic acquisition, engagement, calls to action—and are consistently placed into one of the columns, as shown in Figure 5.11.

There are two ways to add a widget:

- You can navigate to a report and click the Add To Dashboard link at the top of the page, as described for label R in Figure 4.4 in the previous chapter. If you choose this method, you can add the report to an existing dashboard or create a new one.

- Within an existing dashboard, you can create a new widget by selecting the + Add Widget button at the top of the dashboard report. Figure 5.12 shows the resulting pop-up display

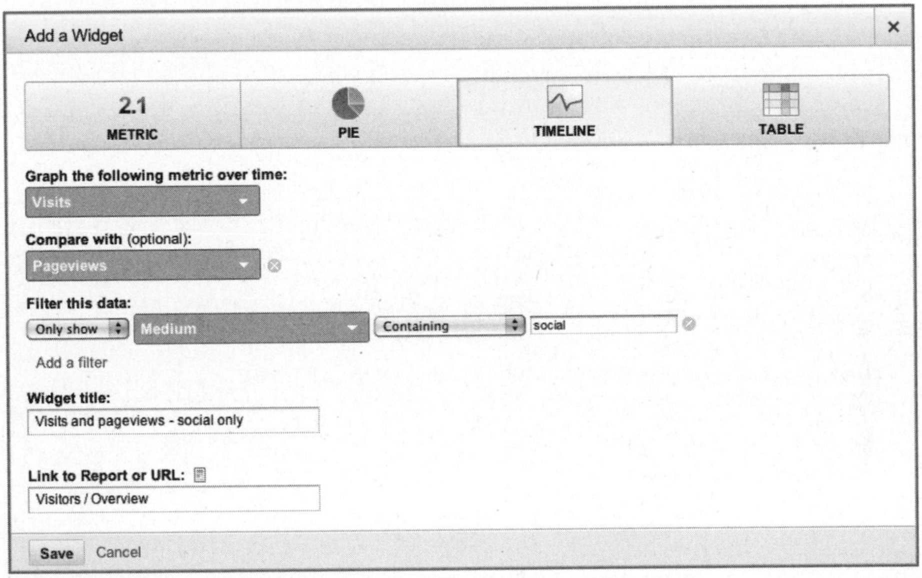

Figure 5.12 Adding a new dashboard widget

Working my way down through Figure 5.12, the first selection is to choose a widget type from the four available. In this example, Timeline is selected and the remaining settings refer to this—the other widgets operate in a similar way. Figure 5.13 highlights what the widget types look like on the dashboard.

Timeline widget

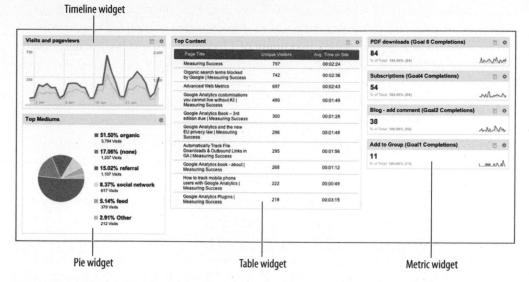

Pie widget   Table widget   Metric widget

Figure 5.13 Dashboard widget types

For a Timeline chart, up to two metrics can be plotted alongside each other with two y-axis scales. Optionally, a filter can be applied to the data. As shown in Figure 5.12, visits and pageviews are to be plotted over time for social media visits only (filtered by medium). The remaining items are to name the widget and optionally add a direct link to the full report.

> **Note:** Applying a widget filter is not the same as applying an advanced segment. That is, it is hit based, not visit based. Consider the following example: You apply a widget filter of `Page URL = homepage.php`. This will include data only for that specific page URL—no other data from the same visit is included. Conversely, for an advanced segment based on the same page URL criteria, if one page during a session matches, the entire session data (visit) is included. That is, pages that do not match the criteria will show in the report because they are part of a visitor's session that included a match. Advanced segments are discussed in detail in Chapter 8, "Best Practices Configuration Guide."

The widget naming is straightforward, though I recommend you include a brief filter description if this option is applied—otherwise it is difficult to discern the name of the widget from the dashboard view. The link to the full report is a clever piece of technology that auto-populates with a shortcut as you type. For example, type the word *visit* to get yourself familiar with the technique.

A key point to emphasize is that a dashboard is configured on a per-user basis. That is, the contents are specific to your login and cannot be adjusted by others.

Top Standard Reports

The following sections are not intended as a definitive list of the only reports you should look at. Rather, they are suggestions to take you beyond the initial visitor volume numbers that you will see. Reviewing these reports for your organization will give you an understanding of visitor behavior before you map your organization's stakeholders and determine what key performance indicators to use for benchmarking your website.

The reports in this chapter are not listed in any particular order, except for the first one, which is an important development for digital marketers (released summer 2011) that deserves special attention. Before reading this chapter, review Chapter 4 to ensure that you get the most out of using the reports.

Multi-Channel Funnels

As discussed in Chapter 3, "Google Analytics Features, Benefits, and Limitations," the default attribution model for Google Analytics is to give credit for a conversion, or a transaction, to the last referral campaign. As you will have appreciated, that is a simplification of what can happen in reality. That is, typically a visitor will come to your website a number of times before they are ready to convert, and each visit can be via a different referrer. Multi-Channel Funnels is a suite of reports that helps you understand the full referral path and what impact *each* referral has on the final conversion. I consider two reports here—Assisted Conversions and Top Conversion Paths.

Assisted Conversions Report

Consider a person looking for a new product or service who is ultimately looking to buy or contact you online. In this scenario, many people start their search on Google looking for general information—they do not yet know the name of the product or company they are looking for and perhaps are not familiar with the exact product terminology. In a "research" frame of mind, they typically select organic links to improve their knowledge because these links are ranked by their corresponding website's content and link value (the number of other websites that link to them). A second visit to your site may come from a review site. Once a decision is made to commit to a purchase or make contact with a supplier, people are then more likely to click an ad for their third visit because these ads have strong call-to-action incentives.

Assuming this results in three visits to your website and a conversion takes place on the third visit, the Multi-Channel Funnels report will show the complete, three-step referral path and will also monetize the first interaction, the last interaction, and any steps in between (assists). Figure 5.14 shows an example assisted conversion report for a site that has monetized goals and an e-commerce shopping cart.

Figure 5.14 Multi-Channel Funnels assisted conversion report

In Figure 5.14, the summary row (label A) immediately tells you that more than one referral contributed to the final conversion. In this example, there are 34 assisted conversions. If the revenue for these conversions—from a mixture of goal values and transactions—is assigned to the assist referrals, their total value is $106, whereas if all the revenue is assigned to the last interaction, the value is $721.

The last column provides a very insightful ratio: The number of assisted referral conversions divided by the number of last click referrals. In this example, the overall value is 0.17. This is a measure of how important assists are to the overall digital marketing plan. A value close to 0 indicates that this channel functioned primarily as the final conversion interaction. A value close to 1 indicates that this channel functioned equally in an assist role and as the final conversion interaction. The more this value exceeds 1, the more this channel functioned in an assist role.

> **Note:** Clarifying Figure 5.14, label A, the total number of goal completions plus transactions (if applicable) is 195, of which 34 had assists from other referrals. That is, it is not 195 + 34 goal completions.

The data table below the chart in Figure 5.14 shows the breakdown of these metrics on a per-channel basis. It is interesting to note that paid advertising (row 6) plays a higher assisting role for this example website than it does as a last click interaction (label B). This shows how simplistic last click conversion analysis is. If only the last click was given credit, paid advertising would be substantially undervalued. In fact, this is applicable for all the referral mediums shown, except for social network—though it should be noted that the conversion numbers are very low toward the bottom of the table.

By default, the Assisted Conversions report shows your referral data grouped into the color-coded dimension named *channels*. These are analogous to referral mediums—as discussed in the sidebar "Glossary of Terms" in Chapter 1, "Why Understanding Your Web Traffic Is Important to Your Business." The exception is the channel named Social Network, which is an advanced segment compiled from over 150 social network sites. You can change the referral dimension shown using the links above the data table (label C). You can also create your own custom channel grouping—either from scratch or using an existing channel group as a template. An example of this is discussed in Chapter 11, "Real-World Tasks."

By default, the Multi-Channel Funnels reports show you data for all conversions from all referral sources. The setting by label D allows you to modify this—for example, viewing data from only AdWords visits. Likewise, you may wish to see data for transactions only or for a specific goal.

As with other reports in Google Analytics, you can apply segmentation to your Multi-Channel Funnels reports. Elsewhere, this is termed Advanced Segments—see Figure 4.4, for example. Within the Multi-Channel Funnels reports it is called Conversion Segments (label E in Figure 5.14). The principal of segmentation is exactly the same in both cases. An example of using a conversion segment for a Multi-Channel Funnels report is discussed in Chapter 11. Advanced Segments are discussed in Chapter 8.

Figure 5.14, label F, shows a message you may see in your Multi-Channel Funnels reports. This is an automatic warning that is displayed if you have a profile filter applied to your report. Essentially, profile filters either remove or manipulate your collected data. Clearly such filters could have a major impact on how representative Multi-Channel Funnels reports can be, hence the warning message.

The general guidance is to use an unfiltered profile for analysis of Multi-Channel Funnels reports—you should always have an unfiltered profile as your data backup! However, filters that do not exclude the referral source, medium, or campaign values of your visitors are okay to use. Similarly, filters that rewrite page URLs, making them readable for example, or rewrite referral mediums for affiliates or social network visits, are usually safe to use. Similarly, filters that exclude entire visits—such as, exclude internal staff, exclude all visits from France, and so on—are usually safe.

In summary, although it is best to avoid profile filters when viewing Multi-Channel Funnels reports, when considered alongside the accuracy of the technique itself (see sidebar), as long as you are not removing visits based on referral data, your data should be fine. Profile filters are discussed in detail in Chapter 8.

The Accuracy of Multi-Channel Funnels

Multi-Channel Funnels reports are generated from conversion paths logged at Google Analytics during the 30 days prior to each conversion or transaction. For this, the unique ID of each visit is required—this is obtained from the Google Analytics __utma cookie. Because a cookie is involved, the same accuracy caveats as described in Chapter 2, "Available Methodologies and Their Accuracy," apply here. That is, visitors who delete their cookies between visits and those who use multiple devices for their browsing will not have accurate Multi-Channel Funnels reports.

If your site sells or provides high-value items, bear in mind that these incur a longer consideration time for purchasers to commit. The higher the value, the more likelihood this could span more than 30 days. If so, you will not see the full referral path of your visitors, the initial steps being missing.

The Multi-Channel Funnels reports also highlight the need for a thorough process for implementing accurate and reliable campaign tracking. This is a critical step if you advertise your website, promote it on social networks, conduct email marketing, or work with affiliates and partners. Campaign tracking is discussed in Chapter 7, "Advanced Implementation."

Top Conversion Paths

This report shows the conversion paths your customers or leads took on their way to converting. An example is shown in Figure 5.15. Looking at this report allows you to see what interactions exist between referrers. In this example, numerous table rows show that "direct" referral visits are combined with another channel. This is interesting because a direct visitor by definition is already familiar with the website URL. Yet email, paid advertising, and organic search still play a role in driving the conversion for these visitors.

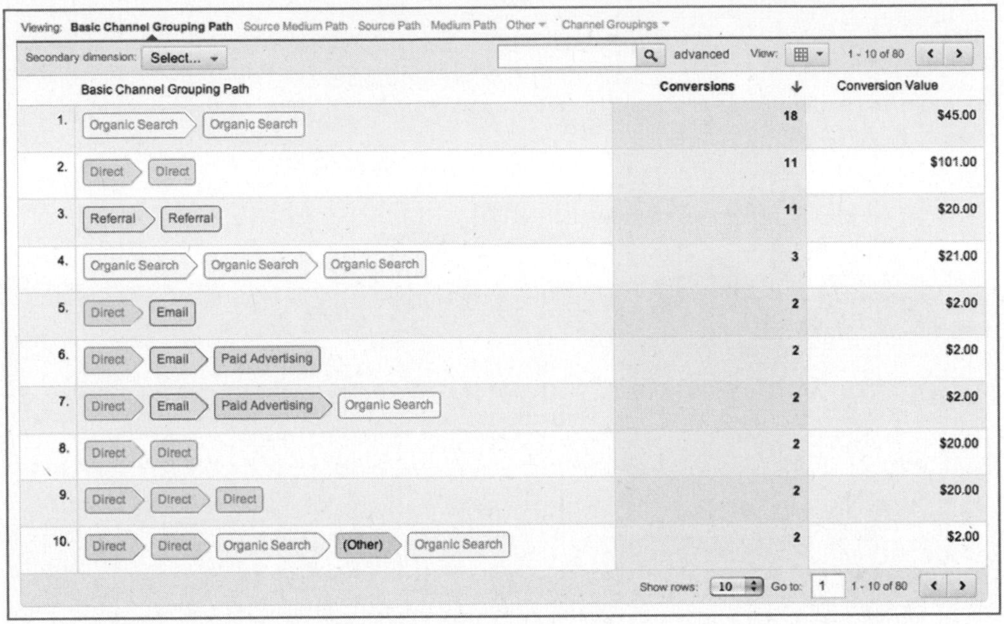

	Basic Channel Grouping Path	Conversions	Conversion Value
1.	Organic Search > Organic Search	18	$45.00
2.	Direct > Direct	11	$101.00
3.	Referral > Referral	11	$20.00
4.	Organic Search > Organic Search > Organic Search	3	$21.00
5.	Direct > Email	2	$2.00
6.	Direct > Email > Paid Advertising	2	$2.00
7.	Direct > Email > Paid Advertising > Organic Search	2	$2.00
8.	Direct > Direct	2	$20.00
9.	Direct > Direct > Direct	2	$20.00
10.	Direct > Direct > Organic Search > (Other) > Organic Search	2	$2.00

Figure 5.15 Top Conversion Paths report (also shown in the color insert)

Considering only last-click-wins analysis, the report shown in Figure 5.15 shows that email and paid advertising would be given credit for only one conversion each. Yet they played a role in three and two conversions, respectively. This report therefore allows you to obtain a more holistic view of how all your digital marketing efforts contribute and interact with each other.

Although not shown here, the same options as shown in Figure 5.14, labels A through F, are available in the Top Conversion Paths report—with a nice little addition: the Path Length drop-down menu, shown in Figure 5.16. This deserves a special mention because of the neat, at-a-glance information it provides. Apart from the ability to change the path length shown in the report, set as 2 Or More by default, this clever item displays a summary table and chart of conversions by path length. Immediately, this allows you to understand the impact of referrer path length on goal conversions. For example, in Figure 5.16 it shows that a significant proportion of conversions have 10 or more referrers!

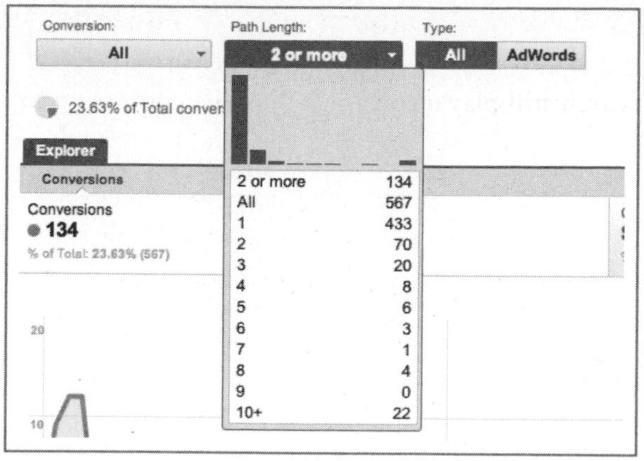

Figure 5.16 Multi-Channel Funnels Path Length view

Important Notes for Multi-Channel Funnels

There are important considerations to take into account when interpreting your Multi-Channel Funnels reports:

- Multi-channel funnels data is compiled from unsampled data and is based on all conversions and transactions.

- Historically, multi-channel funnels data is available back to January 2011.

- Multi-channel funnels reporting is delayed by up to two days due to the amount of processing required to generate the reports.

- Google Analytics records up to 5,000 interactions per conversion path. There is no limit to the number of unique conversion paths that can be recorded.

- A conversion path is created for each conversion and transaction recorded. For example, repeat conversions by the same visitor are shown as different paths.

- Assisted/Last Interaction Conversions ratio: If a channel assisted multiple times in the path of a single conversion, only one conversion is included in the ratio as an assisted conversion. If a channel both assisted and served as the last interaction for a given conversion, the channel is only credited as a last interaction conversion for the ratio.

How Direct Visits Are Treated

In the Multi-Channel Funnels reports, if a person converts on your site during a "direct" visit, the conversion is attributed to the "direct" channel. This differs from other Google Analytics reports in which the conversion is attributed to the previous nondirect campaign or source, if there is one. The default behavior is described in the section "The Default Attribution Model" in Chapter 3.

Social Interactions

Social engagement is the ability to track the actions of people who click your social love buttons. These are the small social network icons that you can add to your website: Like (Facebook), Tweet (Twitter), Google +1 (Google), Share (LinkedIn), and so forth. These are important interactions for website marketers because they indicate a very strong engagement. That is, a visitor appreciated your content so much that they are prepared to tell their friends, colleagues, and acquaintances. It's the equivalent of word of mouth marketing, with the added potential of becoming viral—and it's free.

Google Analytics has the following reports available in the Visitors > Social section:

Engagement How many visitors click one of your love buttons and their associated metrics (pages per visit, time on site, per-visit value, conversion rate, e-commerce revenue, and so on) compared with those who are not socially engaged with you.

Action This is the action provided by the love button, and its value will depend on the social network used and your implementation of its button. Available options include Like, Dislike, Tweet, Share, +1.

Pages The pages where the action took place. This report has a very useful pivot table view set as default that shows the source and action on a per-page basis.

An example Social Action report in shown in Figure 5.17. In this case, Twitter is the preferred social source. With this information you can adjust your social marketing budget accordingly.

To get the most out of this report, ensure that you are familiar with the section "Navigating Your Way Around: Report Layout" in Chapter 4.

Visitors: Location

The Visitors > Demographics > Location report shows you where your visitors come from, enabling you to identify your most lucrative geographic markets. Visually stunning, the map overlay is also an extremely powerful report—it gets across the information you need to know at a glance. The displayed maps are color-coded by density—the darker the color, the higher the reported metric, such as more visits or revenue. A density key is shown in the bottom-left corner, and you can mouse over the regions, countries, or cities to view top-level metrics.

Geographic information is extremely powerful for targeting your online marketing activities. For online marketing, Google AdWords (and other pay-per-click networks) enables you to geotarget your advertisements. In this respect, the locations report of Google Analytics can be used in two ways: to identify new locations for potential online campaigns and to measure the effectiveness of existing geotargeted campaigns.

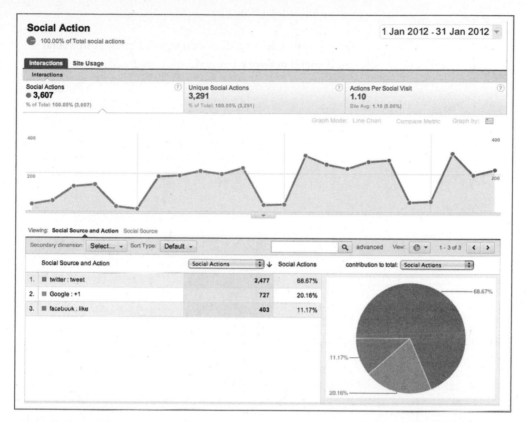

Figure 5.17 Example Social Action report

To illustrate its ability, consider the two charts in Figure 5.18—shown for the same profile and date range. Figure 5.18a shows the visitor information, whereas Figure 5.18b shows the e-commerce conversion rate data from the same visitors. As you can see, the map densities are quite different.

Within the map, use your mouse to click and zoom in from world view to country, regional, and city level and along the way examine visitor statistics from that part of the world. You zoom out by using the breadcrumb navigation located just above the summary row of data at the top of the report. Below the displayed map is the tabulated data for the selected region, with the additional option of selecting a continent and subcontinent. For each location, you can cross-segment your visitors against other metrics, such as referral source, medium, language, and so on, by using the Secondary Dimension drop-down. For example, once you have found your location of interest, you can cross-segment to view which mediums are popular with your visitors there—as shown in Figure 5.19.

Figure 5.18 Geographic density of (a) visits and (b) goal conversions rate for the same data set (also shown in the color insert)

As with all reports shown in this chapter, to get the most out of this report, ensure you are familiar with the section "Navigating Your Way Around: Report Layout" in Chapter 4.

E-commerce: Overview Report

The e-commerce section is a suite of reports that enable you to identify top-performing products and revenue sources and to trace transactions back to a specific campaign—right down to the keyword level. Individual product data can be viewed and grouped (referred to as categories), and loyalty and latency metrics (the number of days to transact, the number of visits to transact) are available. Such information is critical for a successful product-by-product search-engine marketing initiative as well as for determining what products to stock and your pricing strategy.

 Note: Even if you do not have an e-commerce facility, you should still monetize your website by adding goal values. Monetizing a non-e-commerce website is discussed in detail in Chapter 11, "Real-World Tasks."

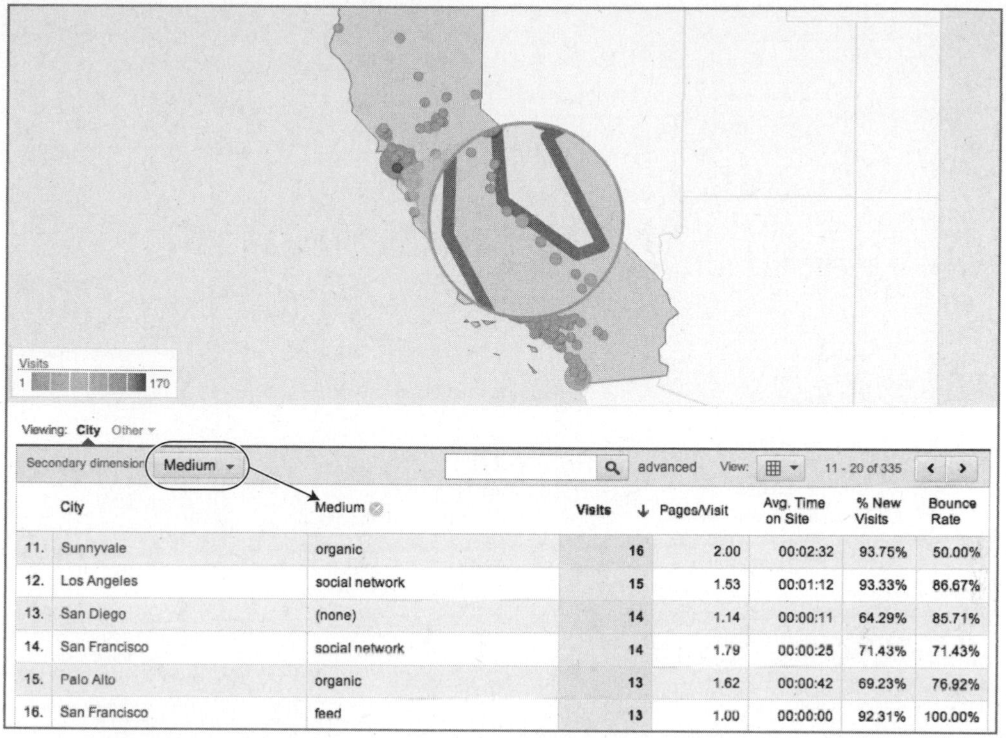

Figure 5.19 Segmenting geographic visitors using a secondary dimension

From the initial Conversions > E-commerce > Overview report (see Figure 5.20), a wealth of information is provided for you to feast on. These are the details that are driving your website transactions. From here, select a top revenue source from the left-hand table to view its detail in the right-hand table; products are selected by default. Click one of the top-performing products to view its individual report and then cross-segment, by selecting a secondary dimension, against other fields, such as referral source, campaign name, keywords, and so on. Alternatively, to view all products, select the View Full Report link at the bottom of the report highlighted in Figure 5.20.

Motion Charts

Motion charts are a great aid for data visualization. They turn static, dry, two-dimensional data tables into something that is interesting and even exciting to look at—a rare phenomenon in the world of data analysis! Most important, motion charts animate data against time, so that you can see how multiple metrics evolve. A static version is shown in Figure 5.21.

E-commerce Overview

1 Jan 2012 - 31 Jan 2012 ▾

100.00% of Total visits

Overview

Metric: E-commerce Conversion Rate   Compare Metric   Graph by:

20.00%   20.00%

10.00%   10.00%

~∿∿ **4.08%** E-commerce Conversion Rate

~∿∿ **23** Transactions

~∿∿ **$247.00** Revenue

───∿─ **$10.74** Average Value

~∿∿ **23** Unique Purchases

~∿∿ **23** Quantity

Top Revenue Sources

Product	>
Product SKU	
Product Category	
Source/Medium	

Product	Quantity	% Quantity
Enhanced Listing: 24/7 PLUMBER	2	8.70%
Enhanced Listing: 1st Format Loft Conversions	1	4.35%
Enhanced Listing: 24/7 PLUMBING & HEATING.	1	4.35%
Enhanced Listing: Ancestree Research	1	4.35%
Enhanced Listing: Animal Kickboxing	1	4.35%
Enhanced Listing: Castle Garage Doors	1	4.35%
Enhanced Listing: Cuckmere Corrections	1	4.35%
Enhanced Listing: Jones Britain	1	4.35%
Enhanced Listing: Law Tutor London	1	4.35%
Enhanced Listing: Mindshare Marketing	1	4.35%

view full report

Figure 5.20 A typical E-commerce Overview report

A motion chart is not a report in itself. Rather, it's an animated view of an existing report. Hence, you can access motion charts from most Google Analytics reports by selecting the Graph Mode button at the top of the chart (refer to Figure 4.4, label C3). When a report is animated, five dimensions are plotted: x-axis, y-axis, data point size, data point color, and time. Because of the difficulty in describing how all of these interact on paper, I strongly encourage you to view the official YouTube demonstration on the Google Analytics channel at www.youtube.com/watch?v=D4QePIt_TTs.

 Note: The voice behind many Google Analytics demonstrations on YouTube is Alden DeSoto. You can view one of his many talents (and other Google Analytics team members) at www.youtube.com/watch?v=nimrc-uG7UY.

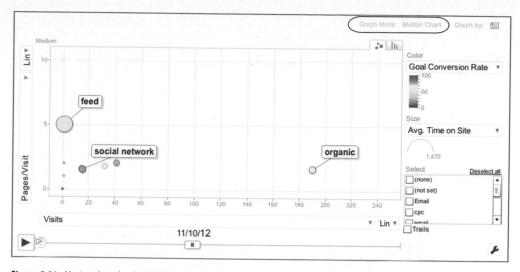

Figure 5.21 Motion chart for the Traffic Sources Medium report (also shown in the color insert)

In the example in Figure 5.21, the five dimensions for each data point are as follows:

- Visits—shown on the y-axis
- Pages per visit—shown on the x-axis
- Goal conversion rate—color
- Average time on site—bubble size
- Time—displayed as a time slider below the chart (paused on January 10)

The signals for success in this motion chart are data points that are up and to the right, have a large bubble size, and appear hot (red in color). This informs you of any mediums that are driving high volumes of traffic, with strong engagement (in terms of pages per visit and time on site), and conversions. If and when that happens, how long such a situation lasts, and how each medium compares over time are key pieces of information that are practically impossible to ascertain from a static set of data tables.

There are many more features of motion charts that you should explore. For example, you can plot x- and y-axis on a log scale (used when the range of displayed values is very broad), adjust the speed of an animation, plot trails for each data point, zoom in on a particular chart area, alter the opacity of data points to highlight those of most importance, and even change the presentation from a bubble chart to a bar chart—though I have always preferred the bubble chart format.

At first, the motion of multiple metrics moving across the screen can make your eyes glaze over; it can even be mesmeric. "It's pretty, but what's it telling me?" is often the initial response from users. However, once you get familiar with following the different metrics, you'll learn how to spot unusual events that require further investigation.

The key to getting the most from this report is selecting long time periods (greater than a month) and repeatedly viewing the animation in slow motion. After three or four run-throughs, you should notice any activity of interest. Select Trails and adjust the opacity to focus on certain data points accordingly. Remember that a motion chart is a visualization tool—that is, the precursor for further analysis.

Tip: Ensure that you use all five dimensions of the motion chart available to you—even if fewer are required. For instance, I often use the color and bubble dimensions as duplicates to highlight a significant change. In the example in Figure 5.21, if the average time on site is not a metric of interest, I would also use the bubble size for the goal conversion rate. That way, higher conversion-rate data points are double highlighted with a large bubble and warmer color. The more you can make important data stand out, the better.

Goal and Funnel Reports

As discussed throughout this book, goal reporting (conversions) is an important measurement for your organization. Regardless of whether you have an online retail facility or not, measuring goal conversions is the de facto way to ascertain whether your website is engaging to your visitors and therefore a key component of measuring success.

In addition to measuring your goal conversion rate, the Conversions > Goals > Goal URLs report enables you to view the specific URLs that trigger the reporting of a goal. This is particularly useful when a wildcard is used to define the goal, such as, for example, *.pdf. In this case, the Goal URLs report will list all the PDF downloads that trigger the reporting of that defined conversion.

Also within this section, the Reverse Goal Path report considers the last three steps (pages) visitors took before reaching a goal. This is an excellent place to look for visitor paths that could be considered for *funnel analysis*.

Goal Conversions versus Goal Completions

Say, for example, one of your website goals is *.pdf—that is, the download of any PDF file. A visitor arrives on your website and downloads five PDF files. Google Analytics will count this as one goal conversion (not five, as you might expect). The rationale for this is that visitors can convert only once during their session, which makes sense.

To view the total number of PDF downloads and which files they were, you can either view the Conversions > Goals > Goal URLs report or, if you wish to cross-segment the data, go to the Content > Pages report and use the table filter to display only PDF files.

Funnel analysis (sometimes referred to as *path analysis* by other vendor tools) is a subsection of the Goals report. Some goals have clearly defined paths that a visitor takes to reach the goal. An obvious example is an e-commerce checkout process; others include newsletter sign-ups, registration subscriptions, reservation systems, and brochure requests. Not all goals have a defined path, but if yours do, then it is useful to visualize how your visitors traverse them (or not) to reach the goal. The Funnel Visualization report helps you do just that, and an example is shown in Figure 5.22 taken from the Conversions > Goals > Funnel Visualization section.

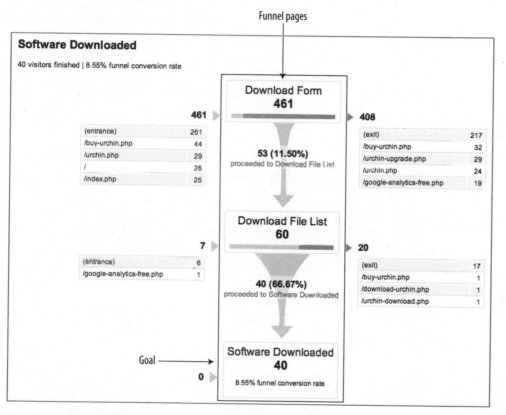

Figure 5.22 A three-step Funnel Visualization report (also shown in the color insert)

The pages of a funnel a visitor is expected to pass through (as defined by your configuration) to reach the goal are in the central section highlighted in Figure 5.22—in this example, to download software. The tables to the left are entrance pages into the funnel. The tables to the right are exit pages out of the funnel steps—that is, where visitors go when they leave the funnel page. The exit pages listed can be other pages within your website or the report can show the visitor leaving the site completely. A well-defined funnel should have the vast majority of visitors passing downward into a minimum number of funnel steps.

Funnel visualization enables you to assess how good your funnel pages are at persuasion—that is, how good they are at getting visitors to proceed to the next step, getting closer to approaching conversion. A funnel with pages optimized for persuasion and conversion should have a minimal number of exit points (pages to the right of the funnel), thereby leading to a high conversion rate. A detailed funnel analysis is considered in the section "Funnel Optimization Case Study" in Chapter 11.

Visitor: Mobile Report

Google Analytics tracks all visitors to your website, whether they come via a mobile, laptop, desktop, or any other Internet-enabled device that can execute JavaScript and set cookies. Mobile devices include smartphones and tablets such as the iPad, the Samsung Galaxy Tab, and so forth. Because the user experience of accessing a website via a mobile device is not the same as via a desktop or laptop, Google has a dedicated report section just for such visitors—found in the in the Visitors > Mobile section.

The mobile Overview report provides the information required to understand the differences between mobile visitors and those from regular computers. Metrics such as pages per visit, time on site, per-visit value, conversion rate, e-commerce revenue, and so forth can be compared for the two visitor types. This report looks very similar to other Google Analytics reports, except the data is for the two segments of Mobile = Yes and Mobile = No. Therefore, I show the Visitors > Mobile > Devices report (Figure 5.23).

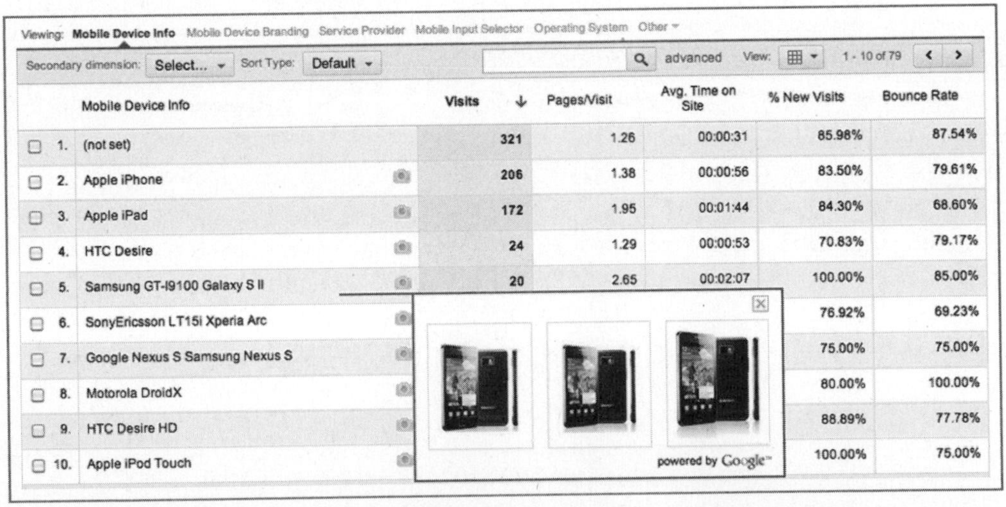

Mobile Device Info		Visits ↓	Pages/Visit	Avg. Time on Site	% New Visits	Bounce Rate
☐ 1.	(not set)	321	1.26	00:00:31	85.98%	87.54%
☐ 2.	Apple iPhone	206	1.38	00:00:56	83.50%	79.61%
☐ 3.	Apple iPad	172	1.95	00:01:44	84.30%	68.60%
☐ 4.	HTC Desire	24	1.29	00:00:53	70.83%	79.17%
☐ 5.	Samsung GT-I9100 Galaxy S II	20	2.65	00:02:07	100.00%	85.00%
☐ 6.	SonyEricsson LT15i Xperia Arc				76.92%	69.23%
☐ 7.	Google Nexus S Samsung Nexus S				75.00%	75.00%
☐ 8.	Motorola DroidX				80.00%	100.00%
☐ 9.	HTC Desire HD				88.89%	77.78%
☐ 10.	Apple iPod Touch				100.00%	75.00%

Figure 5.23 Mobile devices report

The report shown in Figure 5.23 lists the mobile brand and device name as the dimension. In addition, clicking the small camera icon next to the device name displays a pop-up with images of the selected device—as shown for Samsung. Other interesting dimensions that can be selected include Mobile Input Device (such as touch screen, clickwheel, joystick) and Screen Resolutions (from the Other drop-down menu option). You can also select screen resolutions as a secondary dimension.

To get the most from this report, ensure that you are familiar with "Navigating Your Way Around: Report Layout" in Chapter 4.

> **Note:** No additional Google Analytics setup is required to track visitors from smartphones or tablets. However, if your site needs to cater to users of older-generation feature phones and their WAP protocol, you will need to implement server-side tracking. This is discussed in "Tracking Mobile Visitors" in Chapter 6, "Getting Started: Initial Setup."

Traffic Sources: Search Engine Optimization

The vast majority of reports in your Google Analytics account are generated from data of visitors actually viewing your content. That is, they are *on-site* analytics reports. The Search Engine Optimization reports are an example of combining this with *off-site* data, which is data points Google captures prior to a visitor coming to your site. The following off-site metrics are examples that could be shown in your Search Engine Optimization reports:

- Impressions—the number of times any URL from your site appeared in Google's search results viewed by a user, not including paid AdWords search impressions

- Average Position—the average ranking of your website URLs for the query or queries

This information comes from an import of data from your Google Webmaster Tools account (www.google.com/webmasters). Essentially, Webmaster Tools is a set of tools from Google to assist you in the management and promotion of your website in Google's organic results. In other words, it's information about your pages' visibility on Google search properties, so it's an important set of reports.

> **Note:** The differences between onsite and offsite web analytics are discussed in Chapter 1.

To view your Search Engine Optimization reports, you will need to have a Google Webmaster Tools account and integrate it with your Google Analytics account. This is described in Chapter 6. Assuming you have done this, a key report from this section is the Queries report, shown in Figure 5.24. These are the keywords used by your visitors on one of Google's search properties (such as google.com or google.co.uk). As you will note from Figure 5.24, I have added a secondary dimension Google Property to the table and sorted descending by the number of click-throughs.

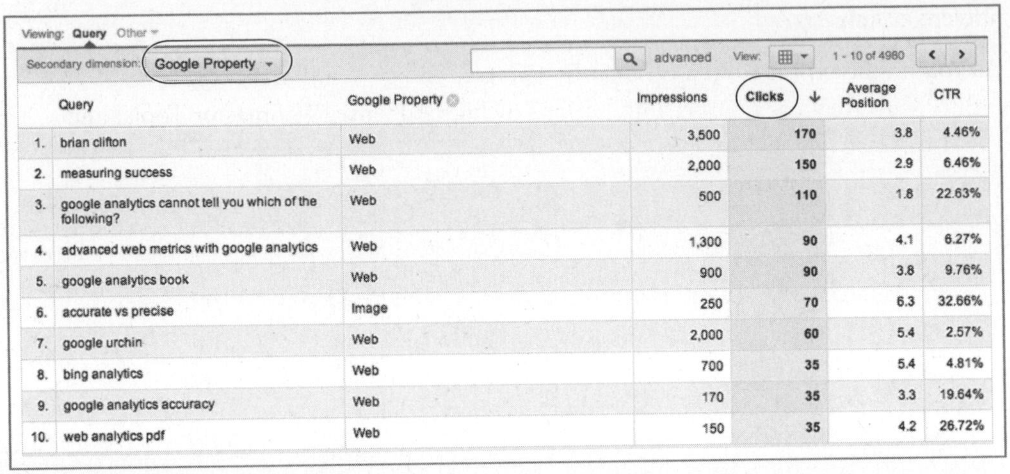

Viewing: Query Other

Secondary dimension: Google Property

advanced View: 1 - 10 of 4980

	Query	Google Property	Impressions	Clicks	Average Position	CTR
1.	brian clifton	Web	3,500	170	3.8	4.46%
2.	measuring success	Web	2,000	150	2.9	6.46%
3.	google analytics cannot tell you which of the following?	Web	500	110	1.8	22.63%
4.	advanced web metrics with google analytics	Web	1,300	90	4.1	6.27%
5.	google analytics book	Web	900	90	3.8	9.76%
6.	accurate vs precise	Image	250	70	6.3	32.66%
7.	google urchin	Web	2,000	60	5.4	2.57%
8.	bing analytics	Web	700	35	5.4	4.81%
9.	google analytics accuracy	Web	170	35	3.3	19.64%
10.	web analytics pdf	Web	150	35	4.2	26.72%

Figure 5.24 Search Engine Optimization report

The Google Property dimension shown in Figure 5.24 can have one of four values: Web Search, Mobile Search, Video Search, or Image Search. From this report, row 6 shows that a significant number of visits (strictly speaking, click-throughs) came from Google image search. That fact alone may be important to the website owner and marketing department.

By viewing the Impressions column and comparing it with the Clicks column, you can see how much of your potential audience you are capturing via your organic rankings—the Click Through Rate (CTR) column provides the ratio. In this example, the CTR highlights that my relatively unique name is capturing only 4.46 percent of the total traffic (table row 1). That could be of concern, only capturing such a small percentage of the market. However, a little further investigation reveals a US basketball coach shares the same name. So I may not be doing so badly with my organic rankings after all.

Data Import Accuracy and Limitations

The data shown in the Traffic Sources > Search Engine Optimization reports is an import from your Google Webmaster Tools account and is subject to the same limitations. That is, data is limited to your top 1,000 daily query terms and top 1,000 daily landing pages. There is also a two-day delay for importing the Webmaster Tools data. As with all data imports, be aware that click-through data may not exactly align with your visit reports. Accuracy considerations are discussed in Chapter 2.

AdWords: Campaigns

As you might expect from a product by Google, Google Analytics integrates tightly with AdWords. Other integrations include AdSense, Webmaster Tools, and FeedBurner. Undoubtedly in the future there will be further integrations with other Google products. In fact, I see this as Google's main challenge moving forward—integrating Google Analytics within all Google products to provide a unified measurement platform for each.

AdWords, being a key component of any digital marketer's armory these days, has a dedicated subsection of reports within the Advertising menu navigation. Assuming you have an AdWords account and it is linked to your Google Analytics account, your AdWords impression, cost, position, and click-through data is imported into this report area.

Note: An AdWords import takes place whenever a report containing AdWords data is generated. This ensures that you always view the latest data and that it will match what you can view directly in your AdWords account.

The power of combining your AdWords account data with Google Analytics is illustrated in Figure 5.25—taken from the Advertising > AdWords > Campaigns report. For example, Figure 5.25 shows the campaign detail with the same column headings and report tabs as for any other visitor type. That is, for each campaign, you can view its performance in terms of site usage, goal conversions, and e-commerce performance. Do not limit yourself to the initial default data shown. Use the full suite of reports features available to you, as described in the section "Navigating Your Way Around: Report Layout" in Chapter 4. You can also drill down and perform the same analysis at the ad group and keyword levels by selecting these reports from the navigation menu.

At the top of Figure 5.25 are buttons to show traffic from visitors who used a high-end mobile (smartphone) or tablet device when clicking your ad. Essentially these are advanced segments for the different device types and allow you to analyze your performance just for those visitor users.

A unique menu tab for AdWords reports is Clicks, shown in Figure 5.26. With the exception of the Revenue Per Click (RPC) and ROI columns, the data in the Clicks report is imported directly from your AdWords account. The revenue is obtained by summing your website's monetized goals and any e-commerce revenue generated by AdWords visitors.

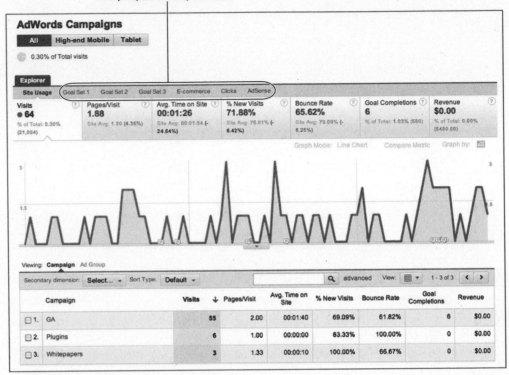

Figure 5.25 AdWords per campaign

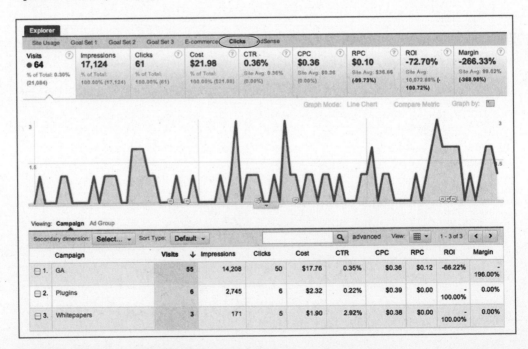

Figure 5.26 AdWords Campaigns report showing the Clicks detail

In addition to tracking your AdWords cost data, you should keep a close eye on your return on investment (ROI). Chapter 11 looks at interpreting this data in more detail.

AdWords: Keyword Report

This report allows you to view the performance of your ads at the keyword level. However, for this example I use it to display the domains of click-throughs from the display network. Digital marketers have the option of displaying ads on either the Google search network (google.com, ask.com, aol.com, and so on), the display network, or both. The display network comprises websites, news pages, and blogs that partner with Google to display targeted AdWords ads. The partner uses AdSense to manage this and shares in some of the click-through revenue.

If you have opted in to displaying your ads on the Google display network, then your Advertising > AdWords > Keywords report will display (content targeting) in the keyword column for such click-throughs—as shown in Figure 5.27 (a table filter is used to show only these visits). To analyze the performance of your content network visits, apply the secondary dimension of Placement Domain to show which website the visitor came from.

At this time it is not possible to view the actual keyword matching that AdSense has performed.

	Keyword	Placement Domain	Visits ↓	Pages/Visit	Avg. Time on Site	% New Visits	Bounce Rate	Goal Completions	Revenue
☐ 1.	(content targeting)	youtube.com	17	1.00	00:00:00	11.76%	100.00%	0	£0.00
☐ 2.	(content targeting)	glasgowonline.co.uk	6	3.00	00:01:12	50.00%	50.00%	2	£0.00
☐ 3.	(content targeting)	smashingwindscreens.co.uk	6	6.17	00:02:15	100.00%	33.33%	4	£0.00
☐ 4.	(content targeting)	streetdirectory.com	5	4.80	00:02:17	60.00%	40.00%	0	£0.00
☐ 5.	(content targeting)	autoinsider.co.uk	4	4.50	00:04:17	50.00%	25.00%	0	£0.00
☐ 6.	(content targeting)	google.com	4	2.50	00:05:52	75.00%	50.00%	0	£0.00
☐ 7.	(content targeting)	ibuckinghamshire.co.uk	4	4.75	00:01:58	75.00%	25.00%	1	£0.00
☐ 8.	(content targeting)	tecca.com	4	1.00	00:00:00	0.00%	100.00%	0	£0.00
☐ 9.	(content targeting)	whocallsme.com	4	4.25	00:03:15	0.00%	0.00%	3	£0.00
☐ 10.	(remarketing/content targeting)	funnygames.co.uk	4	1.00	00:00:00	0.00%	100.00%	0	£0.00

Figure 5.27 AdWords Keywords report showing the referring domain for content network visitors

AdWords: Matched Queries Report

For managing an AdWords account, digital marketers create ads for groups of related search terms. For example, to target visitors to this book's website, I might select the following search terms:

- Web metrics
- Advanced web metrics
- Advanced web metrics third edition
- Advanced web metrics second edition
- Advanced web metrics *any* edition

Assuming the same landing page URL is suitable for each search term, I would create a single ad for all four-plus search terms—there is no need to create separate ads for each term. Within AdWords you achieve this by setting the match type equal to *phrase* for the term "web metrics." In this way, any search query with this phrase will result in my ad being displayed to the user. Incidentally, I could also add negative search terms, so that "web metrics with Yahoo Analytics" does not display my advertisement!

In this case, a single ad targeting multiple search terms, "web metrics" is the *bid term*, whereas the visitor's actual search term that triggers the ad is called the *search term*. You can view the correlation between bid terms and search terms in the Advertising > AdWords > Matched Search Query report, setting the secondary dimension as Keyword—as shown in Figure 5.28. Note that Google Analytics uses the terminology Keyword and Matched Search Query for the AdWords bid term and search term, respectively.

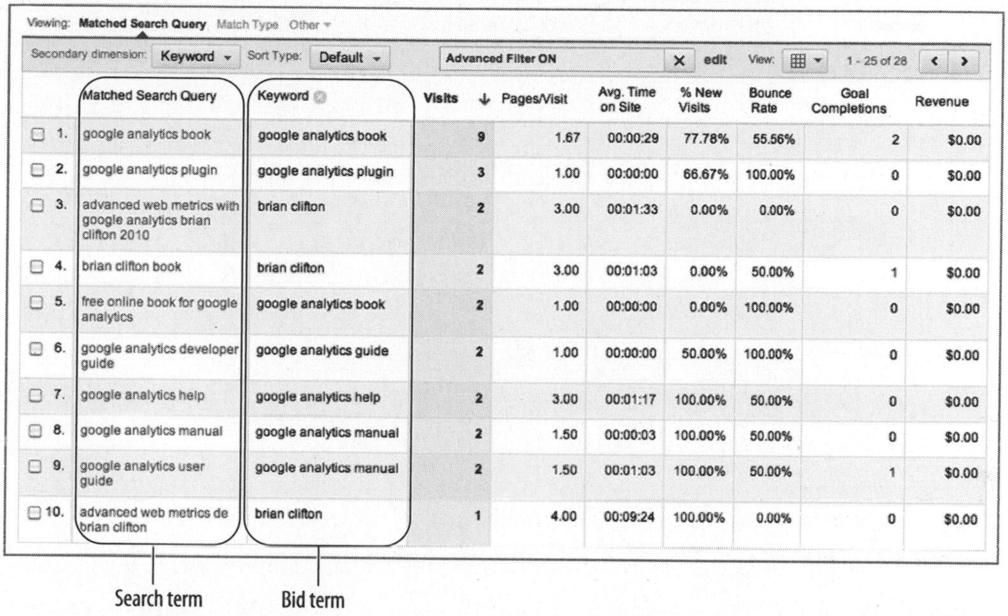

	Matched Search Query	Keyword	Visits	Pages/Visit	Avg. Time on Site	% New Visits	Bounce Rate	Goal Completions	Revenue
1.	google analytics book	google analytics book	9	1.67	00:00:29	77.78%	55.56%	2	$0.00
2.	google analytics plugin	google analytics plugin	3	1.00	00:00:00	66.67%	100.00%	0	$0.00
3.	advanced web metrics with google analytics brian clifton 2010	brian clifton	2	3.00	00:01:33	0.00%	0.00%	0	$0.00
4.	brian clifton book	brian clifton	2	3.00	00:01:03	0.00%	50.00%	1	$0.00
5.	free online book for google analytics	google analytics book	2	1.00	00:00:00	0.00%	100.00%	0	$0.00
6.	google analytics developer guide	google analytics guide	2	1.00	00:00:00	50.00%	100.00%	0	$0.00
7.	google analytics help	google analytics help	2	3.00	00:01:17	100.00%	50.00%	0	$0.00
8.	google analytics manual	google analytics manual	2	1.50	00:00:03	100.00%	50.00%	0	$0.00
9.	google analytics user guide	google analytics manual	2	1.50	00:01:03	100.00%	50.00%	1	$0.00
10.	advanced web metrics de brian clifton	brian clifton	1	4.00	00:09:24	100.00%	0.00%	0	$0.00

Figure 5.28 AdWords Matched Search Query report showing the search term and corresponding bid terms

AdWords: Keyword Positions Report

The AdWords Keyword Positions report tells you what position your AdWords ad was in when the visitor clicked it. In addition, you can drill down and view how your ad conversion rate, bounce rate, per-visit goal value, number of transactions, revenue, and other metrics vary by position, using the Position Breakdown drop-down menu.

In Figure 5.29, the left side of the report table lists the AdWords keywords you have bid on during the specified time frame. Selecting one of these options changes the view on the right to a schematic screen shot of the Google search engine, with the positions your ad was shown at and the number of visits received while in that position. This emulates what the positions would look like on the Google search engine results page.

You might expect that the higher your position in the AdWords auction model, the more visitors you receive. However, this may not always be the case and may not be desirable. For example, high ad positions—especially those displayed at the top of the pages rather than on the side—may get more clicks, but they may be less qualified (poorer quality). Therefore, it's important to study the effect of ad position on other metrics. Figure 5.30 shows the Goal 1 conversion rate and per-visit goal value for a different keyword selected from the same report. As you can see, these metrics show a very different pattern by position compared to the volume of visits by position. The key to success is to strike the right balance between high-quality click-throughs and volume of traffic.

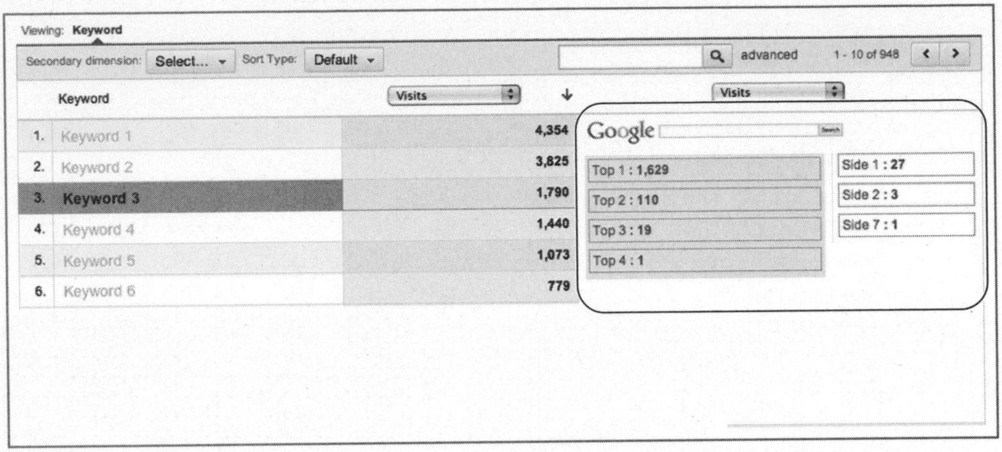

Figure 5.29 AdWords Keyword Positions report

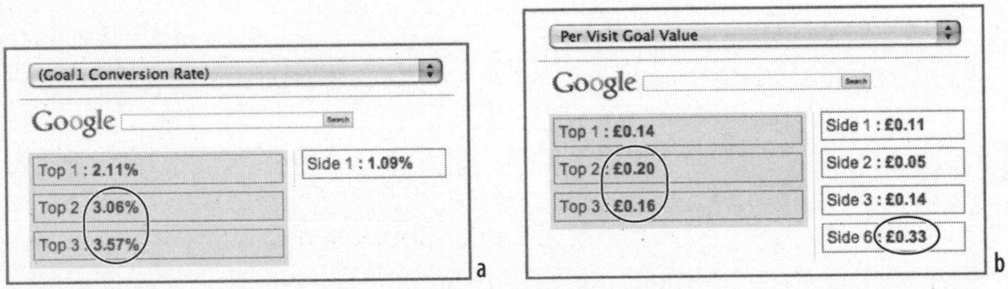

Figure 5.30 AdWords Keyword Positions report for (a) Goal 1 conversion rate and (b) per-visit goal value

Understanding the Average Position Metric

Hal Varian, Google's chief economist, has written a very insightful article on the subject of understanding the average position metric. The post is available from the AdWords official blog:

```
http://adwords.blogspot.com/2011/04/understanding-average-position-
metric.html
```

Content: Navigation Summary

Knowing which pages, and landing pages, are popular on your site is an obvious first step when assessing your website's performance. The common per-page metrics of pageviews, time on site, bounce rate (single-page zero event visits), and percentage of visits that leave from a page (% Exit) are all available in the Content > Site Content > Pages report and the Landing Pages report, respectively. I discuss the use of the Landing Pages report in Chapter 11.

Going beyond the page metrics, another useful report is the Navigation Summary. You get to this from the Pages report by clicking a listed URL (or page title) and then selecting Navigation Summary. An example is shown in Figure 5.31 for the URL /blog/auto-tracking-file-downloads-outbound-links/.

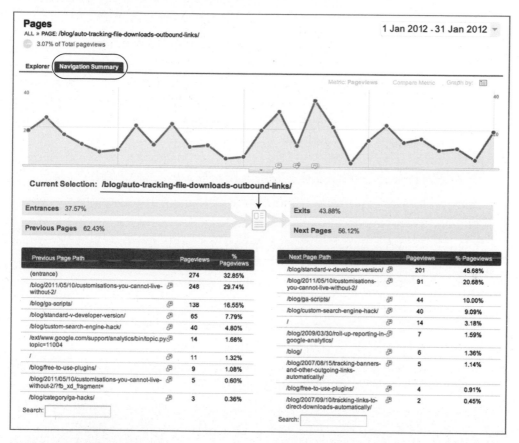

Figure 5.31 Navigation Summary report

At first the Navigation Summary report can appear confusing. However, the key is to focus on the central "page" icon that represents the URL selected. The summary metrics to left of the page icon show the percent of visits that came directly to this page and the remaining percentage that came via another page on this site. The summary metrics to the right of the page icon show the number of visits that left the site completely from this URL and the number of visits that went on to view another page within the site.

Below the summary information is the detail of the previous and next page URLs viewed. This is a great way to understand how traffic has flowed through a specific page URL. By default, the top 10 previous and next URLs are shown in the table. You can drill down below this using the search boxes provided at the bottom. You can view each page URL by clicking the small icon in each row. This opens the page in a new window.

 Note: If you wish to see a more general view of how traffic flows through your website, view the Flow Visualization report as described earlier in this chapter.

Content: Site Speed

No one likes waiting, yet for some reason the tolerance for waiting on the Internet is super low—it's simply too easy to go somewhere else. And people do. A study by Forrester Consulting examining e-commerce website performance and its correlation with an online shopper's behavior found site performance to be a key factor in a consumer's loyalty to a site.

www.akamai.com/html/about/press/releases/2009/press_091409.html

You probably realized this already. However, the report puts some interesting numbers to what our intuition tells us:

- Fifty-two percent of online shoppers stated that quick page loading is important to their site loyalty.

- The speed threshold expected was only 2 seconds.

- Shoppers often become distracted when made to wait for a page to load. Fourteen percent will begin shopping at another site, and 23 percent will stop shopping or walk away from their computer.

- For retail and travel sites, 79 percent of online shoppers who experience a dissatisfying visit are less likely to buy from that site again.

Hence, your site's speed is closely correlated with your revenue, lead generation, visitor engagement, and their loyalty. In view of that, Google has a dedicated report that focuses on the speed of your pages in the Content > Site Speed section. My initial preference is the Performance report shown in Figure 5.32 because it provides a quick overview of any performance issues.

You can view the performance of your individual URLs by clicking on the Explorer link above the summary metrics. The impact of geolocation on your speed can be seen in the Map Overlay section. The general rule of thumb is that the farther away your visitors are from your web servers, the longer the latency of their connection.

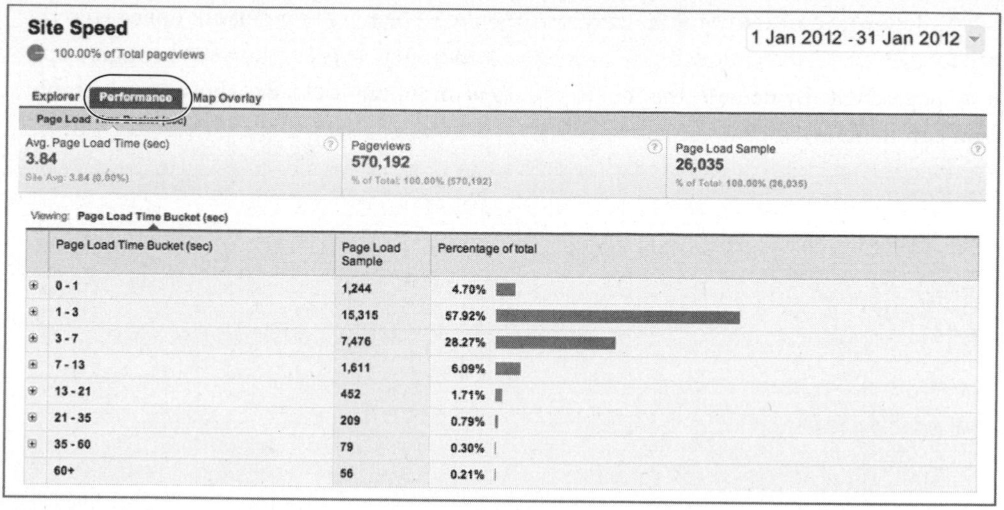

Figure 5.32 Site Speed report

Site Speed Data Sampling

Site speed data is automatically collected for all web properties at a 1 percent sample rate. No changes to your web pages or your GATC are required.

The default sample rate may be adjusted using the _setSiteSpeedSampleRate function. Allowed sample rates range from 0 (to disable site speed tracking) to 10 (maximum allowed sample rate). This is described in the section "Customizing the GATC" in Chapter 7.

Site Search: Usage Report

The Site Search reports contained in the Content section of Google Analytics are dedicated to understanding the usage of your internal search engine (if you have one). For large, complex websites with thousands of product pages, and in some cases hundreds of thousands, having an internal site search engine is critical for a successful visitor experience—no navigational system can perform as well as a good internal search engine in these cases.

At the very least, Site Search reports are a form of market research—every time visitors enter a keyword into your search box, they are telling you exactly what they want to find on your website. Marketers can use this information to better target campaigns. Content creators can use it to improve page titles and descriptions. Product managers can use it as a feedback mechanism for designing new features or adding new products. Hence, a report on the search terms used by visitors on your website is clearly powerful information for your organization.

In addition, understanding where on your website a visitor uses your search box, what page they go to following a search, how long they stay on your site after conducting a search, whether they perform further search refinements, whether they are more likely to make a conversion, and whether their average order value is higher are also vital clues that can help you optimize the visitor experience.

The answers to all these questions can be found in the Content > Site Search section, as shown in Figure 5.33.

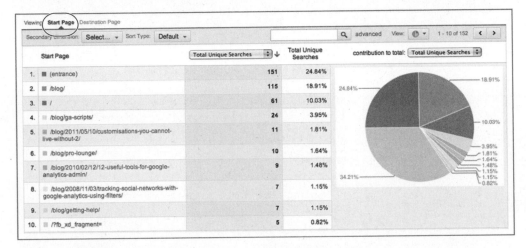

Figure 5.33 Site Search report showing which pages visitors start their search from (also shown in the color section)

Content: In-Page Analytics

The In-Page Analytics report loads a page from your website and then overlays it with the key metrics for each link on that page. It's an excellent visual way to see which links on your website drive traffic, conversions, transactions, and revenue (see Figure 5.34). The default view is to display the percentage of clicks received for each link on a page using a small orange bar next to the link—mouse over a percentage bar chart to see the corresponding pop-up metrics as per label A in Figure 5.34.

You can easily change the metrics displayed using the control drop-down menu at the top of the report—label B. For example, you can show number of goal completions, transactions, revenue, or goal value. You can also set a threshold for visualizations of that metric, such as, for example, clicks with more than 10 percent.

The In-Page Analytics report is a working HTML preview of your website. Hence, you can click any of your links to navigate to that page and view its overlaid statistics. As you may have noticed in Figure 5.34, some metrics are duplicated. For example, the logo at the top-left side and the first link in the top menu (Home) both show 9.1 percent of the clicks from this page. In fact, these two metrics are duplicates because each link points to exactly the same page. Chapter 9 describes how you can customize your links so that the In-Page Analytics repo rt can be used to differentiate links that point to the same URL.

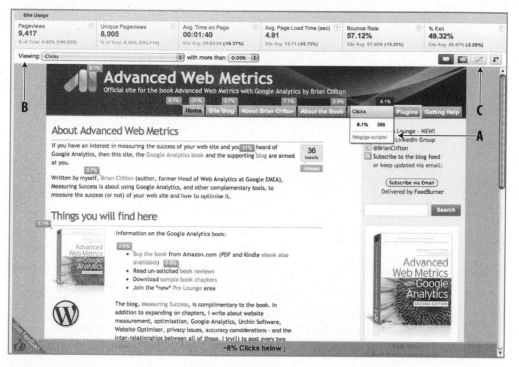

Figure 5.34 In-Page Analytics report (also shown in the color insert)

The control labeled C in Figure 5.34 allows you to show or hide the overlay metrics, color-code the orange bar (blue for low values, red for high, with shades in between), and expand the view to a fuller screen.

Current Limitations of In-Page Analytics

In order for In-Page Analytics to work correctly, the page referenced by each link must exist as an HREF element on the page being viewed. That is, if you use the function _trackPageView for generating virtual pageviews (as described in Chapter 7, "Advanced Implementation"), the In-Page Analytics report will not work. Nor will In-Page Analytics work for pages containing Flash content.

Another example is the submission of forms. A submit button or form tag does not contain an HREF element. Therefore, if you have a goal conversion configured as a form submission, the In-Page Analytics report will not show this as part of the metrics.

Understanding Report Sampling

Report sampling is a process used for sites that generate large volumes of visit data. The rationale is to optimize the report generation and minimize any delays in the building of reports.

Essentially, if Google Analytics is in report sampling mode, it examines only a portion of the collected data for calculating results. Then for displaying the report, Google Analytics automatically scales these numbers back up. For example, if 10 percent of your actual data is used for the sample calculation, metrics such as number of visits and number of pageviews are multiplied by 10 in the displayed report. It's a standard statistical approach when dealing with large volumes of data—a smaller representative subset of data is used to estimate the total values.

 Note: As a rule of thumb, if your site receives fewer than 100,000 visits per month, is it highly unlikely you will come across report sampling.

Note that report sampling is different from data collection sampling, which is discussed in "Customizing the GATC" in Chapter 7. Data collection sampling determines how much data is sent to Google Analytics, and this is under your control. Report sampling happens automatically when a report is generated that exceeds certain thresholds.

Whether your data is automatically sampled or not is determined on a per-report basis. Ultimately this comes down to the volume of data to be processed by your report request—determined by the date range and report type you select in the user interface. For example, the suite of reports contained in the Standard Reporting section of Google Analytics (refer to Chapter 4, Figure 4.3 and Figure 4.4) is generated from *unsampled*, pre-aggregated data tables. Any report request that can be satisfied by using the pre-aggregated data is not sampled.

However, a report request may require a custom data set, such as the use of advanced segments, a secondary dimension, or a custom report. In these cases, if the requested data comes from a web property that exceeds 500,000 visits for the same date range, sampling will take place.

Per-Visit Sampling

Sampling occurs on a per-visit basis at the web property level. That is, Google selects a random sample of visits from each day for a particular web property. Figure 4.1 in Chapter 4 explains the relationship between web properties and profiles. Further information on the report sampling criteria is available at

http://code.google.com/apis/analytics/docs/concepts/gaConceptsSampling.html

To illustrate this, suppose you are viewing the Content > Site Content > Landing Page report, with a secondary dimension of medium selected, and this results in a table with a total of 90,000 visits. Why may such a relatively small data set be sampled?

In this case, you are requesting a custom data set that cannot be obtained from the unsampled, pre-aggregated reports. Therefore, a request to the raw session data is required. Sampling will happen if the total number of visits during the selected date range for this *web property* exceeds 500,000 visits. Note my deliberate emphasis on web property—even if you have a filtered profile excluding most of your traffic, sampling is taken at the web property level.

To indicate that a report is generated from sampled data, Google Analytics displays a yellow notification box at the top of the screen stating, "This report is generated in fast-access mode," as shown in Figure 5.35. Although not explicitly written, this means sampling has taken place.

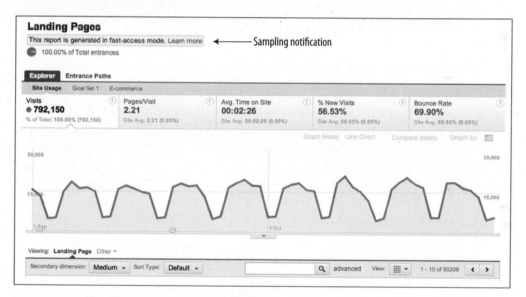

Figure 5.35 Report sampling notification within the user interface

Consider report sampling as a sign of success—that is, you are receiving so many qualified visitors that reporting all their activity becomes a time-consuming and resource-intensive process. However, attempt to minimize when sampling can happen by structuring your data in a way that makes sense. For example, rather than placing everything together, consider spreading your data over different Google Analytics web properties and even separate Google Analytics accounts. Using extra Google Analytics accounts is discussed in "Roll-up Reporting" in Chapter 6.

Note: Google Analytics Premium, the paid-for version of Google Analytics, has a feature that enables you to download unsampled reports in CSV format. Note that within the user interface, the report generation is still subject to the same sampling criteria in order to keep the reports loading fast; that is, a 500,000 visit threshold for custom data requests that cannot be served via pre-aggregated data. Google Analytics Premium is discussed in Chapter 3.

Summary

In Chapter 5, you have learned the following:

How to effectively use the Home area Real-time reporting, intelligence alerts, flow visualization, and dashboards are key areas to be aware of when you have a specific need outside of the standard report set.

Which standard reports are the most useful You have learned about the top reports that can help you understand visitor behavior and provide a starting point for further detailed analysis and optimization.

How to understand report sampling You have learned how data sampling may impact the numbers you see in your reports and how to mitigate against such impacts.

Implementing Google Analytics

Part III provides a detailed description of everything you need to do in order to collect visitor data—from creating an account to installing the tracking code in a best-practice manner.

We also look at the configuration of goals, funnels, filters, and visitor segmentation. Finally, the last chapter in this section, Chapter 9, "Google Analytics Customizations," is a workaround chapter for when you have specialized requirements.

If you are a webmaster or web developer, this section is for you. However, in keeping with this book's philosophy, the content is not aimed at programmers, so technicalities are kept to a minimum. You should, though, at least be familiar with HTML and JavaScript.

In Part III, you will learn the following:

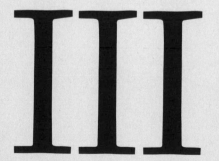

Getting Started: Initial Setup

Even if you already have a Google Analytics account, I recommend that you review this chapter; it contains important considerations for structuring your data. This chapter is all about getting the basics right—creating an account in the right place (stand-alone or linked to AdWords), tagging your pages, becoming familiar with the concept of multiple profiles, and ensuring that you track AdWords visitors and import the concomitant impression and cost data for such visitors. If you are with an agency or hosting provider, you need to bear in mind a couple of additional points, which are described in this chapter.

In Chapter 6, you will learn:

To create your Google Analytics account and add the tracking code to your pages

To back up your web traffic data to a local server

To use profiles in conjunction with accounts

To use roll-up reporting and collecting data into multiple accounts

To set up agency client accounts

To link Google Analytics with Google AdWords, AdSense, Webmaster Tools and Feedburner data

To track mobile visitors to your site

To answer common implementation questions

Creating Your Google Analytics Account

Opening a Google Analytics account and performing a base setup is straightforward. An initial setup enables you to receive data that you can use to begin to understand your website traffic. The time required to do this varies depending on your expertise and familiarity with HTML, your website architecture, and the level of access you have to your web pages. Setting up one website can take as little as an hour or as long as a full working day.

However, it is important to manage your expectations. The initial collection of data is only the first step in understanding your visitor traffic. Configuring your Google Analytics account to your specific needs (see Chapter 7, Chapter 8, and Chapter 9) is what will give you the most insight. Nonetheless, collecting the base data first will give you initial information with which you can fine-tune your setup, so it's important to get the foundations right.

You can open a Google Analytics account in one of two ways. If you have an AdWords account, it makes sense to do it there so that your campaigns can automatically be tracked and cost and impression data imported. Click the Tools And Analysis tab at the top of your AdWords account area, as shown in Figure 6.1a. If you do not have an AdWords account, visit the stand-alone version at www.google.com/analytics and begin the sign up, as shown in Figure 6.1b. These versions of Google Analytics are identical and you can switch between the two. That is, if you manage AdWords, you can still use the stand-alone version.

If you use the stand-alone version, note that the email address you use to create the account is your Google login. A Google login account is a registered email address for a single sign-on for any Google-hosted service. It gives you access to Google Analytics and other Google services such as AdWords, Gmail, Google Groups, personalized search, your personalized home page, and more. If you've used any of these services before, you already have a Google login. If you have multiple Google logins, choose the one you most frequently use. That way you will be automatically signed into Google Analytics if you have previously signed in to another Google service.

AdWords Users—a Special Case

If you have a Google AdWords account, it is important to create your Google Analytics account from within the AdWords interface. This enables you to quickly and easily link the two—that is, automatically import your AdWords cost data and be able to log into Google Analytics via your AdWords account interface. You will also be able to log in via the stand-alone interface if you wish.

If you have created a stand-alone Google Analytics account first and then wish to link to your AdWords account, ensure that your AdWords administrator login address is also a Google Analytics administrator. Then when you click the Analytics tab within AdWords, you will be given the option to link your two accounts.

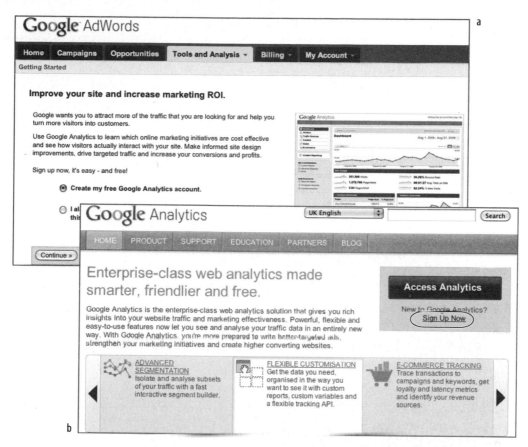

a

b

Figure 6.1 Creating a Google Analytics account from (a) within AdWords or (b) via the stand-alone interface

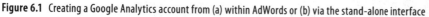

Gmail Addresses Are Not Recommended

You can register and use any email address, such as your company email address, as your single sign-on Google login. It does not have to be a Gmail account. In fact, it is preferable to use your company email address so that users and administrators are easily identified and managed. The only requirement is that the email must belong to an individual and not a mailing list. Further information is available at www.google.com/accounts.

Once you have your Google login, follow the instructions during the Google Analytics sign-up process. Essentially, there is only one page to complete for opening a Google Analytics account, and that involves providing your basic information and agreeing to the Terms of Service. See Figure 6.2.

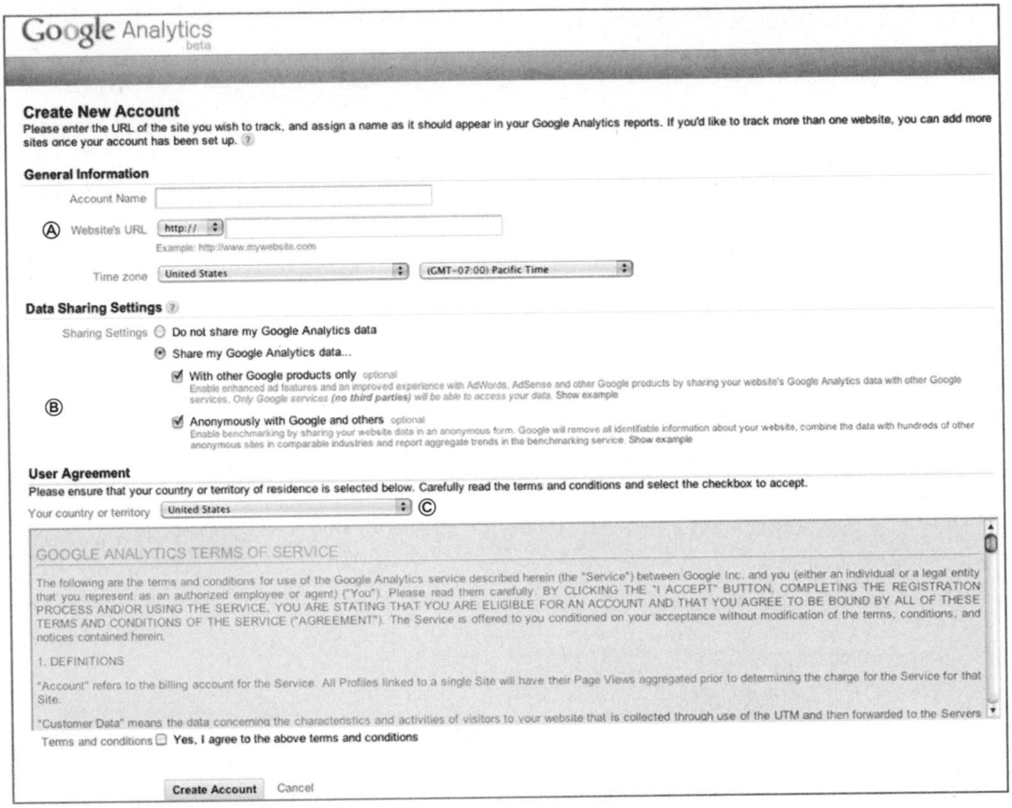

Figure 6.2 The one-step Google Analytics account creation process

General Account Information

This is straightforward information to provide with only one item I wish to point out—time zone setting (part A of Figure 6.2). If your account is not connected with an AdWords account, you can adjust your time zone setting whenever you wish, on a per-profile basis (a profile is a report set, discussed later in this chapter in "Using Accounts, Web Properties and Profiles").

However, if your account is connected to AdWords, then the time zone setting of your AdWords account takes precedence and is applied to your entire Google Analytics account—that is, for *all* profiles and *all* web properties. Moreover, once set, it is fixed and cannot be changed—either in AdWords or in Google Analytics. Clearly this has important implications if you are managing Google Analytics for international websites where times zones differ.

If this describes your situation, review the section of this chapter titled "Choosing between Roll-up Reporting and Multiple Profiles or Multiple Web Properties." If you are operating your website and AdWords account in only one time zone, go ahead and set this here.

Configuring Data-Sharing Settings

Within Google Analytics you have the option of sharing your data with Google (part B of Figure 6.2). By default, Share My Google Analytics Data is selected. As you might expect, by sharing your data with Google, there are some benefits for your account. Note that data is shared with Google only—not any third parties. Two sharing options are available:

• With Other Google Products Only

• Anonymously With Google And Others

According to Google, the first option helps improve the products and services it provides your organization. The rationale is that products such as AdWords, AdSense, Ad Planner Publisher Center, and Website Optimizer can be improved and better integrated within Google Analytics if such data is shared. That is certainly a strong incentive if you use any of those products.

If you choose the anonymous data-sharing option, Google will remove all identifiable information about your website and then combine your data with other anonymous sites in comparable industries. Previously Google offered a Benchmarking report so you could compare yourself with other anonymous and aggregated websites in your sector. That report has been removed and replaced with a quarterly benchmarking newsletter.

Unless you operate in a monopoly situation or have only a small number of competitors, I recommend enabling both data-sharing options. You can always opt out of these at a later date.

> **Note:** You are able to opt in or out from data sharing at any time. However, if you opt out, previously shared data is not removed. Google's position on privacy is discussed in Chapter 3, "Google Analytics Features, Benefits, and Limitations."

Accepting the Terms of Service

Once you are comfortable with your data sharing options, ensure that you select the correct country or region (the one closest to you) from the drop-down menu of the User Agreement section (part C of Figure 6.2). This ensures that you are shown the correct terms of service that you agree to in order to complete the account-creation process.

Of course, I advise you to read this carefully—it is actually quite easy to read and to the point (not full of legal jargon). An important part of the Google Analytics terms of service to emphasize is item 7 (US version), which covers privacy. At all times you should be aware that you cannot use Google Analytics to collect any personally identifiable information.

Tagging Your Pages

The most important part of the sign-up process is the final setup screen, which identifies your unique tag to be placed on all your pages. This is referred to as the Google Analytics Tracking Code (GATC). It is the use of this single tag to collect visitor data—the exact same tag for every page—that makes Google Analytics so easy to install.

Understanding the Google Analytics Tracking Code

The GATC is a snippet of JavaScript that is pasted into your pages. The code is hidden and acts as a beacon for gathering visitor information and sending it to Google Analytics data-collection servers. An example is given in Figure 6.3.

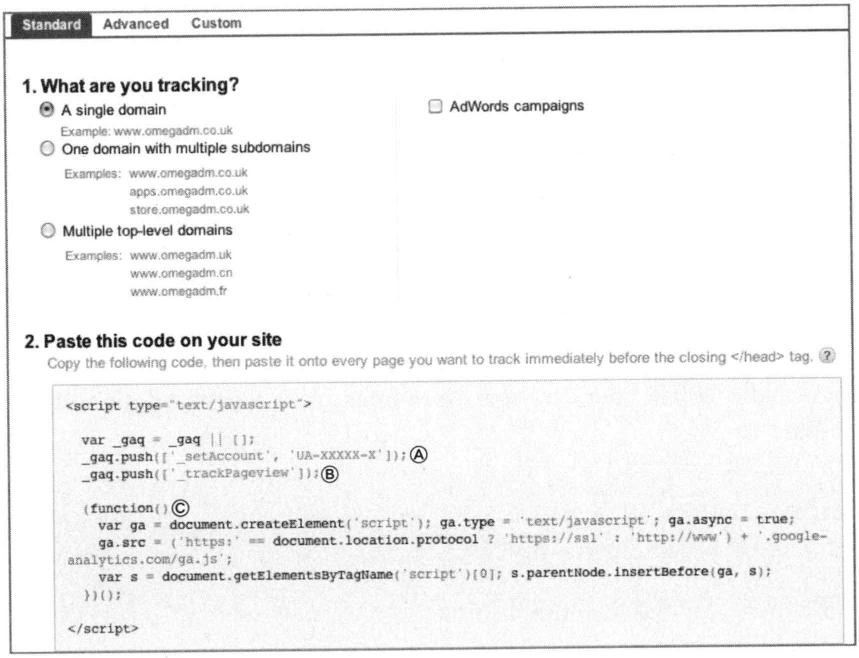

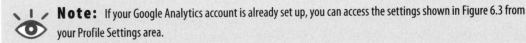

Figure 6.3 Typical GATC to add to your pages

Note: If your Google Analytics account is already set up, you can access the settings shown in Figure 6.3 from your Profile Settings area.

The purpose of the GATC was schematically described in Figure 3.2 in Chapter 3. Here I discuss the code in a little more detail. Essentially, there are three parts:

(A) Your unique account ID, in the form UA-*XXXX-XX* This is unique for each Google Analytics account and must be used exactly as quoted or your data will be sent to another account. This can happen accidentally (an implementation typo) or deliberately (people injecting their URL into your reports in the hope you will click through and view their advertising). You can use a filter to prevent the latter, and I discuss this in Chapter 8, "Best Practices Configuration Guide."

(B) The call of the JavaScript routine _trackPageview This is the workhorse of Google Analytics. Essentially, the line _trackPageview collects the URL of the pageview a visitor loads in their browser, including associated parameters such as browser type, language setting, referrer, and time stamp. Cookies are then read and set, and this information is passed back to Google data-collecting servers. The _trackPageview function is discussed in detail in Chapter 7.

(C) The call of a master JavaScript file from Google servers The master file, ga.js, contains the necessary code to conduct data collection. This file is approximately 18 KB in size, although once it is called it is cached by the visitor's browser and available for all subsequent pageviews. It is also the exact same file for all Google Analytics accounts. Therefore, if your visitor has recently visited another website that also has Google Analytics installed (highly likely), the ga.js file may not be requested at all because it is already present in their cache.

Although this section of the GATC looks verbose, it is simply detecting whether to load ga.js via a standard HTTP web request or via the HTTPS (encrypted) protocol. This autodetection means you do not have to change anything should your visitors access secure areas of your website, for example, to enter credit card details.

You will notice from the JavaScript shown in Figure 6.3 that the GATC is written in asynchronous code. That is, it's loaded in *parallel* with your page. When this method is used, load times for the .js file are improved and any latency reduced.

While you can also load the GATC using the standard (traditional) JavaScript convention, that is, in *series* with your page, the async method allows for improved tracking accuracy. This is because you can safely place the GATC in the <head> part of your HTML without it interfering with the rest of your page loading. For example, should there be a delay in communicating with Google servers, the async code simply waits until it is ready. However, if the standard (non-async) GATC is used, any delay from Google servers would hold up the loading of the rest of your page. You can get around this by placing the standard GATC at the bottom of your pages, but that creates another caveat—visitors who are quick at clicking to another page will not get tracked if the GATC has not loaded. The use of the async GATC avoids these issues altogether.

The _gaq object is what makes the asynchronous syntax possible. It acts as a queue, which is a first-in, first-out data structure that collects API calls until ga.js is ready to execute them. To add something to the queue, the _gaq.push method is used.

The Anatomy of the GATC

Understanding the details of the JavaScript code of the GATC is not required, or necessary—you simply need to know how to communicate with it. However, I include details here for developers who have an interest in such things. If that does not describe you, feel free to ignore this sidebar!

Using the example shown in Figure 6.3, the anatomy of the code is as follows:

```
var _gaq - gaq || [];
```

This line creates a JavaScript array. If _gaq is already defined, the script will continue to use that variable; if not, it creates a new array instead.

```
_gaq.push()['setAccount','UA-XXXXX-X'] ;
_gaq.push()['trackPageview'] ;
```

While the master file, ga.js, is loading, two commands are pushed (queued) onto the array. The first sets the account ID where your data will be stored. The second captures the page URL being loaded. When ga.js finishes loading, it replaces the array with the _gaq object and executes all the queued commands. Subsequent calls to _gaq.push resolve to this function, which executes commands as they are pushed.

```
(function () { ....}) ();
```

This injects a new script element in the document to load ga.js (where all the tracking and communication with Google happens). This code is immediately invoked as the page loads. This is wrapped inside an anonymous function to avoid any namespace conflicts.

Note: The code examples of this book only consider the async version of the GATC.

Notice in Figure 6.3 that there are alternatives to the GATC depending on your requirements: These are shown in the top tabbed menu as Standard, Advanced, and Custom. Essentially, if you have a single domain name that requires tracking (for example, www.mysite.com), the Standard GATC is what you need. The other variations are for when you have a site where visitors can pass between subdomains (for example, www.mysite.com to helpdesk.mysite.com) or third-party domains (for example, www.mysite.com to www.payment-gateway.com). I cover the Advanced and Custom variations in "Customizing the GATC" in Chapter 7, "Advanced Implementation."

Migrating from *urchin.js* to *ga.js*

Prior to December 2007, the file referenced by the GATC was called `urchin.js` and contained different code from that of `ga.js`. If you are still using `urchin.js`, you should migrate to the newer `ga.js` code. To get your new tracking code, you'll need to have administrator access to the Google Analytics account. Follow these steps:

1. Log in to your Google Analytics account.

2. For each profile, click the Settings icon.

3. Click the Tracking Code menu tab.

4. Follow the onscreen instructions for adding the new tracking code (`ga.js`).

Deploying the GATC—Tagging Pages

Next, all that is required is for you to place the GATC on your pages. This is often referred to as page tagging. If you have a relatively small website in terms of number of pages, you can copy and paste the GATC into your HTML. Alternatively, if you have built your website using a template or content management system (CMS), simply add the GATC to your master template or header file. The recommended placement is just above the `</head>` tag at the top of the page. This will improve tracking accuracy because the `ga.js` file will be loaded first. Should there be a delay in communication with Google servers (`google-analytics.com`), the GATC simply waits until it is available. There is no interference with the rest of your page loading.

Once your pages are tagged, you should start to see data in your account within 4 hours. However, for new accounts, it can take up to 24 hours, so be patient at this stage!

An important aspect of the deployment of your GATC is that it must be pasted onto *all* of your pages. As described in Chapter 2, "Available Methodologies and Their Accuracy," missing page tags is a common issue that casts doubt over the validity of your data. Apart from incorrect visitor and pageview counting, you may see your own website listed as a referrer, referrer information may be missing altogether (usually overwritten), there may be overly long or short time onsite and time-on-page metrics, unusual values for bounce rates may be shown, and many other peculiarities may be present.

The greater the percentage of missing page tags, the greater the inaccuracy. As a guide, I aim for a minimum of 98 percent deployment of the GATC. That is, 98 percent of all your pages should have the GATC present for you to have confidence in your reports. Less than this requires investigation. Ninety-five percent is acceptable for large sites where a lot of content may not be available to the visitor (previous design, deprecated content waiting to be removed, and the like), though my point is that deployment must be very high. If you have less than 90 percent deployment, then don't even bother looking at your reports—fix the problem first. Table 6.1 lists available tools that can help you troubleshoot the deployment of your GATC. Other troubleshooting tools are listed in Appendix B, "Useful Tools."

▶ **Table 6.1** Tools to help troubleshoot your GATC deployment

Tool Name	Comment
WASP (Web Analytics Solution Profiler)	A Firefox plug-in that detects the setting of the GATC cookies plus 300 other analytic tools. Works on a page-by-page (free) or site-scanning (paid) basis: www.webanalyticssolutionprofiler.com.
ObservePoint	Paid Software as a Service (SaaS) vendor. Detects the setting of the GATC cookies plus Omniture's cookies. Works as a site-scanning and monitoring/alert tool: www.observepoint.com.
Accenture Digital Diagnostics (formerly Maxamine)	Paid Software as a Service (SaaS) vendor. High-end site diagnostic tool: www.accenture.com/Global/Consulting/Marketing_ and_Sales_Effectiveness/Digital/Transformation_Suite/ AMSDiagnostics.htm.

Although having a CMS is a more reliable way to insert your GATC, you still need to ensure that it includes all newly created pages—not always taken into account by default—and any pages that do not use your standard template. If you do not have a content management system, there are alternatives for automatically tagging your pages. Two of these are Apache mod_layout and PHP auto_prepend_file.

Mod_layout is a loadable module (similar in principle to a plug-in) for the Apache web server. It can be used to tag your pages as visitors request them. If you use Apache, ask your development team or hosting provider to install the mod_layout loadable module from http://tangent.org. Once the module is implemented, the Apache web server will automatically insert your GATC on every page it serves. Note that this means exactly that, *every* page served, so you should add exclusions to those files where the GATC is not required, such as robots.txt, cgi-bin files, and so forth.

A full description of mod_layout is beyond the scope of this book, but an example configuration for your httpd.conf file is given in the following snippet. In this example, two file types are ignored (*.cgi and *.txt) and the file contents of utm_GA.html (the GATC content—as per Figure 6.3) are inserted just above the </head> tag of the HTML page being served:

```
#mod_layout directives
LayoutMergeBeginTag </head>
```

```
LayoutIgnoreURI *.cgi
LayoutIgnoreURI *.txt
LayoutHeader /var/www/html/mysite.com/utm_GA.html
LayoutMerge On
```

> **Warning:** If your pages use the CAPTCHA method (http://en.wikipedia.org/wiki/CAPTCHA) of generating security images to protect your site from automated form submission, test that your security image still loads. If not, you may need to exclude the embedded file that calls the security image from mod_layout.

If your pages are PHP generated (filenames ending in .php), then you can use the auto_prepend_file directive. This specifies the name of a file that is automatically parsed before the main file. The file is included as if it was called with the PHP require() function. The directive can be included in your php.ini configuration file (therefore applied to *all* files and hosts on your server) or more specifically in an .htaccess file in your website root directory, as follows:

```
<IfModule mod_php5.c>
    php_value include_path ".:/usr/local/lib/php"
    php_value auto_prepend_file "/home/www/utm_GA.html"
</IfModule>
```

In this way, the file utm_GA.html, the file containing your GATC, is automatically prepended to the top of all your PHP web pages—before the HTML <html> tag. Strictly speaking this is not the correct placement; all content should be placed within your <html> and </html> tags. However, the GATC still works, and this method is a useful workaround if you have no immediate alternative available. Note that the full path is used to define the utm_GA.html location. In this way, all subdirectories also receive the GATC without further modification. If you wish to avoid this, define a relative path.

> **Note:** Because auto_prepend_file is applicable only to PHP files, you do not have to exclude non-PHP files such as robots.txt. If other file types do require the GATC, you will need to add this manually. You also do not need to worry about other included PHP files receiving a double page tag. For example, if you use <? include("/includes/navigation.php"); ?> within your pages to build your navigation menu, navigation.php will not be tagged.

If you are a Wordpress user, there are several plug-ins available to help you automatically insert your GATC onto your pages. Similarly, there are plug-ins available for popular content management systems:

```
http://wordpress.org/extend/plugins/search.php?q=google+analytics
```

http://drupal.org/project/google_analytics

http://extensions.joomla.org/extensions/site-management/site-analytics/4300

Back Up: Keeping a Local Copy of Your Data

Keeping a local copy of your Google Analytics data can be very useful for your organization. For example, Google currently commits to keeping data for up to 25 months, enabling you to compare monthly reports spanning three years. That is adequate for most users, but what if you wish to retain your data longer? Also, because Google will not pass raw data to third parties, you will need an alternative if your web visitor data must be audited. Publishing sites often require this because third-party auditing is an independent way of verifying their advertiser rate cards for potential advertisers.

The technique is to modify the GATC so that it simultaneously sends your visitor data to your web server logfiles as well as to Google Analytics data-collection servers. This is a one-line modification of the GATC as highlighted:

```
<script type="text/javascript">
var _gaq = _gaq || [];_
_gaq.push(['_setAccount', 'UA-12345-1']);
_gaq.push(['_setLocalRemoteServerMode']);
_gaq.push(['_trackPageview']);

(function() {
var ga = document.createElement('script'); ga.type =➡
'text/javascript'; ga.async = true; ga.src = ('https:' ==➡
document.location.protocol ? 'https://ssl' : 'http://www') + '.google-➡
analytics.com/ga.js';
var s = document.getElementsByTagName('script')[0];
s.parentNode.insertBefore(ga, s);
})();
</script>
```

The consequence of this modification is an additional request for a file named __utm.gif from your web server when your GATC is loaded. This is a 1 × 1–pixel transparent image that Google Analytics uses to append its information into your web server logfiles. Create the file for yourself and upload it into your document root, that is, where your home page resides.

Because all web servers log their activity by default, usually in plaintext format, you should see the presence of additional __utm.gif entries in your logfile almost immediately after making this change. These correspond to the visit data as seen by Google Analytics. Also, your web server must log cookie information. If you do not see cookie values in your logfiles, check the specified log format of your web server. A correctly working Apache logfile line entry should appear as follows:

```
79.79.125.174 advanced-web-metrics.com - [03/Jan/2010:00:17:01 +0000] "GET
/images/book-cover.jpg HTTP/1.1" 200 27905 "http://www.advanced-web-
metrics.com/blog/2008/02/16/accuracy-whitepaper/" "Mozilla/5.0 (Windows; U;
Windows NT 6.0; en-GB; rv:1.9.0.15) Gecko/2009101601 Firefox/3.0.15
(.NET CLR 3.5.30729)"
"__utma=202414657.217961957.1257207415.1257207415.1257207415.1;
__utmb=202414657.1.10.1257207415; __utmc=202414657;
__utmz=202414657.1257207415.1.1.utmcsr=google.co.uk|utmccn=(referral)|
utmcmd=referral|utmcct=/imgres; session_start_time=1257207419839"
```

Note that this is a single line in your logfile, beginning with the visitor's IP address and ending with the GATC cookie values.

Defining a Logfile Format for Apache

Apache can be configured to log data in a variety of custom formats. The important part for Google Analytics is the logging of cookie information. I recommend using the full NCSA log format in your httpd.conf file, as shown here:

```
LogFormat "%h %v %u %t "%r" %>s %b "%{Referer}i" "%{User-➡
Agent}i" "%{Cookie}i"" combined
```

Note the use of double quotes throughout. In addition, this statement must be a single line in your configuration file.

For Microsoft IIS, the format can be as follows:

```
2010-01-01 01:56:56 68.222.73.77--- GET /__utm.gif
utmn=1395285084&utmsr=1280x1024&utmsa=1280x960 &utmsc=32-
bit&utmbs=1280x809&utmul=en-us&utmje=1&utmce=1&utmtz=-0500&utmjv=1.3&
utmcn=1&utmr=http://www.yoursite.com/s/s.dll?spage=search%2Fresultshome
1.htm&startdate=01%2F01%2F2010&man=1&num=10&SearchType=web&string=looking
+for+mysite.com&imageField.x=12&imageField.y=6&utmp=/ 200 878 853 93 - -
Mozilla/4.0+(compatible;+MSIE+6.0;+Windows+NT+5.1;+SV1;+ .NET+CLR+1.0.3705;
+Media+Center+PC+3.1;+.NET+CLR+1.1.4322) - http://www.yoursite.com/
```

In this example, the log entry starts with the visitor's timestamp and ends with the website hostname.

In both examples, the augmented information applied by the GATC is the addition of *utm** name/value pairs. This is known as a *hybrid data-collection method* and is mentioned in Chapter 2.

Note that there are overhead considerations to keeping a local copy of visitor data, and we discussed these in Chapter 3. Because web server logfiles can get very large very quickly and swamp hard disk space, I generally do not recommend keeping a local copy of your data unless you have a specific reason for doing so. That said, maintaining a local copy of your Google Analytics data does provide you with the option to do the following:

- Maintain greater control over your data—for auditing purposes, for example
- Troubleshoot Google Analytics implementation issues
- Process historical data as far back as you wish—using Urchin software
- Reprocess data when you wish—using Urchin software

Let's look at these benefits in detail:

Maintain greater control over your data   Some organizations feel more comfortable having their data sitting physically within their premises and are prepared to invest in the IT resources to do so. You cannot run this data through an alternative web analytics vendor because the GATC page tag information will be meaningless to anyone else. However, you do have the option of passing your data to a third-party auditing service. Some website owners use third-party audit companies to verify their visitor numbers—useful for content and publishing sites that sell advertising and therefore need to validate their rate cards.

Warning: Be aware that when you pass data to a third party, protecting end-user privacy (your visitors') is your responsibility, and you should be transparent about this in your privacy policy.

Troubleshoot Google Analytics implementation issues   A local copy of Google Analytics visit data is very useful for troubleshooting complex Google Analytics installations. This is possible because your logfile entries show each pageview captured in real time. Therefore, you can trace whether you have implemented tracking correctly—particularly nonstandard tracking such as PDF, EXE, and other download files types and outbound exit links. See Appendix B for more troubleshooting tools.

Process historical data as far back as you wish—using Urchin software   As mentioned previously, Google Analytics currently stores reports for up to 25 months (though Google has so far made no attempt to remove older data). If you want to keep your reports longer, you should purchase Urchin software and process your local data as far back as you wish. The downloadable software version runs on a local server and processes your web server logfiles. Urchin also provides complementary reports to Google Analytics, as described in Chapter 3.

Reprocess data when you wish—using Urchin software With data and the web analytics tools under your control, you can apply filters and process data retroactively. For example, say you wish to create a separate profile just to report on blog visitors. This is typically done by applying a page-level filter—including all pageview data from the /blog directory. For Google Analytics, reports are populated as soon as that profile filter is applied—that is, from that point forward. For Urchin software, you can also reprocess older data to view the blog reports historically.

Using Accounts, Web Properties, and Profiles

A Google Analytics profile is a set of configuration parameters that define a report for a particular web property. You need at least one web property and one profile to view your visitor data. Figure 6.3 showed the last step of creating a new Google Analytics account. Following the click of the Continue button, Google Analytics automatically creates your first web property and profile, and this is all you need to get started viewing reports.

However, as you may have guessed, you can configure Google Analytics to provide reports for multiple web properties and multiple profiles. You may even have access to multiple Google Analytics accounts—for example, in an agency scenario where you look after numerous client accounts. The relationship between the different levels—account, web property, and profile—is shown in Figure 6.4.

Figure 6.4 shows a user having access to two Google Analytics accounts. Each account contains two web properties (websites). A set of Google Analytics reports is generated for each profile. For this example, there are six sets of Google Analytics reports—four of which are created by applying filters on the report data. The structure of each report is identical—it is the data contained within each that will differ. This will depend on the web property and filter to which the report is applicable.

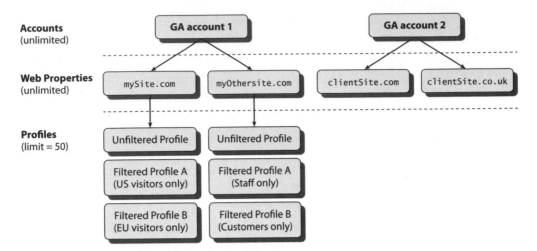

Accounts (unlimited)

GA account 1

GA account 2

Web Properties (unlimited)

mySite.com

myOthersite.com

clientSite.com

clientSite.co.uk

Profiles (limit = 50)

Unfiltered Profile

Unfiltered Profile

Filtered Profile A (US visitors only)

Filtered Profile A (Staff only)

Filtered Profile B (EU visitors only)

Filtered Profile B (Customers only)

Figure 6.4 The relationship between Google Analytics accounts, web properties, and profiles

For a particular Google Analytics account, users can be granted access to a single profile for a single web property, a group of profiles across multiple web properties, or all web profiles in all web properties.

Account Management Considerations

Ensure that you are aware of the following points for managing your Google Analytics account:

- There is a limit of 50 profiles for any given web property.

- Provide administrative access wisely. If you want to provide administrative access to other users of an account, those users will be able to see and modify all profile data for all websites being tracked in the account.

- You cannot migrate historical data from one account to another. Thus, if you set up an account for a web property and then later want to move tracking to a separate account, you cannot migrate the data from the old account to the new account.

- You cannot transfer profiles or web properties to other accounts. However, you may exchange accounts between users, for example, in an agency scenario where the agency initially configures the account on behalf of the user.

Creating a New Profile

Consider a profile as a configuration setup that defines the report contents for a particular web property. Typically you create additional profiles for your organization when you have different functions or divisions within your business. Having content in multiple languages is an obvious choice for generating additional profiles. It makes sense for such segmented content to have a set of dedicated reports just for their needs. However, if you are an AdWords user and have multiple AdWords accounts, review "Choosing between Roll-up Reporting and Multiple Profiles or Multiple Web Properties" later in this chapter before creating new profiles.

Another scenario for which having additional profiles can be beneficial is a single website with split responsibilities—for example, for customer support as well as product marketing. Customer support usually has a very different objective for the user experience compared with the rest of the website. For example, they may wish to minimize the time on site (customers finding answers they are looking for quickly) and reduce goal conversions (less contact with the expensive call center), whereas the marketing department will wish to increase these for their section. Hence, it is better to have separate profiles for this scenario so the various teams can focus on their objectives.

> **Tip:** Additional profiles are created in order to apply filters to your report data. By definition, filtered profiles have had their data sets altered. To protect yourself from errors and provide an unperturbed reference profile, always maintain a master profile with no filters applied in your account. This is shown in Figure 6.4.

Creating a profile for the same web property requires no changes to your GATC. Using Figure 6.5 as your guide, you create an additional profile for a web property by clicking the settings icon (top right of your screen) and selecting the Profile Settings tab menu. Click + New Profile from the right side of the screen. From here, you simply name your new profile. Use a meaningful name such as "US only visitors" so you will recognize at a glance what information this report set contains.

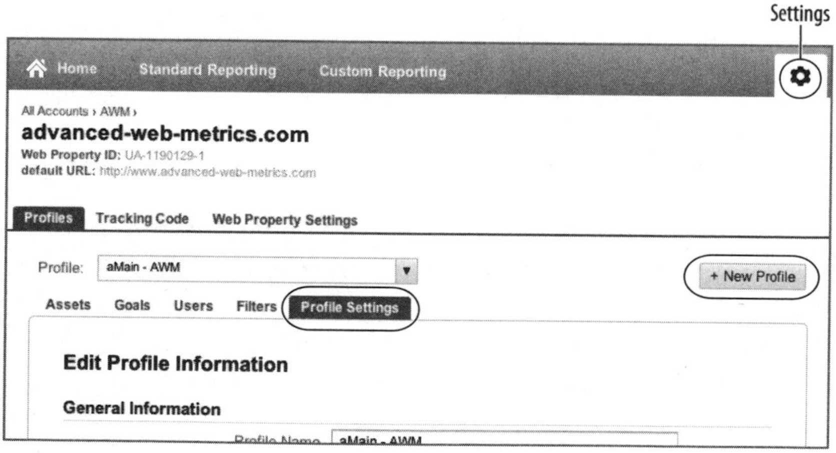

Figure 6.5 Creating an additional profile

Note that profiles are listed alphabetically by default in Google Analytics. While you can reorder the list with a click, it can be useful to use numbers in your profile names so that they are always listed in your own prioritized order—for example, "01 US only visitors," "02 EU only visitors," and so forth. Otherwise the EU profile would appear first by default.

With a separate profile in place, the next step is to apply filters to the data. The use of profile filters is described in the section "Profile Segments: Segmenting Visitors Using Filters" in Chapter 8, "Best Practices Configuration Guide."

An Important Note on Profile Aggregation

Once you have defined your profiles, you cannot produce an aggregate report at a later date; that is, you cannot roll up the individual profiles. The strategy, therefore, is to produce an aggregate profile first and then use filters to generate the separate profiles. Alternatively, you can add an extra GATC and collect the data into a separate Google Analytics account, as described in the section "Roll-up Reporting" later in this chapter.

Creating a New Web Property

Create a new web property when you have multiple websites that you would like to track in the same Google Analytics account, such as, for example, content targeted at different markets (mysite.com and mysite.ca, or mysite.fr and mysite.nl, and so on). You may also have product-specific websites that belong to the same organization (productA.com, productB.com, and so forth) or operate subdivisions that have their own website. For these scenarios, it makes sense to have a set of dedicated reports within the same Google Analytics account. You achieve this by creating web properties.

Warning: Be sure you have the authority to add additional websites to your Google Analytics account—see "Agencies and Hosting Providers: Setting Up Client Accounts" later in this chapter.

Remember from earlier in this chapter ("General Account Information") that if your Google Analytics account is connected to a single AdWords account, the time zone setting of your AdWords account is applied to your entire Google Analytics account—that is, for *all* profiles and *all* web properties. All AdWords cost data will also be in a single currency. Therefore, before creating a new web property, ensure that you review the section "Choosing between Roll-up Reporting and Multiple Profiles or Multiple Web Properties" later in this chapter.

If you are operating your websites and AdWords account in only one time zone and in a single currency, go ahead with creating your additional web properties. To do this, ensure that you are in the root level of your account settings—click the settings icon at the top right of your browser window, then select your account name in the top left menu links. In Figure 6.5, this is shown as All Accounts > AWM. Clicking the account name, AWM in my example, takes you to the root level account settings as shown in Figure 6.6. Click the + New Web Property button, and enter your web property details as shown in Figure 6.7.

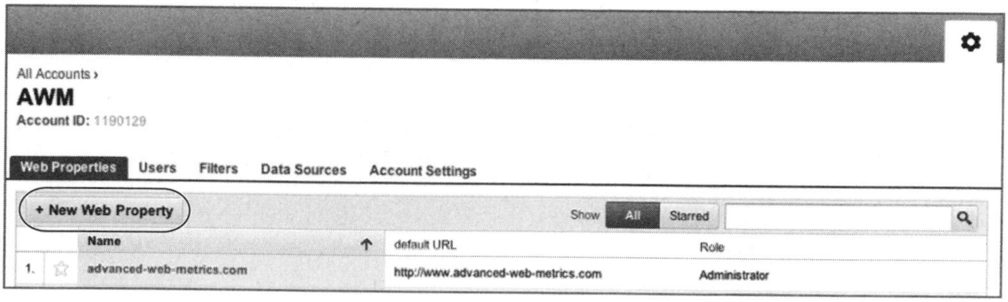

Figure 6.6 The root level account settings

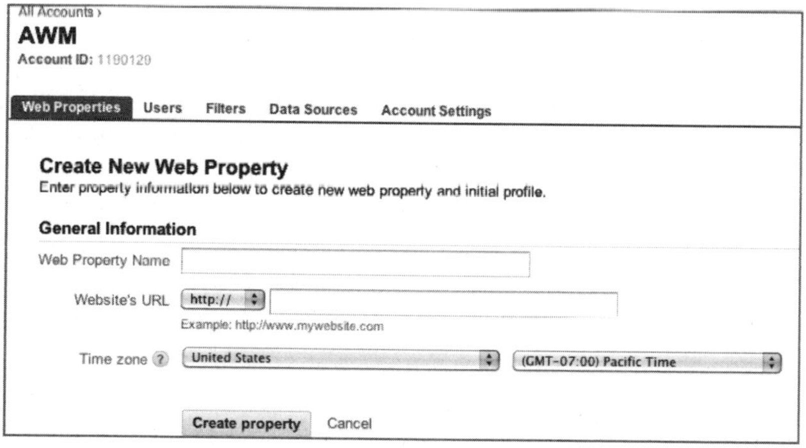

Figure 6.7 Creating an additional web property

I recommend that the hostname of the website in question is used as the web property name. For example, for the site `http://www.mysite.com`, use `www.mysite.com`. This gives you the option to differentiate subdomains such as `m.mysite.com` and `blog.mysite.com` and removes the clutter of `http://`. Of course, if you do not intend to use subdomains, then use only `mysite.com` for the web property name.

Creating a New Account

You create a new account when you wish to keep your web properties and profiles separate from each other. This can be because you are an agency with separate client accounts or because your additional web properties operate in different time zones and in different currencies—AdWords or transactional revenue. If the latter case describes your situation, review the section "Choosing between Roll-up Reporting and Multiple Profiles or Multiple Web Properties" later in this chapter before creating new accounts.

To create a new Google Analytics account, go to your account administration area—from the screen shown in Figure 6.6, click All Accounts in the top left menu links. This takes you to the screen shown in Figure 6.8. Then click the + New Account button. You will be taken to the same screen shown in Figure 6.2. Enter the information for the account as you did previously.

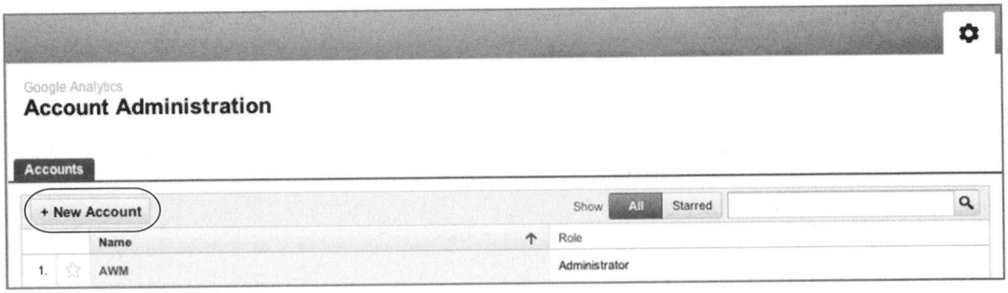

Figure 6.8 Creating a new Google Analytics account from within an existing account

Currently the maximum number of accounts you can create from *within* Google Analytics is 25. However, there is no limit to the number of Google Analytics accounts you can create or have access to.

Roll-up Reporting

Roll-up reporting is not a standard feature in Google Analytics. However, with a little extra coding, you can have stand-alone reports for specific (product- or region-dedicated) websites and a roll-up report to provide a global overview.

Consider the following scenario: You have semi-autonomous country offices that have brand- or product-specific websites suitable for their particular market needs. These sites have their own AdWords account and operate in different time zones and use different currencies (AdWords spend or transactional revenue). Because of these specific needs, it makes sense to have separate, stand-alone Google Analytics accounts for each website. That way, segmentation, referral analysis, and e-commerce revenue (or lead generation) can be analyzed accurately and in detail.

However, global HQ also needs a high-level overview of *all* web visitor activity. You can achieve this by having a single catch-all Google Analytics account with all data from all websites aggregated together—a roll-up report. So long as the GATC deployment is managed centrally for consistency, this solution provides both autonomy for your country- or product-specific websites and a big-picture reporting view on all website activity for HQ. Each can manage its own reporting needs without affecting the other.

The principle of roll-up reporting is straightforward—you create additional Google Analytics accounts and add multiple GATCs to your web pages. One specifies the individual account, and the other is for the roll-up account. Schematically this is shown here for two websites:

```
<script>
    1. Track the pageview or event for siteA into its individual account
    2. Track the pageview or event for siteA into the roll-up account
</script>
```

Although I describe this technique as adding multiple GATCs, a full additional GATC is not added to your pages, just a second tracker object. An actual GATC, with the second tracker object highlighted, is as follows:

```
<script type="text/javascript">
var _gaq = _gaq || [];_
_gaq.push(['_setAccount', 'UA-12345-1']);
_gaq.push(['_trackPageview']);
_gaq.push(['t2._setAccount', 'UA-67890-1']);
_gaq.push(['t2._trackPageview']);


(function() {
var ga = document.createElement('script');
ga.type = 'text/javascript'; ga.async = true;
ga.src = ('https:' == document.location.protocol ? 'https://ssl' : ➡
'http://www') + '.google-analytics.com/ga.js';
var s = document.getElementsByTagName('script')[0];
s.parentNode.insertBefore(ga, s);
})();
</script>
```

Note that I have kept the original format for the default tracker object. That is, it has no name. The second tracker object is named t2. You can choose any names you wish—for example t1, t2 or firstTracker, secondTracker and so forth—though it pays to be as clear as possible.

Deploy this multi-tracker object GATC across all your websites. For each stand-alone website (siteA, siteB, and so on), modify only the default tracker _setAccount line to use your specific UA account number for that website. The roll-up account information, t2, remains the same for each site—in this case UA-67890-1, though of course that needs to be changed to your roll-up account number.

In this way, the folks in the marketing department at global HQ can log into Google Analytics account UA-67890-1 for their roll-up report and filter, segment, or configure as required. Country- or product-specific offices can log into UA-12345-1 and modify as they wish without impacting the global roll-up report.

Note: For a full implementation, you also need to consider e-commerce tracking as well as the impact of numerous caveats that this approach has. This is discussed in more detail in Chapter 9, "Google Analytics Customizations."

Choosing between Roll-up Reporting and Multiple Profiles or Multiple Web Properties

For the vast majority of implementations, multiple profiles will be the most appropriate choice, such as, for example, if you have one website, use a single AdWords account, and transact in a single currency and time zone. You would create profiles to segment your data—perhaps by location, language, visitor type (customer versus prospect), or website section visited—and for this you need to ensure that any associated e-commerce or AdWords data is shown consistently across all profile reports. Creating profiles by applying filters will enable you to do this efficiently, without any modification of your GATC. By default, all e-commerce and AdWords data is applied to all profiles in your account.

If you have multiple websites but still operate in a single time zone (or at least very similar) and single currency, add your websites as multiple web properties in your Google Analytics account. Create profiles for your web properties as needed.

Roll-up reporting answers very specific requirements of enterprise clients. Use roll-up reporting when you operate in different time zones and currencies and have multiple AdWords accounts. Use roll-up reporting if you have autonomous offices or departments that wish to manage their own reporting needs while you maintain control over data integrity (that is, the GATC deployment across the enterprise) so that all offices can compare apples with apples.

Having a stand-alone Google Analytics account gives each department control over who has account access (such as web and marketing agencies) and provides a set of reports and configurations without the obfuscation of other departments. You also overcome the limit of 50 profiles per web property.

Note that roll-up reporting of accounts is a nonstandard feature of Google Analytics that requires modification of the GATC. This is discussed in more detail in Chapter 9.

Agencies and Hosting Providers: Setting Up Client Accounts

It is tempting to think that Figure 6.4 shows an excellent route for agencies and hosting providers to take on behalf of their clients—that is, have all client reports in one Google Analytics account. However, in accordance with the Google Analytics terms of service (found on www.google.com/analytics), any party setting up Google Analytics on behalf of clients must set up a separate Google Analytics account for each business entity. This is the same way AdWords operates and should therefore be familiar to existing AdWords agencies.

Other limitations include the constraint of 50 profiles per Google Analytics web property. Also, if you import AdWords data, time zone settings and currency labels are fixed for *all* profiles in your account; if you have an e-commerce setup, by default e-commerce data is applied to *all* profiles in your account. Clearly, these are undesirable effects. Even with filters in place to counter them, there is always a real possibility that one client's data will end up in another client's report. At best, this muddies the metrics; at worst, it's a breach of your client's confidentiality.

For agencies (or hosting providers) to move efficiently between different client accounts, Google Analytics has a feature similar to the My Client Center feature of AdWords. As long as you use the same Google login for each Google Analytics account you create or manage, you will see a drop-down menu on the left side of your report interface. This lists all the accounts, web properties, and profiles to which you have access, as shown in Figure 6.9.

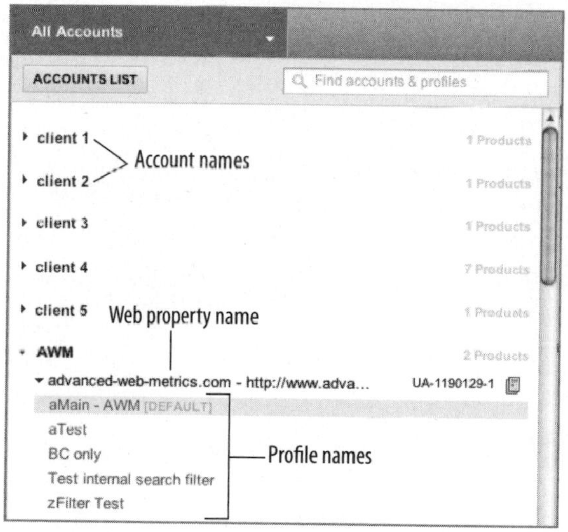

Figure 6.9 The Accounts area is the equivalent of the My Client Center feature for AdWords.

Note: More information on the My Client Center feature of AdWords can be found here at `http://adwords.google.com/support/bin/answer.py?answer=7725`.

As described earlier in this chapter, you can create a maximum of 25 accounts from within your Google Analytics account. However, there's no limit on the number of Google Analytics accounts that can be associated with your Google login. That is, any number of clients can add your Google login email address as their administrator or report viewer, and these will appear in your accounts drop-down menu.

If you need to create more than 25 Google Analytics accounts, set up a secondary Google login for yourself and use it for creating further Google Analytics accounts.

Once they're created, you can then add your primary Google login as an administrator and have the account appended to your Accounts drop-down list.

Integrating with Your AdWords Data

If you're an online advertiser, chances are good that you are using Google AdWords as part of your marketing mix. AdWords is a way of targeting text ads to visitors who are using the Google search engine by the keywords they use. That way, your advertisement is displayed to people who are actually looking for something related to your product. AdWords are also shown in a similar way on Google partner sites such as Ask.com, AOL.com, and the AdSense network. Importing your AdSense data is discussed later in this chapter for the benefit of AdSense users.

Google AdWords is an extremely effective and efficient way of marketing online because the auction system used is based on how many visitors click your ad rather than just its display. Hence, this method of advertising is referred to as pay-per-click (PPC) or cost-per-click (CPC). Yahoo! Search Marketing, Microsoft adCenter, Miva, and Mirago operate similar advertising networks. Google Analytics can track visits and conversions from all of these.

As you might expect, Google Analytics, being a part of Google, offers enormous benefits when it comes to integrating data from its AdWords pay-per-click network. Getting your AdWords data in is simply a matter of checking two check boxes—one in your AdWords account, the other in your Google Analytics account. These are shown in Figures 6.10 and Figure 6.11 respectively.

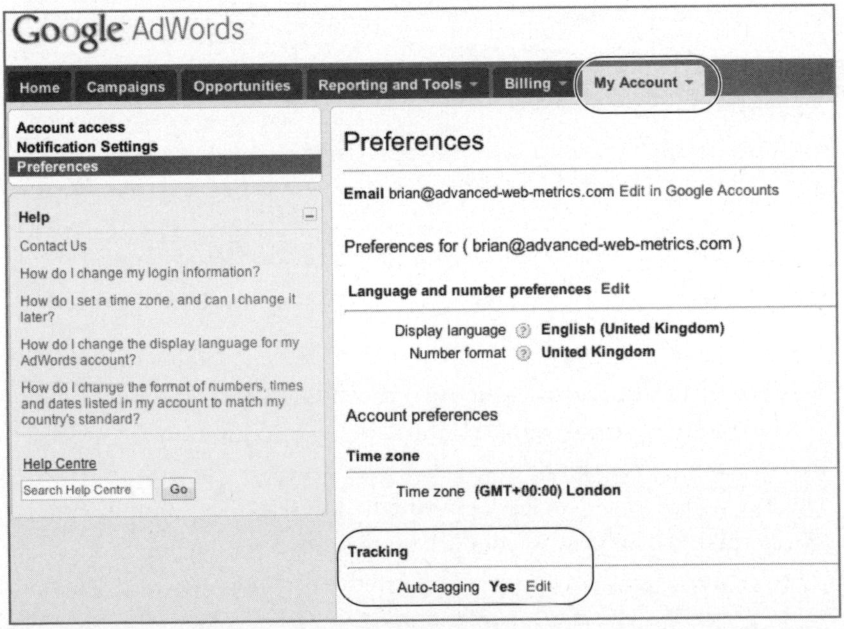

Figure 6.10 Setting auto-tagging within your AdWords account

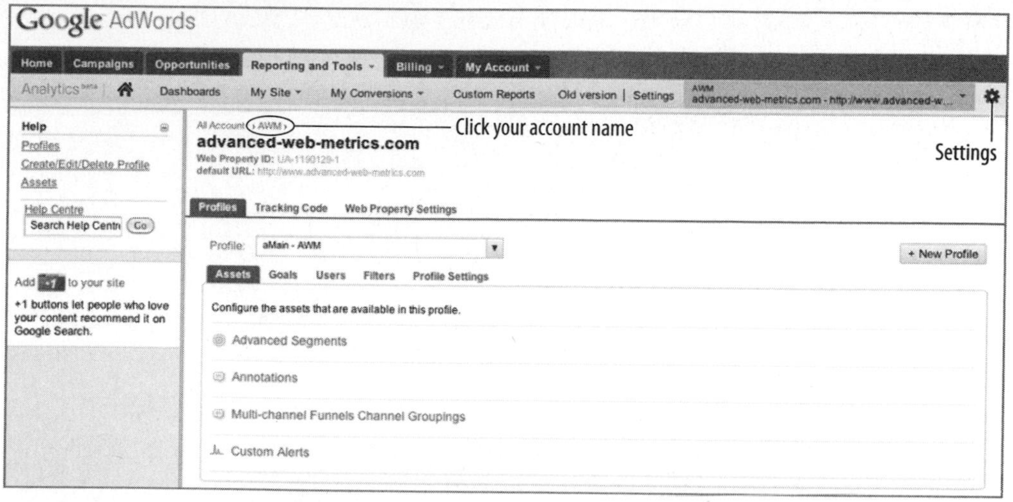

Figure 6.11 Accessing Google Analytics profile settings within AdWords

Before you start, make sure that you're using a Google login that has access to both your Google Analytics and AdWords accounts and is an administrator login for the Analytics account. From within your AdWords account, follow these steps.

First, set up auto-tagging for your AdWords visitors. This ensures that any click-throughs from your ads are correctly attributed to AdWords:

1. Go to the My Account > Preferences area.
2. Click the Edit link under Tracking (see Figure 6.10).
3. Select the box labeled Destination URL Auto-Tagging and then save your changes.

Then import your AdWords account data to allow the display of your AdWords impressions, clicks, and cost data in your Google Analytics reports:

4. Click the Reporting And Tools tab and choose Google Analytics
5. Select the settings icon on the top right (see Figure 6.11). This takes you to the settings screen for your default profile. Select your account name from the menu link on the top left. In this example, this is AWM.
6. Select the Data Sources tab and click the Link Accounts button, shown in Figure 6.12. The result is the pop-up box shown in Figure 6.13.
7. You can then select which profiles will receive the AdWords data. Place a check in the check box by each profile name, and select Continue.

That's it! All your AdWords data (impressions, clicks, cost) will automatically be imported into your account and applied to the profiles you selected in step 7. If you later change your mind, you can adjust which profiles receive AdWords data in the same Data Sources tab of your account settings. You can even unlink an entire AdWords account from your Google Analytics account.

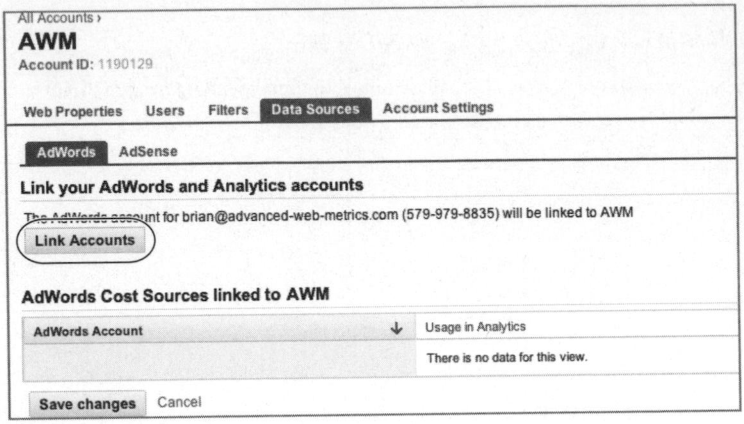

All Accounts ›

AWM
Account ID: 1190129

Web Properties   Users   Filters   **Data Sources**   Account Settings

AdWords   AdSense

Link your AdWords and Analytics accounts

The AdWords account for brian@advanced-web-metrics.com (579-979-8835) will be linked to AWM

(Link Accounts)

AdWords Cost Sources linked to AWM

AdWords Account	↓	Usage in Analytics
		There is no data for this view.

Save changes   Cancel

Figure 6.12 Linking your AdWords account to your Google Analytics account

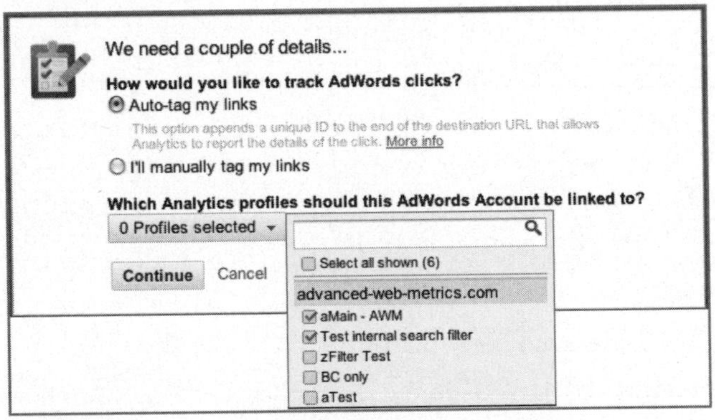

We need a couple of details...

How would you like to track AdWords clicks?
◉ Auto-tag my links
　This option appends a unique ID to the end of the destination URL that allows
　Analytics to report the details of the click. More info

○ I'll manually tag my links

Which Analytics profiles should this AdWords Account be linked to?

0 Profiles selected ▾   [🔍]

Continue   Cancel

☐ Select all shown (6)

advanced-web-metrics.com
☑ aMain - AWM
☑ Test internal search filter
☐ zFilter Test
☐ BC only
☐ aTest

Figure 6.13 Integrating AdWords data on a per profile basis

Imported data is shown in the Advertising > AdWords section of your reports (an example AdWords report is shown in Chapter 5, "Reports Explained"). The import of AdWords data is continuous. That is, the data is pulled from your AdWords account whenever you request the report in the user interface.

With auto-tagging enabled (step 3 in place), you will notice an additional parameter showing in the landing page URLs of your AdWords ads should you click through to them. Here's an example:

www.mysite.com/?gclid=COvQgK7JrY8CFSUWEAodKEEyuA

The gclid parameter is a keyword-specific parameter unique to your account. AdWords appends this for Google Analytics tracking, and it must remain in place when visitors arrive on your website in order for them to be detected as AdWords visitors. If the gclid parameter is missing or corrupted, then the visitor will be incorrectly assigned as "google (organic)" as opposed to "google (cpc)."

Importing Cost Data from Multiple AdWords Accounts

A new Google Analytics feature (from August 2011) allows you to import cost data from multiple AdWords accounts—for example, if you are running separate campaigns for your products or you have separate agencies managing separate campaigns for you. To do so, log in to your other AdWords accounts and repeat the procedure described in steps 1 through 7 in the section "Integrating with Your AdWords Data."

Note that if you have multiple AdWords accounts in different time zones, you should not combine them into a single Google Analytics account. This is because you need to set one time zone for your entire Google Analytics account. If combined with AdWords, then Adwords automatically takes precedence. This cannot later be changed.

Also, there may be currency implications to consider. That is, you may need to ensure that the currency used in your AdWords account matches the one used in your Google Analytics profile. Make sure you review the section "Roll-up Reporting" in this chapter and consider your options carefully before importing data from multiple AdWords accounts.

Note: As described here, it is straightforward to import data from multiple AdWords accounts into one Google Analytics account and conversely to import one AdWords account data into multiple Google Analytics accounts. However, the actual linking of accounts—that is, being able to log in to your Google Analytics reports from *within* AdWords—can only take place from one AdWords account.

Testing after Enabling Auto-Tagging

As discussed in "Why PPC Vendor Numbers Do Not Match Web Analytics Reports" in Chapter 2, third-party ad-tracking systems can inadvertently corrupt or remove the tracking parameter required by Google Analytics AdWords tracking. For example, systems such as Adform, Atlas Search, Bluestreak, DoubleClick, and Efficient Frontier use redirection URLs to collect visitor statistics independently of your organization. These may inadvertently break the AdWords gclid. Therefore, after enabling auto-tagging, always test a sample of your AdWords ads by clicking through from a Google search results page.

If the test fails, then contact your third-party ad-tracking provider because there may be a simple fix. For example, your AdWords auto-tagged landing page URL may look like this:

```
http://www.mysite.com/?gclid=COvQgK7JrY8CFSUWEAodKE
```

If a third-party tracking system is used for redirection, it could end up as this:

```
http://www.redirect.com?http://www.mysite.com/?gclid=COvQgK7JrY8CFSUWEAodKE
```

Notice the two ?—this is invalid because you cannot have two question marks in a URL. Some systems may allow you to replace the second ? with a # so the URL can be processed correctly. This has to be done within the third-party ad tracking system, not within AdWords. Another workaround is to append an encoded dummy variable to your landing page URL, as shown here:

```
http://www.mysite.com/%3Fdum=1
```

AdWords auto-tagging will then append the `gclid` as

```
http://www.mysite.com/%3Fdum=1&gclid=COvQgK7JrY8CFSUWEAodKEEyuA
```

so that when you use your third-party ad-tracking system the URL becomes the following:

```
http://www.redirect.com?http://www.mysite.com/%3Fdum=1&gclid= ➡
COvQgK7JrY8CFSUWEAodKEEyuA
```

This will work. That is, the URL will retain the `gclid` parameter for Google Analytics tracking in the correct format. You can then exclude the tracking of the dummy variable in the Google Analytics configuration settings by adding it as an "Exclude URL Query Parameters" (see Figure 8.1 in "Initial Configuration" in Chapter 8).

> **Note:** If you already have parameters in your landing page URLs, you do not need to add a dummy parameter. However, you will need to change your ? to its encoded equivalent, %3F.

Integrating with Your AdSense Data

If you're an online publisher, you may be using Google's AdSense product. AdSense is the tool that allows you to display Google ads on your own website, thereby sharing in the click-through revenue. The clever part of AdSense is that the ads displayed on your site are targeted to your content. For the most part these are contextual advertising, though advertisers can also target to specific websites. By these methods, the ads shown are more suited to your audience's interests. The result is that you focus on building engaging high-quality content, while Google takes care of the technology for displaying relevant advertisements to your readers. For more information about AdSense, see `http://adsense.google.com`.

Note: AdWords advertisers control whether they wish to display their ads on sites running AdSense. From an advertiser's perspective, this is known as opting in to the Google Display Network within their AdWords account.

Similar to importing your spend and impression data from AdWords as described in the previous section, you can also import your AdSense earnings, impression, and content performance data. Within your AdSense account Home area, select the link Integrate Your AdSense Account With Google Analytics, shown in Figure 6.14.

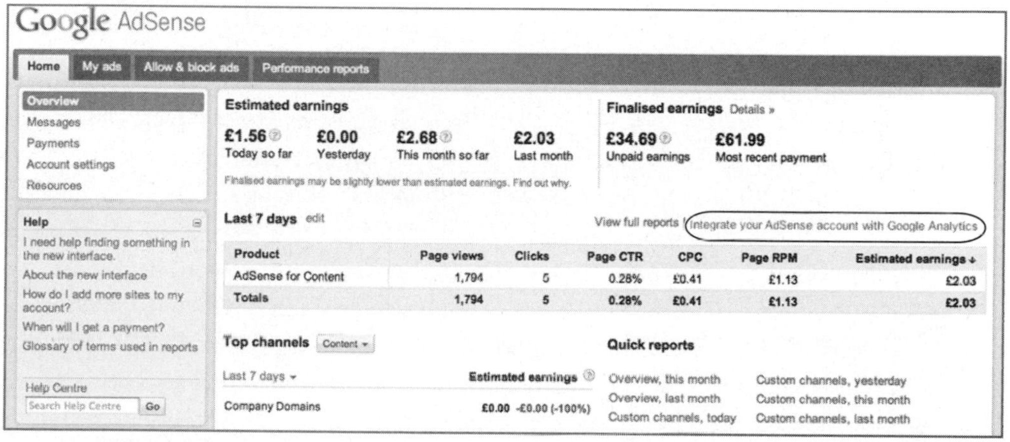

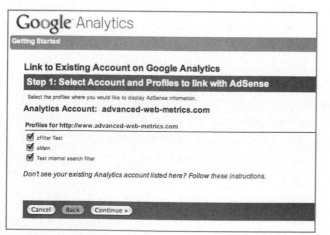

Figure 6.14 Integrating AdSense with Google Analytics

The following screen allows you to either create a Google Analytics account or select an existing one. If you choose the latter, ensure that the AdSense account login you are using is also listed as an administrator within your Google Analytics account before proceeding. If you have done this, AdSense then connects to your Google Analytics account and displays its profiles (see Figure 6.15).

Figure 6.15 Selecting Google Analytics profiles to receive AdSense data

Assuming you are managing only a single website domain in your Google Analytics account, select the profiles you wish to import your AdSense data into. Generally, this will be for all your profiles and so no changes are required to your GATC.

If you manage multiple domains, with AdSense displaying ads across your entire network of sites, you will need to decide which domain is the primary domain for your data import. The primary domain does not require any changes to its GATC, but secondary domains will require changes. Therefore, you should choose the most complex GATC profile as your primary domain so that you minimize changes. See also the Help Center article at

www.google.com/support/analytics/bin/answer.py?answer=92625

If you are required to select a primary domain, the following screen will display the code snippets to update your GATC. Finally, click Continue to complete the linking process. Doing so immediately creates a new section in your Google Analytics reports in the Content > AdSense section. AdSense data (impressions, clicks, revenue) will automatically be imported into your account.

Bear in mind that the import takes place once per day (usually in the middle of the night Pacific time) and is for the period minus 48 to 24 hours in arrears from 23:59 the previous day. The reason for this delay is to allow time for the AdWords fraud-detection algorithms to work through your account. You should also be aware of data import discrepancies, as discussed in Chapter 2 in the section "Why PPC Vendor Numbers Do Not Match Web Analytics Reports."

Note: It is currently not possible to import multiple AdSense account data into a single Google Analytics account.

Integrating with Your Webmaster Tools Data

If you are active with search engine optimization (SEO), you will most likely have a Google Webmaster Tools account—www.google.com/webmasters/tools. Google Webmaster Tools allows you to gain an insight into how Google "sees" your site from an organic (non-advertising) point of view; that is, what pages it finds during a Googlebot crawl, errors found, who links to your content, what user queries on its search engine return pages from your site and your ranking for those queries, and a great deal more useful information for optimizing your site. In many ways, Webmaster Tools data is similar to that contained in your AdWords account, but it's for organic search only.

If you do not have a Webmaster Tools account, simply create one (it's free!) and then integrate with your Google Analytics account as follows:

1. From the home page on your Webmaster Tools account, click Manage Site next to your website, and then click Google Analytics Property (see Figure 6.16).

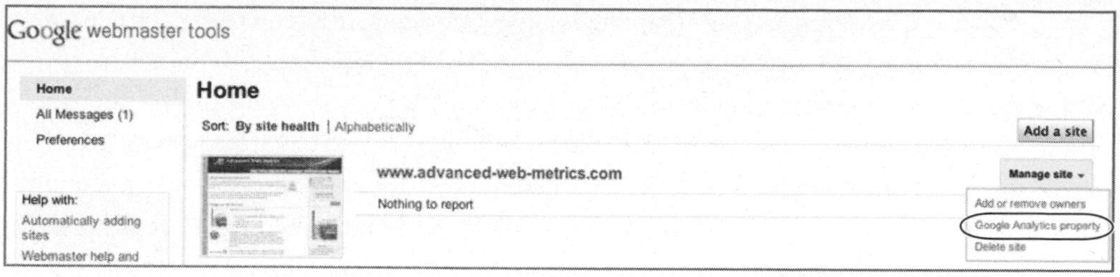

Figure 6.16 Integrating Google Analytics from within Webmaster Tools

2. Click the web property you wish to link and save.

Alternatively, within Google Analytics you can visit your web property settings and integrate the Webmaster Tools data (see Figure 6.17). Select the Edit link and click the web property you wish to link and save.

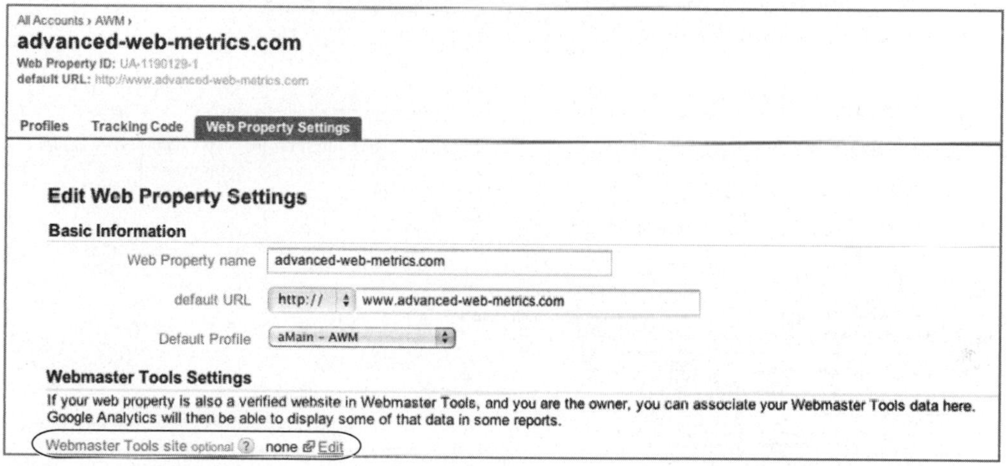

Figure 6.17 Integrating Webmaster Tools from within Google Analytics

Once it's set up, your Webmaster Tools data will show in your Google Analytics reports in the Traffic Sources > Search Engine Optimization section. An example report is shown in Chapter 5.

Integrating with Feedburner

Feeds are a way for websites large and small to distribute their content well beyond just visitors using web browsers. Feeds provide a method of subscription to a website's content that is delivered automatically via a web portal, newsreader, or email. For the consumer, subscribing to feeds makes it possible to review a large amount of online content in a short time—they do not need to visit each individual website, or page, to get the updates they are interested in. For the publisher or blogger, feeds provide instant distribution of your content and the ability for readers to subscribe.

From a tracking point of view, the issue is that feed subscribers do not need to visit your website to read your content. Hence no GATC and therefore no tracking of these highly engaged readers takes place (they subscribed, so by definition they are highly engaged), unless, that is, they click through to your website. You encourage this by being clever with how you produce and distribute your content—providing snippets of information in your RSS feed that entice readers to click through to your site for the full article (these are truly engaged visitors!).

However, once on your website and tracked in the normal way, such visitors cannot be correctly attributed to your feed—either the reader itself is not a referrer or, if it is, the specific details of which article drove the visitor to your site are lost. This problem is *partially* overcome if you use Google's Feedburner service to distribute your content (`http://feedburner.google.com`). Essentially, you set Feedburner to automatically modify your feed's RSS content for you so that click-throughs can be correctly attributed. This is achieved by Feedburner appending campaign parameters to your article title at the point of distribution.

Note: Note my deliberate emphasis on the issue of visitor attribution only being partially overcome by Feedburner. At present, only the article *title* within your feed receives campaign parameters. Other links within your content do not receive campaign parameters and so any click-throughs from these are likely to be labeled as being direct visitors. This is a current limitation of the Feedburner integration.

Note: The issue of being able to correctly attribute non-standard referral visitors is discussed in Chapter 7, "Advanced Implementation." Specifically, refer to Table 7.3.

Within your Feedburner account, select your feed and navigate to the Configure Analytics" section (see Figure 6.18). Then activate "Track clicks as a traffic source in Google Analytics" save.

That's all that's required. From this point forward, readers of your feed content who click through on your article or page title to your website will be tracked and correctly attributed to Feedburner, with the specific feed detail (article) also reported. You view such visits in your Traffic Sources > All Traffic report. Look for feedburner as a campaign source, as shown in Figure 6.19.

If you wish, you can customize the labels used for the attribution by inserting Feedburner's variables in the campaign tracking parameters. However, the default parameters work sufficiently for most users. Campaign tracking is discussed in Chapter 7.

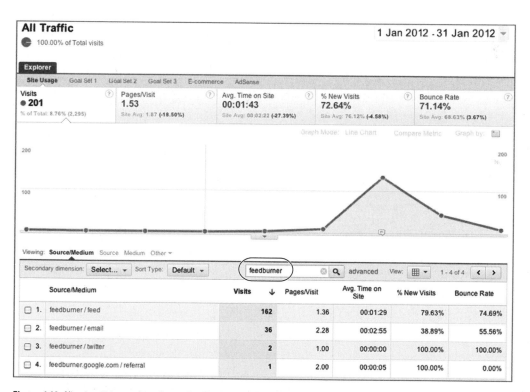

Figure 6.18 Integrating Feedburner data with Google Analytics

Figure 6.19 Viewing visits resulting from a Feedburner distributed feed

Tracking Mobile Visitors

At the end of 2010, smartphones outsold PCs for the first time; 94 million PCs versus 100 million smartphones were sold:

    www.guardian.co.uk/technology/2011/jun/05/smartphones-killing-pc

According to a comScore report, nearly 7 percent of all Internet content consumed in the United States in August 2011 was via a mobile device, up +0.6 percent on the previous quarter:

    www.comscore.com/Press_Events/Presentations_Whitepapers/2011/Digital_Omnivores

Although still a small percentage, the boundary between desktop and mobile Internet access is rapidly changing, essentially because mobile devices are getting much smarter.

Smartphones today have the same computational power of a desktop from just a few years ago. Their web browsers are very similar to desktop versions and implement the same popular JavaScript engines. Hence, smartphone users can navigate "desktop"-designed websites, and these visitors will be tracked by default in Google Analytics—using a standard GATC implementation. An example mobile visitors report is shown in Chapter 5. The tracking of users interacting with mobile apps is covered in Chapter 12.

Tip: Although smartphone users can navigate your desktop version of your website, you should optimize their experience by having a specific style sheet to cater to them. For example, it can be used to remove unnecessary graphics, simplify navigation items, and reorganize the content of a page so that it is easier to read on a small screen.

Mobile Visitors Have Different Expectations

Clearly a mobile user is also a desktop user; however, when they're using a mobile device, the same users' expectations can be very different. For example, by definition mobile users are rarely in an ideal environment to sit, relax, and read content at their leisure on a large, easy-to-view screen with a full ergonomic keyboard. Typical requirements are to quickly find local information—venues, addresses, timetables, contact details.

Mobile connections (and browser rendering) are usually much slower than for desktops, so there is even less patience from the user for slow-loading pages. Battery life and screen standbys (power savers) also contribute to the sense of urgency. Mobile users also rarely close their browser—there is no need to. Hence, time on site and bounce rates can be heavily skewed.

Because of these differences, if mobile website traffic is a significant proportion of your overall traffic volume (say greater than 20 percent), I recommend that you track these visits in a separate profile to your desktop site. This is achieved using a profile filter and is discussed in the section "Profile Segments: Segmenting Visitors Using Filters" in Chapter 8.

Server-Side Tracking for Mobile Sites

As stated earlier, visits from smartphone users are tracked by Google Analytics by default—no changes are required to your GATC or account configuration. This will be the case for the vast majority of website owners. However, some websites need to cater to users of older-generation "feature" phones and their WAP protocol. Such "mobile sites" are built more simply than their desktop counterparts and are lighter on system resources to accommodate the technical limitations of these devices. Consequently, there are two important considerations when tracking a WAP mobile site:

- A mobile website built for feature phones is a very different website (and experience) from your desktop version. Therefore, use a different Google Analytics account or profile for its data collection.

- A regular GATC implementation is not suitable for a mobile site because most feature phones cannot run JavaScript and do not set cookies, both of which are required by the standard GATC. Also, the master tracking file itself (ga.js) is 18 Kb, which is considered heavy for the limitations of a feature phone.

Because of these, Google Analytics can be implemented with a server-side snippet of code that does not use JavaScript and is specifically developed for feature phone tracking. This is referred to as the Google Analytics for Mobile Package—a library ported to PHP, JSP, ASP.NET, and Perl that can be used to track simple traffic from mobile website pageviews. The package, and details of its usage, is available at the following location:

http://code.google.com/mobile/analytics/docs/web/

The following is an example server-side implementation for a page using PHP. There are two steps. First insert the following code before the <HTML> tag:

```php
<?php
  // Copyright 2010 Google Inc. All Rights Reserved.

  $GA_ACCOUNT = "MO-3635138-14";
  $GA_PIXEL = "/ga.php";

  function googleAnalyticsGetImageUrl() {
    global $GA_ACCOUNT, $GA_PIXEL;
    $url = "";
    $url .= $GA_PIXEL . "?";
    $url .= "utmac=" . $GA_ACCOUNT;
    $url .= "&utmn=" . rand(0, 0x7fffffff);
    $referer = $_SERVER["HTTP_REFERER"];
    $query = $_SERVER["QUERY_STRING"];
    $path = $_SERVER["REQUEST_URI"];
```

```php
      if (empty($referer)) {
        $referer = "-";
      }
      $url .= "&utmr=" . urlencode($referer);
      if (!empty($path)) {
        $url .= "&utmp=" . urlencode($path);
      }
      $url .= "&guid=ON";
      return str_replace("&", "&amp;", $url);
    }
?>
```

 Note: The server-side tracking method can be implemented only on dynamic pages—that is, not placed on static HTML pages. This is because the script needs to perform dynamic processing of HTTP headers for referral information and cache-buster parameters.

Then add the server-side generated image snippet into the page source just before the HTML </body> tag:

```php
<?php
  $googleAnalyticsImageUrl = googleAnalyticsGetImageUrl();
  echo '<img src="' . $googleAnalyticsImageUrl . '" />';
?>
```

Why Not Use Server-Side Tracking for All Tracking Requirements?

For many a web developer, the potential use of server-side code as an alternative tracking method to the client-side GATC is an attractive proposition—visitors do not have to wait for the ga.js file to load, JavaScript does not need to be enabled on the visitor's browser, and all the tracking code is controlled in house. Google can be used as just a data repository.

However, the Google Analytics for Mobile Package can track only simple pageviews. It cannot track events, custom variables, e-commerce data, or social interactions. Therefore, server-side tracking is suitable only for feature phone/WAP sites. Also consider that the limitations just described for the GATC method are actually not that limiting—see the list item "Will tagging my pages with the GATC slow them down?" in the next section.

Common Pre-implementation Questions

Installing Google Analytics, as with any other web analytics tool, requires a commitment from you as a website owner—be it the hiring of expertise to achieve a best practice implementation or the use of your own time in reading this book and doing it yourself. Clearly you will want to know if the Google Analytics tool is right for you before investing in such a process.

Assuming you have already had an initial demonstration of the user interface, the following are answers to common questions I regularly receive from people about to decide on their Google Analytics commitment.

Who uses Google Analytics? The number of Google Analytics users is of the order of millions of accounts. However, in my experience only a very small fraction of these have a best practice implementation. Well-known brands that are Google Analytics users are shown at

www.advanced-web-metrics.com/blog/who-uses-google-analytics

Can I store visitor data locally? Yes. By adding a modification to your GATC, you can store a copy of the information sent to Google Analytics in your own web server log files. This is described earlier in this chapter. However, the data will make sense only if processed using Google Urchin software. Urchin is discussed in Chapter 3.

What visitors cannot be tracked? Google Analytics is able to track *all* visitors to your website. However, by default there are only four channel groupings, called *mediums*. These are direct, organic, search (paid and organic), referral. To augment them and to ensure precise measurement, you will need to implement campaign tracking, as discussed in Chapter 7.

What about tracking non-pageviews? In addition to tracking standard pageviews, Google Analytics can track error pages, file downloads, clicks on mail-to links, partial form completion, outbound links, error pages, Flash, and object interactions. This can be via a virtual pageview technique or event tracking. See Chapter 7 for further details.

Can we use an existing tracking tool with Google Analytics? Yes. Google Analytics will happily sit alongside any other page-tagging, logfile, or web analytics solution. As long as there are no JavaScript errors on your web pages, Google Analytics will collect visitor information independently. Similarly, for tracking paid campaigns, Google Analytics variables are simply appended to your existing landing page URLs—regardless of whether another vendor also has tracking variables.

Can we track visitors across different websites? Yes. You can track whether a visitor traverses many website domains owned or managed by you—for example, a visitor passing from www.mysiteA.com to www.mysiteB.com. Typically this happens if you process credit card information with a third-party payment gateway such as WorldPay, PayPal, SecureTrading, or something similar. Tracking across the two sites is achieved by ensuring that the links to the subsequent domains are modified to include a JavaScript function call to either _link (when using an href link) or _linkByPost (when using a form). This is discussed in detail in the section "Tracking E-commerce Transactions" in Chapter 7. Google Analytics cannot be used to track visits across websites that you do not control or manage.

What is the processing limit of Google Analytics? The free version of Google Analytics will process up to 10 million data hits per month per account. A data hit is a pageview, an event, or a transaction item. Generally speaking, unless you have a highly complex event tracking setup, the free limit is good for 10 million pageviews per month— approximately 50,000 visits per day. If you go beyond this you will need to implement data collection sampling, as discussed in Chapter 7.

Google Analytics Premium, the paid-for version, allows for up to 1 billion data hits per month per account. Putting that into perspective, only a handful of users globally receive that amount of traffic. Google Analytics Premium is discussed in Chapter 3.

Can the list of search engines be customized? Yes. Niche search engines or regional specific ones can be added. The defaults can be renamed if you wish. Customizing the list of search engines is discussed in Chapter 9.

Can we track transactions on a third-party payment gateway? Yes, provided you are able to add your GATC to your template pages hosted on the third-party site. Even if you cannot do this, there are workarounds. Ensure that you use either _link (when using an href link) or _linkByPost (when using a form) when linking to the third-party payment gateway website. This is discussed in detail in the section "Tracking E-commerce Transactions" in Chapter 7.

How often does Google Analytics process my data? Putting the feature of real-time reporting aside (discussed in Chapter 5), this depends on the volume of traffic to your site. If visits to your site number fewer than 50,000 data hits per day (hit = pageview + any associated events), reports can be processed within minutes. Between 50,000 and 1 million hits per day and reports are typically 3 to 4 hours in arrears. If you have more than 1 million hits per day, reports are processed once per day. Note that these timings are approximate based on empirical evidence.

If you are running Google Analytics Premium, all processing is guaranteed to be completed within 4 hours. The Premium product is discussed in Chapter 3.

Can I track the login names of my visitors? No. The tracking of personally identifiable information is strictly forbidden in the Google Analytics terms of service. See section 7 (US version) of the terms of service documentation: www.google.com/intl/en/analytics/tos.html.

How does Google Analytics attribute credit for a conversion? By default, credit for a conversion is given to the last clicked referrer. However, the Multi-Channel Funnels report shows all referral paths for a visitor who converts. Multi-channel funnels are discussed in Chapter 5.

Do I own the data in Google Analytics? If you are a user of Google Analytics Premium, your service-level agreement clearly identifies your organization as the owner of the collected data. If you use the free Google Analytics product, this is not the case. From a client perspective, having data ownership typically means the ability to ring-fence data and either delete it or bring it within your own organization should you choose.

With the free Google Analytics product, data is replicated and distributed over the entire cloud of Google servers and data centers (estimated at over 1 million machines). Isolating a particular data set is therefore not offered for the free product. The Premium product is discussed in Chapter 3.

How long after creating an account can I expect to see data? Once your pages are tagged, you should start to see data in your account within 4 hours. However, for high-traffic websites, it can take up to 24 hours.

Do we have to modify the GATC in order to cross-segment data? No. Cross-segmentation is built into the Google Analytics product by drilling down into data when clicking links within the various reports. In addition, cross-segment drop-down menus exist in most reports.

Does Google Analytics use first-party cookies, and what happens if the visitor disables them? All Google Analytics data is collected via first-party cookies only. The GATC loads JavaScript into your site from google-analytics.com. Because it is your site that executes the JavaScript, all cookies are first party. You can view them in your browser privacy settings.

If cookies are disabled or blocked by a visitor, their data will not be collected.

Is the AdWords gclid auto-tagging parameter unique? Yes, the gclid parameter is unique for each keyword in your AdWords account.

Can Google reprocess my historical data? Google cannot currently reprocess historical data, so it is important to always have a default catch-all profile with no filters applied in case you introduce an error in your filters and lose data. Filters are discussed in Chapter 8.

How long does Google keep my data? For the standard version of Google Analytics, your data is retained for 25 months. If you use Premium (the paid-for version), data is guaranteed for 36 months. The Premium product is discussed in Chapter 3.

Can we customize the reports and dashboards? Yes. Custom reporting allows you to design one-of-a-kind reports to fit your specific needs. For example, perhaps you would like to see total goal completions by day of the month or view how affiliate sales are going. These are not standard reports in Google Analytics, but you can build them yourself using the custom report interface (see Chapter 9). You can also build your own dashboards either by adding a specific report to your dashboard, or building custom dashboard widgets (see Chapter 5).

Can I schedule a report to be emailed to me or a colleague regularly? Yes, each report has an Email link. The feature includes a scheduler to automate future emailings.

Can I import cost data from third parties? No. At present, importing cost data from third parties is not possible (for example, from Yahoo! Search Marketing or email marketing platforms). Note that all visitors are still tracked in the same way as other visitors are—using campaign variables appended to the landing page URLs. However, cost or impression data cannot be imported. If this is important to you, consider the option of exporting your Google Analytics data into the third-party system via the export API. This is discussed in Chapter 12.

How many goals can I track? By default, you can track up to 20 goals in Google Analytics and group them into categories. A goal can be defined as a pageview URL (or wildcard), an in-page event (or wildcard), a time-on-site threshold such as greater than 60 seconds, or a number-of-pages-per-visit threshold. By creating more profiles, you could also track additional goals. However, if you have numerous goals—for example, you have a PDF library you wish to track—it is better to have a pseudo e-commerce configuration. That is, you trigger a virtual transaction for each goal completed. That way, each goal is considered a product, and the entire e-commerce reporting section of Google Analytics is available to you. See the section "Monetizing a Non-E-commerce Website" in Chapter 11 for further details.

Can I monetize goals? Yes. You can assign a goal value within the goal configuration section of the Admin area of your Google Analytics account. In fact, this is strongly encouraged, particularly for non-e-commerce sites, so that you may see the intrinsic value of your website. Also see "Monetizing a Non-E-commerce Website" in Chapter 11.

Is there a relationship between the Google Analytics map overlay and the geotargeting options available in AdWords? Yes, the geo-IP database used for both services is the same, so you can use the map overlay information presented in Google Analytics to measure existing AdWords geotargeted campaigns or to help target new markets.

Does Flash break Google Analytics? No. Flash actions can be tracked, but it requires your input—that is, you need to implement event tracking within your FLA file. Chapter 7 discusses this in detail.

Can YouTube video plays be tracked? Yes, if the video is embedded into your pages. Tracking is achieved by communicating with the YouTube Player API as discussed in Chapter 7.

Will tagging my pages with the GATC slow them down? The GATC calls the ga.js file, which is approximately 18 KB in size, from Google servers. The ga.js file is the same for every page you tag on your site. Therefore, once a visitor has downloaded the file from their initial pageview, it will be cached on their machine—so no further requests for the file are required. In addition, the ga.js file is the same for all users of Google Analytics. If a visitor to your website has previously visited another website running Google Analytics tracking (highly likely), then the ga.js file will already be cached on their machine or Internet service provider's caching server. The result is an industry-leading minimal download time for tagging your pages.

In addition the GATC implementation uses asynchronous JavaScript that loads the ga.js file in the background. This means there is no interference with the rest of your page loading.

Are gclids still valid if accounts are not linked? No. If your Google Analytics account is not linked to your AdWords account, AdWords visitors will not be tracked correctly.

Therefore, if you use AdWords, you need to link your accounts in order to track visitors correctly.

Will using Google Analytics directly affect the ranking of my natural search results, ad quality score, or ad placement? No. There are a great number of myths, conspiracy theories, and—to be frank—rubbish written about this on various forums and blogs. As a search marketer, Xoogler (ex-Googler), and now web consultant, I have seen both sides of the "Google fence," and that has been fascinating. I know from my experience as a senior manager at Google that individual website data, from Google Analytics or any other product, is not used to affect your natural search results, ad quality score, or ad placement. Of course, Google wants to improve its products for you—both as a website owner and as a general web user. To that end, aggregate data from multiple sources and across many web properties is used to improve them.

Can Google Analytics track search engine robots? No, not unless the robot can execute JavaScript and set cookies. Most search engine robots cannot do either of these. In particular, Googlebot does not do these and cannot execute the GATC. Similar to the previous question, there are many myths and rumors about Googlebot being able to execute JavaScript. However, as I'm writing this, this is not the case. If you wish to track robot activity, you can use Urchin software, as described in Chapter 3, or for Googlebot specifically, use Google's Webmaster Central (www.google.com/webmasters). Note that apart from being aware that a robot has visited your website, there is little further information to be gained from analyzing search engine robot activity than what Google's Webmaster Central can already provide.

Summary

In Chapter 6, you have learned the following:

How to get started You learned how to create your Google Analytics account either as part of your AdWords account or via the stand-alone version.

How to deploy the tracking code I explained the functions of the GATC code and how to deploy it; I also showed the help that server-side-delivered page tags can offer in simplifying the process.

How to back up and store data locally You learned how to back up traffic data in your local web server logfiles to give you greater flexibility, and I discussed the options for Google Analytics troubleshooting, auditing, and reprocessing.

The difference between accounts and profiles I showed you how to use accounts, profiles, and roll-up reports and what to consider if you are setting up accounts on behalf of clients as an agency or hosting provider.

How to import AdWords data I demonstrated how to link Google Analytics with your Google AdWords account and the importance of testing the auto-tag feature, especially when using AdWords in conjunction with a third-party tracking tool that employs redirects.

How to import AdSense data You learned how to link Google Analytics with your Google AdSense account.

How to integrate with Feedburner and Webmaster Tools You learned how to link Google Analytics with your Google Feedburner and Webmaster Tools accounts.

How to track mobile visitors You learned how to track visitors from mobile sites that cater to feature phones and that require no extra work if your visitors are only smartphone users.

How to manage expectations You learned the answers to common implementation questions.

Advanced Implementation

Now that you understand the basics of getting your web visitor data into Google Analytics, this chapter looks at the more advanced setup considerations you may require. I discuss capturing e-commerce transactions, tagging your marketing campaigns, and tracking events (those actions on your website that are not standard pageviews).

In addition, you'll learn how to customize the Google Analytics Tracking Code (GATC) for your specific needs. For example, do you want to convert dynamic URLs into something more readable? Do you use multiple domains or subdomains? Do you have nonstandard requirements such as changing time-out settings, controlling keyword preferences, or setting sampling rates? All these scenarios and more are covered here.

In Chapter 7, you will learn:

To use the `_trackPageview` function to create virtual pageviews

To capture e-commerce transactions

To track online marketing, including social media campaigns

To track events such as Flash interactions and YouTube plays

To customize the GATC for your specific needs

_trackPageview: the Google Analytics Workhorse

As discussed in Chapter 6, "Getting Started: Initial Setup," the final part of the GATC is a call to the JavaScript routine _trackPageview. This is the main function for tracking a page within Google Analytics. _trackPageview sets up all the required cookies for the session and submits the data to the Google servers. Table 7.1 lists the cookies that Google Analytics sets. You can view these values by using the preferences settings of your browser—typically located in your privacy setup.

▶ **Table 7.1** The five cookies Google Analytics uses

Cookie Name	Time to Live, Type	Purpose
__utma	24 months, first-party	Stores domain and visitor identifiers such as, for example, unique ID, time stamp of initial visit, number of sessions to date.
__utmb	30 minutes, first-party	Stores session identifiers. Used to detect session expiration.
__utmc	Session, first-party	Created for backward compatibility with urchin.js and is no longer used by ga.js.
__utmv	24 months, first-party	Stores custom label. That is custom variables added with the _setCustomVar function (see Chapter 9).
__utmz	6 months, first-party	Stores campaign variables such as, for example, referrer, keyword (if search engine), medium type (CPC, organic, banner, email).

When viewing your Google Analytics cookies, you will notice that all values are preceded by a hash of the host.domain name of the host on which the GATC is located on (taken from the document.domain DOM property). The hash value is a fixed-length numerical value that represents your website. For example, a hash of www.mysite .com might be 202414657, and hence a value of the __utmv cookie could be 202414657 .staff%20user. Similarly, for www.yoursite.com, the hash could be 195485746, with a __utmv cookie of 1954857467.subscriber%20user. Notice that the hash values are both nine digits in length, despite the domain length being different. This is the purpose of the hash. The domain-hashing functionality in Google Analytics uses this number to check cookie integrity for visitors.

If you have multiple subdomains, such as www.mysite.com and support.mysite .com, and you want to track users who pass across both of them, you need to modify how cookies are set by Google Analytics. Similarly, you also need to make changes if you pass visitors to other third-party domains that you control, such as from www .mysite.com to www.myproductsite.com. These special cases are discussed later in this chapter in the section "Customizing the GATC."

With an understanding of how _trackPageview works, you can leverage it to track virtual pageviews and file downloads, as discussed next.

Tracking Unreadable URLs with Virtual Pageviews

If you have a site that includes a shopping cart or has more than a few dozen pages of content, chances are good that you are using dynamic URLs. In this context, these are pages generated on-the-fly (that is, the visitor requests them by clicking page links) as opposed to prebuilt static HTML content. This is how a content management system operates.

Dynamic URLs work by using a server-side scripting language, such as CGI-PERL, PHP, ASP, or Python, that pulls nonformatted information into a common design template. Usually, URL parameters define the page content. You can tell if you are using dynamic URLs by your page names. Static URLs have page filenames ending in `.htm` or `.html`. Dynamic ones have names that end in `.cgi`, `.pl`, `.php`, `.asp`, or `.py`. That does not mean all page names ending in `.php` are generated dynamically. However, if your website URLs also include a query (?) symbol followed by parameters such as name/value pairs, they are most likely dynamic URLs, as shown in the following three examples:

Example 1—a static URL:

```
http://www.mysite.com/local/product101.html
```

Example 2—a dynamic URL with one parameter:

```
http://www.mysite.com/catalogue/product.php?sku=123
```

Example 3—a dynamic URL with three parameters:

```
http://www.mysite.com/catalogue/product.php?sku=148&lang=en&sect=suede
```

In the dynamic examples, the query parameters `sku`, `lang`, and `sect` define the content of the page within a design template.

Note: Some web servers may use an alternative to ?, such as #, to define dynamic URL parameters.

For the purposes of Google Analytics, a URL structure is shown in Figure 7.1. The URL is broken down into its constituent parts here:

- Protocol: `http://`
- Hostname: `www.mysite.com`
- Directory: `/catalogue`
- Filename: `product.php`
- Query parameters: `sku=123&lang=en&sect=leather`
- URI: `/product.php?sku=123&lang=en&sect=leather`

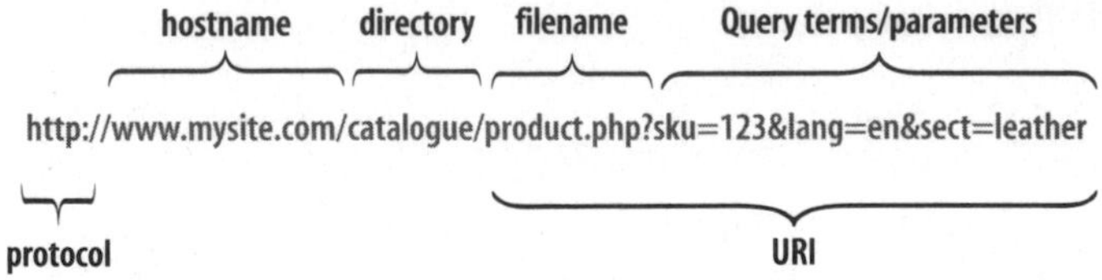

Figure 7.1 Parts of a URL

For this scenario, the query terms used in the vast majority of cases are completely meaningless to the human reader; they are present in order to communicate with your database. Even if your URLs are static, they may still be meaningless to you, as shown in Example 1 earlier. To help those who are using reports, it is preferable to have reader-friendly URLs where possible. In fact, it can make a huge difference for an analyst's engagement with your data, bringing clarity and ease of use to the reports.

Google Analytics can generate reader-friendly URLs by rewriting query terms and meaningless path and filenames as product names or descriptions and display them in your reports as virtual URLs, that is, virtual pageviews.

By default, Google Analytics tracks your viewed pages by calling the JavaScript routine _trackPageview in the GATC. As described in Chapter 6, the standard GATC calls _trackPageview without any additional values. As such, Google Analytics records the URI directly from your browser address bar and displays it in the reports as the pageview. You can override this behavior by modifying the _trackPageview call to create virtual pageviews. For example, using the URL in Figure 7.1, these could be:

```
_gaq.push(['_trackPageview', '/catalogue/products/english/leather/➡
brown tassel shoe']);
_gaq.push(['_trackPageview', '/catalogue/products/english/leather/➡
blue tassel shoe']);
_gaq.push(['_trackPageview', '/catalogue/products/english/suede/➡
high heeled boot']);
```

The additional quoted string contains the virtual pageview and path. This overrides the default URI value. When virtual pageviews are used, reports become much easier to read and interpret. As long as the additional text begins with a forward slash, virtual pageview names may be organized into any virtual directory style structure you wish. This does not mean all query terms and page URLs should be rewritten—only those that are important in identifying specific pages because some parts may be required for reporting on other information such as internal site search.

You can manually modify the additional text for _trackPageview on each page, or you can use the variables present within your web environment, such as your shopping cart or content management system, to build a more meaningful virtual URL. A good webmaster or web developer will be able to set this up quickly. At the very least, simply using what is already available in the example in Figure 7.1, you could have the following:

```
_gaq.push(['_trackPageview', '/catalogue/products/eng/leather/➡
prod code 123']);
```

Clearly, this is not the finished article, but it is a lot more readable to your report users than the original. As stated previously, you should use this technique only to rewrite URLs that are necessary to you. In addition, you should discuss the full consequences with your webmaster. For example, it is not necessary or desirable to rewrite the following:

```
http://www.mysite.com/search?q=shoes
```

In this example, the URI relates to an onsite search query that you will want to view in your Site Search reports. Rewriting this will break those reports. If your URL contains a mix of variables, some of which you want to overwrite and some you do not, then include the variables you wish to keep in the virtual pageview. For example, consider the following dynamic URL that contains a Site Search query term plus other dynamic variables:

```
http://www.mysite.com/search?q=shoes&lang=en
&sect=leather
```

As a virtual URL, this could be written as follows:

```
_gaq.push(['_trackPageview', '/products/eng/leather/?q=shoes']);
```

Here, the original q=shoes query is written back into the virtual pageview, enabling you to view Site Search reports as normal. As with all URLs, if you wish to write query variables in your virtual pageviews, then use the standard convention—a question mark (?) to begin the variable definition and an ampersand (&) to separate multiple name/value pairs.

> **Note:** A consequence of using virtual pageviews is that they will break the In-Page Analytics reports because the page doesn't exist in the real world. If this feature is important to you, then don't rewrite your URLs. However, you'll likely find that the greater clarity virtual pageviews bring to the reporting of complex URLs far outweighs the loss of this feature.

Tracking File Downloads with Virtual Pageviews

By default, Google Analytics will not track your file downloads (for example, PDF, EXE, DOC, XLS, ZIP) because these pages cannot be tagged with the GATC. However, it is easy to track these by modifying the download link on your web pages using the virtual pageview technique just described.

In the following example, the link itself within your web page is modified, not the GATC. Here is the original HTML link that cannot be tracked:

```
<a href="mydoc.pdf">Download a PDF</a>
```

This new link is tracked in the virtual /downloads directory:

```
<a href="mydoc.pdf"
onclick="_gaq.push(['_trackPageview','/downloads/mydoc.pdf']);">
Download a PDF</a>
```

Tracking Partially Completed Forms with Virtual Pageviews

Virtual pageviews can also be used to track the partial completion of forms. This is particularly useful if you have long (more than 10 fields) or multipage forms, such as registration forms or feedback surveys. Using virtual pageviews in this way enables you to see where visitors bail out before getting to the Submit button. This is achieved using the Funnel Visualization report, as discussed in the section "Goal and Funnel Reports" in Chapter 5, "Reports Explained."

In order to accomplish this, use the onBlur event handler to modify your HTML form fields as follows:

```
<form action="cgi-bin/formhandler.pl" method="post" name="theForm">
<input type="text" name="firstname" onBlur="➡
if(document.theForm.firstname.value != '');_gaq.push(['_trackPageview'➡
, '/forms/signup/firstname'])">


<input type="text" name="lastname" onBlur="➡
if(document.theForm.lastname.value != ''); _gaq.push(['_trackPageview'➡
, '/forms/signup/lastname'])">


<input type="text" name="dob" onBlur="➡
if(document.theForm.dob.value != ''); _gaq.push(['_trackPageview'➡
, '/forms/signup/dob']) ">


<input type="text" name="address1" onBlur="➡
if(document.theForm.address1.value != ''); _gaq.push(['_trackPageview'➡
, '/forms/signup/address1']) ">
.

.

</form>
```

The if() != '' statement is included to confirm that each form field has content before the virtual pageview is created. Of course, not all form fields will be compulsory to the visitor, so use the if statement appropriately.

> **Warning:** The virtual pageviews tracked in this example are labels that enable you to confirm whether a field has been completed—they are not personal information submitted by the visitor. It is against the Google Analytics terms of service to track personally identifiable information. For more information, see www.google .com/analytics/tos.html.

Virtual Pageviews versus Event Tracking

Using virtual pageviews to track file downloads, or partial form completion, inflates your pageview count because obviously these are not real pageviews. Therefore, consider carefully your use of them.

If the action you are tracking can be considered as analogous to a pageview, then the virtual pageview technique is valid. In my opinion, this is the case for readable file downloads (PDF, DOC, XLS, PPT, and the like) and partial form completion. My hypothesis is that such content is readable in the same way as other HTML pages from your site—the reader is agnostic to the file format and so such virtual pageviews are comparable with all other pageviews on your site.

The alternative approach is to use Event Tracking, as discussed later in this chapter. Events are reported separately from pageviews and so are not easy to compare with pageview content. My recommendation is therefore to use Event Tracking only where the action being tracked is in no way related to a pageview; that is, the visitor is not accessing a page of readable content but instead is, for example, downloading ZIP and EXE files or interacting with a video or animation file. See the section "Event Tracking" later in this chapter for examples.

Tracking E-commerce Transactions

Before describing how to capture e-commerce data, consider the salient points to take into account when collecting visitor transactional data:

Currency formatting and labels The values reported for item price and transaction totals do not respect any currency formatting. For example, the first instance of either a comma or a period indicates a fractional value. Therefore, use 1495.00 (or 1495,00) for the captured amount and not 1,495.00 because the latter would be reported at 1.495. A currency label can be displayed in your reports, such as, for example, $, £, € (24 currency symbols are available). However, the value is currency agnostic. That is, the currency is purely a label for display purposes.

Google Analytics with multiple currencies Because transaction and item values are currency agnostic (see the previous list item), you need to give special consideration if your website allows visitors to purchase in multiple currencies or if you are running multiple websites with localized currency values.

If you allow purchases in different currencies, capture only one fixed value for Google Analytics and use the appropriate label in your reports. For example, if you sell an item for £39.00, €49.00, and $59.00, choose only one of these values for Google Analytics, irrespective of what your visitor pays with. Of course, you can perform an exchange rate calculation on each item to unify the currency and then forward this to Google Analytics, but that will confuse your marketing department, which will need to back out exchange rate fluctuations in order to ascertain whether a campaign is successful or not.

Similarly, if you are running multiple websites with localized currency values, then these will not be converted into the single currency label you have set for each profile. Best practice is therefore to use one Google Analytics account for each localized website. This makes sense when you consider that each localized website is also likely to be running in its own time zone and its own AdWords campaigns, where the cost data is also localized. To generate an aggregate report of all local websites, add a second GATC to your pages with transactional data unified to a single currency. Chapter 6 discusses this scenario in more detail in the section "Roll-up Reporting."

Maintaining your back office systems Google Analytics is not a substitute for your back office or customer relationship management system—there will always be discrepancies between these two data sources. For example, JavaScript-disabled browsers, blocked or deleted cookies, multiple visitor clicks, Internet connection blips, returned orders, implementation mistakes, and so on all add error bars when it comes to aligning web visitor data with order fulfillment systems. As a rule of thumb, counting transactions in Google Analytics usually differs between 5 and 10 percent from other systems. Accuracy considerations are discussed in Chapter 2, "Available Methodologies and Their Accuracy," in the section "Comparing Data from Different Vendors."

Instead, use Google Analytics E-commerce reports to measure the effectiveness of your marketing campaigns and your website's ability to convert a visitor into a customer.

Importing customer data into your CRM system Google Analytics does not collect any personally identifiable information, and it is against the terms of service to attempt to collect such information. However, it is possible to pass Google Analytics cookie data, along with the transaction detail, to your CRM system. In this way, for example, your back office system can contain information on how your customers arrived at your website and how long it took them to make their first purchase and so forth. This is discussed in Chapter 12 in the section "Extracting Google Analytics Information."

With these points in mind, the first step is to get your visitor transactional data into Google Analytics, and I discuss this process next.

Capturing Secure E-commerce Transactions

Google Analytics supports a client-side data-collection technique for capturing e-commerce transactions. With some straightforward additions to the GATC on your purchase receipt page, you can configure Google Analytics to record transaction and product information. The following is an example GATC to do this:

```
<script type="text/javascript">
var _gaq = _gaq || [];_
_gaq.push(['_setAccount', 'UA-12345-1']);
_gaq.push(['_trackPageview']);

_gaq.push(["_addTrans",
"1234",                     // unique order ID - required
"Mountain View Book Store", // affiliation code or store name
"89.97",                    // total value - required
"6.30",                     // tax
"5"                         // shipping
]);

_gaq.push(["_addItem",
"1234",                     // order ID - must match above - required
"DD44-BJC",                 // SKU code (stock keeping unit) - required
"Advanced Web Metrics",     // product name - required
"Web, Technical",           // category name
"29.99",                    // unit price - required
"3"                         // quantity - required
]);

_gaq.push(['_trackTrans']);

(function() {
var ga = document.createElement('script');
ga.type = 'text/javascript'; ga.async = true;
ga.src = ('https:' == document.location.protocol ? 'https://ssl' : ➡
'http://www') + '.google-analytics.com/ga.js';
var s = document.getElementsByTagName('script')[0];
s.parentNode.insertBefore(ga, s);
})();
</script>
```

For this example, three additional lines have been added within the GATC:

- The transaction line, as defined by _addTrans, which is a list of comma-separated values delimited by quotation marks
- The product item line, as defined by _addItem, which is a list of comma-separated values delimited by quotation marks

- A call to the JavaScript function _trackTrans, which sends the transaction and item information to Google Analytics

The order of these lines within your GATC is important, so maintain the order shown here on your receipt page.

As shown in the code example, both _addTrans and _addItem can be written on multiple lines for clarity. Conversely, they can also be written on a single line, which may be an easier format for you to use with transactions containing multiple items:

```
_gaq.push(["_addTrans", "1234","Mountain View Book Store",➡
"89.97","6.30","5"]);
_gaq.push(["_addItem", "1234","ISBN-1118168445",➡
"Advanced Web Metrics","Web","29.99","2"]);
_gaq.push(["_addItem", "1234","ISBN-9780321344755",➡
"Don't Make me Think","Web","29.99","1"]);
```

For each transaction, there should be only one _addTrans entry. This line specifies the total amount for the transaction and the tax and shipping amounts. For each item purchased, there must be an _addItem line. That is, two purchased items require two _addItem lines, and so forth. Item lines contain the product names, codes, unit prices, and quantities. The variable values required are shown in Table 7.2. You obtain these from your e-commerce shopping system.

▶ **Table 7.2** E-commerce parameter reference guide

Variable	Description
Transaction Line Variables	
order-id	Your internal, unique order ID number
affiliation	Affiliation or store name (optional)
total	Total value of the transaction
tax	Tax amount of the transaction (optional)
shipping	The shipping amount of the transaction (optional)
Item Line Variables	
order-id	Your internal, unique order ID (must match the transaction line)
sku-code	Product stock-keeping unit code (must be unique for each product)
product-name	Product name or description
category	Category name of the product (optional)
price	Unit price of the product
quantity	Quantity ordered

If you don't have data for a certain variable, leave the quotation marks for the variable empty (with no spaces). For example, if you have no affiliate network, shipping is included in the purchase price, and you do not use categories, you would use the following:

```
_gaq.push(["_addTrans", "1234","","89.97","6.30",""]);
_gaq.push(["_addItem", "1234","ISBN-1118168445",➡
"Advanced Web Metrics","","29.99","2"]);
_gaq.push(["_addItem", "1234","ISBN-9780321344755",➡
"Don't Make me Think","","29.99","1"]);
```

The Importance of Unique Order IDs

It is important to use unique order IDs (consisting of numbers or text or a mixture of both) for each transaction. Otherwise, separate transactions that have the same order ID will be compounded, rendering the data meaningless. This can happen to you if customers inadvertently multiple-click the final purchase button. For best practice, prevent this behavior. Following is a JavaScript example:

```
<script>
var firsttime;
function validator(){
 if (firsttime == "Y"){
   alert("Please wait, your payment is being processed.");
   return (false);
 }
 firsttime = "Y";
 return (true);
}
</script>
```

Paste the above code into the <head> area of your HTML page that contains the final e-commerce checkout link or button. Then within your HTML of the same page, modify your submission form as follows:

```
<FORM METHOD="POST" ACTION="authorize.cgi" onSubmit= ➡
"return validator()">
```

The onSubmit event handler will prevent multiple submissions of the form, thus preventing Google Analytics from capturing any duplicate transaction IDs.

If your purchase form already has an onSubmit event handler, append the validator call as follows:

```
<FORM METHOD="POST" ACTION="authorize.cgi" onSubmit= ➡
"return checkEmail; return validator()">
```

E-commerce Guidelines

Keep in mind these guidelines when implementing e-commerce tracking.

The SKU code is a required parameter for every item that is added to the transaction. If a transaction contains multiple items and the SKU is not supplied for every item, a GIF request is sent only for the last item added to the transaction for which the SKU is provided. In addition, if your inventory has different items with the same SKU, and a visitor purchases both of them, you will receive data for only the most recently added. For this reason, you should make sure each item you offer has a unique SKU.

If you are implementing e-commerce tracking and using a third-party payment gateway, you will need to configure cross-domain tracking as well. See the section "Transactions via a Third-Party Payment Gateway."

Transactions via a Third-Party Payment Gateway

If your website initiates a purchase checkout process on a separate store site (for example, if you send customers from www.mysite.com to a payment gateway, such as www.secure-site.com), you need to make additional changes to your web pages. This is because Google Analytics uses first-party cookies for best-practice purposes. As discussed in Chapter 2, only the domain that sets first-party cookies can read or modify them—a security feature built into all web browsers by default. You can overcome this and pass your Google Analytics first-party cookies to your third-party domain with the following two-step method.

- First, you will modify the GATC on all your pages—on both your primary site and all store site pages. This is to allow cookie information to be shared.

- Second, any link or button that causes the visitor to traverse across sites requires modification.

Note: Strictly speaking, the first step is required only on two pages—the ones that pass over and receive the first-party cookies. Typically, this is the last page of the checkout process that occurs on www.mysite.com and the entry page visitors use to complete their checkout on www.secure-site.com. However, by using the same GATC throughout your website, you minimize any potential errors, particularly if you later add further crossover links to your pages; that is, additional ways for visitors to check out via the third-party payment gateway. By defining only one GATC, you provide a simple level of future-proofing your tracking requirements.

Modify your GATC as follows:

```
<script type="text/javascript">
```

```
var _gaq = _gaq || [];
_gaq.push(['_setAccount', 'UA-12345-1']);
_gaq.push(['_setDomainName', 'mysite.com']);
_gaq.push(['_setAllowLinker ', true]);
_gaq.push(['_trackPageview']);

(function() {
var ga = document.createElement('script');
ga.type = 'text/javascript'; ga.async = true;
ga.src = ('https:' == document.location.protocol ? 'https://ssl' : ➡
'http://www') + '.google-analytics.com/ga.js';
var s = document.getElementsByTagName('script')[0];
s.parentNode.insertBefore(ga, s);
})();
</script>
```

The modified GATC does two things: _setDomainName forces the domain hash
of the Google Analytics cookies to be explicitly set to the given string and sets the
cookie's host to be the same value. The use of setAllowLinker then allows cookies to be
pushed from one domain to the next.

Warning: In previous editions of this book and in the Google online documentation up until August
2011, _gaq.push([' setDomainName', 'none']) was the recommended setting. Although it's now
deprecated, if you are already using this, it is important to keep it in place. This is because Google Analytics checks
the domain hash when reading cookies directly. If you remove this, cookies from returning visitors will be ignored
because the hash values will not match the new cookies set. For this reason, sites that are already set with _gaq
.push(['_setDomainName', 'none']) should not be modified.

The second step is to modify the web page on www.mysite.com that calls the third-
party gateway site, in one of two ways:

Link method If your website uses a link to pass visitors to the third-party site, modify it
to look like this:

```
<a href="https://www.secure-site.com/?store=parameters"
onclick="_gaq.push(['_link', this.href]); return false;">
Continue to Purchase</a>
```

With this method, you are passing the Google Analytics cookies to the receiving
domain by appending them to the URL string. If you see __utma, __utmb, and __utmc
parameters in your third-party landing page URL, then this has worked.

Form method If your website uses a form to pass visitors to the third-party site, then modify the form as follows:

```
<form method="post" action="http://www.secure-site.com/process.cgi"
onSubmit="_gaq.push(['_linkByPost', this]);">
```

With this method, the Google Analytics cookies are passed to the receiving domain via the HTTP headers. This will work even for forms with `method="GET"`. You can verify that this has worked by viewing the HTTP headers sent in Firefox using the add-on LiveHTTPheaders (`http://livehttpheaders.mozdev.org`).

I recommend using the first `_link` method to test to see whether your setup is correct; that is, you can see your cookie values in your third-party landing page URL. Then switch to the `_linkByPost` method if required.

What to Do When a Third-Party Gateway Does Not Allow Tracking

If your third-party payment gateway does not allow you to modify its payment pages—that is, add your GATC—you cannot directly capture completed transactions. However, there are workarounds, as detailed in the following sections.

Use a Page Callback

Use a page callback to your website from the third-party gateway site. The callback is a page the visitor is automatically returned to on your site when the transaction completes successfully. Many payment gateways offer this feature.

Provided this page is unavailable to visitors other than via the callback, you can place your e-commerce variables on the same page. They are under your control because the callback page is hosted within your website. An important step of this method is to ignore the third-party site as referrer. By doing so, you maintain the original referrer details in the purchaser's cookie. Otherwise, all purchasers will show their referrer as being from `www.secure-site.com`. To avoid this, do one of the following:

- Add a line of code to the GATC of the callback page:

  `_gaq.push(['_addIgnoredRef', 'secure-site.com']);`

  This should be placed just before the call to `_trackPageview`.

- Alternatively, append utm_nooverride=1 to the callback URL:

  `www.mysite.com/purchase-callback.php?utm_nooverride=1`

When you use either of these methods (you can even use both to be double sure), e-commerce data will align closely with that of your third-party gateway company. I recommend this method whenever available. If you cannot use this approach, there are workarounds (as described next). However, seriously consider changing your third-party payment partner. There are numerous solutions that are flexible enough to appreciate that tracking e-commerce performance is an important element of the purchasing process.

Track The Purchaser's Intent

For a basic approximation of a transaction, use an onClick or onSubmit event handler at the point where visitors are just about to click away to the payment gateway. Using one of these methods, call the _trackTrans function and capture the transaction details. The addTrans and addItem calls also must be configured on the same page.

An example call via a link would be as follows:

```
<a href="https://www.secure-site.com/?store=parameters" onclick="➡
_gaq.push(['_link', this.href]); return false;">
Continue to Purchase</a>
```

The obvious caveat with this method is that you are not tracking completed transactions but the intent to complete. Perhaps the visitor's credit card details are declined, or they change their mind at the last minute before completing payment. Whatever the reason, your Google Analytics E-commerce reports will only be a rough guide to transaction activity and are unlikely to align well with reports from your third-party gateway company.

Create a Server-Side Transaction Hit

A transaction is registered with Google Analytics when the _addTrans function is called from a page. It is also possible to create a transaction data hit by server-side methods, that is, with no pageview required. Essentially, the server processing the confirmed purchase generates the GIF request (data stream) required by Google Analytics.

The GIF request is a long URL request to google-analytics.com containing parameters that define the data sent. Here is an example of part of a GIF request:

```
http://www.google-analytics.com/__utm.gif?utmwv=4&utmn=769876874&utmhn=
example.com&utmcs➡
=ISO-8859-1&utmsr=1280x1024&utmsc=32-bit&utmul=en-us&utmje=1&utmfl➡
=9.0%20%20r115&utmcn=1&utmdt=GATC012%20setting%20variables&utmhid➡
=2059107202&utmr=0&utmp=/auto/GATC012.html?utm_source=www.gatc012.org➡
&utm_campaign=campaign+gatc012&utm_term=keywords+gatc012&utm_content➡
=content+gatc012&utm_medium=medium+gatc012&utmac=UA-30138-1&utmcc=➡
__utma%3D97315849.1774621898.1207701397.1207701397.1207701397.1%3B...
```

The definitions of the GIF request parameters are available at the following location:

```
http://code.google.com/apis/analytics/docs/concepts/gaConceptsOverview.
html#gifParameters
```

By populating this URL with the correct parameters for your transaction, your server can register the data with Google Analytics without the need for a confirmation pageview. The downside of this method, however, is that apart from requiring the help of a good web developer, the e-commerce tracking code is hidden from view. That means you will always have to keep that helpful developer close at hand for troubleshooting purposes.

Tracking Negative Transactions

All e-commerce organizations have to deal with product returns at some point, whether because of damaged or faulty goods, order mistakes, or other reasons. It is possible to account for these within your Google Analytics reports by processing a *negative transaction*. However, I don't recommend this for two reasons:

Aligning web visitor data with internal systems does not yield perfect results. A negative transaction usually takes place well after the original purchase, therefore in a different reporting period. This is generally more confusing than simply leaving the returned transaction in your reports.

Returns are not representative of your marketing or website effectiveness. If I search for "running shoes" and then make a purchase from your website, that is a perfectly good transaction—one that reflects the effectiveness of your website and your marketing campaigns.

If subsequently I decide I don't like the shoes and return them, this would be because of the product, perhaps a quality issue. That is separate from the effectiveness of your marketing; just because I return my running shoes does not mean that no further marketing investment should be made for that product.

For completeness, I include how to process a negative transaction here.

First, create an internal-only version of your completed purchase form that can be edited for the negative details. The form should be edited in a text editor and *not* loaded in a browser at this stage; otherwise, it will trigger the code. To remove an order, edit as follows.

For the _addTrans line:

- Use the same *order-id* for the transaction as the one used for the original purchase.
- Ensure that the *total* value is negative.
- Ensure that the *tax* and *shipping* variables are negative.

For the _addItem line:

- Use the same *order-id* for the transaction as the one used for the original purchase.
- Ensure that the *price* value is positive.
- Ensure that the *quantity* value is negative.

Process the form details by loading the modified copy of your order receipt page into your browser. This will call the _trackTrans function as if it were a regular purchase.

By this method, you will still be able to see the actual transaction and the duplicate negative transaction when you select the days on which each of these transactions was recorded. However, when you select a date range that includes both the original and the negative transaction, the transaction will not be included in the total revenue reported.

Campaign Tracking

Of all the setup and implementation advice I provide in this book, showing you how to correctly track your marketing activity is probably the most important. Typically, your traffic acquisition costs are greater than the cost to develop and build and maintain your website. Therefore, knowing which marketing campaigns are effective and determining which of them produce a positive return on investment is a key requirement of any web analytics tool.

By default, Google Analytics reports on traffic from three referral types (mediums):

Organic Visits from organic (free) search engine listings such as Google, Yahoo!, Bing, and Baidu

Referrals Visits from people who have clicked a link on another site, such as affilaite1 .com, partner2.com, or Facebook.com

Direct Visits from people who have remembered your web address and typed it directly into their browsers

If you do nothing other than install the GATC on your pages, visits from these three referral mediums will show in your reports, along with concomitant information such as the name of the search engine, keywords used (organic), and website address (referral). However, if you use campaign tracking, a much richer report emerges. Figure 7.2 compares the marketing performance of a default report and one where campaign tracking has been implemented. A similar report can be viewed to see how this relates to revenue or goal conversions.

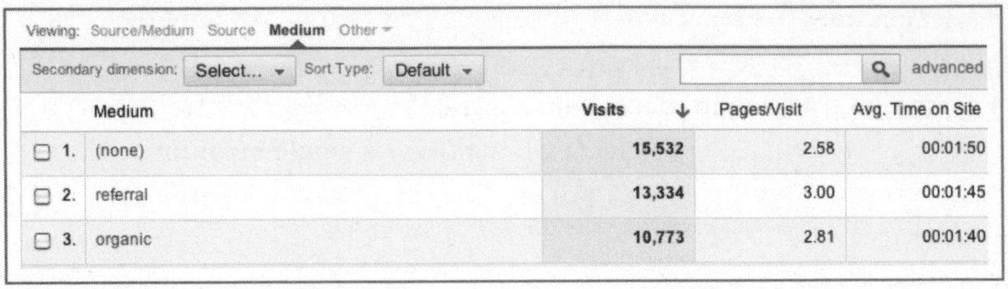

Viewing: Source/Medium Source **Medium** Other

Secondary dimension: Select... Sort Type: Default advanced

	Medium	Visits	Pages/Visit	Avg. Time on Site
1.	(none)	15,532	2.58	00:01:50
2.	referral	13,334	3.00	00:01:45
3.	organic	10,773	2.81	00:01:40

a

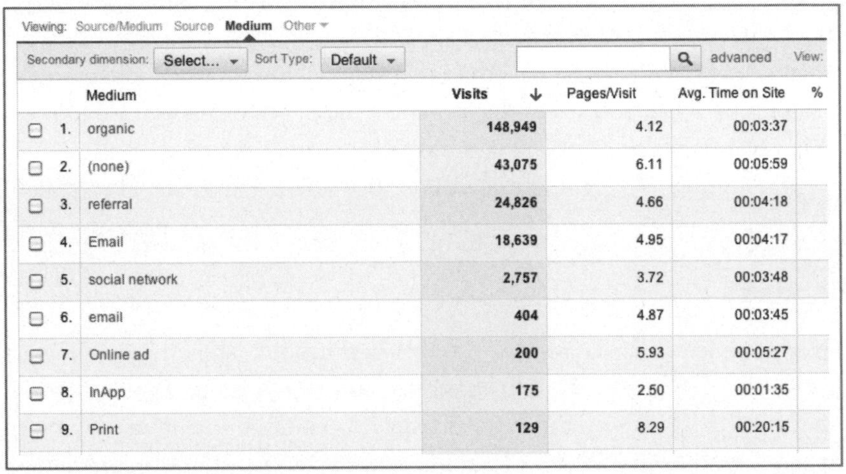

Viewing: Source/Medium Source **Medium** Other

Secondary dimension: Select... Sort Type: Default advanced View:

	Medium	Visits	Pages/Visit	Avg. Time on Site	%
1.	organic	148,949	4.12	00:03:37	
2.	(none)	43,075	6.11	00:05:59	
3.	referral	24,826	4.66	00:04:18	
4.	Email	18,639	4.95	00:04:17	
5.	social network	2,757	3.72	00:03:48	
6.	email	404	4.87	00:03:45	
7.	Online ad	200	5.93	00:05:27	
8.	InApp	175	2.50	00:01:35	
9.	Print	129	8.29	00:20:15	

b

Figure 7.2 Comparing (a) the default marketing report with (b) one that uses campaign tracking

The technique for gaining such rich marketing reports is the use of campaign tracking parameters in your landing page URLs. A *landing page* is the destination page on which you want visitors to enter your website following a click-through on a referring website. In most cases, you can control what destination page your visitors arrive at (land on) by specifying the URL. For example, if you have a link on a product portal directory that specializes in all things widget, then you may decide to point your link URL to a specific product landing page such as `www.mysite.com/widgets.htm` as opposed to your generic home page. That way, you improve the experience for visitors who click through by showing them a specific page relevant to their interests.

For the product portal directory example, nothing more is required. You will see how many visitors and conversions are received from that website in your Traffic Sources > Sources > Referrals report. However, what if you also have a paid banner advertisement on the portal directory? Without the use of campaign tracking parameters in your landing page URLs, you will not be able to differentiate visits from these two visitor types—referral click-throughs and banner click-throughs—because they come from a single source.

Campaign tracking also allows you to correctly track visitors from social network sites such as Facebook and Twitter. This is important because many different conversations may be taking place about your products and brand. Without campaign tracking, all you see in your reports are referral visitors from the social network site in question. With campaign tracking in place, you can track visits from a specific social campaign and even aggregate all social referrals together as a single medium so they can be compared against the performance of other mediums, such as organic, paid search, and email visitors.

Another use of campaign tracking is to track a visitor who does not click a web page to reach your website but instead reaches it, for example, through email marketing or by clicking from within a document such as brochure.pdf because neither a PDF document nor a user's email program can receive a GATC.

I illustrate all these examples in the following sections. However, you should first understand how to set up your campaign tracking.

> **Note:** With a little lateral thought, you can also apply campaign tracking to track the performance of *offline* marketing campaigns. This is discussed in Chapter 11, "Real-World Tasks."

Adding Campaign Parameters to Your Landing Page URLs

The principle and process are straightforward—you append additional Google Analytics parameters to the end of your URLs. Following are two examples (which will be discussed in more detail) of tagging landing pages for use in paid campaigns on the Yahoo! Search Marketing network:

Example static landing page

Original landing page URL:

```
http://www.mysite.com/widgets.htm
```

The landing page URL with campaign parameters:

```
http://www.mysite.com/widgets.htm?➡
utm_source=yahoo&utm_medium=ppc&utm_term=widgets
```

Example dynamic landing page

Original landing page URL:

```
http://www.mysite.com/widgets.php?prod=101
```

The landing page URL with campaign parameters:

```
http://www.mysite.com/widgets.php?prod=101&➡
utm_source=yahoo&utm_medium=ppc&utm_term=widgets
```

> **Note:** Do not add campaign parameters to your AdWords campaigns. This is done for you automatically (see "Integrating with Your AdWords Data" in Chapter 6).

Whether you wish to track pay-per-click networks, social media campaigns, banners, links within documents, or email marketing, the same variables are applied in this straightforward way. If you don't use campaign tracking parameters, visitors from these to your site are still being tracked. However, the referrer information is not known, and so it becomes aggregated with other sources, as shown in Table 7.3.

▶ **Table 7.3** Visitor attribution with and without the use of campaign tracking

Referral	Example Attribution with Campaign Tracking in Place	Attribution without Campaign Tracking
Paid search (other than AdWords)	cpc	Labeled as "organic search" with specific campaign information lost.
Social network site	social media	Labeled as "referral" and buried in your reports among other referrers.
Display ad	banner	Labeled as "referral" and buried in your reports among other referrers.
Affiliate	affiliate	Labeled as "referral" and buried in your reports among other referrers.
Email marketing	email	Labeled as "direct" with no information about which particular email generated the visit. If web mail is used, the visit will be labeled as referral.
Links from within documents (e.g., PDFs)	docs	Labeled as "direct" with no information about which particular document generated the visit.

In Table 7.3, I deliberately use the term *example attribution* in the column heading because it is you who defines what exact label shows within your reports. For example, by default in the AdWords reports, paid search is listed as medium=cpc (cost-per-click). You may wish to follow this format for your other paid search campaigns or perhaps use ppc (pay-per-click) to differentiate from AdWords.

There are certain links that do not require campaign tracking. For instance, you should not use this method for organic (nonpaid) links from search engines, and it isn't necessary to use this with links that come from referral sites where your link listing is free, such as web portals—these will correctly show in your referral reports.

 Warning: Do not attempt campaign tracking for internal links (links within your website). Doing so will cause Google Analytics to restart the session for the same visitor. That is, the visit will be double-counted with new referrer details, and you will not be able to trace back any subsequent transactions or goal completions to the original referrer. Instead, use custom variables for this purpose, as explained in the section "Labeling Visitors, Sessions, and Pages" in Chapter 9, "Google Analytics Customizations."

When you are adding campaign tracking to your landing page URLs, there are five Google Analytics parameters to consider, shown in Table 7.4.

▶ **Table 7.4** Landing page campaign variables

Tag Variables	Condition	Description
utm_source	Required	Used to identify a particular search engine, newsletter, or other referral source
utm_medium	Required	Used to identify a medium such as, for example, CPC, PPC, banner, email, PDF, DOC, or XLS, etc.
utm_term	Optional	Used for paid search to note the keywords being targeted for a particular ad
utm_content	Optional	Used for version testing to distinguish different content, such as for example, ads that link to the same landing page
utm_campaign	Recommended	Used to identify different strategic campaigns from the same source-medium combination, such as, for example, for an email newsletter using "spring promotion" or "summer promotion"

As previously shown, campaign links consist of a URL address followed by a ? (or & if you have existing parameters) and two or more of your campaign variables. Appending these additional variables to your landing page URLs overrides any browser-detected referral information, that is, document.referrer. It is this that enables Google Analytics to differentiate visitors—for example, between an organic visitor from Yahoo! and a banner visitor from Yahoo! or between a direct visitor and one who clicked an email link. Because up to five variables are allowed, the URLs can appear complicated. To get you started, and to avoid worrying about the exact syntax, use Google's URL Builder tool at

www.google.com/support/googleanalytics/bin/answer.py?answer=55578

The URL Builder tool creates the campaign-tracked links for you—you simply copy and paste the resultant URL as your ad landing page URL. Once you understand the structure of the campaign-tracked URLs, you may want to switch to using a spreadsheet of these for bulk upload into your pay-per-click account or other management system.

Note: If you are using a third-party ad-tracking system to track click-throughs to your website, your visitors will be passed through redirection URLs. If this describes your scenario, be sure to test your landing page URLs because redirection may break them. You can test by clicking the resultant combined link (ad-tracking link plus campaign-tagged link). See "Testing after Enabling Auto-Tagging" in Chapter 6 for further details.

The examples in the following sections demonstrate the best ways to tag the five most common kinds of online campaigns: banner ads, email campaigns, social media campaigns, paid keywords (pay-per-click), and links within digital documents. Note that each landing page URL is specific to the campaign you create it for—do not use it anywhere else!

Banner Ads

Consider the following hypothetical marketing scenario on the AOL.com website: You have a graphical banner for branding purposes and an organic listing from the nonpaid listings. AOL has informed you that the banner will display only when a visitor searches for the term "shoes"; in this case the banner campaign is about *Sprint shoes*. These are two different campaigns that are from the same referral domain name (reported as aol.com) and can refer a visitor to your website.

Using the URL Builder tool, shown in Figure 7.3, you can differentiate visitors from banner click-throughs by supplying the resultant campaign-tracked landing page URL to the person or agency setting up your AOL banner. It is not necessary (or possible) to tag your AOL organic listing because it will be detected automatically.

If you were then to run the same banner ad but on a different website or portal—Yahoo! for example—only the value of utm_source would change (to Yahoo). It's important to ensure that the other parameters remain the same so the performance of the banner campaign can be compared across all other placements.

Note: Even if your banner is placed on a social media site, such as Facebook, the medium parameter value remains banner so that you can compare the performance of all banners side by side.

Email Marketing

Continuing with the previous example, suppose you also plan to run a monthly email newsletter that begins in July 2012. The newsletter is for the shoe department and concerns a summer promotion. You want to ensure that all click-throughs from the email campaign are tracked in your Google Analytics reports.

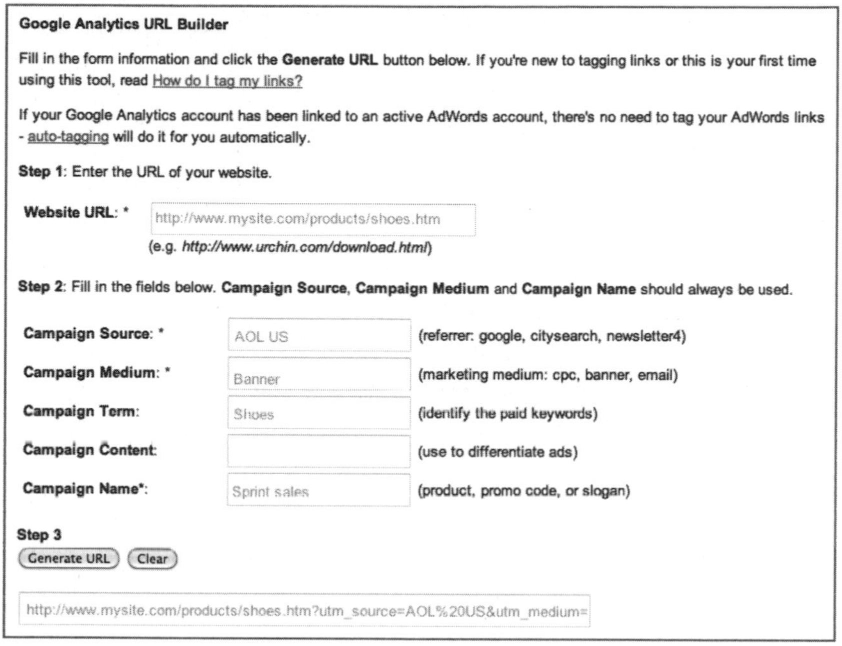

Google Analytics URL Builder

Fill in the form information and click the **Generate URL** button below. If you're new to tagging links or this is your first time using this tool, read How do I tag my links?

If your Google Analytics account has been linked to an active AdWords account, there's no need to tag your AdWords links - auto-tagging will do it for you automatically.

Step 1: Enter the URL of your website.

Website URL: * http://www.mysite.com/products/shoes.htm
(e.g. *http://www.urchin.com/download.html*)

Step 2: Fill in the fields below. **Campaign Source**, **Campaign Medium** and **Campaign Name** should always be used.

Campaign Source: *   AOL US   (referrer: google, citysearch, newsletter4)

Campaign Medium: *   Banner   (marketing medium: cpc, banner, email)

Campaign Term: Shoes   (identify the paid keywords)

Campaign Content: (use to differentiate ads)

Campaign Name*:   Sprint sales   (product, promo code, or slogan)

Step 3
(Generate URL) (Clear)

http://www.mysite.com/products/shoes.htm?utm_source=AOL%20US&utm_medium=

Figure 7.3 Campaign tracking banner ad URLs

To add to the mix, your marketing department also wants to compare the effectiveness of changing the product image used in the email. They would like to know whether visits and conversions vary depending on the image used in the sent emails (this is the basis of A/B split testing).

You can track these two email campaigns by using the example landing page URLs shown in Figure 7.4. In both cases, the Campaign Content field is used to differentiate the email formatting. You then supply the resultant campaign-tracked landing page URL to the person setting up your email marketing.

You may have numerous links within the same email message that point to different landing pages on your website. Therefore, you'll need to adjust each landing page URL accordingly. For example, shoes.htm may become boots.htm. However, the tracking parameters will remain the same.

As for the banner campaign previously described, if you were to send the same campaign email but to a different audience (a different segment of your mailing list database, for example), only the value of utm_source would change (for example, to US_westcoast). The other parameters remain the same so the performance of the email campaign can be compared across all recipient segments.

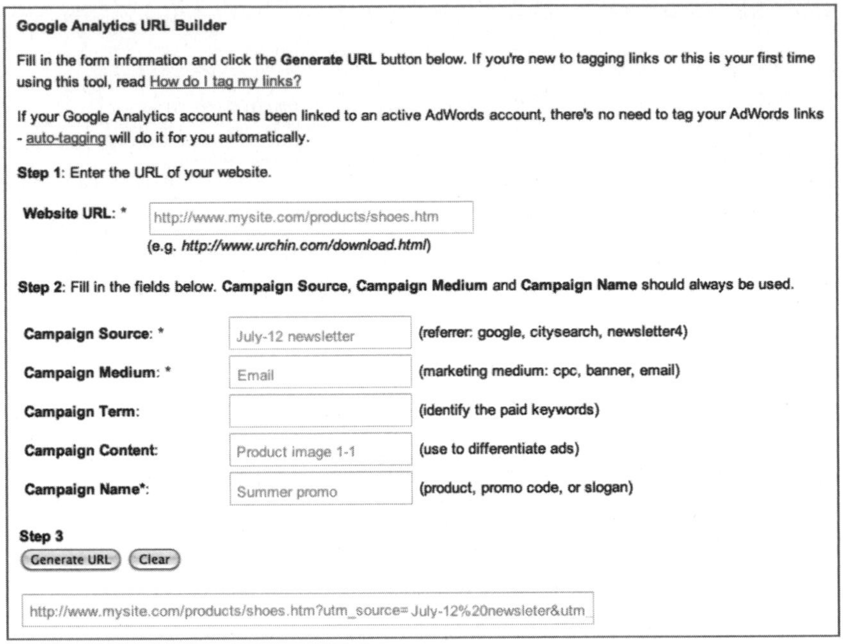

Google Analytics URL Builder

Fill in the form information and click the **Generate URL** button below. If you're new to tagging links or this is your first time using this tool, read How do I tag my links?

If your Google Analytics account has been linked to an active AdWords account, there's no need to tag your AdWords links - auto-tagging will do it for you automatically.

Step 1: Enter the URL of your website.

Website URL: *   http://www.mysite.com/products/shoes.htm
(e.g. *http://www.urchin.com/download.html*)

Step 2: Fill in the fields below. **Campaign Source**, **Campaign Medium** and **Campaign Name** should always be used.

Campaign Source: *   July-12 newsletter   (referrer: google, citysearch, newsletter4)

Campaign Medium: *   Email   (marketing medium: cpc, banner, email)

Campaign Term: (identify the paid keywords)

Campaign Content: Product image 1-1   (use to differentiate ads)

Campaign Name*:   Summer promo   (product, promo code, or slogan)

Step 3
Generate URL   Clear

http://www.mysite.com/products/shoes.htm?utm_source= July-12%20newsletter&utm

a

Google Analytics URL Builder

Fill in the form information and click the **Generate URL** button below. If you're new to tagging links or this is your first time using this tool, read How do I tag my links?

If your Google Analytics account has been linked to an active AdWords account, there's no need to tag your AdWords links - auto-tagging will do it for you automatically.

Step 1: Enter the URL of your website.

Website URL: *   http://www.mysite.com/products/shoes.htm
(e.g. *http://www.urchin.com/download.html*)

Step 2: Fill in the fields below. **Campaign Source**, **Campaign Medium** and **Campaign Name** should always be used.

Campaign Source: *   July-12 newsletter   (referrer: google, citysearch, newsletter4)

Campaign Medium: *   Email   (marketing medium: cpc, banner, email)

Campaign Term: (identify the paid keywords)

Campaign Content: Product image 1-2   (use to differentiate ads)

Campaign Name*:   Summer promo   (product, promo code, or slogan)

Step 3
Generate URL   Clear

http://www.mysite.com/products/shoes.htm?utm_source=July-12%20newsletter&utm

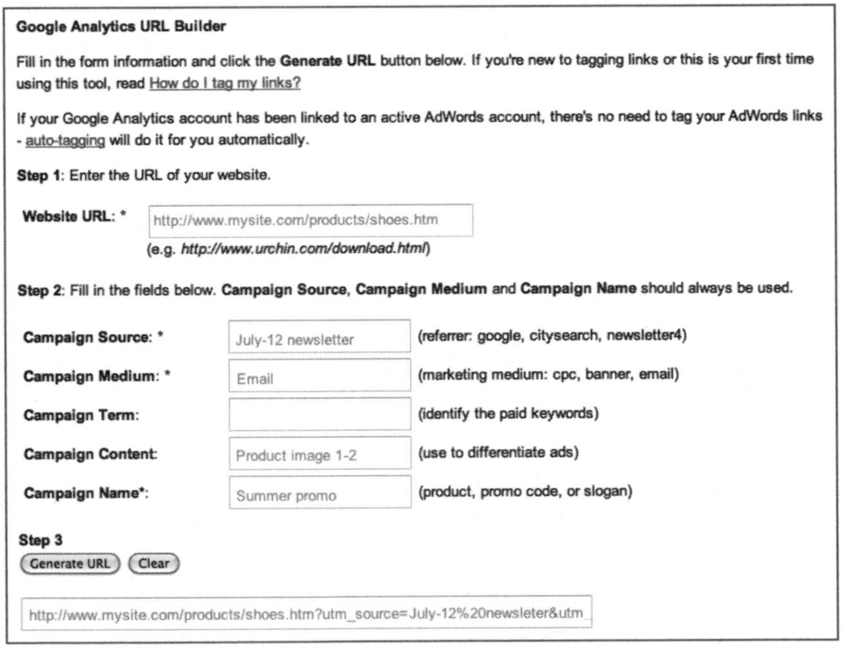

b

Figure 7.4   Campaign tracking an email campaign containing a split test: (a) product image 1, (b) product image 2

Social Media

Campaign tracking for social media campaigns is required for two reasons. First, according to public statements from Facebook (www.facebook.com/press/info .php?statistics) and Twitter (http://blog.twitter.com/2010/09/evolving-ecosystem .html), approximately 50 percent of consumers of content on Facebook and Twitter do so via mobile. Assuming these users access the site via the most convenient route—that is, use an app rather than using their mobile web browser—no referral information is available when the reader subsequently clicks through to your website (an app isn't a web referrer). Second, a click-through to your site may not take place on the social network site on which the link was originally placed—a visitor may reshare your link on another social network of their choice. For example, a URL shared on LinkedIn may be tweeted.

To ensure that you are able to track the impact of your social campaign (or conversation), you append campaign parameters to your landing pages in the usual way, as shown in Figure 7.5.

For the same campaign running across different social media sites, replace the utm_source parameter. Following the example shown in Figure 7.5, if you were to run the same campaign on LinkedIn, then you would replace utm_source=linkedin, and so forth.

URL shorteners are often used on social networking sites, particularly on Twitter, where space is a premium, and sites where it is not possible to hide your campaign parameters within HTML anchor text (that is, when your full URL is displayed in ugly plain text beginning http://). If you use a URL shortener, such as bit.ly, tinyurl.com, or goo.gl, ensure that you add your campaign parameters *before* you shorten it.

Paid Search

As discussed earlier, Google automatically tags your paid keywords from AdWords campaigns so you don't have to. However, campaigns running on other paid networks do require tagging. Otherwise, a paid visitor will be reported as an organic (nonpaid) visitor with the campaign information lost. Figure 7.6 shows an example URL Builder for pay-per-click Yahoo! Search Marketing visitors.

You supply the resultant tagged landing page URL to the person setting up your pay-per-click campaigns. You should use a similar approach for other pay-per-click accounts that you run—for example, Microsoft adCenter. The only difference is that the Campaign Source field would be set as adCenter (or any phrase you wish to use to identify such visitors).

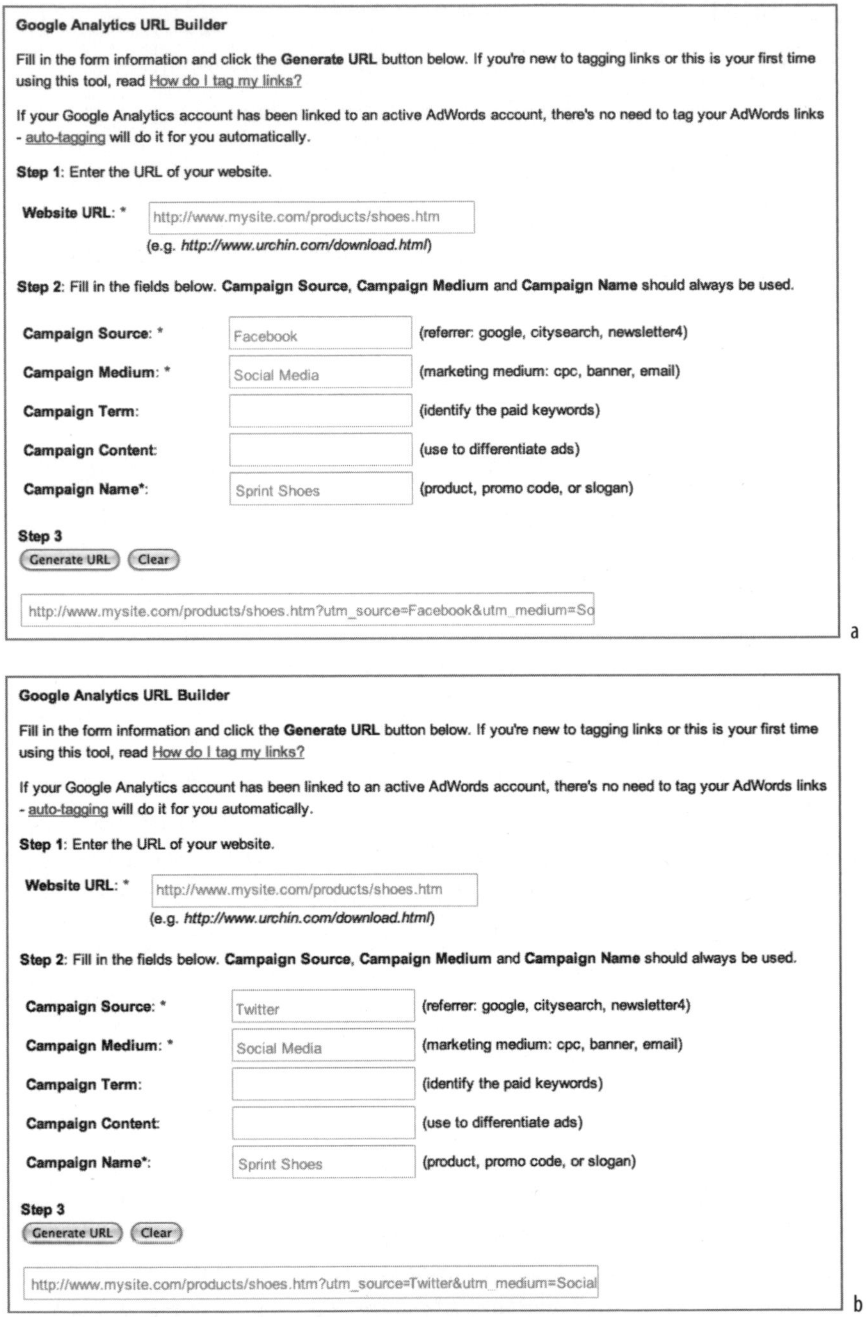

Google Analytics URL Builder

Fill in the form information and click the **Generate URL** button below. If you're new to tagging links or this is your first time using this tool, read How do I tag my links?

If your Google Analytics account has been linked to an active AdWords account, there's no need to tag your AdWords links - auto-tagging will do it for you automatically.

Step 1: Enter the URL of your website.

Website URL: *   http://www.mysite.com/products/shoes.htm

(e.g. *http://www.urchin.com/download.html*)

Step 2: Fill in the fields below. **Campaign Source**, **Campaign Medium** and **Campaign Name** should always be used.

Campaign Source: *	Facebook	(referrer: google, citysearch, newsletter4)
Campaign Medium: *	Social Media	(marketing medium: cpc, banner, email)
Campaign Term:		(identify the paid keywords)
Campaign Content:		(use to differentiate ads)
Campaign Name*:	Sprint Shoes	(product, promo code, or slogan)

Step 3
Generate URL   Clear

http://www.mysite.com/products/shoes.htm?utm_source=Facebook&utm_medium=So

a

Google Analytics URL Builder

Fill in the form information and click the **Generate URL** button below. If you're new to tagging links or this is your first time using this tool, read How do I tag my links?

If your Google Analytics account has been linked to an active AdWords account, there's no need to tag your AdWords links - auto-tagging will do it for you automatically.

Step 1: Enter the URL of your website.

Website URL: *   http://www.mysite.com/products/shoes.htm

(e.g. *http://www.urchin.com/download.html*)

Step 2: Fill in the fields below. **Campaign Source**, **Campaign Medium** and **Campaign Name** should always be used.

Campaign Source: *	Twitter	(referrer: google, citysearch, newsletter4)
Campaign Medium: *	Social Media	(marketing medium: cpc, banner, email)
Campaign Term:		(identify the paid keywords)
Campaign Content:		(use to differentiate ads)
Campaign Name*:	Sprint Shoes	(product, promo code, or slogan)

Step 3
Generate URL   Clear

http://www.mysite.com/products/shoes.htm?utm_source=Twitter&utm_medium=Social

b

Figure 7.5 Campaign tracking for social media: (a) Facebook; (b) Twitter

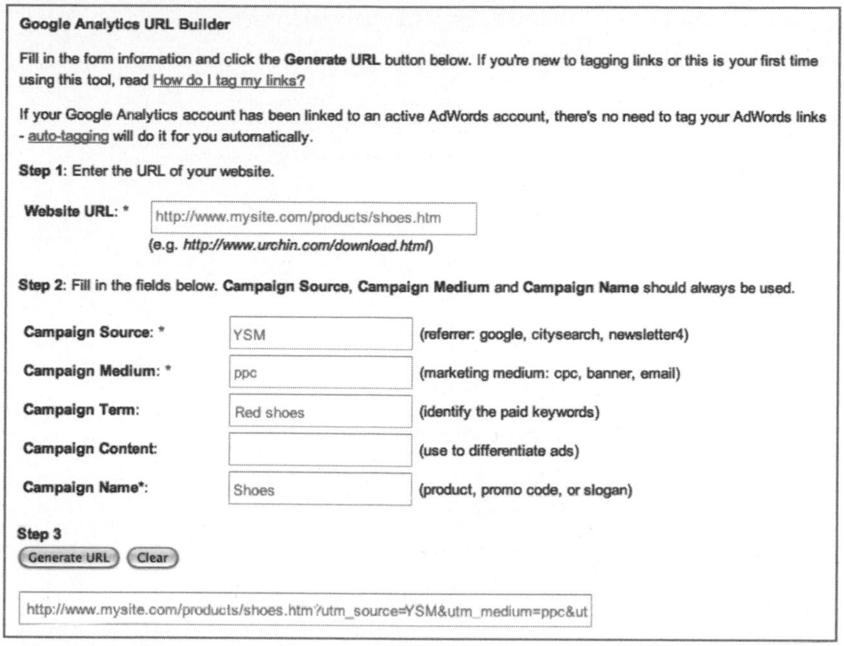

Figure 7.6 Campaign tracking paid search

> **Note:** Google AdWords auto-tagging always labels AdWords visitors as medium=cpc (cost-per-click). You may wish to continue this labeling convention for Yahoo! Search Marketing, Microsoft adCenter, and other pay-per-click networks so they are reported together when viewing Medium reports. However, because AdWords is so prevalent for online advertising, I have found it useful to group all other pay-per-click networks as medium=ppc (or any other alternative label) and treat them as if they were a separate medium. This enables them to be compared against AdWords as a whole.

Embedded Links within Digital Documents

If you host non-HTML content on your website, such as catalogue.pdf, spec-sheet .doc, or price-matrix.xls, you probably have links within those documents that point back to your website. By using campaign tracking parameters, you can track visits that result from those documents, which in turn will enable you to monetize your digital collateral. Without this, visitors from your digital documents are labeled as direct—that is, they are grouped together with visitors who typed the URL directly into their browser or bookmarked your site from a previous visit.

Using the method shown in Figure 7.7 ensures that links from your digital collateral are given credit for referring visitors to your website. Supply the resultant landing page URL to the people who create such documents. Alternatively, coach your content creators to use the URL Builder tool themselves. That way, they will be tracking links as an integral part of their content creation and design process.

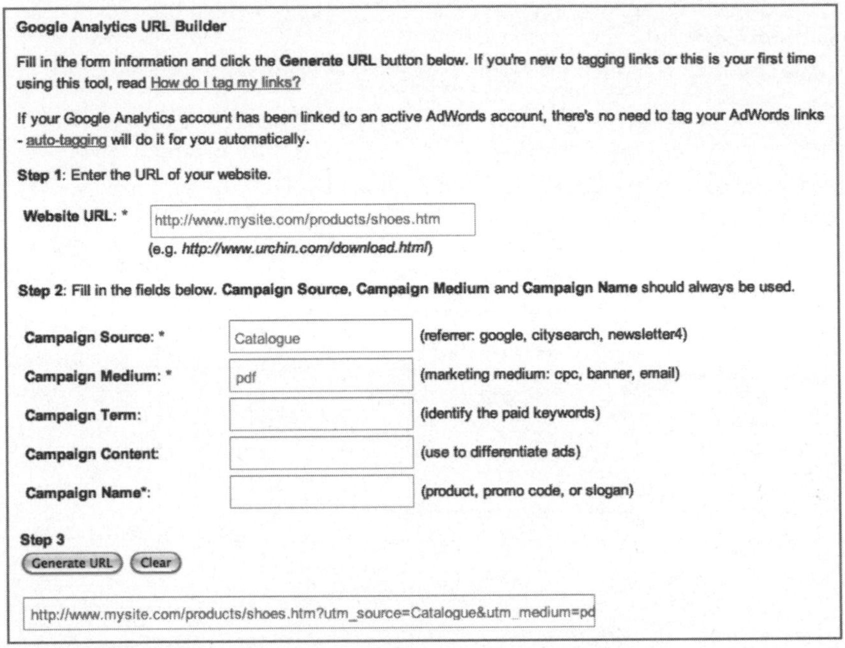

Google Analytics URL Builder

Fill in the form information and click the **Generate URL** button below. If you're new to tagging links or this is your first time using this tool, read How do I tag my links?

If your Google Analytics account has been linked to an active AdWords account, there's no need to tag your AdWords links - auto-tagging will do it for you automatically.

Step 1: Enter the URL of your website.

Website URL: *   http://www.mysite.com/products/shoes.htm
                    (e.g. http://www.urchin.com/download.html)

Step 2: Fill in the fields below. **Campaign Source**, **Campaign Medium** and **Campaign Name** should always be used.

Campaign Source: *   Catalogue   (referrer: google, citysearch, newsletter4)

Campaign Medium: *   pdf   (marketing medium: cpc, banner, email)

Campaign Term: (identify the paid keywords)

Campaign Content: (use to differentiate ads)

Campaign Name*:   (product, promo code, or slogan)

Step 3
(Generate URL) (Clear)

http://www.mysite.com/products/shoes.htm?utm_source=Catalogue&utm_medium=pd

Figure 7.7 Tagging embedded links within digital collateral

Creating Custom Campaign Fields

If you have been using another tracking methodology or tool, you may have already manually tracked your landing page URLs for paid campaigns, banners, email, and digital collateral. Rather than disregard these or append the additional Google Analytics variables, it is possible to configure Google Analytics to recognize your existing tags. As stressed previously, this is not required for AdWords tracking.

Add the following highlighted code to your GATC, replacing orig_name with the variable name that you are currently using. If no original value exists, then omit that line from your GATC.

```
<script type="text/javascript">
  var _gaq = _gaq || [];
  _gaq.push(['_setAccount', 'UA-12345-1']);
  _gaq.push(['_setCampNameKey', 'orig_campaign']);    // default: utm_campaign
  _gaq.push(['_setCampMediumKey', 'orig_medium']);    // default: utm_medium
  _gaq.push(['_setCampSourceKey', 'orig_source']);    // default: utm_source
  _gaq.push(['_setCampTermKey', 'orig_term']);        // default: utm_term
  _gaq.push(['_setCampContentKey', 'orig_content']);  // default: utm_content
```

```
_gaq.push(['_trackPageview']);

(function() {
var ga = document.createElement('script');
ga.type = 'text/javascript'; ga.async = true;
ga.src = ('https:' == document.location.protocol ? 'https://ssl' : ➡
'http://www') + '.google-analytics.com/ga.js';
var s = document.getElementsByTagName('script')[0];
s.parentNode.insertBefore(ga, s);
})();
</script>
```

At a minimum, orig_source and orig_medium are required. If these are not present in your current landing page URLs, you need to include the Google Analytics equivalents.

Best Practice Tips for Campaign Tracking

What you place in the campaign tracking parameters is exactly what you see in your reports, capitalization and misspellings included, so consistency is important. For example, if you decide on utm_medium=email, this syntax should always be used—not utm_medium=Email, or utm_medium=e-mail—because these will each be shown in your reports separately. Ditto for the other tracking parameter fields. Otherwise you make it difficult to determine the success, or not, of the channel or campaign you are running.

Following on from this, ensure that campaign tracking parameters are readable by the end user, the person(s) who need to interpret the reports.

When running a campaign across multiple marketing channels (mediums), keep the name of the campaign consistent while changing the other parameters. Keeping campaign centric allows you to easily compare the performance of your campaigns as a whole. Consider it the central pivot for your marketing data.

Think of the utm_medium parameter as your roll-up or categorization parameter. That is, keep the number of mediums at a manageable level. My recommendation is that the number of different mediums should not exceed 10, but the number of sources and campaigns will be much larger.

With a fixed number of utm_medium names and a well-defined utm_campaign naming convention, marketers often have difficulty deciding what to use for the utm_source parameter. Think of this as the data source of where your visitors will be coming from when they click on your campaign. In most cases, this will be the name of the website where your campaign is being displayed. The exceptions to this are email marketing and digital documents. For email marketing, your utm_source is the data source you are using, that is, the name of the database table containing the recipients (for example,

"US prospects" or "US customers"). For digital documents the source is the filename of the document.

Event Tracking

Google Analytics is capable of tracking any browser-based event, including Flash and JavaScript events. Think of these as *in-page* actions from visitors that do not generate a pageview. However, when considering event tracking, also bear in mind the possibility of virtual pageviews, as discussed earlier in this chapter.

Event activity is reported separately from your pageview activity. The following list includes examples of in-page events:

- Any Flash-driven element, such as a Flash website or a Flash movie player
- Embedded Ajax page elements, such as onClick, onSubmit, onReset, onMouseOver, onMouseOut, onMouseMove, onSelect, onFocus, onBlur, onKeyPress, and onChange
- Page gadgets
- File downloads
- Exit and outbound links

An important consideration when tracking events is the impact on page bounce rates. With no events being tracked, a bounce is a single page visit. This is generally considered a bad experience for the visitor—they came, viewed one page, and left. The theory is that if your site content is good and relevant to the visitor, then surely they will want to read more than one page from you! Hence, pages with high bounce rates are a strong indicator that something is wrong with that process. The caveat to this theory is that you are not writing the perfect one-page article. See "Content Creator KPI Examples" in Chapter 10, "Focusing on Key Performance Indicators," for further discussion on bounce rates.

Now consider a visitor arriving on a page to view or interact with your Ajax widget or Flash movie. While viewing only a single HTML page, it is entirely possible that a visitor can have a great user experience. Event tracking allows you to measure this because a single page with any triggered event is no longer considered a bounce. You then use other metrics to ascertain if the experience is a good one or not, such as the number and type of events per visit. Of course, if the bounce rate for that page remains high, then you know your widget or Flash movie is not a good match for your visitors.

Bounce rates are popular key performance indicators used for optimizing websites. These are discussed in the section "Content Creator KPI Examples" in Chapter 10 and in the section "Identify and Optimize Poor Performing Pages" in Chapter 11.

Note: Tracked events can be used to define a conversion goal and can also be monetized—either as a whole or on a per-event basis. However, at present it is not possible for a funnel to be defined by an event.

Setting Up Event Tracking

Event Tracking reports are available by default in the Content section of Google Analytics. Therefore, no configuration changes to your account are necessary. However, you are required to modify your page or application to collect event-driven data and populate the reports. To do this, follow these two steps:

1. Define your event reporting structure.
2. For each event, call the _trackEvent function in your web page or application source code.

To understand how to define your events, I describe these steps in reverse order.

The _*trackEvent* Function

Event Tracking uses standard JavaScript method calls and provides a hierarchy data model of categories, actions, labels, and values. These parameters (Table 7.5) map directly to elements in the Analytics Reports interface.

▶ **Table 7.5** _trackEvent parameters

Parameter	Condition	Description
category	Required	The name you supply for the group of objects you want to track.
action	Required	A string that is uniquely paired with each category and commonly used to define the type of user interaction for the web object, such as a visitor's mouse click.
optional_label	Optional	A string to provide additional dimensions to the event data. Note that any spaces used in the label parameter must be encoded as %20.
optional_value	Optional	An integer that you can use to provide numerical data about the user event, such as time or a dollar amount.
optional_nonInteraction	Optional	The nonInteraction setting defines whether an event is treated as non-interaction; that is, not affecting user engagement metrics such as, for example, bounce rate. When this is set to true, the event is non-interacting. When left undefined, it defaults to false.

The following example illustrates how you might use the event tracking method to record a user interaction with a video play link on your page:

```
<a href="#" onClick="_gaq.push(['_trackEvent','Category-name',➥
'Action-name', 'Label-name', 'Value-integer']);">Play video</a>
```

Any text-string value can be used for the event parameters, though if optional_value is used, this must be an integer. In practice, the values could be as follows:

```
<a href="#" onClick="_gaq.push(['_trackEvent', 'Video', 'Play',➥
'Birthday Party']);">Play</a>
```

In this scenario, the report for events would display *Video* as the category, *Play* as the action, and *Birthday Party* as the label (there is no value in this example). If for some reason you did not wish to count such an event as an interaction, you would use the following, omitting the value parameter:

```
<a href="#" onClick="_gaq.push(['_trackEvent', 'Video', 'Play',➡
'Birthday Party',,true]);">Play</a>
```

An example Event Tracking report is shown in Figure 7.8.

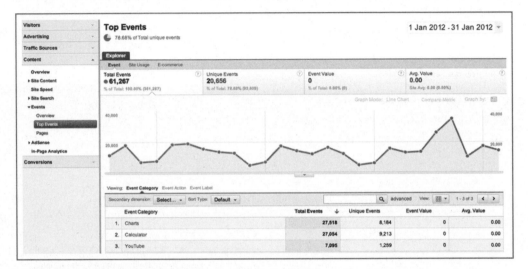

Figure 7.8 Event Tracking overview report showing three event categories

The _trackEvent Limits

Because events can rapidly accumulate for a visitor's session (imagine tracking every mouse movement!), there is a limit to the number of events that can be tracked per visit. As I am writing this, the maximum is 500 combined GATC requests—both events and page views.

There is also a limit to the number of events that can be captured at any one time, and this is controlled by the use of tokens. The rate-limiting system starts a user with 10 tokens and awards a new token every 5 seconds. A maximum of 10 tokens can be accumulated. Therefore, sending out a burst of events will exhaust the 10 available tokens immediately and send out only a maximum of one event hit per 5 seconds until the event is slowed down long enough for the user to accumulate more than one token. Therefore, consider the following guidelines:

- Avoid scripting a video to send an event for every second played and other highly repetitive event triggers.
- Avoid excessive mouse movement tracking.
- Avoid time-lapse mechanisms that generate high event counts.

Defining Your Event Reporting Structure

Because of the setup flexibility for event tracking, it is important to first plan your desired reporting structure and then test it before implementing it. As mentioned earlier, this is really your first step once you understand the structure of the event tracking implementation.

In the following examples, I use the interaction of a visitor viewing a movie file to illustrate event tracking because this is a straightforward general concept to follow and helps with comprehending the data structure. The specific case of tracking embedded YouTube videos is described later in this chapter.

Defining Event Categories

A category represents the root level of the hierarchical structure of event tracking, and you can use this structure in any way to suit your needs. Typically, you will use the same category name multiple times in order to group metrics under a given category. For example, you might track user interaction on two separate controls, Play and Pause, on a single video interface as follows:

```
_gaq.push(['_trackEvent', 'Video', 'Play', 'Birthday Party']);
_gaq.push(['_trackEvent', 'Video', 'Pause', 'Birthday Party']);
```

You can also track events for different video files in the same category:

```
_gaq.push(['_trackEvent', 'Video', 'Play', 'Xmas 2011']);
_gaq.push(['_trackEvent', 'Video', 'Play', 'Xmas 2012']);
```

This allows you to see aggregate data for the category Video as well as being able to drill down into action and label details, as schematically shown in Figure 7.9.

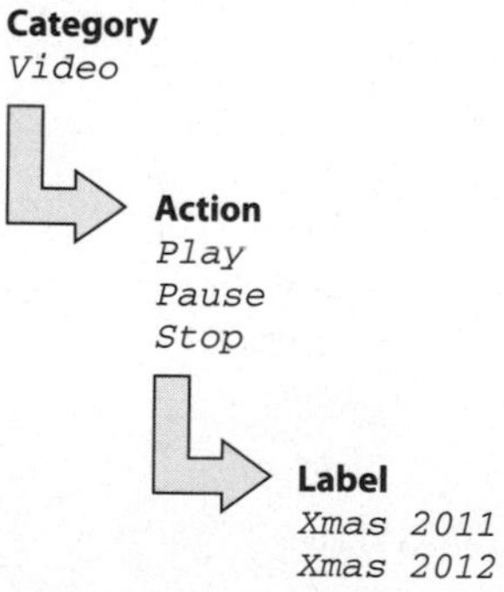

Category
Video

     Action
     Play
     Pause
     Stop

          Label
          Xmas 2011
          Xmas 2012

Figure 7.9 Schematic hierarchical structure of event tracking

Perhaps you would like to categorize your videos in a different way:

```
_gaq.push(['_trackEvent', 'Videos 2011', 'Play', 'Xmas']);
_gaq.push(['_trackEvent', 'Videos 2012', 'Play', 'Birthday']);
_gaq.push(['_trackEvent', 'Downloads', 'Click', 'Birthday 2012']);
```

In this scenario, you can view the total combined event count for all three categories. The Total Events metric counts all categories supplied in your implementation. However, you will not be able to view combined metrics for all videos separately from downloads because detailed event metrics are combined under their respective categories.

Syntax for Event Tracking Parameters

Be aware of the following syntax requirements that apply to all event text parameters (category, action, play):

- If you plan to use the same parameter name in multiple locations on your site, be careful to correctly reference it. For example, if you call your video tracking category Video and later use the plural, Videos, you will have two separate categories for video tracking.

- If you decide to change the parameter name of an object that has already been tracked under a different name, for example, the historical data for the original name will not be reprocessed, and you will have metrics for the same event listed under two categories.

- The text-string values you define for your event parameters are case sensitive. That is, the category Video will be reported separately from video, the action Play will be reported separately from play, and so forth.

Tip: If you manage an e-commerce site with events related to your shopping categories (for example, an introduction Flash animation for each of your store sections), consider matching your event categories to your store categories. This way you will be able to compare the performance of your events on a per-shopping-section basis—a common requirement for e-commerce managers.

Defining Event Actions

Typically, the action parameter defines the interaction or event that you wish to capture from a visitor. Using the video example, these would be as follows:

- Play—button clicks
- Stop—button clicks
- Pause—button clicks

You could also use the following event actions:

- Time—how much of the video is watched, how much of the game is played, how long it takes to add to cart, and so on
- Resize, or zoom—manipulating an image

- Select, change, drag, or drop—manipulating an object such as, for example, a graphing widget
- Click—click-through on a download link or a banner advertisement

Usually, defining the action parameter for Event Tracking is straightforward because in most cases it is the physical action of the visitor's interaction. The exception in the previous examples is Time.

Importantly, action names can be used to either aggregate or differentiate user interaction. Consider the last example that has an action named Click for both the Downloads category and the Banners category. The Event Actions report will contain *all* interactions with that same name, that is, no differentiation of clicks for Banners or Downloads. You can view a detailed breakdown of the Click action by category in the next report level. However, the point is that if you use the action Click indiscriminately across your Event Tracking implementation, the usefulness of that segment will be diminished in the reports.

As you probably have realized, the action value of Click, although useful for aggregation reports, is not particularly meaningful. An alternative approach is to differentiate the two types of click actions. For the download link, you could use the document file type as the action parameter. In this way, your reports for the Downloads category would be broken out by file type (PDF, DOC, XLS, and so on), with the filename detail as the label. See Figure 7.10a.

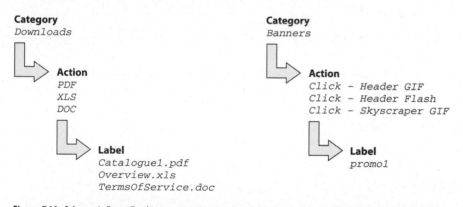

Figure 7.10 Schematic Event Tracking report structure for (a) file downloads and (b) banner click-throughs

Similarly, for the Banners category, you could use the banner type or version to differentiate the same ad in different formats. In this way you can compare overall banner events with other events as well as distinguish different creative formats, such as animated versus static, for example. See Figure 7.10b.

Both aggregating and differentiating action names have their advantages, and it's a matter of personal choice which method you use. Generally, it usually comes down to how your business is structured. If you have a video directory, download catalogue, or much library-type content, you will probably wish to differentiate actions—by video genre or file type, for example. If you have a small collection of disparate actions (two Flash demos, one how-to video guide, three download files), then it makes sense to aggregate the actions so that each event performance can be compared against the other.

Unique Events Are Incremented by Unique Actions

Any time a visitor interacts with an object tagged with a particular action name, the initial interaction is logged as one unique event for that action name. Any additional interaction with the same action name for that user's visit will not contribute to the unique event calculation for that particular action. This is the case even if the visitor leaves that object and begins to interact with another object tagged via the same action name.

This has two significant consequences in the reports. First, suppose a user interacts with the Play action from two unique video players tagged with separate categories. The Event Actions reports for Play will list one unique event even though the user engaged with two unique players. Second, each category's Action report will list one unique action because there is indeed one unique event per category-action pair.

Defining Event Labels—Optional

With labels, you can provide additional information for events that you want to track, such as the movie title in the previous video examples or the name of a file when you're tracking downloads. If you have multiple events with the same category and action names, use the label parameter to differentiate.

Defining Event Values—Optional

The event values parameter differs from the others in that it is an integer used to assign a numerical value for a tracked event (all other parameters are text strings). For example, you could use it to provide the play time (how much of a video has been watched in seconds, minutes, or a percentage), load time (how long a page takes to download), or revenue (a monetary value assigned to a triggered event). Examples of these are discussed in upcoming sections.

Defining an Event Non-interaction—Optional

Setting the non-event parameter as true prevents the event from affecting user engagement metrics, such as, for example, bounce rate. Although rare, there are cases where you may wish to consider this. For example, you may want to track a visitor's interaction with an image carousel on a landing page. The visitor clicking forward or backward through the carousel could be an event you wish to track yet you don't want to affect the bounce rate calculation because the action is not a strong signal of engagement unless the visitor actually selects one of the images.

> **Note:** In recent years there has been a growth spurt of rich Internet applications (RIAs) such as Flash, Flex, Air, and Silverlight. This means that the tracking of events, by any web analytics tool, is still nascent. To keep up-to-date on the technicalities of this feature in Google Analytics, I recommend the online documentation at `http://code.google.com/apis/analytics/docs/tracking/eventTrackerOverview.html`

Tracking Flash Video and Animation as Events

Unless you have built your entire website content in Flash (why?), most Flash user interactions can be considered events rather than virtual pageviews. However, this is not a hard-and-fast rule. Consider the benefits, or not, of both prior to implementing. Here I explain only how to track Flash user interactions as Google Analytics events. The use of virtual pageviews is discussed earlier in this chapter.

The technique you choose to track Flash events will be determined by two factors:

- What software you use to generate the Flash FLA file; more specifically, the version of ActionScript you use
- The type of Flash development you perform; that is, occasional Flash development as part of a larger website project or development as a dedicated Flash professional

> #### Different Versions of ActionScript
>
> The method for tracking Flash events differs depending on whether you are coding in the legacy ActionScript 2 or the latest ActionScript 3. ActionScript was first included in Flash Player 5, with version 3 introduced in 2006 as part of Flash Player 9 and upward. If you are developing your Flash applications in Flash CS3 or higher, you are using ActionScript 3.
>
> I recommend you use ActionScript 3 wherever possible because it is better designed to handle Flash browser communications and is therefore more robust for event tracking. I consider only ActionScript 3 in this book.

Using ActionScript 3

For this example, I assume you have the standard GATC on your HTML pages and that you are embedding a Flash SWF movie file with a Play button. You wish to track clicks on the Play button as an event with category name Video, action name Play, and label name Toy Story 3.

Essentially there are three steps to follow:

1. Add an external class reference within your FLA file. This is a one-time call:

```
import flash.external.ExternalInterface
```

2. Modify the button or link within your FLA file and pass the associated category, action, label, and value parameters to be displayed in the reports:

```
myBtn.addEventListener(
MouseEvent.CLICK, ➡
ExternalInterface.call(_gaq.push(['_trackEvent', ➡
'Video', 'Play', 'Toy Story 3', '9']));
```

3. Modify the HTML where the SWF file is embedded:

```
<object ...
    <param name="allowScriptAccess" value="always" />
    <!-- {...REMAINING OBJECT CONTENT...}   -->
    <embed ...
      allowScriptAccess="always"
      <!-- {...REMAINING EMBED CONTENT...}   -->
    </embed>
</object>
```

That's all there is to it. Other Flash buttons can have their events defined in a similar way, such as Stop and Pause. Multiple videos can be tracked by passing different labels. Thus, to track three movies, your video Flash object might be reported schematically as shown in Figure 7.11.

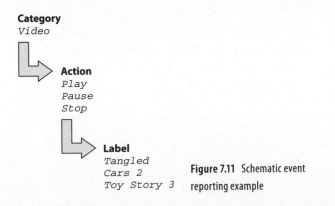

Category
Video

Action
Play
Pause
Stop

Label
Tangled
Cars 2
Toy Story 3

Figure 7.11 Schematic event reporting example

Extending the Flash example further, when the video is placed on the web page, you can use FlashVars parameters to provide *label* and *value* input values for your SWF file, making it generic and easy to reuse. FlashVars is the Flash counterpart to a URL query string. That is, it's a way to pass variables from HTML to a Flash movie.

Variables passed via FlashVars are placed into the _root level of the Flash movie, as shown in the following example:

```
<object classid="clsid:D27CDB6E-AE6D-11cf-96B8-444553540000"➥
codebase="http://download.macromedia.com/pub/shockwave/➥
cabs/flash/swflash.cab#version=7,0,19,0" width="300" height="400">
    <param name="FlashVars" value="label=Toy%20Story%203&value=9" />
    <param name="movie" value="movie1.swf" />
    <param name="quality" value="high" />
    <embed src="movie1.swf" FlashVars="label=Toy%20Story%203&value=9"➥
quality="high" pluginspage="http://www.macromedia.com/go/getflashplayer"➥
type="application/x-shockwave-flash" width="300" height="400"></embed>
</object>
```

This makes your ActionScript code within the player generic and reusable—you reuse the same code for each movie with the necessary parameters picked up from FlashVars. This is a particularly useful technique if, for example, you have hundreds (or thousands) of video files that you don't wish to create individual SWF files for.

These variables are stored in the parameters property of the LoaderInfo class associated with the DisplayObject. To utilize these values in your FLA file, use the following format:

```
myBtn.addEventListener(
MouseEvent.CLICK, ExternalInterface.call(_gaq_push(['_trackEvent',➥
'Video', 'Play']), root.loaderInfo.parameters.label,➥
root.loaderInfo.parameters.value));
```

For the same three movies, your video Flash object might be reported schematically as shown in Figure 7.12.

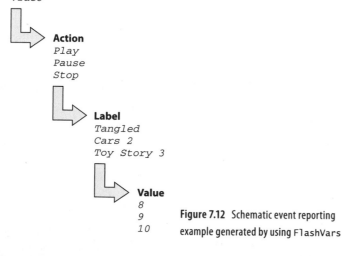

Category
Video

Action
Play
Pause
Stop

Label
Tangled
Cars 2
Toy Story 3

Value
8
9
10

Figure 7.12 Schematic event reporting example generated by using FlashVars

Event Tracking for Flash Professionals

The previous examples allow you to track Flash actions as events on a per-event basis when the need arises. Typically, you use these techniques when you are embedding your SWF file into a page that already contains the GATC. It is the simplest method if you are a webmaster and want to communicate Google Analytics tracking requirements to a third-party Flash designer.

However, if you develop Flash applications full-time yourself, the previous methods of constantly coding each action can become laborious. Therefore, you can use the gaforflash software component available at http://code.google.com/p/gaforflash/. This is an ActionScript 3 API for Google Analytics data collection, developed under an open-source initiative with Adobe Systems Inc. It can simplify the tracking of your Flash content in a number of situations, such as these:

- When you have a large number of embedded Flash files on HTML pages
- When you are creating a stand-alone Flex application or Flash-only site hosted on an HTML page
- When you are distributing your Flex/Flash application where you have no control over where the file will be placed

> **Note:** Currently, Flash tracking is available for any Flash content embedded in a web page. Tracking of data sent from Adobe Air or Shockwave or via the Flash IDE is not supported at this time.

To get started, download and install gaforflash from http://code.google.com/p/gaforflash/. The installation is as straightforward as copying, or importing, the class files (SWC) into the relevant directory where your Flash or Flex installation can read them. Then you will have two ways of tracking your Flash events, Bridge mode or AS3 mode.

Bridge mode is the most common method because it is utilized when a GATC is already embedded within the HTML. It provides a simple wrapper to all the ga.js functions using the ExternalInterface class, as previously described. Everything else is managed from within Flash itself. In Bridge Mode, gaforflash will call ExternalInterface (or getUrl if ExternalInterface is blocked for some reason) in the background. The following code is an example of Bridge mode in use:

```
import com.google.analytics.AnalyticsTracker;
import com.google.analytics.GATracker;
var tracker:AnalyticsTracker = new GATracker(this, "UA-12345-1", ➡
"Bridge", false);
_gaq.push(['_trackPageview','/Movies']);          // track virtual pageview
_gaq.push(['_trackEvent','Video','Play','Toy Story 3', 9]); // track event
```

AS3 Mode provides a method of bypassing any Flash-JavaScript communication issues. This is particularly relevant if your SWF file is to be deployed on different domains; that is, sites using third-party content because often such sites do not allow the ExternalInterface method. In AS3 Mode, you do not require a GATC to be present within your HTML—it is an implementation of Google Analytics tracking written entirely in ActionScript. As a result, all Google Analytics interactions are generated from within the Flash object. The following code is an example of AS3 Mode use:

```
import com.google.analytics.AnalyticsTracker;
import com.google.analytics.GATracker;
var tracker:AnalyticsTracker = new GATracker(this, "UA-12345-1", "AS3",➡
false);
_gaq.push(['_trackPageview','/Movies']);              // track virtual pageview
_gaq.push(['_trackEvent','Video','Play','Toy Story 3', 9]);  // track event
```

Unless you are developing the same Flash content for deployment on multiple domains, you will most likely use gaforflash in Bridge Mode.

There is a great deal more to gaforflash that is beyond the realm of this book. I hope by scratching the surface I have whetted your appetite for its capabilities. If you are a Flash developer, check out the following location for the latest developments:

http://code.google.com/apis/analytics/docs/tracking/eventTrackerOverview.html

Flash Cookies and Privacy Considerations

In AS3 Mode, Google Analytics cookies are stored with other Flash cookies. However, they are not controlled within a user's browser but are part of the Flash Player install on your machine, known as Shared Objects. A fuller description is provided at Wikipedia:

http://en.wikipedia.org/wiki/Local_Shared_Object

Because a user's browser does not control Shared Objects, there are important privacy implications of using this method. Chapter 2, "Available Methodologies and Their Accuracy, and Chapter 3, "Google Analytics Features, Benefits, and Limitations," discuss the privacy issues of web analytics and Google Analytics, respectively. The key to a best-practice implementation of your tracking methodology is to be transparent in how you handle visitor privacy and provide visitors with clear instructions for how to opt out of such tracking.

From a user's perspective, Flash Shared Objects can be managed using the Adobe Flash Player Settings Manager at

http://www.macromedia.com/support/documentation/en/flashplayer/help/
settings_manager.html

A number of Firefox add-ons, such as BetterPrivacy, can provide similar functionality.

Tracking Banners and Other Outgoing Links as Events

If you publish advertising banners or links on your site that refer visitors to other websites, you have two options for tracking: tracking the click-through as a virtual pageview or tracking the click-through as an event. Both options allow you to monetize the click action; the merits of each are discussed earlier in this chapter in "Virtual Pageviews versus Event Tracking." In this section I consider only event tracking, with the category defined as Exit Points.

For an animated GIF or other non-Flash banner ad, modify the outgoing link as follows:

```
<a href="http://www.advertiser-site.com" onClick= ➡
"_gaq.push(['_trackEvent','ExitPoints', 'Click', 'advertisername - Ad ➡
version A', 4]) "><img src="bannerA.gif"></a>
```

Note that a value of 4 has been assigned to this event, which is a click-through. The equivalent code used within a Flash banner, assigned with a higher monetary value, is as follows:

```
myBtn.addEventListener(
MouseEvent.CLICK, ExternalInterface.call(_gaq.push(['_trackEvent', ➡
'Exit Points', 'Click', 'advertisername - Ad version B', 5]));
```

For both examples, it is possible to view and segment the event reports both by the advertiser's name and the ad version, such as, for example, header banner versus skyscraper.

Note: In addition to the code shown, you will need to set `import flash.external.ExternalInterface` in your FLA file and `allowScriptAccess` in your HTML—as described previously in "Tracking Flash Video and Animation as Events."

However, I prefer to use action names to distinguish object elements. For example, rather than aggregate the event action Click for all outbound link types, go one step further and differentiate between click-throughs on Flash and GIF banners.

For GIF banner event tracking, use this:

```
<a href="http://www.advertiser-site.com"
onClick="_gaq.push(['_trackEvent','Exit Points', 'Click - GIF banner', ➡
'advertisername - Ad version A', 4])"><img src="bannerA.gif"></a>
```

Use this for Flash banner event tracking:

```
myBtn.addEventListener(
MouseEvent.CLICK, ExternalInterface.call(_gaq.push(['_trackEvent', ➡
'Exit Points', 'Click - FLASH banner', 'advertisername - Ad ➡
version A', 5]));
```

To wrap up this series of outbound click tracking, for an outbound link, use link event tracking:

```
<a href="http://www.advertiser-site.com"
onClick="_gaq.push(['_trackEvent','Exit Points', 'Click - link', ➥
'linkURL', 1) ">View our Partner</a>
```

Note: For a Google Analytics plug-in that automatically sets up outbound links found on a page as events, see Appendix B, "Useful Tools."

Tracking Mailto: Clicks as Events

The mailto: link is another outgoing link that can be tracked in exactly the same way as described previously. I discuss it here separately simply to emphasize the importance of tracking mailto: clicks—particularly for websites that are not e-commerce websites, where any action that can bring a visitor closer to lead generation for you has an intrinsic value. As your sales department follows up on these contacts, you will be able to assess the conversion rate and average order value of such leads and therefore monetize the mailto: onClick event. Modify your mailto: links as follows:

```
<a href="mailto:mail@mysite.co.uk"
onClick="_gaq.push([_trackEvent','Exit Points', 'Click - email', ➥
'mail@mysite.co.uk']) ">mail@mysite.co.uk</a>
```

Add a monetary value to this event as desired.

Tracking Embedded Video from YouTube

Videos are commonly shared on the Web via YouTube. YouTube allows you to upload your video content and hosts your files for you as a free service. In additional to sharing content with other YouTube visitors as a potential viral marketing medium, you can embed your YouTube video files back into your own website.

Although you cannot modify the YouTube video player directly with your events, you can interact with YouTube's player API. The player API allows a site owner to control how videos look and are controlled when embedded on their website. The JavaScript API exposes Play and Pause buttons and the like as external calls to which you can attach events. Although they cannot be extended to track video interactions on www.youtube.com, interactions with the video embedded within your site can be tracked.

Note: As I am writing this, the iFrame player API described in this section is a beta feature that Google has stated represents the next stage of the YouTube Player API. In addition, the iFrame method allows YouTube to display video content in HTML5 format when a Flash player is not available on the user's device, such as on Apple mobile devices (iPhone, iPad). This is the main advantage of the iFrame player API over the other available API methods.

The following example code is a modification of that shown on
http://code.google.com/apis/youtube/getting_started.html#player_apis
The code embeds a YouTube video (videoeId = a-I5VXDpbSQ) in a page within an iFrame. As highlighted in the code example, two nonstandard calls are made—both setting a Google Analytics event. That is, an event is set when a visitor clicks the video play icon, and another event is set when the video has completed. For both cases, the URL of the actual YouTube video is captured as the event label.

```html
<!-- 1. The <div> tag will contain the <iframe> (and video player) -->
    <div id="player"></div>

    <script>
      // 2. This code loads the IFrame Player API code asynchronously.
      var tag = document.createElement('script');
      tag.src = "http://www.youtube.com/player_api";
      var firstScriptTag = document.getElementsByTagName('script')[0];
      firstScriptTag.parentNode.insertBefore(tag, firstScriptTag);

      // 3. This function creates an <iframe> and YouTube player after the
      // API code downloads. Change the dimensions and videoId accordingly
      var player;
      function onYouTubePlayerAPIReady() {
        player = new YT.Player('player', {
          height: '200',
          width: '300',
          videoId: 'a-I5VXDpbSQ',
          events: {
            'onReady': onPlayerReady,
            'onStateChange': onPlayerStateChange
          }
        });
      }

      // 4. The API calls this function when the player's state changes.
      // This is where you set Google Analytics event tracking.
      function onPlayerStateChange(event) {
        if (event.data == YT.PlayerState.PLAYING) ➡
{_gaq.push(['_trackEvent', 'YouTube','Play', player.getVideoUrl() )}
        if (event.data == YT.PlayerState.ENDED) ➡
{_gaq.push(['_trackEvent', 'YouTube','Completed', player.getVideoUrl() )}
      }
    </script>
```

Figure 7.13 shows the results of the YouTube iFrame implementation. In this case it reveals that 30% of visitors who started to watch a video actually viewed it to completion (12,837 + 42,512).

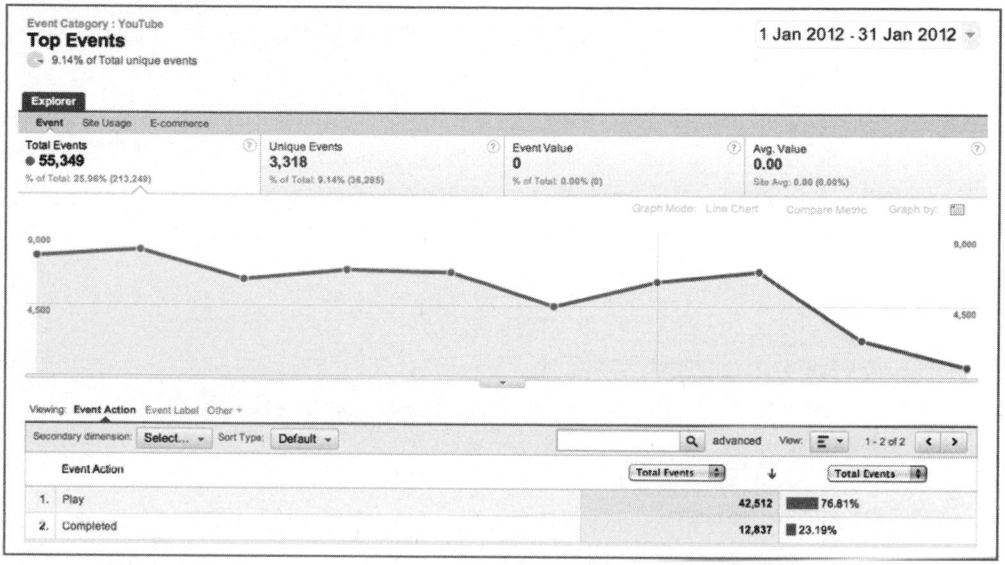

Figure 7.13 YouTube embedded video tracking showing 30% of visitors watching to completion

In addition to the actions of Play and Completed, it is possible to capture other YouTube player changes of state, such as, for example, YT.PlayerState.PAUSED, YT.PlayerState.BUFFERING, or YT.PlayerState.CUED. However, I have found little business value in capturing these as events. A metric of interest that is currently not available via the YouTube APIs is the percentage of a video played before the visitor exits the page. Modifying the example code to call a timer function when the video is started and triggering a Google Analytics event when the page is exited (using window .onunload) is straightforward for a good webmaster to achieve. The key is to group timings into buckets—for example, visitors watched 10%, 20%, 30%, and so forth of a video.

Customizing the GATC

As discussed in Chapter 6, in the section "Understanding the Google Analytics Tracking Code," for the majority of websites, you will not need to make any customizations to your GATC—you will use the example code presented in the Standard tab of Figure 6.3, accessed from the Profile Settings area of your account (click the Check Status link). However, the following sections describe some of the available options you can use should the need arise.

Note: The GATC is updated regularly by Google. As such, the exact syntax of the following examples is likely to change. To keep on top of GATC changes, view the ga.js change log at

http://code.google.com/apis/analytics/docs/gaJS/changelog.html

Subdomain Tracking

This is a simple one-line change to your GATC. As such, you can automate the change required by selecting "One domain with multiple subdomains" in your profile Tracking Code settings, as shown in Figure 7.14. The following is a description of why the change is required and what it achieves. You should also consider the filter to differentiate your different subdomains (discussed in Chapter 8).

All Accounts › advanced-web-metrics.com ›

http://www.advanced-web-metrics.com
Web Property ID: UA-1190129-1
default URL: http://www.advanced-web-metrics.com

Profiles | **Tracking Code** | Web Property Settings

Tracking Code Configuration

Tracking Status Information

Web Property Name   http://www.advanced-web-metrics.com

Website URL   http://www.advanced-web-metrics.com

Web Property ID   UA-1190129-1

Tracking Status   **Tracking Installed**   Last checked: 01-Feb-2012 11:01:26 PST

Standard | Advanced | Custom

1. What are you tracking?

○ A single domain
   Example: www.advanced-web-metrics.com

◉ One domain with multiple subdomains
   Examples: www.advanced-web-metrics.com
            apps.advanced-web-metrics.com
            store.advanced-web-metrics.com

○ Multiple top-level domains
   Examples: www.advanced-web-metrics.uk
            www.advanced-web-metrics.cn
            www.advanced-web-metrics.fr

☐ AdWords campaigns

2. Paste this code on your site

Copy the following code, then paste it onto every page that you want to track immediately before the closing </head> tag. ⑦

```
<script type="text/javascript">

var _gaq = _gaq || [];
_gaq.push(['_setAccount', 'UA-1190129-1']);
_gaq.push(['_setDomainName', 'advanced-web-metrics.com']);
_gaq.push(['_trackPageview']);

(function() {
  var ga = document.createElement('script'); ga.type = 'text/javascript'; ga.async = true;
  ga.src = ('https:' == document.location.protocol ? 'https://ssl' : 'http://www') + '.google-analytics.com/ga.js';
  var s = document.getElementsByTagName('script')[0]; s.parentNode.insertBefore(ga, s);
})();
</script>
```

Figure 7.14 Automated GATC modification for tracking subdomains

Google Analytics uses first-party cookies, which means collected information is associated with your fully qualified hostname—for example, `www.mysite.com`. Only your fully qualified hostname can read or set its first-party cookies. This is a built-in security feature of all web browsers.

A *subdomain* is one that is a part of the parent domain. In this example, the parent domain is `mysite.com`, so www is actually a subdomain of `mysite.com`. Other example subdomains include `secure.mysite.com`, `store.mysite.com`, `en.mysite.com`, and so on.

> **Note:** Any name can be used as a subdomain name as long as it contains only alphanumeric characters and the hyphen (-). Of course, you can use a subdomain only if your DNS has been configured for it.

The default behavior when you set up Google Analytics is that subdomains are tracked in separate profiles—as described in Chapter 6 in the section "Using Accounts, Web Properties and Profiles." As a consequence, by default Google Analytics tracks visitors that traverse your different subdomains as referrers. For example, `www.mysite.com` becomes a referrer of `secure.mysite.com`. That can be valuable information in itself, but the original referrer (for example, a keyword search on `www.google.com`), which is captured and reported on `www.mysite.com`, cannot be transferred into your reports for `secure.mysite.com`. If this was for a transaction, you would know how your visitors found you (via reports for `www.mysite.com`) but would have no information on how your *customers* found you (original referrer lost in reports for `secure.mysite.com`).

Fortunately, modifying this behavior for your own domains is straightforward. You achieve this by combining all your subdomain data under the one parent domain. To accomplish this, set your parent domain in the GATC so that the Google Analytics first-party cookies can be shared across your subdomains, as highlighted here:

```
<script type="text/javascript">
  var _gaq = _gaq || [];
  _gaq.push(['_setAccount', 'UA-12345-1']);
  _gaq.push(['_setDomainName', 'mysite.com']);
  _gaq.push(['_trackPageview']);

(function() {
var ga = document.createElement('script');
ga.type = 'text/javascript'; ga.async = true;
ga.src = ('https:' == document.location.protocol ? 'https://ssl' : ➦
'http://www') + '.google-analytics.com/ga.js';
var s = document.getElementsByTagName('script')[0];
s.parentNode.insertBefore(ga, s);
})();
</script>
```

Note: This is the same modification if you have sub-subdomains. You do not need to do anything more than calling _setDomainName with your root domain name (mysite.com in my example). By this method, cookies set using _setDomainName as a.com are accessible from a.com, b.a.com, c.b.a.com, and d.c.b.a.com.

This way all subdomains of mysite.com can read, write, or edit the __utm cookies that Google Analytics uses. No further GATC modifications are required. However, as you may have realized, both subdomains are now aggregated, meaning that visits to www.mysite.com/index.html and secure.mysite.com/index.html will show in your reports as the same page—that is, both /index.html. In addition, you will not know how many visits your www site referred to your secure site. Correct these by applying the filter, as shown in Figure 7.15.

Add Filter to Profile

Choose method to apply filter to Website Profile
Please decide if you would like to create a new filter or apply an existing filter to the Profile.
- ◉ Create **new** Filter for Profile **OR** ○ Apply **existing** Filter to Profile

Filter Information

Filter Name: Insert Hostname

Filter Type: ○ Pre-defined filter ◉ Custom filter

- ○ Exclude
- ○ Include
- ○ Lowercase
- ○ Uppercase
- ○ Search and Replace
- ◉ Advanced

Field A -> Extract A: Hostname | (.*)

Field B -> Extract B: — | (.*)

Output To -> Constructor: — | /$A1$B1

Field A Required: ◉ Yes ○ No

Field B Required: ○ Yes ◉ No

Override Output Field: ◉ Yes ○ No

Case-sensitive: ○ Yes ◉ No

Figure 7.15 Filter to differentiate identical subdomain page names

Note: The filter shown in Figure 7.15 will make In-Page Analytics reports inoperable and may require you to modify your goal settings accordingly. However, I find the loss of the In-Page Analytics report is more than compensated by the greater insight that applying this filter provides.

By using this filter, page names will include your subdomains, allowing you to differentiate accordingly. For example, in the Content > Site Content > Pages report will be www.mysite.com/index.html and secure.mysite.com/index.html, respectively.

The use of filters is discussed in detail in Chapter 8.

Multiple Domain Tracking

As discussed in the previous section, web browsers have built-in security features that prevent the sharing of first-party cookies with other domains. If your website passes a visitor to different parent domains, then this needs special consideration.

Consider the following example: Your main website is www.mysite.com and you host regional variations (language, currency, and so on) on different parent domains such as www.mysite.co.uk. Both sites are tagged with your GATC. By clicking a link from a search results page on www.google.com, for example, a visitor arrives on www.mysite.com. Next, they click the option to select your regional version at www.mysite.co.uk. A conversion is then made on this site.

Note: Google Analytics cannot track visitors traversing the Web to unrelated domains. It can only track visitors across domains that you own or control and to which you can add your GATC.

By default, the visitor converting at www.mysite.co.uk will be reported as a referral visitor from www.mysite.com. The original referral information (search at www.google.com and associated search keywords) is lost because the cookie information cannot follow the visitor to the third-party domain. This is analogous to the situation described earlier for subdomain tracking.

If you maintain separate Google Analytics profiles for these two websites, then all page metrics (time on site, page depth, bounce rate, and so on) will be counted separately—in this example, a one-page visit for www.mysite.com and $x - 1$ page visits for www.mysite.co.uk. On the other hand, if you have configured data for both websites to be collected into a single profile (that is, you used the same GATC on both domains), then your page metrics will be skewed with overinflated numbers of single-page visits for www.mysite.com. Clearly, this is not the outcome you want.

The solution for tracking visitors across multiple sites is to maintain the session by transferring cookies across the multiple domains. There are two methods of achieving this, depending on how you forward visitors to your other domains—either by a link or via a form submission. These are the same as those discussed earlier (see "Transactions Via a Third-Party Payment Gateway") because in both cases first-party cookies need to be handed over to a third-party domain.

Regardless of which method you use, you will need to modify your GATC on the pages where a visitor leaves one domain and enters another. In the example given, this would be the home pages of www.mysite.com and www.mysite.co.uk, respectively. However, for this scenario it is common to have multiple pages where this can happen. Therefore, I recommend you make the GATC modification to *all* pages for *all* your domains to ensure consistency of your visitor tracking. The modification required for the two websites is shown in the following highlighted code. On www.mysite.com, use this:

```
<script type="text/javascript">
  var _gaq = _gaq || [];
  _gaq.push(['_setAccount', 'UA-12345-1']);
  _gaq.push(['_setDomainName', 'mysite.com']);
  _gaq.push(['_setAllowLinker ', true]);
  _gaq.push(['_trackPageview']);


(function() {
var ga = document.createElement('script');
ga.type = 'text/javascript'; ga.async = true;
ga.src = ('https:' == document.location.protocol ? 'https://ssl' : ➡
'http://www') + '.google-analytics.com/ga.js';
var s = document.getElementsByTagName('script')[0];
s.parentNode.insertBefore(ga, s);
})();
</script>
```

On www.mysite.co.uk, use this:

```
<script type="text/javascript">
  var _gaq = _gaq || [];
  _gaq.push(['_setAccount', 'UA-12345-1']);
  _gaq.push(['_setDomainName', 'mysite.co.uk']);
  _gaq.push(['_setAllowLinker ', true]);
  _gaq.push(['_trackPageview']);


(function() {
var ga = document.createElement('script');
ga.type = 'text/javascript'; ga.async = true;
ga.src = ('https:' == document.location.protocol ? 'https://ssl' : ➡
'http://www') + '.google-analytics.com/ga.js';
var s = document.getElementsByTagName('script')[0];
s.parentNode.insertBefore(ga, s);
})();
</script>
```

The two GATCs are identical except for the different values for _setDomainName. The use of _setDomainName forces the domain hash of the __utm cookies to be set to the string given and sets the cookies' host to the same value. The next line, `_setAllowLinker`, allows the cookie name/value pairs to be either transferred or received.

> **Note:** In previous editions of this book and in the Google online documentation up until August 2011, `_gaq.push(['_setDomainName', 'none'])` was the recommended setting. Although it's now deprecated, if you are already using this, it is important to keep it in place. This is because Google Analytics checks the domain hash when reading cookies directly. If you remove this, cookies from returning visitors will be ignored because the hash values will not match the new cookies set. For this reason, sites that are already set with `_gaq.push(['_set-DomainName', 'none'])` should not be modified.

As for subdomain tracking, these detailed GATC changes can be automated from your profile Check Status area by selecting Multiple top-level domains, as shown in Figure 7.16.

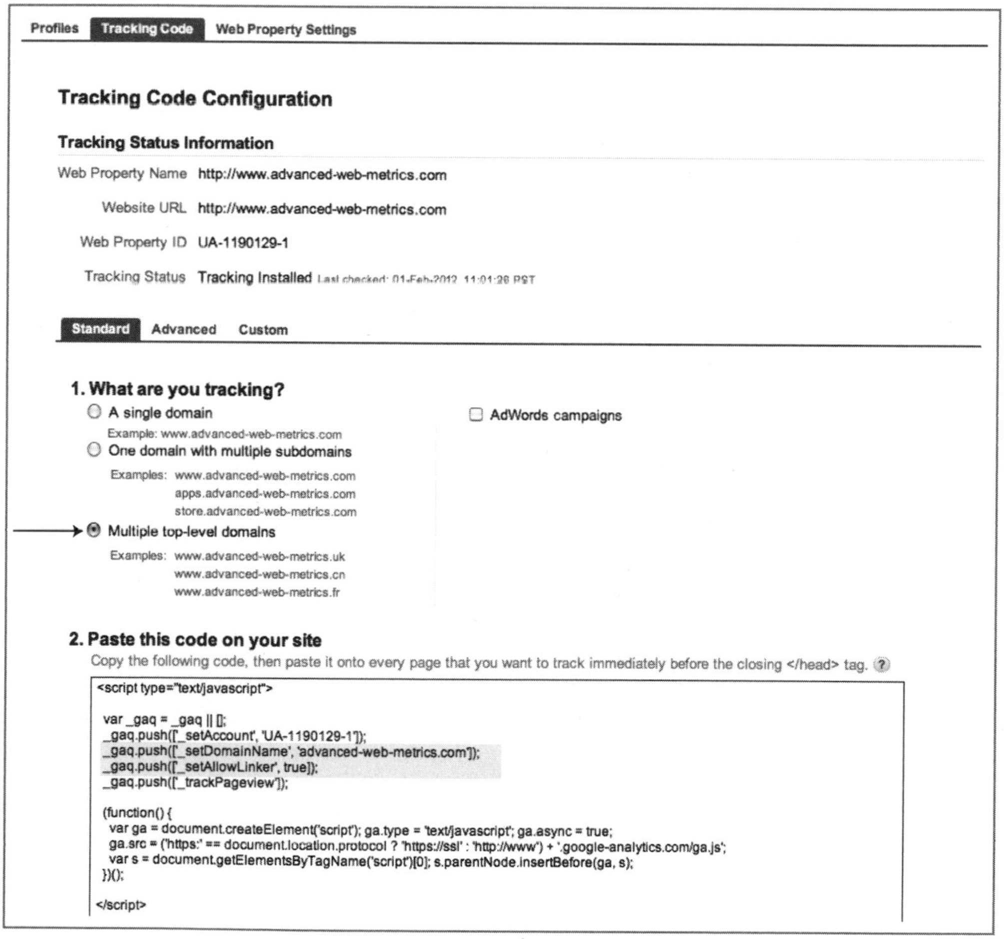

Figure 7.16 Automated GATC modification for tracking across multiple domains

With your pages modified, you then amend the link, or form, your visitors use to navigate between the domains, as described next.

Method 1: Track a Visitor across Domains When Using a Link

Use this method when you are passing visitors to another domain using a standard hyperlink. Within your web pages, modify all links to your other domains as follows:

```
<a href="http://www.mysite.co.uk" onclick="_gaq.push(['_link', this.href]);
return false; ">
Go to our UK web site</a>
```

With this method, the Google Analytics cookies are "pushed" to the receiving domain by appending them to the URL string (HTTP GET). If you see __utma, __utmb, and __utmc parameters in the URL of the landing page, then this has worked.

 Note: Note the use of return false; here. This ensures that for visitor browsers that have JavaScript disabled, the href link will be followed without error. Of course, if JavaScript is disabled, Google Analytics tracking won't occur, but the modified link will still work.

Method 2: Track a Visitor across Domains When Using a Form

Use this method when you are passing visitors to another domain using a form. Within your web pages, modify all form references to your other domains as follows:

```
<form method="post" onsubmit="_gaq.push(['_linkByPost', this]);">
```

If you already have an onSubmit validation routine, you append the cross-domain modification to your existing function call as follows:

```
<form method="post"
onsubmit="validate_routine(this);_gaq.push(['_linkByPost', this]);) ">
```

With this method, the Google Analytics cookies are "pushed" to the receiving domain via the HTTP headers (HTTP POST). This will work even for forms where method="GET". You can verify if this has worked by viewing the HTTP headers sent in Firefox using the add-on LiveHTTPheaders (http://livehttpheaders.mozdev.org).

The GATC Setup Wizard

The changes illustrated in Figures 7.14 and 7.16 are examples of using the GATC setup wizard. That is, they are changes required to your tracking code that Google Analytics can automatically provide for you—without the need for you to manually edit page code.

In this section, I'll show you how to track visitors that traverse subdomains or multiple domains. The required changes are all contained within the Standard tab menu of the GATC setup wizard. As you will have noticed, there are also Advanced and Custom menu tabs.

The Advanced menu provides additional instructions that affect your GATC, such as, for example, how to import data from AdWords, how to track paid campaigns for non-AdWords pay-per-click accounts, how to use Urchin in conjunction with Google Analytics, and so forth. These are discussed in the relevant sections of this book. Neither the Standard nor Advanced GATC code can be edited from within the wizard.

The Custom menu is an area where you can manually edit the GATC within the wizard and save it for later reference. For all menu tabs, you can distribute the required code via email. The text supplied for you to do this is obtained by selecting Optional: Email These Instructions.

Tracking Visitors across Subdomains and Multiple Domains

Until August 2011, this was a special scenario when you have visitors traversing both subdomains *and* third-party domains within their visit. Consider the following example:

- A visitor goes to www.mysite.com.
- Next the visitor clicks a link to blog.mysite.com.
- Then the visitor decides to purchase a product and so clicks the shopping cart link, which sends them off to www.shoppingcart.com/widgets.

Previously this required an additional change to the GATC (_setAllowHash). This is no longer required. Configuring your GATC as described in this section for "Multiple Domain Tracking" will take care of this scenario.

However, although _setAllowHash is now deprecated, if you are already using it, it is important to keep it in place. This is because Google Analytics checks the domain hash when reading cookies directly. If you remove this, cookies from returning visitors will be ignored because the hash values will not match the new cookies set. For this reason, sites that are already set with _gaq.push(['_setAllowHash', 'false']) should not be modified.

Additional Customization Options

The following sections are not intended to cover an exhaustive list of GATC customizations. Rather, they cover the ones most commonly used. Refer to the following online documentation for more customization options:

http://code.google.com/apis/analytics/docs/gaJS/gaJSApiDomainDirectory.html

http://code.google.com/apis/analytics/docs/gaJS/gaJSApiBasicConfiguration.html

http://code.google.com/apis/analytics/docs/gaJS/gaJSApiSearchEngines.html

Controlling Time-Outs

You can control two cookie time-outs from within your GATC: the session time-out and the campaign conversion time-out.

By default, a visitor's session (visit) times out after 30 minutes of inactivity, so if a visitor continues browsing your website after 31 minutes of inactivity, that visitor is counted as a returning visitor. The original referral information is maintained as long as a new referral source was not used to continue their session.

The 30-minute rule is the unwritten standard across the web analytics industry. However, there may be instances when you wish to change this. Typical examples include when your visitors are engaging with music or video or reading lengthy documents during their visit. The latter is a less-likely scenario because visitors usually print large documents and read them offline. However, music and video sites are common examples in which visitors set and forget their actions only to return and complete another action on your site when the content has finished playing.

If inactivity is likely to last longer than 30 minutes for a continuous visit, then consider increasing the default session time-out as follows:

```
<script type="text/javascript">
  var _gaq = _gaq || [];
  _gaq.push(['_setAccount', 'UA-12345-1']);
  _gaq.push(['_setSessionCookieTimeout', 3600000]); // set to 1 hour
  _gaq.push(['_trackPageview']);

(function() {
var ga = document.createElement('script');
ga.type = 'text/javascript'; ga.async = true;
ga.src = ('https:' == document.location.protocol ? 'https://ssl' : ➡
'http://www') + '.google-analytics.com/ga.js';
var s = document.getElementsByTagName('script')[0];
s.parentNode.insertBefore(ga, s);
})();
</script>
```

 Note: In Google Analytics, time is measured in milliseconds. Therefore, 30 minutes = 1,800,000 milliseconds, 1 hour = 3,600,000 milliseconds, and so forth.

Another time-out that you can adjust is the length of time for which Google Analytics credits a conversion referral. By default, the campaign conversion time-out is six months (15,768,000,000 milliseconds), after which the referral cookie (__utmz)

expires. For example, you may wish to reduce this value when you are paying a commission to affiliates. You can achieve this as follows:

```
<script type="text/javascript">
  var _gaq = _gaq || [];
  _gaq.push(['_setAccount', 'UA-12345-1']);
  _gaq.push(['_setCampaignCookieTimeout', 2592000000]); // set to 30 days
  _gaq.push(['_trackPageview']);

(function() {
var ga = document.createElement('script');
ga.type = 'text/javascript'; ga.async = true;
ga.src = ('https:' == document.location.protocol ? 'https://ssl' : ➡
'http://www') + '.google-analytics.com/ga.js';
var s = document.getElementsByTagName('script')[0];
s.parentNode.insertBefore(ga, s);
})();
</script>
```

The value of the campaign conversion time-out can also be increased. However, it doesn't make much sense to go beyond six months due to the increased risk that the original cookie information will be lost, making your conversion referral data less reliable. See "Issues Affecting Visitor Data When Using Cookies," in Chapter 2.

> **Note:** There is a third time-out value you can control: the visitor cookie. By default, the visitor cookie is set to expire after two years. If you prefer, you can change the expiration date using the following setting within your GATC: _gaq.push(['_setVisitorCookieTimeout',63072000000]);, where the number represents the number of milliseconds in two years. However, I do not see any value in changing this and so do not recommend using it.

Setting Ignore Referrer Preferences

You can configure Google Analytics to treat certain referrers as direct traffic (that is, not as a referral). This is important if visitors are arriving at your site from a third-party domain and you do not want this referrer information to be recorded in your Google Analytics reports. This is a common scenario if you are an e-commerce site and your purchasers are processed via a third-party payment gateway that you are unable to track. It is described earlier in this chapter in the section, "What to Do When a Third-Party Gateway Does Not Allow Tracking."

Use _addIgnoredRef to treat a referral as direct, as shown here:

```
<script type="text/javascript">
```

```
    var _gaq = _gaq || [];
    _gaq.push(['_setAccount', 'UA-12345-1']);
    _gaq.push(['_addIgnoredRef', 'www.payment-gateway.com']);
    _gaq.push(['_trackPageview']);

(function() {
var ga = document.createElement('script');
ga.type = 'text/javascript'; ga.async = true;
ga.src = ('https:' == document.location.protocol ? 'https://ssl' : ➡
'http://www') + '.google-analytics.com/ga.js';
var s = document.getElementsByTagName('script')[0];
s.parentNode.insertBefore(ga, s);
})();
</script>
```

The default behavior of Google Analytics is for direct traffic not to overwrite any existing campaign information. So if a purchaser originally came to your site via a Google organic search with the search term "widget purchase," this will be maintained and shown in your reports with the direct reference dropped. Only if there is no previous campaign information will *direct* be written into your reports as the referral source.

Site Speed Sample Rate

Using the Content > Site Speed report is discussed in Chapter 5, in the section "Top Standard Reports". The report is generated from sampled data set at default sample rate of 1 percent. However, the default sample rate may be adjusted using the _setSiteSpeedSampleRate function. Allowed sample rates range from 0 (to disable site speed tracking) to 10 percent (maximum allowed sample rate). This is set as follows:

```
    <script type="text/javascript">
    var _gaq = _gaq || [];
    _gaq.push(['_setAccount', 'UA-12345-1']);
    _gaq.push(['_setSiteSpeedSampleRate', 10]);
    _gaq.push(['_trackPageview']);

(function() {
var ga = document.createElement('script');
ga.type = 'text/javascript'; ga.async = true;
ga.src = ('https:' == document.location.protocol ? 'https://ssl' : ➡
'http://www') + '.google-analytics.com/ga.js';
var s = document.getElementsByTagName('script')[0];
s.parentNode.insertBefore(ga, s);
```

```
})();
</script>
```

Google Analytics restricts the site speed collection hits for a single web property to either 1 percent of visitors or 10,000 hits per day—whichever is the greater. Unless you have high traffic volumes, for example above 100,000 pageviews per day, I recommend you set _setSiteSpeedSampleRate to its maximum value (10) in order to provide the most accurate site speed report.

Note: The effect of _setSiteSpeedSampleRate only affects the calling page. If you have pages where site speed data collection is important, you can set the value at 10 on these pages, and 0 on less important pages. That way, you stay below the daily threshold of 10,000 visits or 1 percent of visitors.

Anonymize IP Addresses

In some parts of the world, most notably Germany, an IP address is considered personally identifiable information. Therefore, collection of this information is illegal without the explicit consent of each individual. Google Analytics captures IP addresses by default for the purposes of reporting geolocation information, so if you conduct business in Germany you must use the _anonymizeIP function to anonymize your visitors' IP addresses.

The _anonymizeIP tells Google Analytics to anonymize the information sent by the tracker objects by removing the last octet of the IP address prior to its storage. The function is used as follows:

```
<script type="text/javascript">
  var _gaq = _gaq || [];
  _gaq.push(['_setAccount', 'UA-12345-1']);
  _gaq.push(['_anonymizeIP']);
  _gaq.push(['_trackPageview']);

(function() {
var ga = document.createElement('script');
ga.type = 'text/javascript'; ga.async = true;
ga.src = ('https:' == document.location.protocol ? 'https://ssl' : ➡
'http://www') + '.google-analytics.com/ga.js';
var s = document.getElementsByTagName('script')[0];
s.parentNode.insertBefore(ga, s);
})();
</script>
```

Note that this will slightly reduce the accuracy of geolocation reporting.

Sampling: Controlling Data Collection

By default, Google Analytics collects pageview data for every visitor. However, the Google Analytics terms of service (www.google.com/intl/en/analytics/tos.html) state that the available limit for the free version is 10 million data hits per month—a hit is the summation of all pageviews, events, and transaction items. If your traffic volumes regularly go beyond this limit you have two options: Upgrade to the paid-for version of Google Analytics, called Premium (discussed in Chapter 3) or sample your data collection so that you fall below the terms of service threshold.

 Note: Rather than cutting off your data collection when you reach the 10 million hit threshold, Google will politely send you an email asking you to upgrade to the Premium product or introduce data collection sampling. That means the onus is on you to stay within the terms of service. Of course if you ignore the emails, Google may enforce collection sampling from its side or even terminate your account.

Note that the data volume limit is applied at the account level. That means separating out your data into multiple web properties or profiles will not reduce your data volume count. A possible solution is to use the roll-up reporting technique described in Chapter 6. That is using multiple Google Analytics accounts. However, in most cases, if you are exceeding the data threshold, you will need to employ data collection sampling.

To achieve this, specify a sampling collection rate in your GATC using the _setSampleRate function, as shown here:

```
<script type="text/javascript">
  var _gaq = _gaq || [];
  _gaq.push(['_setAccount', 'UA-12345-1']);
  _gaq.push(['_setSampleRate', '25']);
  _gaq.push(['_trackPageview']);


(function() {
var ga = document.createElement('script');
ga.type = 'text/javascript'; ga.async = true;
ga.src = ('https:' == document.location.protocol ? 'https://ssl' : ➡
'http://www') + '.google-analytics.com/ga.js';
var s = document.getElementsByTagName('script')[0];
s.parentNode.insertBefore(ga, s);
})();
</script>
```

A sample rate of 25 percent means that every fourth visitor is counted for Google Analytics tracking. Therefore, if you are receiving around 36 million data hits per month, the sample rate will bring you below the threshold limit.

Data sampling takes place at the *visitor* level—entire visit activity is dropped, and if the excluded visitor returns to your site later, they will again be excluded. This ensures that there is integrity in trending and reporting even when sampling is enabled because unique visitors remain included or excluded from the sample.

> **Note:** The automatic sampling of report data is discussed in Chapter 5 in the section "Understanding Report Sampling."

Don't Look for Small Needles in Giant Haystacks

The data sampling techniques employed by Google Analytics are statistically valid—they originate from standard statistical theory. As with all sampling methods, the sample size is important—the larger it is, the more accurately the sample will reflect the true picture. The use of _setSampleRate is recommended only when you receive more than 10 million data hits per month. Therefore, by definition this is a very large sample size.

However, problems do arise when you attempt to drill down within large data sets to find a much smaller data set—for example, within 10 million pageviews, trying to find visit data that only accounts for a handful of viewed URLs. The analogy is that of finding a needle in a giant haystack. With sampling enabled, there is a possibility of the needle not even appearing in the sample. If you know those pages must exist in the data—perhaps you are testing your own visit activity—you can come to the conclusion that the report is wrong. This is a statistically invalid assumption in the same way that it is invalid to say that such a minute proportion of visit activity can have an impact on your business.

Summary

In Chapter 7, you have learned the following:

Leveraging tagging and tracking Having read this far, you will have now completed the following actions:

- Tagged all of your website pages with the GATC
- Tagged your campaign landing pages to capture visitors from email marketing, social media, banners, paid search, and so forth
- Adjusted your setup for tracking file downloads, events, and embedded YouTube video tracking
- Modified your checkout completion page for the capture of e-commerce transactions

With all that in place, your installation is complete. Take an initial look at some of your reports and get comfortable with using them, as described in Part II, "Using Google Analytics Reports."

Using the `_trackPageview` function to create virtual pageviews You have learned how to modify the Google Analytics workhorse function to report more meaningful URL names as well as track those not captured by default.

Capturing e-commerce transactions We discussed how to capture transactional information both on your site and if you are using a third-party payment gateway.

Tracking online campaigns You learned how to use campaign variables to identify and differentiate online campaigns from traditional digital marketing and social media.

Tracking in-page interactions as events You can now use the Google Analytics Event Tracking feature to capture actions separately from pageviews, including Flash movie interaction.

Customizing the GATC for your specific needs You learned to modify the default behavior of Google Analytics when your needs are more specialized.

Best Practices Configuration Guide

Having read the first seven chapters of this book, you should now have your Google Analytics account set up and collecting quality data. To help you gain a better understanding of visitor behavior and get the most out of your data, this chapter will assist you with your configuration.

By following the recommended steps, you will gain real insight into the performance of your online presence. If you don't follow the steps, reread this chapter. Seriously, this information is too important to skip over without implementing the suggested configurations—particularly goals and funnels.

No modifications of the Google Analytics Tracking Code (GATC) or your pages are required here. However, you will need administrator access to your Google Analytics account to use this chapter.

In Chapter 8, you will learn:

Best practices for configuring Google Analytics

The importance of defining goals and funnels

The importance of visitor segmentation

How to use filters and advanced segments

How to set up your own intelligence alerts

Initial Configuration

It is important that the marketer and webmaster work together to understand each other's needs. The marketer will be building the marketing strategy, and that requires working in conjunction with the webmaster to implement the necessary configuration changes. If you are a part of a large organization, then it is you as the analyst who manages and oversees this part of the project. Unless you are performing all three roles yourself, collaboration is the key to success here.

Once you have established your first Google Analytics web property and profile—created as part of your initial account-creation process—there are a few options you should configure in the first instance, as shown in Figure 8.1. To access this area from your initial login area, click the Settings icon at the top-right corner of your reports, then select the Profile Settings tab.

In Figure 8.1, in the area labeled A, the time zone and country options were set at the time of account creation. You can adjust them here, though bear in mind that if you have linked your account to your AdWords account, your AdWords settings take precedence and this cannot be changed—either in AdWords or Google Analytics. The consequences of this, particularly if you have multiple AdWords accounts, are discussed in the section "Roll-up Reporting" in Chapter 6, "Getting Started: Initial Setup."

The remaining options allow you to enter your default page, exclude any URL query parameters for which reports are not required, and set the localization of currency. These are explained next.

Setting the Default Page

The default page is the web page your server defaults to when no page is specified—that is, the your home page. This is usually `index.html`, `index.htm`, `index.php`, or `default.asp`, but it can be anything your web hosting company or webmaster has specified. Once you enter your default page, Google Analytics is able to combine visits to `www.mysite.com` and `www.mysite.com/index.html`, which are in fact the same page, and report them both as `/index.html`.

If the default page is not specified, then these examples are reported as two separate pages, which is not desirable. However, some content management systems are rigorous with link definitions and are configured so that it is not possible for this scenario to arise. The result is that your default page name is hidden. If that describes your website, then I recommend leaving the default page field empty. This is to simplify your reports—showing root directory pages simply as / rather than `/index.html`. It's a data visualization preference I have.

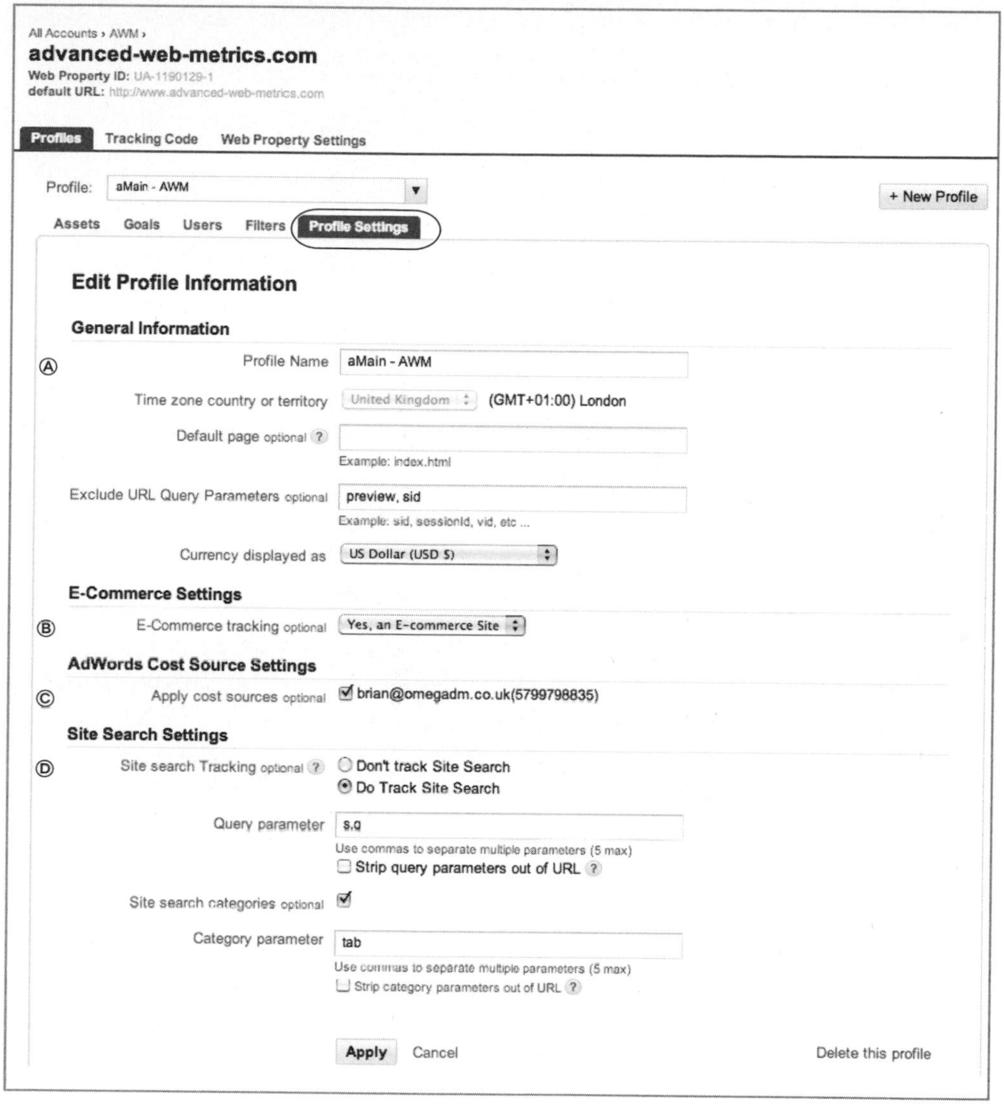

Figure 8.1 Initial profile setup options

Excluding Unnecessary Parameters

If your site uses unique session IDs or displays other query parameters in your URLs that are of no interest to you, you can exclude these parameters by entering them in the Exclude URL Query Parameters field (see Figure 8.1, the area labeled A). In fact, it is best practice to do this because it can dramatically reduce the amount of superfluous data collected, making reports faster loading and easier to read. Enter the variable name that you wish to exclude as it appears in your URLs. Variable name/value pairs follow a query symbol (?) in your URL and are separated by ampersands (&). Enter the name part you wish to exclude here—the part before the equal sign (=).

An example URL with a unique session ID is as follows:

```
www.mysite.com/BookingSystem/Action.do;jsessionid=QQQRTlkWyhJC016s18JYwN2
```

Specifying the *jsessionid* as the excluded parameter will shorten this into a more manageable URL for your reports and reduce the amount of unnecessarily collected data.

Excluding Parameter Mitigates Data Sampling

Google Analytics is restricted to providing reports for up to 10 million pageviews per month. This is stated in the terms of service. If you go above this limit, Google will send out email reminders to account administrators requesting that you sample your data collection so that you remain within the terms of service. For example, if you receive 20 million pageviews per month, Google will advise that you set a data collection sample rate of 50 percent.

Sampling data is statistically valid—10 million visits is a very large sample size. However, you can mitigate the need for sampling by ensuring that you exclude unnecessary query parameters. Setting your data collection sample rate is discussed in the section "Customizing the GATC" in Chapter 7, "Advanced Implementation."

Currency Setting

The display currency you set and see in your reports—for transaction revenue, AdWords cost data, or monetized goals—is for display purposes only. It does not represent any real currency or take into consideration any exchange rates. That is, Google Analytics treats the currency setting as a label only.

For example, if you trade in US dollars and you accidentally set your profile currency setting to Japanese yen (it's next in the drop-down list), the exact same numerical amount will be displayed in your reports, just the label will be incorrect. This affects all report revenue and cost metrics.

Enabling E-commerce Reporting

If your site has an e-commerce facility, you will want to see this data in your reports so that you can follow the complete visitor journey from referral source and pages viewed to checkout and payment confirmation. Selecting Yes, An E-Commerce Site, as shown in Figure 8.1 in the area labeled B, enables this reporting; you will see it as a separate menu item on the left side of the reports and as an additional tab within most report tables. If you do not have an e-commerce website, keep the default selection of Not An E-Commerce Site.

Note that enabling e-commerce provides additional reports within your account. Selecting this feature does not enable Google Analytics to collect the e-commerce data for you. To do this, you need to apply additional tracking code to the receipt page of your checkout system—see "Tracking E-commerce Transactions," in Chapter 7.

AdWords Cost Source Settings

Once you import your AdWords data, you can apply the import on a per-profile basis. The area shown in Figure 8.1 in the area labeled C, is where you set this. If you have linked multiple AdWords accounts to your Google Analytics account, you will see multiple cost sources here. Linking your account with AdWords is described in the section "Integrating with Your AdWords Data" in Chapter 6.

Enabling Site Search

If your site has an internal search engine to help visitors locate content, you will want to see how this facility affects your visitors' experience. Capturing internal search terms is an important asset when tuning your website. For example, it can reveal misspellings, synonyms, partial matches, or just plain different descriptions.

To do this, first select Do Track Site Search, as shown in Figure 8.1 in the area labeled D. This enables an additional Google Analytics report menu that can be found in the Content > Site Search section.

With this feature enabled, you need to define which query parameter in your URLs contains the visitor's site search term. You can usually discover this quickly by performing a site search yourself and looking for your search term in the result page URL. This is typically of the form ?q=mykeyword or &search=mykeyword. For these examples, the query parameter names are q and search, respectively. Google Analytics uses these values to determine that a visitor has made a search and which search terms were used. In the example in Figure 8.1 in the area labeled D, the query parameters are s and q.

Notice also that there is an option to strip your defined site search query parameters from the URL after site search processing has been completed. This can be helpful if those query parameters are of no further use to you for the purpose of Google Analytics reporting. However, those parameters may be important for defining your goals, your funnel steps, or your filters (see the sections "Goal Conversions and Funnels" and "Why Segmentation Is Important" later in this chapter). Site search query parameters could also be important if you are using virtual pageviews to aid in the reading of your reports (discussed in the section "_trackPageview: The Google

Analytics Workhorse" in Chapter 7). Therefore, you should strip query parameters only if absolutely necessary.

Google Analytics Site Search also provides the option to define categories. Use this if your site search facility allows visitors to select a category for their search. For example, a retail site may have categories such as Menswear, Ladies' Wear, and so on. A real estate website may have categories such as Apartments, Condos, Houses, and so forth. Categories help visitors find information easier by focusing their search. Understanding how categories compare is often the initial step when assessing the performance of your internal site search engine.

As with defining the site search query parameter, category parameters are obtained from the results page URL—for example, ?cat=menswear or &sect=condo. For these examples, the category parameter names are cat and sect, respectively. As with your defined query parameter, you can also strip your defined category parameters from the URL after site search processing has been completed. However, for the same reasons, strip query parameters only if absolutely necessary.

What If My URLs Don't Contain Site Search Parameters?

For this situation you can employ virtual pageviews to insert the parameters for you. If your site search results page contains the visitor's query term as an environment variable (for example, *%searchterm*), then you can use this as a virtual pageview. The following example is a modified GATC to achieve this:

```
<script type="text/javascript">
var _gaq = _gaq || [];_
_gaq.push(['_setAccount', 'UA-12345-1']);
_gaq.push(['_trackPageview','/site search/?q=%searchterm']);

(function() {
var ga = document.createElement('script');
ga.type = 'text/javascript'; ga.async = true;
ga.src = ('https:' == document.location.protocol ? 'https://ssl' : ➥
'http://www') + '.google-analytics.com/ga.js';
var s = document.getElementsByTagName('script')[0];
s.parentNode.insertBefore(ga, s);
})();
</script>
```

In this example I have created a virtual pageview with a query parameter of q and its value set as the environment variable *%searchterm*. You can then use q as your site search query parameter as if this were the physical URL. The use of virtual pageviews is discussed in the section "_trackPageview: The Google Analytics Workhorse" in Chapter 7.

Tracking Zero Results for Site Search

A common requirement when assessing the effectiveness and performance of a site search facility is the ability to track which search terms generate zero results. Returning zero results is a particularly bad user experience that often leads to an automatic dismissal—the visitor moves on to another website.

That reaction is fair enough if you do not have the products or services the visitor is looking for. However, I regularly find that this is not the case. On the contrary, for some reason internal site search is frequently added to a site as an afterthought with little attention given to the quality of its performance, despite the obvious fact that users rely heavily on search when using the Web. Hence, many visitors leave a website with the mistaken belief that it cannot cater to their needs.

Capturing zero results allows you to distinguish between good and bad user experiences. To achieve this, use a category parameter labeled zero in your search result URL when this happens, as in this example:

```
www.mysite.com?q=widget&tab=zero
```

Ensure that you have added the category parameter tab (or other name) to your configuration, as shown in Figure 8.1. Then when you view your Site Search reports, you will have a dedicated category just for analyzing zero search results.

Goal Conversions and Funnels

As emphasized throughout this book, collecting data is only the first step in understanding the visitor performance of your website. Google Analytics has more than 100 built-in reports by default; that's impressive for fine-grain analysis, but it can be quite daunting to absorb all of this information, even for experienced users. In fact, I recommend you don't even attempt to do so.

Instead, you can distill visitor information by configuring Google Analytics to report on goal conversions. Think of goal conversions as *specific* measurable actions that can be applied to every visit. The path a visitor takes to reach a goal is known as the funnel; this is shown schematically in Figure 8.2. As you can see, the number of visitors entering the funnel process decreases at each step.

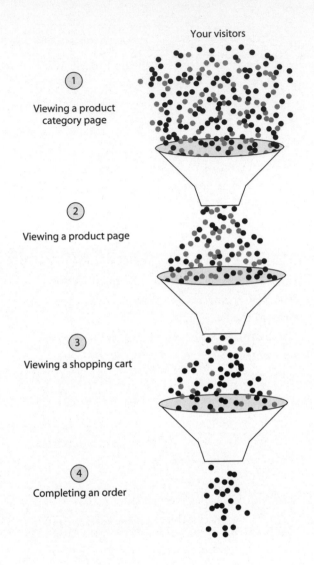

Figure 8.2 Schematic funnel and goal process

The Importance of Defining Goals

Defining your website goals is probably the single most important step of your configuration process because it enables you to define success. Goal conversions, also referred to as simply *goals* or *conversions*, are any actions or engagements that build a relationship with your visitors. An obvious goal for an e-commerce site is the completion of a transaction. However, even without e-commerce, your website has goals, such as, for example, the completion of a feedback form, a subscription request, leaving a comment on a blog post, downloading a PDF white paper, viewing a special-offers page, or clicking a `mailto:` link. Goal conversions are the de facto way to ascertain whether your website is engaging with your visitors. They are your "success" metrics.

A goal is typically the reason why you put up a website in the first place: Was it to sell directly, to generate leads, to keep your clients or shareholders up-to-date, to provide centralized product updates, or to attract new staff? As you begin this exercise, you will realize that you actually have many website goals.

Also consider that goals don't have to include the full conversion of a visitor into a customer—that is obviously very important, but it's only part of the picture. If your only goal is to gain customers, then how will you know just how close noncustomers came to converting? You can gain insight into this by using additional goals to measure the building of relationships with your visitors. For example, for most visitors arriving on your website, it is unlikely they will instantly convert, so the page needs to *persuade* them to go deeper—that is, get them one step closer to your goal. Table 8.1 lists some example goals.

▶ **Table 8.1** Sample website goals

Non-E-commerce Goals	Examples
Visitors downloading a document	Brochure, manual, white paper, price list (file types include PDF, XLS, DOC, PPT, etc.)
Visitors looking at specific pages or sections of pages	Jobs, price list, special offers, login page, admin page, location and contact details, terms and conditions, help desk or support area
Visitors completing a form	Login, registration, feedback form, subscription
Visitor engagement	Adding a blog comment, completing a survey, submitting a forum post, adding or editing their user profile, uploading content, rating an article
Visitor thresholds	Staying on the site longer than *XX* seconds, viewing more than *YY* pages
Transaction completed	Credit card thank-you page
Transaction failed	Credit card rejection page
Visitors entering shopping system	Adding to cart, getting to step *x* of *y*, using a promotional code or not

Further Reading on Designing Goal-Driven Websites

Bryan Eisenberg, his brother Jeffrey Eisenberg, and Lisa T. Davis have written extensively on the persuasion process technique and coined the phrase *persuasion architecture*. Their book on the process is *Waiting for Your Cat to Bark: Persuading Customers When They Ignore Marketing* (Thomas Nelson Publishers, 2006).

Another worthwhile read when considering website goals and funnels is the excellent book *Don't Make Me Think* by Steve Krug (New Riders, 2005). It's a commonsense approach to web usability written in an easy-to-read and humorous way.

Apart from the goals shown in Table 8.1, your website may possess negative goals—that is, goals for which you would like to decrease or minimize the conversion rate. For example, if onsite search is an important aspect of your website navigation structure, then minimizing the number of zero search results returned for a query is a valid ambition. Perhaps minimizing the number of searches per visitor is also an indication of an efficient onsite search tool; the theory could be that fewer searches conducted means visitors are finding what they are looking for more quickly. Negative goals are common for product-support websites—that is, when the best visitor experience is for the least amount of engagement, such as time on site or page depth.

Defining and measuring goals is the basis for building your key performance indicators (KPIs). Chapter 10 defines and discusses KPIs in more detail, but essentially they enable you to incorporate web data into your overall business model.

Your Google Analytics Profile Can Be Configured for Up to 20 Goals

Your website should be focused enough that 20 goals cover your requirements. If they don't, then look again at the number of goals you wish to measure. An obvious efficiency is to use wildcards—for example, *.pdf rather than individual PDF filenames.

If you truly need more than 20 goals to measure your website effectiveness, read "Monetizing a Non-E-commerce Website" in Chapter 11, which is applicable for all non-e-commerce goals.

What Funnel Shapes Can Tell You

Many website owners and marketers want to see a 100 percent goal conversion rate. In the real world, that just isn't feasible. In fact, it is not as desirable as you might think. Consider your funnel as acting like a sieve, qualifying visitors along the way. As with the offline world, it is important to qualify your web visitors so that your support or returns department is not swamped with calls from disappointed customers. Therefore, losing visitors via your funnel is not necessarily a bad thing.

Conversely, if you have verified all the qualifications before the visitor enters the funnel, then you would expect a high conversion rate. The outcome is highly dependent on how good your funnel pages are at doing their job—that is, persuading visitors to continue to the next step. Consider each funnel step as a "micro-conversion" toward the "macro-conversion" of achieving a goal completion. Figure 8.3 shows example schematic funnel shapes.

Note: A detailed funnel analysis for a website is performed in Chapter 11.

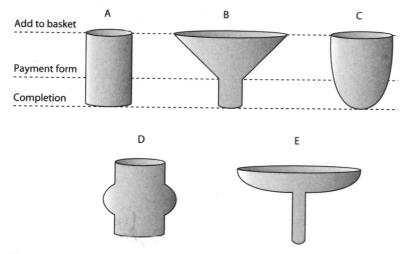

Add to basket

Payment form

Completion

Figure 8.3 Schematic conversion funnel shapes

Here's the explanation for Figure 8.3:

Shape A The impossible 100 percent conversion rate.

Shape B The most common funnel shape, showing a sharp decrease in visitors until the payment form step. Assuming there are no hidden surprises for the visitor at this point, the vast majority of visitors who reach this point should convert.

Shape C A well-optimized conversion-funnel process, with only a gradual decrease in visitors. This is the optimum shape you will wish to obtain for all your funnels.

Shape D An ill-defined funnel—visitors are entering the funnel midway through the process.

Shape E A poorly converting funnel with a serious barrier to progress.

The most common shapes I have come across are B, D, and E. Shape A occurs only for a small section of an overall funnel process (if at all). Shape C is very rare—optimizing your funnels to approach this shape is where your greatest opportunity lies.

The Goal Setup Process

To set up your goals, log in to your Google Analytics account and click the settings icon (top right of your reports) for the profile you want to add a goal to. Then select the Goals section, as shown in Figure 8.4. Here you can define up to 20 goals. You can also group your goals into four categories (5 goals per category). Grouping similar goals together in the same category provides easier report interpretation. Apart from this, there is no other difference.

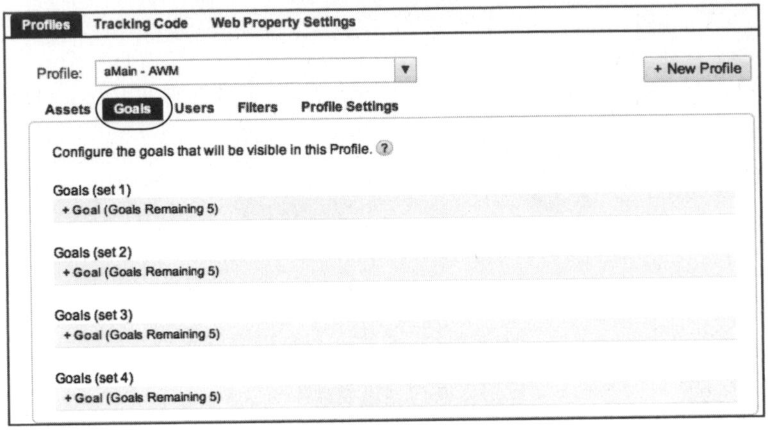

Figure 8.4 The Goals section of an account profile

In the Goals section, click + Goal for a goal set. This takes you to the screen shown in Figure 8.5—I assume you will choose Set 1.

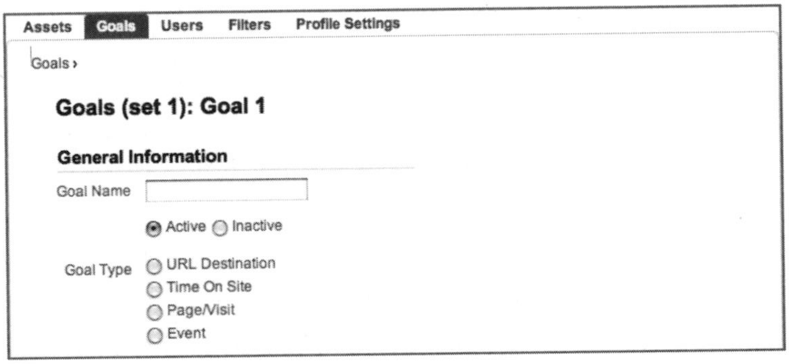

Figure 8.5 Initial goal-configuration screen

General Information

In this area you name your goal, activate or deactivate it, and define what constitutes a goal.

Goal Name First, define a Goal Name that you will recognize when viewing reports. Examples include Email sign-up, Article AB123 download, Inquiry form sent, and Purchase complete. Ensure that the goal is Active, and then select a Goal Type from the options URL Destination, Time On Site, Page/Visit, and Event.

Goal Type Time On Site and Page/Visit are *threshold* goal types. With these, you can specify a value that the web visit must be greater than, less than, or equal to in order to trigger a goal match, such as, for example, Time On Site greater than 5 minutes, Page/Visit greater than 10. These could indicate strong interest from visitors whom you wish to identify. However, think carefully before reaching a conclusion on threshold goals; you should correlate with other data because a high Time On Site or Page/Visit value could mean your visitors are lost or confused and cannot find what they are looking for.

For the purposes of this example, select URL Destination as the Goal Type, which then expands out the screen as per Figure 8.6.

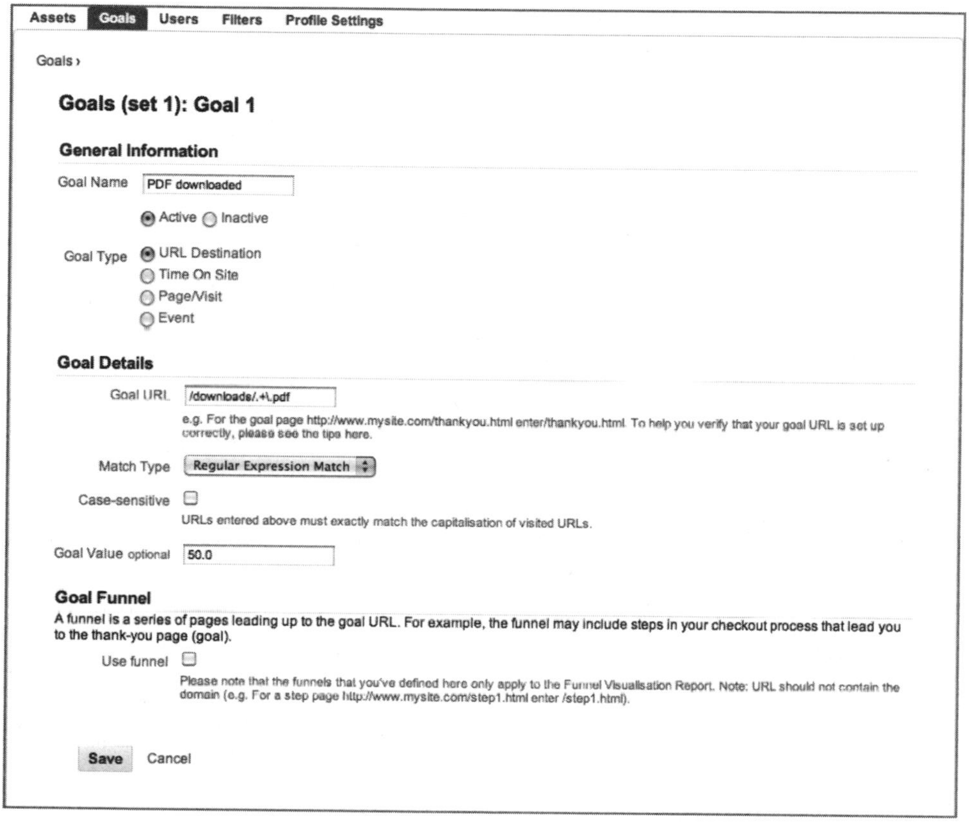

Figure 8.6 Second goal-configuration screen

Goal Details

In this area you indicate how Google Analytics identifies a goal and associate a value, if applicable, when the goal is triggered.

Goal URL This is a page URL that can be reached only by achieving a goal. Clearly, if your goal page can be reached by visitors who have not completed the goal, then your conversion rates will be inflated and not representative. Although this is listed as the first step in the Goal Details section, ensure that you understand the match type, described next, before you complete this field.

Note: The goal URL should not contain the domain.

Match Type Before entering the URL Destination value, you need to decide on how Google Analytics will perform the match.

The match type determines how your defined URLs are matched. There are three ways to achieve this: Exact Match, Head Match, and Regular Expression Match.

Exact Match This means exactly what it says—the exact URL of the page you want to define. No dynamic session identifiers and no wildcards can be used here, so it is best to cut and paste the URL from the address bar of your browser to define your goal.

Head Match If your URL destination is always the same but is followed by a unique session identifier or other parameters, use the Head Match filter and omit the unique values. For example, if the URL for a particular page is

```
http://www.mysite.com/checkout.cgi?page=5of5&id=9982251615
```

but the id varies for every user, enter

```
http://www.mysite.com/checkout.cgi?page=5of5
```

Regular Expression Match This uses regular expressions to match your URL Destination—for example, wildcards and metacharacters. This is useful when the URL, query parameters, or both vary between users:

```
http://sports.mysite.com/checkout.cgi?page=5of5&id=002
http://news.mysite.com/checkout.cgi?page=5of5&language=fr&id=119
```

To match against a single goal for this example, you would use the regular expression .+page=5of5+. to define the constant element, in this case, one or more characters, followed by the string *page=5of5*, followed by one or more characters. If you are unfamiliar with the use of regular expressions, see the overview provided in Appendix A.

Head Match and Exact Match are by far the most common ways to define simple goal and funnel steps, but e-commerce systems often require the use of regular expressions.

Case Sensitive If you want to differentiate URL Destinations that are identical except for the fact that one uses uppercase characters and the other uses lowercase characters—for example, productx.html and productX.html—then you should check the Case Sensitive check box. Most people do not change this, but it is there if needed.

Goal Value For non-e-commerce goals, Google Analytics uses your assigned goal value to calculate ROI, Per Visit Value, and other revenue-related metrics. The goal value is a constant value that is applied to all goal-completed URLs for each goal.

A good way to value a goal is to determine how often the visitors who reach the goal become customers. If, for example, your sales team can close 10 percent of people who request to be contacted and your average transaction is $500, then you might assign $50 (10 percent of $500) to your Inquiry form sent goal. Conversely, if only 1 percent of mailing list sign-ups result in a sale, then you might assign only $5 to your Email sign-up goal.

Goal Funnel

If you are using the goal type URL Destination, you have the option to add a funnel. Define these by clicking Use Funnel and proceed to the section "The Funnel Setup Process." Otherwise, save your goal setup now.

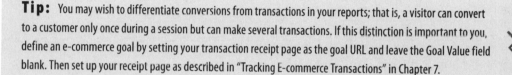

> **Note:** Monetizing goals is discussed in detail in "Monetizing a Non-E-commerce Website" in Chapter 11.

> **Tip:** You may wish to differentiate conversions from transactions in your reports; that is, a visitor can convert to a customer only once during a session but can make several transactions. If this distinction is important to you, define an e-commerce goal by setting your transaction receipt page as the goal URL and leave the Goal Value field blank. Then set up your receipt page as described in "Tracking E-commerce Transactions" in Chapter 7.

Events Defined as Goals

An alternative goal type is an event—a goal that is triggered when an event is matched. An example is shown in Figure 8.7 for a visitor who has watched a YouTube video to completion.

When tracking an event, you can configure up to four parameters—the event category, action, label, and value (the setup of event tracking is discussed in Chapter 7). Any of these can be used to trigger the event as matching a goal. When using multiple matches, as shown in Figure 8.7, the matching parameters must all occur for the goal to be triggered. That is, for this example, the event category name must equal YouTube *and* the action name must equal Completed. If only one of those parameters matches, the goal will not be captured.

An important difference in the setup of event goals, compared to other goal types, is that an event goal value can be set at the point the event is triggered within your pages as opposed to within the goal configuration area. This is useful if the goal value varies depending on your visitor's actions. For example, watching the same video in a different part of your website may have a higher value to your business.

By implementing an event value within your pages, as opposed to within the goal configuration area, you can use a *dynamic* goal value. If this describes your event tracking setup, select Use The Actual Event Value for the goal value section (Figure 8.7). Otherwise, you can set a constant value.

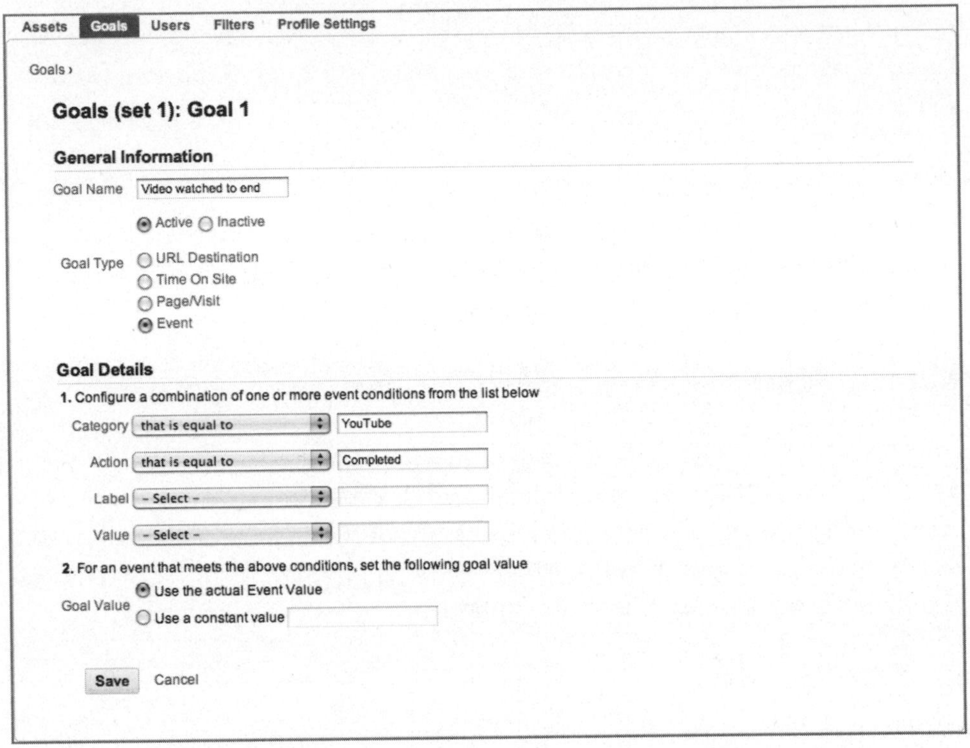

Figure 8.7 Configuring a video event as a goal

> **Tip:** If you are creating event values within your pages but do not wish to assign a goal value for your events, select Use A Constant Value and enter 0.

The Funnel Setup Process

If you are using the goal type URL Destination, you have the option to add a funnel. Use this if you have a well-defined path that you expect visitors to take on their way to your goal URL. A checkout process is an obvious e-commerce example, though you may also have funnels for non-e-commerce goals, such as a subscription sign-up.

You may specify up to 10 page URLs in a funnel. Defining these pages enables you to see which pages lead to goal abandonment and where visitors go next. For an e-commerce goal, these pages might be the Begin Checkout page, Shipping Address Information page, and Credit Card Information page—a four-step funnel, that is, three funnel steps plus the goal conversion. Each step of the funnel has its own conversion rate that you can focus on.

Use Funnels Where Appropriate

Not all URL Destination goals have funnels. That is, not all conversions are achieved by visitors following a clearly defined linear path. An obvious linear path to conversion is an e-commerce shopping cart. You should certainly configure a defined funnel to analyze such a process.

However, for non-e-commerce conversions, consider carefully whether a funnel is necessary. For example, if there are many paths to achieve a PDF download, then analyzing this with a funnel would be pointless at best and misleading at worst. It would make more sense to define the goal without a funnel. If knowing the path that leads to such downloads is a key element of measuring your website's success, then consider the Flow Visualizations report as discussed in Chapter 5, "Reports Explained."

Figure 8.8 shows two funnel configuration examples—one for a nontransactional site, where the goal is a PDF file download, and one for an e-commerce shopping cart. Notice for the e-commerce funnel example, I have ended the URL match for steps 1 and 2 with `?catid=` and `?prodid=` respectively. The `id` values, such as `www.mysite.com/shop/category.aspx?catid=101`, are not important for the funnel configuration. By omitting them, I am grouping together all product and category URLs. An example Funnel Visualization report is shown in Figure 8.9.

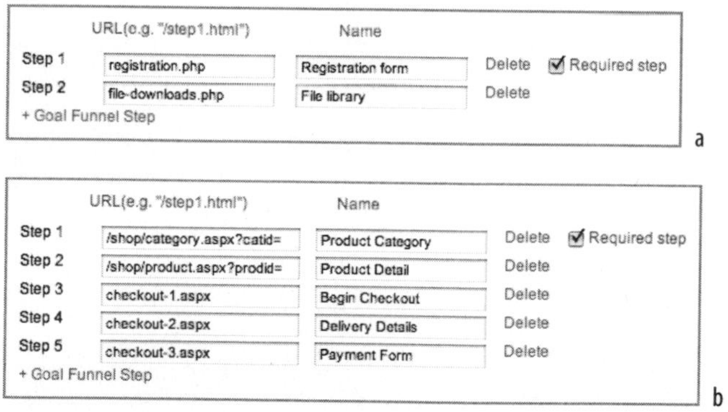
URL(e.g. "/step1.html")
Name
Step 1
registration.php
Registration form
Delete
Required step
Step 2
file-downloads.php
File library
Delete
+ Goal Funnel Step
a
URL(e.g. "/step1.html")
Name
Step 1
/shop/category.aspx?catid=
Product Category
Delete
Required step
Step 2
/shop/product.aspx?prodid=
Product Detail
Delete
Step 3
checkout-1.aspx
Begin Checkout
Delete
Step 4
checkout-2.aspx
Delivery Details
Delete
Step 5
checkout-3.aspx
Payment Form
Delete
+ Goal Funnel Step
b

Figure 8.8 (a) Example three-step funnel configuration for a nontransactional goal, and (b) example six-step funnel configuration for an e-commerce checkout. Note that the final goal page is not shown.

Note: Whichever match type you selected for URL Destination is continued throughout the funnel configuration. For example, if you selected Regular Expression Match, this is the same match type for each funnel step. Therefore, ensure that you check your funnel URLs for correctness—for example, escaping periods in filenames. See Appendix A for an overview of regular expressions.

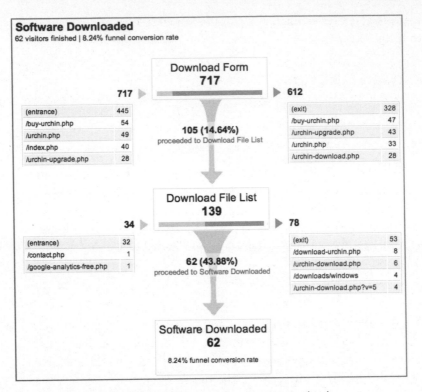

Software Downloaded
62 visitors finished | 8.24% funnel conversion rate

Download Form
717

717 ▷   612 ▷

(entrance)	445
/buy-urchin.php	54
/urchin.php	49
/index.php	40
/urchin-upgrade.php	28

(exit)	328
/buy-urchin.php	47
/urchin-upgrade.php	43
/urchin.php	33
/urchin-download.php	28

105 (14.64%)
proceeded to Download File List

Download File List
139

34 ▷   78 ▷

(entrance)	32
/contact.php	1
/google-analytics-free.php	1

(exit)	53
/download-urchin.php	8
/urchin-download.php	6
/downloads/windows	4
/urchin-download.php?v=5	4

62 (43.88%)
proceeded to Software Downloaded

Software Downloaded
62

8.24% funnel conversion rate

Figure 8.9 A three-step Funnel Visualization report for a nontransactional goal

Funnel Backfill Behavior

It is important to define a funnel only where a clear linear path exists and where funnel steps cannot be skipped. If a funnel page is skipped by a visitor, Google Analytics will backfill the missing data as if the visitor had gone through those steps. Consider a scenario in which you have four funnel steps: S1 > S2 > S3 > S4. A visitor entering the funnel at S2 and going directly to S4 will show as also progressing through S3 via the Google Analytics backfill. The backfill auto-completes any missing steps between the visitor's funnel entry point and last step.

What Is a Required Step?

As you can see in Figure 8.8, there is a check box labeled Required Step next to the first funnel step. If this check box is selected, users reaching your goal page without traveling through this funnel page will not be counted as conversions in the Funnel Visualization report. Hence, the required step can be an important differentiator.

For example, consider visitors accessing a password-protected area of your website. You wish to define two goals:

- New sign-ups for access to this area
- The login of existing users

Both sets of visitors complete their action by arriving on the same page—the password-protected home page. This means the goal URL page must be defined the same way for each circumstance. However, the initial step is different. Therefore, you should use the Required Step check box to differentiate the different types of goals in this scenario.

> **Note:** Using the required step to differentiate goals with the same URL will show only in reports that have funnel visualization in them. Other goal reports will show the same conversion rate for both examples because only the funnel path differentiates them.

Tracking Funnels for Which Every Step Has the Same URL

You may encounter a situation where you need to track a visitor's progress through a funnel that has the same URL for each step. For example, your sign-up funnel might look like this:

Step 1: Sign Up

```
www.mysite.com/sign_up.cgi
```

Step 2: Accept Agreement

```
www.mysite.com/sign_up.cgi
```

Step 3: Finish

```
www.mysite.com/sign_up.cgi
```

To get around this, call the _trackPageview function to track virtual pageviews within each step, as discussed in "Tracking Unreadable URLs with Virtual Pageviews," in Chapter 7. For example, within the GATC of the pages in question, you create virtual pageviews to be logged in Google Analytics as follows:

```
_gaq.push(['_trackPageview','/funnel_G1/step1.html'])
_gaq.push(['_trackPageview','/funnel_G1/step2.html'])
_gaq.push(['_trackPageview','/funnel_G1/step3.html'])
```

With these virtual pageviews now being logged instead of sign_up.cgi, you can configure each step of your funnel as follows:

Step 1: Sign Up

```
/funnel_G1/step1.html
```

Step 2: Accept Agreement

/funnel_G1/step2.html

Step 3: Finish

/funnel_G1/step3.html

Why Segmentation Is Important

For you to understand the importance of segmentation, we first need to examine how averages are used in web analytics. When discussing averages, we are generally referring to the arithmetic mean that is computed by adding a group of values together and dividing by the total number of values in the group. It's used in mathematics to approximate the statistical norm or expected value.

The arithmetic mean works well when the distribution under consideration is close to normal, that is, Gaussian or bell shaped. For normal distributions, the average value is also the most common (modal) value. For example, assuming a normal distribution for visitor time onsite, if the average time is calculated at 95 seconds, then it is also true to say the average visitor spends 95 seconds on your website. However, this is not true when the distribution is not normal—see Figure 8.10. That is, for the graphs labeled b and c, it is not true to say that the average visitor spends 95 seconds on your site. The concept of "average visitor" is not applicable unless the distribution is close to normal.

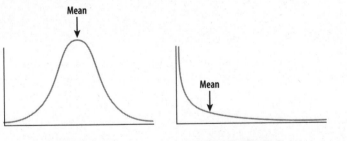

a) Normal distribution   b) Long tall distribution   c) A random distribution

Figure 8.10 Sample visitor distributions for time spent onsite

Figure 8.10 shows that for nonnormal distributions, a typical visitor will not exhibit the average (mean) behavior; in other words, not stay on the site for the mean length of time.

Plans based on average assumptions are wrong on average.

—FROM "THE FLAW OF AVERAGES" BY SAM SAVAGE, www.stanford
.edu/%7Esavage/faculty/savage/Flaw%20of%20averages.pdf

For the random distribution in the graph labeled c in Figure 8.10, quoting the mean value for the time spent onsite is misleading because the distribution indicates that many types of behavior are being exhibited. Perhaps the difference is indicating a mix of personas on your website—visitors, customers, blog readers, demographic differences, geographic differences. Whatever the reason, simply reporting an average is a blunt metric, and it is precisely the reason you rarely see averages reported in Google Analytics. When averages are reported, they are segmented—for example, shown for a specific page URL.

In summary, the mean is sensitive to outliers—data points that are numerically distant from the rest of the data. A frequent cause of outliers is a mixture of distributions, which may be distinct subpopulations (groups of visitors with different intentions). Therefore, when looking at averages, it is important to segment.

Within Google Analytics, there are three ways to segment your visitors:

- As you drill down through your reports (clicking data links)
- Using filters to provide a dedicated profile
- Using the Advanced Segments drop-down menu located at the top of your report screen

Drilling down into your data is intuitive and self-explanatory—as discussed in Chapter 4, "Using the Google Analytics Interface," and Chapter 5, "Reports Explained." Therefore, the next sections describe how to segment based on using profile filters or advanced segments.

Choosing Advanced Segments versus Profile Filters

Profile filters and advanced segments are complementary features to segment your visitors. Often I use both, first discovering segments within reports using the Advanced Segments menu. This is a quick and efficient method because I segment the data immediately and can look back at historical data using the same segment. Then if required, I use profile filters to create dedicated report sets just for that segment.

I consider profile filters a longer-term segmentation technique—a permanent way of segmenting visitors. Though profile filters can be changed or removed at any time, the main difference is that once data is segmented out, for example, removing the filter does not restore historical unfiltered data. The removed segment is permanently lost. Advanced segments, on the other hand, allow you to apply and remove segments *without* removing data. Table 8.2 compares the usage of each and suggests when one method may be more appropriate than the other.

▶ **Table 8.2** Advanced segments versus profile filters

Advanced Segments	Profile Filters
Modify a report view at the visit level.	Modify incoming data at the pageview level to create separate profiles (reports).
Applied to current and historical data.	Applied only to new data from the time the filter is created.
Instantaneous results. Once they're created, you can view segmented data in your reports immediately.	Aimed at longer-term usage where once set, the segment is unlikely to change.
Allow the use of conditional values on metrics, such as, for example, greater than, less than.	Only text string matches can be included. No numerical conditionals are available.
Set up by report users, making them safe. No data can be lost.	Set up by administrators because data can be permanently deleted.
Can test a hypothesis immediately.	Take 3–4 hours for data to populate reports.
Combine statements to meet multiple conditions.	Use cascading filters for combination effect.
Set on a per-user basis. Segments can be shared with other report users but cannot be used to hide data.	Set on a per-profile basis, therefore access to segmented data can be controlled separately from other wdata.
Regular expression statements are not limited, though the total combined for a segment with multiple statements must not exceed 30,000 characters.	Regular expression statements are limited to 255 characters.

In summary, use profile filters to remove "noise" segments from your reports, such as your own staff visitors or your agency, which can be excluded from your target audience. Apply profile filters when the segment defined is a long-term one and unlikely to change—for example, your country offices wish to analyze only visits from within their region, or your support department wishes to focus only on help desk visitors. Use profile filters when you wish to control the level of access, such as providing paid search data to an external agency.

Conversely, use advanced segments when you are drilling down to understand visitor behavior—for example, comparing the performance of a particular marketing campaign against another, viewing mobile visitors versus desktop visitors, or determining whether customers browse differently from noncustomers. Apply advanced segments when you need to use conditional operators, such as visitors who spend more than 30 seconds on site or visitors who spend more than $100 per transaction.

Profile Segments: Segmenting Visitors Using Filters

Everything discussed so far in this book has been concerned with the collection of good-quality data—ensuring that the report numbers are as comprehensive, accurate, and informative as possible. We will now consider the removal of data using filters.

Profile filters are applied to the information coming into your account to manipulate the final data in order to provide specialized profiles (reports). By filtering, you gain a better understanding of visitor types to avoid interpreting an average of averages. In this case, think of it as segmenting out the "noise," or outliers. For example, you may want to remove visits to your website from your own employees because the number of such visits can be significant, especially if your website is set as the default home page in their browsers.

In addition to having a data-cleansing role, profile filters can provide dedicated segmented reports. For example, if you run an overseas office, they may wish to have their own siloed set of reports relevant to their specific market, such as Asian visitors only or UK visitors only. That way, their conversion rates and ROI metrics will more accurately reflect their true value rather than including visits from other regions.

To segment your visitors into separate profiles, you apply filters to the data. Filters are applied on new data only. That is, a profile filter cannot affect historical data, and it is not possible to reprocess your old data through the new filter.

> **Note:** Profile filters are not the same as table filters, as discussed in Chapter 4, "Using the Google Analytics Interface."

> **Best Practice Tip: Keep a Profile without Filters**
>
> Always keep raw data intact. That is, keep your original profile and apply new filters to a duplicate profile in your account. That way, if you make a mistake in applying a new filter, you always have the original profile to fall back on.
>
> Using this method, data will be imported simultaneously into both your original and the new report profile. Note that any existing filters applied to the first profile will not be copied, so you will need to reapply them using the Filter Manager. Creating new profiles is discussed in Chapter 6.

Creating a Profile Filter

To create a profile filter, log in to your Google Analytics account as an administrator, click the settings icon (top right of the report screen) for the profile you wish to add a filter to, and then select the Filters menu tab as shown in Figure 8.11. To create a new filter, click + New Filter to take you to the screen in Figure 8.12. Note that once you have created your filter, you will be able to apply it to other profiles within your account.

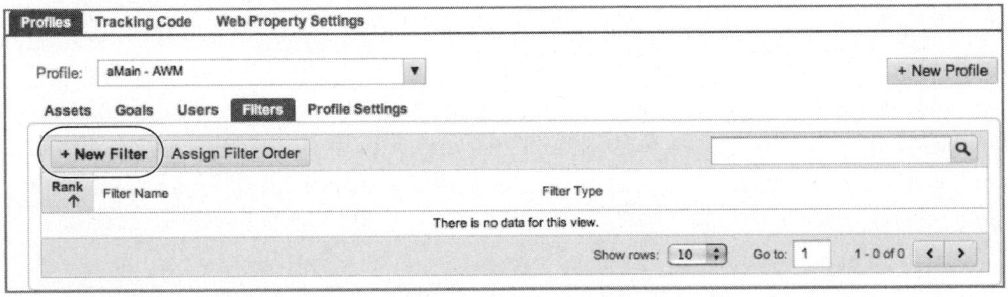

Figure 8.11 Adding a new profile filter

Google Analytics provides you with predefined filter types as well as numerous options for a custom filter:

- Predefined filters provide a quick and easy way to accomplish some of the most common filtering tasks, as shown in Table 8.3. Creating a predefined filter is covered online in "How do I create a predefined filter?"

  www.google.com/support/googleanalytics/bin/answer.py?answer=55496

- A custom filter allows for more advanced manipulation of data, and these are listed in Table 8.4. Creating a custom filter is covered online in "How do I create a custom filter?"

  www.google.com/support/googleanalytics/bin/answer.py?answer=55492

A custom filter is used in most of the following filter examples.

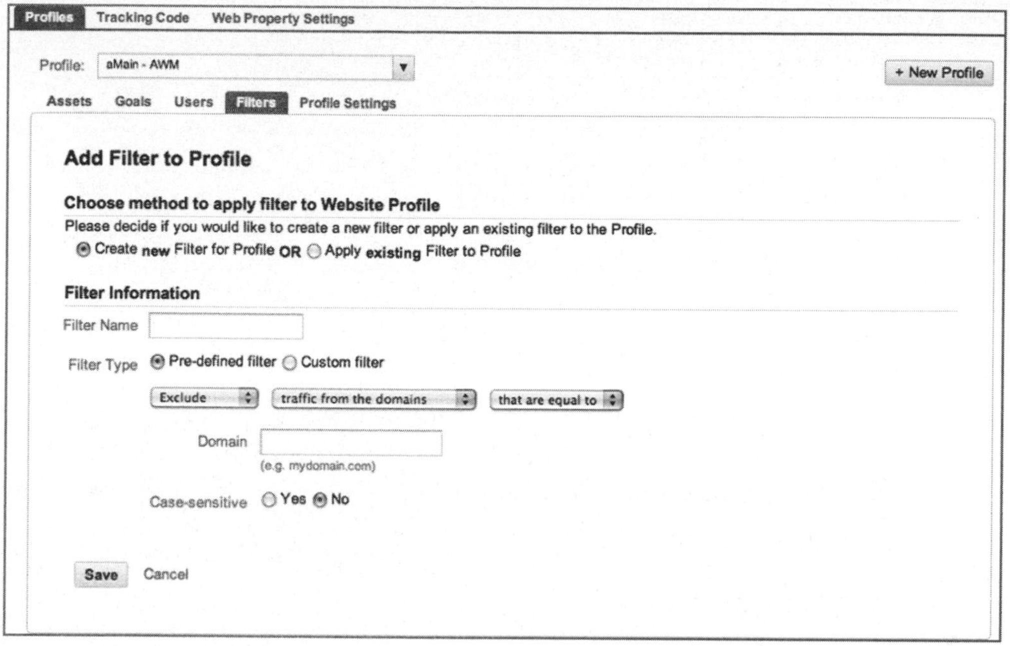

Figure 8.12 Creating a new profile filter

► **Table 8.3** Predefined filters

Filter Type	Filter Name	Description
Include and exclude	Traffic from the domains	Includes or excludes traffic from a specific domain, such as an ISP or company network.
Include and exclude	Traffic from the IP address	Includes or excludes clicks from certain sources. You can enter a single IP address or a range of addresses.
Include and exclude	Traffic to the subdirectories	Includes or excludes visitors viewing only a particular subdirectory on your website, such as `www.mysite.com/helpdesk`.

► **Table 8.4** Custom filters

Custom Filter	Description
Exclude Pattern	This type of filter excludes log file lines (hits) that match the filter pattern. Matching lines are ignored in their entirety; for example, a filter that excludes Netscape will also exclude all other information in that log line, such as visitor, path, referral, and domain information.
Include Pattern	This type of filter includes logfile lines (hits) that match the filter pattern. All non-matching hits are ignored, and any data in nonmatching hits is unavailable.
Uppercase/ Lowercase	Converts the contents of the field into all uppercase or all lowercase characters. These filters affect only letters, not special characters or numbers.

Continues

Custom Filter	Description
Search & Replace	This simple filter can be used to search for a pattern within a field and replace it with an alternate form.
Advanced	This type of filter enables you to build a field from one or two other fields. The filtering engine will apply the expressions defined in the two Extract fields and then construct a field using the Constructor expression. See Chapter 9, "Google Analytics Customizations," for examples of advanced custom filters in use.

Understanding Filter Logic

If the filter being applied is an exclude filter and the pattern matches a data record, then the pageview entry is thrown away and Google Analytics continues processing with the next data record. If the pattern does not match, then the next filter is applied (if there is one) to that data record. This means that you can create either a single exclude filter with multiple patterns separated by pipe characters (|) or multiple exclude filters with a single pattern for each. Here are some examples:

Single exclude filter Exclude all traffic from 217.158.66.33 | 21.7.158.67.1

In English this means exclude traffic from one IP address OR the other. This can also be achieved using two separate filters processed one after the other:

Filter 1 of 2 Exclude all traffic from 217.158.66.33

Filter 2 of 2 Exclude all traffic from 21.7.158.67.1

 Note: Filter patterns must not be longer than 255 characters. An overview of constructing regular expressions is given in Appendix A.

Include filters are applied with the reverse logic. When an include filter is applied, the data entry is thrown away if the pattern does *not* match the data. This is an important distinction if you apply multiple include filters because then the data entry must match *every applied include filter* in order for the data entry to be saved.

For example, if you apply an include filter for your internal (staff) visitors using your network IP address, it would not make sense to then add an additional include filter for, say, all Google search visitors. The combination will not result in reports of internal visitors plus Google visitors. The report will be only for internal visitors, assuming this filter is applied first, because everything else is discarded during processing at that point.

As for the case of exclude filters, to include multiple patterns for a specific field, create a single include filter that contains all of the individual expressions separated by pipe characters (|).

Custom Filters: Available Fields

Building your own custom filter allows you go way beyond the default filters preconfigured in Google Analytics. Essentially, you can filter on any available data field present in your reports.

Table 8.5 and Table 8.6 list all available fields and their purposes. Table 8.5 lists the regular fields—those automatically captured by Google Analytics—and Table 8.6 lists the user-defined variables whose values are determined by your implementation of Google Analytics, such as, for example, landing page campaign parameters, e-commerce fields, and so on.

Examples of using these for a custom filter are discussed in the next section, "Five Common Profile Filters."

▶ **Table 8.5** Regular field list

Filter Name	Description
Request URI	Includes the relative URL (the piece of the URL after the hostname). For example, for `http://www.mysite.com/requestURL/index.html?sample=text`, the request URI is `/requestURL/index.html?sample=text`.
Hostname	The full domain name of the page requested. For example, for `http://www.mysite.com/requestURL/index.html?sample=text`, the hostname is `www.mysite.com`.
Referral	The external referrer, if any. This field is populated only for the initial external referral at the beginning of a session.
Page Title	The contents of the `<title>` tags in the HTML of the delivered page.
Visitor Browser Program	The name of the browser program used by the visitor.
Visitor Browser Version	The version of the browser program used by the visitor.
Visitor Operating System Platform	The visitor's operating system platform.
Visitor Operating System Version	The visitor's operating system version.
Visitor Language Settings	The language setting in the visitor's browser preferences.
Visitor Screen Resolution	The resolution of the visitor's screen, as determined from the browser program.
Visitor Screen Colors	The color capabilities of the visitor's screen, as determined from the browser program.

Continues

Filter Name	Description
Visitor Java Enabled?	Whether Java is enabled in the visitor's browser program.
Visitor Flash version	The version of Flash installed in the visitor's browser program.
Visitor IP Address	The visitor's IP address.
Visitor Geographic Domain	The visitor's ISP (for example, aol.com or aol.co.uk for AOL users), derived from the geographic database.
Visitor ISP Organization	The ISP organization registered to the IP address of the user. This is the ISP the visitor is using to access the Internet.
Visitor Country	The visitor's geographic country location obtained by information registered with the IP address.
Visitor Region	The visitor's geographic region or state location, obtained by information registered with the IP address.
Visitor City	The visitor's geographic city location, obtained by information registered with the IP address.
Visitor Connection Speed	Deprecated. The visitor's connection speed, obtained by information registered with the IP address.
Visitor Type	Either New Visitor or Returning Visitor, based on Google Analytics identifiers.
Custom Field 1	An empty, custom field for storage of values during filter computation. Data is not stored permanently in this field but can be used by subsequent filters.
Custom Field 2	An empty, custom field for storage of values during filter computation. Data is not stored permanently in this field but can be used by subsequent filters.

▶ **Table 8.6** User-defined variables

Filter Name	Description
Campaign Source	The resource that provided the click (e.g., Google). This variable is automatically generated for AdWords hits when auto-tagging is turned on through the AdWords interface.
Campaign Medium	The medium used to generate the request (e.g., organic, cpc, or ppc). This variable is automatically generated for AdWords hits when auto-tagging is turned on through the AdWords interface.
Campaign Name	The name given to the marketing campaign or used to differentiate the campaign source (e.g., October Campaign). This variable is automatically generated for AdWords hits when auto-tagging is turned on through the AdWords interface.
Campaign Term	The term used to generate the ad from the referring source or campaign source, such as a keyword. This variable is automatically generated for AdWords hits when auto-tagging is turned on through the AdWords interface.
Campaign Content	Typically defines multivariate or split testing or is used to disseminate campaign target variables in an advertising campaign. This variable is automatically generated for AdWords hits when auto-tagging is turned on through the AdWords interface.

Continues

Filter Name	Description
Campaign Code	Can be used to refer to a campaign lookup table (not yet implemented in Google Analytics).
User Defined	Deprecated. A custom variable name for use by the end user.
E-Commerce Transaction ID	A unique ID variable correlated with a designated transaction.
E-Commerce Transaction Country	Deprecated. Used to designate the country defined by the transaction process; obtained by information registered with the IP address.
E-Commerce Transaction Region	Deprecated. Used to designate the region defined by the transaction process; obtained by information registered with the IP address.
E-Commerce Transaction City	Deprecated. Represents the city where the commerce transaction occurred; obtained by information registered with the IP address.
E-Commerce Store or Order Location	Describes the store or affiliated site processing the transaction (e.g., US store, UK store, Affiliate123).
E-Commerce Item Name	The name of the item purchased.
E-Commerce Item Code	The identifier or code number corresponding to the item purchased. Commonly referred to as the stock-keeping unit (SKU) code.

Note: There are a number of fields listed in Table 8.5 and Table 8.6 that are now deprecated. I list them here for completeness because the fields still exist in the current profile filter configuration screen.

Five Common Profile Filters

The following list highlights, in no particular order, the five most common filters applied by most users of Google Analytics. The majority are custom filters:

Include only your website's traffic At the very least you should apply this filter to all your profiles.

Exclude certain known visitors For example, exclude your employees, your web agency, and so on.

Segment by geographical location Make it easy for your country managers by creating profiles of visitors relevant only to them.

Segment by visitor campaign, medium, or referrer source Visitors from different referrers may have different objectives.

Segment by content Visitors viewing particular sections of your website may display different behavior, such as, for example, purchase versus support sections.

These filters are discussed in more detail in the following sections. Before studying these, you should be familiar with regular expressions—see in Appendix A, "Regular Expression Overview."

Including Only Your Website's Traffic

This custom filter ensures that your data, and *only* your data, is collected into your Google Analytics profile. For example, it is possible for another person to hijack your GATC, placing the same code onto their own pages. This can happen deliberately or accidentally and is incredibly easy to do. A person simply copies your GATC by viewing your HTML source code. The consequence is that third-party traffic contaminates your results. Using the include filter shown in Figure 8.13 results in only traffic to mysite.com being reported. Note the backslash character (\) used to escape the delimiter character (.). This is an example of using regular expression syntax. Simply substitute mysite.com for your domain using the escape character for each . in your domain.

Assets	Goals	Users	**Filters**	Profile Settings

Add Filter to Profile

Choose method to apply filter to Website Profile
Please decide if you would like to create a new filter or apply an existing filter to the Profile.
◉ Create new Filter for Profile **OR** ○ Apply existing Filter to Profile

Filter Information

Filter Name   Only mysite.com traffic

Filter Type   ○ Pre-defined filter ◉ Custom filter

    ○ Exclude
    ◉ Include
    ○ Lowercase
    ○ Uppercase
    ○ Search and Replace
    ○ Advanced

Filter Field   Hostname

Filter Pattern   mysite\.com

Case-sensitive   ○ Yes ◉ No

Figure 8.13 Filter to include only your website's traffic

Of course, it may be desirable to collect data from multiple websites you control into one profile. In that case, add the multiple domains in the filter pattern separated with pipe characters—for example, mysite\.com|mysite\.co\.uk.

Tip: In my view, the filter to include only your website's traffic is the most important filter to apply to your profiles and is a required first step for a best practice configuration. It ensures that your data remains clean and prevents GATC hijacking—spammers use it to get their URLs in your reports in the hope you will click through to view ads. If you apply only one filter to your account, make sure it is this one.

Excluding Certain Known Visitors

Excluding visits from staff, your search marketing agency, or any known third parties, such as your web developers, is an important step when creating your profiles. These visitors generate a relatively high number of pageviews in areas that will greatly impact key metrics, such as your conversion rates.

For example, employees who have their browser home page set to the company website will show in your reports as returning visitors every time they open their browser—and most likely as one-page visitors. Remember that the GATC deliberately breaks through any caching, so it's important to exclude employee visits from those of potential customers. Similarly, web developers heavily test checkout systems for troubleshooting purposes. These will also trigger GATC page requests, and most likely these will be for your goal-conversion pages. You should therefore exclude all such visits from your reports.

Excluding known visitors is straightforward if the visitor connects to the Internet via a fixed IP address. If this is the case, select the predefined filter Exclude Traffic From The IP Addresses from the Filter Manager, as shown in Figure 8.14a.

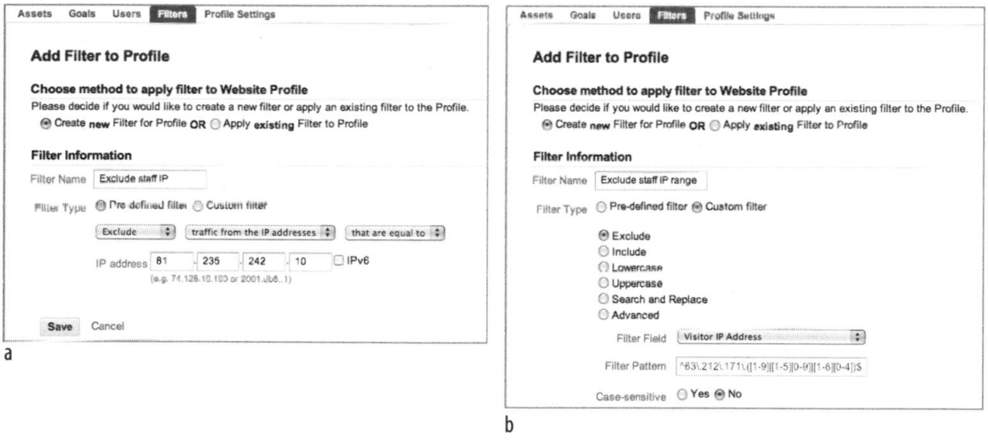

Figure 8.14 Excluding visitors from a known IP address (a) for a single IP address and (b) for an IP range

The example shown in Figure 8.14a is suitable for a single IP address or when you have a handful of IP addresses to exclude (set up multiple exclude filters for this). However, for an IP range, use a custom filter with a regular expression. For example, excluding the IP range 63.212.171.1–64 is shown as a custom filter in Figure 8.14b. For clarity, the regular expression is ^63\.212\.171\.([1-9]|[1-5][0-9]|[1-6][0-4])$. See Appendix A for an overview of regular expressions.

Tip: To help you build regular expressions for IP ranges, Google has an excellent IP Address Range Tool you can use at www.google.com/support/analyticshelp/bin/answer.py?answer=1034771.

What If Visitors Do Not Have a Fixed IP Address?

This is often the case for home users, where the Internet service provider (ISP) assigns a different IP address each time the home user connects; this can also happen during a connected session. The solution is to use a custom variable (_setCustomVar) in conjunction with a custom exclude filter. The Custom Variables feature is described in Chapter 9 in "Labeling Visitors, Sessions, and Pages."

The principle is that you direct known visitors you want to exclude to a hidden page (not used by regular visitors) that contains a JavaScript label within the GATC. The label is stored as a persistent cookie on that visitor's computer and forms part of their pageview data. An exclude filter is then used to remove any pageview data that contains this label.

To assign a custom label to visitors, call the function _setCustomVar within the GATC on your hidden page as follows:

```
<script type="text/javascript">
var _gaq = _gaq || [];_
_gaq.push(['_setAccount', 'UA-12345-1']);
_gaq.push(['_setCustomVar',1,'Exclude Visitor','Dynamic IP',1]);
_gaq.push(['_trackPageview']);

(function() {
var ga = document.createElement('script');
ga.type = 'text/javascript'; ga.async = true;
ga.src = ('https:' == document.location.protocol ? 'https://ssl' : ➡
'http://www') + '.google-analytics.com/ga.js';
var s = document.getElementsByTagName('script')[0];
s.parentNode.insertBefore(ga, s);
})();
</script>
```

In this way, only one visit to, for example, www.mysite.com/hiddenpage.htm is required to label the visitor until the cookie expires (24 months)—assuming the label cookie is not overwritten or deleted. Note that in this example, _setCustomVar is called with a name of Exclude Visitor and value (label) of Dyanmic IP. However, any value can be used for these, though it pays to have an easy-to-follow format. With each pageview from your dynamic IP visitor now labeled, you are ready to apply the filter required to exclude those visits from your profile (Figure 8.15).

 Note: The index of the custom variable used in this example is set to 1. You will need to ensure that this index is free and not being used for any other custom variable, otherwise it may be overwritten. You can check what custom variables are being set by viewing your Visitors > Demographics > Custom Variables reports.

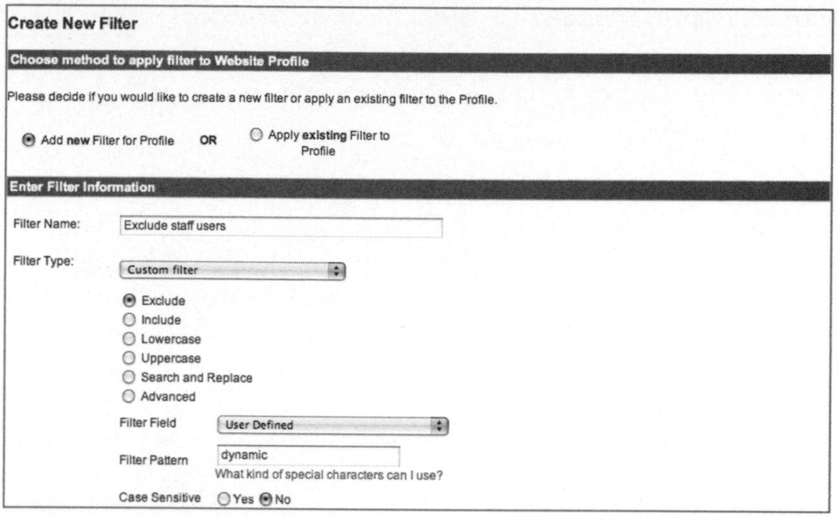

Figure 8.15 Excluding labeled visitors

Segmenting by Geographical Location

Google Analytics performs an excellent job of showing you the countries from which your visitors are accessing your website. It even groups them into regions (continents, such as Americas, Europe, Asia, Oceania, Africa) and subregions (Northern Europe, Central Europe, Eastern Europe, Southern Europe). For example, refer to Chapter 5. However, if your organization operates specifically in certain markets, you may want to create a profile that focuses on reporting visitors from just those countries. For example, North America (Canada and the United States) or BRIC Region (Brazil, Russia, India, China) can be included in a separate profile; the latter is shown by the filter in Figure 8.16.

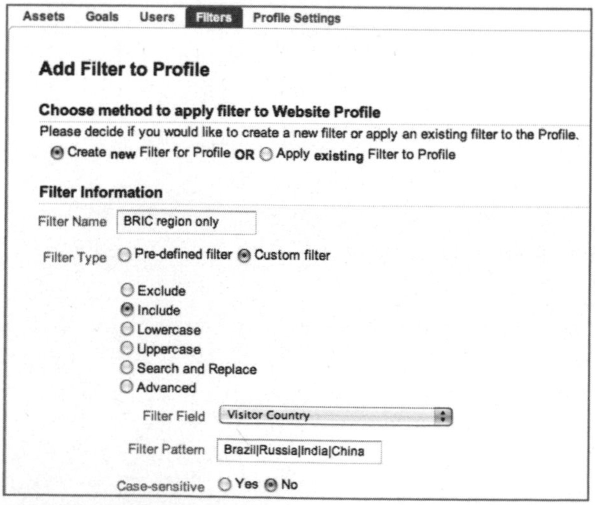

Figure 8.16 Segmenting visitors by country

By this method, country managers can better focus on the metrics without having to constantly remove out irrelevant visits. For clarity, the regular expression is Brazil|Russia|India|China. See Appendix A for an overview of regular expressions.

Segmenting by Campaign, Medium, or Referrer Source

As with the use of other filters discussed, Google Analytics already does an excellent job of displaying different campaigns, mediums, or source referrers. However, in some scenarios it can be helpful to have a profile with dedicated reports for them to help you optimize them better. For example, if you have a search marketing agency helping you with paid search, you may wish to isolate just your paid search visitors for their view. Similarly, if you employ an email marketing agency, you can isolate just email referrals. Having a separate profile gives you control over the report access, allowing you to filter out noise and protect other potentially confidential data.

How you construct this filter depends on how you have set up your campaign landing page URLs (see "Campaign Tracking" in Chapter 7). The values you assigned for utm_source, utm_medium, and utm_campaign need to match the following filter fields:

- Campaign Name
- Campaign Source
- Campaign Medium

To filter Google-only visitors, both paid and nonpaid, into a separate profile, apply the filter shown in Figure 8.17.

If you wish to track AdWords-only visitors, and this is the only paid search network you are running, apply the filter as shown in Figure 8.18. (I have assumed you have auto-tagging enabled in your AdWords account.)

If you are running other paid search networks (Microsoft adCenter, Yahoo! Search Marketing, and so on) and they are labeled as utm_medium = cpc, you will need to apply both filters (shown in Figure 8.17 and Figure 8.18) in order.

Assets   Goals   Users   **Filters**   Profile Settings

Add Filter to Profile

Choose method to apply filter to Website Profile

Please decide if you would like to create a new filter or apply an existing filter to the Profile.

◉ Create **new** Filter for Profile **OR** ○ Apply **existing** Filter to Profile

Filter Information

Filter Name   Google visitors only

Filter Type   ○ Pre-defined filter ◉ Custom filter

○ Exclude
◉ Include
○ Lowercase
○ Uppercase
○ Search and Replace
○ Advanced

Filter Field   [Campaign Source ▼]

Filter Pattern   google

Case-sensitive   ○ Yes ◉ No

Figure 8.17   Filter to include only Google visitors

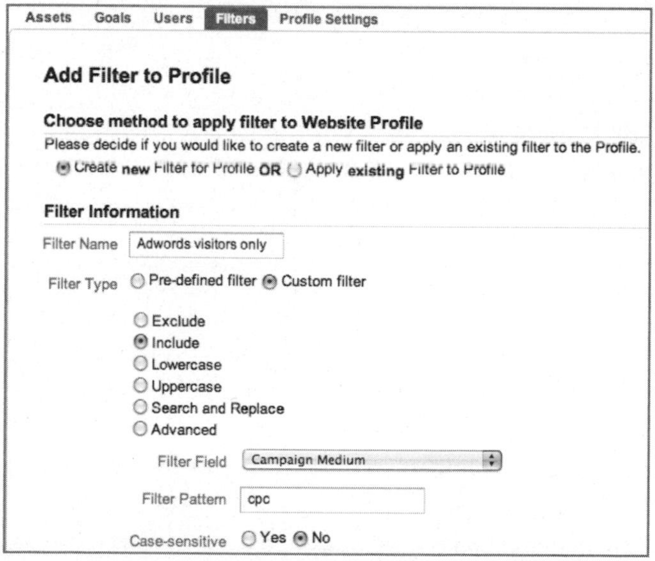

Assets   Goals   Users   **Filters**   Profile Settings

Add Filter to Profile

Choose method to apply filter to Website Profile

Please decide if you would like to create a new filter or apply an existing filter to the Profile.

◉ Create **new** Filter for Profile **OR** ○ Apply **existing** Filter to Profile

Filter Information

Filter Name   Adwords visitors only

Filter Type   ○ Pre-defined filter ◉ Custom filter

○ Exclude
◉ Include
○ Lowercase
○ Uppercase
○ Search and Replace
○ Advanced

Filter Field   [Campaign Medium ▼]

Filter Pattern   cpc

Case-sensitive   ○ Yes ◉ No

Figure 8.18   Filter to include only AdWords visitors

Note: If you tag all other pay-per-click campaigns, such as Yahoo! Search Marketing, Microsoft adCenter, Miva, and so on, with utm_medium=ppc, then the filter shown in Figure 8.18 on its own would be sufficient to segment Google AdWords visitors from other paid search networks. I use this technique because Google AdWords is so prevalent for online marketing. Being able to compare AdWords visitors against all other pay-per-click networks as a whole can be very useful.

Figure 8.19 shows how to segment only email visitors—that is, those visitors who have clicked a link to your website within an email message, assuming you set up such links as `utm_medium=email`.

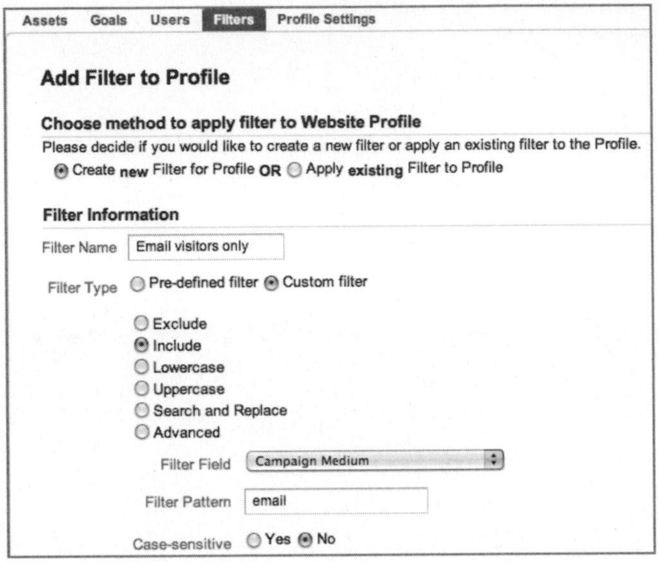

Figure 8.19   Filter to include only email visitors

As you can see, segmenting by campaign, source, or medium is as simple as knowing what these values are in your corresponding landing page URLs and then applying them as field values to your include and exclude filters.

Segmenting by Content

Often within one website you will be trying to satisfy the needs of very different visitors, such as, for example, product purchase versus product support or corporate information versus customer information. Effectively measuring such different needs requires the setting of very different goals for each section, hence the creation of separate profiles using filters. Figure 8.20 is an example filter that segments by content—in this case, a support blog.

Of course, the success of this filter depends on you having a well-ordered website directory structure on which to filter content. If you do not, it is possible to achieve a virtual structure by using virtual pageviews, as described in "`_trackPageview`: The Google Analytics Workhorse," in Chapter 7.

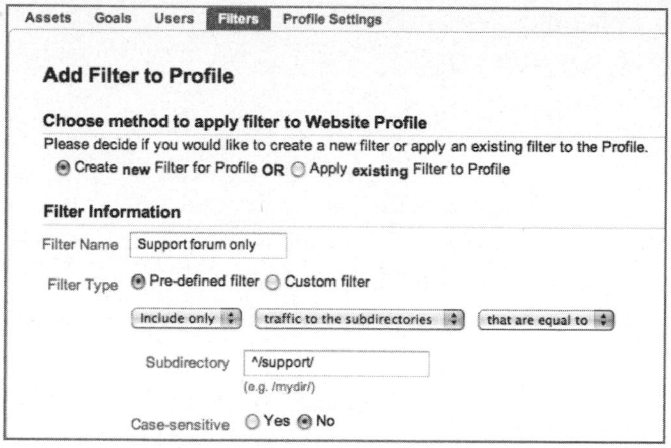

Figure 8.20 Filter to include only blog visitors

Assigning a Filter Order

By default, a profile's filters are applied to the incoming data in the order in which the filters were added. However, you can easily modify the order from your Profile Settings > Filters page, using the Assign Filter Order button from within your profile settings (shown in Figure 8.11). This shows the current filter order with the ability to move any filter up or down in the list (see Figure 8.21). The order in which filters are applied is important, for example, if the filters described in Figure 8.17 and Figure 8.18 are to be combined.

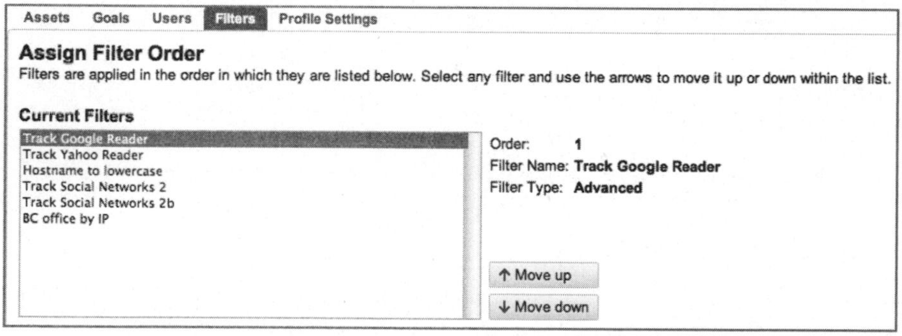

Figure 8.21 Assigning filter order

Report Segments: Segmenting Visitors Using Advanced Segments

The Advanced Segments menu allows you to segment your data *within* your reports. Unlike with profile filters, you do not have to create separate profiles for an advanced segment because it leaves your original data untouched. Whereas profile filters modify data on the pageview level, advanced segments change a report's view of the data at the visit level.

Note: To reiterate, advanced segments work on entire visits. For example, if you create an advanced segment equal to "Page Title matches *X*," the result shows you all visits in which pages with the title *X* were viewed, including all other pageviews that occurred during those visits.

The majority of Google Analytics reports contain an Advanced Segments drop-down menu at the top left of the screen (it's labeled O in Figure 4.4). By default, All Visits is selected. If you click this option, the area beneath it expands, as shown in Figure 8.22. This is where you can select, create, and manage your advanced segments.

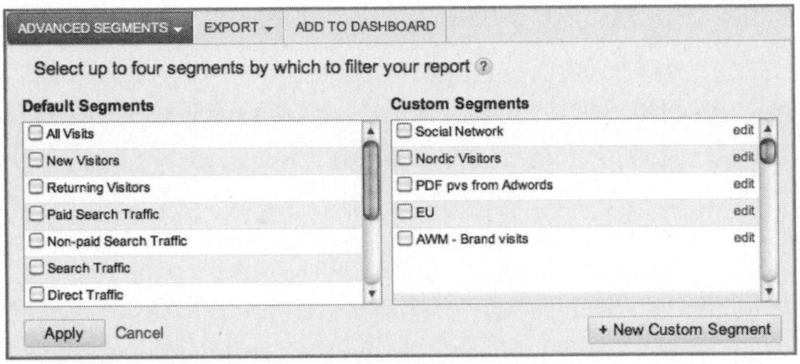

Figure 8.22 Advanced Segments management area

As you can see from Figure 8.22, two options are available: Default Segments includes segments that are prebuilt and ready for immediate use; Custom Segments allows you create your own advanced segment for specific needs. The Custom Segments area will be empty if you have not previously created any.

Default Advanced Segments

As the name suggests, Google has included a number of prebuilt advanced segments for you to use:

All Visits No segmentation applied.

New Visitors Visitors who have not been to your site before, assuming they have not deleted their Google Analytics cookies since their last visit, or returning visitors using a different computer or browser. Definition: Visitor type matches exactly "New Visitor."

Returning Visitors Visitors who have previously viewed your site using the same device and browser. Definition: Visitor type matches exactly "Returning Visitor."

Paid Search Traffic Definition: Visitor referral medium matches exactly any of the following: cpc, ppc, cpa, cpm, cpv, or cpp.

Non-paid Search Traffic Any visit whose referral medium is set to organic. Definition: Visitor medium matches exactly "organic."

Search Traffic Both paid and nonpaid searches. Definition: Visitor referral medium matches exactly any of the following: cpc, ppc, cpa, cpm, cpv, cpp, or organic.

Direct Traffic Visitors who typed your web URL directly or used a browser bookmark to arrive at your site. These could also be visits missing campaign information. See Chapter 7 for a description of campaign tracking. Definition: Visitor referral medium matches (none).

Referral Traffic Visitors who followed a link from other site (not a recognized search engine) to arrive at yours. Definition: Visitor referral medium matches exactly "referral."

Visits with Conversions Your highest-value visitors. Definition: Visits with total goal completions greater than 0.

Visits with Transactions Your customers. Definition: Visits with transactions greater than 0.

Mobile Traffic Visits from smartphones and tablet devices. Definition: Mobile matches exactly "Yes."

Non-bounce Visits Visits that consisted of more than one page or one page plus an event. See Chapter 7 for a definition of event tracking. Definition: Visits with bounce equal to 0.

This is not intended to be an exhaustive list, though it is very handy for common segmentation requirements. Check off the segments you want to select—currently limited to a maximum of four at any one time, and click Apply to finish. Your graph and tables reflect the segmented data, as shown in Figure 8.23.

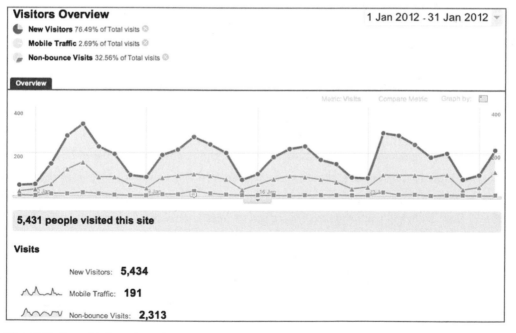

Figure 8.23 Comparing three advanced segments

Custom Advanced Segments

Although the default segments are useful, the real power of this feature is in its ability for you to be creative and discover the segments that are important to you. To create your own custom segment, from the screen shown in Figure 8.22, select + New Custom Segment. For this example, we will create a custom segment of *visits with two or more unique purchases* (purchased 2 or more unique items in their transaction). Follow these steps, as shown in Figure 8.24:

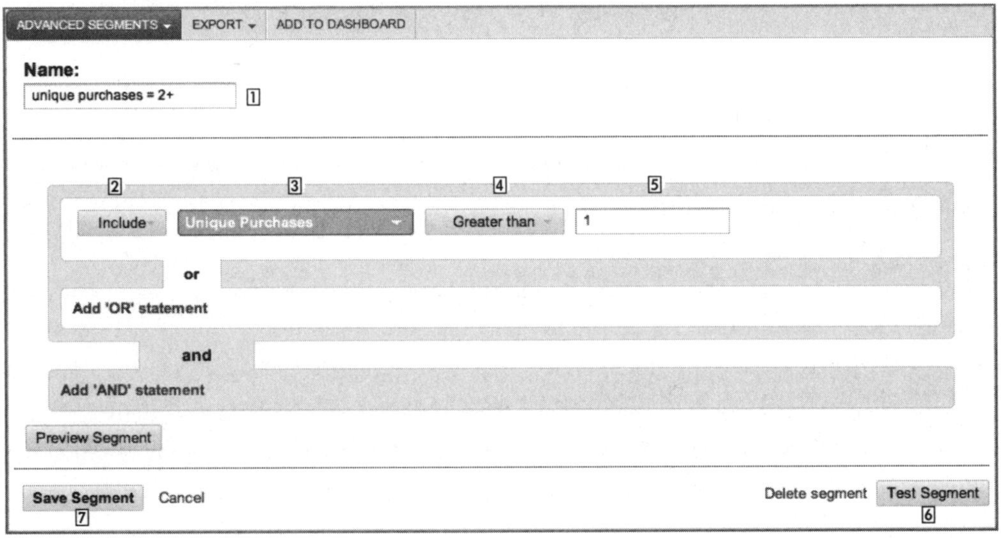

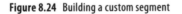

Figure 8.24 Building a custom segment

1. Name your segment with an informative name.

2. Select Include as the segment type.

3. Scroll to the Unique Purchases metric in the dimension/metric drop-down menu (the list is alphabetically sorted), or search for the word *unique* in the query field at the top of the list.

4. Select the Unique Purchases metric and set the condition to Greater Than.

5. Enter the comparison value for the segment. In this example, enter **1** in the value field.

6. Test each segment to make sure conditions make sense for the segment you defined. Click Test Segment to view the effect once the advanced segment is applied.

7. Assuming the test is successful, save your new segment.

Once saved, your new advanced segment is available to use as a check box in the Custom Segments area, shown in Figure 8.22. You can manage (edit, copy, delete) your custom segments from your profile settings page, under Assets, as shown in Figure 8.25.

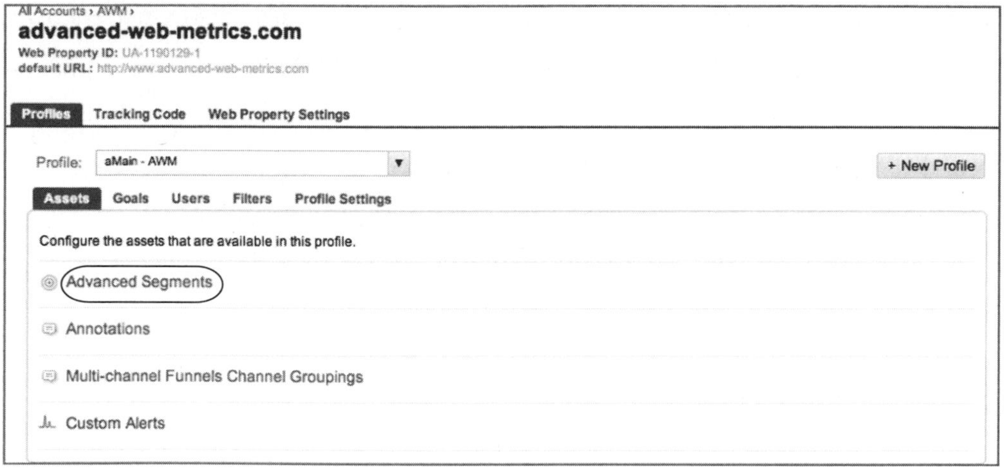

Figure 8.25 Managing your custom segments

Dimensions versus Metrics

Two types of data are represented in Google Analytics reports: dimensions and metrics (refer to Figure 4.5). Dimensions are typically listed in the left column vertically and metrics are typically listed along the top horizontally. Dimensions are text strings that describe an item. Think of them as names, such as page URL, page title, hostname, browser type, connection speed, transaction ID, product name, and so on. Metrics are numbers such as, for example, time on page, time on site, bounce rate, and purchase total. The conditional operators less than and greater than can be applied only to metrics.

Example Custom Segments

Advanced segments can be incredibly powerful when it comes to drilling down into your data. It can seem like an endless supply of permutations and combinations is available. Which specific advanced segments meet your needs will be determined by your website type (lead generation, e-commerce, corporate information, content publisher, and so on) and the value such segments bring to your organization. The following four examples are ones that I commonly use.

Segmenting Customers from Visitors

Segments that differentiate your customer visits from those that are not customers are important because often you will wish to analyze these two visitor types separately. You have two options to achieve this. The simplest approach for a transactional website is to segment visitors who purchase during their visit. A default segment is available for this: Visits with Transactions. As described earlier, this is defined as visits where the number of transactions is greater than zero.

However, an improvement on this is to segment visitors who have purchased from your website at *any* time during their relationship with you. You achieve this by applying a visitor-scoped label at the point of their purchase confirmation. Essentially, a persistent cookie is set when a purchase is made—for example, purchaser—and this is updated for any subsequent purchases. By this method you can segment your customers and view their behavior on your site, even if they do not purchase, by applying the custom segment shown in Figure 8.26.

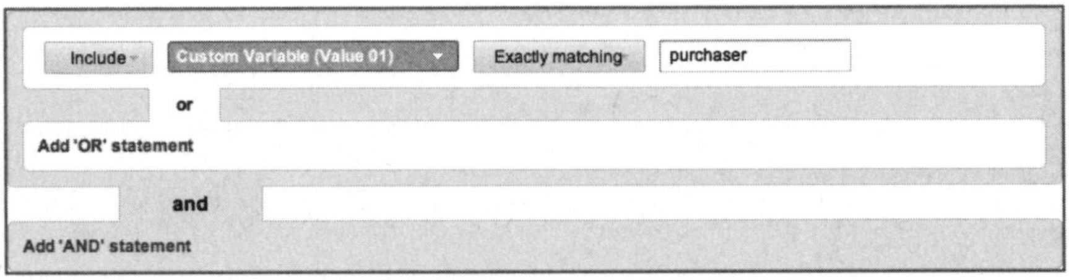

Figure 8.26 A custom segment to differentiate e-commerce customers

The method is also applicable for a nontransactional site. That is, set a visitor-scoped label at the point of an engagement that is a strong indicator for them becoming a customer (for example, when a PDF brochure is downloaded, a contact form submitted, or subscription request confirmed). If you have all of these as engagement options, you could use the same label to aggregate all your potential customers together or use different labels and apply multiple OR conditions to group them into one custom segment. The latter is shown as an example in Figure 8.27.

Visitor labeling is described in "Labeling Visitors, Sessions, and Pages" in Chapter 9.

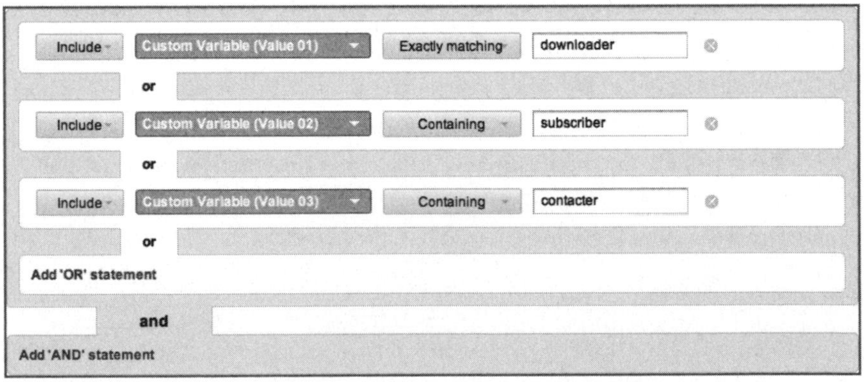

Figure 8.27 A custom segment to differentiate non-e-commerce potential customers

Segmenting Social Network Visits

In Google Analytics, all visits that originate from a social network website are tracked in the same way as any other referrals to your site. That is, they are grouped together with the plethora of visits from all the other referral links to your site. Because social networks can significantly impact your search engine rankings as well as rapidly create a buzz around your brand, studying this segment can be very revealing.

Figure 8.28 groups the social networks that are relevant to www.advanced-web-metrics.com as a single segment using a regular expression to match a list of social referrer sources:

```
facebook|feedburner|twitter|^t\.co|wikipedia|stumbleupon|groups\.google|
groups\.yahoo|linkedin|technorati|newsgator|PRweb|econsultancy|
searchengineland|hootsuite|webmasterworld
```

Figure 8.28 A custom segment highlighting social network visits

In addition, in Figure 8.28 I have set an OR condition to match if the campaign medium is set to social network. By default all social network visits are labeled as medium=referral in your Google Analytics reports. However, if you are using campaign tracking for your social media strategy, as specified in Chapter 7 (see Figure 7.5a and Figure 7.5b), then the OR condition will pick these up also.

You will want to build your own regular expression list around the networks that are important to you. As a starter, include the first four from my list. Note that you could create separate matching conditions, using the OR operator, in the same way as shown in Figure 8.27. That is a perfectly valid way, though I chose a regular expression because this list can become long.

Note: Key performance indicators (KPIs) for social network visits are covered in Chapter 10.

Grouping Visits from a Geographic Region

Google Analytics does an excellent job of showing geographically where your visitors come from. However, there are times when you need to group visitors as a single segment. For example, if you have North, South, and Central American offices, you may want to group visits from those regions. If you operate only on the East Coast, you may want to group visitors from relevant cities. You can apply this as well to Europe, the Middle East, Asia, and Africa.

Figure 8.29 shows a segment generated for Nordic customers. I use OR to match the country field with AND to ensure that this is for customers rather than all visits. Notice in this case that I did not use Matches Regular Expression to build a single-condition field. Instead, I explicitly entered each country as a separate match. This can be useful for troubleshooting purposes; that is, you can explicitly match each field and test to ensure that you receive the expected result. Then you can combine the fields as a regular expression if required.

Figure 8.29 A custom segment grouping customers from the Nordic region

Segmenting Branded Search Visits

The number of people who arrive on your site as a result of knowing your brand name is an important segment. This includes visitors who type in your brand names or product names on search engines and click through to your site—for both paid and organic searches. Figure 8.30 is an example of reporting on a brand segment for this book.

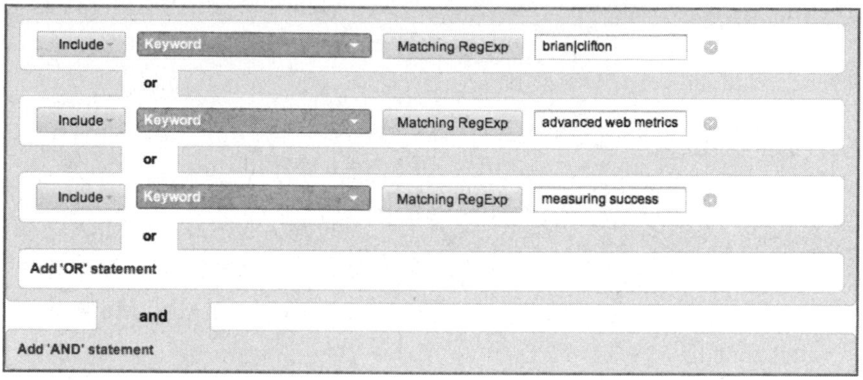

Figure 8.30 A custom segment grouping all brand-related visits

Although I could have used a single regular expression to simplify the matching, I deliberately separated these into three groups: brand name matches (author name), product name matches (book name), and blog name matches. If you have a large number of brand names to match on, it can be useful to group your matches in this way to simplify understanding the advanced segment construction. A common use of this is when your brand or product is known by a different name in other languages.

When Organic Keywords Are Not Provided

For logged-in users of Google organic search —that is, visitors who are logged into their Google account when performing an organic search (such as logged into Gmail in a different browser window/tab)—their keyword terms are not available in your reports. Search terms from such visitors will show as (not provided) in Google Analytics.

See the official announcement of this "feature":

```
http://googleblog.blogspot.com/2011/10/making-search-more-secure.html
```

Note: KPIs for brand engagement are discussed in the section "Marketer and Communication KPI Examples" in Chapter 10.

Creating Custom Intelligence Alerts

As described in Chapter 5, the Google Analytics intelligence engine monitors your website's traffic to detect significant statistical variations and then generates alerts when those variations occur. They are a powerful way of highlighting what traffic patterns have changed on your site. However, you do need to view the reports in order to see the alerts.

To improve on this, custom intelligence alerts not only allow you to specify your own alert criteria, they also have the ability to send an email when the alert triggers—so you do not need to view your reports to be aware of the change. As you can imagine, there are myriad possibilities for this feature, so it's important that you focus on alerts that may not get picked up by automatic alerts. Otherwise, you end up being swamped with email alerts and quickly suffer from alert blindness.

You set up custom intelligence alerts by clicking the profile settings icon (top right of the report screen) and selecting Custom Alerts from your profile Assets tab—see Figure 8.25.

The following are two example custom intelligence alerts that I often use. The first example is shown in Figure 8.31. This simply alerts me if there has been a sudden traffic spike. I define a traffic spike as being 30 percent greater than the same day the previous week. If your traffic regularly varies by large amounts week on week, consider specifying a visit number as a threshold instead, with the condition set to Increases By More Than. For example, you could use a number 30 percent higher than what you would normally expect for a peak day.

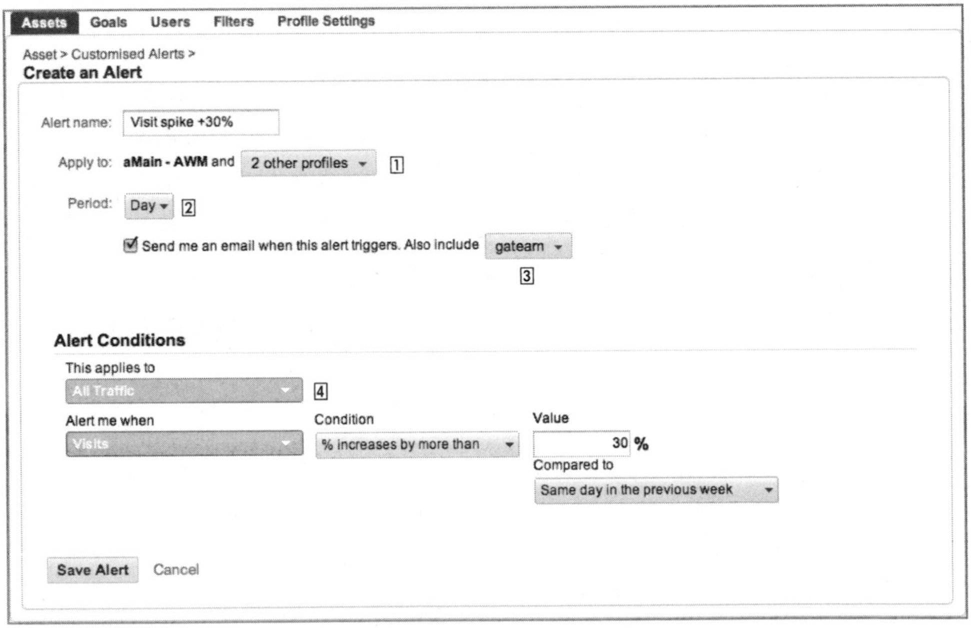

Figure 8.31 A custom intelligence alert for traffic spikes

Some important features to note from Figure 8.31:

1. The alert can be applied to multiple profiles. These can be any profile you have access to, including those within other Google Analytics accounts.

2. You can specify the alert period to compare with traffic day on day, week on week, or month on month.

3. An email can be sent when the alert triggers. This can be to yourself and others.

4. The alert condition can be applied to all visits, or to any other dimension, as well as any predefined advanced custom segment.

> **Tip:** I also recommend a custom alert to warn you when traffic drops significantly. Simply change the condition shown in Figure 8.31 to % Decreases By More Than.

The second example, shown in Figure 8.32, alerts the marketer when revenue from a new online campaign is generated. Generally speaking, traffic from a new campaign is expected and therefore not considered alert material. However, revenue indicates success, and so it's something much more important to be aware of! It also provides a quick indication of the time lag between a campaign launching and when it begins to generate revenue.

If you are a nontransaction site, substitute the alert metric Revenue, for the Goal Conversion Rate.

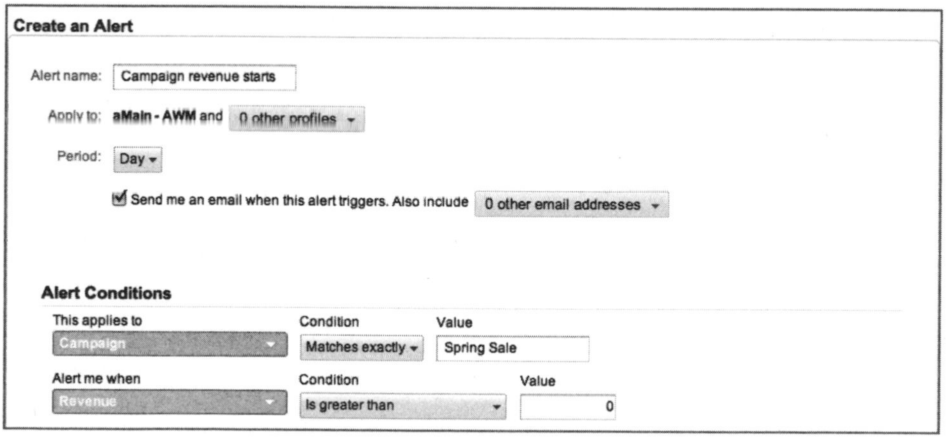

Figure 8.32 A custom intelligence alert for revenue from a new campaign

Summary

In Chapter 8, you have learned the following:

Perform initial configuration You have learned how to set the initial configuration of your account, including localization, e-commerce, and Site Search settings.

Configure goals Configuring goals provides you with conversion and engagement rates. You have learned how to identify and set goals in order to benchmark yourself.

Configure funnels Funnels enable you to see what barriers exist on the path to achieving a goal. We discussed how to configure funnels and the significance of their shapes.

Configure segmentation Filtering keeps your data clean and, along with the Advanced Segments component, is the method of segmenting visitors:

- Setting up filters to maintain the integrity of your data
- Segmenting data to gain a deeper understanding of visitor behavior
- Using filters for data cleansing as a method for long-term segmentation
- Using advanced segments as an efficient way to focus on visitor types

Configure custom intelligence alerts Intelligence alerts make you aware of significant change. By customizing them, you define what constitutes a significant change and can be alerted via email.

Google Analytics Customizations

Out of the box, Google Analytics is a powerful weapon to add to your armory of search marketing, customer relationship, and other business-management firepower. With only a single page tag required to collect data, it is straightforward to set up, and with the addition of some filters, you can really gain insight into your website performance.

If at this stage the reports answer all of your questions, that's great. However, you may find yourself asking further questions that are not answered by default in your reports. Fear not— you can still achieve a great deal more insight with a little bit of lateral thought; Google Analytics is incredibly flexible in that respect.

In Chapter 9, you will learn:

To customize the list of recognized search engines

To label and sessionize visitors for better segmentation

To track error pages and broken links

To gain a greater insight into your pay-per-click tracking

To improve site overlay, conversion, and e-commerce reports

Why Customize an Existing Product?

Google Analytics is a great product, but it does need to cater to the needs of a wide variety of report end users, such as traditional e-commerce sites, to publishers' sites, blogs, forums, corporate sites, informational sites, and lead-generation sites. Because of this diversity, certain compromises have to be made by the Google Analytics development team, as is the case for any web analytics product, hence the need for a customization chapter to provide potential workarounds for you.

There are four approaches to customizations:

- Build custom reports in the user interface (uses existing data points). This is the method to choose when you can view the data in your reports but it's cumbersome to get at, with multiple drill-downs and cross-referencing required.

- Modify the GATC (creates new data points). Use this method when the data point is not present in your reports, such as the labeling of visitor types. Because the GATC is written in standard JavaScript, there are numerous ways it can be altered or customized. A good webmaster should be able to do this for you without too much trouble.

- Use filters to rewrite dimensions (modifies existing data points). Filters allow you to manipulate the data, such as combining multiple dimensions by adding referral source information to transaction IDs for example.

- Or a combination of all the above.

Google Analytics customizations help you delve deep into analysis. To do that, you need to think laterally and be creative with applying filters, segments, and so forth. Some examples in this chapter do require a strong understanding of JavaScript and HTML. The examples provided are only a sample of what you can achieve. Feel free to experiment and share your own experiences on the book blog site: www.advanced-web-metrics.com/blog.

Positioning and Updates of GATC Customizations

When modifying the GATC, note that the placement of the code edits is important. Therefore, ensure that you follow the placement instructions carefully. The general rule is that edits to the GATC must take place before the all-important _trackPageview call because it is this call that sends your modifications to the data collection servers (or _trackEvent if you are using that method to capture your customization).

In addition, the exact syntax of the GATC is constantly in flux. Therefore, if you apply these customizations, or build your own, subscribe to the Google Analytics changelog feed at

http://code.google.com/apis/analytics/community/gajs_changelog.html

Updates to the customizations in this chapter will be made available at www.advanced-web-metrics.com/chapter9.

Custom Reports

A custom report is a way for you to control the display and organization of the types of information already available in Google Analytics but in a way that is most relevant to you. It's difficult to describe in print, so I describe four common custom report examples for you to experiment with. The first three customizations are for reports that are not currently available in Google Analytics. The fourth example is an improvement on what is currently shown in Google Analytics for AdWords managers:

- Day parting
- Unique visitors by page
- Affiliate performance
- Improved AdWords layout

Building a custom report is similar to building an advanced segment or advanced table filter. That is, you populate placeholder fields with either the dimension or metric name you wish to display. These are shown in the section "Custom Advanced Segments" in Chapter 8, "Best Practices Configuration Guide," and in the section "Table Filters (Advanced)" in Chapter 4, "Using the Google Analytics Interface." If you are unfamiliar with the difference between dimensions and metrics, review those sections first because they allow you to quickly see how to find information. In fact, you may even find what you are looking for without having to create a custom report (as often happens). However, if that is not the case for you, go to the Custom Reports navigation item and select New Custom Report, shown in Figure 9.1.

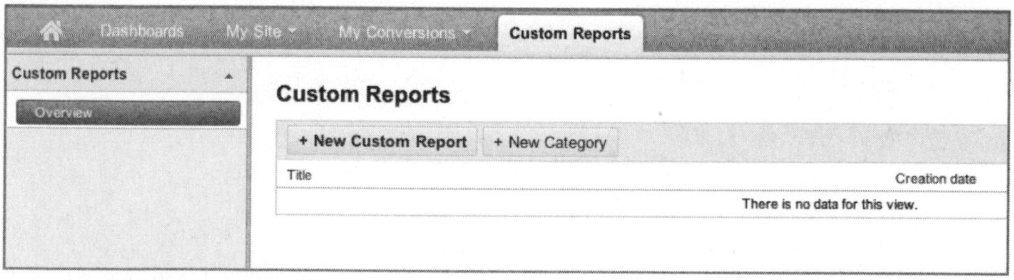

Figure 9.1 Creating a custom report

Day-on-Day Custom Report

As you will have noticed from viewing almost all Google Analytics reports, the data-over-time chart is an obvious way to see how your data has evolved over a set time period. By combining it with advanced segments and table filters, you can drill down and view signals above the noise. However, the chart is linear. That is, it's a chart showing day-to-day differences. It does not show how all Mondays compare with all Tuesdays, and so forth. This custom report allows you to do just that so you can compare *day-on-day* performance. If some of your marketing is scheduled at regular intervals—for example, a weekly email campaign that goes out every Tuesday morning—this custom report will help you understand its impact.

The setup for this report is shown Figure 9.2. In Figure 9.2, note the dual usage of the dimension Day of week. This is deliberate, so that at first you can compare data for all days of the week side by side, as shown in Figure 9.3a. Then, by drilling down on a particular day, you can compare only that day of the week over time—as show in Figure 9.3b.

Note in Figure 9.3 that days of the week are numbered in the reports from 0 to 6, representing Sunday through Saturday.

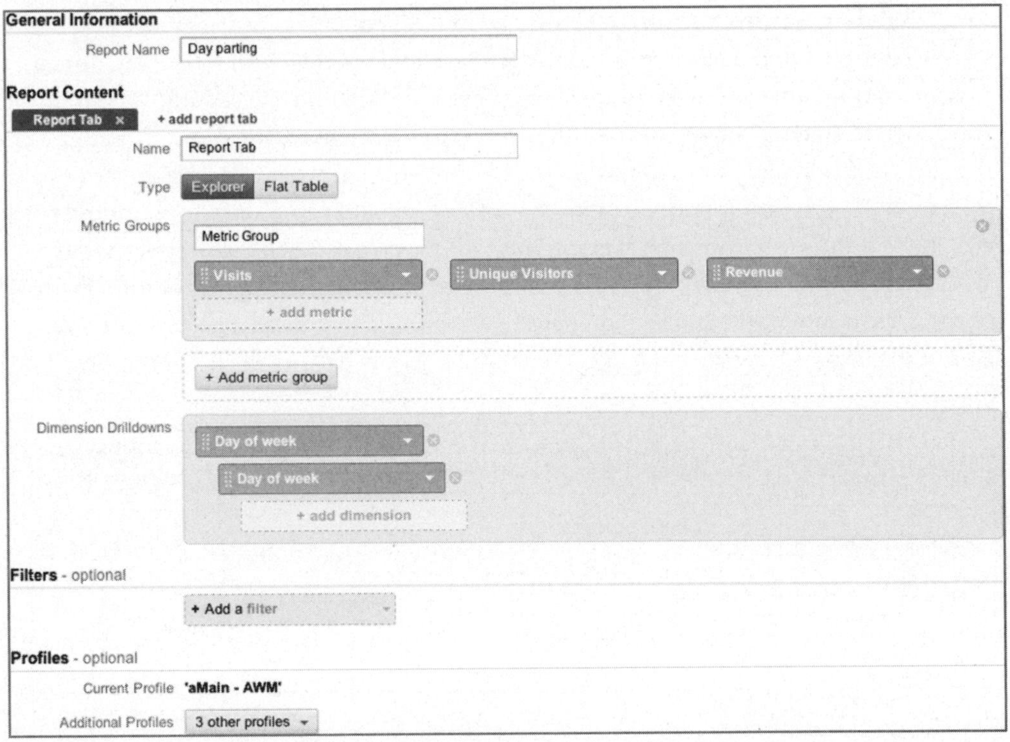

Figure 9.2 A custom report set up to allow day-on-day comparisons

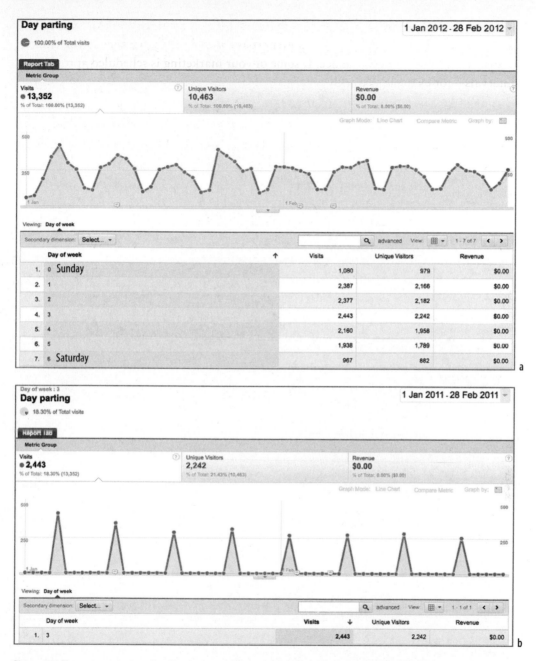

Figure 9.3 The custom report produced by the setup of Figure 9.2: (a) Days of the week, (b) Wednesdays only

Unique Visitors by Page

As discussed in the section "Data Misinterpretation: Lies, Damned Lies, and Statistics," in Chapter 2, "Available Methodologies and Their Accuracy," counting unique visitors for a website is fraught with caveats and therefore results in an inaccurate number. It is why you rarely see reports in Google Analytics that include the unique visitor metric. Instead, where possible use the visit metric. That said, content publishers—sites such as www.nyt.com, www.bbc.com, and www.cnn.com that deliberately encourage regular visits to their site—rely on the use of unique visitors as a success metric. This is because it more closely aligns with their actual readership—people who may visit the site every day or even multiple times per day.

The custom report setup shown in Figure 9.4 allows you to view unique visitor counts next to your content. For this customization, I copied the format of the default Content > Site Content > Pages report and substituted the metric Unique Visitors for Pageviews. The result is a report that is much more visitor-centric, presenting a better representation of readership than the default Pages report, as shown in Figure 9.5.

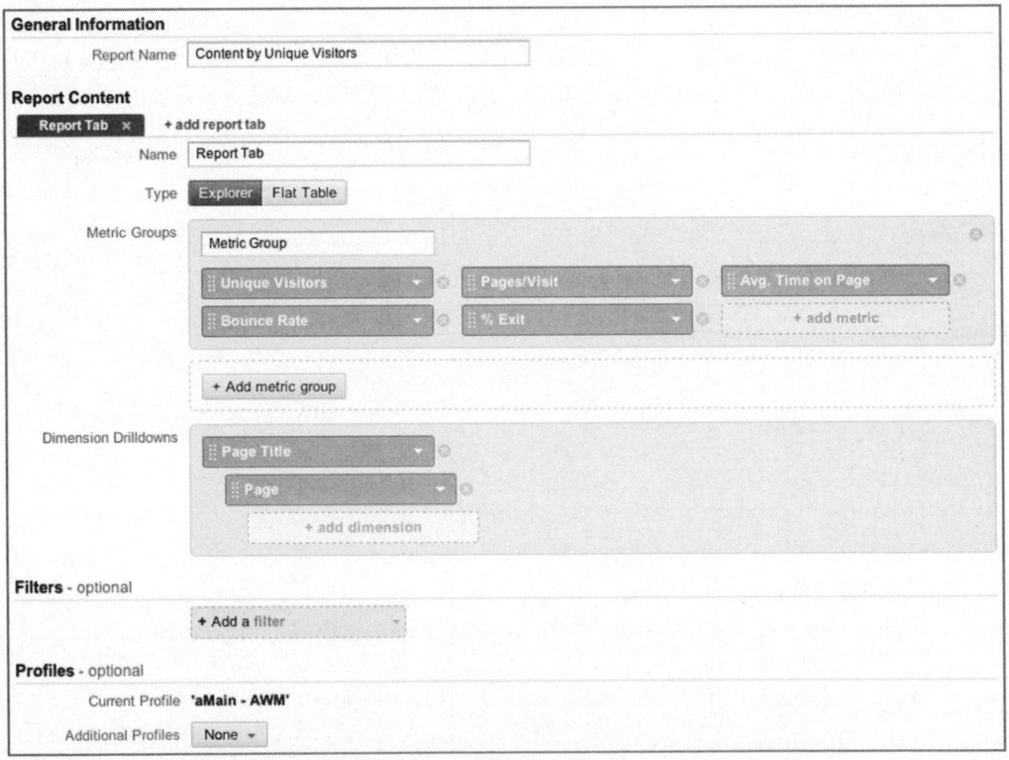

General Information

Report Name   Content by Unique Visitors

Report Content

Report Tab ×   + add report tab

Name   Report Tab

Type   Explorer   Flat Table

Metric Groups   Metric Group

Unique Visitors   Pages/Visit   Avg. Time on Page

Bounce Rate   % Exit   + add metric

+ Add metric group

Dimension Drilldowns   Page Title

Page

+ add dimension

Filters - optional

+ Add a filter

Profiles - optional

Current Profile   'aMain - AWM'

Additional Profiles   None ▾

Figure 9.4   A custom report setup for reporting content performance on a per-visitor basis

Figure 9.5 Making the Pages report visitor-centric after applying the custom report of Figure 9.4

Affiliate Performance

If you make use of affiliates to drive sales or leads to your website, you can capture the affiliate name as part of your e-commerce tracking. However, at present, reporting of affiliate performance is very limited in Google Analytics. It is only available as a secondary dimension in the E-commerce > Transactions report. Because each transaction is reported separately, it is difficult to roll up the performance of all revenue from a particular affiliate. In fact, it is a manual process, and only revenue, tax, and shipping metrics are available.

The custom report shown in Figure 9.6 improves this so that affiliates have a dedicated performance report revealing the total number of transactions and average value (average order value) for each affiliate in addition to their total revenue, as shown in Figure 9.7.

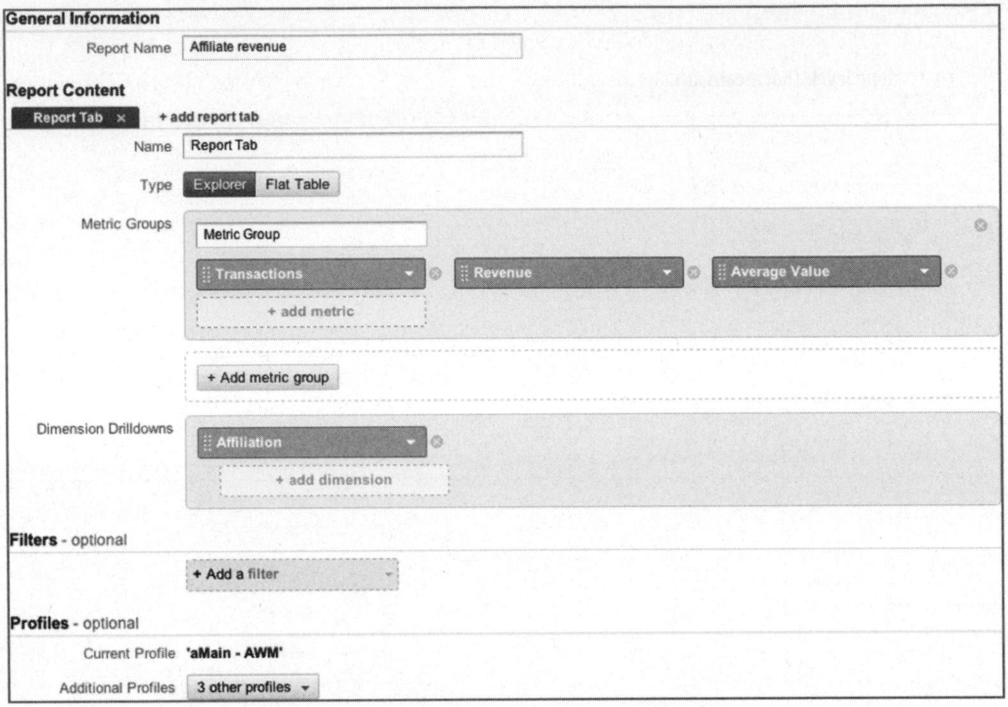

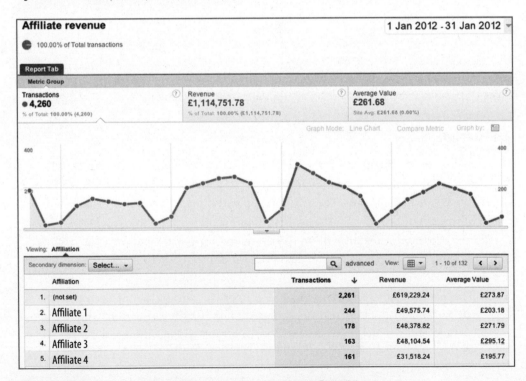

Figure 9.6 A custom report setup for affiliate reporting

Figure 9.7 Affiliate performance report from applying the custom report in Figure 9.6

> **Note:** At present, Google Analytics captures the affiliate name only at the transaction level, not at the purchased item level. That means affiliate performance for specific product items or product categories is not available. The section "Tracking E-commerce Transactions," in Chapter 7 describes how to capture e-commerce data.

Better AdWords

When you're viewing the performance of your AdWords campaigns, the default reports of Google Analytics show your campaign and keyword performance under the Clicks menu tab, shown in Figure 9.8. As you can see, the report includes all the AdWords cost and impression data and associated advertising metrics. However, goal and e-commerce data from AdWords visitors is reported separately in its respective menu tabs. Obviously, the separation of cost and return metrics is not ideal and often results in a frustrated clicking back and forth between the various menu tabs.

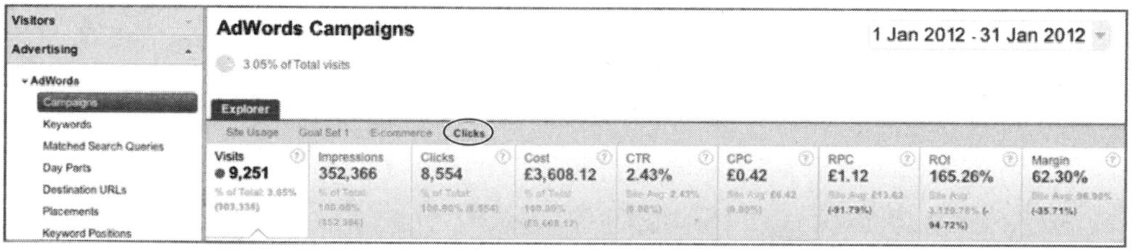

Figure 9.8 The default AdWords report

A better layout is to report your AdWords data *alongside* your e-commerce and goal data. The custom report shown in Figure 9.9 illustrates this for e-commerce, and a similar layout can be created for your goals. The combined report is shown in Figure 9.10 (see page 325).

Managing Custom Reports

You can create, edit, share, and delete your custom reports. If you have a large number of custom reports (for example, an agency-type scenario with different customizations per client), group your custom reports into categories. Click the New Category button as shown in Figure 9.1. Creating a custom report is covered in the previous section, and editing it is self-explanatory. I cover only sharing and deleting here.

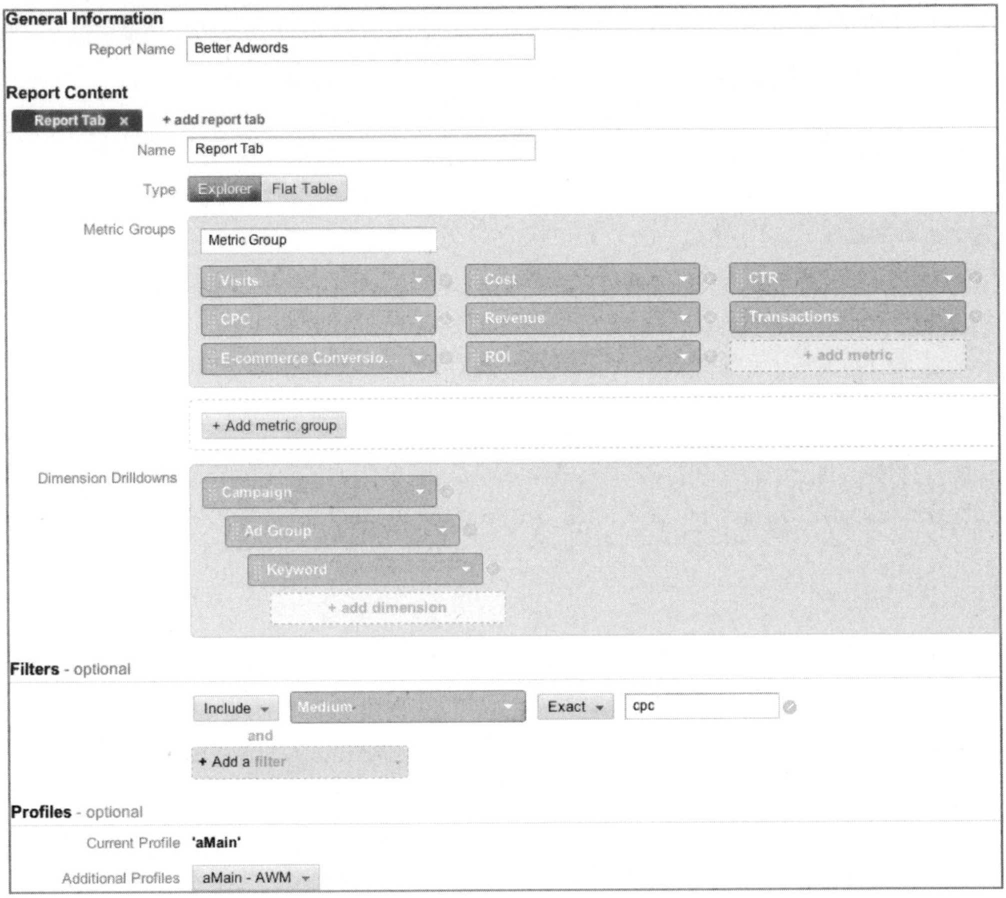

Figure 9.9 A custom report setup for displaying AdWords data alongside e-commerce data

All custom reports are created on a *per-user* login basis, that is, for your login only. However, what if you are a third-party agency or consultant and you need to provide custom reports to your clients? There are two powerful features that allow you apply your custom report elsewhere:

- Within the custom report Overview section, you can share a custom report. This allows you to copy and paste a link in an email. Once the recipient clicks the link, your custom report will be created within their account, ready for saving and applying to profiles they have access to. Use this method if you do not have access to the Google Analytics account that you wish to apply your custom report to (see Figure 9.11).

- Select Additional Profiles when creating or editing a custom report. This allows you to apply your custom report to any profile you have access to, including profiles within other Google Analytics accounts. This is shown at the bottom of Figure 9.2.

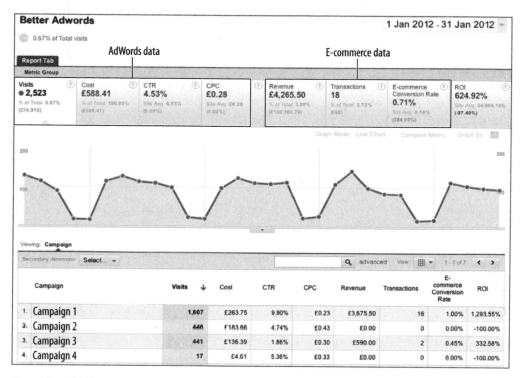

Figure 9.10 AdWords performance report from applying the custom report in Figure 9.9

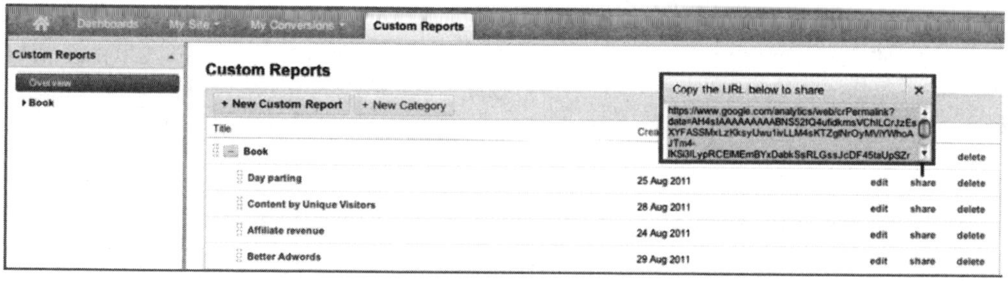

Figure 9.11 Managing custom reports

Deleting a custom report is also self-explanatory. However, a note of caution—deleting it results in the custom report being deleted from *all* profiles you have set in your Additional Profiles settings. Unless you are absolutely sure you have no need for a custom report, it is better to remove it from showing in other profiles by unchecking it in the Additional Profiles drop-down list.

Note: The allowed limit is 100 custom reports per user.

Customizing the List of Recognized Search Engines

Google Analytics currently identifies visitors from the following 37 search engines in your reports. The target audience, if specific, is shown in parentheses:

- About
- Alice
- AlltheWeb
- AltaVista
- AOL
- Ask
- Baidu (China)
- Bing
- CNN
- Daum (Korea)
- Ekolay (Turkey)
- Eniro (Sweden)
- Google (all search domains)
- Kvasir (Norwegian)
- Live (now Bing)
- Lycos
- MSN
- Mama
- Mamma
- Mynet (Turkey)
- Najdi (Slovenia)
- Naver (Korea)
- Netscape
- Onet
- Ozu (Spain)
- PCHome (China)
- Search
- Sesam (Norway)
- Seznam (Czech)
- Szukacz (Poland)
- Terra
- Virgilio (Italy)
- Voila (France)
- Wirtulana Polska (Poland)
- Yahoo!
- Yam (Taiwan)
- Yandex (Russia)

Removing Unwanted Search Engines

In the list of search engines, Search is actually a catchall name for all fully qualified domain names containing the word *search*. For example, in addition to www.search.com, it will match the subdomain search.anysite.com, or even your own internal site search search.mysite.com. In some cases, you may wish to exclude these from the report of search engines. Traffic from sites that are excluded are counted as direct traffic instead. To achieve this, use the _addIgnoredRef() method to remove a website from the referrer list, as in the following example:

```
_gaq.push(['_addIgnoredRef', 'search.anysite.com']);
```

A real-world usage of this technique is shown in the section "What to Do When a Third-Party Gateway Does Not Allow Tracking," in Chapter 7. In that case, the purpose was to ignore the third-party site as a referrer, therefore preserving the original visitor's referral cookie.

Although Google Analytics adds new recognized search engines to this list regularly, there are a great many more search engines in the world—language- and region-specific search engines as well as niche search engines, such as price comparison and vertical portals (for example, I use a list of over 250 search engines when working for clients that span multiple markets). It is therefore possible to append or completely rewrite the list of recognized search engines, as described in the following sections.

Making Search Engines Region-Specific

If you manage search engine optimization (SEO) for your organization or clients, regional differences are important. For example, if you are conducting SEO for a North American audience, knowing if visitors come to your site via a search on google .com, google.ca, or google.co.mx can be important to you. And it's more important in Europe, which is a more fragmented market: google.co.uk, google.de, google.fr, and so forth. It's the same for the Middle East, Asia, Asia-Pacific, and so on. Essentially, if your SEO is targeting different countries, understanding regional differences is a key requirement of your work.

As listed previously, by default Google Analytics tracks 37 search engines, in aggregate. That means, for example, that all Google domains are tracked as a single entity—google. The same for Yahoo!, Bing, and all other search engines. So you don't know if a visitor from a Google search came from google.com or google.co.uk, or any other Google/Yahoo!/Bing domain for that matter.

To overcome this limitation, add region-specific domains to your GATC. A before-and-after example of applying this customization is shown in Figure 9.12. As you can see, the increased granularity of search engine data is quite dramatic.

The method for this customization is to add the following line to your GATC for each search engine:

```
_gaq.push(['_addOrganic', 'new_search_domain', 'query_name', opt_prepend]);
```

In this line, new_search_domain is the domain name of the search engine and query_name is the parameter label containing the visitor's query terms; opt_prepend is an optional Boolean parameter, which if set to true means the newly defined search engine is prepended to the default list and if set to false means the search engine is appended to the list (if not set, false is assumed).

There are two straightforward steps to achieve this.

1. Conduct a search on the region-specific search engine you wish to track, such as google.co.uk, and view the resultant URL. For example, searching for "brian clifton" produces the following search results:

```
http://www.google.co.uk/#hl=en&cp=9&gs_id=q&xhr=t&q=brian+clifton&pf=p
&sclient=psy&newwindow=1&source=hp&pbx=1&oq=brian+cli&aq=0&aqi=g5&aql=
&gs_sm=&gs_upl=&bav=on.2,or.r_gc.r_pw.&fp=87c57dfcd1b2b35=1280&bih=619
```

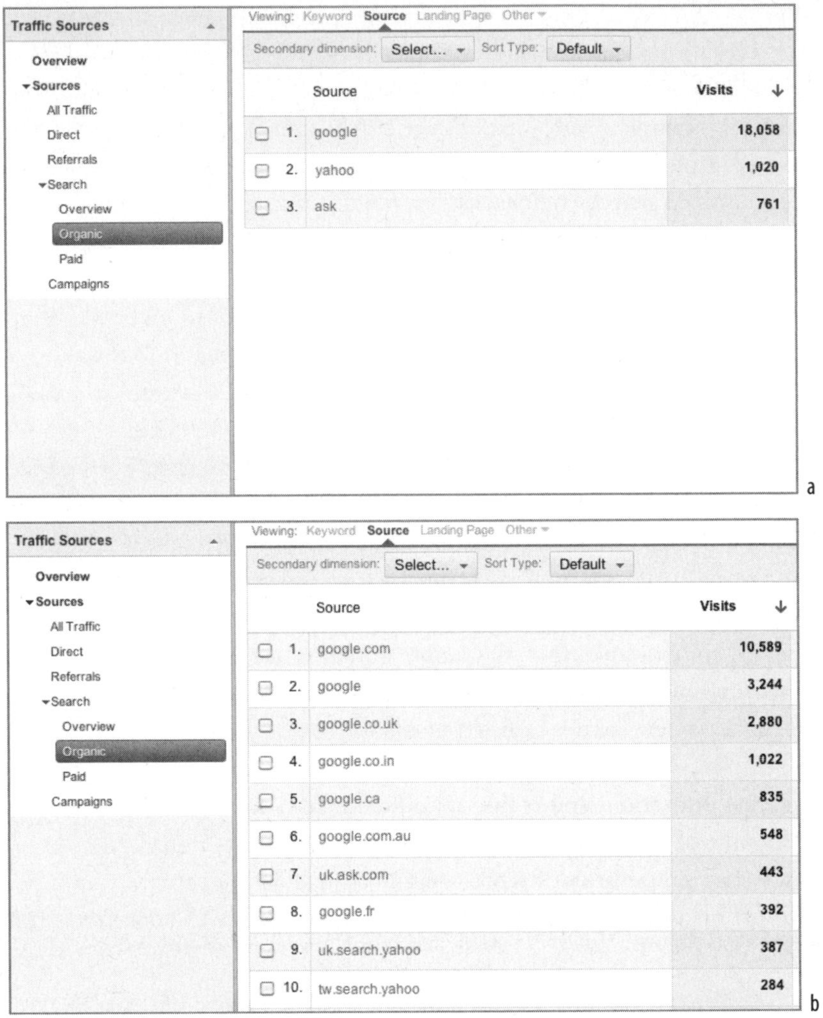

Figure 9.12 The (a) before and (b) after effect of separating out regional search engines

2. From this URL, `new_search_domain` = google.co.uk and the `query_name` = q. Add the following code to your page GATC:

```
_gaq.push(['_addOrganic', 'google.co.uk', 'q', true]);
```

Because the default list of search engines already contains generic entries for google, yahoo, and so on, it is important that regional variations are prepended. That is, `opt_prepend` should always be set to `true`. Expanding my regional list, I have the following code:

```
_gaq.push(['_addOrganic', 'google.co.uk', 'q', true]);
_gaq.push(['_addOrganic', 'google.com.mx', 'q', true]);
_gaq.push(['_addOrganic', 'uk.search.yahoo', 'p', true]);
```

A complete GATC containing these changes would be as follows:

```
<script type="text/javascript">
  var _gaq = _gaq || [];
  _gaq.push(['_setAccount', 'UA-12345-1']);

  _gaq.push(['_addOrganic', 'google.co.uk', 'q', true]);
  _gaq.push(['_addOrganic', 'google.com.mx', 'q', true]);
  _gaq.push(['_addOrganic', 'uk.search.yahoo', 'p', true]);
  _gaq.push(['_trackPageview']);

(function() {
var ga = document.createElement('script');
ga.type = 'text/javascript'; ga.async = true;
ga.src = ('https:' == document.location.protocol ? 'https://ssl' : ➥
'http://www') + '.google-analytics.com/ga.js';
var s = document.getElementsByTagName('script')[0];
s.parentNode.insertBefore(ga, s);
})();
</script>
```

Adding New Search Engines for SEO

Suppose visitors from the BBC search engine and the Russian search engine Rambler are important to your website's marketing success. Because neither is part of the default search engine list, such visitors will show as referrals in your reports from bbc .co.uk and rambler.ru respectively, and the visitor's search keywords will be lost. The method to have these recognized as search engines and keywords captured is similar to the two-step process described in the previous section:

1. Conduct a search on the bbc.co.uk and ramabler.ru websites and view the resultant URLs. For example, searching for "brian clifton" produces the following search results:

```
http://www.bbc.co.uk/search/?q=brian%20clifton
http://nova.rambler.ru/search?btnG=%D0%9D%D0%B0%D0%B9%D1%82%D0%B8%21&query=
brian+Clifton
```

2.   To capture these URLs and keywords as search engines, add the following code to your page GATC, just prior to your _trackPageview call:

```
_gaq.push(['_addOrganic', 'rambler.ru', 'query', true]);
_gaq.push(['_addOrganic', 'bbc.co.uk', 'q', true]);
```

I tend to always set opt_prepend = true to account for any future changes Google may apply to its list of default search engines. In this way, your own list is always processed first.

The important step is to view the URL of a query on the search engine itself and extract the name of the variable containing your keywords. You can continue to add other search engines as needed by creating additional _addOrganic lines.

> **Note:** The SEO plug-in located at www.advanced-web-metrics.com/plugins contains the BBC, Rambler, and many other niche engines from around the world.

Labeling Visitors, Sessions, and Pages

Labeling is way of grouping visitors of similar types, or behavior, together using a common label. A frequent example is to label your customers to segregate them from non-customers; that is, people visiting your site who have purchased from you before versus those who have never purchased from you, regardless of their intent for their current visit. This is achieved using a visitor label (it is a persistent cookie) that remains with the visitor for each subsequent visit.

The power of the Custom Variables feature is that in addition to the visitor level, you can also label sessions (with the label lasting for the duration of the current visit) and pages and even define multiple instances of all three. To help understand this, consider the following example: A publisher, a newspaper website, wishes to know which section of its site is most popular: Sports, Music, or Current Affairs. In addition, the publisher wants to know how visitors interact with various types of calls to action during their visit—do they click an ad, rate an article, or comment on an article, for example? And is the visitor a paying subscriber or an anonymous visitor?

This example demonstrates all three levels of interaction (hierarchies) for using custom variables: page, session, and visitor labels. These are known as the variable *scope* and are illustrated schematically in Figure 9.13.

Understanding scope is important because each custom variable is restricted to one particular scope level. From Figure 9.13, you can see that the custom variable set at the visitor level has only one value for that visitor. Set at the session level, it can have three values because there are three sessions in this example. At the page level, each page can have its own associated custom variable—nine in total in this case. Table 9.1 illustrates how custom variables work, dependent on their scope.

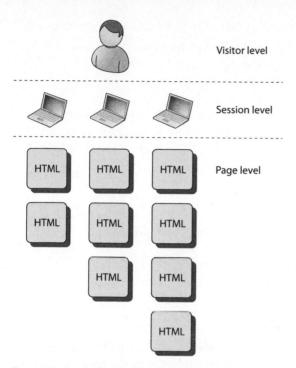

Visitor level

Session level

Page level

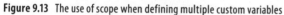

Figure 9.13 The use of scope when defining multiple custom variables

Note: I use the terms *custom variable* and *custom label* interchangeably. The correct terminology from Google Analytics is *custom variable*. However, I find that the term *custom label* is easier to understand and convey to a stakeholder audience, especially when lots of other variables are being discussed.

▶ **Table 9.1** Custom variables by scope

Level	Duration	When Sharing a Slot with Other Custom Variables	Number Allowed
Page level	A single pageview, event, or transaction call.	The last page-level variable to be called on a page is the one applied to that page.	For any web property (collection of pages), many unique page-level variables can be set and slots can be reused, limited only by the number of hits in a given session.
			For any single page, you can set up to 5 simultaneous custom variables.

Continues

Level	Duration	When Sharing a Slot with Other Custom Variables	Number Allowed
Session level	The visit session of the visitor.	The last session-level variable called in a session is the one used for that session. For example, if `login=false` for slot #1 at the beginning of the session and `login=true` for slot #1 later on, the session is set to `true` for `login`. Overrides any previously set page-level variable called *in the same session*. For example, if slot #1 is first used for `category=sports` and then for `login=true` for a session, `category=sports` is ignored.	For any web property, you can create as many distinct session-level custom variables as can be defined—up to the 50,000 unique aggregate table limit that exists in Google Analytics today. For any given user session, you can set up to 5 session-level variables.
Visitor level	The life of the visitor cookie. When set, applies to all visits onward (but not to previous visits or the current visit).	The last visitor-level variable set for a visitor is the one applied to the visitor. Overrides previously set custom variable types called *in the same session*.	For any web property, you can create up to 5 distinct visitor-level variables.

Note: The combined length of the strings used for the name/value parameters must not exceed 128 bytes each. For Latin character sets, this limit corresponds to 128 characters but is reduced for double-byte character sets, that is, Chinese, Japanese, and Korean. The length is checked before URL encoding.

If you define your labels and scopes appropriately, all of these metrics can be viewed at a glance within your Visitors > Demographics > Custom Variables report. An example is shown in Figure 9.14, which is taken from this book's website. In this case, a page-level custom variable is used to differentiate the two types of pages on the website—blog articles and regular content pages. Every page on the site has a page-level custom variable defined. As you can see, blog articles are much more popular in terms of visits than other content pages.

Of course, if the entire website content was nicely grouped in directories such as /pages and /blog, then it would be straightforward to view this information in your Content > Site Content > Pages report. However, that is rarely the case for any website.

In this example, pages are hosted in the root directory and various other subdirectories (and even sub-subdirectories), making it impossible to group content by its directory hierarchy. The use of page-level custom variables enables this.

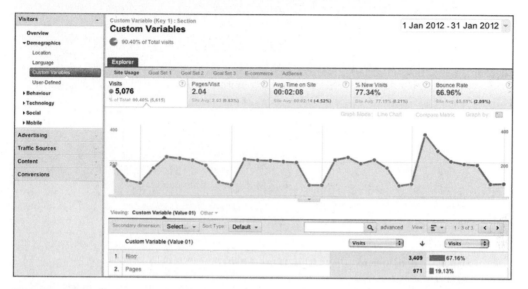

Figure 9.14 Example Custom Variables report

Implementing Custom Variables

You can add a custom label by using the function _setCustomVar() within the page where the label is applied, as shown in the following example:

```
_gaq.push(['_setCustomVar', index, name, value, optional_scope ]);
```

The parameters are defined as follows:

index The slot for the custom variable. This is a number whose value can range from 1 to 5, inclusive. A custom variable should be placed in one slot only and not be reused across different slots. The purpose is to allow multiple variables for the same scope.

name The name for the custom variable. This is a string that identifies the custom variable and appears in your top-level Custom Variables report—for example, "Section name", "Membership type", "Gender", and so on.

value The value for the custom variable. This is a string that is paired with a name. You can pair a number of values with a custom variable name. For example, for name=Section, values could be "Sports", "Music", and "Current Affairs".

optional_scope The scope defines the level of user engagement with your site. Available values are 1 (visitor level), 2 (session level), and 3 (page level). When left undefined, the custom variable scope defaults to page-level interaction.

Note: The current limit on the number of custom variable slots (index value) is five. Therefore, if you define three page-level custom variables on a page and then wish to add session- and visitor-level custom variables for the same page, you are limited to two, that is, using slots 4 and 5.

It's important that you place _setCustomVar before the _trackPageview call of your GATC so that it gets delivered in the GIF request sent by _trackPageview. The following defines a page-level custom variable with the name Section and a value of Sports Pages and assigned to index=1:

```
<script type="text/javascript">
  var _gaq = _gaq || [];
  _gaq.push(['_setAccount', 'UA-12345-1']);
  _gaq.push(['_setCustomVar', 1, 'Section', 'Sports Pages', 3]);
  _gaq.push(['_trackPageview']);

(function() {
var ga = document.createElement('script');
ga.type = 'text/javascript'; ga.async = true;
ga.src = ('https:' == document.location.protocol ? 'https://ssl' : ➡
'http://www') + '.google-analytics.com/ga.js';
var s = document.getElementsByTagName('script')[0];
s.parentNode.insertBefore(ga, s);
})();
</script>
```

This works when you know the value of the custom variable in advance. That is, it does not depend on a visitor's action such as onClick or onSubmit. As stated at the beginning of this chapter, placement of GATC modification is important. Therefore, if visitor action is required to set your custom variable, you must separate your GATC so that _setCustomVar is called within your HTML *before* _trackPageview (or _trackEvent), as in this example:

```
<head>
<script type="text/javascript">
  var _gaq = _gaq || [];
  _gaq.push(['_setAccount', 'UA-12345-1']);
  _gaq.push(['_trackPageview']);

(function() {
var ga = document.createElement('script');
```

```
ga.type = 'text/javascript'; ga.async = true;
ga.src = ('https:' == document.location.protocol ? 'https://ssl' : ➡
'http://www') + '.google-analytics.com/ga.js';
var s = document.getElementsByTagName('script')[0];
s.parentNode.insertBefore(ga, s);
})();
</script>
</head>

<body>
    .
    .

<a href="rate_product.php;" onclick="_gaq.push(['_setCustomVar', 3,➡
'Engagement', 'Contributor', 2]);_gaq.push(['_trackEvent','dummy-ignore',➡
'ignore']);">Rate this product</a>
    .
    .

</body>
```

In this example, a session-level custom variable is defined with the name Engagement and a value of Contributor and is assigned to index=3. This is set only when a visitor clicks the Rate This Product link. A dummy event (or pageview) must also be set after the click; otherwise the custom variable is not captured by Google Analytics. Moving the _trackPageview call to the bottom of the page would not work because it would execute when the page has finished loading—yet the visitor will still be reading the content, deciding on their actions.

For any single page, you can track up to five custom variables, each with a separate slot. This means that you could assign four additional custom variables on this same page. The content placed in the name or value parameter can be any label you wish, though you should use only alphanumeric characters (as well as the space character) to avoid any potential encoding issues. The content you set will be displayed in the Visitors > Custom Variables report and can be cross-segmented as per other metrics.

Note: Once you have set up a custom variable, you can use the _gaq.push(['_deleteCustomVar', index]); method to remove it should you no longer require it (where index is the index of the custom variable to delete). For example, you might use it if a visitor label is a temporary label that requires confirmation by a visitor's further action and the visitor does not complete the action.

Tracking Error Pages and Broken Links

With an out-of-the-box install of Google Analytics, you will not be tracking error pages or broken links on your website. This is because by default you probably have not added the GATC to your error pages. After all, how can you track a page that does not exist? To enable this, you need to add the GATC to the error-page templates that are delivered by your web server. A webmaster will typically do this. The GATC will then track your error-page URLs as if they were any other pageview request. That is the caveat: Without modification, error pages are reported as regular pages, not as errors, making them difficult to detect in your reports! You can highlight and separate error pages by modifying the GATC on your error page templates as follows.

Typically, a web server allows you to define a template for each error status code. For example, to track missing pages on your site, modify the standard GATC on your 404 template page as shown here:

```
<script type="text/javascript">
  var _gaq = _gaq || [];
  _gaq.push(['_setAccount', 'UA-12345-1']);
_gaq.push(['_trackPageview','/error 404/' +document.location.pathname➡
+document.location.search']);


(function() {
var ga = document.createElement('script');
ga.type = 'text/javascript'; ga.async = true;
ga.src = ('https:' == document.location.protocol ? 'https://ssl' : ➡
'http://www') + '.google-analytics.com/ga.js';
var s = document.getElementsByTagName('script')[0];
s.parentNode.insertBefore(ga, s);
})();
</script>
```

This is an example of the virtual pageview technique as discussed in Chapter 7. It allows you to create the virtual directory /error 404/ and the full path to the error page filename (URI), plus any query terms used. You modify other error templates in a similar way:

```
_gaq.push(['_trackPageview','/error 500/' +document.location.pathname➡
+document.location.search']);
```

Using this technique enables you to differentiate error pages from other pageviews within your Google Analytics reports. Resultant entries for error pages will show in your Content > Site Content > Pages report as, for example, /error 404/noexisting-page.htm. This provides you with two very important pieces of information: the type of error (error code) and the URL of the page that produced it.

Web Server Status Codes

These are the status codes, defined in the HTTP 1.0 specification, returned by your web server in its headers (see www.w3.org/Protocols/Overview.html).

2xx Success

The requested action was successfully received and understood:

- 200 OK
- 201 Created
- 202 Accepted
- 203 Provisional Information
- 204 No Response
- 205 Deleted
- 206 Modified

3xx Redirection

Further action must be taken in order to complete the request:

- 301 Moved Permanently
- 302 Moved Temporarily
- 303 Method
- 304 Not Modified

4xx Client Error

The request contains bad syntax or is inherently impossible to fulfill:

- 400 Bad Request
- 401 Unauthorized
- 402 Payment Required
- 403 Forbidden
- 404 Not Found
- 405 Method Not Allowed
- 406 None Acceptable
- 407 Proxy Authentication Required
- 408 Request Timeout

Continues

338 ■

Web Server Status Codes *(Continued)*

5xx Server Error

The server could not fulfill the request:

- 500 Internal Server Error
- 501 Not Implemented
- 502 Bad Gateway
- 503 Service Unavailable
- 504 Gateway Timeout

Figure 9.15 shows an example Pages report for the error pages. Note that the report uses the table filter to highlight the errors, that is, bubble them up to the top of the report table. This is important because error pages are usually buried at the bottom of your pageview listings—assuming they are a small fraction of the total!

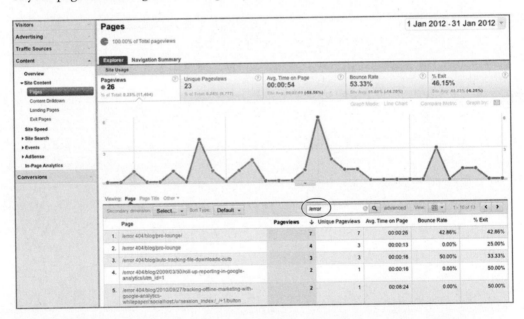

Figure 9.15 Viewing error pages

Tip: Knowing your error page URLs is clearly important, yet they typically appear at the bottom of your Top Content report—possibly hundreds of pages deep. To ensure that your web design and development team follows up on errors, set the table filter to `error` (as shown in Figure 9.15) and schedule this report to be emailed to them on a daily or weekly basis. Emailing reports is discussed in the section "Email Reports," in Chapter 4, "Using the Google Analytics Interface."

Of course, once you have identified error pages, you will want to know which links within your website point to them; that is, you will want to identify broken links. From the report shown in Figure 9.15, click any of the listed error pages to get the detail for that specific page, and then select the Navigational Summary menu tab. The result is a list of pages that your visitors were on just prior to clicking through and receiving the error page, as well as where they went after seeing the error page, as shown in Figure 9.16.

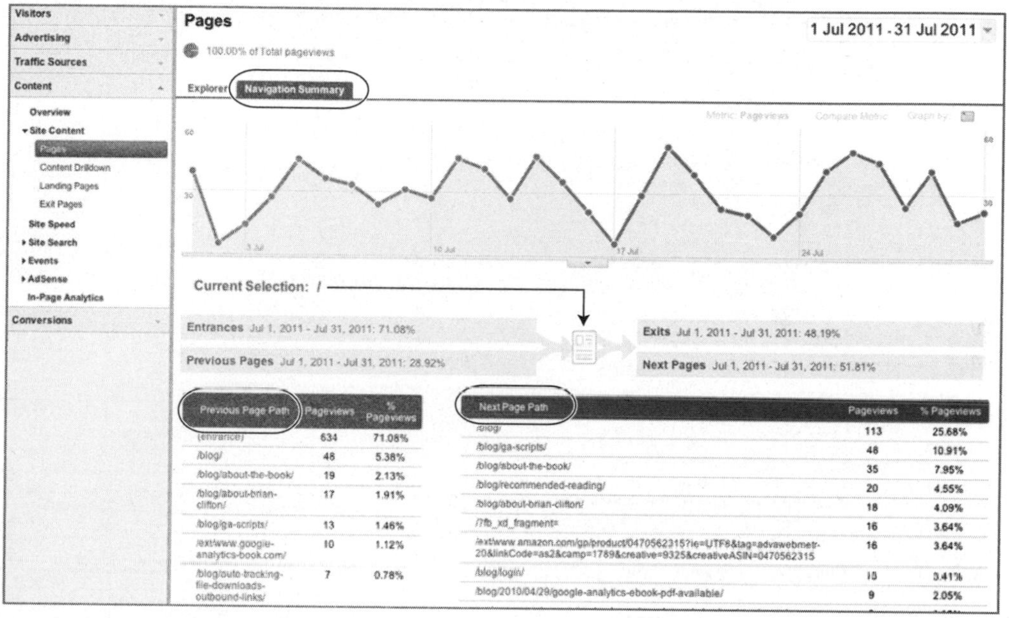

Figure 9.16 Pages leading to and from an error page

What if you cannot use a different GATC in your error templates? Some host providers and even large corporations can be stuck in a one-size-fits-all control panel or content management system where it is not possible (or too difficult) to have a different GATC on their error templates. If this describes your scenario, it may still be possible to track your error pages, so long as the error page title contains a hint that it is actually an error page being displayed. Most Apache configurations do this by default, as shown in Figure 9.17.

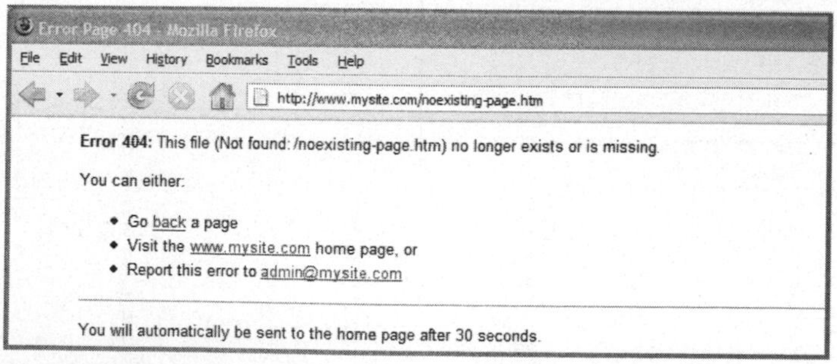

Figure 9.17 Typical 404 "not found" error page returned from the Apache web server

Because the error page template displays its error code in the HTML `<title>` tag, you can apply a filter to differentiate errors from other pageviews in your reports, as shown in Figure 9.18.

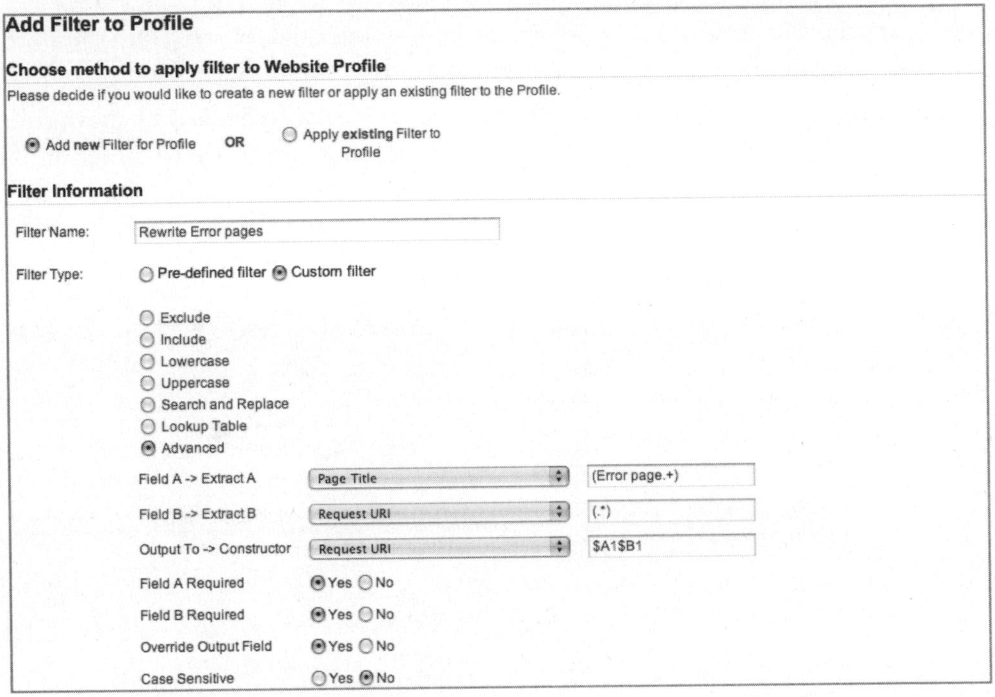

Figure 9.18 Filter to highlight error pages

In plain English, the filter is described as follows:

- Check whether the page title contains the phrase "Error page." If so, extract the page title and the page URI entries.
- Combine the page title and page URI entries, and overwrite the original page URI field.

Differentiating Pay-Per-Click Network Partners

As well as displaying ads on their own search properties, pay-per-click networks often partner with other websites to display their advertisements, sharing revenue from resultant ad click-throughs with the partner. An example is the relationship between Google and Ask.com. Ask.com is an independent search engine with its own search technology for displaying organic search results (formally known as Teoma). However, for paid search, Ask.com partners with Google AdWords. If you advertise on AdWords, then your advertisement will also appear on the Ask.com website. In this way, pay-per-click partner networks are a great additional distribution channel for your advertisement, enabling you to reach a wider audience.

By default, reports in Google Analytics group all pay-per-click partner click-throughs for AdWords as google / cpc. For example, you will not see pay-per-click visitors who originate from Ask.com labeled as such—just google / cpc, as shown in Figure 9.19. The same is also true for other pay-per-click networks such as Bing and Yahoo!, which distribute their ads to AltaVista, Lycos, HotBot, A9, and others.

Figure 9.19 Different paid networks

In addition, if your AdWords strategy spans more than one geography, for example, google.se and google.com, Google Analytics groups all such click-throughs as google / cpc.

Being able to view which partner site, or which specific Google domain, your AdWords visitors come from can help you optimize your advertising approach. If this level of detail is important to you, use two cascading filters (one applied after the other) to show more fully where your pay-per-click visitors are originating from, as shown in Figure 9.20.

In plain English, Figure 9.20 reads as follows:

1. For every pageview, where the medium is defined as cpc or ppc, extract the Referral domain, omitting the http:// text and anything after the next slash (/). Copy the contents of this match to Custom Field 1.

2. Append the referring domain to the Campaign Source variable and overwrite it.

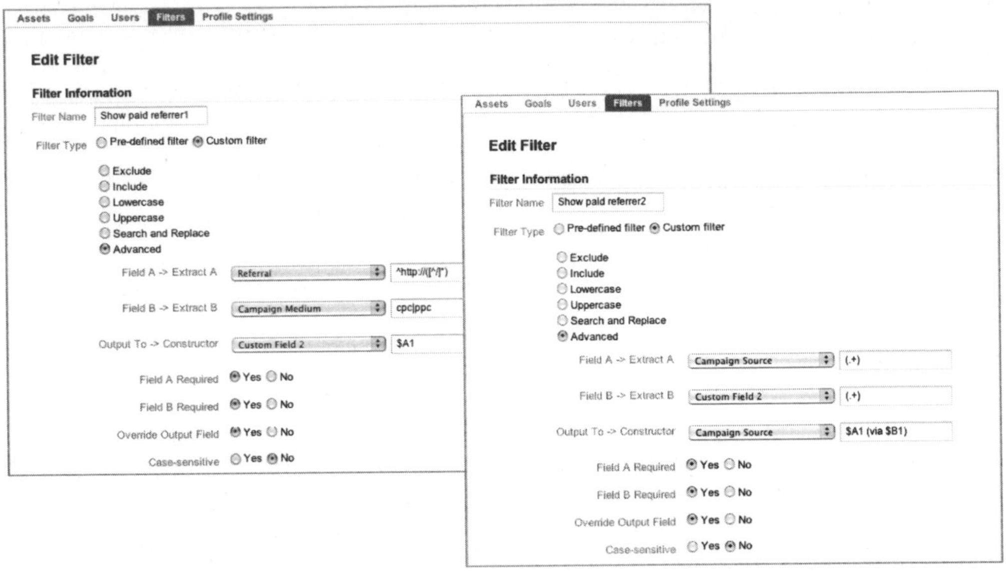

Figure 9.20 Filters to include the original referrer from different pay-per-click networks

Combining Pageview Fields with Session Fields

There is a slight caveat when working with the filters described in Figure 9.20: They combine a per-pageview field (Referral) with a per-session field (Campaign Source). A pageview field is populated with every pageview recorded by Google Analytics, whereas a session field is set, usually at the start of the session, and then maintained throughout a visitor's time on the site.

For example, each time a pageview is viewed, the page title, URL, and referral are updated to match the current page, but the session fields (returning visitor versus new visitor indicator, or campaign name, for example) are the same regardless of the page currently being viewed. Referral is a pageview field, in that each pageview will have its own unique referral, whereas Campaign Source will have the same value across the entire session.

Because cookies can be altered during a session—for example, visitors can remove them or firewalls can restrict them—it is possible that applying an additional profile filter may alter a session field within a visitor's session. This can cause a data misalignment, potentially resulting in an unpredicted data value showing in the reports. This is rare, but it occasionally happens.

Notice that both filters A and B must be executed in order for the filter to work. The result is a report that lists both the original referral and the Google Analytics–defined campaign source, as shown in Figure 9.21.

Search Engine Relationships

The relationships among search engines (paid and nonpaid), directories, and portals are quite complex—as the chart illustrates. To understand the relationship chart, try viewing only Google's relationships; Google provides organic search results for AOL and Netscape. AdWords results are displayed on AOL, Netscape, Ask.com, and many portal sites (via AdSense); Google receives directory results from DMOZ. The other search engines have similar multiple relationships.

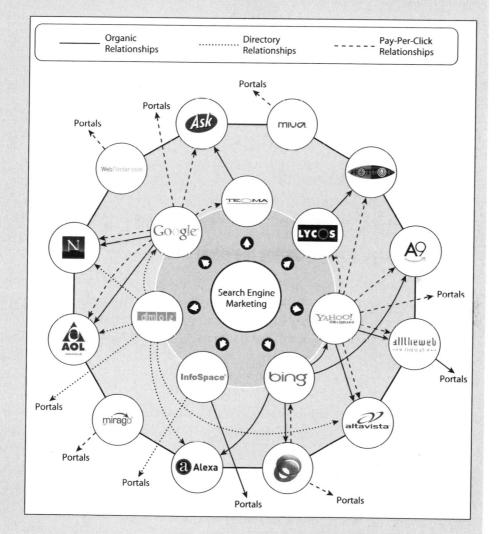

A color-coded, interactive version is available at

www.advanced-web-metrics.com/search-relationship-chart.

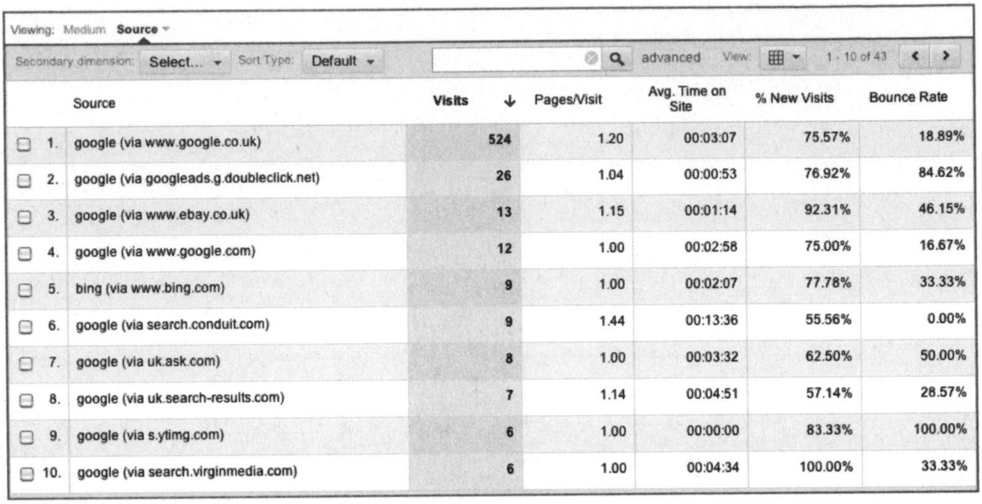
Viewing: Medium Source
Secondary dimension: Select... Sort Type: Default advanced View: 1 - 10 of 43

	Source	Visits	Pages/Visit	Avg. Time on Site	% New Visits	Bounce Rate
1.	google (via www.google.co.uk)	524	1.20	00:03:07	75.57%	18.89%
2.	google (via googleads.g.doubleclick.net)	26	1.04	00:00:53	76.92%	84.62%
3.	google (via www.ebay.co.uk)	13	1.15	00:01:14	92.31%	46.15%
4.	google (via www.google.com)	12	1.00	00:02:58	75.00%	16.67%
5.	bing (via www.bing.com)	9	1.00	00:02:07	77.78%	33.33%
6.	google (via search.conduit.com)	9	1.44	00:13:36	55.56%	0.00%
7.	google (via uk.ask.com)	8	1.00	00:03:32	62.50%	50.00%
8.	google (via uk.search-results.com)	7	1.14	00:04:51	57.14%	28.57%
9.	google (via s.ytimg.com)	6	1.00	00:00:00	83.33%	100.00%
10.	google (via search.virginmedia.com)	6	1.00	00:04:34	100.00%	33.33%

Figure 9.21 Showing the referral URLs from pay-per-click networks

As you can see, the structure of the report in Figure 9.21 is a referral source list of the form *`ppc network source, (via referring website)`*. The report shows visitors from the Google AdWords partner network, including ask.com, images.google.com, conduit.com, visadropbox.co.uk, and mywebsearch.com. Without these filters in place, the level of detail is limited to a single aggregate entry of `google`.

In-Page Analytics: Differentiating Identical Links

The In-Page Analytics report is an excellent way to visualize what links your visitors are clicking and which ones have the most value; that is, drive conversions. However, by default, if you have numerous links on a page all pointing to the same destination URL, the same metrics are shown for each link in the In-Page Analytics report. You are unable to differentiate multiple links to the same URL. This can happen, for example, if you have an image link, a menu link, and a content link on a category page, all pointing to `productA.html`.

An example of this is shown in Figure 9.22, which shows this book's website with three pairs of links highlighted. Each pair points to the same URL—Home, Site Blog, and About Brian Clifton, respectively. Because these are pairs of identical URLs, the site overlay report for these links shows identical metrics. However, by modifying each URL slightly with a different query parameter, we can differentiate these links:

```
http://www.mysite.com/?linkid=topLogo
http://www.mysite.com/?linkid=topMenu
http://www.mysite.com/blog/?linkid=topMenu
http://www.mysite.com/blog/?linkid=contentText
http://www.mysite.com/brian-clifton.htm?linkid=topMenu
http://www.mysite.com/brian-clifton.htm?linkid=contentText
```

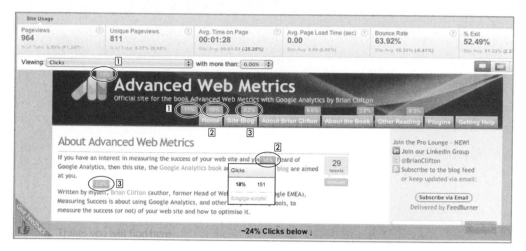

Figure 9.22 Book website with three pairs of identical links

If the links you wish to differentiate already contain query parameters, simply append your differentiator as follows, for example:

```
http://www.mysite.com/blog/?cat=plugins&linkid=topMenu
```

With this method, your In-Page Analytics report will be able to clarify whether a content text link has more of an impact than an image logo link or menu link to the same page. However, bear in mind that when applying this method and viewing other reports, such as the Content > Site Content > Pages report, you will need to sum the pageview data for these links to determine the page total. To overcome this limitation, use a separate profile for these reports. That is, one profile with all your links to the same page differentiated, as described previously, and another profile that strips out the differentiators. The Exclude URL Query Parameters setting in your profile settings can do this for you. See the section "Initial Configuration" in Chapter 8.

Matching Transactions to Specific Referral Data

As discussed in Chapter 1, "Why Understanding Your Web Traffic Is Important to Your Business,"and Chapter 2, "Available Methodologies and Their Accuracy," web analytics is about identifying trends, so you shouldn't get hung up on precise numbers. Understand the strength and accuracy limitations of your data and get comfortable with it. For Google Analytics, Google's strong stance on privacy means that individuals are not tracked and all data is reported at the aggregate level.

However, for e-commerce transactions, e-commerce and marketing managers usually desire a little more detail. Without identifying individuals, the following customization enables you to view your transaction list and identify which referrer source, medium, and keywords were used by the purchaser to find your website in the first place; that is, it combines four dimensions together in one report. By default, Google Analytics allows only two dimensions to be combined.

Note: This technique was originally discussed in an article by Shawn Purtell from ROI Revolution

www.roirevolution.com/blog/2007/05/matching_specific_transactions_to_specific_keyword.html

and is reproduced here with permission.

The customization works by cascading three advanced filters as follows:

Filter 1 Figure 9.23 shows the first filter, which grabs the campaign source and medium of a visit and places them in a custom field.

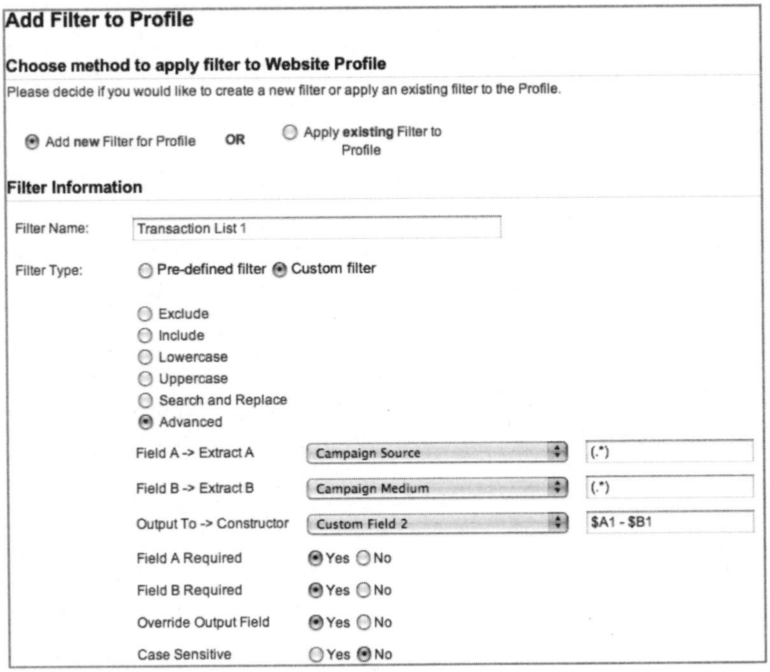

Add Filter to Profile

Choose method to apply filter to Website Profile

Please decide if you would like to create a new filter or apply an existing filter to the Profile.

○ Add **new** Filter for Profile   OR   ○ Apply **existing** Filter to Profile

Filter Information

Filter Name: Transaction List 1

Filter Type: ○ Pre-defined filter ● Custom filter

    ○ Exclude
    ○ Include
    ○ Lowercase
    ○ Uppercase
    ○ Search and Replace
    ● Advanced

Field A -> Extract A | Campaign Source | (.*)
Field B -> Extract B | Campaign Medium | (.*)
Output To -> Constructor | Custom Field 2 | $A1 - $B1
Field A Required   ● Yes ○ No
Field B Required   ● Yes ○ No
Override Output Field   ● Yes ○ No
Case Sensitive   ○ Yes ● No

Figure 9.23 Capturing the campaign source and medium and storing them in a custom field

Filter 2 Figure 9.24 shows the second filter, which adds the keyword to the custom field. The custom field then contains the referrer source, medium, and keyword.

Filter 3 Figure 9.25 shows the third and final filter, which takes the custom field created and appends it to the transaction order ID. This matches sources with specific transactions.

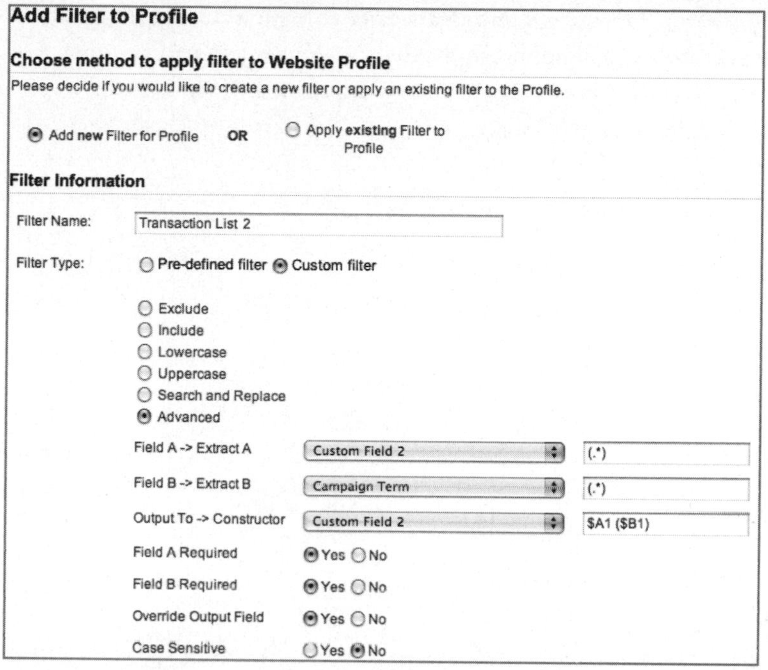

Add Filter to Profile

Choose method to apply filter to Website Profile

Please decide if you would like to create a new filter or apply an existing filter to the Profile.

◉ Add **new** Filter for Profile   **OR**   ○ Apply **existing** Filter to Profile

Filter Information

Filter Name: Transaction List 2

Filter Type: ○ Pre-defined filter ◉ Custom filter

    ○ Exclude
    ○ Include
    ○ Lowercase
    ○ Uppercase
    ○ Search and Replace
    ◉ Advanced

Field A -> Extract A	Custom Field 2	(.*)
Field B -> Extract B	Campaign Term	(.*)
Output To -> Constructor	Custom Field 2	$A1 ($B1)
Field A Required	◉ Yes ○ No	
Field B Required	◉ Yes ○ No	
Override Output Field	◉ Yes ○ No	
Case Sensitive	○ Yes ◉ No	

Figure 9.24 Appending the referral keyword to the custom field

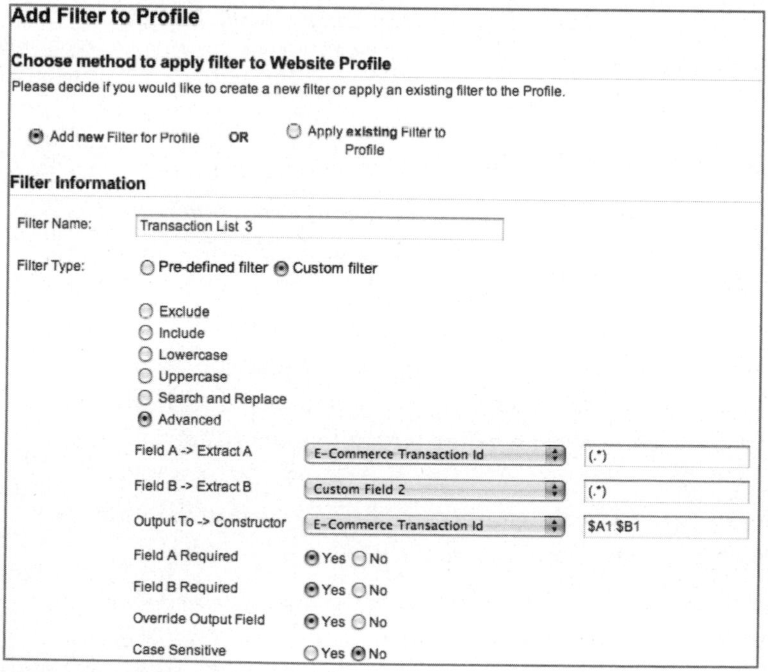

Add Filter to Profile

Choose method to apply filter to Website Profile

Please decide if you would like to create a new filter or apply an existing filter to the Profile.

◉ Add **new** Filter for Profile   **OR**   ○ Apply **existing** Filter to Profile

Filter Information

Filter Name: Transaction List 3

Filter Type: ○ Pre-defined filter ◉ Custom filter

    ○ Exclude
    ○ Include
    ○ Lowercase
    ○ Uppercase
    ○ Search and Replace
    ◉ Advanced

Field A -> Extract A	E-Commerce Transaction Id	(.*)
Field B -> Extract B	Custom Field 2	(.*)
Output To -> Constructor	E-Commerce Transaction Id	$A1 $B1
Field A Required	◉ Yes ○ No	
Field B Required	◉ Yes ○ No	
Override Output Field	◉ Yes ○ No	
Case Sensitive	○ Yes ◉ No	

Figure 9.25 Appending the custom field information to the transaction ID

Of course, the order of the filters is important, and this should be maintained as described. When done correctly, the cumulative result is a Conversions > Ecommerce > Transactions report that is transformed from just showing the list of transaction IDs to including details of the referring source, medium, and keyword, as shown in Figure 9.26. The format is as follows:

```
Transaction-ID referral source - medium (keywords)
```

Figure 9.26 Matching specific transactions to specific keywords

Tracking Campaign Links to File Downloads

What if your campaigns send visitors directly to a file that does not accept the GATC JavaScript page tag? This can be the case with email marketing or other specialized types of campaigns whereby visitors are referred directly to a PDF, EXE, ZIP, DOC, XLS, or PPT download—or any other file type that is not a website landing page. Without the GATC in place, Google Analytics will not detect a visitor from such a campaign. However, you can address this challenge by creating an intermediate landing page to capture the campaign variables *before* forwarding the visitor to the actual file download.

Figure 9.27 shows an example intermediate landing page generated by a link from an email message that points to the following URL:

```
www.mysite.com/forwarder.php?file=catalogue.pdf&utm_source=sales&
utm_campaign=first-followup&utm_medium=email
```

As you can see, the URL contains a list of parameters that includes the filename to be downloaded (catalogue.pdf) and Google Analytics campaign parameters, as discussed in Chapter 7. Table 9.2 describes the individual elements.

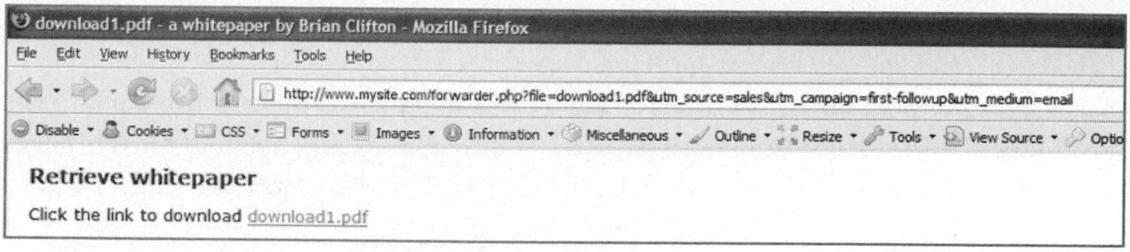

Figure 9.27 Example use of an intermediate landing page for file downloads

► **Table 9.2** URL breakdown for Figure 9.27

Element	Description
`forwarder.php`	Name of the web page that will redirect the visitor to the correct file
`catalogue.pdf`	Name of the file requested by the visitor
`utm_source`	Campaign source identifier
`utm_medium`	Campaign medium identifier
`utm_campaign`	Campaign name identifier

In this example, the forwarding page, `forwarder.php`, contains your GATC with the following code in the HTML `<head>` section tag:

```
<script type="text/javascript">
   var filename=("<? echo $_GET['file']; ?>") ? ➥
    "<? echo $_GET['file']; ?>" : "";
   var source=("<? echo $_GET['utm_source']; ?>") ? ➥
    "<? echo $_GET['utm_source']; ?>" : "";
   var medium=("<? echo $_GET['utm_medium']; ?>") ? ➥
    "<? echo $_GET['utm_medium']; ?>" : "";
   var campaign=("<? echo $_GET['utm_campaign']; ?>") ? ➥
    "<? echo $_GET['utm_campaign']; ?>" : "";
   window.onload = trackFile();

   function trackFile(){
      if (filename) {
         fullPath = "/downloads/direct/" +filename+ "?utm_source="➥
          +source+ "&utm_medium="+medium+ "&utm_campaign=" +campaign;
         _gaq.push(['_trackPageview', fullPath]);
         window.location = "http://" +document.domain +"/"+ filename
      }else{
         alert('No download file specified');
      }
   }
</script>
```

The purpose of the script is to immediately redirect the visitor to the specified download file using window.location. However, before doing so, it sets a virtual pageview for Google Analytics to track and report on and also appends campaign variables, captured from the landing page URL. No other content is required for this page, although as Figure 9.27 shows, also providing the option of a download link is good practice in case the redirect fails for some reason.

The beauty of this method is that you can view each file download as a pageview in your Google Analytics reports with the referral campaign, medium, and source correctly attributed to the referring campaign. See Figure 9.28.

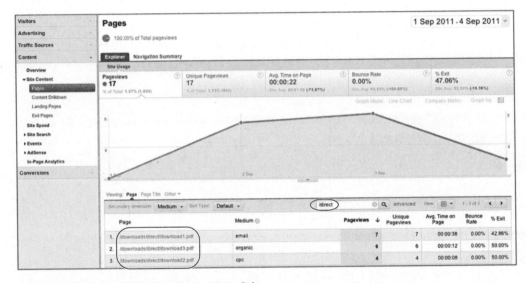

Figure 9.28 File download report from direct campaign links

In addition, forwarder.php will be listed with all the aggregate referral information; however, you might want to remove this page from your reports with an exclude filter to prevent double counting because it is effectively a nonpage.

Tracking Campaign Links to Third-Party Websites

You can use the same technique (Tracking Campaign Links to File Downloads) for tracking email marketing where links within the email point to third-party websites. That may sound counterintuitive—why conduct email marketing that takes the reader elsewhere? However, for highly decentralized organizations, it is sometimes necessary to send people to other websites within the organization that aren't tracked by the marketing department sending the email.

Using Events Instead

Although PHP is used in the example, the technique is equally applicable for any server-side web-scripting language you might use, such as ASP, .NET, CGI-Perl, Python, and so on. It is also easy to modify for tracking file downloads as events. Essentially, you modify the line

```
_gaq.push(['_trackPageview', fullPath]);
```

to something similar to the following example:

```
_gaq.push(['_trackEvent', 'File downloads', source, filename]);
```

See Chapter 7 for details on event tracking.

Changing the Referrer Credited for a Goal Conversion

Defining goals for your website is discussed in Chapter 7. By default, Google Analytics gives credit for a conversion to the last referrer a visitor used. For example, consider the following search scenario for a user who visits your website by way of a different referrer each time:

- Google organic search—visitor leaves your website (referrer 1).
- Google paid search—visitor leaves your website (referrer 2).
- Facebook referrer—visitor converts (referrer 3).

All visit referrals are tracked, with credit for the conversion given to referrer 3. This is the case except when the last referrer is direct—that is, the visitor uses their bookmark or types your URL directly into their browser address bar, for example:

- Google organic search—visitor leaves your website (referrer 1).
- Google paid search—visitor leaves your website (referrer 2).
- Facebook referrer—visitor leaves your website (referrer 3).
- Direct (bookmark)—visitor converts (referrer 4).

Credit for the conversion is still given to referrer 3. That makes sense because it is most likely referrer 3 that led to the bookmarking (or remembering) of your website address. In Chapter 5, "Reports Explained," I discuss the Multi-Channel Funnels reports. Multi-channel funnels show the referral path of conversions, that is, connecting referral sources when multiple visits occur prior to conversion (referrer 1 > referrer 2 > referrer 3 > referrer 4). But what if you wish to ignore one of those referrers? In the next section, you'll see why this can be important and how to do it.

Ignoring a Referrer for a Conversion

Why ignore a referrer? Consider, for example, an online marketing campaign using AdWords to drive visitors to your site. The call to action is a newsletter subscription. Before the subscription can be accepted, you require the visitor to confirm their email address by clicking a link in a confirmation email triggered by their sign-up. This is standard best practice to ensure that subscribers are real people who intended to subscribe.

If you were to use a standard link for confirmation within your email—that is, without any campaign tracking parameters—and the visitor is using a webmail client such a Gmail, Yahoo! Mail, or Hotmail, the confirming visitor will have a new referral source/medium combination set, such as, for example, `mail.google.com/referrer`, `mail.yahoo.com/referrer`, `mail.live.com/referrer` and so forth. These overwrite the AdWords campaign information that originally drove the visitor to your site. Even with campaign parameters appended to your email link URL, the situation is the same. Clearly, such click-throughs are not part of the visitor's referral journey, and you will wish to ignore this in your reports.

How Many People Use Webmail?

According to information collated by Mark Brownlow of Email Marketing Reports, webmail is used by some 800 million people world-wide:

`www.email-marketing-reports.com/metrics/email-statistics.htm`

The vast majority of these are personal accounts. However, business products such as Google Apps provide Gmail access to some 40 million business users according to Google's Chairman, Eric Schmidt:

`http://techcrunch.com/2011/09/01/eric-schmidt-google-apps-has-40m-users-adding-5k-new-companies-per-day/`

You can ignore the last referrer of a visitor by appending your landing page URLs with the `utm_nooveride=1` parameter. When Google Analytics detects the `utm_nooverride=1` parameter, it retains the previous referrer campaign information. That is, only if there are no existing campaign variables will new ones be written. The key here is to be consistent; that is, all "system" emails, such as those for confirming subscriptions and password resets, should have landing page URLs with `utm_nooveride=1`. That way, referral and campaign details that are driving visitors to your website are maintained while the email referrer details are ignored. For example, within your emails use links such as these:

```
http://www.mysite.com/confirm_account.php?id=1098746453svxg&utm_nooveride=1
http://www.mysite.com/reset_passwd.php?id=9887ndhcg765430&utm_nooveride=1
```

Note that if all your visitors used a standard mail application (that is, not web-mail), this technique would not be needed. However, increasingly, webmail cloud services are being used by people, so this is an important step to implement.

Although email follow-ups are the most common use of this technique, there may be other scenarios where you wish to use this method. If so, simply append the utm_nooverride=1 parameter to the landing page URL.

Roll-up Reporting

Roll-up reporting was initially discussed in Chapter 6. In summary, roll-up reporting answers the requirements of a very specific type of enterprise client; that is, autonomous offices or departments that wish to manage their own reporting needs (typically for region-specific domains—the United States, Europe, Asia, and so on) separately from HQ, which requires a bigger picture of all activity.

The principle to achieving this is to add multiple GATCs to your pages—more accurately described as adding a second tracker object. In this way, each autonomous office logs into its own stand-alone Google Analytics account while HQ logs into a "catchall" Google Analytics roll-up account. Each manages its own reporting needs without impacting the other. However, there are a number of caveats to this method, and these more-advanced issues are highlighted here. First, though, review the initial details of the section "Roll-up Reporting" in Chapter 6 before proceeding.

Tracking Roll-up Transactions

If yours is a transactional site, special consideration is required for e-commerce because you will need to call the e-commerce tracking code for each account—once for your stand-alone account and once for your roll-up account. So _addTrans, _addItem, and _trackTrans are required for both your default and second tracker objects. Schematically you need to add the following to your transaction receipt or confirmation page (see Chapter 7 for help with e-commerce tracking):

```
_gaq.push(['_addTrans', enter transaction values as an array ]);
_gaq.push(['_addItem', enter item values as an array ]);
_gaq.push(['_trackTrans']);

_gaq.push(['t2._addTrans', copy of transaction values from above]);
_gaq.push(['t2._addItem', copy of item values from above]);
_gaq.push(['t2._trackTrans']);
```

And that's it except for the following implications.

Implications of the Roll-up Technique

The following implications sound daunting at first, but in many cases they are not. Apart from unifying your e-commerce data (the second item that follows), you probably will not drill down deep enough in a roll-up report for these implications to be noticed. However, you should be aware of them.

Pageview aggregation Pageviews on your different websites that have the same page title or name (for example, index.htm, contact.htm) will be aggregated. That is, you will see only one entry in your roll-up report for index.htm and contact.htm, with the sum of their pageviews. Generally for roll-up reporting, this is not a problem because the account is used to get the bigger picture, or aggregate overview. However, if you still need the page name detail, apply the filter shown in Figure 7.15 of Chapter 7. This is the same filter for differentiating pageviews from subdomains.

Transactions in different currencies Similar to pageview aggregation, e-commerce data will be aggregated. That is, if you have transactions in different currencies, the revenue totals become meaningless at the aggregate roll-up level. Thus, dollars, pounds, euros, and so on are all combined regardless of exchange rates. Therefore, for your roll-up account, unify your transaction data into a single base currency. This base currency should remain fixed so that long-term comparisons can be made. Don't change this to reflect currency exchange rates.

Time zone alignment If your stand-alone accounts operate in different time zones, ignore time-of-day reports in the roll-up account. They won't make sense!

AdWords ROI in different currencies If you run AdWords accounts in different currencies for your stand-alone Google Analytics account, ignore the ROI and margin metrics from the Traffic Sources > AdWords reports. They won't make sense!

Cookie manipulation The roll-up reporting method results in cookies being shared between both your stand-alone and roll-up Google Analytics accounts. Therefore, any cookie manipulation on one—changing time-out values or expiry date, for example—results in changes impacting both sets of reports. This issue can arise, for example, if you have an agency collecting data for its own internal purposes (stand-alone account). They may wish to experiment, not realizing the wider impact. If this happens, a great deal of time and money can be wasted trying to troubleshoot data anomalies. Therefore, ensure that such changes are managed centrally. One option is to use the Custom tab of the GATC setup wizard, as discussed in the section "Customizing the GATC" in Chapter 7.

Improvement Tip: Simplify with Pageview Roll-up

If you have dozens or even hundreds of product micro sites, you may wish to simplify your roll-up pageview reports even further. Rather than collecting detail of every page URL on each micro site into the roll-up account, "concertina" this into a per-site view. That is, roll up your pageviews.

In this way, instead of having page A = 300 views, page B = 200 views, page C = 100 views, and so on, you would have pageview for www.mysite.com = 600, www.mysite2.com = 130, and so on. This simplifies the Top Content report so that you see overall pageview volumes on a per-site basis. You can use the following GATC modification for simplifying pageview reports:

```
<script type="text/javascript">
  var _gaq = _gaq || [];
  _gaq.push(['_setAccount', 'UA-12345-1']);
  _gaq.push(['t2._setAccount', 'UA-98765-1']);
  _gaq.push(['_trackPageview']);                      // maintain pageview detail
  _gaq.push(['t2._trackPageview', location.host]);    // roll-up pageviews


(function() {
var ga = document.createElement('script');
ga.type = 'text/javascript'; ga.async = true;
ga.src = ('https:' == document.location.protocol ? 'https://ssl' : ➥
'http://www') + '.google-analytics.com/ga.js';
var s = document.getElementsByTagName('script')[0];
s.parentNode.insertBefore(ga, s);
})();
</script>
```

Summary

In Chapter 9, you have learned the following:

Customizing the list of recognized search engines You have learned to add new and regional variations to the default search engine list so that you can differentiate visitors from, for example, google.com and google.co.uk, among others.

Labeling You know how to apply labels via the use of custom variables to visitors, sessions, and pages, allowing you to group these for better segmentation and analysis.

Tracking error pages and broken links You can now identify and highlight things that don't work on your site so they can be fixed quickly.

Tracking referral URLs from pay-per-click networks You understand which niche pay-per-click sites are driving traffic and conversions for you when they are part of a greater network.

Differentiating links to the same page (site overlay) I discussed how the performance of a link differs by its format and placement on a page.

Matching transactions to specific keywords You learned how to determine which source, medium, and keywords are driving revenue at the specific transaction level.

Tracking campaign links to file downloads You saw how to ensure that a link in an email leading directly to a file download is tracked.

Changing which referrer is given credit for a conversion You can now manipulate the referrer attribution model to credit the first referrer or the last referrer or capture both.

Using roll-up reports You learned how to use roll-up reports for catchall overviews of multiple websites.

Using Visitor Data to Drive Website Improvement

Reporting, although important, is only half the story. The real power of web analytics lies in what you do with the data. Having a clear understanding of visitor behavior enables you to identify bottlenecks in conversion processes and marketing campaigns so you can improve them. That is, you can turn inert data into actionable information.

Part IV is about using data, from determining the most important metrics of performance (how to measure success) to optimizing pages, processes, and online and offline marketing campaigns. In addition, integrating Google Analytics data with third-party applications is a recent phenomenon that is on the increase.

In Part IV, you will learn the following:

Google Analytics in Color

Color is extremely helpful when viewing large amounts of information. Within Google Analytics it is used to differentiate sections of your reports, add clarity, provide emphasis, and show value and pain points. Color is an integral part of the information architecture, which I think the Google Analytics team has designed well.

This section lets me show the most important images in color. I also encourage you to read this book while viewing your own Google Analytics reports so that you can interact with your data while I describe the detail.

Figure 4.4 is a key screen shot for understanding the Google Analytics user interface—it has a typical structure that most reports follow. Ensure that you are familiar with the use of its features (labels A to R).

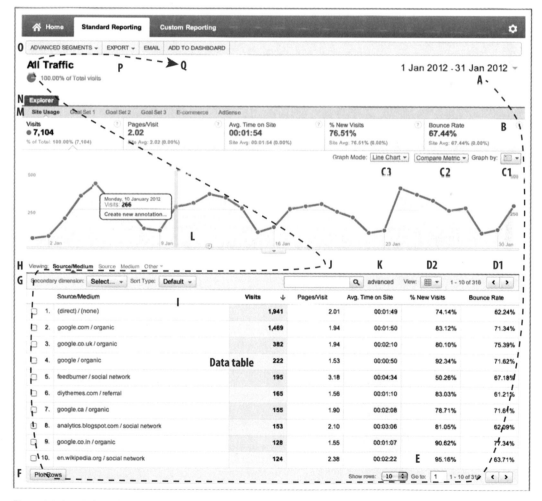

Figure 4.4 A typical Google Analytics report with guideline path

Reports contain two types of information—metrics (numbers) and dimensions (text). These are color-coded green and blue in Figure 4.5. Throughout Google Analytics, there are many instances where you can select dimensions and metrics. Therefore, it is important that you understand the difference.

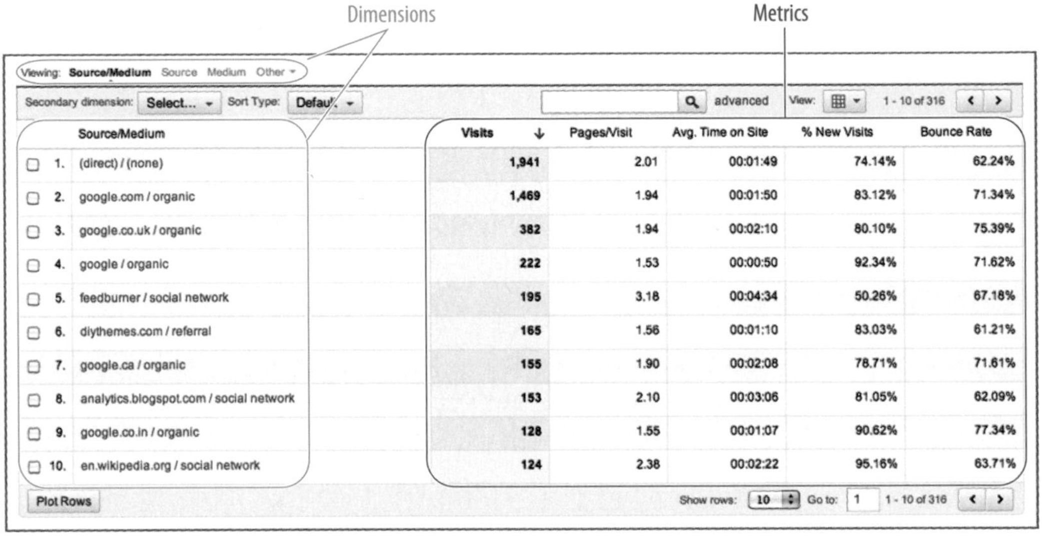

Figure 4.5 The difference between dimensions and metrics: green = dimensions; blue = metrics

Using a secondary dimension allows you to cross-reference your data. For example, the source/medium of a visitor by visitor type, as shown in Figure 4.13, allows you to understand the differences between new and returning visitors based on how those visitors find your site.

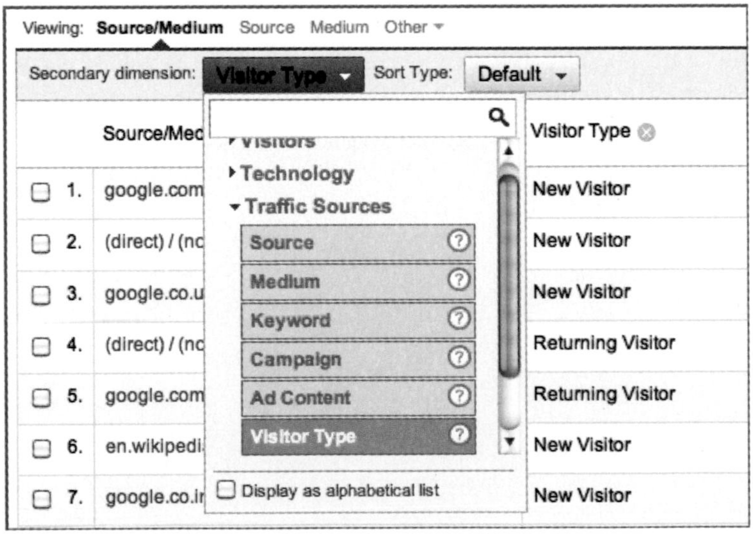

Figure 4.13 Viewing a secondary dimension

Figure 4.7 shows Google Analytics color-coding data by date (compare to past) and performance (an improvement or not). Metrics that improve are shown in bold green, while those that decrease are in bold red. The Bounce Rate metric is the exception because a decrease in this metric is considered a good thing.

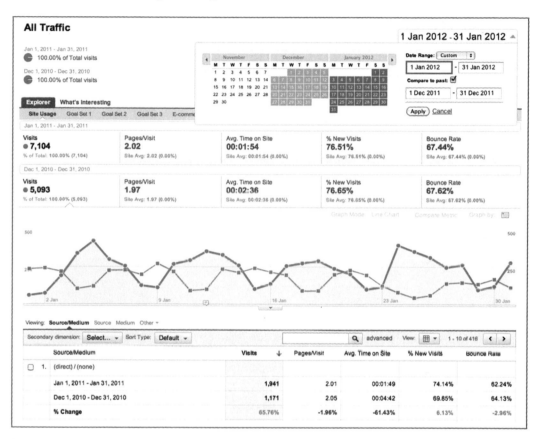

Figure 4.7 Comparing two date ranges

The "comparison" view of table data, as shown in Figure 4.10, is a great way to quickly identify which dimensions (in this example, referral mediums) are your significant traffic contributors. Green bars show those that are above the table average, with red bars indicating those that are below the table average. Besides traffic volume, other metrics can be viewed in this way, for example, goal conversion rate, transactions, revenue, per visit value, and so forth.

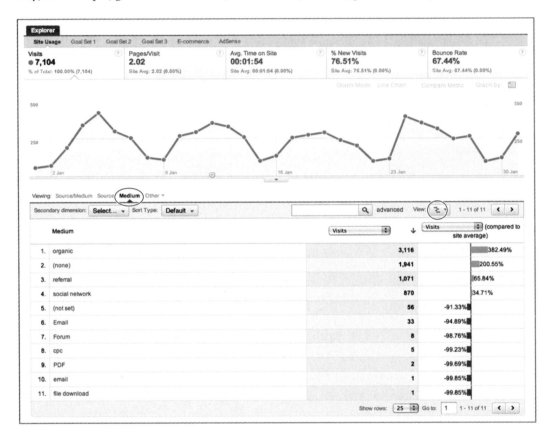

Figure 4.10 Comparison view

Figure 4.15 shows the building of an advanced table filter to show only visit data from visitors that arrive from referral links (for example, partner sites) and social networks who also spend at least 3 minutes on your site and have a conversion rate of greater than 10 percent. Note the color coding of dimensions and metrics.

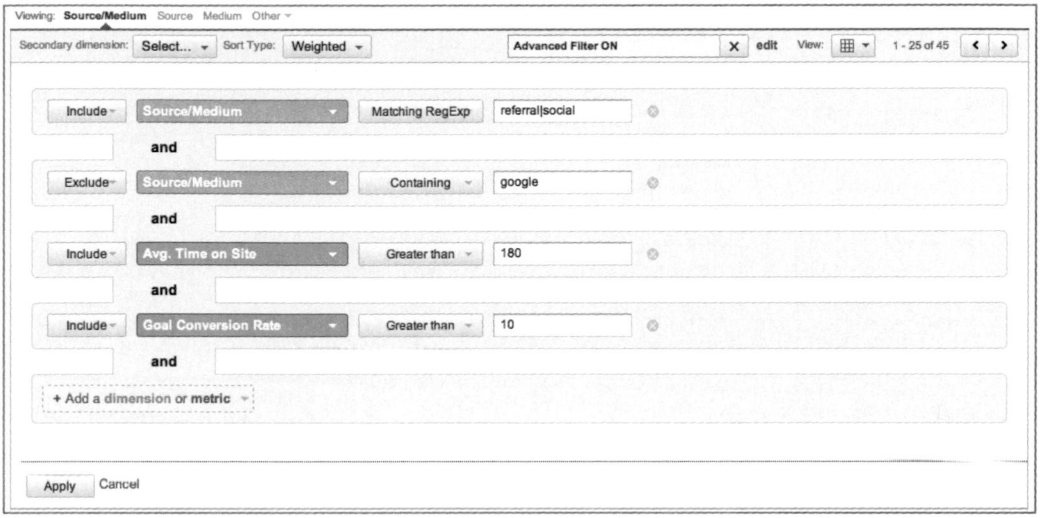

Figure 4.15 An advanced search filter for complex table filtering

Real-time reports, as shown in Figure 5.2, display a 30-minute window of your website traffic, updated within seconds. It is an excellent resource for testing new campaigns and monitoring time-sensitive performance—for example, a new product announcement, news article, or TV ad.

Figure 5.2 A real-time report showing up-to-the-second view of referral sources

The Intelligence Events Overview report, shown in Figure 5.3, is your alert system that flags important changes in your traffic patterns that may otherwise have gone unnoticed.

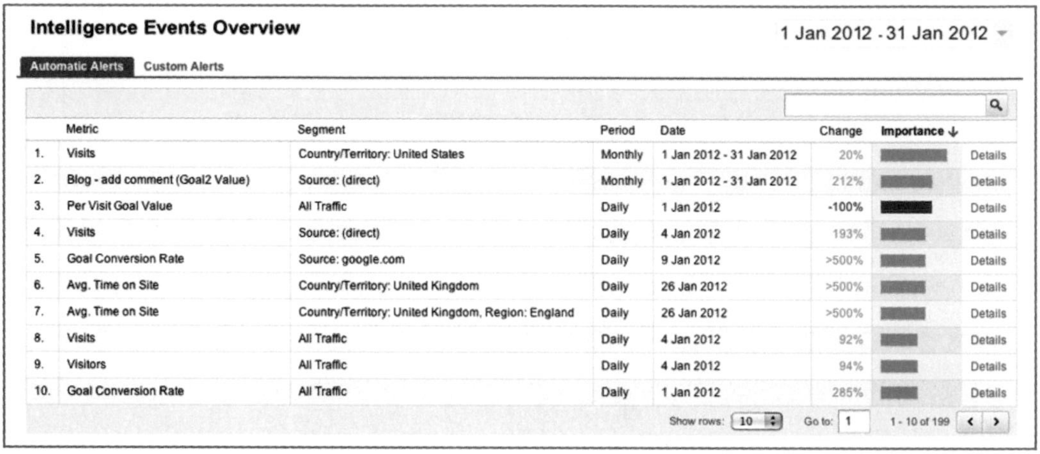

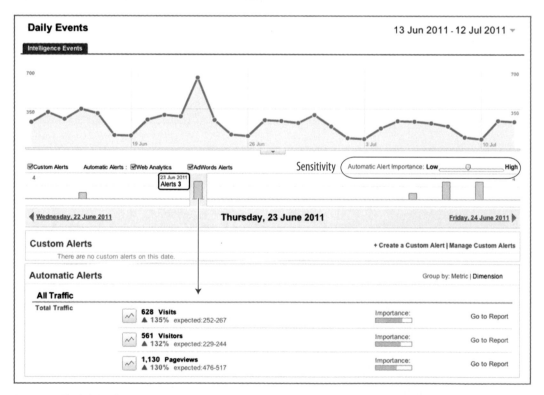

Figure 5.3 The Intelligence Overview report

Clicking through on one of the alerts shown in Figure 5.3 shows the report in Figure 5.4. The report details the important factors that triggered the alert.

Figure 5.4 The daily intelligence report

Flow visualization, shown in Figure 5.7, allows you to view how traffic flows around your website. Unlike path analysis from other vendor tools, a *node* is not a single page but rather a collection of similar pages that Google Analytics has grouped together. This technique greatly improves your ability to understand *flow* rather than individual paths, which are meaningless.

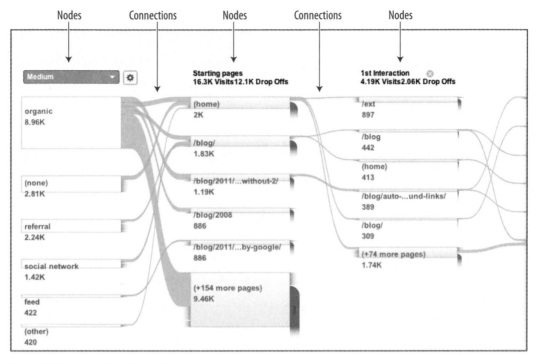

Figure 5.7 An example Flow Visualization report

Multi-Channel Funnels is a new report suite that allows you view all the referral sources that have contributed to a conversion—as opposed to last click wins. Figure 5.14 shows the level of detail and customization features available. In particular, you see the value of referral sources based on whether they only assisted in the conversion process or were the last click in the conversion chain.

Figure 5.14 Multi-Channel Funnels assisted conversion report

As part of the Multi-Channel Funnels suite of reports, Figure 5.15 shows how different mediums have contributed and interacted for those visitors that converted—that is, completed a goal or transacted. For example, rows 5 through 7 reveal that email follow-ups are an important part of the marketing mix, a fact that is lost if only the "last click wins" scenario is considered.

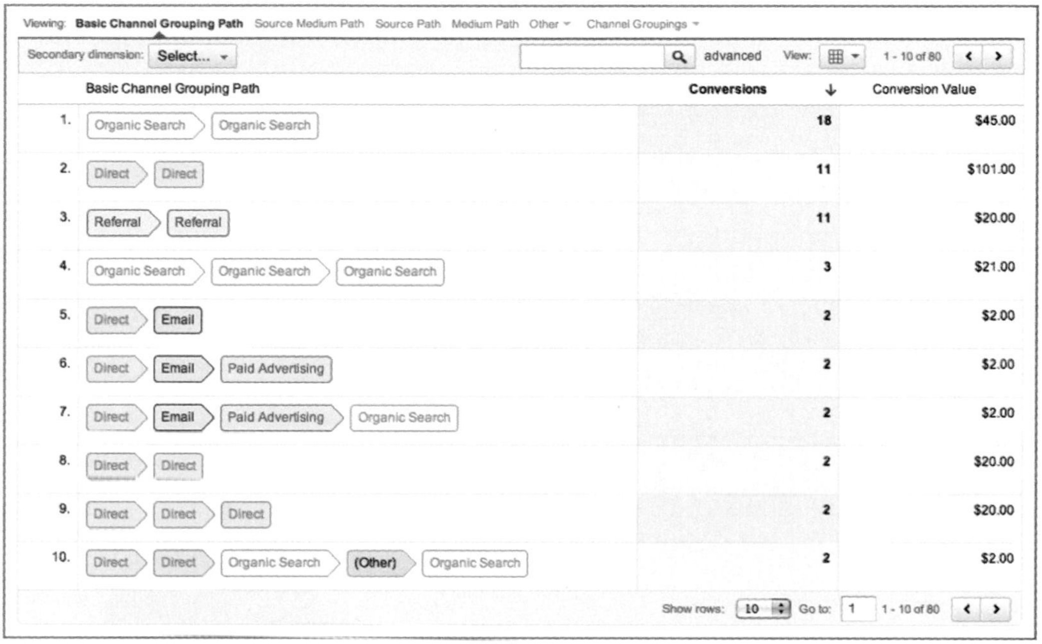
Viewing: Basic Channel Grouping Path Source Medium Path Source Path Medium Path Other Channel Groupings

Secondary dimension: Select... advanced View: 1 - 10 of 80

	Basic Channel Grouping Path	Conversions	Conversion Value
1.	Organic Search > Organic Search	18	$45.00
2.	Direct > Direct	11	$101.00
3.	Referral > Referral	11	$20.00
4.	Organic Search > Organic Search > Organic Search	3	$21.00
5.	Direct > Email	2	$2.00
6.	Direct > Email > Paid Advertising	2	$2.00
7.	Direct > Email > Paid Advertising > Organic Search	2	$2.00
8.	Direct > Direct	2	$20.00
9.	Direct > Direct > Direct	2	$20.00
10.	Direct > Direct > Organic Search > (Other) > Organic Search	2	$2.00

Show rows: 10 Go to: 1 1 - 10 of 80

Figure 5.15 Top Conversion Paths report

The Social Actions report of Figure 5.17 shows the level of social interactions with your content; that is, do people tweet, share, like, and rate your content, and if so, what is the preferred social network for your visitor demographic?

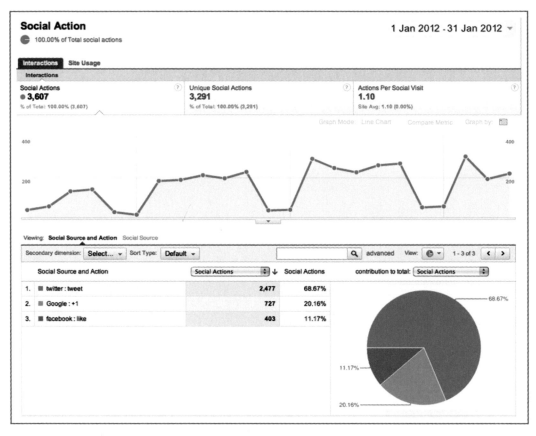

Figure 5.17 Example Social Actions report

The geographic density maps of Google Analytics are an excellent way of visualizing your data when location is important. You can zoom in to continent, subcontinent, country, and even regional level. Figure 5.18 compares the visit density of US visits to the goal conversion rate density. For this example website, location is clearly an important factor in success.

Figure 5.18 Geographic density of (a) visits and (b) goal conversions rate for the same data set

Motion charts animate your data. I recommend you regularly view this report to spot important changes. By animating with motion charts, you can view how up to four metrics of a dimension vary over time. For example, for the dimension `referral source`, show how traffic volume, page depth, goal conversion rate, and average time on site vary over time, as shown in Figure 5.21. The visualization technique is an excellent way to spot significant changes over time—something that is practically impossible to do with the default static view of data.

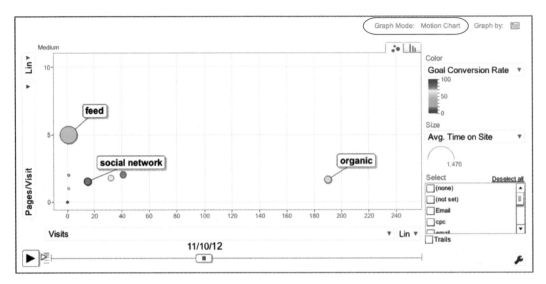

Figure 5.21 Motion chart for the Traffic Sources Medium report

Figure 5.33 shows how your internal search engine (site search report) is performing. In this example, it shows the number of searches performed, broken down by which page the visitor performed the search from. Clicking through each page URL reveals the search terms used.

	Start Page	Total Unique Searches	Total Unique Searches	
1.	■ (entrance)	151	24.84%	
2.	■ /blog/	115	18.91%	
3.	■ /	61	10.03%	
4.	/blog/ga-scripts/	24	3.95%	
5.	■ /blog/2011/05/10/customisations-you-cannot-live-without-2/	11	1.81%	
6.	■ /blog/pro-lounge/	10	1.64%	
7.	■ /blog/2010/02/12/12-useful-tools-for-google-analytics-admin/	9	1.48%	
8.	/blog/2008/11/03/tracking-social-networks-with-google-analytics-using-filters/	7	1.15%	
9.	■ /blog/getting-help/	7	1.15%	
10.	■ /?fb_xd_fragment=	5	0.82%	

Figure 5.33 Site Search report showing which pages visitors start their search from

Funnel visualization is a technique used to optimize well-defined linear paths on your website—for example, a checkout process or subscription sign-up—as shown in Figure 5.22.

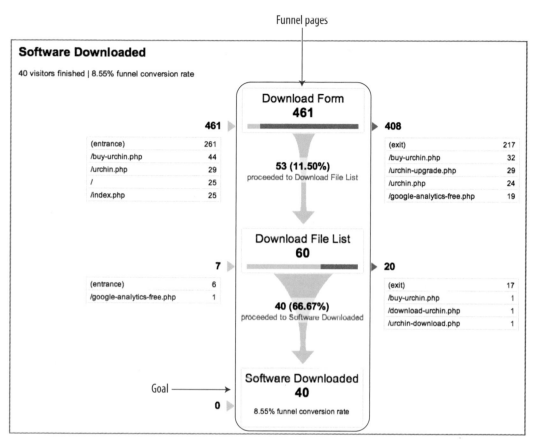

Figure 5.22 A three-step Funnel Visualization report

Figure 5.34 is a visual map of the performance of links within a page. The site overlay shows (for this example) where your visitors are clicking. Other performance metrics can also be used, such as goal conversion rate, transactions, value metric, and so forth.

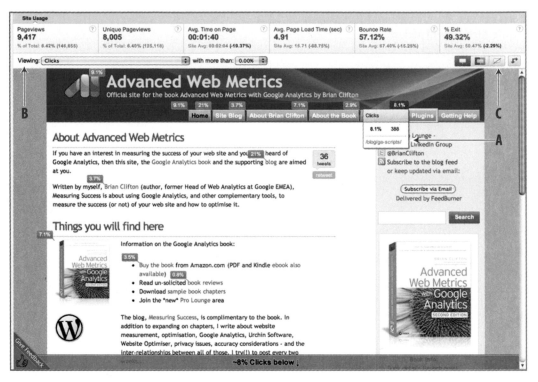

Figure 5.34 In-Page Analytics report

Sometimes you need to focus your audience's attention (and even yourself!) on a specific set of data values or a customized group of metrics—typically these are your key performance indicators. For these, export your data, either manually as a file download or automatically using the API, and import into an Excel spreadsheet for further manipulation, as is shown in Figure 10.1.

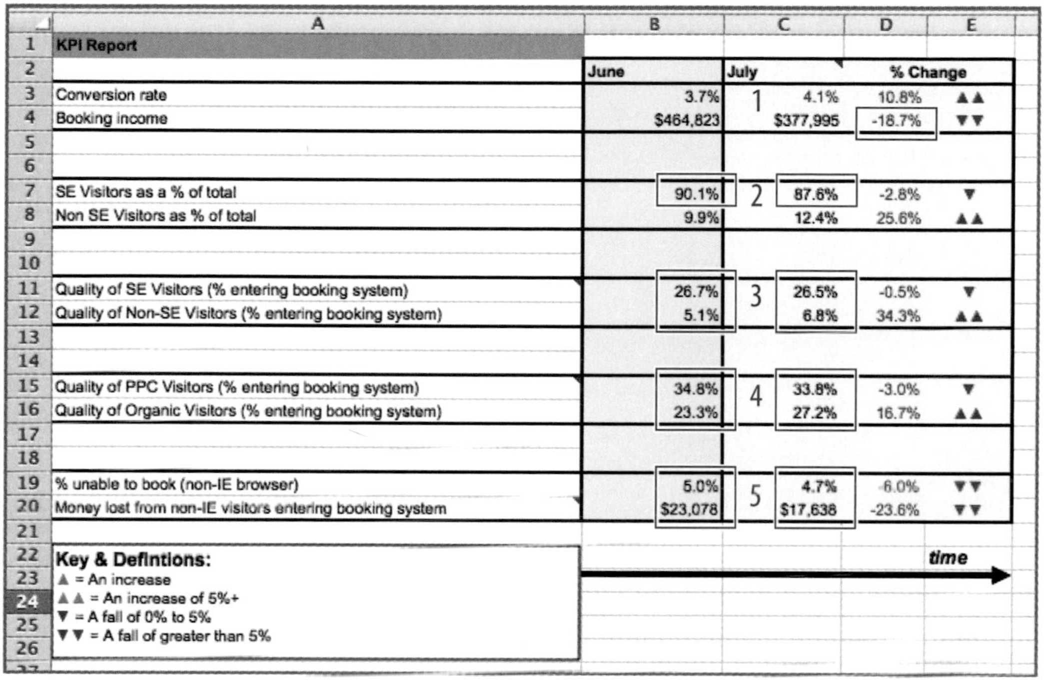

	A	B	C	D	E
1	KPI Report				
2		June	July	% Change	
3	Conversion rate	3.7%	1 4.1%	10.8%	▲▲
4	Booking income	$464,823	$377,995	-18.7%	▼▼
5					
6					
7	SE Visitors as a % of total	90.1%	2 87.6%	-2.8%	▼
8	Non SE Visitors as % of total	9.9%	12.4%	25.6%	▲▲
9					
10					
11	Quality of SE Visitors (% entering booking system)	26.7%	3 26.5%	-0.5%	▼
12	Quality of Non-SE Visitors (% entering booking system)	5.1%	6.8%	34.3%	▲▲
13					
14					
15	Quality of PPC Visitors (% entering booking system)	34.8%	4 33.8%	-3.0%	▼
16	Quality of Organic Visitors (% entering booking system)	23.3%	27.2%	16.7%	▲▲
17					
18					
19	% unable to book (non-IE browser)	5.0%	5 4.7%	-6.0%	▼▼
20	Money lost from non-IE visitors entering booking system	$23,078	$17,638	-23.6%	▼▼
21					
22	Key & Defintions:				*time*
23	▲ = An increase				
24	▲▲ = An increase of 5%+				
25	▼ = A fall of 0% to 5%				
26	▼▼ = A fall of greater than 5%				

Figure 10.1 Example KPI report for a travel website using Excel

A powerful addition to the Multi-Channel Funnels reports that are discussed in Chapter 5 is the ability to build a custom channel grouping, as shown in Figure 11.18. In the example shown, the custom channel will compare the use of brand versus generic keywords from search engine visitors; that is, when there are multiple visits to achieve a conversion, what is the relationship between the referral search terms for each visit?

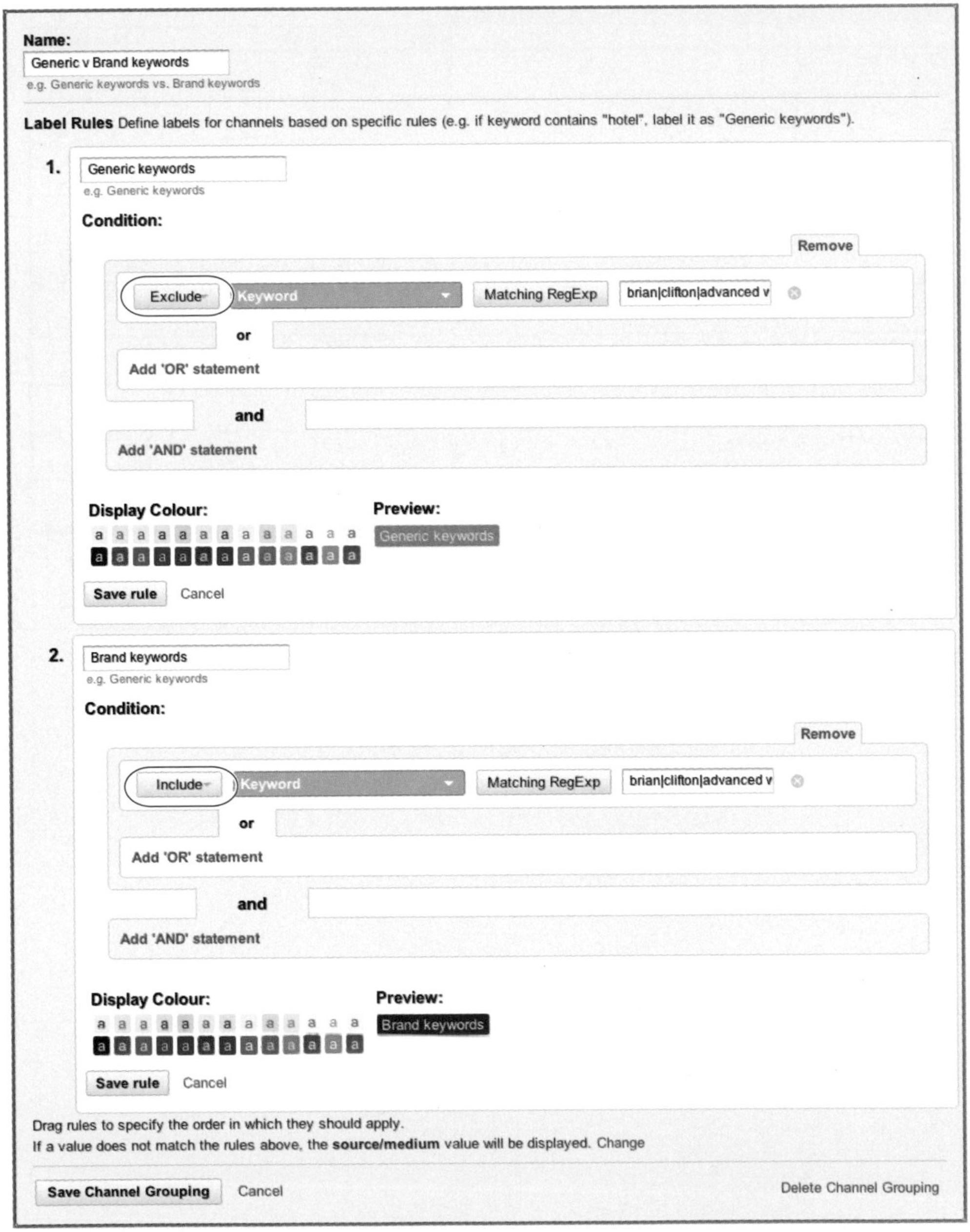

Name:

Generic v Brand keywords

e.g. Generic keywords vs. Brand keywords

Label Rules Define labels for channels based on specific rules (e.g. if keyword contains "hotel", label it as "Generic keywords").

1. Generic keywords

e.g. Generic keywords

Condition:

Remove

Exclude▾ Keyword ▾ | Matching RegExp | brian|clifton|advanced v ⊗

or

Add 'OR' statement

and

Add 'AND' statement

Display Colour: **Preview:**

a a a a a a a a a a a a   Generic keywords
a a a a a a a a a a a a

Save rule   Cancel

2. Brand keywords

e.g. Generic keywords

Condition:

Remove

Include▾ Keyword ▾ | Matching RegExp | brian|clifton|advanced v ⊗

or

Add 'OR' statement

and

Add 'AND' statement

Display Colour: **Preview:**

a a a a a a a a a a a a   Brand keywords
a a a a a a a a a a a a

Save rule   Cancel

Drag rules to specify the order in which they should apply.
If a value does not match the rules above, the **source/medium** value will be displayed. Change

Save Channel Grouping   Cancel   Delete Channel Grouping

Figure 11.18 Custom channel grouping set up for search engine visitors using brand terms versus generic terms

Focusing on Key Performance Indicators

By now you understand what web analytics tools can do, how to set up Google Analytics using best practices, and how to navigate its interface so that you feel comfortable with the data.

What we have discussed so far has been fairly straightforward—dare I say easy? The next step, providing key performance indicators (KPIs), *is the difficult part—not from a technical perspective but purely in terms of communication.*

KPIs enable your colleagues to focus on the parts of their online strategy that are most effective at increasing visitors, leads, conversions, and revenue for the business. The key for large organizations is delivering different KPI reports to each stakeholder and ensuring that these are hierarchical.

10

In Chapter 10, you will learn:

To set objectives and key results

To select and prepare KPIs

To present hierarchical KPIs

About example KPIs segmented by stakeholder job roles

About KPIs for a Web 2.0 environment

Setting Objectives and Key Results

To summarize the story so far, the best-practice implementation principles are as follows:

- Tag everything—get the most complete picture of your website visitors possible.
- Clean and segment your data—apply filters.
- Define goals—distill the 100-plus reports of Google Analytics into performance benchmarks.

If you have followed these steps, that's excellent. However, the usual problem is that few other people in your organization know what you've done or appreciate your work. To many people, you have created a set of nice charts and reports. Even if they don't say it aloud, they may be thinking, "So what?"

The unfortunate truth is that you will have wasted your time unless you can get the buy-in to use the visitor data to drive business decisions and be the focal point for instigating change on your website. With your initial understanding of your visitor data, this is your next step—that is, to set key performance indicators for your website and align these with the objectives and key results (OKRs) of your organization. For this you need to bring in stakeholders from the other parts of the business.

What Is a Stakeholder?

Stakeholders can be internal or external to your organization; for example, a search marketing agency can be a stakeholder that's external to your organization. They can be actively involved, or they may be end users of your reports attempting to make strategic business decisions from it. In this context, stakeholders are senior managers who have the organizational authority to allocate resources (people, budget) and can prioritize change. They are the people who make or break a change.

This is precisely why you need stakeholders on board. As discussed in Chapter 1, "Why Understanding Your Web Traffic Is Important to Your Business," web measurement is all about providing the foundation and yardstick for instigating change.

Most people are using web analytics as a benchmark: how did we do yesterday, and how are we doing today? Smart people are actually analyzing to optimize their website. The advanced people are using Web data to optimize all of their marketing.

—Jim Sterne, founding director and chairman
of the Web Analytics Association

OKRs are about understanding your business goals. This is an important prerequisite before you delve into the specific KPIs for your website. Essentially, you need to ensure that the two are in alignment, and setting OKRs prepares the way. Once you have your list of OKRs, the business language of your organization, you can use them to build your KPIs, the analyst language of your website.

The process of defining your OKRs consists of four steps:

1. Map your stakeholders.
2. Brainstorm with them.
3. Set your OKRs.
4. Distill and refine your OKRs.

Step 1: Map your stakeholders. Who are your stakeholders? They may be marketing, sales, PR, operations, web development and design agencies, e-commerce managers, content creators—even the CEO. Of course, it may be only the CEO, but if not, select one person from each department as the key contact for initial discussions. Your first choice may not end up being the right person, but you can change that later. The important thing is to get people on board from those departments. A key initial stakeholder is the person or department responsible for your Google Analytics implementation. If changes to your setup are required, this person should be involved from the start so they understand the vision and direction of your other stakeholders. This person can advise you on what can and cannot be done, understands the pain points, and can advise on alternative strategies as needed.

Your key contacts are the individuals who represent the interests of that department within your organization. They can canvass opinion from the rest of the organization on your behalf; in other words, they do not have to be the most senior people in their departments, though they should have a strategic and overview role, such as managerial. Try to make this a two-way street, with you setting the scene with your initial data and thoughts on the current situation and stakeholders providing their perspective on how it fits with their department. For example, they may provide information from customer relationship management (CRM) systems, call center figures, web server performance, and so on.

Step 2: Brainstorm with your stakeholders. Determine their requirements and expectations, and, more important, manage these to ensure that your project is a success. Accomplish this by arranging regular meetings with your stakeholders. For the first meeting, bring everyone together and aim to get a consensus of opinion. This should focus on what is currently happening—not whether it is good or bad, but rather what information is available. By the end of the session, you and your stakeholders should start to understand each other with respect to terminology, what data can be collected, and its accuracy and limitations.

For the second and subsequent meetings, meet with each stakeholder separately. In broad terms, you will be guiding the stakeholder as to what information can be gleaned from your reports and how it can be useful to the business. The trick is to get them to realize the opportunity that data insights can bring, so take some ideas into the meeting with you. Often your stakeholders will ask for more information, or possibly less, but usually they want to see data cross-referenced against other metrics—something to prepare for the next meeting. This brainstorming process usually takes one or two meetings and is an important period in which to manage expectations, such as timeline and budget.

Step 3: Set your OKRs. With expectations managed and stakeholders on board and feeling engaged with the project, you should be ready to ask the question, "What is the objective of our website from your specific point of view?" With this, ask them to define what performance constitutes good and what constitutes bad. If you can answer those three questions from each stakeholder, you have done a great job. The key, and often the difficulty, is to delve below the obvious macro objectives of generating more overall revenue, sales leads, and traffic volumes. Those of course will be dealt with, but it's the layers of detail below this that impact on those, and that's what you need to find out. Don't worry if you need a few more meetings to achieve this. Every organization is different. But try not to let this process drag on or you risk losing momentum. The process taking place is not set in stone and can be reviewed and modified in six months or whenever necessary.

Encourage your stakeholders to give measurable answers to your objectives question or suggest some yourself; these form the *results* part of the OKRs. The following are example OKRs I have come across:

- A Main Street retail store carries tens of thousands of products. It is not feasible to have all of these on its e-commerce-enabled website because some are not cost-effective to ship, for example. By analyzing the site's transaction and feedback data (the objective), it wishes to select the most popular product categories for the focus of its online efforts (the result).

- A home furniture store that does *not* have a transactional website produces a printed catalog each year (at great expense). However, which products make it into the printed version is a mixture of experienced guesswork and luck, based largely on the whims of fashion trends. By analyzing the interests of its web visitors (objective), it wishes to better predict and select with greater confidence which items should go into their next catalog (result).

- A gaming company wants to understand which is the next hot market to establish operations in. By understanding the geographies and language demographics of its web visitors (objective), it wishes to select candidate markets for further research and tests (result).

- A waste disposal company wishes to emphasize the environmental friendliness of its work on its corporate website. But what are visitors who visit a waste disposal website interested in (objective)? Understanding this will enable the company to better tailor content to get its environmental message across (result).

- A government information site, a nonprofit, is struggling to cope with the inquiry volume of its visitors and has requested an investment in new support staff. However, the funding department wants to know whether this is a cost-effective option or whether they should alter how their website operates, such as provide more self-help articles (objective). The web team needs to understand which visitor actions are of most value to support their funding request (result).

Step 4: Distill and refine your OKRs. With a long list of objectives and key results from your stakeholders (such lists are always long to start with), distill it down to the five most important OKRs for each. This should be your maximum because it is likely that each OKR will require more than one KPI to measure it. Therefore, focusing your efforts on the five most important OKRs will stand you in good stead because managers generally cannot cope with a long list of directives to act on. Where possible, group OKRs and keep them directional by avoiding the temptation of overspecifying.

Selecting and Preparing KPIs

Google Analytics is your free data-gathering and reporting tool, but it will not optimize your website for you. That requires smart people (you!) to analyze, interpret, and act on the reported findings. To act on your Google Analytics information—that is, instigate changes—you need to present your findings in a clear, understandable format to stakeholders. These are a diverse group of people who sit at different levels in your organization—all the way up to the board, one hopes. That's the caveat: Presenting web analytics data outside of your immediate team is a challenge because most businesspeople simply do not have the time to understand the details that such reports offer.

To communicate your story effectively to your stakeholders, create reports in a format and language that business managers understand—that is, KPI reports. These are abridged versions of your web analytics reports, usually summarized in Microsoft Excel or PowerPoint.

What Is a KPI?

Web analytics aside, organizations around the world use key performance indicators to assess their performance. Also sometimes referred to as key success indicators (KSI) or balanced score cards (BSC), KPIs are used in business intelligence to appraise the state of a business. Once an organization has set its OKRs, it needs a way to measure progress. Key performance indicators are those measurements.

Similarly, in web analytics, a key performance indicator is a web metric that is essential for your organization's online success. The emphasis here is on the word *essential*. If a 10 percent change—positive or negative—in a KPI doesn't make you sit up and call someone to find out what happened, then it is not well defined. Good KPIs create expectations and drive action, and because of this they are a small subset of information from your reports.

When considering your KPIs, bear in mind the following:

- Try to use monetary values where possible; everybody understands $$$.

- If not a monetary value, use a ratio, percentage, or average rather than the raw number. This allows data to be presented in context.

- A KPI needs to be temporal, that is, time bound. This highlights change and its speed.

- A KPI drives business-critical actions. Many things are measurable, but that does not make them key to your organization's success.

Use KPIs to put your data into context. For example, saying "We had 10,000 visitors this week" provides a piece of data, but it is not a KPI because it has no context. How do you know whether this number is good or bad? A KPI based on this data could be "Our visitor numbers are up 10 percent month on month." This is a temporal indication that things are looking good over the time span of one month. In this example, the raw number should still be part of the KPI report, but it is not the KPI itself.

For the reasons just given, the vast majority of KPIs are ratios, percentages, or averages. However, sometimes a raw number can have a much greater impact. Consider the following examples:

- Our website lost 15 orders yesterday because our e-commerce server was down for 34 minutes.

- We lost $10,000 in potential revenue last week because our booking system does not work for visitors who use Firefox.

- We spent $36,000 last month on PPC keywords that did not convert.

Clearly, knowing what fraction of the total these numbers represent is important, but the impact of the raw numbers themselves is far greater at obtaining action and therefore should be the KPI .

The key point is that you should develop KPIs relevant to *your* particular business and *your* stakeholders. Any metric, percentage, ratio, or average that can help your organization quickly understand visitor data and is in context and temporal should be considered a KPI.

Preparing KPIs

Most of the hard work of preparing KPIs consists of defining OKRs—the dialogue you had with your stakeholders in obtaining the business objectives of your company. The key results used to establish OKR success are in fact your KPIs; you just need to turn these into actual web metrics that are available to you.

Sometimes (actually, quite often) discussing KPIs with stakeholders instills fear in your colleagues. They think you are performing the web equivalent of a time and motion study that is going to spotlight their deficiencies and single them out as not doing a good job. That fear is understandable: Being measured is not a comfortable feeling. However, my approach has always been to dispel that image. Evangelize web analytics KPIs as the tools to help your stakeholders shine and be rewarded for their efforts. Wield a carrot, not a stick.

The art of building and presenting a KPI report lies in being able to distill the plethora of website visitor data into metrics that align with your OKRs. For small organizations, having a report of 10 KPIs aligning with 10 OKRs is usually sufficient. For organizations with many stakeholders, having only one KPI report will not cover the requirements of your entire business—there are simply too many stakeholders to reach a consensus about what the KPI short list should contain. Therefore, ensure that you tailor your KPI reports to specific needs by having individual stakeholder and hierarchical KPI reports.

Here is a six-point KPI preparation checklist:

1. Set your OKRs.

   I repeat this here because of its importance. Identifying your stakeholders, discussing their needs, and being aware of the overall business plan for your organization enables you to put in place relevant metrics. This is an essential first step to ensure that your KPIs align with the business objectives of your organization. Otherwise, you are just a hit counter monkey—looking backward and not forward.

2. Translate OKRs into KPIs.

   This means setting specific web metrics against the business OKRs. Some metrics will be directly accessible from your Google Analytics reports; for example, if your e-commerce department says they want to "increase the amount of money each customer spends," then you will look for the average order value (AOV) from within the e-commerce section and monitor this over time. However, not all KPI metrics can be obtained in this way; sometimes segmentation is required or the multiplication or division of one number by another. Table 10.1 is a useful translation tool.

Stakeholder OKR	Suggested KPIs
To see more traffic from search engines	Percentage of visits from search engines
	Percentage of conversions from search engine visitors
To sell more products	Percentage of visits that add to shopping cart
	Ratio of visits that complete the shopping cart over the number that started
	Percentage of visits in which shopping cart is abandoned at position X in the process
To see visitors engaging with our website more	Percentage of visits that leave a comment, click a love button (Facebook Like, Twitter Follow, Google +1, etc.) or download a brochure
	Percentage of visits that complete a Contact Us form or click a mailto link
	Average time on site per visit
	Average page depth per visit
To cross-sell more products to our customers	Average order value
	Average number of items per transaction
To improve the customer experience	Percentage of visits that bounce (single-page visits)
	Percentage of internal site searches that produce zero results
	Percentage of visits that result in a support ticket being submitted

3. Ensure that KPIs are actionable and accountable.

   For each translated KPI, always go back and ask the stakeholder, "Who would you contact if this metric fell by 10 percent?" and "Who would you *formally* congratulate if it rose by 10 percent?" If a good answer for both is not forthcoming, then the suggested KPI is not a good one to include in your short list. I emphasize the word *formally* because this is a good way to focus the minds of your stakeholders on KPIs that lead to actions. A formal recognition could be a department-wide email bulletin or a performance bonus—that usually does the trick.

4. Create hierarchical KPI reports.

   Ensure that each recipient of your KPI report receives only the data they need; the more relevant the information presented, the more attention and buy-in you will gain. It follows that a chief marketing officer will need a different, though similar, KPI report than a marketing strategist or account manager.

5. Define partial KPIs.

   A frequently requested OKR is to increase the website conversion rate, usually sales or leads. This is often straightforward to measure, but it is also black and white—the visitor either converts or doesn't. By providing partial KPIs, also known as micro conversions, you can preempt your stakeholder's next question: "Why is the conversion rate so low?" I refer to these as partial KPIs because they relate to the partial completion of a full KPI. For example, if the conversion is to purchase, then adding an item to the shopping basket is a partial KPI—it's the first step of the conversion process. Here are some similar partial KPIs:

- Reaching a certain point in a checkout process
- Adding additional items (up-sell products) to the shopping cart
- For a multipage subscription form, the completion of step x of y
- Navigating to the download area or special offers section
- Completing an onsite search successfully, that is, nonzero results

Tip: Tracking partially completed forms is discussed in the section "Tracking Partially Completed Forms with Virtual Pageviews" in Chapter 7, "Advanced Implementation."

6.   **Consolidate.**

After forming a list of required KPIs for each stakeholder, consolidate them by looking for overlaps. The point of KPIs is to focus on the metrics that are important to your business. To be significant, each KPI should represent at least 10 percent of the whole—so no more than 10 KPIs are allowed. If a single KPI is much less than 10 percent in importance, then drop it or consolidate it into a more important one. I cannot emphasize the importance of having no more than 10 KPIs. Having more than 10 will cost you the interest of your stakeholders by your third report!

Remember that initial KPI reports are not set in stone—they can and should evolve as your audience learns to understand the metrics of their website and develop their actions to effect change. Review your KPI short list quarterly, at the very least, and refine the six steps described here as required.

Tip: As part of your role as a web analyst, you might also want to include KPIs that are not part of your Google Analytics reports—for example, search engine rankings, notes of any offline campaigns or PR, website updates, new product launches, user feedback, news and events that impact your business, server uptime, and response speed. All of these can help explain what you see and therefore add value to your data.

Presenting Your KPIs

The best way to present KPI reports is by using Microsoft Excel or a similar spreadsheet program. Every strategist, manager, or executive is familiar with the spreadsheet format and recognizes its layout immediately. It is far better to present your KPI reports using Excel than to try to teach a new interface (Google Analytics) to old hands. In addition to using Google Analytics, you may be collecting data from different sources, such as visitor surveys or search engine–ranking reports. Combining all of them into one familiar interface will make it easy for everyone to understand the material you are presenting.

Figure 10.1 is an example KPI report for an online marketing executive containing 10 key metrics. Color coding (using Excel's conditional formatting) and arrows have been used to highlight positive and negative changes, with a threshold of 5 percent used to "double highlight" values.

	A	B	C	D	E
1	KPI Report				
2		June	July	% Change	
3	Conversion rate	3.7%	4.1%	10.8%	▲▲
4	Booking income	$484,823	$377,995	-18.7%	▼▼
5					
6					
7	SE Visitors as a % of total	90.1%	87.6%	-2.8%	▼
8	Non SE Visitors as % of total	9.9%	12.4%	25.6%	▲▲
9					
10					
11	Quality of SE Visitors (% entering booking system)	26.7%	26.5%	-0.5%	▼
12	Quality of Non-SE Visitors (% entering booking system)	5.1%	6.8%	34.3%	▲▲
13					
14					
15	Quality of PPC Visitors (% entering booking system)	34.8%	33.8%	-3.0%	▼
16	Quality of Organic Visitors (% entering booking system)	23.3%	27.2%	16.7%	▲▲
17					
18					
19	% unable to book (non-IE browser)	5.0%	4.7%	-6.0%	▼▼
20	Money lost from non-IE visitors entering booking system	$23,078	$17,638	-23.6%	▼▼
21					time
22	Key & Defintions:				
23	▲ = An increase				
24	▲▲ = An increase of 5%+				
25	▼ = A fall of 0% to 5%				
26	▼▼ = A fall of greater than 5%				

Figure 10.1 Example KPI report for a travel website using Excel (also shown in the color insert)

All the data shown in Figure 10.1 is readily available from within Google Analytics, but using a spreadsheet to combine exactly what data elements your stakeholder wants to see enables you to deliver a concise report within a familiar interface.

Tip: Once you have built your KPI spreadsheet, you may wish to have its metrics refreshed automatically each time it is viewed—or applied to a different profile or Google Analytics account. To achieve this, read Chapter 12, "Integrating Google Analytics with Third-Party Applications." You can download an automated example of the spreadsheet used in Figure 10.1 from the book blog site at www.advanced-web-metrics.com/chapter10. The spreadsheet is updated with API calls and can be edited. With thanks to Mikael Thuneberg.

The stakeholder (online marketer for a travel website) who receives the KPI report shown in Figure 10.1 is interested in the performance of his online marketing efforts—SEO and PPC—specifically, the propensity to book a vacation.

Interpreting the KPI report from Figure 10.1:

1. Online revenue is down 18.7 percent for July compared with June.

Action: Check whether the drop in online revenue is a seasonal fluctuation experienced across the whole business or unique to the online channel. Note that despite the fall in revenue, the conversion rate is up by 10.8 percent.

2. Approximately 90 percent of all visitors who arrive at the website do so from search engines.

   Action: Ninety percent of visitors arriving via a search engine appears at first glance to be too high a figure; share this statistic with the rest of the marketing department for discussion. Is this the result of a great search engine marketing strategy or are other channels not working very well?

3. Visitors from search engines are almost five times more likely to enter the booking system than non-search-engine visitors.

   Action: See 2.

4. Visitors from pay-per-click sources are 24 to 49 percent more likely to enter the booking system than organic search engine visitors.

   Action: Increase the budget for pay-per-click campaigns—they work! However, PPC may be working better here because of failings with organic search optimization. For example, are the organic landing pages meeting the expectation of the visitor, or perhaps are they too generalized? Regardless, in the short term, raising the pay-per-click budget makes sense.

   Because the website booking engine does not work with non–Internet Explorer web browsers, the website is losing $17,000 to $23,000 per month.

   Action: Set up a meeting with the web development department to investigate an improved booking engine that will work with other major web browsers.

As you can see, significant action points are required as a result of the KPI report presented. Without this data being shown in such a clear and concise way, discovering the action points from the wealth of Google Analytics reports available would be like finding a needle in a haystack and they could even be missed.

As the volume of KPI data increases over time, plot your KPIs to spot long-term trends.

Tip: Consider delivering your KPI reports on a quarterly basis if you are a corporate or governmental organization and monthly if your website is a key part of your business model. If you are a transactional e-commerce site, certain stakeholders will want to receive reports weekly, even daily for very high-volume websites. Consider which report frequency is realistic for you. If your organization cannot take action on a daily basis, particularly your web development and design team, then daily KPI reports do not make sense. Bear in mind the issues discussed under "Understanding Web Analytics Data Accuracy," in Chapter 2, "Available Methodologies and Their Accuracy."

Presenting Hierarchical KPIs via Segmentation

There are hundreds of potential KPIs for your business. Which ones are relevant to your organization is an important discussion you will need to have with your company stakeholders. A key point stressed earlier is that you must deliver hierarchical KPI reports. That is, KPI reports for the chief marketing officer will differ from those for departmental managers, and they will differ from those for the account managers and strategists within each department.

For example, the CMO of a retail site would want to see the average conversion rate, average order value, and cost per acquisition. A marketing strategist would like to see this same information segmented by referral medium type (paid search versus organic search versus social media referrals versus email marketing and so on). Without wishing to insult any chief marketing officer's intelligence, segmentation detail is generally too much information and is not required in order to give direction to the team, that is, to balance the investment of TV, radio, print, and digital marketing. However, it is required for the digital strategists to be effective in their role.

Detailed KPIs are obtained by segmentation, and a great deal of segmentation is available within the Google Analytics interface. As described in Chapter 4, "Using the Google Analytics Interface," rather than use a menu-style navigation system, Google Analytics encourages you to drill down through the data itself, automatically cross-segmenting by each click-through of the reports. Where applicable, you will often see a drop-down menu for further analysis. For example, Figure 10.2 highlights the numerous ways to cross-segment visitors by displaying a secondary dimension. In addition, using Advanced Segments allows you to segment data at the visit level.

Most segmentation for KPI building involves the visitor type, referring source, or visitor geography. Segmenting on-the-fly via the user interface is a great tactic for quickly understanding the behavior of different visitor segments. Once you have identified the key ones that affect your website, you may wish to create specific profiles that report on only these. Having dedicated segmented reports enables you to investigate visitor behavior in greater detail, more efficiently, and more quickly. Segmentation is discussed in detail in the section "Why Segmentation Is Important" in Chapter 8, "Best Practices Configuration Guide."

Figure 10.3 illustrates this model for an e-commerce website. Both the marketing strategist and head of department have six KPIs. That does not mean six metrics each, because that would be oversimplifying. For example, the head of department will wish to review sales performance by both volume and revenue; that is, the highest-selling products by quantity may not be the most profitable. For the marketing strategist, each KPI is further subdivided by referral source (segmented).

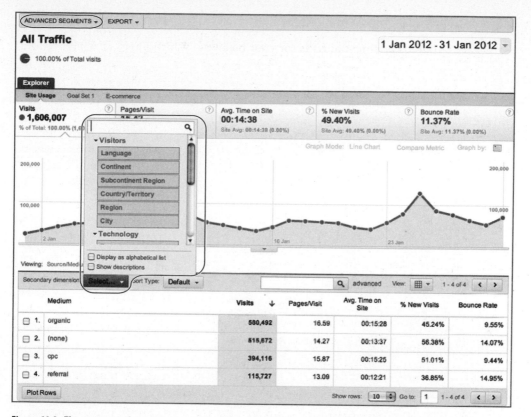

Figure 10.2 The two types of segmentation within reports: showing a secondary dimension; using advanced segments

**Marketing Strategist
(reviewed daily)**

1. Average sales per day
   (by referral source*)

2. Average conversion rate
   (by referral source)

3. Average order value
   (by referral source)

4. Average per visit value
   (by referral source)

5. First visit customer index
   (by referral source)

High data volume → Low data volume

**Head of Department
(reviewed weekly)**

1. Average sales per day
   (by quantity and revenue)

2. Average conversion rate per day

3. Category names accounting for
   80% of revenue

4. Top three product names
   (by quantity and revenue)

5. Average order value

6. Average per visit value

* Referral source values are organic search, PPC, social media, email, banners, referral link, direct.

Figure 10.3 Hierarchical example e-commerce KPI with differences highlighted

In addition, each recipient does not review these KPIs in isolation—the marketing strategists have their weekly meeting with the head of department. Hence there is a strong overlap in metrics. Highlighted in Figure 10.3 are the ones that do not overlap. For example, even if the three top-selling products change on a daily basis, the marketing strategist cannot take action. Therefore this is not on their KPI list. Instead, product selection and promotion is a decision the head of department will make, following a review of seven days' worth of data. Thus this KPI is on the head of department's list.

Explanations of the KPIs shown in Figure 10.3 are included later in this chapter.

Performing segmentation for hierarchical KPIs is a fine balance between obtaining clarity about visitor behavior and generating information overload. Clearly, Google Analytics offers a great number of segmentation options. However, whenever you segment data, you multiply the information reported—double it, triple it, and so on. This is clearly contrary to the purpose of KPI reporting. Therefore, you should apply a good deal of thought and investigation prior to segmenting. For example, ask yourself, "How is this going to enhance my understanding of visitors, and what will I do with such information?" If you are not satisfied with your own answers, don't overload yourself with more segmented data.

Benchmark Considerations

KPIs are important to drive improvement for your *own* website. Although it is obviously interesting and insightful to compare how your website is performing against those of your peers and competitors, in my opinion it is a mistake to place too much emphasis on external industry benchmarks. These can be misleading and often end up with you finding the benchmark that fits your story, giving a false impression of success.

KPIs vary greatly by business sector—for example, retail, travel, technology, B2B, finance, and so on. Even within subsectors there is wide variance: Think flights versus vacations or food retail versus clothing retail. Even comparing against your competitors with *identically defined goals* is fraught with gross approximations. The exact path that visitors will take to complete a goal and the quality of their user experience along the way will vary for every website. Slight changes in these can have a major impact on conversion rates. I deliberately emphasize the phrase *identically defined goals* here because definitions from different organizations can become blurred. For example, retail managers will often wish to differentiate existing customer visits from noncustomer visits. Quoting an average conversion rate across an industry can therefore be misleading.

Also, consider that e-commerce conversion rates can be measured in a variety of ways:

- The number of conversions × total number of visits to the website
- The number of conversions × total number of visitors to the website

- The number of conversions × total number of visits that add to cart
- The number of conversions × total number of visitors who add to cart

In the preceding list you can also substitute the word *transactions* for *conversions*. That is, a visitor may complete a purchase and enjoy the experience so much that they return to make an additional purchase within the same visit session. Depending on the web analytics tool used and the preference of the organization, that can be defined as one conversion with two transactions or two conversions with two transactions.

> **Note:** For the preceding scenario, Google Analytics would show one conversion and two transactions because the visitor has converted to a customer and this can happen only once during their session.

The following list includes some other onsite factors that can greatly affect conversion rates, and therefore muddy the waters for benchmarking:

- Your website's search engine visibility (organic and paid search listings).
- Your website's social media visibility (Facebook, Twitter, LinkedIn, Google+, and so forth).
- You website's usability and accessibility. (Is your site easy to navigate?)
- Whether a purchase requires registration up front. It's exasperating to see how many sites require this. Put it at the end of the transaction process.
- Your page response and download times. Page bloat is a conversion killer.
- Page content quality and imagery. These should be up to a professional standard.
- The use of trust factors such as safe-shopping logos, a privacy policy, a warranty, use of encryption for payment pages, client testimonials, and so on.
- The existence of broken links or broken images. These destroy the user experience.
- Quick and accurate onsite product searching.
- Whether your website works in all major browsers.

As you can see, comparing apples with apples is complicated. By all means, benchmark yourself against your peers. It can be an interesting and energizing comparison. However, I emphasize the need for internal benchmarking as the main driver for your website's success.

KPI Examples by Job Role

Rather than produce a dictionary-style list of every potential KPI metric, I have focused on a small group that require a little more thought in preparation (that is, they cannot be simply plucked from your Google Analytics reports) or require further explanation.

This is not intended to be an exhaustive list; rather, it is a sample to demonstrate how KPIs are defined and used. KPIs tell an easy-to-follow story. The story you need to tell will be very specific to your organization and your stakeholder relationships.

For job roles, I have grouped and differentiated the KPIs into five stakeholders: e-commerce manager, marketing and communications manager, social media manager, content creator, and webmaster. These should not be considered mutually exclusive, though. For example, marketers want to know the bottom line and e-commerce managers need to prioritize. As discussed previously, the level of segmentation applied will determine the hierarchy. As a web analyst, your role covers all of the above with regular deep dives to support your stakeholders.

Last, there is almost always more than one way to discover the KPI information within Google Analytics, and quite often the data points lie within several overlapping reports. In the following examples, I list the most obvious or most likely way to access the data.

Note: In Google Analytics, goal conversions and revenue (if you have monetized your goals) are reported separately from purchaser (e-commerce) conversions and revenue. Metrics that require the total revenue use the e-commerce plus goal revenue amounts.

E-commerce Manager KPI Examples

An e-commerce site probably has the most potential KPIs to choose from because the main goal (purchase) is relatively easy to measure and the site objective (driving visitors into the shopping-cart system) is so clearly defined. Google Analytics has an entire section dedicated to the reporting of e-commerce activity. However, most of my KPIs come from other reporting areas.

Looking beyond visitor volume, the following KPIs are suggested for an e-commerce manager:

- Average conversion rate
- Average value (a.k.a. average order value).
- Average per-visit value
- Average ROI
- Customer on first visit index

Average Conversion Rate

This is a high-level metric that every retailer watches with a keen eye in the offline world and is very easy to identify for online transactions. However, although useful, the conversion rate quoted in your reports is a blunt metric—for example, see Figure 10.4 (taken from the Conversion > E-commerce > Overview report). The calculation by Google Analytics is straightforward: the number of transactions divided by the total number of visits (expressed as a percentage). For example, 1,054 transactions from 346,193 web visits is a conversion rate of 0.30 percent.

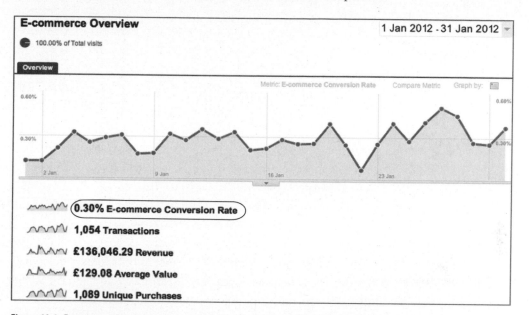

Figure 10.4 E-commerce Overview report graphing the conversion rate KPI over time

However, this calculation includes *all* visitors to your website, even those who came for the wrong reasons and therefore have no intention of purchasing. To provide more insight, it would be useful to remove such visitors. You can achieve this by looking at your site-wide bounce rate. For example, if your site bounce rate for the same time period is 20 percent, the number of "prospect" visitors is actually 276,954 (0.8 × 346,193) and your conversion rate recalculates as 0.38 percent—27 percent higher than reported.

For a partial KPI, you can further refine your conversion rate by including only those visits that begin the purchase process, such as add to cart. This tells you how good your checkout process, rather than your entire site, is at converting. Replace the denominator by the number of visits that get to page 1 of your checkout system (from your Content > Site Content > Pages report). Similarly, to measure how good your site's content is at driving conversions, your calculation would be number of visits that add to cart divided by total number of visits that do not bounce.

Average Value

Like the average conversion rate, the average value (often referred to as the average order value) is an important high-level KPI that retailers watch closely. It is listed here because it is such an important metric for e-commerce managers. However, it is straightforward to calculate, and it can be obtained directly from your Google Analytics reports, as shown in Figure 10.4.

Average Per-Visit Value

Understanding the average value per visit to your website is a strong KPI. Every visit has a value to your organization. Even if a visitor does not purchase, you can monetize your goals to evaluate your lead generation, registrations, and downloads. These all contribute to being able to differentiate your visitors and therefore target them better in future campaigns.

Knowing the value of your visitors and segmenting these by referral source and campaign (as well as other dimensions) is a powerful aid to both your e-commerce and marketing departments. By default, Google Analytics measures two types of per-visit value: per-visit goal value (based on the value of your goals) and per-visit value (based on e-commerce transaction data). These can be obtained directly from your reports. Figure 10.5 shows both types (taken from the Traffic Sources > Sources > All Traffic report). You add the two together for the *overall average per-visit value* KPI. Visitors who achieve neither a monetized goal nor a purchase will have a zero value for that visit.

Figure 10.5a and Figure 10.5b show the respective per-visit values segmented by medium in the tables and graphed against overall traffic. From Figure 10.5a, you can see that the per-visit goal value increases when overall visitor traffic is low (on the weekends). It appears from this that people research information during the week yet commit to a monetized goal on the weekends. Direct visitors, that is from medium = none, have the higher value by far when it comes to goal conversions. However, for transactions (Figure 10.5b), the situation is quite different—the most valuable visitors are from referral sites. The transaction pattern also matches the traffic volume pattern, more or less. Understanding why this difference arises is an important next step for this site.

Note: Although you can define up to four different goal sets, the overall goal conversion rate and per-visit goal values are not set-specific. That is, the calculation is based on all defined goals.

Average Return on Investment

Return on investment (ROI) is a KPI that all business managers understand. It tells you how much, as a percentage, you are getting back for every dollar you spend acquiring visitors. For clarity, the formula used for calculating return on investment in Google Analytics, expressed as a percentage, is

$$\text{ROI} = (\text{revenue} - \text{cost}) / \text{cost}$$

where cost is the amount spent acquiring Google AdWords visitors—currently Google AdWords is the only cost data that can be imported into Google Analytics. For example, if for every $1 you spend on AdWords, you get $2 back in sales from your website, your ROI would be 100 percent. If you received $3 back for the same outlay, your ROI would be 200 percent, and so forth. Obviously, you want to maximize your ROI—the greater this number, the better.

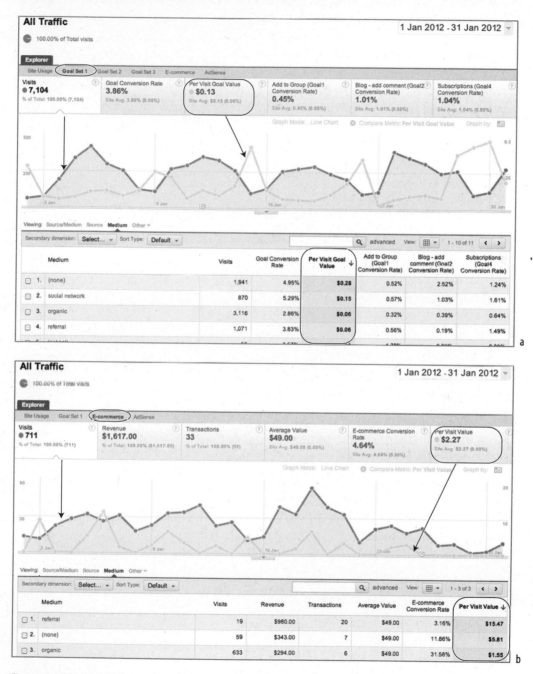

Figure 10.5 Obtaining (a) the per-visit goal value and (b) the per-visit value

A negative ROI means you are losing money: Your costs of acquisition are greater than your returns. However, when launching a new AdWords campaign, ROI is likely to be negative until repeat visitors or brand awareness starts to grow and leads to more conversions (see Figure 10.6). Reaching the break-even point (0 percent ROI) could take hours, days, weeks, or even months, depending on many (visitor-centric, online, offline) factors. For mature campaigns, keep your ROI above 0 percent unless there is a clear reason not to do so. For example, you may be a new entry in the market and want to buy market share to gain customers at a later date.

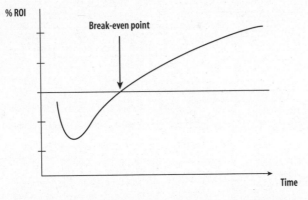

Figure 10.6 Possible change in ROI over time for a new AdWords campaign

Within Google Analytics you can drill down to view ROI reports for AdWords at three levels: Campaign, Ad Group, and Keyword. Figure 10.7 shows data at the Ad Group level (taken from the Advertising > AdWords > Campaigns report). The report table clearly shows that although the Ad Group for "Auto-track plugin" has a very low click-through rate (CTR), it has the highest ROI by far at 239.53 percent. That is to say, for every dollar invested in the "Auto-track plugin" Ad Group, an average of $3.40 is returned—a pretty good investment, though reasons to explain (and therefore improve) the low CTR should be investigated. From the data graph, Figure 10.7 also shows that the overall AdWords ROI was not always positive during January, with a four-day period when costs were higher than returns. That seems odd to appear during the middle of a campaign and so should be investigated further—perhaps there was an error in the AdWords account setup.

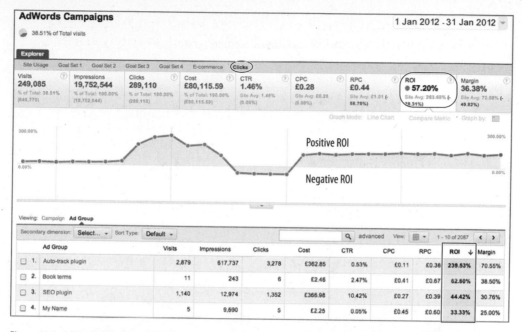

Figure 10.7 AdWords ROI report shown for each Ad Group

Of course, ROI is a top-level indication of performance from your total income. It does not take into account what profit margin you make on your sales. Nor does it take into account the volume of transactions or visitors received. For example, a high ROI campaign may be so specific that it generates only a small revenue. A lower ROI (less-specific) campaign may in fact produce greater revenue because of the higher visitor volume it generates.

Modifying ROI to take into account profit margins is further discussed in the section "Optimizing Your Search Engine Marketing" in Chapter 11, "Real-World Tasks."

Customer on First Visit Index

Use this KPI when you are evaluating the impact of promotion codes, discounted pricing, and trust factors—those things that can help convert a new visitor into a new customer on their first visit. It answers the question, "What is the likelihood of a new visitor becoming a customer on their very first visit?"

You may notice from your reports a high proportion of transactions generated by new (first-time) visitors, as per Figure 10.8 (taken from the Visitors > Behavior > New vs. Returning report). But how does that relate to the *number* of first-time visitors? Take Figure 10.8, for example: Although it is correct to say that 72.73 percent of transactions are from new visitors, it is not true to also interpret this as 72.73 percent of new visitors are generating your transactions—unless the number of new visitors to the site is also exactly 72.73 percent. It could be that only a small percentage of new visitors are generating your income.

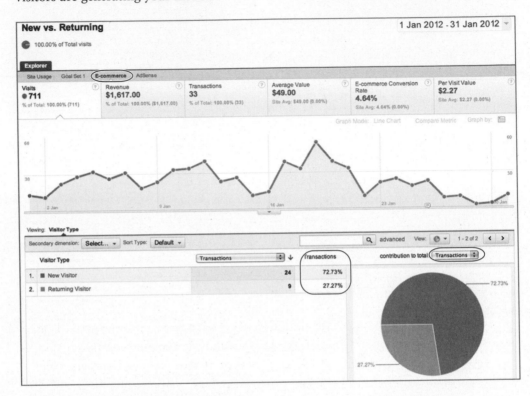

Figure 10.8 Percent transactions from new visitors

The customer on first visit index KPI allows you to understand this relationship better. It is defined as follows:

$$\text{customer on first visit index} = \frac{\text{percentage transactions from new visitors}}{\text{percentage of new visitors}}$$

From the data in Figure 10.8 and knowing the percentage of new visitors, the value is calculated as follows:

customer on first visit index = 72.73 / 86.22

customer on first visit index = 0.84

Interpretation: A value of 1.0 indicates that a new visitor is equally likely to become a customer as a returning visitor. A value less than 1.0 indicates that a new visitor is less likely to become a customer than a returning visitor, and a value greater than 1.0 indicates that a new visitor is more likely to become a customer than a returning visitor.

Hence, for this example business, this KPI shows that a new visitor is 16 percent less likely to purchase than a returning visitor. Would new visitors be more likely to purchase on their first visit if the product cost was reduced? Following this KPI allows you to highlight any impact of promotion codes, discounted pricing, and trust factors on your site's propensity to convert.

Marketer and Communication KPI Examples

Bringing good-quality visitors—that is, qualified leads—to your website is the bread and butter of your marketing and communications (marcomm) department. Putting offline marketing to one side, the "bringing" part is achieved with online marketing. Working alongside this is the managing of communications between an organization and its public (often referred to as public relations). The toolbox for your department may include any or all of the following sources: search engine optimization (free search rankings), pay-per-click advertising (paid search), social network interactions (Facebook, LinkedIn, Twitter, Google+, forums, blogs, and so forth), press releases, banner advertising, affiliate networks, links from site referrals, and email marketing.

In this section and the following subsections, I focus on the needs of the digital marketing team. Although I dislike separating, and therefore siloing the communications team, I focus on social media KPIs in the section "Social Media KPI Examples" later in this chapter.

Determining which traffic is qualified means looking at the conversion rates, campaign costs, revenue generated (e-commerce or goal values), and ROI. KPIs for the marketing department therefore overlap strongly with KPIs for the e-commerce manager. An important difference is that marketers look not only at transaction rates but also at goal conversions because these build visitor relationships that, it is hoped, will later lead to purchases. In addition, understanding the levers that drive a KPI and correlating them with departmental campaigns and activity is a key requirement. Note that because e-commerce conversions have been discussed in the previous section, only KPIs related to goal conversions are considered here.

Understanding Campaign Tracking

It is important that you fully understand campaign tracking when considering marketing and communication KPIs because the setup and management of this will be *your* responsibility. Don't worry, as you can discover in Chapter 7, campaign tracking is a nontechnical process. However, it does require "ownership," and this is best placed with the marketing team; in other words, do not delegate this to your IT department.

In most cases, online marketing and social media are grouped under the general marketing and communications department. It is therefore critical here to use hierarchical KPIs to differentiate those members of your audience who specialize with the online channel from generalists who need to consider it against other channels. Looking beyond the overall visitor volume to a site, the following KPIs are suggested for marketers:

- Percentage brand engagement
- Conversion quality index
- Average ROI by campaign type
- Percentage of new versus returning visitors (or customers)

Percentage Brand Engagement

In his blog at www.webanalyticsdemystified.com, Eric T. Peterson describes brand engagement as the brand index KPI. Visitors who know your brand and have arrived at your site because of it have, by definition, engaged with you. This KPI is defined as follows:

$$\text{percentage brand engagement} = \frac{\text{number of visits with search terms containing brand names} + \text{number of direct visits}}{\text{total number of visits from search engines} + \text{number of direct visits}}$$

Note that when referring to search terms here, I am referring to search engine referral keywords, both paid and free search. Direct-access visits are also included because these are people who know your website address and therefore your brand. I have assumed a best practice implementation of campaign tracking and that you have excluded access of your own staff from your reports (see "Profile Segments: Segmenting Visitors Using Filters," in Chapter 8).

A percentage brand engagement report is not yet directly available within Google Analytics, but it is straightforward to calculate from two other reports. First, from the Traffic Sources > Sources > Search > Overview report, select keyword from the dimension menu and use the table filter to enter your regular expression of brand keywords. In my case, I used the table filter Keyword "Matching RegExp" brian|clifton|advanced web metrics|measuring success, where the pipe character (|) represents the logical operator OR (see Figure 10.9a). This includes my effective business name, Brian Clifton, and product names, Advanced Web Metrics and Measuring Success (the book and the supporting blog respectively). The number of direct visits is taken from the Traffic Sources > Sources > Direct report (see Figure 10.9b).

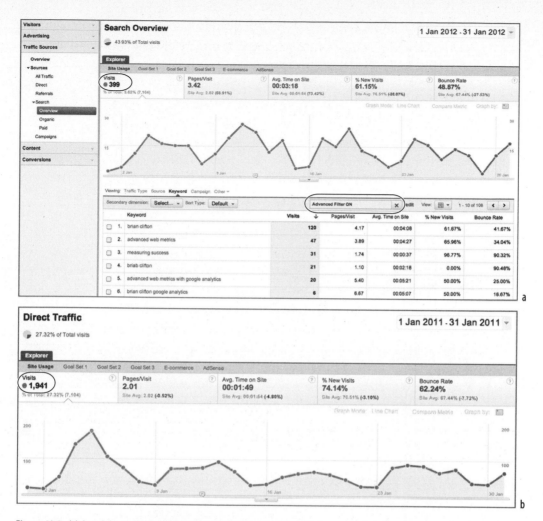

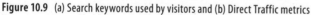

Figure 10.9 (a) Search keywords used by visitors and (b) Direct Traffic metrics

Constructing Regular Expressions

Because a maximum of 255 characters is allowed within the table filter box, you should construct your regular expression with some thought. For example, in Figure 10.9a, the brand term I am actually looking for is "Advanced Web Metrics with Google Analytics"—one example brand name for the book website. However, I shorten this to "advanced web metrics" because this will pick up both terms and any other brand terms containing this phrase. It is also unlikely to match any non-brand terms. The result is a significant saving of repeated text. Further examples of the use of regular expression is given in Appendix A, "Regular Expression Overview."

Once you have filtered this way, you could define an advanced segment to keep these terms permanently at hand for easy comparison. Advanced segments have much greater character limits for constructing regular expressions (see Table 8.2). Using advanced segments and profile filters is discussed in Chapter 8.

Using the data from Figures 10.9a and 10.9b and knowing that the total number of search engine visitors to this example website is 3,121 (taken from the Traffic Sources > Search Engines report), the calculation is as follows:

percentage brand index = (399 + 1941) / (3121 + 1941)

percentage brand index = 46.23%

This illustrates how important branding is for my site (www.advanced-web-metrics.com). It may be that I would wish to increase this metric (a common request from marketers and brand managers), though often you may actually wish to reduce this. That is, you would want to increase the volume of traffic from visitors who are new to your brand.

By selecting a Goal Set tab within the reports of Figures 10.9a and 10.9b, you can also quickly calculate the brand index KPI on a per-goal basis.

Conversion Quality Index

Viewing a breakdown of visitors by referrer is an extremely effective set of KPIs for the marketer. For example, what's driving your traffic acquisition—email marketing, organic search, paid advertising, social networks, affiliates, or your offline marketing? Going beyond visitor volumes, the conversion quality index (CQI) is all about measuring how well targeted your campaigns are at driving conversion on your website.

For example, suppose 50 percent of your visitors are from AdWords (labeled in your reports as google / cpc), but only 20 percent of conversions are from this campaign source. That's an underperforming campaign because given two equally targeted campaigns, each producing 50 percent of your visitor traffic, both should produce 50 percent of your conversions. If one outperforms the other by generating more than its share of conversions, then by definition that campaign must be better targeted.

> **Note:** The introduction of the Multi-Channel Funnels feature in August 2011 (discussed in Chapter 5, "Reports Explained") certainly adds another dimension to the use of the Conversion Quality Index. That is, some campaigns can heavily assist but not drive the final conversion. However, given two or more equally targeted campaigns, this is unlikely, though still possible. Therefore, in conjunction with calculating your CQI, observe your Multi-Channel Funnels reports to see if this is the case for you. If a campaign medium is driving visits but not conversions, remove this medium from your CQI calculation.

The conversion quality index, shown here, enables you to view these differences so you can better understand the effectiveness of your visitor-acquisition strategy:

$$CQI_{\text{referrer X}} = \frac{\text{percent goal conversion}_{\text{referrer X}}}{\text{percent visits}_{\text{referrer X}}}$$

This report does not yet exist in Google Analytics. However, it is easy to calculate from the available reports using the data in Figure 10.10 (taken from the Traffic Sources > Sources > All Traffic report). The values from these reports are then used to populate the rows of Table 10.2. Think of this as dividing one chart by the other in order to standardize the data. In this example, I have selected referral "medium" for the quality index. If individual campaign detail is important to you, drill down into a specific source to obtain these numbers.

Interpretation for the conversion quality index KPI: A value of 1.0 tells us that a visitor from the referral is as likely to convert as a visitor from any other. A value of less than 1.0 indicates that a visitor is less likely to convert than a visitor from any other referral, and a value of greater than 1.0 indicates that a visitor is more likely to convert than a visitor from any other referral. As a marketer, you should be aiming for a value of 1.0 for each referral setup. Column D of Table 10.2 normalizes the CQI to the highest value.

By using this method, three distinct types of referral performance are highlighted:

High performing Social network, direct (medium = none)

Medium performing Referrals, organic search

Low performing All other referral mediums, including email, forum, AdWords (CPC), and PDF documents

▶ **Table 10.2** Conversion quality index (CQI)

Campaign	A % Visits (Figure 10.10a)	B % Conversions (Figure 10.10b)	C Conversion Quality Index (B/A)	D CQI Normalized
Organic	43.86	32.48	0.74	0.54
Direct	27.32	35.04	1.28	0.93
Referral	15.08	14.96	0.99	0.72
Social network	12.25	16.79	1.37	1.0
Email	0.46	0.00	0.00	0.00
Forum	0.11	0.00	0.00	0.00
CPC	0.07	0.00	0.00	0.00
PDF	0.03	0.00	0.00	0.00

Viewing the data of Table 10.2 for the site advanced-web-metrics.com, we can see that social network and direct visitors are the highest performers. That is, they have the greatest engagement level. Effectively, these visitors are punching way above their weight in terms of propensity to convert—an observation that is completely missing from any Google Analytics reports.

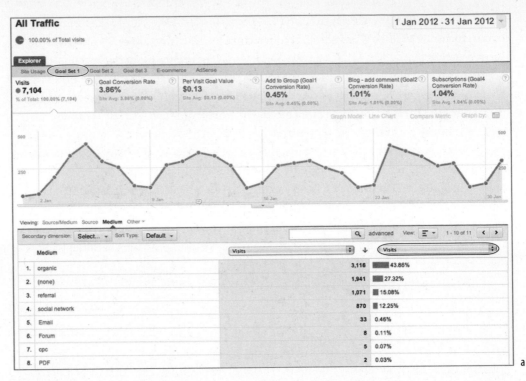

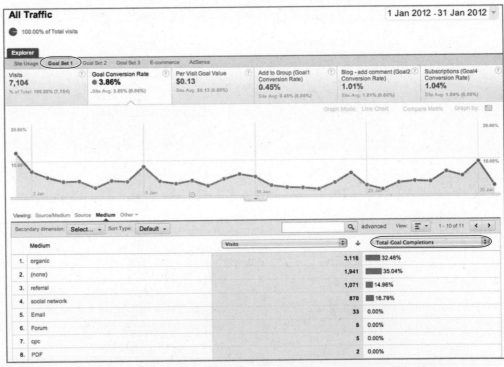

Figure 10.10 (a) Number of visits as a percentage by referral medium and (b) conversion rates as a percentage by referral medium

What is also interesting from the CQI analysis is the very low performance of email, forum, CPC (AdWords) and PDF referrals. At first glance you would wish to drop these campaigns. The large caveat with this hypothesis is very low visit numbers for these (only five visits for CPC). Hence, disregard such conclusions until more data is collected. (I left these in to highlight the need to keep raw numbers close at hand when calculating KPIs that are averages, ratios, or percentages.)

Assuming you have enough conversion data (at least hundreds of goal completions for each data row) to mitigate random fluctuations, the conversion quality index is a valuable KPI against which to benchmark your referrals. It allows marketing managers to ask the question, "Does the distribution of our marketing budget match our conversions?" If, for example, little of your budget is being spent on social media participation, then you know from Table 10.2 that this source provides a great goal conversion rate for you and so should be exploited further.

Why Is Organic Search Showing Such a Low CQI?

Organic search is often touted as been a very good source of quality traffic—the visitor is proactively searching for your content after all. However, even after eliminating data rows that provide fewer than 100 visits from Table 10.2, the results still show that visitors from organic search engines perform the worst. From experience, provided its normalized CQI is above 0.7, I tend not to worry about this because of the ubiquitous nature of search and the popularity of Google as a search engine.

For example, people will arrive at your website through a search for all sorts of reasons that may not be relevant to your business, including job search, competitive research, clients searching for contact details, spammers, misspellings, and misassociations (Omega watches versus Omega Couriers, for example). This can lead to high volumes of organic referral traffic from search engines that are not qualified, which unfortunately is difficult to avoid if you are actively promoting yourself via search engine optimization.

If your normalized organic CQI is lower than 0.7 of your best performing campaign, bring in the person responsible for search engine optimization of your site and discuss the approach being used, that is, its keyword focus.

Average ROI by Campaign Type

This KPI is the same as the one discussed for e-commerce managers and shown in Figure 10.7. I list it here for completeness.

Percentage of New versus Returning Visitors (or Customers)

Knowing whether new or returning visitors are driving your website metrics is an important top-level guide to the success of your online marketing strategy—see Figure 10.11 (taken from the Visitors > Behavior > New vs. Returning report). If your marketing focus is on acquiring new visitors, then you would expect a greater proportion of these. If you focus on visitor retention, then you would expect the number of returning visitors to be higher.

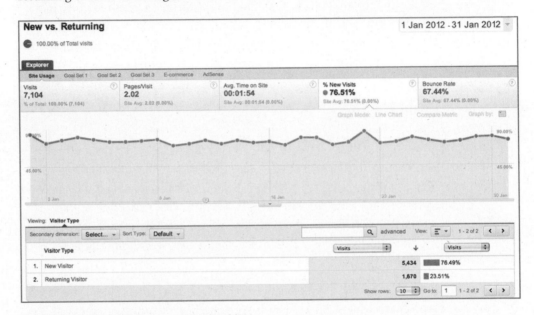

Figure 10.11 Understanding new versus returning visitors

Unless you are embarking on a new online marketing initiative, these metrics should remain fairly stable. Generally speaking, the more proactive your organization is at search engine marketing, the higher the percentage of new visitors—typically, 70 percent plus. Exceptions to this are customer-support websites and content-publishing websites that have a more even mix of new versus returning visitors.

Be careful when interpreting changes in percentage of visitor types. For example, a decrease in percentage of new visitors could in fact be due to an increase in percentage of returning visitors rather than any change in your new-visitor acquisition strategy. To check, compare different date ranges and examine the raw numbers.

In addition to traffic volume, you can view the ratio of new versus returning customers—provided you are labeling visitors who purchase, as described in Chapter 9, "Google Analytics Customizations." By this method, select your customer label in the Visitors > Demographics > Custom Variables report and cross-segment by visitor type.

Social Media KPI Examples

Social media communication has a strong overlap with the digital marketing department. In fact, often the social media campaign is precisely to market to a potentially large audience. However, if done well (and it is often done very badly), social media communication can go way beyond the reach of digital marketing and build strong relationships with users. So much so that users can inadvertently become evangelists for your products and services, spreading the good news virally—without requesting a cent in return! It can of course also work the other way round; that is, spreading bad news or a bad experience, very quickly.

Essentially, social media communication attempts to influence active participants by putting your side of the story out there, be it to announce something new and newsworthy, to defuse criticism, or to provide comment on an existing story. You do this by interacting with others, instigating discussions, and responding to conversations on sites where people engage with each other. Beyond the high profile examples of Facebook, Twitter, Google+, and LinkedIn, there are numerous others. According to Wikipedia (`http://en.wikipedia.org/wiki/List_of_social_networking_websites`), there are 76 social websites with more than 1 million registered users.

Whichever conversational approach you use, the key to success is to always have more content as a follow-up on your *own* website. That way, interested visitors are likely to click through from the social networking site onto yours. In doing so, what is happening away from your website (and therefore difficult to measure and compare) becomes trackable within Google Analytics. Therefore, a visitor from a social media network simply becomes another visitor segment that you can analyze.

This is a key point I wish to emphasize: *Social media visitors are simply another segment of visitors*, as per the many other visitor segments you will be defining in Google Analytics, such as search engine visitors, visits resulting from email marketing, and so forth. Hence, the KPIs you use to benchmark such visitors remain the same as for other segments. That is, are they driving sales, leads, downloads, conversions?

Tracking Social Conversations That Happen Off Site

As discussed in Chapter 1, Google Analytics is an onsite web measurement tool—it tracks visitors who visit your website. If people discuss your company or products elsewhere, for example on Yahoo! Groups, Facebook, or Twitter, you cannot measure it (or even know it is taking place) with Google Analytics. You need different tools for this, as shown in Figure 1.3.

However, the key to measuring social media success is to interact with the conversations and provide a link for further information back to your website with campaign tracking parameters in your landing page URL. That way, those social media users that are truly engaged with your message will click through to your site. When they do so, Google Analytics will report which particular social network and specific conversation they came from.

So if social media visits are simply another visitor segment, why do we need a KPI section in this chapter for them? For tracking visitors from a social network, we don't. However, as a producer of content on your website, you have the possibility of initiating social conversations yourself. You do this by providing the opportunity for your visitors to easily reference your page, or site, on their social network—such as a button that enables a tweet of your content, a Facebook Like button (which is added to the visitor's Facebook wall), a Google +1 button, and many other potential buttons to suit your audience preferences. Collectively, I refer to such buttons as *love buttons*, and examples are shown in Figure 10.12.

Figure 10.12
Examples of social
media love buttons

These small icons should be embedded within your key pages—that means those that have real informative content (not product pages, checkout pages, or similar hard-sell content). If you run a blog on your site, group or forum, review or rating system, or any other form of user-generated content, these are good places to position your love buttons. Then, if people are genuinely interested in your content, there is a strong chance they will wish to share it with their friends and colleagues—finding good content on the Internet is hard enough as it is! Love buttons make doing so a simple process for the visitor, sometimes just one click.

As you will no doubt have already concluded, interactions with such buttons are a key engagement point—visitors are using their word of mouth to spread your message. Gold dust for any marketing or PR manager!

Percentage Love Button Usage

Because clicks on these are links to outbound links, that is, links that take the visitor away from your website to their social network account (usually via a pop-up window), you will need to ensure that they are set up in your implementation. See the Campaign Tracking section of Chapter 7, "Advanced Implementation." Assuming they are in place, tracking the percentage usage of such buttons is straightforward because there is a dedicated Google Analytics report for you in the Visitors > Social section of your reports, either in aggregate (all buttons) or broken down by each button type—see Figure 10.13.

Using these reports also lets you obtain broader social media KPIs:

- The number of social actions (retweets/Likes/Google +1/Shares) per page of your site. Calculate this by taking the total number of social actions and divide by the number of pages on your site that contain a love button.

- The ratio of social actions to community size. For example, the number of page tweets per 1,000 Twitter followers, or the number of Shares per 1,000 LinkedIn connections.

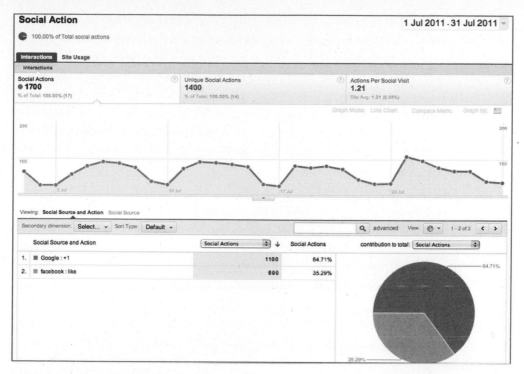

Figure 10.13 Breakdown of visitors who clicked a love button

Content Creator KPI Examples

If you create content—that is, you are an author, journalist, or copywriter for a content-driven website—then audience engagement is your goal. How long people spend reading your content and how much of it they consume are key indicators for measuring engagement.

Essentially, there are three categories of content-driven websites:

Product and organization information Examples include corporate website information, product review sites, blogs, help-desk support, online training sites, and so on.

Advertising-based content These include free-to-read content websites that derive revenue from selling advertisements (banner or text ads) alongside content. Examples include cnet.com, myspace.com, and most TV, newspaper, and magazine websites such as nytimes.com, ft.com, and cnn.com. Some blogs also embed contextual advertising within their articles—for example, using AdSense.

Subscription-based content As an alternative to deriving income from advertising, content-driven websites can offer subscription-based content; that is, you pay as a subscriber to access the material (or perhaps a more complete version of an article). Examples include jupiterresearch.com, econsultancy.com, forrester.com, and many daily newspaper sites.

The latter two categories I classify as publishers, and they usually employ both methods of generating revenue. As a publisher, if you provide advertising-based content, then you have a dilemma: If you write the perfect article to fit on one page, visitors will read that single page, be satisfied, and move on to another site or activity. They will be single-page visitors. However, single-page visits are not good for business when you derive your revenue from advertising. To increase your revenue, you want visitors to read more pages so that they are exposed to more advertisements (greater inventory), increasing the likelihood that they will click one. That makes your website more attractive to advertisers.

Regardless of your content site's business model, greater engagement with your visitors is the key. Consequently, content managers are always looking at ways to include complementary subject matter with each article or page to encourage this. Clearly for content sites, visit volume—the number of visits per day, week, or month— is an important KPI, along with how this varies over time. However, the following sample KPIs focus on helping you measure engagement:

- Bounce rate
- Percent engagement
- Average time on site and pageviews per visit
- Advertisement performance
- Percent new versus returning visitors
- Percent high, medium, low visitor recency

Bounce Rate

A *bounce* in Google Analytics terminology is a one-page, zero-action visit—that is, a visitor arrives on your website, views one page, has no further action, and then bounces off to another site or closes their browser. It's an important, very-easy-to-understand KPI that every stakeholder wishes to reduce. Bounced visitors have no value to your business (assuming you have a well-crafted article that entices further click-throughs) and are important to minimize because an e-commerce manager wishes to maximize revenue. Web analysts love analyzing bounce rates—such a simple metric that can be so telling for web performance.

The bounce-rate calculation can vary for different web analytics vendors, so I clarify the formula here for Google Analytics:

$$\text{percentage bounce rate}_{\text{page X}} = \frac{\text{number of single page visits with zero actions}_{\text{page X}}}{\text{number of entry page visits}_{\text{page X}}}$$

I emphasize the use of the term *zero actions*. By *action*, I mean any non-pageview action that can be tracked by Google Analytics—such as an event (file download, Flash movie interaction, and so on) or e-commerce transaction. See Chapter 7 for further details on e-commerce and event tracking.

Note: Labeling a visitor, as described in Chapter 9, is not defined as an action in this context.

The average website bounce rate (a weighted average of all your page bounce rates) is quoted in numerous places throughout Google Analytics reports (for example, in the Content Overview report). To view the bounce rate for a particular page, view the Content > Site Content > Pages report, shown in Figure 10.14. Because bounce rates can vary quite widely from page to page, I maintain focus by using an advanced filter in Figure 10.14 to exclude outliers (very high or very low bounce rates and pages with low pageview traffic). The filter is shown in Figure 10.15.

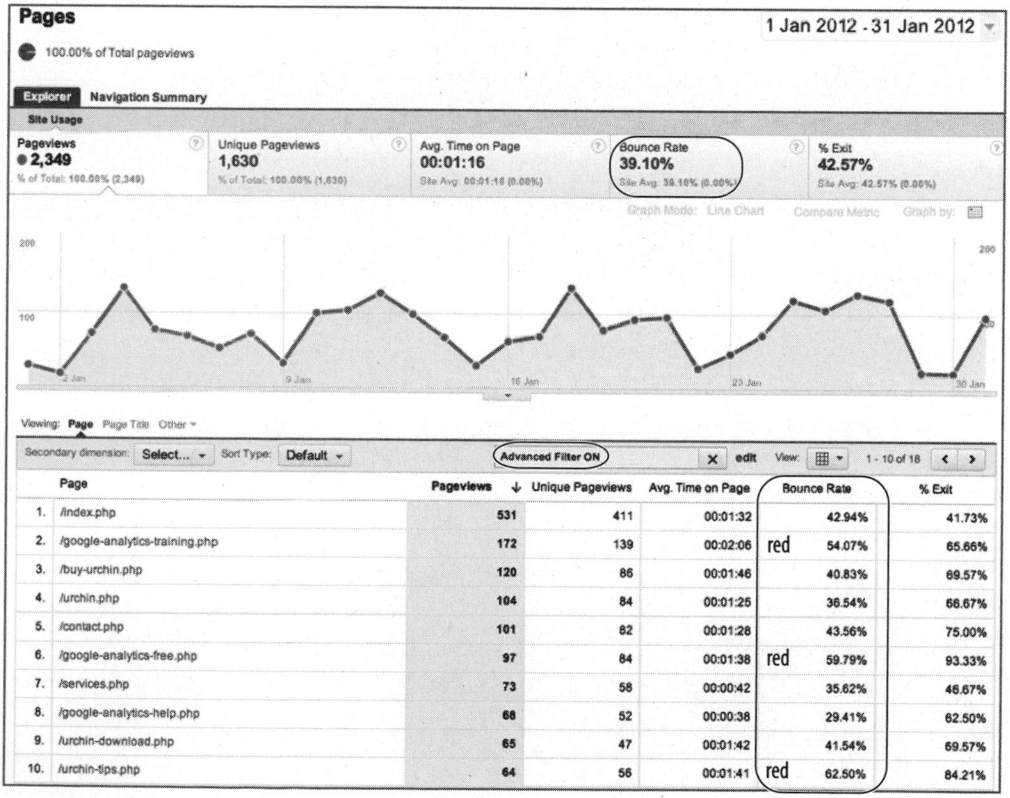

	Page	Pageviews	Unique Pageviews	Avg. Time on Page		Bounce Rate	% Exit
1.	/index.php	531	411	00:01:32		42.94%	41.73%
2.	/google-analytics-training.php	172	139	00:02:06	red	54.07%	65.66%
3.	/buy-urchin.php	120	86	00:01:46		40.83%	69.57%
4.	/urchin.php	104	84	00:01:25		36.54%	66.67%
5.	/contact.php	101	82	00:01:28		43.56%	75.00%
6.	/google-analytics-free.php	97	84	00:01:38	red	59.79%	93.33%
7.	/services.php	73	58	00:00:42		35.62%	46.67%
8.	/google-analytics-help.php	68	52	00:00:38		29.41%	62.50%
9.	/urchin-download.php	65	47	00:01:42		41.54%	69.57%
10.	/urchin-tips.php	64	56	00:01:41	red	62.50%	84.21%

Figure 10.14 Top Content report using an advanced filter to focus on bounce rates

Include ▾	Bounce Rate ▾	Greater than ▾	10	⊗
	and			
Include ▾	Bounce Rate ▾	Less than ▾	100	⊗
	and			
+ Add a dimension or metric ▾				

Figure 10.15 The advanced table filter used to exclude outliers in the bounce rate report

From a content creator's point of view, a high percentage of bounced visitors means poor engagement. But what constitutes a high bounce rate? I use a traffic-light system as follows.

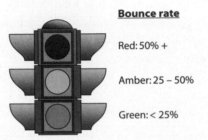

Bounce rate

Red: 50% +

Amber: 25 – 50%

Green: < 25%

High bounce rate pages (red, greater than 50 percent) obviously need to be prioritized for review. Perhaps there is out-of-date content or errors on the page. If you cannot find a reason for a visitor's bounce, consider culling the content—remove pages that have a high bounce rate. After all, producing and maintaining content has a cost. If visitors are not interested in reading more than one page from you, then maybe the content is not relevant to your website.

Medium bounce rate pages (amber, 25–50 percent) hopefully constitute the bulk of your Top Content report. Thus, it can be some time before you optimize these for improvement—lower bounce rates.

Low bounce rate pages (green, less than 25 percent), although performing well, should not be ignored. Target them for new promotions, major news updates, or key announcements because they have the greatest traction with your visitors.

> **Note:** Anil Batra has written a report on typical industry bounce rates by surveying 80 companies across five industry sectors. Bearing in mind my caveats of external benchmarking discussed earlier in this chapter, his report makes interesting reading and is free to download from www.anilbatra.com/digitalmarketing/bounce-rates.asp.

Percentage Engagement

Percent engagement has the opposite meaning of bounce rate. However, it is not simply the inverse of the bounce rate calculation. That is, just because a visitor does not bounce does not mean they are engaged—that would be far too simplistic.

Apart from visitors reading your content, how else could you determine their engagement? Examples include downloads, subscriptions, article ratings, blog comments, social share (Tweet, Facebook Likes, Google +1, Digg, StumbleUpon, and so on), and visitors who provide unsolicited feedback in some other way. Whatever the method, visitors who connect with your website are a valuable metric of engagement. Expressed as a percentage, the calculation is as follows:

$$\text{percentage engaged visits} = \frac{\text{total number of engagements}}{\text{total number of visits}}$$

Google Analytics tracks all data at the aggregate level, so it is best to track this KPI on a per-visit basis rather than a per-visitor basis. Hence, it is not possible to determine whether a small number of visitors—for example, one visitor—is making all the engagements. Such a scenario is highly unlikely but something to bear in mind.

If all of your engagements are defined as goals, a simple way to obtain this KPI is to view the Conversions > Goals > Overview report, shown in Figure 10.16.

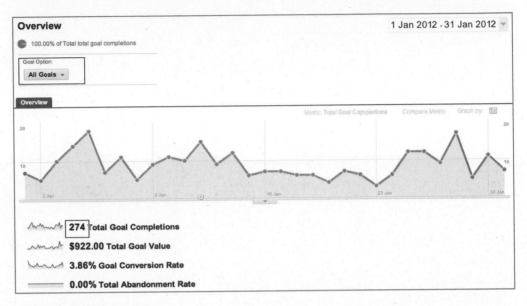

Figure 10.16 Goal conversion rates

The Goals Overview report shows the number of goal completions, or engagements. Divided by the total number of visits (taken from Figure 10.11), the percent engaged visits for this example data is as follows:

percentage engaged visits = 274 / 7104

percentage engaged visits = 3.85%

Why not simply use the conversion rate that is directly reported in Figure 10.16? Although the numbers appear the same in this example (3.85% versus 3.86%), they are in fact different calculations. The conversion rate calculation uses *unique conversions*. That is, in Google Analytics a visitor is defined as converting only once during their session even though they may have completed numerous goals.

In my example, I have assumed that visitors clicking your social media love buttons (see the preceding section, "Social Media KPI Examples") are also defined as goals, which I recommend they should be. In this case, defined as an event goal by setting category = social media in the goal configuration area (see Chapter 8 for details on goal setup). In this way, all engagements are considered equal. However, you can also differentiate by selecting particular goals from the Goal Option drop-down menu shown in Figure 10.16. In addition, Google Analytics reports the percent socially engaged KPI directly—see Figure 10.17 (taken from the Visitors > Behavior > New vs. Returning report).

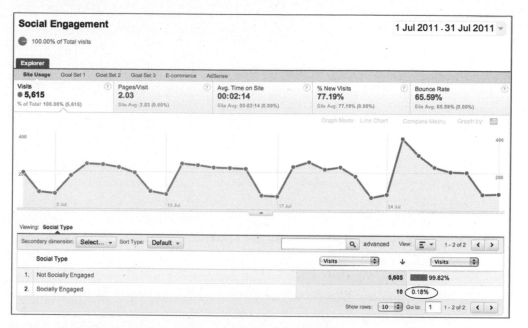

Figure 10.17 The percent socially engaged KPI is reported directly in Google Analytics

If some of your engagements are not defined as goals, you can still find these metrics (as URLs or events) in your reports. Use advanced table filters to quickly find these numbers.

Percent Engaged Visitors

It is possible to be clever here and use the `_setCustomVar()` function as a label to track whether a visitor has engaged with your website (see "Labeling Visitors, Sessions, and Pages," in Chapter 9 for the use of visitor labeling). The KPI could then be changed to percentage engaged visitors by substituting for the number of visits:

$$\text{percentage engaged visitors} = \frac{\text{total number of engaged visitors}}{\text{total number of visitors}}$$

This can be further refined by either labeling the visitor on a per-session basis (only labeled as engaged or not during each visit) or persistently (remembering previous engagement label on subsequent visits). The total number of engaged visitors shows in the Visitors > Demographics > Custom Variables report.

Average Time on Site and Pageviews per Visit

The average time on site is the length of time visitors spend interacting with your website, and it is a good base metric to help you understand whether your visitors are engaging with your site. All content creators want to increase this KPI—assuming, of course, the visitor experience is a good one.

The calculation is straightforward, though it is worth mentioning how it is determined. To calculate the time on site, Google Analytics uses the difference in time between the last and first pageview a visitor requests (or event if you are also tracking these). Note that times are measured when the page or event is *requested*, not when a visitor leaves a page. That complicates matters when the page in question is the last one visited—you know when the visitor made the request but not when they left. Perhaps the visitor opened another site in a new browser window or new browser tab or just minimized their browser while continuing with other work. These are very common scenarios resulting in the tracking session being closed by a cookie time-out, which is set at 30 minutes by default in Google Analytics, though it can be adjusted; see "Customizing the GATC" in Chapter 7. Having a final pageview last 30 minutes would clearly skew the time-on-site metrics. To avoid the situation, Google Analytics ignores the last pageview for all time-on-site calculations. In fact, this is a common approach throughout the web analytics industry.

The depth of visit—that is, the average pages per visit—is closely related to the time on site. If one increases, you would expect the other to also increase. Hence, they are displayed together in your Google Analytics reports. For example, if your depth of visit KPI causes you to ask further questions, you should also refer to the time on site. It could be that a low average pages per visit KPI is a bad thing. However, if these visitors also display a high time on site or trigger other on-page events such as watching a Flash movie clip, then it could be good thing.

As with all KPIs, don't use the site-wide average because that is too broad to be useful. A more informative view is to compare how these vary by visitor segment. For example, compare average time on site and pages per visit for new versus returning visitors or by referring traffic sources. To illustrate this, Figure 10.18 shows how these vary by referring source medium (taken from the Traffic Sources > Sources > All Traffic report). An interesting observation is that visitors from a print ad campaign have a very low pages per visit and low time on site, whereas visitors from social network sites have much higher rates. Initial thought—drop the print ad and invest the money saved into social media activities; marketing is changing!

By comparing segments for these KPIs, you can better tailor your website content, advertising, and overall usability for each visitor type. If you believe your content is already well structured and intuitive to use (everyone initially thinks that about their website), yet the average time on site or page depth is low, then consider how you are acquiring your visitors. Examine whether they are qualified visitors and whether the landing page they first arrive at is suitable for them.

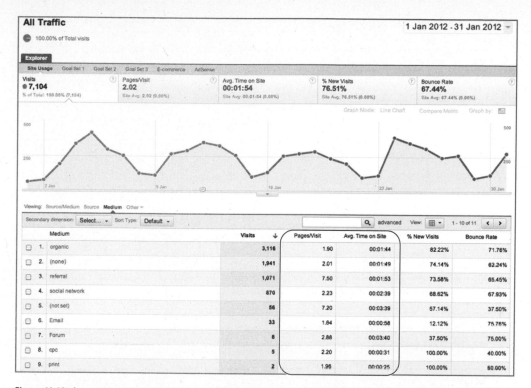

Figure 10.18 Average time on site and pages per visit by referring source medium

A Higher Time on Site or Page Depth Is Not Always a Good Thing

It's difficult to tell if a higher value for these metrics is a good thing or not. On the one hand, spending more time on your site and viewing more pages could mean visitors are highly engaged and interested in your content; on the other, they could be confused and lost in your navigation. Therefore, take care before drawing conclusions from these metrics. Always attempt to cross-reference with other KPIs that can provide further insight—particularly bounce rate and engagement KPIs.

Advertisement Performance

If you are an AdSense user—that is, you are displaying Google advertising alongside your content and benefiting from a share of the advertising revenue—there is a set of Google Analytics reports dedicated just for you. Assuming you have followed the integration steps described in Chapter 6, "Getting Started: Initial Setup," the Content > AdSense report contains a host of KPI metrics, all of which can be of use straight out of the box—see Figure 10.19.

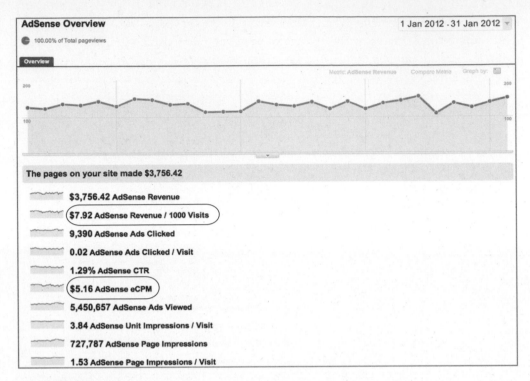

Figure 10.19 AdSense report

I always prefer monetized KPIs, so the AdSense Revenue / 1,000 Visits and the AdSense eCPM metrics are particular favorites from this report. These two metrics tell you how much advertising revenue you are making from AdSense click-throughs per 1,000 visits and per 1,000 AdSense page impressions, respectively. Clearly you will want to increase these.

Because AdSense is contextual- or interest-based advertising, the key to improving these metrics is to provide good-quality content (isn't it always!) so that Google's ad network can find a relevant ad match. The stronger that correlation, the more relevant the ad will be and hence the more likely a visitor will click it.

If you are not an AdSense user, then a little more work is required to obtain these metrics for yourself. Assuming your advertisements lead a visitor to an external website, you will need to track these outbound links as discussed in Chapter 7, either as virtual pageviews or as events. With this tracking in place, performing calculations is straightforward using the Content > Site Content > Pages report (virtual pageviews) or from the Content > Events > Top Events report (events), as shown next.

$$\text{Number of advertisements clicked per 1000 visits} = \frac{\text{total number of advertisements clicked}}{\text{total number of visits}} \times 1000$$

Extending the method, you can obtain your advertising revenue per 1,000 visits by multiplying this value by the average value of your advertising sales. You can even differentiate ad formats; that is, you can take into account your rate card and have a different advertising revenue per 1,000 visits for each format, by using the technique described in Chapter 7 in "Tracking Banners and Other Outgoing Links as Events."

The reason for multiplying the average by 1,000 is that this metric is usually very small and does not convey the information as well as a KPI. In addition, advertising rate cards for content and media sites are usually priced according to a cost-per-thousand-impressions model (CPM—cost per mille; *mille* is Latin for *thousand*). Having this KPI with the same multiplier is clearly beneficial to help establish your rate card.

If you feel these KPIs are low, then investigate the quality, quantity, relevance, and placement of advertisements.

Note: For non-AdSense users, these calculations do not take into account that a single visit could produce all advertisement click-throughs—an unlikely scenario, but something to bear in mind if you spot a large anomaly.

Percent New versus Returning Visitors

This KPI is the same as the one discussed for e-commerce managers and shown in Figure 10.11. I list it here for completeness.

Percent High, Medium, Low Visitor Recency

Recency is defined as the amount of time that passes between sequential visits—that is, when were the current visitors last on your site? From experience, many people struggle to understand what recency is telling them or how to interpret the chart. Maybe it is because the terminology is not widely used in business. Nonetheless, it is an essential metric for measuring engagement. The report in Figure 10.20 illustrates this (taken from the Visitors > Behavior > Frequency & Recency report). Note that I have applied an advanced segment = returning visitors. This makes sense when considering recency—the time period since the *last* visit—because new visitors are not relevant in this instance.

Interpreting the chart in Figure 10.20 of the returning visits made in the period shown, the vast majority (52.40 percent) of them are for the same day, 9.94 percent also visited one day before, 4.67 percent visited two days ago, and so on. For visitor recency KPI reports, group this chart into high, medium, and low categories. The boundaries for each group will depend on your business model, though I tend to use the following:

- High = within one week
- Medium = between 8 and 30 days
- Low = more than 30 days

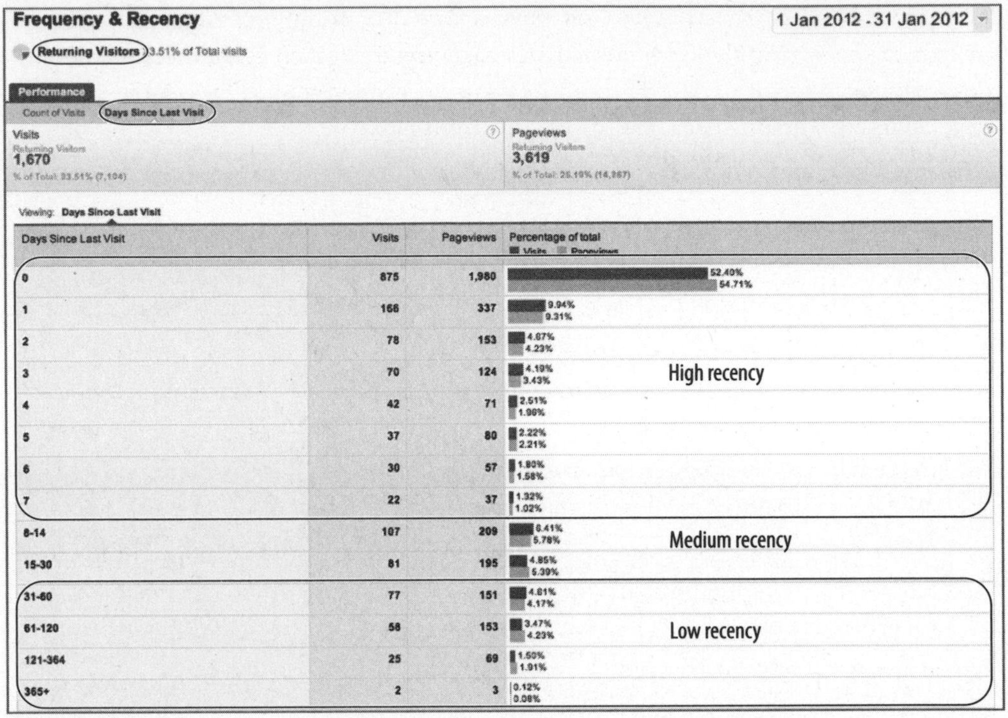

Frequency & Recency 1 Jan 2012 - 31 Jan 2012

Returning Visitors 33.51% of Total visits

Performance

Count of Visits | Days Since Last Visit

Visits
Returning Visitors
1,670
% of Total: 33.51% (7,104)

Pageviews
Returning Visitors
3,619
% of Total: 25.19% (14,367)

Viewing: Days Since Last Visit

Days Since Last Visit	Visits	Pageviews	Percentage of total (Visits / Pageviews)	
0	875	1,980	52.40% / 54.71%	High recency
1	166	337	9.94% / 9.31%	
2	78	153	4.67% / 4.23%	
3	70	124	4.19% / 3.43%	
4	42	71	2.51% / 1.96%	
5	37	80	2.22% / 2.21%	
6	30	57	1.80% / 1.58%	
7	22	37	1.32% / 1.02%	
8-14	107	209	6.41% / 5.78%	Medium recency
15-30	81	195	4.85% / 5.39%	
31-60	77	151	4.61% / 4.17%	
61-120	56	153	3.47% / 4.23%	Low recency
121-364	25	69	1.50% / 1.91%	
365+	2	3	0.12% / 0.08%	

Figure 10.20 Visitor recency chart

In all examples, the higher the recency, the better; that is, the fewer days between previous visits, the more engagement you have. For e-commerce websites, this could be the amount of time between visit and purchase. However, not all sites exhibit this behavior; high-value purchase items tend to have long visitor recency because visitors take longer to consider their purchase.

Note: According to a July 2007 ScanAlert report, online shoppers take an average of 34 hours and 19 minutes from their first visit to purchase.

Webmaster KPI Examples

Your webmaster department includes the people responsible for keeping your website up and running smoothly. Therefore, they need to know the expected visitor load on their servers. They also need to advise your design and content-creation departments on visitor profiles from a technical perspective, such as which browsers are most commonly used and what language settings visitors have on their computers. This is how the industry of web analytics got started—webmasters wanting to know "how many?"

Webmaster KPIs are usually nonhierarchical because of their technical importance and intended audience: technical people for whom high-level summary indicators raise more questions. For this audience, you may also consider bringing in other nonvisitor metrics to supplement the Google Analytics pageview data, such as web server uptime, server response speed, bandwidth used, and so on. These are not considered here.

Sample KPIs for webmasters include the following:

- Volume of visitors, visits, and pageviews
- Percentage of visitors without English language settings
- Percentage of visitors not using Microsoft Internet Explorer
- Percentage of visitors waiting too long for a page load
- Percentage of visitors receiving an error page
- Internal search performance and quality

Volume of Visitors, Visits, and Pageviews

This is a classic base metric that enables webmasters to quickly get a handle on the volume of traffic the website receives. Such metrics are important in determining the load on your web servers and network infrastructure and the potential importance of your website compared to other parts of your business. For example, if you measure your customer base in the thousands and one week you suddenly received 100,000 visits, your business needs to know about this!

The following metrics can be obtained directly from the Visitors > Overview report:

- Average number of visits per time frame
- Average number of unique visitors per time frame
- Average number of pageviews per time frame
- Average pageviews per visit

For such metrics, collect data over long periods to diminish the effects of large fluctuations. If you are a B2B website, the number of visits per day averaged over a week will be skewed by the weekend. In this case, it would be better to consider the average over the working week (Monday through Friday).

Percentage of Visits without English Language Settings

The more insight you have about your website visitor demographics, the better, and this KPI strongly overlaps with the goals of the marketing department. The visitor language setting is an excellent way of determining your international reach and whether your content matches this. Of course, if your main website language is not English, then simply replace the KPI name "English" with the appropriate language.

You can view the distribution of visitor languages directly from the Visitors > Demographics > Languages report (see Figure 10.21). You will need to do some grouping here because all language types are reported. For example, British English (en-gb) is reported separately from American English (en-us). Similarly, Spanish, Portuguese, and

French have different variations, as do many other languages. It is therefore important to group (or not) different language versions according to your requirements. To view grouped data, use an advanced segment as per Figure 10.22.

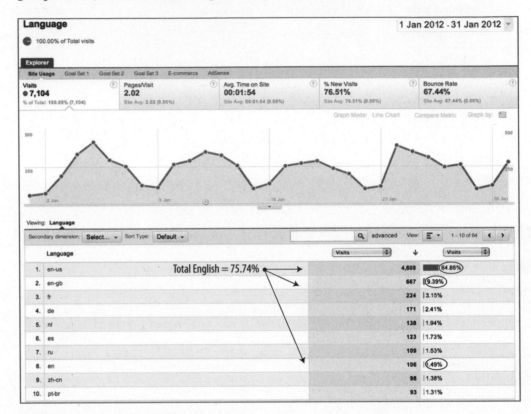

Figure 10.21 Distribution of visitor language settings

Figure 10.22 Advanced segment for grouping English language visits

 Note: Don't infer too much from the difference between en-gb and en-us because a great many non-US users have their browser settings set as en-us by default and never bother to change this. For example, I noticed that when I access my Google Analytics reports, I do so in US English. In over two years I have not bothered to change this to UK English.

From Figure 10.21 you might assume that the vast majority of visitor language requirements (75.74 percent) are accounted for. However, you should always assess this further. For example, viewing the Goal Set tabs, all things being equal, you would expect that the same proportion of conversions should occur for English visitors as for non-English visitors (if not higher). If that is not the case, there may be an opportunity for you to market in other languages. Also compare this table for new versus returning visitor segments. If foreign visitors feel you are not catering to their language needs, they are unlikely to return, and comparing your language distribution for returning visitors will reveal this.

> **Note:** An excellent resource for comparing Internet world statistics is www.internetworldstats.com. See, for example, www.internetworldstats.com/stats7.htm, where English accounts for 26.8 percent of world Internet usage (May 2011), down 2 percent in the last two years.

Percentage of Visits Not Using Microsoft Internet Explorer

Microsoft has contributed hugely to the proliferation of the Internet because of its ubiquitous operating systems and free browser software (Internet Explorer). However, times are changing—the once-dominant use of the software giant's products is being eroded by alternative operating systems from Apple and Ubuntu (Linux for the desk/laptop) and the abundance of browsers such as Firefox, Opera, Safari, and Chrome.

Various web browsers and operating systems render web pages differently. This means pages can look different from what was intended or not even work—the browser usually has the greatest impact here. Despite the use of Internet Explorer being globally estimated at 53 percent (see the sidebar "The Price of Incompatibility"), it still amazes me to visit websites of well-known brands that cannot process orders from non–Internet Explorer visitors. An example of this is posted at www.advanced-web-metrics.com/blog/2010/11/17/how-much-money-does-easyjet-lose/. Simply put, they are losing out on significant revenue and damaging their brand reputation to boot. Perhaps it is because testing web pages on different browsers and operating system platforms is a laborious job for webmasters and therefore rarely prioritized.

Whatever the reasons, you can access this KPI at a glance from the Visitors > Technology > Browser & OS report, shown in Figure 10.23. Knowing what your visitors use to access your website enables you to prioritize resources effectively. As you can see from Figure 10.23, the majority of visitors to this example site do not use Internet Explorer (81.32 percent).

In this case, having the website working well in MS Internet Explorer, Chrome, and Firefox is important, accounting for 90 percent of all visits. In addition, you should assess this further by viewing the Goal Set tabs. For example, visitors from MS Internet Explorer and visitors from Firefox should result in approximately the same conversion rates. If not, then likely your website does not work equally well for both browsers. Taking this a step further, you can also drill down on a browser type and view individual browser version details.

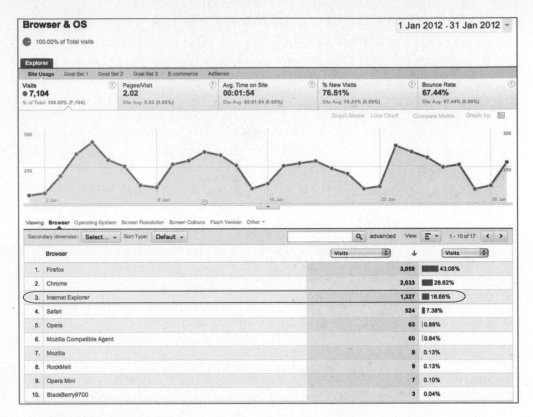

Figure 10.23 Visitor browser types

The Price of Incompatibility

Browser market share data from Net Applications for July 2011 (`http://marketshare.hits-link.com/browser-market-share.aspx?spider=1&qprid=0`) shows a global average of 47 percent of non–Internet Explorer users (up from 33 percent two years ago). Assuming these visitors behave in the same way as Internet Explorer visitors (there is no reason to suppose otherwise for the same website), that equates to an 89 percent loss of revenue if your website cannot work in these browsers (100/53). Even if your percentage of visitors not using Internet Explorer is lower than the global average, say only 20 percent, that is still 25 percent (100/80) of your money left on the table. A crime in my view!

Putting this into perspective, consider the percentage gains your marketing department is trying to squeeze out from optimizing online marketing campaigns—typically an additional 1 to 2 percentage point improvement, an order of magnitude smaller.

With browser standards now well established, there really is no excuse for not making your website work well in all browsers that have double digit usage by your visitors.

Percentage of Visitors Waiting Too Long for a Page Load

Slow-loading pages are a frustrating experience for any web user. It could be your overbloated landing pages or the visitor's Internet connection. Whatever the bottle-neck may be, the speed at which visitors access your content has obvious implications for webmasters. A study by Forrester Consulting for Akamai Technologies (September 2009) revealed that 2 seconds is the threshold in terms of an average online shopper's expectation for a web page to load (www.akamai.com/html/about/press/releases/2009/press_091409.html). In addition, its report reveals that 79 percent of online shoppers who experience a dissatisfying visit are less likely to buy from that site again. Interestingly, its similar study of 2006 revealed a 4-second rule—web users are becoming less tolerant of slow page loads. Whether you have a transactional website or not, I suggest the 2-second rule be applied to your web pages.

The Site Speed report, as discussed in Chapter 5, is an excellent place to view the impact of individual page load time on your site. However, to use page-load time as a KPI, select the Performance tab as shown in Figure 10.24 (taken from the Content > Site Speed report). Your threshold may vary, though I suggest that reducing the percentage of visitors waiting longer than 3 seconds should be your KPI. From Figure 10.24, this is 30.2 percent.

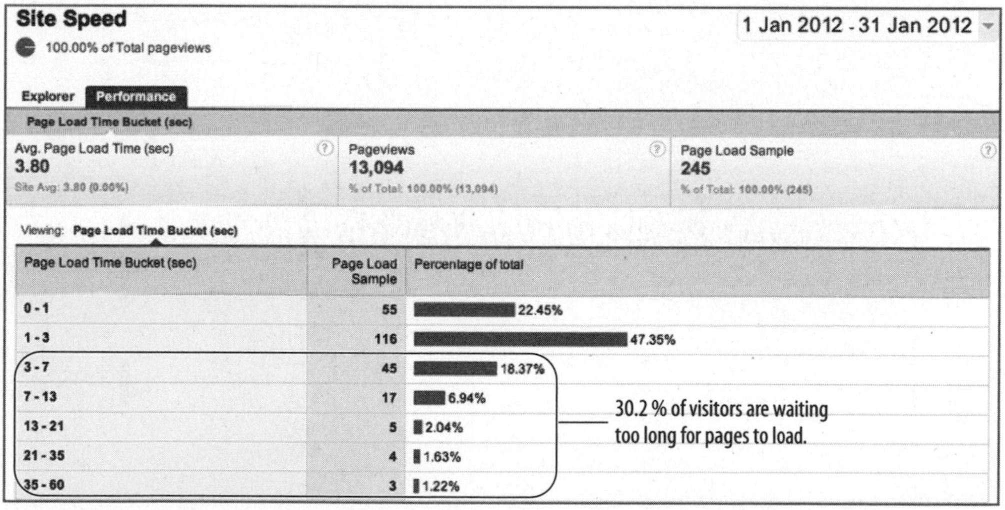

Figure 10.24 Site Speed Performance report

Percentage of Error Pages Served

This is an obvious metric any webmaster would wish to minimize. It is defined as follows and quoted as a percentage:

$$\text{percentage error pages served} = \frac{\text{total number of error pages served}}{\text{total number of pageviews served}}$$

Tracking error pages is discussed in "Tracking Error Pages and Broken Links" in Chapter 9. You track them as virtual pageviews so they can be viewed in your Content > Pages report. A target for this KPI could be to maintain this level at less than 0.1 percent of your total pageviews.

Internal Search Performance

Onsite search is now so important for large websites that it has become an integral part of the navigation system. Even for smaller sites, a good internal search engine can improve the user experience and hence your bottom line, so measuring the internal search experience is a key metric.

Important site search KPIs are available in the Content > Site Search > Overview report, shown in Figure 10.25.

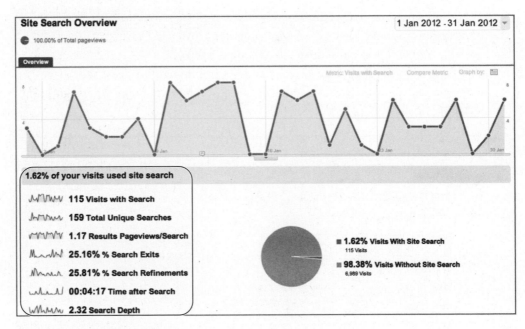

Figure 10.25 Site Search Overview report

The report in Figure 10.25 is a great starting point to evaluate your site search performance. For example, from this report you obtain the following:

- Percentage of visits that use site search (1.62 percent).
- Average number of search results viewed per search (1.17).
- Percentage of people exiting the site after viewing search results (25.16 percent).
- Percentage of people conducting multiple searches during their visit (25.81 percent). This excludes multiple searches for the same keyword.
- Average time on site for a visit following a search (00:04:17).

- Average number of pages visitors view after performing a search (2.32). If this is fewer than 1, then a significant number of visitors searching are not going beyond your results page.

Other important KPIs for site search include how visitors who use this facility compare with those who do not. For example, are site search visitors more likely to convert, spend more money, spend more time on site, or view more pages—that is, less likely to bounce? You can see these rates by viewing the Content > Site Search > Usage report, as shown in Figure 10.26.

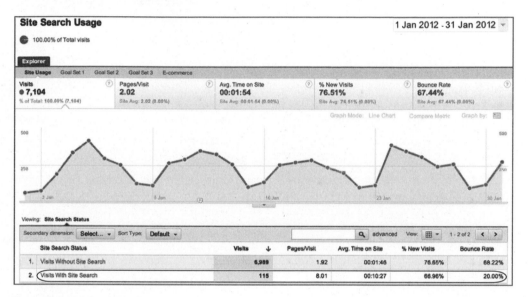

Figure 10.26 Site Search Usage report

From Figure 10.26, you can see that visitors who use the site search facility do indeed behave quite differently from those who do not. The Pages/Visit and Average Time on Site metrics are more than four times as high, while Bounce Rate is significantly lower. In addition, although not shown, the Goal Conversion rate for site search users is double that of those who do not use site search. From this report, site search clearly has a positive impact on the user experience for this example site, assuming the quality of the search results is good (see later in this section).

Note: Be aware that when selecting different metrics from the drop-down menu, the row order (and color key) may change depending on which is the highest value. For example, Visits With Site Search may be displayed as the first row when revenue is selected but as the second row when bounce rate is selected. This is the same behavior for all reports. That is, the highest value is always displayed first in the data table by default, something that still catches me out sometimes!

Why Site Search Visits May Not Have Zero Bounce Rates

A lower bounce rate is expected for site search visitors because by definition visitors who perform an onsite search will view at least two pages—one to conduct the search and one to view the results. So why is the bounce rate not zero?

Two common explanations are that your search result pages are indexed by the search engine robots and therefore can be accessed directly from a Google search, for example, and visitors can bookmark search results and therefore view them directly at a later date. For both of these scenarios, if the visitors do not view any further pages from you (or trigger any events), they are counted as bounced visits.

To compare site search usage against visits that do not search the site, take the site search metric and divide by the equivalent non–site search metric. This provides you with the ratio of how much more valuable (or not) site search is for your site. For example, Figure 10.27 shows that for the Per Visit Goal Value metric, visits that use site search are 23 percent more valuable than those that do not (0.16 / 0.13). Other useful metrics for this calculation are Conversion Rate, Revenue, and Number of Transactions, if applicable.

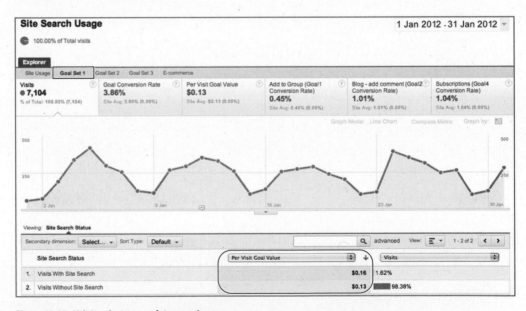

Figure 10.27 Valuing the impact of site search usage

Internal Search Quality

Determining your site search's result quality is harder to ascertain. Without asking your visitors what they think (survey integration is discussed in Chapter 12), a useful KPI is the number of zero-result search pages delivered. The theory is that searches producing zero results reflect a poorly configured internal site search engine.

Tracking zero results for site search is discussed in Chapter 8. Essentially, a different URL is required for search terms that generate a zero result than for those that do not. I use the Category field for this, as shown in Figure 10.28 (taken from the Content > Site Search > Search Terms report). From this example data, you can see that 17.61 percent of visits that used the search facility received a zero result. You can investigate this further by clicking the zero category label and viewing the search terms that generated this result. Measuring the success of site search is described in Chapter 11.

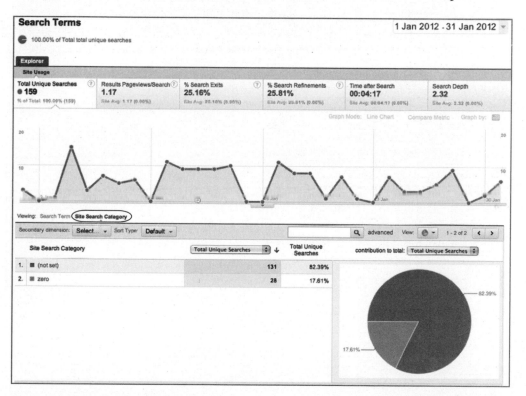

Figure 10.28 Percentage of zero search results

Note that it is possible that zero site search results could also be due to acquiring poor-quality traffic, though I have not considered this possibility here.

Using KPIs for Web 2.0

Web 2.0 is a phrase attributed to Tim O'Reilly (see www.oreillynet.com/lpt/a/6228 and www.oreillynet.com/pub/a/oreilly/tim/news/2005/09/30/what-is-web-20.html). In effect, it is a buzzword for the next generation of browser applications. According to Wikipedia, "Web 2.0 is a term often applied to a perceived ongoing transition of the World Wide Web from a collection of websites to a full-fledged computing platform serving web applications to end users. Ultimately Web 2.0 services are expected to replace desktop computing applications for many purposes."

The irony is that the technology that drives Web 2.0 is part of the original Web 1.0 technology and has been around for many years—that is, JavaScript and XML. Thus, Web 2.0 does not refer to any technical advancements of the Web or the Internet infrastructure it runs on but refers to changes in the way the medium is used. That's not to devalue the significance of Web 2.0, because this major shift in how users participate and surf the Web is driving the second generation of interactive web applications.

Example Web 2.0 Sites

Here are some excellent examples of Web 2.0 websites with RIAs:

Google Maps: `maps.google.com` (Ajax)

Google Mail: `mail.google.com` (Ajax)

Yahoo! Mail: `mail.yahoo.com` (Ajax)

Google Docs: `docs.google.com` (Ajax)

YouTube: `www.youtube.com` (Flash and Ajax)

Photosynth: `photosynth.net` (Silverlight)

MobileMe: `www.mobileme.com` (Ajax)

Flickr: `www.flickr.com` (Ajax)

Silverlight Showcase: `silverlight.net/showcase/` (Silverlight)

As you can see, Google is a great proponent of Web 2.0 technologies. In fact, Google Analytics itself is a prime example—combining Flash and Ajax.

Web 2.0 applications are usually built using Ajax (asynchronous JavaScript and XML) techniques. Similar to LAMP and DHTML, Ajax is not a technology in itself but a collection of technologies and methodologies combining JavaScript, XML, XHTML, and CSS. Another Web 2.0 technology is Flash. As with Ajax, it has been around for over 12 years but has only recently emerged as something more than just cool animation, with its ability to stream video and interact with XML.

Other technologies include Adobe Flex, Adobe AIR, and Microsoft Silverlight as well as HTML5—the latest version of HTML, which can achieve a great deal of animation and may even supersede the proprietary Flash format one day (in fact, iPhones, iPads, and the latest version of Windows Mobile no longer support Flash in favor of HTML5). Collectively, all these technologies are referred to as rich Internet applications (RIAs).

Why the Fuss about Web 2.0?

The techniques employed when developing a website using Web 2.0 technologies separate the components of data, format, style, and function. Instead of a web server loading a discrete page of information combining all those elements, each element is pulled separately. This has tremendous implications when it comes to defining KPIs because the concept of a pageview all but disappears.

For example, load `http://maps.google.com` in your browser and navigate to your hometown (usually in the format of "town, country"). Then zoom in and out and pan around by dragging the map. You can also change to satellite view or a hybrid of that and map view. It is difficult to describe this in words, but if you try it out you very quickly get the idea.

Google Maps is an excellent example of the power and interaction of a Web 2.0 website. When you load the first page, there is an initial delay while a JavaScript file is downloaded in the background. This is the controlling file that interacts with your mouse instructions. Note that the page and controlling JavaScript file are only loaded once. Then, as you interact with the map (zoom, pan around, and so on), further data is requested on-the-fly and inserted into the existing page. (The page URL does not change while you do this; the web page itself has become part of the delivery process.) By contrast, a traditional Web 1.0 website would require the reloading of the page to insert each additional map image.

This is an example of a visitor requesting one HTML page yet interacting in many different ways—perhaps creating dozens of actions or events (zooming and panning around) and gaining significant benefit from the experience. Clearly, using only pageview data for your KPIs is not going to work if your website contains RIAs.

> **Note:** Tracking Web 2.0 websites is not an issue for Google Analytics. These websites can even be monetized. See "Event Tracking" in Chapter 7.

Web 2.0 sites are still relatively rare, but they can have a huge impact. For example, not many people are unaware of Google Maps, Yahoo! Mail, and YouTube. The key to their growing success is that the user experience is "cool." Visitors find and interact with content quickly and without waiting for page refreshes. I often refer to Web 2.0 as drag-and-drop technology.

Consider the screen shot from YouTube shown in Figure 10.29. The six areas highlighted are actions or events that the visitor can interact with; that is, they are not pageviews. Essentially, the visitor can multitask with all of these on the same page (only one pageview).

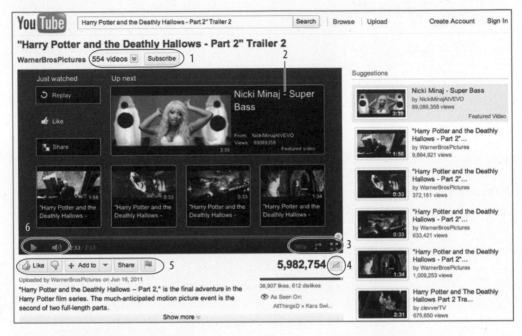

Figure 10.29 Visitor engagements on YouTube

As the number of Web 2.0 RIA sites grows, the requirement to define KPIs for them grows. Rather than think in terms of pageviews, analysts need to think in terms of actions and events that indicate engagement. In other words, what actions do you want your visitors to perform in order to classify an engagement?

Another implication of Web 2.0 has been the proliferation of user-generated content (UGC) sites—collectively referred to as social networks. Examples include Twitter, YouTube, Facebook, Google+, Myspace, Bebo, Orkut, and the plethora of Blogger and WordPress blogs. Measuring visitors from social networks is straightforward because they are tracked just like any other visitor to your site. The caveat is that without segmentation or rewrite filters, such visitors are buried deep within all your other referral traffic. Chapter 8 discusses how to bubble these up in your reports in the section "Example Custom Segments."

KPIs for Web 2.0 are actually no different from existing KPIs for a Web 1.0 world. True, you may be tracking them as events rather than pageviews; however, beyond visitor volume and transactions numbers, key metrics boil down to engagements, that is, determining how strong your virtual relationship is with your anonymous visitors. Engagement is exactly what savvy marketing managers and content creators are already focusing on with Web 1.0 technologies. If that describes you (I hope it does if you have read this far), any changes planned for your site involving RIAs or UGC will be easy for you to accommodate within your existing KPI strategy.

We discussed engagement in detail in the section "Content Creator KPI Examples." The principle is the same for RIAs and UGC. Without changing your analytical thinking, the following current KPIs are suited to a Web 2.0 environment:

- Percentage of visitors with content interaction—for example, zoom, pan around, view next message, customize

- Percentage of visitors triggering an event—for example, play, pause, next, upload, advertisement click-through, drag to cart

- Percentage engagement—for example, subscribe, register, comment, rate, Facebook Like, Google +1, retweet, and so forth

Summary

In Chapter 10, you have learned the following:

Setting objectives and key results Setting OKRs is an important prerequisite for aligning KPIs with your business, allowing you to manage expectations and gain the support of the business as a whole.

Defining KPIs based on business goals We discussed selecting and preparing KPIs by translating OKRs into actionable and accountable metrics, allowing success metrics from the Web to be incorporated into the rest of the business.

Making KPIs easy to understand You learned how to present KPIs in a clear format that business managers recognize and understand.

Defining KPIs by stakeholder job roles We examined KPI examples by job role to help you get started with important metrics.

Understanding the new KPIs You learned how Web 2.0 and rich Internet applications are changing metrics and KPI definitions.

Real-World Tasks

By now you may find your eyes glazing over at the scale of the project you have undertaken. However, Google Analytics is one of the easiest web analytics tools to configure, use, and understand. This chapter includes real-world examples of tasks most web analysts regularly need to perform. By presenting them, I hope to demystify the complexities of web analytics. As long as you dedicate the time and resources, you will find that this isn't rocket science. Even better, you will have a profound impact on the performance of your organization's website.

The tasks presented here are not intended to be an exhaustive or definitive list; rather, their purpose is help you obtain useful information you can act on. Acting on your data is the single most important aspect of web analytics, yet it is this aspect that most people stumble with.

In Chapter 11, you will learn:
To identify and optimize poor-performing pages
To measure the success of internal site search
To optimize your search engine marketing
To monetize a non-e-commerce website
To track offline marketing
To use Website Optimizer

Identify and Optimize Poor-Performing Pages

With all that visitor data coming in, one thing you will want to do is optimize your pages for the best possible user experience. Often the improvements are straightforward—for example, fixing broken links, changing landing page URLs to match the visitor's intent, or aligning page content with your advertising message. But which pages should you optimize and how? If your website has more than a handful of pages, where do you start?

Traditionally for web analytics solutions, identifying pages that underperform from the plethora of other pageview data has been a difficult task. However, Google Analytics has several resources and reports to help you. The following highlights the two areas I most commonly turn to:

- Landing pages (bounce rates)
- Funnel visualization

Using Landing Pages (Bounce Rates)

As the name suggests, the Content > Site Content > Landing Pages report shows the most popular entrance pages for your visitors (Figure 11.1). Note the weighted sort that I have applied to ensure that the volume of traffic—that is, visits—is taken into account when sorting by bounce rate (weighted sort is discussed in Chapter 4, "Using the Google Analytics Interface").

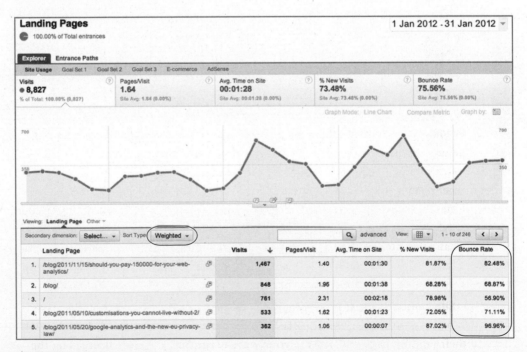

Figure 11.1 Landing Pages report

For this report, the bounce rate is the *key* metric; if visitors are arriving at the landing page and then leaving the site after viewing only that one page with no other action or event triggered, it is poor engagement. If a landing page has a high bounce rate, it means that the content of that page did not meet the visitors' expectations. Beyond looking for page errors, you need insight as to what the visitors' expectations were, which means looking at the referral details.

> **Note:** My definition of a single pageview with no other action or event constituting poor engagement assumes you are not writing the perfect one-page article. Even if you are, you should be soliciting a further action from your visitors, such as, for example, click to rate, add a comment, a subscription, a share, or a Like on their social network and so forth. If you do not do this, how will you define success? In fact, how will you ever know if your efforts are being appreciated or worthwhile?

What constitutes a high bounce rate is discussed in the section titled "Content Creator KPI Examples" in Chapter 10, "Focusing on Key Performance Indicators." My rule of thumb is to define *high* as a bounce rate of greater than 50 percent for nonpublisher websites. Publishing sites such as newspapers, book publishers, and blogs that do not require a user login generally have higher bounce rates—there is simply less incentive for visitors to click through.

Exercises for Bounce Rate Optimization

Once you have a list of your 10 worst-performing landing pages—as defined by high bounce rate weighted by traffic volume, bring in your marketing or agency team to discuss improvements. Include a member of your sales team and your customer service department in the meeting, and ask them to bring a list of the five most common questions customers ask. Then spend a morning brainstorming. The following describes a three-step approach for doing this.

Map marketing campaigns to landing pages   As an initial exercise, ask the teams to map out the campaigns that *should* be driving visits to these landing pages. I emphasize the word *should* because sometimes something outside of your organization's control—for example, a news story—can be driving your traffic and your team should also be aware of these. Hopefully, a strong overlap is apparent between your team's knowledge and where your visitors are coming from. That is, the marketing team has campaigns running that are targeting the pages on your list, including organic search engine optimization campaigns. The important lesson from this exercise is in understanding why visitors arrive on these landing pages and what are the drivers for their doing so.

Check that visitor expectations align with landing page message   In your next meeting, discuss how to improve visitor engagement; that is, how to encourage visitors to click through beyond their landing page and explore your website further, therefore decreasing the bounce rate. As a team, view each landing page from your list in a browser. The important question to answer is: Does the landing page match the expectations of the marketing campaigns for it? Perhaps the pricing is wrong, or a special offer is outdated? Are there any errors—images not loading, spelling or grammatical errors? Are your landing pages slow to load? All of these are very off-putting to potential customers.

 Tip: When you view your landing pages in a browser, ensure that you use an external route to your server, one that goes via the Internet as if you are a regular visitor and not via your local network. That way you will view your pages as your visitors do—experiencing the same errors and time delays. Also, ensure that you have cleared your browser's cache.

Define the landing page purpose and optimize. For your third team meeting, examine the purpose of each landing page. All landing pages have a purpose, and that is to help drive goal conversions. This is why you should not use your home page as a campaign landing page—it is too generic and ill focused. The purpose of your home page is to define your brand, not drive conversions directly. An obvious purpose is to present product information, but it may also be providing trust and credibility for your organization as well as managing the visitor's expectations.

Summary of Methodology

The exercises just described are excellent for getting your teams thinking about the purpose of a page in relation to its marketing rather than focusing on its marketing in isolation, which is often the case. Bounce rate is a powerful metric for understanding content performance, and I find it is often underutilized. The following is a summary of the points discussed in this section:

- Use weighted sort to obtain your list of poor-performing landing pages from the Content > Site Content > Landing Pages report. Focus on the top 10 worst performing landing pages by bounce rate, and bring in your marketing team and agency for a meeting.

- Map out the current campaign strategy for the listed pages. Understand what should be driving traffic to them. See if this matches your report. For example, if 50 percent of your marketing budget for a landing page is for paid search, does that landing page receive approximately 50 percent of its traffic from that source?

- Load each landing page in your browser, and check what the visitor's expectation will be. Does the messaging of the campaign align with that of the landing page? Are there any errors or omissions? Do pages load quickly? Improve as required. Ensure that your home page is not being used as a campaign landing page. If it is, assign a dedicated page for it, or build one.

- View the content of each landing page and determine how to increase its engagement. Ask the team what its purpose is in relation to your goals and how the purpose can be strengthened. Add or modify the conversion contributing factors.

- Where page improvements are not obvious, consider showing alternatives to a small sample of your visitors by using an A/B or multivariate testing tool—see "An Introduction to Google Website Optimizer" later in this chapter.

Conduct this entire exercise quarterly. For example, you may select 10 pages in the first quarter, followed by the next 10 in the second quarter, and so forth. Consider that most websites obey the 20/80 rule; that is, 20 percent of content is responsible for 80 percent of revenue or leads. Therefore, you should find your optimization efforts being rewarded quickly.

For assessing bounce rates in detail, the key dimensions to review are the entrance sources and entrance keywords—because these refer to your visitors' expectations before arriving on your website. Exercises for doing this are discussed next.

Assessing Entrance Sources

As the term suggests, *entrance sources* are the referring websites and campaigns that lead visitors to your site—for example, search engines, paid advertising, social networks, affiliates, and email links. An example report for a website home page is shown in Figure 11.2.

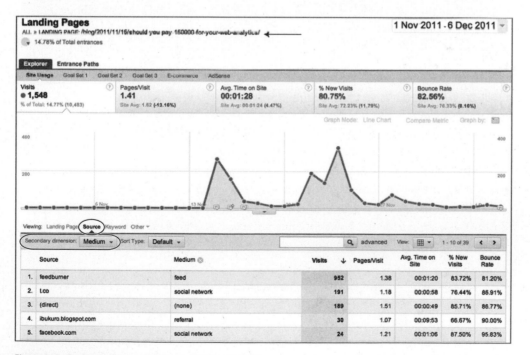

Figure 11.2 Entrance sources report for a specific landing page

Discuss this report with your marketing team by considering the following perspectives:

- Offline marketing initiatives
- Paid search campaigns
- Search engine optimization (SEO)
- Social network participation
- Email marketing

In the report shown in Figure 11.2, the source labeled (direct) in row 3 could be the result of offline marketing efforts whereby people have seen your ad and remembered your web address. If you observe a high bounce rate from this source, then look at how you are targeting visitors by offline methods. A common mistake is to send visitors for a specific campaign to a generic home page, leading to poor traction with the visitor. Later in this chapter I discuss how to overcome this (see "Tracking Offline Marketing").

Note: The label (direct) will also be applied to visitors who bookmark your website (add to favorites) and any non–web referral link that has not been set up correctly, such as email links, mobile apps, and embedded links within PDF files. To ensure that these are tracked, refer to "Campaign Tracking" in Chapter 7, "Advanced Implementation."

From the report shown in Figure 11.2, identify any paid search campaigns. Pay-per-click advertising is an excellent way to target search engine visitors with a specific message (ad creative) and specific content (landing page URL). Any high bounce rates observed from these sources should be investigated immediately because they reflect poor targeting or a misaligned message. A common mistake is using time- or price-sensitive information in your ad creative that is outdated when the visitor clicks through. Therefore, you should review your ads carefully.

In addition, are your ad landing page URLs targeted for your campaigns? Avoid the use of your generic home page as a landing page URL—use a more specific one. Another area to look at is how you target your visitors with geotargeting; for example, do your pricing and delivery options match the expectations of visitors from different locations? These are discussed later in this chapter in "Optimizing Your Search Engine Marketing."

From an SEO perspective, think in terms of the visitor experience because ultimately this is what search engines are trying to emulate with their ranking algorithms. For high-bounce-rate pages from organic search visitors, view the source code and read the content within the HTML `<title>` and `<meta name="description"...>` tag sections.

Are these in alignment with the rest of your page content? This is important because it is the only information about your organization a visitor sees on a search engine results page—the text of the clickable link is taken from your page title tag, while the snippet of text underneath is taken from your meta description tag. Hence, these are important qualifiers for visitors before clicking through to your site. Discuss with your marketing team making adjustments to these HTML tags. Most Content Management Systems (CMSs) allow you to do this without having to edit source code.

Also consider link referrals from other websites. Following a link from another website that turns out to be out of context is obviously a poor experience and waste of time for the visitor (it can also have a negative impact on your SEO rankings). If you find referral links with high bounce rates, use the Traffic Sources > Sources > Referrals report to investigate further. From there you can identify the referring site and view the exact page that visitors clicked through to arrive on your website. Sometimes a simple, polite email to the webmaster of the referring site can pay you dividends. Specify that you want to ensure that links are in context and point to a relevant, specific landing page on your website. Provide any necessary details in your email.

Assessing Entrance Keywords

The Entrance Keywords report focuses on those visitors who have used search engines to arrive on your website—both paid and nonpaid (organic) search engines. In effect, this report is direct market research—visitors are informing you of exactly what content they expect to see on the page they arrive at on your site. Click the Keyword dimension shown in Figure 11.2 to extend the report, as shown in Figure 11.3.

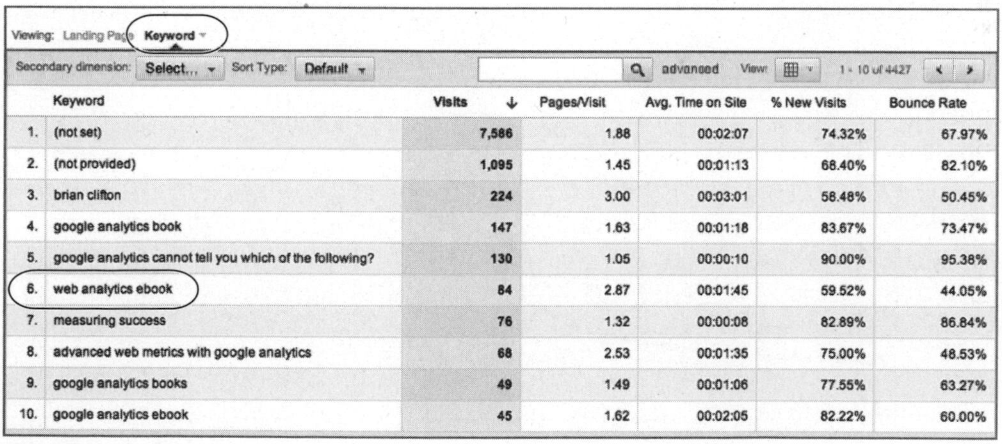

	Keyword	Visits ↓	Pages/Visit	Avg. Time on Site	% New Visits	Bounce Rate
1.	(not set)	7,586	1.88	00:02:07	74.32%	67.97%
2.	(not provided)	1,095	1.45	00:01:13	68.40%	82.10%
3.	brian clifton	224	3.00	00:03:01	58.48%	50.45%
4.	google analytics book	147	1.63	00:01:18	83.67%	73.47%
5.	google analytics cannot tell you which of the following?	130	1.05	00:00:10	90.00%	95.38%
6.	web analytics ebook	84	2.87	00:01:45	59.52%	44.05%
7.	measuring success	76	1.32	00:00:08	82.89%	86.84%
8.	advanced web metrics with google analytics	68	2.53	00:01:35	75.00%	48.53%
9.	google analytics books	49	1.49	00:01:06	77.55%	63.27%
10.	google analytics ebook	45	1.62	00:02:05	82.22%	60.00%

Figure 11.3 An Entrance Keywords report

As with the Entrance Sources report, high bounce rates here (greater than 50 percent) are an indicator that something may be amiss with your online marketing. Assuming your web server performance is not an issue, look at your visitor targeting, message alignment, and page relevancy, as described in the previous section.

Following this, consider the Entrance Keywords report as an opportunity to build page content around the listed keywords. For example, in Figure 11.3, row 6 for www.advanced-web-metrics.com shows a search term of *web analytics ebook*, yet I had not considered the term *ebook* in my content—instead I had been referencing the terminology as PDF. I now know *ebook* is an important term to my visitors and so have been including it ever since on relevant pages.

This is an example of where viewing low-bounce-rate pages can also provide important information (row 6 shows a relatively low bounce rate). Generally speaking, you will focus your efforts on analyzing high-bounce-rate pages because these are the ones killing your visitors' user experience. However, it's important to look at both ends of the spectrum when searching for insights.

Funnel Optimization Case Study

As discussed in Chapter 5, "Reports Explained," funnel analysis is an important process that helps you recognize barriers to conversion on your website, including the checkout process. I have often seen how understanding the visitor's journey within a website, followed by subsequent changes to improve the process, can lead to dramatic improvements in conversion rates and therefore the bottom line. For example, the fourfold increase in bookings for a travel website, shown in Figure 11.4, was the result of the following funnel optimization case study.

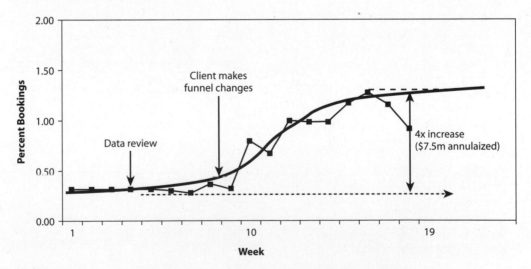

Figure 11.4 Conversion rate improvement for a travel website before and after funnel optimization

Billions of Dollars Left Abandoned

According to 2010 data from Forrester Research Inc.

`www.internetretailer.com/2010/09/28/key-profit-indicators-point`

the average shopping cart abandonment rate for US online retailers is 55 percent. In other words, the transaction revenue obtained by site owners is approximately half of what customers are willing to spend and are in the process of spending. That is, on average US retailers leave $1 of the money on the table for every $1 collected! It is an incredible amount statistic when you consider that US online retail is predicted to be worth $279 billion by 2015. See

`http://techcrunch.com/2011/02/28/forrester-online-retail-industry-in-the-us-will-be-worth-279-billion-in-2015)`

Schematic funnel shapes and their meanings are discussed in the section "What Funnel Shapes Can Tell You" in Chapter 8, "Best Practices Configuration Guide." An ideal funnel process would schematically look like Figure 11.5, where there is a gradual decrease in visitors (width of funnel) because of self-qualification through the various steps (height of funnel). The process of self-qualification could be by, for example, price, feature list, delivery location, stock availability, and so on.

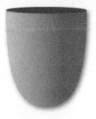

Figure 11.5 An ideal schematic wine goblet funnel shape

For this travel website case study, Figure 11.6 schematically illustrates the checkout process (booking a vacation).

The customer follows these steps:

1. Search for a vacation rental.
2. View search results.
3. Check the availability of rental.
4. Book the trip.
5. Confirm the booking.
6. Make payment.
7. Receive confirmation of payment.

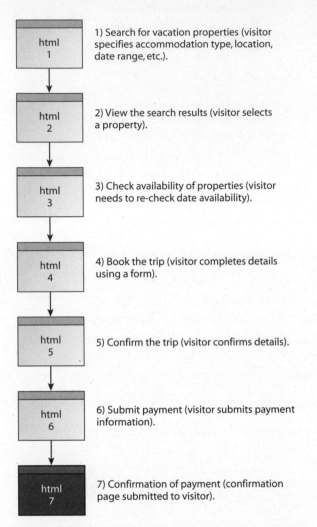

1) Search for vacation properties (visitor specifies accommodation type, location, date range, etc.).

2) View the search results (visitor selects a property).

3) Check availability of properties (visitor needs to re-check date availability).

4) Book the trip (visitor completes details using a form).

5) Confirm the trip (visitor confirms details).

6) Submit payment (visitor submits payment information).

7) Confirmation of payment (confirmation page submitted to visitor).

Figure 11.6 Schematic funnel process for the travel website case study

Figure 11.7 is the actual funnel process reported in Google Analytics for the travel website using the Conversions > Goals > Funnel Visualization report.

 Note: I am quite biased when it comes to travel websites. On the whole, they tend to be poorly built from a user's viewpoint. They are pretty, with a lot of colorful images and inspiring photographs, but I never seem to have a good experience when it comes to actually booking my travel plans, let alone a great one. However, as a wise person (@AnderssonSara) once said to me, "Your biggest obstacle is also your greatest opportunity."

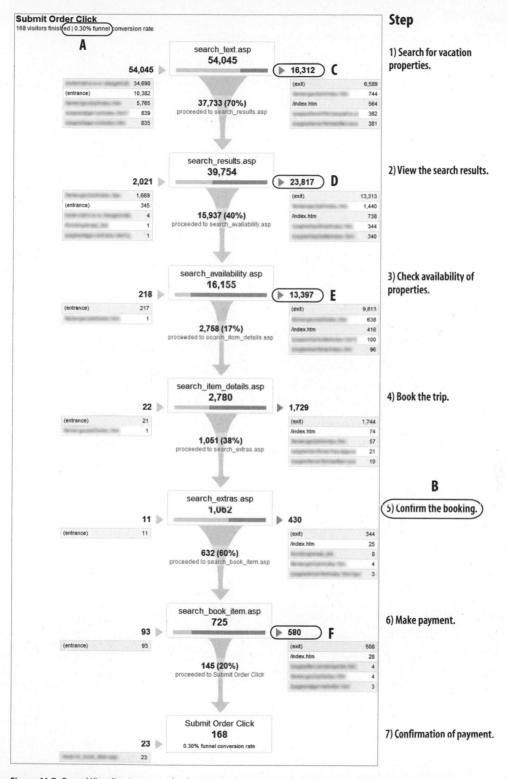

Figure 11.7 Funnel Visualization report for the travel website case study (page names obfuscated for anonymity)

Issues with the Funnel Presented

The steps from the funnel visualization in Figure 11.6 are discussed in the context of the following six issues, indicated by the large letters in Figure 11.7:

Issue A The most obvious metric that stands out in Figure 11.7 is the end conversion rate—a woefully poor 0.30 percent. Put another way, 99.70 percent of all visitors abandon the booking process. Considering the cost of acquiring those visitors by both paid and nonpaid search, that means a very, very negative return on investment.

> **Note:** Although this funnel example is an extreme case, it never ceases to amaze me that online purchase rates can be so low and are accepted as such. For example, the e-tailing group 10th Annual Merchant Survey, April 2011, shows that the most common US merchant conversion rates are between 1.0 and 2.9 percent (see the chart in Figure 1.5 in Chapter 1, "Why Understanding Your Web Traffic Is Important to Your Business"). Surely we can do better than having 97 plus percent of visitors leave a website without conversion? I hope that having read this far, you will agree that it is laudable and entirely possible to improve this percentage significantly.

Issue B Looking at the entire booking process, the length of the funnel, at seven steps, appears overly long. From user experience experiments, it is widely known that users do not like long checkout processes. That's obvious to anyone who uses the Web! The most effective method to reduce cart abandonment is to streamline the number of steps in the process, and this is applicable here. On inspection, step 5 (confirm the booking) is superfluous because all booking details are displayed at each preceding step.

Issue C The process begins with the search_text.asp page. This is the page where visitors search for their vacation rental (hotel, villa, apartment). From this page, 30 percent drop out of the funnel.

Issue D Following step 1, the search results page (step 2) loses 60 percent of remaining visitors; over half of these (13,313) exit the site completely.

Issue E Looking at the check-availability page (step 3), 83 percent of remaining visitors drop out of the funnel; again, the vast majority are site exits (60 percent). This is clearly a pain point and should be red-flagged as a problem page.

Issue F The next steps in the system have similar problems, but the killer is step 6, which is when payment details from the visitor are requested. Out of the 725 visitors who have had the stamina and persistence to get through what is obviously a difficult process, 80 percent of them (580) abandon at this final step; the vast majority leave the website completely.

Seeing the result of these issues represented schematically, we observe a funnel shape more like what is shown in Figure 11.8, with two clear pain points in the process, step 3 and step 6, that lead to large-scale abandonment.

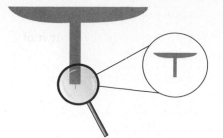

Figure 11.8 Stacked champagne glass schematic funnel shape

Action Points from the Funnel Optimization

Understanding the real-world funnel process of Figure 11.7 and its problems took less than one hour because the data is so clearly presented. Of course, correcting such issues obviously takes longer; you need to understand why this happened. This is something that web analytics tools cannot do; they cannot tell you why visitors are abandoning your booking process.

To address this, you could deploy a feedback system—a survey that pops up when a visitor abandons the booking process or leaves your website. Example survey tools include Clicktools, Kampyle, SurveyMonkey, and UserVoice. However, if your visitors are leaving because of a bad experience, they usually won't want to spend further time on your site explaining what went wrong. That said, any feedback from visitors *within* your shopping cart system who are abandoning is gold dust and worth pursuing. See Chapter 12, "Integrating Google Analytics with Third-Party Applications," for an example integration with the Kampyle feedback system.

Putting aside having to deploy a feedback survey system, a little lateral thought and visiting your own website as if you were a potential customer can go a long way. For example, in this scenario I focused on steps 3 and 6, where the vast majority of visitors were abandoning the booking process. This led to the development of four key recommendations for improvement:

Improve the availability checker page. Step 3 (the availability checker) indicates either a total lack of accommodation availability, in which case the website owners should turn down the visitor acquisition tap and save marketing budget, or a malfunction in the process of selecting available dates.

Lack of availability was not an issue. When I viewed the availability checker manually, no errors were found, but the process was quite clunky and difficult to interpret. For example, dates themselves were nonclickable. Instead, date-selection controls were located below the fold of the page—that is, not visible without scrolling down.

Correct the layout of the payment form. Step 6 (the payment form) required some additional thought. Although the form was considered to be overly long at seven steps, it did not make sense that such persistent visitors would bail out en masse at the penultimate step (visitors were aware of their progress by the numbering of the steps—for example, with the heading "Step X of Y"). To test for problems, I tried the process of booking a vacation myself.

What I immediately discovered when clicking to submit my dummy payment details was an error page. In addition, the error page did not indicate what caused the problem. Using the Back button, I checked all the required fields and tried again—same error page, no message indicating what the error was. This process was repeated many, many times with no further insight. It really did appear to be a mystery as to why I could not complete my payment.

In fact, the problem was staring me in the face. The credit card type (Amex, Visa, MasterCard) was preselected as Amex by default. However, the HTML drop-down list for selecting the card type was not aligned with the other form fields—it was to the extreme right of the page, while everything else was left aligned.

Despite repeatedly testing the payment system and staring frustratedly at the page, I simply didn't see the right-aligned card selector. I was filling in all my details correctly and hadn't noticed the default setting for the credit card as Amex while I was using Visa. In fact, I hadn't noticed the card type drop-down list at all.

Now the explanation of large-scale abandonment at step 6 is clear. Visitors were receiving the error page, which was probably the straw that broke the camel's back after such a difficult and torturous booking process, and so they simply abandoned the site.

Streamlining the Checkout Process

Although selecting your card type on a payment form is almost always a manual process, it is possible to automate this and remove any potential errors. You can do this by using the initial digits of the card number, as shown in the following table:

Card Types	Prefix	Number of digits
American Express	34, 37	15
Diners Club	300 to 305, 36	14
Carte Blanche	38	14
Discover	6011	16
EnRoute	2014, 2149	15
JCB	3	16
JCB	2131, 1800	15
MasterCard	51 to 55	16
Visa	4	13, 16

Track error pages. Part of the difficulty in identifying the problem visitors were experiencing in step 6 was that the subsequent error page was not being tracked. Had it been, using the methods described in Chapter 9, "Google Analytics Customizations," the investigation could have taken place much more quickly.

Show clear instructions in your error pages. Even if an investigation into the low conversion rate had not been undertaken, visitors could have corrected the payment problem themselves—that is, if they were told what the problem was. Clearly this is not a solution to the problem, but it is certainly better than slamming the door in their face with nothing more informative than "Error—please try again."

Summary of Funnel Optimization

Presenting these findings to the client was groundbreaking. They had hired and fired several search engine marketing agencies in the belief that they were receiving poorly qualified leads, resulting in such a low (0.3 percent) conversion rate. In fact, the problem was entirely on their site: a poor user experience. Once the problem was fixed, their conversion rate jumped fourfold, with a concomitant revenue increase of millions of extra dollars per year. I should have billed by commission!

Funnel analysis shows both the power and the weakness of web analytics as a technique for understanding visitor behavior on your website. The power is in identifying the problem areas during a typical path visitors take; for that, your web analytics is capable of telling you what happened and when. That in turn enables you to focus your efforts on improving the particular problem page. The weakness of web analytics is that it does not tell you why visitors made the choices they did. To understand why visitors behave in an unanticipated way, you need to investigate—either directly yourself (try a checkout or booking on your own website) or by conducting a survey or usability experiment.

Tip: If *usability experiments* is a new term for you, don't contact a specialist agency until you check out these excellent books by Steve Krug: *Don't Make Me Think* (New Riders, 2006) and *Rocket Surgery Made Easy* (New Riders, 2010).

Measuring the Impact of Site Search

Site search is the internal search engine of your website that visitors often substitute for a menu navigation system. For large websites with hundreds or thousands of content pages (sometimes hundreds of thousands), internal search is a critical component for website visitors, enabling them to find what they are looking for quickly. Internal search engines generally use the same architecture as an external search engine such as Google. In fact, the major search engine companies sell their search technology to organizations. See, for example, the Google Search Appliance:

www.google.com/enterprise/search/gsa.html

Important site search KPIs were discussed in the section "Webmaster KPI Examples" in Chapter 10. In addition to the Site Search Overview report (refer to Figure 10.25), one of the things you will want to know is what keywords visitors are typing once they arrive on your website. The idea is that once you know these keywords, you include them (or exclude them if they are not relevant to you) in your paid and organic campaigns as well as ensure that landing pages are optimized for them. This is discussed in the section "Optimizing Your Search Engine Marketing" later in this chapter. Example site search terms are shown in Figure 11.9, taken from the Content > Site Search > Search Terms report.

	Search Term	Total Unique Searches ↓	Results Pageviews/Search	% Search Exits	% Search Refinements	Time after Search	Search Depth
1.	logfile	141	1.25	77.30%	2.27%	00:01:59	0.94
2.	outbound links	95	1.15	68.42%	0.92%	00:03:11	1.04
3.	seo	63	1.11	28.57%	11.43%	00:03:43	2.17
4.	downloads	52	1.15	53.85%	3.33%	00:03:27	1.48
5.	async	45	1.07	35.56%	0.00%	00:15:28	2.24
6.	crm	41	1.02	48.78%	0.00%	00:04:55	1.78
7.	emetrics	39	1.08	94.87%	0.00%	00:00:17	0.05
8.	facebook	27	1.00	37.04%	0.00%	00:00:01	0.96
9.	filters	23	1.09	69.57%	0.00%	00:03:07	0.91
10.	first referrer	22	1.41	27.27%	6.45%	00:07:23	3.32

Viewing: **Search Term** Site Search Category — Secondary dimension: Select... ▾ Sort Type: Default ▾ — Advanced Filter ON ✕ edit View: 1 - 10 of 1538 ‹ ›

Figure 11.9 Site Search Terms report showing keywords used

Note: The value of the Site Search Terms report shown in Figure 11.9 should not be underestimated. Visitors on your website are actually telling you what they would like to see, in their own language, using their own terminology. Perhaps you assumed "widgets" was the commonly known name of your product, but you find out that people are searching for "gadgets," or people are looking for "widgets with feature X," which your manufacturing team hadn't thought of. It's analogous to your potential customers walking into your store or office and providing you with direct feedback—without you having to ask or worry about infringing on visitor privacy.

The Revenue Impact of Site Search

Beyond looking at site search terms used, how do visitors who use your site search facility compare to those who do not? I illustrate this with two screen shots taken from the Content > Site Search > Usage reports (Figure 11.10 and Figure 11.11).

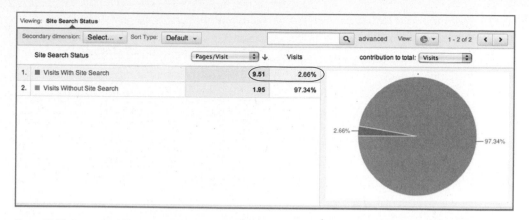

Figure 11.10 Pages per visit comparison of visitors who use site search and visitors who do not

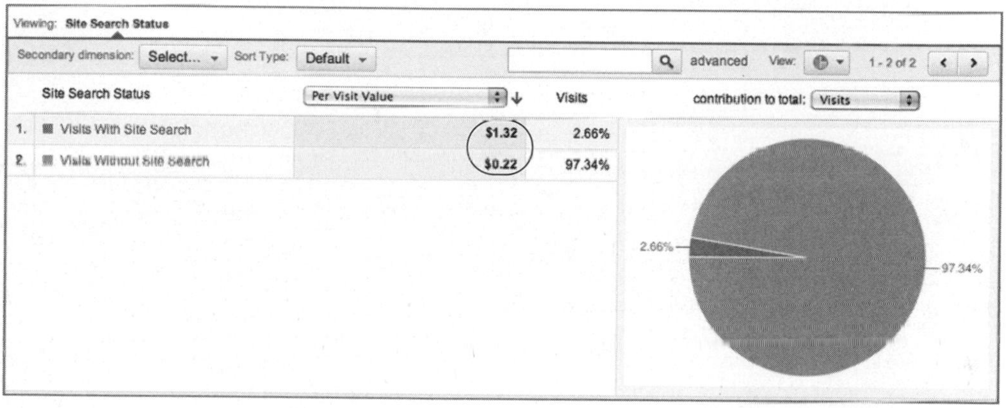

Figure 11.11 The per visit value difference from using site search

In Figure 11.10, you can see that the percentage of visits resulting in a site search is low at only 2.66 percent. However, the Pages/Visit metric for those visitors is almost five times higher compared to those who did not perform a search. Hence, a better user experience is inferred for those visitors.

Other key metrics can be selected from the drop-down list for comparison. A particular favorite of mine is the Per Visit Value (or Per Visit Goal Value if yours is a nontransactional site), as shown in Figure 11.11. For this metric to be available, ensure that you are in a Goal Set or E-commerce section of your reports—refer to label M of Figure 4.4 in Chapter 4 if needed.

Per visit values measure the value of a visitor. That is, did a visitor go on to complete a transaction or monetized goal? The higher the per visit value or per visit goal value for a visitor using site search, the more important that function is to the value of your website. I am assuming that where a visitor has come from, their referral source, is not a factor in whether they use site search or not.

From Figure 11.11, a visitor who uses site search is six times as valuable as a visitor who does not. For this example site, increasing the usage of the site search feature is clearly going to have a positive impact on the site. Armed with this information, meet with your web development team (those responsible for your internal site search engine) and discuss with them what plans they have for developing and growing the site search service. Before doing so, use the following formula to calculate the revenue impact that site search is having on your website:

$$\text{Revenue Impact of Site Search} = \left(\begin{matrix} \text{Per Visit Value} \\ \text{with Site Search} \end{matrix} - \begin{matrix} \text{Per Visit Value} \\ \text{without Site Search} \end{matrix} \right) \times \begin{matrix} \text{Number of Visits} \\ \text{with Site Search} \end{matrix}$$

Using Figure 11.11 and knowing the number of visitors who used site search for this example website (11,463, taken from the Site Search Overview report, not shown), the calculation is

$$\text{revenue impact of site search} = (1.32 - 0.22) \times 11,463 = \$12,609 \text{ per month}$$

To put this value into context, it represents only 2.66 percent of the total traffic to the site. If site search participation can be increased, say to a around quarter of all visits, their value becomes $126,000 per month—a very significant amount. This may at first sound like an unbelievable target. However, I have achieved these types of gains with several e-commerce site search facilities.

What If Site Search Has a Negative Revenue Impact?

In the previous examples, site search was shown to be clearly beneficial for the site, but what if the metrics are reversed—that is, visitors who use site search have *lower* Per Visit and Per Visit Goal Values than those who don't. This would result in a negative revenue impact of site search—its use is costing you money!

It is possible that such a result could be valid. That is, in some scenarios, finding information can best be served by a directory-type structure of navigation rather than a search engine—for example, a visitor looking for location-specific information or where jargon may be a barrier to know what to search for. However, I have found this to be rare.

Instead, a negative revenue impact of site search usually indicates an issue with the quality of the results returned. So far, we have assumed that your internal site search engine is working well, producing accurate and informative results regarding visitors' searches—the visitor just needs to be encouraged to use it. Unfortunately, most often this is not the case. There can be two reasons for this to happen:

- Your site search cannot find content to match the visitor's query.
- The results returned by your site search are of poor quality.

Other Metrics for Comparing the Performance of Site Search

Other key metrics can be selected from the drop-down list shown at the top of the table in Figure 11.1. These are as follows:

Goal Conversion Rate

$$\text{goal conversion rate} = \left(\frac{\text{number of conversions}}{\text{number of visits}}\right) \times 100$$

Revenue

$$\text{revenue} = \text{goal value} + \text{e-commerce value}$$

Average Value

$$\text{average value} = \frac{\text{goal value} + \text{e-commerce value}}{\text{number of conversions} + \text{number of transactions}}$$

E-commerce Conversion Rate

$$\text{e-commerce conversion rate} = \left(\frac{\text{number of transactions}}{\text{number of visits}}\right) \times 100$$

Per Visit Value

$$\text{per visit value} = \frac{\text{goal value} + \text{e-commerce value}}{\text{number of visits}}$$

To get a handle on whether the first reason is valid, look at the zero results produced by your site search engine. The method for tracking zero results is discussed in Chapter 8. Assuming you have used the same setup, select the label Zero from your Content > Site Search > Search Terms Category report. This reveals the keywords used that generated a zero result—as per Figure 11.12.

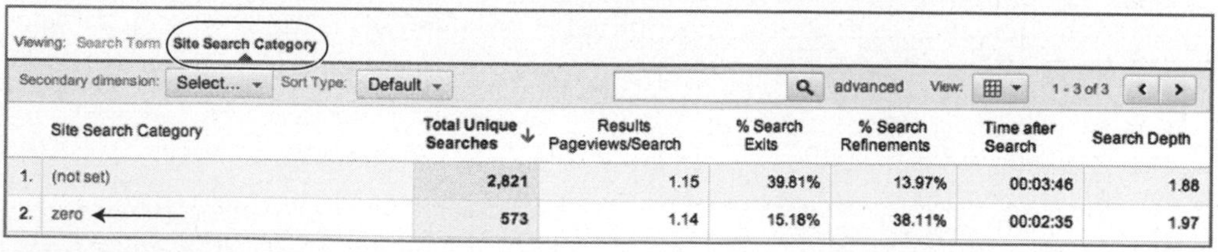

	Site Search Category	Total Unique Searches ↓	Results Pageviews/Search	% Search Exits	% Search Refinements	Time after Search	Search Depth
1.	(not set)	2,821	1.15	39.81%	13.97%	00:03:46	1.88
2.	zero ←	573	1.14	15.18%	38.11%	00:02:35	1.97

Viewing: Search Term **Site Search Category**

Secondary dimension: Select... ▾ Sort Type: Default ▾   🔍 advanced   View: ▦ ▾   1 - 3 of 3 ‹ ›

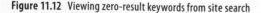

Figure 11.12 Viewing zero-result keywords from site search

Export this list into Excel, and highlight the keywords that are directly related to your website content. Meet with your web development team to ascertain why such relevant terms produce zero results. Maybe you have overlooked misspellings, regional differences (think "holiday" versus "vacation"), or visitors using terminology they are not familiar with. However, it may be that there is a problem with how your site search engine works or is configured. Is it picking up newly created or modified pages? Can it index PDF files? How is it ranking results?

Identifying the second reason—poor quality results returned by your site search—is harder to ascertain quantitatively. As discussed in Chapter 1, web analytics tools are great at telling you what happened on your website and when. But they cannot tell you why it happened. To understand the *quality* of a user's experience, you need to either ask your visitors (deploy a feedback survey) or put yourself in your visitors' shoes and go through the experience yourself. I recommend the latter method in the first instance—in fact, you should be regularly visiting your site to test the visitor experience.

Poor-quality results are indicated by a negative value, or a low value, of your revenue impact of site search combined with low frequency of zero results. This is the case when your site search returns irrelevant results, such as, for example, reams of press releases—useful for the media though not interesting for the vast majority of your visitors, or when site search returns product sales information when the visitor is looking for help and support information. Investigate this further by looking at the number of search exits (visitors who exit following a search) and search depth (the number of pages viewed after a search). Review the section "Webmaster KPI Examples" in Chapter 10 and in particular Figure 10.25 as needed.

A high search exit rate and low search depth are indicators of poor site search results. It may mean that the results are either irrelevant or are poorly ranked—too many results with a lower relevancy ranking higher. Perform the searches for your 10 most common keywords and judge for yourself. A simple fix is to allow your visitors to categorize their search requests. For example, using the previously mentioned scenarios, search only within the "product details," "support information," and "press releases" categories.

Summary of Site Search Impact

Site search engines are often installed and configured once and then forgotten—that's a mistake. I often find the greatest opportunity for site improvement, that is, conversion and revenue improvement, is found by looking at its site search performance. Websites evolve rapidly, including new content and new technologies. If site search visitors have a lower revenue impact without good reason, then site search is costing you money. Present this figure to the head of your web team and schedule a meeting to discuss enhancements or a replacement. Showing a dollar amount is a much better motivator than saying, "Our site search is not working effectively."

With your export list of zero-result site search terms, highlight the keywords visitors used that are *not* relevant to your organization but are related to the business you are in. If the number of these is significant (more than a few percent of the total number of unique searches), then meet with your product or service team to discuss their meaning. Perhaps the product team never thought people would want to search for feature X combined with product Y. Your site search data could provide valuable insight into this. For example, an action item may be to build a specific landing page for product XY to gain further feedback from those visitors.

Optimizing Your Search Engine Marketing

If you own a commercial website, then you want to drive as much qualified traffic to it as possible. Online marketing options include search engine optimization (nonpaid search, also known as organic search), paid search advertising (text ads, also referred to as pay-per-click or cost-per-click), email marketing, display advertising (banners), and social network participation (comments and links left on sites such as Twitter, LinkedIn, Facebook, forums, blogs, and so on).

All of these visitor acquisition methods have a cost—either direct with the media owner or indirect in management fees—though there is nothing stopping you as a do-it-yourself enthusiast. Optimizing your marketing campaigns using Google Analytics data can achieve cost savings and expose significant opportunities for your business. The following sections focus on the essential steps for optimizing your search engine marketing (SEM), both paid and nonpaid, including the following:

- Keyword discovery (paid and nonpaid search)
- Campaign optimization (paid search)
- Landing page optimization and SEO (paid and nonpaid search)
- AdWords day parting optimization (paid search)
- AdWords ad version optimization (paid search)

Keyword Discovery

When optimizing for SEM, one of the things you will constantly be on the lookout for is ideas for adding new, relevant keywords to your campaigns. These can be broad (for example, *shoes*), bringing in low-qualified visitors in the hope they will bookmark your page or remember your brand and website address for later use, or very specific (for example, *blue suede shoes*), which are highly targeted to one of your products and could lead to an immediate conversion on a visitor's first visit.

Several *offsite* tools are available to help you conduct keyword research:

- Google AdWords Keyword Tool (https://adwords.google.com/select/KeywordToolExternal)
- Wordtracker (www.wordtracker.com)

These enable you to discover what people are searching for on the Web as a whole (hence the term *offsite tool*) that may be related to your products or services and in what numbers. The tools help you determine which search keywords are most frequently used by search engine visitors and then help you identify related keywords, synonyms, and misspellings that could also be useful to your marketing campaigns. Clearly, being language and region specific is important; for example, *tap* and *holiday* are terms used in the UK that in the United States are more commonly known as *faucet* and *vacation*, respectively.

> **Note:** The differences between offsite and onsite web analytics are discussed in Chapter 1, "Why Understanding Your Web Traffic Is Important to Your Business."

In addition to these offsite tools, your Google Analytics reports contain a wealth of onsite information that can help you hunt for additional suitable keywords. There are two areas to look at: search terms used by visitors to find your website from a search engine and internal site search queries, that is, those used by visitors within your website.

Farming from Organic Visitors

The Traffic Sources > Sources > Search > Organic report is dedicated to referral keywords—keywords used by visitors who come from all organic search engines (see Figure 11.13). As an initial exercise, export all of your organic keywords. Compare them with those targeted by your paid campaigns from the Traffic Sources > Sources > Search > Paid report. Organic terms that are not in your paid campaigns are excellent candidates to be added to your pay-per-click account. After all, you will wish to maximize your exposure to relevant search terms.

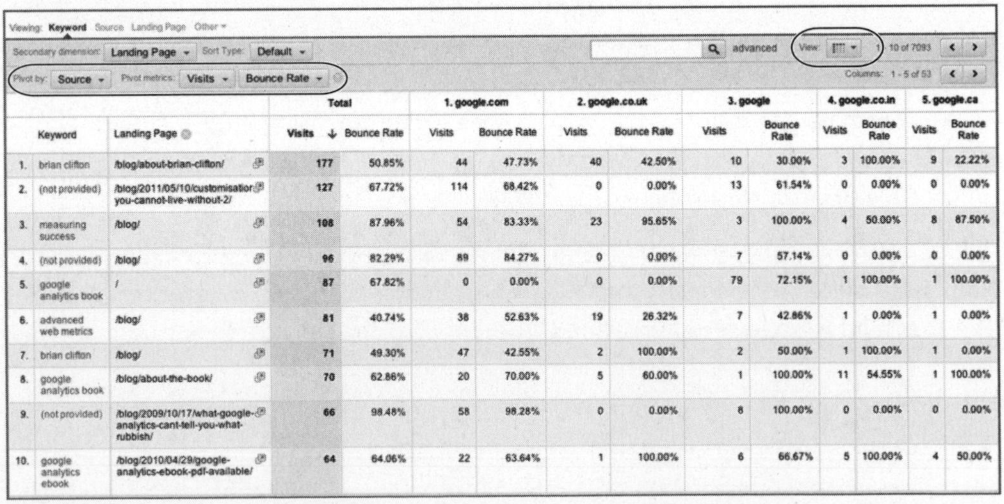

			Total		1. google.com		2. google.co.uk		3. google		4. google.co.in		5. google.ca	
	Keyword	Landing Page	Visits ↓	Bounce Rate	Visits	Bounce Rate	Visits	Bounce Rate	Visits	Bounce Rate	Visits	Bounce Rate	Visits	Bounce Rate
1.	brian clifton	/blog/about-brian-clifton/	177	50.85%	44	47.73%	40	42.50%	10	30.00%	3	100.00%	9	22.22%
2.	(not provided)	/blog/2011/05/10/customisation-you-cannot-live-without-2/	127	67.72%	114	68.42%	0	0.00%	13	61.54%	0	0.00%	0	0.00%
3.	measuring success	/blog/	108	87.96%	54	83.33%	23	95.65%	3	100.00%	4	50.00%	8	87.50%
4.	(not provided)	/blog/	96	82.29%	89	84.27%	0	0.00%	7	57.14%	0	0.00%	0	0.00%
5.	google analytics book	/	87	67.82%	0	0.00%	0	0.00%	79	72.15%	1	100.00%	1	100.00%
6.	advanced web metrics	/blog/	81	40.74%	38	52.63%	19	26.32%	7	42.86%	1	0.00%	1	0.00%
7.	brian clifton	/blog/	71	49.30%	47	42.55%	2	100.00%	2	50.00%	1	100.00%	1	0.00%
8.	google analytics book	/blog/about-the-book/	70	62.86%	20	70.00%	5	60.00%	1	100.00%	11	54.55%	1	100.00%
9.	(not provided)	/blog/2009/10/17/what-google-analytics-cant-tell-you-what-rubbish/	66	98.48%	58	98.28%	0	0.00%	8	100.00%	0	0.00%	0	0.00%
10.	google analytics ebook	/blog/2010/04/29/google-analytics-ebook-pdf-available/	64	64.06%	22	63.64%	1	100.00%	6	66.67%	5	100.00%	4	50.00%

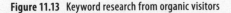

Figure 11.13 Keyword research from organic visitors

When adding keywords used by organic search visitors to your pay-per-click campaigns, consider your current organic search rankings for those terms. For example, if you are number one for your brand or product name in the organic results, should you also add this to your paid campaigns? If you do, you are likely to cannibalize your own free organic traffic.

My recommendation is to *not* bid if you have no pay-per-click competitors for a specific brand term (such as your company name)—otherwise you will be paying for traffic that will already come to you. On the other hand, if your competitors are bidding on your brand terms you should also bid on them, even with your number one organic ranking. The hypothesis is that you receive an additional boost in traffic (a 2 + 2 = 5 effect) by picking up traffic from your competitors. The additional traffic comes from pushing down your competitors' ranking in the paid result and occupying more "shelf space" on the results page itself.

The screen shown in Figure 11.13 is an excellent example of the wealth of information readily available within reports for improving your SEO efforts. In this case I have selected the pivot view to show visits and bounce rates on a per-search-engine basis. The secondary dimension is also used to provide the landing page URL for each keyword. The result is a report of search engines (shown horizontally across the top of the data table) that correlates keywords with landing pages, showing bounce rate and visit metrics. This is information that will surely keep any marketer busy for several hours!

What Does the Keyword (Not Provided) Mean?

Row 4 in Figure 11.13 shows a keyword labeled "(not provided)". This is the entry that Google sets when a visitor conducts a search on a Google property while they were logged into their Google account—for example, a Gmail user who is logged into their mail account and opens another window to perform a search.

Google's reasoning for this is privacy—that is, users often access their email via open Wi-Fi networks, and their search query terms could contain personally identifiable information. When logged in to their Google account, the user's search is encrypted and so not viewable over an open Wi-Fi connection. In October 2011, Google also made the decision to remove any referral keyword information transferred to a website when a user clicks through from a search result. Because the keyword information is removed, this affects all web analytics vendors.

Oddly, this setting does not affect visitors who click ads while logged in and conducting their search. For more discussion on this see

www.advanced-web-metrics.com/blog/2011/10/19/organic-search-terms-blocked-by-google

Farming from Site Search Visitors

If your site has an internal search engine to help visitors find what they are looking for, then this is an excellent feedback mechanism for your marketing department—that is, visitors telling you exactly what they want to see on your website. Your Content > Site Search > Search Terms report is a rich seam of invaluable keyword information for you to mine. We looked at measuring the success of site search in the preceding section and also in Chapter 10, in the section "Webmaster KPI Examples."

From within your Google Analytics account, export your site search keywords and compare them with those in your paid search accounts (pay-per-click). Site search keywords not in your pay-per-click accounts are strong candidates to be added. As described for farming from organic search visitors, when selecting new keywords from your Site Search reports, also check your organic rankings for them. If you have a *relevant* landing page ranked as number one organically for a particular search engine and no pay-per-click competition for that term, I suggest that you do not add that term to your paid campaigns for that search engine. There is no point—you just cannibalize your own free organic traffic.

In addition to comparing keywords from site search with your paid campaigns, also compare them with your nonpaid search terms. Perhaps there are variations in usage or spelling you can take account of in your page content. Perhaps visitors are using relevant keywords after they are on your site that you are not aware of. For example, visitors looking for books may also use keywords such as "how-to guides," "manuals," "white papers," and "tech sheets" on your internal site search. This is a perfect opportunity to build and optimize your website content for those additional, related terms.

Campaign Optimization (AdWords)

After farming for new keywords from organic search engines and site search users, and adding them to your paid campaigns (if applicable) and to the content of relevant pages, the next stage is to ensure that these keywords are optimized—that is, that they give you the best possible chance of conversion.

Within the Advertising side menu is a dedicated section for AdWords. This enables you to drill down into campaign, ad group, and keyword levels for details of conversion rates, return on investment (ROI), margin, and more. As a business entity, you want to invest more in campaigns that produce more conversions and leads for you than in those that merely create visibility for your brand. However, you must take care here because by default Google Analytics gives credit for a conversion to the last referrer. In other words, spending more on campaigns that are reported as generating conversions and culling those that don't may result in you chopping off the head that feeds the tail.

The Multi-Channel Funnels report discussed in Chapter 5 enables you to see the path and interaction of different referral sources that lead to conversion. Therefore, it is important to refer to this report when optimizing all of your marketing efforts. This is discussed in "Attribution Optimization" later in this chapter.

Calculating Your Real ROI

The calculation performed by Google Analytics for the AdWords Return on Investment is very straightforward, as follows:

ROI = (revenue – cost) / cost

Therefore, if the ROI for a keyword is shown in your reports as 500 percent, this means you are receiving a $5 return for every $1 spent on AdWords. Assuming your revenue is $600 from $100 spent, this is calculated as follows:

ROI = (600 – 100) / 100
    = 500%

However, Google Analytics has no idea what margins you operate under, so the default ROI displayed by Google Analytics is misleading. Figure 11.14 shows the default ROI on a per-keyword basis—available in the Clicks area of your reports in the Advertising > AdWords > Keywords section.

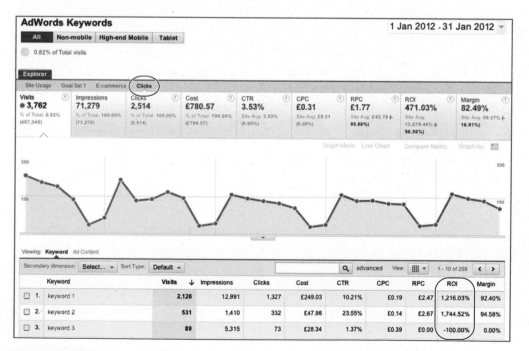

Figure 11.14 The ROI values of AdWords keywords

You will need to factor in your operating profit to get the true ROI figures. For example, assuming the same revenue and cost figures, if your profit margin (excluding marketing costs) is 40 percent, your real ROI is calculated as follows:

$$\begin{aligned} ROI_{real} &= (revenue \times margin - cost) / cost \\ &= (600 \times 0.4 - 100) / 100 \\ &= 140\% \end{aligned}$$

▶ **Table 11.1** Comparing ROI_{real} versus the reported ROI from Google Analytics

	Revenue	AOV	ROI	ROI_{real}
Keyword 1	$3,277.30	$192.78	1,216.03%	426.40%
Keyword 2	$885.00	$147.50	1,744.52%	637.81%
Keyword 3	$0.00	$0.00	–100.00%	–100.00%

Table 11.1 illustrates the importance of taking into account your profit margins when interpreting your ROI values. While the trends will remain the same, the more accurate ROI_{real} values are important because they determine how much money you can bid for competitive terms in order to stay profitable. This is discussed next.

Note that when a keyword does not generate any revenue, its ROI and ROI_{real} values show as –100%.

Note: At the beginning of a campaign launch, your ROI may be negative as you build up brand awareness and visibility for your website. Visitors to a new website (new to them) usually require multiple visits before they convert. However, a negative ROI should be acceptable for only a short period of time—on the order of weeks, depending on your circumstances. See also Figure 10.6 in the section titled, "E-Commerce Manager KPI Examples," in Chapter 10.

The ROI of Other PPC Networks

Within Google Analytics you can track visitors from any search engine, and any referral, right down to campaign and keyword levels. However, at present, cost data can only be imported from AdWords. That is, within your reports, ROI data can be calculated only for AdWords visitors. To perform the same calculations for other marketing channels, export your visit and revenue data to a spreadsheet and merge it with your third-party cost data.

Calculating Your Maximum Bid Amount

Your maximum bid (max bid) is the maximum amount you are prepared to pay for a keyword in the AdWords auction system. The actual amount you pay depends on many factors. For example, how many competitors are also bidding on the same keyword, how effective their ads are at gaining click-throughs, how effective your ads are at gaining click-throughs, how well you retain your visitors—that is, not bouncing them back to AdWords because your landing page failed to meet their expectations. These are the basis of the AdWords Quality Score system.

Being able to calculate your max bid is therefore an important aspect of your AdWords optimization. Your ROI_{real} determines the amount. That is, the ROI_{real} you wish to maintain while bidding will determine the max bid amount. The following is a detailed explanation. Unfortunately, describing the process on paper is cumbersome. However, in Excel the process is quite straightforward. I show this in the next section, "Simplifying the Task."

First, select a ROI_{real} that you are comfortable with—that is, one that drives more traffic to your website while still providing a healthy profit margin for you. For an online retailer this may be 25 percent, for example (making $0.25 profit for every $1.00 spent). With your preferred ROI_{real} set, calculate the maximum amount this allows you to spend on customer acquisition—the maximum cost per acquisition (cpa_{max})—by using the following procedure:

$$cpa_{max} = \frac{\text{average order value} \times \text{margin}}{ROI_{real} + 1}$$

For this example, I use the data for Keyword 1 from Table 11.1. Setting a target ROI_{real} of 25 percent and a profit margin of 40 percent, the calculation is as follows:

$$cpa_{max} = 192.78 \times 0.4 / 1.25$$
$$= \$61.69$$

This is the total cost you are willing to pay for a visitor with keyword 1 in order to achieve an average order of $192.78. Of course, not every visitor who clicks your ad is going to become a customer, so knowing your conversion rate for each keyword, you calculate your maximum cost per click (cpc_{max}) allowed for that keyword. Here I use the e-commerce conversion rate for keyword 1 (0.8 percent), taken from the E-commerce section of the reports (the menu link adjacent to Clicks), though it is not shown.

$$cpc_{max} = cpa_{max} \times (\text{e-commerce conversion rate} / 100)$$
$$= \$61.69 \times (0.8 / 100)$$
$$= \$0.49$$

For this example keyword, you could bid up to $0.49 in AdWords to generate as much traffic as possible and be assured that you will make a gross profit of $1.25 for every $1.00 spent. You will never overbid for your AdWords keywords—even if you reach your cpc_{max} within your AdWords account, you will still maintain a 125 percent ROI_{real}. Because the actual bid you pay in AdWords is determined by the market and is in constant flux, your ROI_{real} is likely to be higher than this for all but your most competitive keywords.

Tip: As you will have noticed from this exercise, the data you are accessing comes from two reports within your Advertising > AdWords > Keywords report—the Clicks and E-commerce reports. Clicking backward and forward between these is obviously cumbersome. Therefore, use the Better AdWords custom report as described in Chapter 9 to merge the relevant data points. One change is required to this custom report—change the dimension from campaign to AdWords keyword.

Note: If you are a nontransactional site, substitute Total Goal Value for Revenue, Per Visit Goal Value for Average Order Value, and Goal Conversion Rate for E-commerce Conversion Rate in the calculations. Your goals will need to be monetized for this to work—see Chapter 8.

Simplifying the Task

The calculations of cpc_{max} appear cumbersome when written on paper, but with a spreadsheet it is actually quite simple, as shown in Figure 11.15. First, you need to export your Advertising > AdWords > Keywords report. However, as explained in the previous tip, the data you require is in two reports—the Clicks and E-commerce reports. To make things easier for you, use the Better AdWords custom report as shown in Chapter 9. This allows you to have all the data in one report (you will need to change the dimension from campaign to AdWords keyword).

	A	B	C	D	E	F
1	# ------------					
2	www.mysite.com			Profit Margin %	40.00	
3	AdWords Keywords:			ROI Real %	125.00	
4	01-Jan-2012	31-Jan-2012				
5	# ------------					
6						
7	# ------------					
8	# Table					
9	# ------------					
10	**Keyword**	**Visits**	**Average Value ($)**	**E-commerce Conversion Rate**	**CPAmax ($)**	**CPCmax ($)**
11	keyword 1	1380	49	0.065217391	8.71	0.57
12	keyword 2	520	55	0.01	9.78	0.10
13	keyword 3	10	34	0.05	6.04	0.30
14	# ------------					

Figure 11.15 Excel spreadsheet to calculate per-keyword cpc_{max}

With the Better AdWords custom report loaded, export the data to a CSV file (or schedule a report email on a regular basis), and open the file in Excel. From this spreadsheet, you require only three columns of data: Keyword, Average Value, and E-commerce Conversion Rate; the rest can be discarded unless you are a nontransactional site—see the previous sidebar note about substituting goal values for transaction values. From the screen shown in Figure 11.15, inputting your profit margin (cell E2) and desired ROI_{real} (cell E3) will display the cpc_{max} (column F).

Note: You can download this Excel template from `www.advanced-web-metrics.com/chapter11`.

As you can see, the cpc_{max} calculation is at the keyword level throughout. However, if you are bidding on large volumes of keywords (I once reviewed an AdWords account with over a million bid terms!), it is more likely that you will be bidding a single cpc amount for groups of keywords—that is, ad groups. In that case, the more focused your ad groups are, the more accurate the cpc_{max} calculation will be.

Attribution Optimization

Multi-Channel Funnels reports are described in the section "Top Standard Reports" in Chapter 5. They allow you to view the entire referral path that visitors use when they convert—that is, not just the last click, as has been traditionally the case. An example of this is shown in Figure 11.16, taken from the Conversions > Multi-Channel Funnels > Top Conversion Paths report.

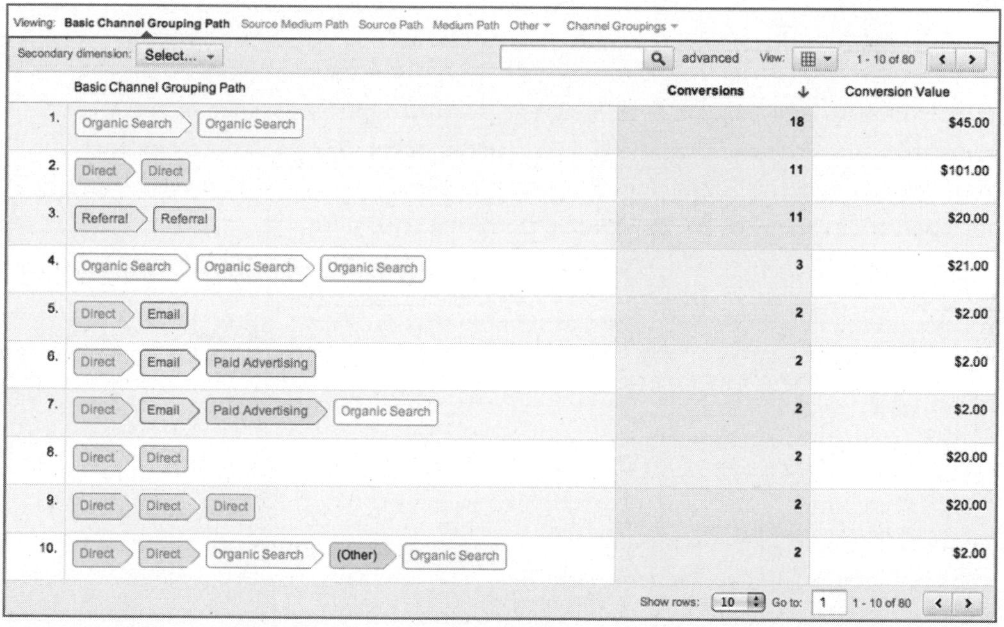

	Basic Channel Grouping Path	Conversions	Conversion Value
1.	Organic Search > Organic Search	18	$45.00
2.	Direct > Direct	11	$101.00
3.	Referral > Referral	11	$20.00
4.	Organic Search > Organic Search > Organic Search	3	$21.00
5.	Direct > Email	2	$2.00
6.	Direct > Email > Paid Advertising	2	$2.00
7.	Direct > Email > Paid Advertising > Organic Search	2	$2.00
8.	Direct > Direct	2	$20.00
9.	Direct > Direct > Direct	2	$20.00
10.	Direct > Direct > Organic Search > (Other) > Organic Search	2	$2.00

Figure 11.16 Top conversion paths report (also shown in the color insert)

Figure 11.16 shows referrers grouped into color-coded dimension named *channels*. These are analogous to referral mediums. The default view is to show the basic channel grouping path. This is an insightful report in itself. However, I encourage you to explore other channels, using the links at the top of the report table—for example, source path, campaign path, and keyword path.

Why Copy the Basic Channel Grouping Template?

The second menu item shown in the drop-down list in Figure 11.17 allows you to copy the existing template used for the basic channel grouping, which is the default display for the Conversions > Multi-Channel Funnels > Top Conversion Paths report. You will need to alter this template if the default report does not match your existing campaign tracking setup. For example, Google Analytics groups together all referrals where `medium=email` as the channel named Email. That is obviously correct, but perhaps in your campaign tracking you have set `medium=e-mail`, `e-mail marketing`, or `e-post` (Swedish). With the default template these will not be grouped together in the Email channel. To do so, copy the basic channel grouping and edit accordingly.

Other common edits to the default grouping include Feed and Social Network. For example, Feed is set to use `medium=feed` by default to detect visits from your RSS feed. Yet you may have custom-tagged your feed as something else—the section "Integrating with Feedburner" in Chapter 6, "Getting Started: Initial Setup," describes how to do this. The channel Social Network is compiled using a list of over 150 social network sites, determined by Google. Although the list is extensive, you may have niche social sites you wish to include with Google's list.

As your knowledge of Multi-Channel Funnels reports grows, you will want to go deeper into understanding the finer correlations that exist. To assist with this, you can create your own custom channel groupings—either from scratch or using an existing channel, as shown in Figure 11.17.

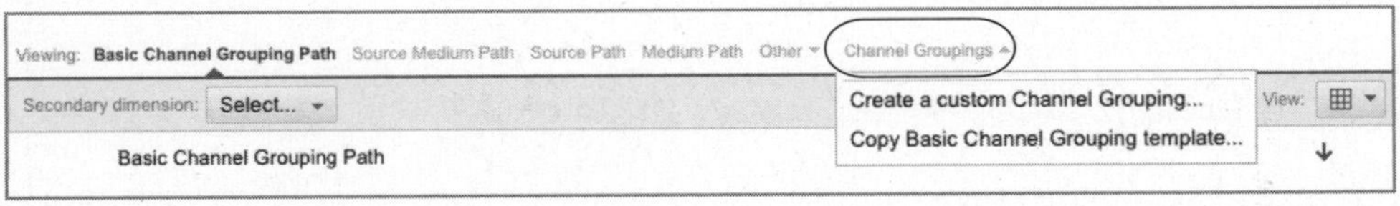

Figure 11.17 Creating your own custom channel grouping

A common custom channel grouping I recommend is to compare brand search terms and generic search terms—that is, search engine visitors who already know of your company or product names versus those who are unaware of you. Knowing what interaction exists between these search engine visits clearly impacts your digital marketing. Figure 11.18 shows an example custom channel grouping for this book's website (advanced-web-metrics.com).

In Figure 11.18, I have used two rules—one using a regular expression to include my specific brand terms. These are `brian|clifton|advanced web metrics|measuring success`. The second rule is the inverse of this, the same regular expression match but with the condition set to exclude my brand terms; that is, every other keyword used by my visitors. You could be more specific here. For example, using "company brand" keywords, "product A brand" keywords, "product B brand" keywords, and so forth.

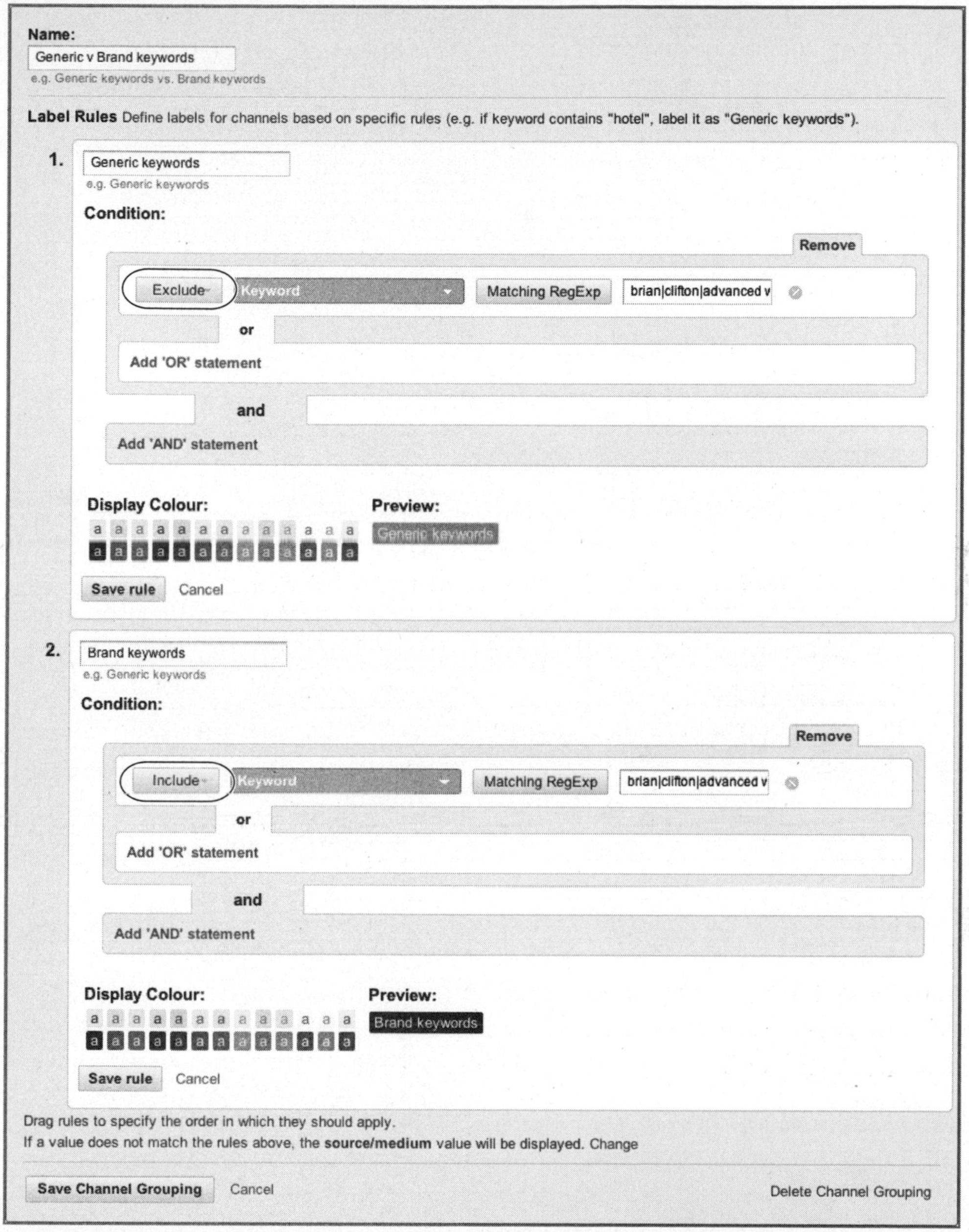

Name:

Generic v Brand keywords

e.g. Generic keywords vs. Brand keywords

Label Rules Define labels for channels based on specific rules (e.g. if keyword contains "hotel", label it as "Generic keywords").

1. Generic keywords

   e.g. Generic keywords

   Condition:

   Remove

   Exclude | Keyword ▾ | Matching RegExp | brian|clifton|advanced v ⊘

   or

   Add 'OR' statement

   and

   Add 'AND' statement

   Display Colour:
   a a a a a a a a a a a a a
   a a a a a a a a a a a a a

   Preview:
   Generic keywords

   Save rule Cancel

2. Brand keywords

   e.g. Generic keywords

   Condition:

   Remove

   Include | Keyword ▾ | Matching RegExp | brian|clifton|advanced v ⊘

   or

   Add 'OR' statement

   and

   Add 'AND' statement

   Display Colour:
   a a a a a a a a a a a a a
   a a a a a a a a a a a a a

   Preview:
   Brand keywords

   Save rule Cancel

Drag rules to specify the order in which they should apply.

If a value does not match the rules above, the **source/medium** value will be displayed. Change

Save Channel Grouping Cancel   Delete Channel Grouping

Figure 11.18 Custom channel grouping set up for search engine visitors using brand terms versus generic terms (also shown in the color insert)

The result of applying my custom channel grouping is the report shown in Figure 11.19. This has branded search terms color-coded as gold and nonbranded search terms color-coded as black and shows conversions where the referral path contains two or more referrals (the default view).

What is interesting to observe from Figure 11.19 is that 51 of 121 transactions have visitor interactions between brand and generic terms, accounting for 21 percent of the revenue. (Note that to illustrate the point, I have used only the data shown for the first 10 conversion paths for this calculation—not the full channel grouping contents of 149 rows).

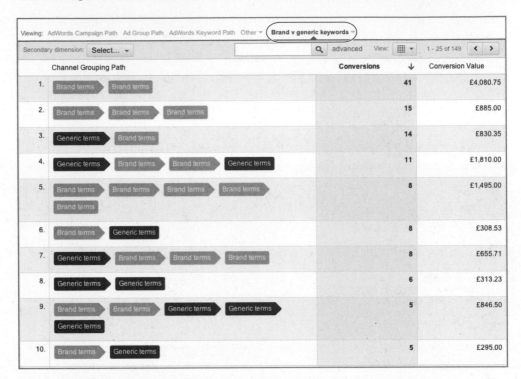

Figure 11.19 Custom channel grouping report produced from Figure 11.18 (also shown in the color insert)

As Figure 11.19 clearly shows a strong interaction between brand and nonbranded search terms, I recommend a further refinement of this method. That is, creating two additional custom channel groupings to differentiate between paid and organic search and between head terms and long-tail keyword terms. See Figure 11.20a and b, for example.

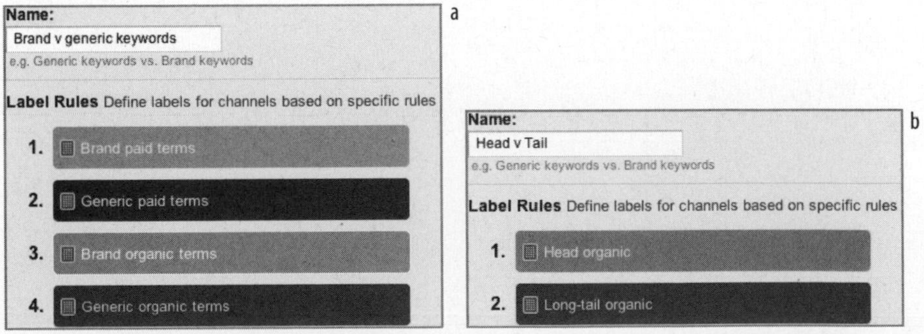

Figure 11.20 Refining your custom channel grouping: (a) differentiating paid versus organic terms and (b) differentiating organic head versus long-tail terms

Landing Page Optimization and SEO

For search engine marketing, a landing page is defined as the page your visitors land on (arrive at) when they click through from a search engine results page. As such, landing pages need to be focused on the keywords your visitors have used—that is, keywords relevant to what they are looking for—and be as close to the conversion point as possible. That way, you give yourself the best possible chance of converting your visitors into customers.

For paid search, controlling which landing page a visitor arrives at is straightforward: You enter the URL in your pay-per-click campaigns. For example, in AdWords, each ad group can have its own unique landing page relevant to the displayed advertisement. For all paid search campaigns, you need to append tracking parameters to your URLs. This is done automatically for you in AdWords, but you must apply this manually for other paid networks (see "Campaign Tracking" in Chapter 7).

Robots.txt

Not all pages on your site are relevant to search engine visitors, such as, for example, your privacy policy or your mission statement to be carbon neutral by the end of this year. Although both are laudable, unless they are a key aspect of your business, consider removing such pages from the search engine indexes—the file `robots.txt` is used to do this.

The use of `robots.txt` stops search engines from indexing pages on your website. If you have an existing page indexed and you add it to your `robots.txt` file as an exclusion, then over time it will be removed from the indexes.

For example, create a text file in the root of your web space named `robots.txt` with the following contents:

```
User-agent: *
Disallow: /images/
Disallow: /offer_codeY.aspx
```

This file tells all search engines that follow the robots exclusion standard (all the main ones do) to not index any files in the directory named `/images` or the specific file named `offer_codeY.aspx`. For more information on the robots exclusion standard, see www.robotstxt.org.

For nonpaid search (organic search), controlling landing pages is much harder to achieve because search engines consider all pages on your website when deciding which are most relevant to a visitor's search query. If you describe a product on multiple pages, then any or all of the pages may appear in the search engine results. However, the highest-ranked page may not be your best-converting page. By optimizing the content of your best-converting page, you can influence its position within the search engine results, thereby gaining a higher position than other related pages from your site. Landing page optimization is therefore a subset of search engine optimization (SEO).

Principles of SEO and Landing Page Optimization

For both paid and nonpaid search visitors, you want to ensure that the landing page is as effective as possible—optimized for conversion—once a visitor arrives. That does not mean the visitor's next step is necessarily to convert from this initial landing page; the landing page could be the beginning of the relationship, with the conversion happening much later or on a subsequent visit. By optimizing the content of your landing pages for a better user experience, you not only increase conversions for all visitor types but also improve your organic search engine rankings. Often the effects of this optimization process can be dramatic.

A key part of the optimizing process is understanding why visitors landed on a particular page of your website in the first place. The keywords they used on the referring search engine tell you this. Within Google Analytics you can view keywords for your top landing pages in a couple of ways:

- From the Traffic Sources > Sources > Search section, select the Organic or Paid report to view the respective keywords from each. Click a keyword, and select Landing Page as the secondary dimension.

- From the Content > Site Content > Landing Pages report, click a landing page and select Keyword as the secondary dimension.

Generally I prefer the latter: focusing on a landing page and viewing which search keywords led visitors to it. This method is referrer agnostic, meaning you cannot tell whether your visitors arrived on a particular landing page by clicking an organic listing or a paid ad. This difference is not important; a visitor arriving on your website by a well-targeted link (paid or nonpaid) should be just as likely to convert regardless of the referrer used.

For the optimal user experience, focus your landing pages on a particular keyword theme, such as a specific product or service. The exception to this would be your home page, which shouldn't be used as a landing page except for your company or brand name keywords.

Keyword theme is a term used in search engine marketing to describe a collection of keywords that accurately describe the content of a page. For example, if you sell classic model cars, keyword themes would center on particular makes and models, such as the following:

classic alpha romeo model car

replica model alpha romeo

classic alpha romeo toy car

Less-product-specific pages—for example, a category page—would use a less-specific keyword theme:

model cars for purchase

classic toy cars for sale

scale model cars to buy

As a rule of thumb, themes generally consist of 5 to 10 phrases per page that overlap in keywords (the preceding examples list three such phrases for each page). Having more than 10 overlapping phrases dilutes the impact and effectiveness of the page, from the perspective of both the user experience and search engine ranking. If you already have a page that targets more than 10 keyword phrases, consider creating a separate page to cater to the additional keywords.

At this stage I am assuming you have been through the process described earlier in this chapter under the heading "Identify and Optimize Poor-Performing Pages." If not, do this first because it ensures that the user experience for each page is optimized; improving the user experience often reaps large rewards. Then, as an exercise, view your top 10 landing pages from your Content > Site Content > Landing Pages report.

For each page listed in the report, click through and select Keyword as the secondary dimension. Print out the top 10 entrance keywords and repeat this process for each of your landing pages. Visit your website and print out each of your top 10 landing pages. That gives you your top 10 landing pages with a list of the top 10 keywords associated with each.

Note: If your Keywords report for each landing page contains hundreds of table rows, it may be because it is poorly focused or targeted. Also, check the landing page URLs specified in your paid campaigns. Are they pointing to the most appropriate pages? If not, change them accordingly.

For each landing page URL, view the two corresponding printouts. Is the page content tightly focused on its listed Entrance Keywords report? This is quite a subjective process, though as a guide, if you read the first three paragraphs (or approximately the first 200 words) of your landing page and you don't come across every one of your top 10 entrance keywords, then the page can be said to be unfocused. The extent of this is relative to the percentage of missing entrance keywords from those first paragraphs; for example, three keywords missed and you can say your page is 70 percent focused.

If you determine that a landing page is unfocused, revise its content, ensuring that all 10 of your top target keywords are placed within the first 200 human-readable words (that is, not part of the HTML syntax). Pay particular attention to placing keywords in your paragraph headings—for example, assuming a target keyword of "blue widget," use a heading of `<h1>Our blue widget selection</h1>`.

Use Text to Display Text—Not Images

Machine-readable text is text that can be selected within your browser and copied and pasted into another document or other application such as Word or TextPad. If you cannot do that, then the text is likely to be a rastered image (GIF, JPG, PNG, and so on) or in another embedded format such as Flash. Often, design agencies prefer the image format when referring to a product or company name so that nonstandard fonts and smoothing or special effects can be applied. However, it is doubtful this has any impact on conversions over plaintext—if images are necessary, use them elsewhere on your pages—not as a substitute for text.

For SEO rankings, machine-readable text is king. The inappropriate use of images or other embedded content as headings will be detrimental to your SEO efforts. Search engines ignore images for ranking purposes, and embedded objects such as Flash can be only partially indexed. To mitigate this, it is good practice to include an `alt` tag (alternative text attribute) for each image to improve the usefulness of your document for people who have reading disabilities. However, it has very little positive impact on search engine ranking. Therefore, where possible, use HTML and CSS to style your text because these are the right tools for the job. Use images to display pictures and Flash for movie or animation effects.

Other prominent areas where you should place your target keywords that are not visible on the page include the title tag and description metatag. Using the same keyword examples, these could be written as follows:

```
<title>Purchase blue widgets from ACME Corp</title>
<meta name="description" content=" ACME Corp, the blue widgets division
of BigCorp, is a US sales and support channel
for the industry-leading blue widget package." />
```

Page title tags are visible by reading the text in the title bar at the top of your browser (usually blue in Windows, silver on a Mac), but visitors generally do not read this on your page because it is located above the browser menu and navigation buttons—separately from your content. However, the title tag is the same text that is listed as the clickable link on search engine results pages and is therefore very, very (deliberate double emphasis) important for SEO ranking purposes. Ensure that each page has a unique title and description tag relevant to its content, with its most important keywords included.

A best practice tip is to also include your target keywords within call-to-action statements and make them hyperlinks to the beginning of a goal process—an Add to Cart page, for example. This is illustrated with the following text examples (the hyperlink text is underlined italic):

Bad SEO example To purchase and get a free gift *click here*.

Good SEO example *Purchase blue widgets* and get a free gift with your first order.

The second example contains three important elements that have proven to be many times more effective than the first (see "An Introduction to Google Website Optimizer," later in the chapter, for ways to test this hypothesis):

- The call-to-action statement contains the target keywords.
- The call-to-action keywords are highlighted as a hyperlink.
- The hyperlink takes the visitor to the start of the goal conversion process.

The techniques described here for optimizing and focusing your landing pages will undoubtedly increase your conversion rates and decrease page bounce rates regardless of visitor referral source. In addition, as a consequence of improving the user experience, such changes also have a significant and positive impact on your search engine rankings. Therefore, once you have optimized the top 10 landing pages, move on to the next 10.

From a paid search point of view, you need to ensure that campaigns point to one of these optimized landing pages—or create new ones. The worst possible thing you can do is use your home page as the landing page. If you take away only one lesson from this section, it should be to avoid this mistake!

A Note on SEO Ethics

When optimizing your landing pages to place keyword phrases in more prominent positions, always consider the user experience. Overly repeating keywords or attempting to hide them (using CSS or matching against the background color, for example), though not illegal, will inevitably result in your entire website being penalized in ranking and possibly removed from search engine indexes altogether—and this can happen at any time without warning, even years later.

Although it is possible to get back into the search engine indexes once you have removed the offending code, this can be a long, drawn-out process that damages your reputation. Essentially, spamming the search engines is not going to win you any friends, either from your visitors or the search engines themselves, so avoid it.

Summary of Landing Page Optimization and SEO Techniques

Optimizing landing pages for better performance is a complicated business; indeed, it's a specialized branch of marketing. However, here is a 10-point summary for you to follow that will give you a solid start:

- Always put your visitors and customers first; design for them, not search engine robots.

- Use dedicated landing pages for your campaigns, for both paid and nonpaid visitors.

- Ensure that landing pages are close to the call to action.

- Structure your landing page content around keyword themes of 5 to 10 overlapping keywords and phrases.

- Place your keyword-rich content near the top of the page, that is, within the first 200 words. Think like a journalist writing for a newspaper, with structured titles, headings, and subheadings that contain keywords.

- Use keywords in your HTML `<title>` tags.

- Use keywords in your anchor links—that is, HTML `<a>` tags.

- Avoid placing text in images or Flash or other embedded content.

- Use a `robots.txt` file to control what pages are indexed by search engines.

- Never "keyword stuff" or attempt to spam the search engines; it's not worth it, and you can achieve better results by legitimate means.

If you have completed all 10 steps and are still thirsting for improvement (pages can always be improved), consider testing alternative page elements, as discussed in "An Introduction to Google Website Optimizer" later in this chapter.

AdWords Day Parting Optimization

By knowing at what time of day visitors are accessing your website, you can better tailor your advertising campaigns to match. For example, if you are a business-to-business website, then most of your visits will probably occur during normal working hours. Rather than display your ads in equal distribution throughout the day, it would make sense to run and maximize your pay-per-click campaigns at around the same time your potential audience is looking on the Web.

Other examples of day parting optimization include targeting magazine readers, who are likely to be online in the early evenings; targeting social networking sites, whose potential audience is most likely to be online from 5:00 p.m. to 1:00 a.m.; and coinciding with radio and TV advertisements, where remembering your website URL can be difficult and so the interested audience may subsequently conduct a search to find your site.

By viewing hourly reports, you can view the distribution of your visitors throughout the day. Hourly visitor reports are available in the Advertising > AdWords > Day Parts report (see Figure 11.21). Of course, time zones should be taken into consideration. For example, if your audience is global, ensure that your reports are first segmented by location—a proxy for time zone.

As with all data analysis, it is important to avoid looking at short time frames such as a single day. Visitors over short periods can vary significantly and randomly, making reports difficult (if not impossible) to interpret. Instead, select a longer period and ensure that the date range includes relevant days of the week for you. For a business-to-business website, for example, select Monday to Friday, or use Friday to Sunday if your target audience is more likely to be looking for your products or services in their leisure time. In addition, try to choose a discrete day range—one that does not overlap with national holidays if that would affect your visitor numbers. Whatever business you are in, also compare weekend visitors to weekday visitors because this can reveal surprising insights.

Figure 11.21 Viewing hourly reports for day parting optimization

From Figure 11.21, which is a business-to-business website with no day parting optimization, you can see that there are very few visitors in the early morning (midnight until 7:00 a.m.), significant numbers climbing to a peak just before lunchtime, a large drop during lunch, and then a steady decline in traffic until the end of the working day around 6:00 p.m. If you have e-commerce reporting enabled, also compare your day parting visitor information with when transactions take place: Go to the E-commerce section (refer to label M of Figure 4.4 to locate this).

Use this information to optimize your paid campaigns by setting ads to display on or around these periods, both when visitors are in a research frame of mind (just visiting) and when they are ready to purchase. Figure 11.22 shows you how to achieve this within the AdWords Ad Schedule page. Not only can you schedule when your ads are displayed, you can also vary your bids for ads on a given time or day. For example, if your default bid is $1.00, you can set a custom percent-of-bid entry for Tuesday from midnight until 7:00 a.m. at 10 percent—that is, your bid for Tuesday only prior to sunrise would be $0.10. By this method, you would be spending money on acquiring paid visitors at periods when they are most likely to be looking and purchasing and at a price that is most advantageous to you. You can customize any day or time period in this way, using 15-minute intervals.

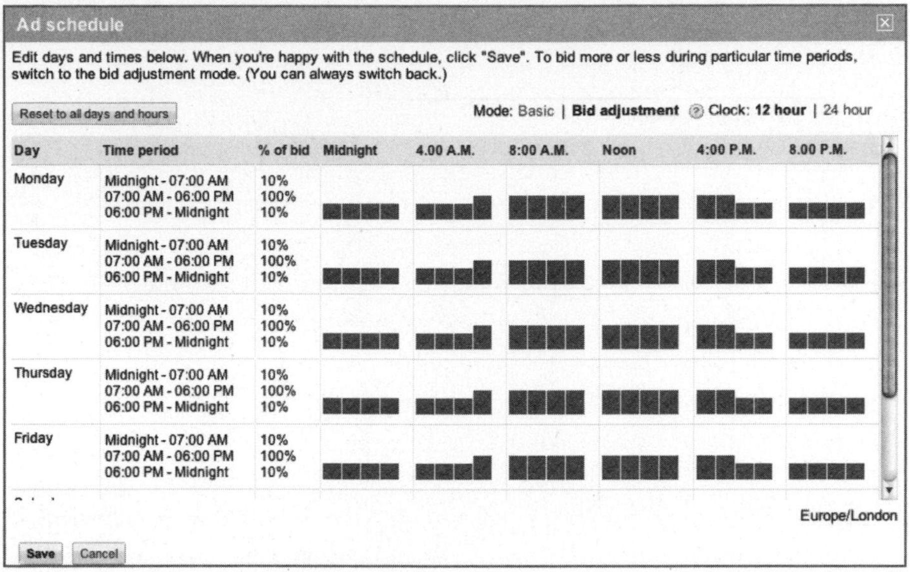

Figure 11.22   Ad scheduling within Google AdWords

Time Zone Considerations

To take advantage of day parting reports, ensure that your paid campaigns are specific to a particular time zone. For example, don't mix your paid campaigns by displaying the same ad to both a US and a UK audience. Time zone settings for AdWords are on a per-account basis. If you have audiences in very different time zones, then create separate AdWords accounts for them.

You can configure time zone settings for Google Analytics on a per-profile basis. However, if you link your Google Analytics account to your AdWords account as described in Chapter 6, then your AdWords time zone and country settings take precedence and you cannot realign them within Google Analytics.

If time zone and other regional specifics (language, currency) are important for you, the best practice advice is to use a one-to-one relationship of Google Analytics and AdWords accounts. You can run an aggregate Google Analytics account by adding an additional GATC to your pages (see the section titled "Roll-up Reporting" in Chapter 6).

AdWords Ad Content Optimization

When creating your pay-per-click campaigns in AdWords, how do you know whether one ad creative is more effective at generating click-throughs than another, similar ad? For example, is the headline "Blue suede shoes" better for you than "Turquoise suede shoes" or "Unique suede shoes"? Of course, you don't know the answer to this, and that's the point: No one does. It's up to your audience to decide. Even after you know the answer, it's like the English summer weather: It can still change quickly and without warning. To determine which ad performs best, use *ad content testing.*

Ad content testing is a method used by pay-per-click networks that enables you to display different ad content for the same target keywords. Within Google AdWords, the method is known as Ad Rotation and there are three ways in which your ads can be rotated:

Rotate Evenly Ads can be rotated in approximately equal proportion to a random selection of visitors—for example, five ads each showing 20 percent of your total impressions. The proportion is approximate because the ad serving favors ads with higher historic click-through rates and quality scores. For more information on AdWords quality scores, see

http://adwords.google.com/support/bin/answer.py?answer=21388

If you are experimenting with the design and content of your landing pages, use this option to ensure that you measure the impact of your landing pages changes.

Optimize For Clicks You can allow AdWords to optimize the display of your ads, favoring the better-performing ones by showing more impressions of the ad that receives more click-throughs. If your landing pages are optimized, select this option to receive the best traffic volumes for your ads.

Optimize For Conversions Show ads expected to provide more conversions. Use this if you have an e-commerce site or a well-defined conversion goal for your AdWords visitors.

My recommendation is to select your ad rotation options in the order shown in the preceding list. That is, first start with setting your ads to Rotate Evenly. Use the resulting visit data to optimize your landing pages. When you are satisfied that your landing pages are performing well, switch your ad rotation setting to Optimize For Clicks. Use this data to understand the visitor engagement differences between your ads. For example, do visitors from one ad spend more time on site, view more pages per visit, complete more goals than from another ad to the same landing page? In particular, do your visitors complete more than one goal, and which are the highest-value goals? It may be that ads that generate the highest number of click-throughs do not necessarily generate the most engagement. That is, you may be receiving more visitors, but of a lower quality.

Figure 11.23 shows the result of using four different ad contents for a specific ad group. To obtain this report, go to the Advertising > AdWords > Campaigns report. Drill down by clicking a particular campaign, then click one of its ad groups. By default, the keywords report will show in the table. Select Ad Content instead, as shown in Figure 11.23.

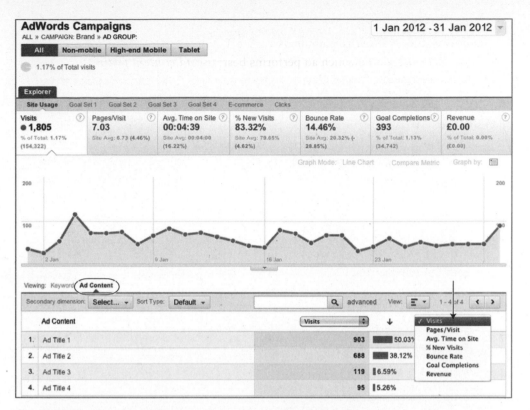

Figure 11.23 The performance of different ad content for the same targeted keywords

As you can see in Figure 11.23, the Ad Title 1 ad is receiving the vast majority of click-throughs from AdWords (set to Optimize For Clicks for this example). From the drop-down menu shown, view other metrics for each ad version. In addition to the Site Usage report, you should view the ad content data in your Goal and E-commerce sections (refer to Label M in Figure 4.4 if needed).

For example, it may be that Ad Title 1 is better for visitor acquisition, but when it comes to visitors interacting with your website, perhaps Ad Title 2 converts better and generates more revenue. If that is the case, then take advantage of this discrepancy and create separate ad groups for each so you can run separate bidding strategies.

Assuming the Goal and E-commerce reports show a trend similar to that in Figure 11.23, you can then either disable (pause) the remaining ad versions and focus all your pay-per-click efforts on Ad Title 1 or switch to Optimize For Conversions, as discussed next.

Warning: Each of the AdWords ad content variations shown in Figure 11.23 has a unique headline (Ad Title). This is defined when you create your ad and is what Google Analytics uses to differentiate ads for the same keywords. Note that it is not yet possible to report on ad variations that use the same headline, differing only in body text. Turning off AdWords auto-tagging and attempting to use manual tracking parameters will not work as an alternative.

Ad Content Optimization for Other PPC Networks

Google Analytics tracks different AdWords ad content with no additional configuration required. Ad content results appear automatically in your reports as long as you have the Google Analytics auto-tagging box checked within your AdWords account (see Chapter 6).

To track ad content for other paid referral sources, such as Yahoo! Search Marketing and Microsoft adCenter, you need to add tracking codes to your landing page URLs as discussed in Chapter 7 in the section "Campaign Tracking." Specifically, the `utm_content` parameter is required to differentiate ad versions.

When to Set Optimize for Conversions

The reason for going through a second step rather than directly to Optimize For Conversions, which you might assume is the best option, is because the result of Optimize For Conversions is very black and white—either a visitor converts or not. Other engagement metrics, such as time on site, bounce rate, time on page, and so forth, are not taken into account. Also, the goal or transaction amount is not considered when serving the ad—just the conversion rate (though the goal and transaction amount is displayed in your AdWords Conversion Tracking reports). These values become important if you have a wide range of values and prices on your site. Optimize For Conversions has no sense of your website value.

If you are an e-commerce site with a narrow range of prices, say within ±50 percent of your average order value, it can make sense to jump straight to Optimize For Conversions after optimizing your landing pages. After all, that is where the money is! To do so requires conversion tracking to be set up in your AdWords account. This is a straightforward import from AdWords, as shown in Figure 11.24.

Note that a goal will be imported only if it has registered at least one conversion in Google Analytics that can be attributed to AdWords. This can be a little bit complicated if you have multiple AdWords accounts linked to Google Analytics because in order for a goal to be imported to multiple AdWords accounts, each of those accounts must have registered at least one conversion from that AdWords account. This is another reason you should use one of the other ad rotation methods first, before switching to Optimize For Conversions.

For Optimize For Conversions to work, you need to have at least 30 conversions in the last 15 days. If there isn't sufficient conversion data to determine which ad will provide the most conversions, ads will rotate using Optimize For Clicks data. For more information about AdWords ad rotation settings, see

http://support.google.com/adwords/bin/answer.py?hl=en&answer=112876

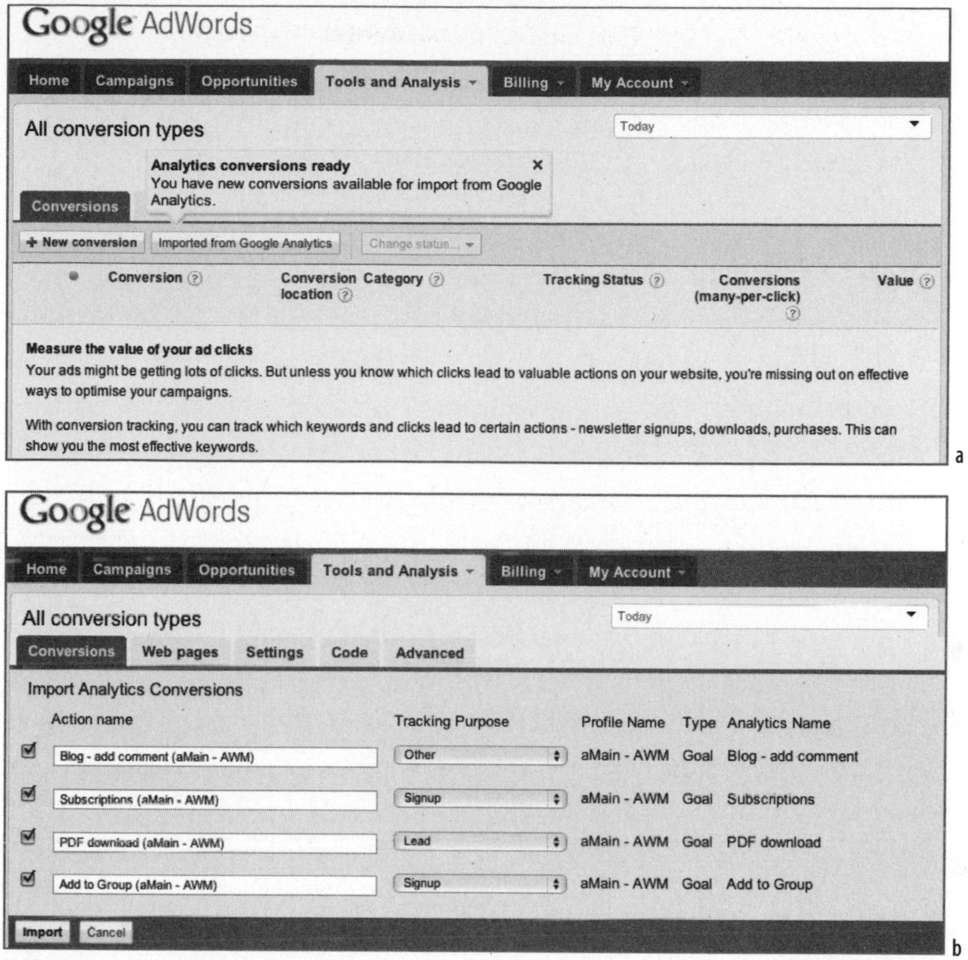

Figure 11.24 Importing Google Analytics goal settings into your AdWords account: (a) initial import screen, (b) setup and confirmation screen

As an aside, you can also use ad version testing for non-pay-per-click campaigns by using the utm_content tracking parameter. For example, if you use a mix of banners for a display campaign, you could test the effectiveness of different formats such as header versus skyscraper or static versus animated. You achieve this by appending utm_content values to the landing page URLs on the banners, such as, for example, utm_content=flash or utm_content=static. If you use the utm_campaign tracking parameter in this way, then also take advantage of using the other campaign tracking parameters available to you (see "Campaign Tracking" in Chapter 7).

Factors to Be Aware of When Importing Your Google Analytics Goals

Depending on when a Google Analytics goal becomes available for AdWords import, AdWords will grab the goal name at that point in time. Therefore, if your Goal was named My Goal 1 and later changed to My Different Goal 1, you may see My Goal 1 when you attempt the import. Once the goal is imported, mouse over the Tracking Status comment bubble to view the Google Analytics goal name and profile so you can verify which goal is which. If you are not happy with the imported goal name, or it has subsequently been redefined in Google Analytics, delete the imported goal and manually configure it by clicking on the + New Conversion button, shown in Figure 11.24a.

If an imported goal is deleted, you will not see it available for import again because technically it has already been imported.

Imported goals can have up to a 48-hour delay. So even if you have registered a conversion for that goal that is attributed to AdWords, it may be 48 hours before you can import that goal into AdWords.

Monetizing a Non-E-commerce Website

For non-e-commerce websites, understanding and communicating website value throughout your organization are key to obtaining buy-in from senior management. After all, you want to make changes to improve your bottom line, but without an associated dollar value, that can be difficult to achieve. By gaining executive support, you will be able to procure investment for content, infrastructure, and online marketing. The problem is that many executives' eyes glaze over when they see yet another set of charts on visitor metrics. "Our site doesn't sell anything, so who cares?" is a common response, and you'll need to address this head on or face a very frustrating job role. Identifying the monetary value of your visitor sessions is a proven way to get executive attention, and it can help keep the company website from becoming just someone's pet project.

Google Analytics provides two mechanisms for demonstrating website monetary value:

- Assigning goal values
- Enabling e-commerce reporting for your non-e-commerce site

The key to both approaches lies in knowing the value of website goal conversions to your business. For example, if a PDF brochure is downloaded 1,000 times and you estimate that one of these downloads results in a customer with an average order value of $250, then each download is worth $0.25 ($250/1,000). If 1 in 100 downloads converts into a customer, then each PDF download is worth $2.50 to you, and so on. Therefore, to attain a monetary value for each goal, you need to ask two fundamental questions: How many goal conversions are required to create a customer, and what is the average lifetime value (LTV) of a customer?

The Google Analytics Conversions > Goals > Overview report shows how many conversions you get to each of your site goals. From this, you'll need to estimate the percentage of goal conversions that result in paying customers. To get the process started, if a visitor's goal conversion provides personal information, such as name and email address, that you can later use as a sales follow-up, I guesstimate 10 percent of these will result in a sale. If no personal information is provided—for example, a visitor clicking a PDF download link—I use 1 percent for my guesstimate of sales. These are just initial guesstimates to start off the conversation with your organization's sales team. This process is not an exact science, and you'll be able to fine-tune later as you collect more information. However, aim to get these numbers formalized within a quarter—if you don't and they continue to change, you will not be able to compare long-term trends.

Determining the average value of a customer *should* be more straightforward. Assuming a customer attributed as a lead from your website has the same value as any other customer, simply ask your sales team for the average LTV of your customers. However, for non-retail businesses, the LTV may not be known. If your business is new or your average customer lifetime is particularly long or difficult to obtain, use the average revenue generated in 12 months per customer as your LTV.

Once you can estimate the value of each of your site goals, it is straightforward to monetize your website—as described next.

> **Tip:** If you are struggling to estimate goal values, start off the process by first evaluating your least-significant goal. Give this a value of 1 (as with assigning all goals in Google Analytics, the actual amount is unitless—the symbols $, £, €, and the like are labels). For more valuable goals, use a multiple of the least valuable one. For example, if your least valuable goal is a PDF download and your next more valuable goal is a subscription request that is five times more valuable to you, then assign goal values of 1 and 5, respectively.

Approach 1: Assign Goal Values Method

This is the simplest of the approaches and requires little or no changes to your website pages. As such, the control of these values is in the hands of the marketers—the best place for them in my opinion! The caveat, however, is that with simplicity comes a lack of flexibility. That is, goal values are fixed on a per-goal basis, though event tracking has a little more flexibility.

Consider that every site has at least one goal; quite often it has several. For a non-e-commerce site there can be PDFs and other files to download, video demonstrations and interviews, brochure requests, quote requests, subscription sign-ups, registrations, account logins, blog comments, social media shares (Tweet, Like, Google +1, and so forth), content ratings, printouts—even the humble `mailto:` link (email address link) can be considered a goal and tracked with Google Analytics.

With your goals defined, assigning a goal value is straightforward. Essentially, all that is required is for an amount (the goal value) to be assigned when the goal is triggered. As described in "Goal Conversions and Funnels" in Chapter 8, there are four goal types:

- URL destination
- Time on site
- Pages per visit
- Event

For the first three, the goal value set is a constant value that is applied to all goal completions. For example, if you determine that a subscription confirmation page is worth $5, then this amount is applied to all subscriptions—even though some subscriptions may be more valuable to you than others. Event tracking is slightly different. In addition to being able to set a constant goal value, you can specify a value at the point when the event is set—so the value can vary for each goal event triggered (see "Event Tracking" in Chapter 7).

Adding values to goals enables you to gain additional metrics in your Google Analytics reports, such as the average per-visit goal value ($/Visit) as shown in the Traffic > Sources section—select a goal set from the report sections (refer to label M in Figure 4.4 if required). In addition, you can view individual and total goal values in the Conversions > Goals > Goal URLs report.

Assigning goal values is a fundamental configuration step and a prerequisite for understanding the value of your nontransactional website. However, you obtain far more detailed reporting by using the technique outlined in the second approach.

Approach 2: Pseudo E-commerce Method

By setting up your nontransactional site as an e-commerce website in Google Analytics, you'll be able to do the following things that are not possible with the Assign Goal Values method:

- Have an unlimited set of goals. Without this goals are limited to 20.
- See the amount of time and number of visits it takes for visitors to convert (see the following sidebar note).
- View a breakdown of how much each "product" (goal) contributes to your website revenue.
- Group goals into unlimited categories. Without this, goals are limited to four categories (goal sets).

- List specific "transactions"—that is, individual goals, rather than collective goals as for the Assign Goal Values method (individual file downloads, for example).

Note: For the Assign Goal Values method, you can view the amount of time and number of visits to conversion using the Conversions > Multi-Channel Funnels > Path Length report. However, there is a current limitation with the report in this respect—you can view these metrics only on an individual goal basis. That is, you cannot roll up all goals to view them as an aggregate whole. The Conversions > E-commerce > Time to Purchase report does not suffer this limitation.

Here is an example to illustrate the last bullet point and the capability the expanded reports will give you. Imagine you are a publisher of content with hundreds of file downloads available. These could be software programs, music files, video downloads, podcasts, or a PDF library, for example. Perhaps you also have multiple subscription types. By enabling e-commerce tracking, more detailed, richer reports are available to you. The caveat, however, is that this method does require changes to your GATC and therefore is more technical—that is, in the hands of your web development team.

Figure 11.25 is an example for a file download catalog site. Note there are a total of 96 different files (products), grouped into categories and monetized. Using this approach, you gain additional aggregate information as well as more specific goal and goal-conversion information. How this is achieved is discussed next.

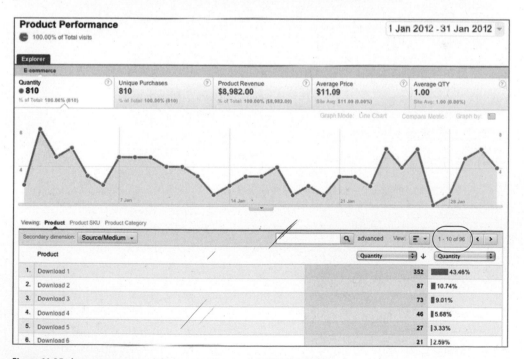

Figure 11.25 An e-commerce report for non-e-commerce goals (file downloads)

Tracking a Non-E-commerce Site as Though It Were an E-commerce Site

The following examples were developed for the corporate website of a global industrial manufacturer. Beyond content updates, investment in the website had trailed off a number of years ago because no one in the organization considered it an opportunity—more of a dot.com necessity. Monetizing visitor actions and hence monetizing the visitors themselves reinvigorated senior executive interest and allowed the digital manager to seek additional budget for further development.

 Note: Before continuing with this section, it's a good idea to review the section "Tracking E-commerce Transactions" in Chapter 7.

Generating Unique Order IDs

In all of the pseudo e-commerce examples given, it is important that you assign a unique order ID to each transaction. An e-commerce system would do this for you automatically. However, here you will need to apply some additional code on your pages. Add the following just above the `</head>` HTML tag of each page that you are tracking with e-commerce fields:

```
<script type="text/javascript">
function getOrderID(){
 // generate a random order id
 var randomnumber = Math.floor(Math.random()*1000);
 var current = new Date();
 var month = current.getMonth()+1
 var timeStamp = current.getFullYear() +month +current.➡
  getDate() + "-" +current.getHours() + current.getMinutes()➡
  + current.getSeconds() +"-" + randomnumber;
 return(timeStamp);
}
</script>
```

With this in place, when the goal page is loaded, a unique order ID is generated of the form *YYYYMMDD-hhmmss-XXX*, where *XXX* is a random number between 0 and 999. This provides tracking of up to 1,000 orders per second and enables you to keep order IDs in a logical structure that can be searched for later within the reports. If you receive significantly fewer than 1,000 orders per day, you can simplify the order ID by removing the *hhmmss* element.

With the script in place, generate an order ID by calling the JavaScript function `getOrderID()`, as shown in the examples.

Essentially, the approach is to tag each goal page with e-commerce tracking information. In summary, the e-commerce fields are a comma-separated set of values as follows:

```
_gaq.push(["_addTrans", "OrderID", "Affiliate", "Total amount",➡
"Tax amount", "Shipping amount"]);
_gaq.push(["_addItem", "OrderID", "SKU", "Product name","Category",➡
"Unit price","Quantity"]);
```

Some of the e-commerce fields will be left blank. For example, assume that one of your goals is for a visitor to click a `mailto:` link. Visitors who click this do not require any tax or shipping amounts to be calculated, so you will not be entering anything for this particular e-commerce field.

There are two steps for implementing this technique: first, defining the e-commerce field values for your goals, and second, calling the function `_trackTrans` so that Google Analytics tracks these when the goal is completed. The following are example goals that we'll track with e-commerce fields:

- Pseudo e-commerce for a `mailto:` goal
- Pseudo e-commerce for a file download goal
- Pseudo e-commerce for a form-submission goal
- Pseudo e-commerce for multiple file-goal downloads

Step 1: Defining Your Pseudo E-commerce Values

For each example, add the e-commerce fields to the page with the goal to be tracked. You must place this after your GATC:

Pseudo e-commerce fields for an email click-through goal Add the following e-commerce fields to the page with the `mailto:` link to be tracked:

```
<script type="text/javascript">
    orderNum = getOrderID();
    _gaq.push(["_addTrans", "orderNum", "", "1", "", ""]);
    _gaq.push(["_addItem", "orderNum", "brian@mysite.com", ➡
    "Email link", "General inquiries", "1", "1"]);
</script>
```

As you can see, several e-commerce fields are blank—you do not require the tax and shipping amounts for someone who simply clicks your email link. A value of $1 and a quantity of 1 have been assigned and categorized under General Inquiries.

Pseudo e-commerce fields for a file download goal In this case, I have used a PDF file as the example. Add the following e-commerce fields to the page with the download link to be tracked:

```
<script type="text/javascript">
    orderNum = getOrderID();
```

```
        _gaq.push(["_addTrans", "orderNum", "", "10", "", ""]);
        _gaq.push(["_addItem", "orderNum", "brochure-2012.pdf", ➡
        "PDF Brochure", "Download", "10", "1"]);
    </script>
```

Here, a PDF download has been categorized as Download and given a value of $10; the quantity remains 1. Note that I have used the filename for the SKU value. If you have multiple PDF files on the same page, then you could categorize them and value each differently, perhaps by language or by content. This is discussed as a special case in the section "Special Case: Pseudo E-commerce Fields for Multiple File Downloads."

Pseudo e-commerce fields for a form submission goal   Add the following e-commerce fields to the page with the form submission to be tracked:

```
    <script type="text/javascript">
        orderNum = getOrderID();
        _gaq.push(["_addTrans", "orderNum", "", "50", "", ""]);
        _gaq.push(["_addItem", "orderNum", document.location.pathname, ➡
        "Form submission", "Subscriptions", "10", "1"]);
    </script>
```

This example assumes a value of $50 per form submission with a quantity of 1 and categorized under Subscriptions. Note that I have used the form page path and file filename for the SKU value.

Step 2: Calling the Function _trackTrans

With your e-commerce fields in place on the pages that contain goals, the second part of the implementation is to decide how to get these values into Google Analytics. This is done using the JavaScript call to the _trackTrans function. For the preceding three examples, use the following calls:

Email click-through goal

```
<a href = "mailto:email@address.com" onClick = "_gaq.push(['_
trackTrans']);">
```

File download goal

```
<a href = "brochure-2012.pdf" onClick = ➡
  "gaq.push(['_trackPageview, '/downloads/brochure-2012.pdf']);
  _gaq.push(['_trackTrans']);">Brochure 2012</a>
```

Form submission goal

```
<form action = "formhandler.php" onSubmit = "_gaq.push(['_trackTrans']);">
```

Note the use of _trackPageview for the second example. This is not directly related to what we wish to achieve, but it should be used as a best-practice technique—that is, capturing the PDF download as a virtual pageview. For more details on virtual pageviews, see "_trackPageview: the Google Analytics Workhorse" in Chapter 7.

Special Case: Pseudo E-commerce Fields for Multiple File Downloads

The preceding file-download example is a simplified case that is useful to illustrate the method. However, if file downloads are important to your website performance, then it is highly likely you will have multiple links to downloads on the same page and the visitor may "purchase" many of them while on that page. This is a special case because the e-commerce event handler needs to be called for *each* file download link. That way, each click on a download link receives a different transaction ID. This is an important requirement because you cannot have multiple items for a single transaction by this method—after all, this is not a real shopping cart. To overcome this limitation, use the following format for each download link:

```
<a href = "brochureA-2012.pdf" onClick =
    "gaq.push(['_trackPageview, '/downloads/brochureA-2012.pdf']);➡
    orderNum=getOrderID();
    _gaq.push(["_addTrans", "orderNum", "", "10", "", ""]);
    _gaq.push(["_addItem", "orderNum", "brochureA-2012.pdf", ➡
    "PDF Brochure", "Download", "10", "1"]);
    _gaq.push(['_trackTrans']);">Brochure A 2012</a>

<a href = "brochureB-2012.pdf" onClick =
    "gaq.push(['_trackPageview, '/downloads/brochureB-2012.pdf']);➡
    orderNum=getOrderID();
    _gaq.push(["_addTrans", "orderNum", "", "5", "", ""]);
    _gaq.push(["_addItem", "orderNum", "brochureB-2012.pdf", ➡
    "PDF Brochure", "Download", "5", "1"]);
    _gaq.push(['_trackTrans']);">Brochure B 2012</a>
```

Here, for the same page, two PDF downloads have been categorized and given values of $10 and $5, respectively. If a visitor clicks both of these files (or repeatedly clicks the same file), then each is tracked as a separate transaction because the function getOrderID() is called on each occasion. Assuming there is a minimal delay in loading the HTML page in question, the transaction IDs for these two files will be very similar—for example, varying only in the *ss-XXX* part of the string *YYYYMMDD-hhmmss-XXX*.

> ### Approach 2 Provides Significant Benefits
>
> By enabling pseudo e-commerce reporting on your non-e-commerce website, you can see at a glance the referring sources that lead to specific product "purchases," time to purchase, visits to purchase, average order value, which keywords convert best, and more.
>
> If you were to use the first approach only, you would need to navigate to each goal page and determine the information separately—and that can be quite tricky with 500 PDF white papers, 10 application downloads, 3 mailing list subscriptions, 2 quote request forms, and a contact-us form!

Tracking Offline Marketing

Having a unified metrics system that can report on key performance indicators from the Web, print, display, radio, and TV—all in one place—and one that can track the correlation between all visitors who start in one channel and cross over into others before converting has been a long-sought analytics nirvana for many a marketer.

Some vendors have attempted to achieve such a system, with varying degrees of success. The barriers of technical difficulty (bringing information from disparate systems together) and issues with data alignment (for example, how do you compare a web visitor who has specifically searched for information to a passive TV viewer?) mean that, to date, few organizations have made such a high-cost and resource-intensive investment.

However, vendors are making many inroads to overcome these difficulties. The open-source nature of Google's application programming interface (API) model for making data accessible goes some way toward making this happen. Google APIs include AdWords, Google Maps, Google Earth, and Google Analytics. With an API, Google Analytics users are able to stream their data directly out and into their own applications—and potentially in the future to import data back into Google Analytics. This could be as simple as real-time updates to KPI tables in Excel or the merging of web data with CRM data. The use of the Google Analytics Core Reporting API is discussed in Chapter 12.

> **Note:** This section assumes you have a strong understanding of Google Analytics Campaign Tracking as described in Chapter 7 and that you understand the principles of URL redirection.

Even without a complete one-stop unified metrics system (will one ever exist?), there is a great deal you can do to track your offline marketing efforts. I explain five such methods here. All are based on the central idea of combining offline campaigns with unique landing page URLs:

Vanity URLs Recommended when you have strong *product* brand awareness, with all web content hosted on a *single* central domain. Examples include Galaxy S, iPad, Castrol, Gillette, Colgate, Aquafresh, Big Mac, Fanta, Snickers, and so on. Requires a technical setup of redirects.

Coded URLs Recommended when you have a strong *company* brand or when your products already have *separate* websites. Examples include IBM, Microsoft, Google, Kellogg's, Kodak, BMW, and any product that relies on model numbers for identification, such as cell phones, cars, printers, and cameras. Requires a technical setup of redirects.

Combining with search Recommended when your brand values are less significant than your product or service values or your target audience is more price oriented than brand oriented. Examples include the vast majority of small to medium-size businesses, the travel industry, the insurance sector, utilities, groceries, and office supplies; that is, industries where there is little brand loyalty. No technical setup required.

Combining with URL shorteners Recommended only for print campaigns and where many links may be required within the same campaign, document, or article. Examples include the publishing industry (newspapers, magazines), white papers, catalogs, and brochures. No technical setup required.

Combining with Quick-Response (QR) codes Recommended only for print campaigns where you wish to engage with a mobile audience. Examples include the publishing industry (newspapers, magazines), billboard advertising, posters, flyers and handouts, and business cards. No technical setup required.

Note: The example names given for tracking offline visitors are for brand recognition only. They do not reflect the actual website architecture or strategies of the sites in question.

Using Vanity URLs to Track Offline Visitors

If your website content is held at www.mysite.com and you have a strong product brand that has greater awareness than your company brand, consider using a vanity URL of www.myproduct.com for your offline campaigns such as television, radio, and print. Use your website (www.mysite.com) only to promote via online marketing.

Clearly, you don't want to build two separate websites to promote to offline and online audiences. Their needs are the same; the only difference is how they find your website. Apart from the resource overhead, you should not build duplicate pages because the search engines will penalize you for this.

To avoid duplicate content, apply permanent redirects to your vanity URLs, such as www.ProductSiteA.com. Redirects on your web server capture the different URLs used by your offline visitors, append tracking parameters, and then automatically forward them through to your main content website, such as www.MainWebsite.com. The process takes a small fraction of a second to perform and shows no visible difference to your offline visitors. They type in a vanity URL (www.ProductSiteA.com) and arrive on your official website (www.MainWebsite.com) with tracking parameters appended. In effect, you are pretending to have product-specific websites for your offline visitors, using this to differentiate, and then redirecting them to your actual content. Schematically this is shown in Figure 11.26.

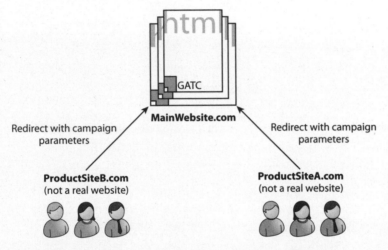

Figure 11.26 Schematic representation of using vanity URLs to track offline visitors

With a redirect in place, you can view offline visitors by identifying the campaign variables used. I illustrate the approach in Figure 11.27, using a fictitious example for Apple. I have assumed that for its products Apple uses ipod.com and iphone.com for all print campaigns, with all content actually hosted on its main apple.com website. The redirects add the following campaign parameters:

utm_source=**Print&utm_medium**=Print&utm_campaign=**iphone5%20launch**

utm_source=**Print&utm_medium**=Print&utm_campaign=**ipod%20classic**

> 👁 **Note:** Although I use Apple as a fictitious example, it is actually using this technique. However, Apple is not a Google Analytics user, and hence it uses different campaign tracking parameters for its redirected URLs.

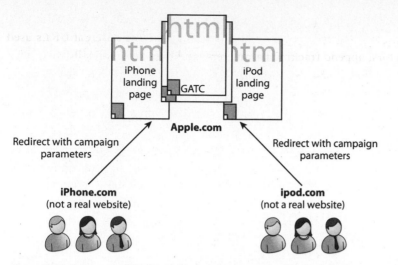

Figure 11.27 Fictitious example of Apple using vanity URLs to track offline visitors

You can then view the performance of all offline print ads in your report where medium is set to Print. An example of what such a report looks like is shown in Figure 11.28.

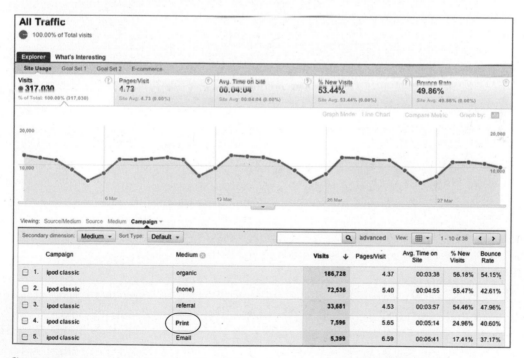

Figure 11.28 Fictitious visit details from an offline (print) campaign tracked using a vanity URL and redirect

Technical Details of Using Redirects for Vanity URLs

Redirects are an important aspect of using vanity URLs because they avoid any duplicate content issues (bad for SEO) and allow campaign variables to be appended to the final URL destination.

Two types of redirects are possible: permanent (status code = 301) and temporary (status code = 302). From a search engine optimization point of view, it is important to apply permanent redirects so that the final destination URL is the one that is indexed by the search engines; otherwise, the search engines ignore the content.

The following is an Apache example of redirecting the vanity URL www.myproduct.com, used only for print campaigns, to the official web address containing the actual content, www.mysite.com. The rewrite code is placed in the virtual host configuration section for www.myproduct.com in the httpd.conf file. Other web servers use a similar method:

```
<VirtualHost>
 ServerName www.myproduct.com
 RewriteEngine on
 RewriteCond %{HTTP_USER_AGENT} .*
 RewriteRule .* http://www.mysite.com/?utm_source=magazineX➥
 &utm_medium=print&utm_campaign=March%20print%20ad [R=301,QSA]
</VirtualHost>
```

The rewrite code requires the mod_rewrite module to be installed. Most Apache servers have this by default (see http://httpd.apache.org/docs/mod/mod_rewrite.html). Ensure that the RewriteRule is contained on one line within your configuration file (up to and including QSA]), and if spaces are required, use character encoding (%20).

In this example, Google Analytics campaign variables are used so that you can uniquely identify the offline campaign. These are then permanently passed on to the official website using the Apache mod_rewrite option. The query string append (QSA) ensures that any other query parameters are also redirected. After a redirect takes place, you should see your campaign variables in the address bar of your browser. If not, the redirect has not worked correctly, and this will need to be resolved.

Using the Vanity URL in Other Offline Campaigns

For the example redirect given, the offline visitor can be identified in your Google Analytics reports anywhere the source, medium, and campaign variables are displayed. In this case, the source is "magazine," the medium is "print," and the campaign is "March print ad." This is effective when the only offline campaign running is a print ad, that is, you can redirect to only one place at a time. If this vanity URL is required for other offline campaigns running at the same time (TV, radio, other print campaigns), then change the utm_source, utm_medium, and utm_campaign tracking variables to the generic text "offline." You then track your offline marketing in aggregate.

Using vanity URLs for managing offline campaigns is very effective, assuming you have multiple domains to use and the product you are selling is not trademarked or protected by someone else, preventing you from using it as part of a domain. Don't use this method if you already have your products hosted on separate websites—see the following section on using coded URLs.

Using Coded URLs to Track Offline Visitors

If there is greater awareness of your company brand than of your products, then consider using coded URLs within your offline campaigns. These are of the following form:

```
www.MainWebsite.com/offer1
www.MainWebsite.com/offer2
```

Coded URLs are unique to your offline campaigns; they are not displayed anywhere on your website and are not visible to the search engines. That means your content should be visible to the search engines, but this will be via a different online-only URL such as `www.MainWebsite.com/productX`,

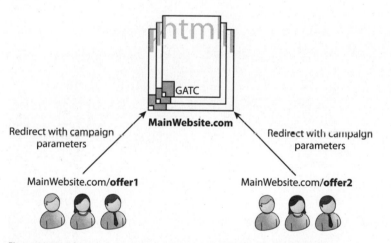

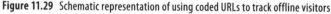

Figure 11.29 Schematic representation of using coded URLs to track offline visitors

By using coded URLs in your offline marketing, you will know that visitors to the subdirectory /offer1 must have come from your offline ad; there is nowhere else to find it. Of course, there is always the possibility that the visitor will remember only your domain (`MainWebsite.com`) and not the specific landing page (offer1) required to distinguish them from direct visitors; this is common for strong brands. It is therefore important that your offline campaign provide a compelling reason for the visitor to remember your specific coded URL. This can be the promotion of special-offer bundles, voucher codes, reduced pricing, free gifts, competitions, unique or personalized products, and so on that are available only by using the specific coded URL you display in your offline campaigns.

A useful tip when employing this technique is to use a landing page URL that can be remembered easily, tying it in with your message and the medium. This sounds like common sense, but you would be surprised what a little thought can achieve for you. For example, for a TV campaign you could consider the following:

```
www.MainWebsite.com/tvoffer
www.MainWebsite.com/10percent
www.MainWebsite.com/getonefree
www.MainWebsite.com/twofourone (or /2for1, /241)
www.MainWebsite.com/xmas
www.MainWebsite.com/sale
```

Identifying with your TV branding slogan or campaign message can be a very effective way of keeping your full URL in the viewer's mind because this associates your website with their viewing activity.

As with the use of vanity URLs, redirecting visitors is required. This enables you to avoid producing duplicate content and appends tracking parameters to the landing page. The only difference here is that the redirection is applied to a subdirectory, not the entire domain. This is desirable if your products are already hosted as separate websites.

I illustrate the approach using the fictitious example advanced-web-metrics.com/25percent. This would be something that I would use as an advertisement flyer—included in welcome packs at relevant digital marketing conferences, for example. The driver for using the full coded URL is the 25 percent discount code available to conference attendees. The URL is not available anywhere on my website. You would only know that it existed if you saw the printed flyer.

To track the impact of such a marketing initiative, the printed URL redirects to a specific landing page with the following campaign parameters added:

```
utm_source=eMetrics%20London&utm_medium=print&utm_campaign=book%20launch
```

Visitors then appear in my Google Analytics reports as shown in Figure 11.30. For each conference event at which I advertise, I simply need to adjust the utm_source campaign value.

Even without redirection, as long as the URLs remain unique to your offline campaigns and are neither shown as links within your website nor indexed by the search engines, you will still be able to measure the number of offline visitors to these specific pages. The purpose of the redirection is to help you compare different campaigns within your Google Analytics reports. This is key for marketers attempting to understand the performance of numerous marketing channels.

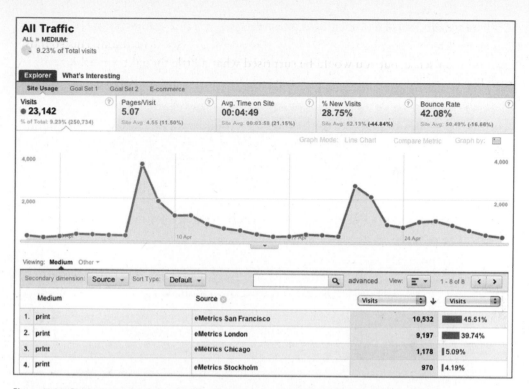

Figure 11.30 Fictitious visit details from an offline (print) campaign tracked using coded URLs and redirects

Redirecting Coded URLs

This example uses the Apache `mod_rewrite` module, which most Apache servers have installed by default. See `http://httpd.apache.org/docs/mod/mod_rewrite.html`.

```
<VirtualHost>
    ServerName www.myproduct.com
    RewriteEngine on
    RewriteCond %{HTTP_USER_AGENT} .*
    RewriteRule /xmas.* /productX/?utm_source=channel123➡
    &utm_medium=tv&utm_campaign=March%20tv%20ad [R=301,QSA]
</VirtualHost>
```

Ensure that the `RewriteRule` is contained on one line within your configuration file (up to and including `QSA]`), and if spaces are required within the URL, use character encoding (`%20`). Adjust your campaign-tracking parameters accordingly—as described in Chapter 7.

Combining with Search to Track Offline Visitors

When your brand values are less significant than your product or service values or your target audience is more price oriented than brand oriented, remembering a URL can be difficult for your potential visitors; your brand is simply not strong enough to gain traction. An alternative technique is to use search as part of your offline message, such as running a radio ad that uses something like "Find our ad on Google by searching for the word *productpromo* and receive 10 percent off your first order."

By creating an AdWords ad just for this campaign, targeting a unique word or phrase that is relevant only to people who have heard your ad, you not only provide a strong incentive for visitors but also directly assign these visitors to a specific offline campaign—this is very difficult to achieve with the two previously described techniques. The process is schematically shown in Figure 11.31.

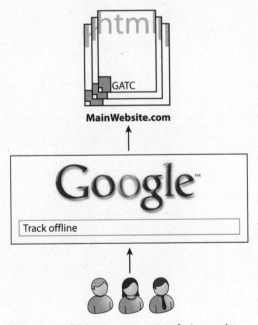

Figure 11.31 Schematic representation of using search to track offline visitors

This extra step of asking your potential audience to first go elsewhere (to a search engine) has two small drawbacks:

- You pay for the click-through on your AdWords ad.

- The visitor is further away from your goal (there is an extra step) and may be distracted by other search results.

However, using a unique search phrase means you should be the only bidder and hence would pay as little as one cent per click-through. For such a small price, the upside is considerable: You have full control of the ad message and landing page URL. That means each campaign (print, TV, display, radio) can have a separate landing page and hence is completely traceable, *without* the need of going to your IT department and asking for redirections to be set up.

Here are some example keywords to use in your AdWords campaign:

- 10percent
- productX101
- whyCompanyName
- 1-800-123-BIKE (your toll free number; United States)
- 207-123-4567 (your telephone number)
- Signal House, London Road (the first line of your address)

Tip: Check your AdWords listing regularly because competitors may pick up your campaigns and start to bid on the same keywords!

I often use this technique when speaking at conferences and events. For example, it would be great if this book and my marketing material were at hand for conference attendees. That way I could refer them to specific chapters and sections whenever I am asked a question that requires a detailed answer. Of course, that is rarely the case. Instead, I can say, "Go online and search for *track offline* to find a white paper from me that discusses this in detail." An example of the search results for this search is shown in Figure 11.32.

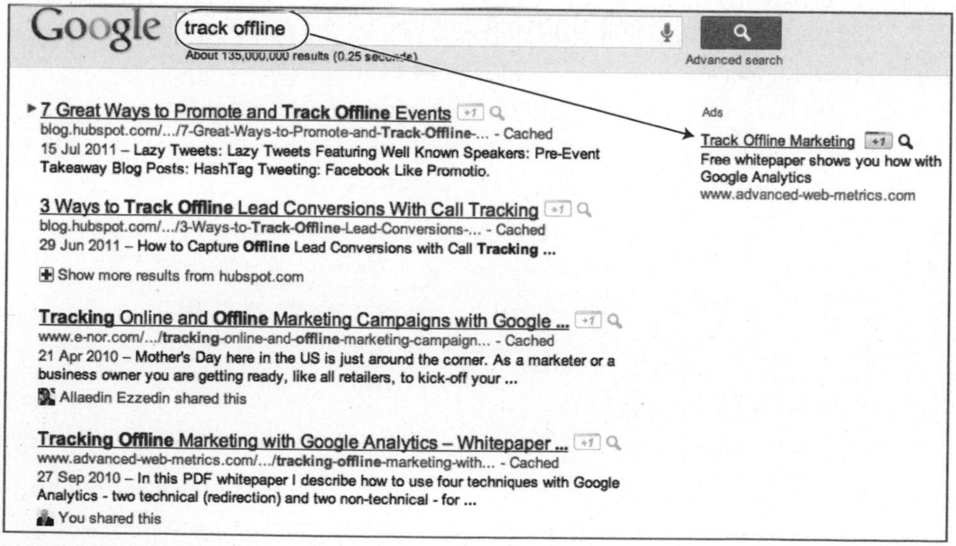

Figure 11.32 Using search to track offline visitors

For this example, all that is required is an AdWords ad configured for the keywords I use and perhaps a few related ones, such as *tracking offline*. The method for doing this would be exactly the same if I were advertising on TV or radio. The beauty of this technique is that I can control the landing page to match the specific campaign at any time. For my example, I would customize the landing page to match the event name and content of where I am mentioning the white paper.

Combining with URL Shorteners

This method is relevant to print publishers and print advertising only, simply because the landing page URL is too complicated to remember to be of use in any other form of offline marketing. As the name suggests, URL shorteners are tools that enable you to shorten a long URL into a short one. Although around since 2002, they became popular with the rise in prominence of Twitter because Twitter has a message limit of 140 characters. Example tools include bit.ly, ow.ly, tinyURL.com, and goo.gl.

Shortening a URL has advantages for marketers because you can include all your campaign tracking parameters *prior* to shortening. That way, two things are achieved—a neater, fixed-length URL and one that is trackable offline. The method is particularly useful when used in social media marketing and engagement—see Chapter 7 for median example of this.

The *New York Times* uses this technique in its print newspapers. The use of a shortened URL avoids the need to print overly long URLs within articles. Crucially, it also provides the means for the newspaper to track reader engagement at a sophisticated level never before possible. For example, printing "Follow this story online at nyti.ms/Byjdi89" potentially enables them to understand which newspaper is being read (they have several), what edition and date the reader saw, which section of the paper, on what page, and which specific article is driving engagement. That has huge implications for content optimization and advertisement placement for the publisher of offline content. Here is an example of the campaign parameters that could be used:

```
utm_source=IHT&utm_medium=newspaper&utm_campaign= ➡
politics&utm_content=page3-col2
```

Note: Although the *New York Times* uses URL shorteners in its print publications, it is not a Google Analytics user.

Combining with Quick Response Codes

Quick response (QR) codes are two-dimensional bar codes, readable by QR scanners, mobile phones with a camera, and smartphones. The code consists of black modules arranged in a square pattern on white background. The information encoded can be text, a URL, or other data. An example is shown in Figure 11.33. For this example, the text encoded is the URL to `advanced-web-metrics.com` with campaign parameters appended.

Figure 11.33 An example QR code with an embedded URL

The technique is applicable to print-based advertising such as newspaper ads, ads in magazines, flyer handouts, billboards, posters, business cards, and so forth—essentially anywhere that a person with a mobile phone is likely to make use of it. Example campaign tracking parameters could be:

utm_source=**book%20flyer**&utm_medium=**print**&utm_campaign=**eMetrics%20London**

> **Note:** The use of QR codes is very popular in Japan. See, for example, the huge LCD billboard at
> `http://en.wikipedia.org/wiki/File:Japan-qr-code-billboard.jpg`

Summary and Case Study

To help guide you through the decision-making process of which method to choose, I describe here the approach I used for this book. That is, I wanted to track whether readers use the URLs provided in the book text to visit `www.advanced-web-metrics.com`. Fortunately, I possess the skills to fully manage the IT requirements of my Apache server. Therefore, all offline tracking methods were available to me: vanity URLs, coded URLs, combining with search, URL shorteners, QR codes.

First, I ruled out combining with search because my offline marketing extends only to print—the book itself. In addition, my target keywords, for example, *Google Analytics*, would attract a very broad and poorly qualified audience. I discarded URL shorteners because my domain name is an important part of my branding. QR codes would occupy too much page space, and in any event I did not see any value in my readers going to the book website via a mobile device. I therefore needed to consider which type of redirection URLs are most suitable—vanity URLs or coded URLs.

For my situation as an author of content wishing to track reader engagement, my brand is the book title and its web address, `www.advanced-web-metrics.com`. My "products" are chapters of this book, and I wish to track reader engagement on a per-chapter basis. Therefore, relatively speaking, I have strong company brand awareness and low product brand awareness (*Chapter 11* is meaningless unless you are aware of the book). Hence I use coded URLs in this book to track *you*. For example, `www.advanced-web-metrics.com/chapter11` redirects to the website with campaign parameters appended, allowing me to view the activity of offline readers in my Google Analytics reports. As you will see if you try this link, I use the parameter `utm_id=81` to differentiate such visitors (campaign parameters are added in the background).

Using these methods, tracking offline marketing activity is relatively straightforward and most important, scalable—1 thousand, 1 million, or 100 million offline visits can be tracked this way. However, despite this, tracking offline marketing efforts has long been a frustrating experience for marketers. Essentially you need a savvy IT person who understands the requirements of marketing and can advise on which of the three methods is the best fit for you on a per-campaign basis—a rare breed indeed.

If that is not available to you, or you are an organization where brand values are less significant than your product or service values, you should combine offline marketing with search marketing. This gives you complete control over tracking without any IT to worry about. Even large brands (for example, Pontiac) have used this technique to great effect.

An Introduction to Google Website Optimizer

Google Website Optimizer is a free web page testing tool that enables you to seamlessly run experiments on your website visitors—comparing either different versions of the same page (A/B testing) or elements within a page, that is, multivariate testing (MVT). The technology displays a test version to your visitors at random, which is maintained throughout their visit. That is, they see only one particular test and are unaware of other versions. Hence, the process does not interfere with your visitors' browsing experience. By defining a goal—analogous to Google Analytics—the test that drives the most goal conversions is the one your visitors prefer. With this knowledge, the idea is that you adopt the winning test page as your permanent content.

Marketers will be familiar with A/B testing—a binary test to compare the effectiveness (usually a conversion rate) of a statistical element, such as one product image versus another. For example, page A is shown to 50 percent of new visitors selected at random, while page B is shown to the remaining 50 percent of visitors. If page A is better at generating conversions than page B, then page A is declared the winner and subsequently shown to all visitors. Another page, or page section, can then be tested, such as product title A versus product title B. Despite its name, you can also perform multiple side-by-side tests, that is, A/B/C/D... tests.

Multivariate testing is used to evaluate multiple page elements such as images, headlines, descriptions, colors, fonts, content, and so on *within* a page in order to understand which combinations provide better conversions. According to Wikipedia (http://en.wikipedia.org/wiki/Multivariate), multivariate statistical analysis describes "a collection of procedures which involve observation and analysis of more than one statistical variable at a time." The key phrase "more than one statistical variable at a time" is what distinguishes MVT from A/B testing.

If you have used AdWords or another pay-per-click search marketing network, you may have already experimented with A/B testing. AdWords ad rotation, discussed earlier in this chapter in the section "AdWords Ad Content Optimization," uses the same statistical methods to display different ad creatives to Google search visitors, where you have more than one ad version available for the same keywords. AdWords ad rotation is a testing technology that compares the performance of different ad versions. Google Website Optimizer extends the methodology for testing page content once a visitor has arrived on your website.

Similar to the launch of Google Analytics, the release of Website Optimizer was a pivotal moment in the short history of the landing page optimization industry. Previously, such tools were complicated to deploy and came with a hefty price tag to implement and use. Google changed that with a simplified setup and free availability to all. Unlike with Google Analytics though, the launch of Website Optimizer in 2007 was the result of internal product development, not an acquisition.

Common Misconceptions

Like all page optimization tools, Google Website Optimizer does have a few limitations. There are, however, many things that have been said and published about Google Website Optimizer that simply aren't true. Here are some of the more common areas of misconception.

Only works for AdWords visitors Google Website Optimizer allows you to run tests on your pages regardless of visitor referral source; it's not just AdWords visitors. You also do not need to be an AdWords advertiser to use it. This misconception came about because when Google Website Optimizer was first released, it was accessible only through the AdWords interface.

Does not run on secure pages Google Website Optimizer code (and the GATC) contains logic that determines whether or not a page is secure or nonsecure and automatically runs the appropriate code for each. Therefore it does not matter whether part of a test, or even the entire test, is contained on SSL pages.

Does not work with dynamic content Google Website Optimizer tests are easiest to set up with static content. However, tests can be set up on pages that include dynamic content, used with sections to swap out CSS, scripts, or other dynamic elements. It is also possible, with more advanced techniques, to have elements persist across pages or even work with server-side delivered content.

Does not allow for multiple conversions The Google Website Optimizer interface asks for the conversion page of the experiment. However, the conversion point is actually determined by the code that is subsequently provided. This means you can have a conversion register on multiple pages or in an onClick or onSubmit event.

AMAT: Where Does Testing Fit?

Consider the following scenario: You have set up your website, initiated marketing to bring relevant traffic, and viewed your visitor reports and you notice that an important page is underperforming. You've identified the problem, and various teams have come up with suggestions to improve the situation. These include changes to the page layout and its design, different product images, snappier headlines, revised descriptive text, and stronger calls to action (bigger buttons!). Now you have to advise which suggestion to pick as the replacement, or should you select all of them?

This common problem can sometimes halt the entire optimization process; people just don't know what to do next—there are too many choices and all (or none) could be right. Often the highest-paid person in the organization (HIPPO) or most vocal person determines the way forward. But the reality is that they know much less about the behavioral patterns of visitors on your website than you do because you look at the data on a regular basis. Are you prepared to put your credibility on the line by taking an educated guess or going with the HIPPO's opinion? That's a dilemma expert consultants as well as novice analysts face.

The answer is you don't need to and shouldn't. Let your visitors decide because theirs are the "expert" opinions you need to listen to. This is precisely where testing comes in. Multivariate and A/B testing are crucial elements that dovetail into the web-marketing life cycle that I refer to as AMAT:

1. Acquire visitors.
2. Measure interactions.
3. Analyze results.
4. Test alternatives.

As Figure 11.34 shows, AMAT allows for a continuous cycle of improvement, providing a measurable process by which you can optimize conversion rates on your website, right down to a page-by-page basis if required.

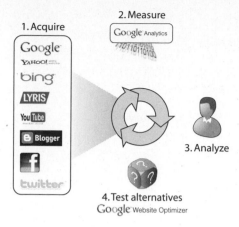

Figure 11.34 The web-marketing life cycle (AMAT)

Choosing a Test Type

At this stage I assume you have been through the process of optimizing poor-performing pages and search engine marketing campaigns—as described earlier in this chapter. Do these first to ensure that you get the basics right before performing a test—there is no point in testing just for the sake of it. Employ testing when you have a fundamental best practice web design and search marketing strategy in place. Otherwise, you waste a great deal of time and effort looking for statistical significance in areas that are basic and can be identified quickly by a good web optimization consultant.

With these in place, next have a clear definition of what page you wish to test. Some practitioners propose "test everything." However, for all but the smallest of websites, that is unrealistic. Instead, focus your efforts on funnel steps to your goal completions and pages with high and low bounce rates.

Funnel steps are the well-defined linear micro-conversions that take the visitor to the end goal—the purpose of your website. High-bounce-rate pages indicate poor performance and are obvious candidates for testing. Low-bounce-rate pages are strong-performing pages that are excellent candidates for testing promotions, new ideas, and so on. Experimenting with any of these can have a huge impact on your website performance—as discussed in "Identify and Optimize Poor-Performing Pages" at the beginning of this chapter.

With a test page defined, log in to your Website Optimization account and click Create A New Experiment. The first thing to decide is what type of test (referred to as *experiment* from now on, with *test* used to describe a particular experiment combination) is most suitable for your needs. As shown in Figure 11.35, you have two choices:

A/B Experiment A/B tests, often referred to as split testing within the industry, allow to you to test two (or more) entirely different versions of a page. Choose this if you are considering a page redesign or new layout or if you simply wish to change one item on a page.

Multivariate Experiment Multivariate tests allow you try multiple combinations of content on the *same* page. Choose this to test combinations simultaneously where the design and layout remain constant.

In both cases you define a conversion goal that signifies success.

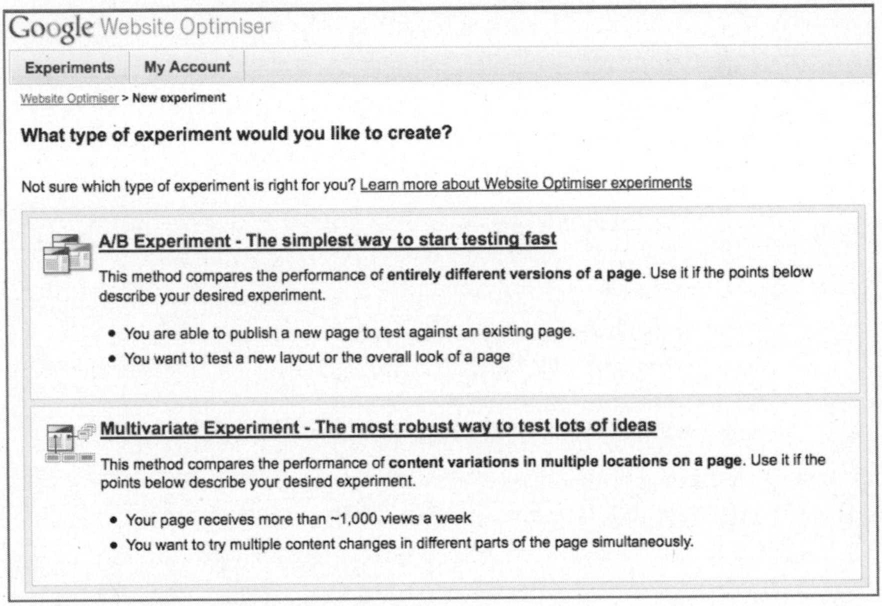

Figure 11.35   Google Website Optimizer initial setup screen

When A/B Experiments Are Appropriate

The great advantage of A/B testing is that it is simple to set up and quick to obtain results and make changes. It is often used to test design layout—for example, should the menu-navigation system be at the top or left side of the page, or is a black-and-white theme preferred to a multicolored alternative? The iterative nature of A/B testing and the few alternatives presented to the visitors (as few as two—the original and an alternative) enable you to gain results quickly. This is particularly useful when answers to macro-questions are required—is version A better than version B or not?

The advantage of A/B experiments diminishes as the number of alternatives grows (A, B, C... Z) because each page must be created and hosted on your servers.

When Multivariate Experiments Are Appropriate

With multiple page elements—for example, multiple product images, titles, and descriptions on the same page—A/B testing is too laborious to implement and too time consuming to obtain results. Another caveat is that A/B testing cannot tell you whether one page element affects the conversion rate of another; for example, what if the product title affects how visitors perceive the product image?

Use multivariate testing to test multiple elements on a page simultaneously. It determines what, if any, correlations exist between elements and evaluates the best combination of all page elements to create a winning recipe—that is, generate more conversions.

The caveat is that multivariate experiments can take a long time to complete as many combinations are generated and each needs to receive significant conversion for the test to be valid. Therefore, multivariate experiments are only suitable for high-traffic websites, that is, websites where you are likely to receive at least *several hundred* conversions over a period of a month.

Use A/B Testing for Dynamic Content

For multivariate (MVT) experiments, Website Optimizer hosts your alternative combinations on Google servers. In this way, when a visitor views a page under test, Website Optimizer replaces the original (control) version of the section you wish to test with one of your alternatives. Because this process takes place on-the-fly, test versions must be defined *within* Website Optimizer.

The advantage of this approach is that it removes a large part of the technical overhead required to perform a multivariate test—a savvy marketer can set up and control an MVT experiment without changes to the website architecture. However, a consequence is realized when the page alternatives depend on dynamic variables, such as the visitor's input prior to the test page being viewed.

For example, consider testing a product-page template of a shopping cart system. Which image, headline, description, and so on are displayed depends on the link the visitor clicked in the preceding product-category page. Website Optimizer has no way to determine which product was selected because this is dynamically generated at the point of click-through. Therefore, you cannot use MVT in this scenario. Instead, perform an A/B test with your alternative combinations.

> **Note:** Depending on what elements you are specifically testing, there are advanced methods allowing you to run MVT tests on dynamically generated content, such as, for example, using server-side logic in conjunction with JavaScript and CSS. In addition, if you use Website Optimizer to inject CSS and JavaScript rather than "content," you can rearrange elements on a page to present different variations to the visitor. However, these are advanced techniques.

Getting Started: Implementing a Multivariate Experiment

In the following sections I consider the setup of a multivariate experiment and two resulting case studies—a retail website (Calyx Flowers) and a large, well-known(!) content publisher (YouTube).

As you may have suspected, there is a close relationship between Website Optimizer and Google Analytics—the conversion data used in Website Optimizer reports comes from the same database system Google Analytics uses. In addition, a modified version of the GATC is used for tracking purposes.

Further Information on Website Optimizer

These sections outline the principles of a Website Optimizer implementation. A fuller description is available from www.google.com/websiteoptimizer with more technical information available at the official Website Optimizer blog:

http://websiteoptimizer.blogspot.com/2009/03/introducing-techie-guide-to-google.html

---

Similar to Google Analytics, Website Optimizer is integrated with AdWords and is accessed from within your AdWords account or directly from www.google.com/websiteoptimizer. Figure 11.35 shows the initial experiment setup screen.

After selecting Multivariate Experiment, you have four steps to complete:

1. Set up a test page and conversion goal.
2. Install JavaScript tags on both pages.
3. Create alternative variations to test.
4. Review and launch.

Step 1: Set Up a Test Page and Conversion Goal

Your choice of a test page is determined during the consideration of test type, described previously. As already mentioned, don't test for the sake of it. Plan your experiments with care or you risk being swamped with even more data (isn't Google Analytics enough for you?). Pages with a high bounce rate or high exit rate are suitable candidates for testing. If you are a transactional site, your checkout funnel is a prime starting point.

For your goal conversion page, you can use the same goal URLs as those defined in your Google Analytics configuration, or define others. An important difference of Website Optimizer goals is that your goal must define success for your *test*—that's not always going to be the same as for Google Analytics, which uses goals to define success of your *website*.

Website Optimizer goals may be virtual pageviews and wildcards; /download/* .pdf and /cgi-bin/*.pl can be defined as goals as long as such files are being tracked by the Website Optimizer tracking script—for example, using an onClick event handler for PDF downloads. You can even define multiple goals on the same page or on subsequent pages. Each conversion is summed and added to the total, though it is currently not possible to weight different goals; all goals are considered equally.

> **Tip:** A conversion goal does not have to immediately follow the test page—it can be much further down the visitor journey. However, bear in mind the longer that path is, the fewer conversions the test will receive and hence the longer the experiment will need to run in order to provide statistically significant results.

Step 2: Install JavaScript Tags on Both Pages

With your test and goal page URLs selected, you need to insert page tags to control the experiment and track the results. Figure 11.36 schematically shows the three different tags required for this. These tags are snippets of JavaScript code that are provided in the Website Optimizer interface during setup. The tracking and conversion scripts are simple modifications of the GATC.

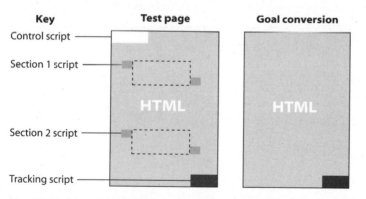

Figure 11.36 Schematic tagging of pages for a multivariate experiment

The three different page tags required are as follows:

Control script The control script governs the progress of the experiment. It contacts Google servers to retrieve appropriate content variations (the actual variations are maintained on Google servers). The control script also ensures that a repeat visitor views the same variation and that multiple views of the same page by the same user do not affect the experiment statistics.

The control script must be placed before any section scripts and before all displayable content. The recommended placement is immediately after the opening <head> tag of the test page.

Section scripts Section scripts are used to define sections of page content that will vary in the experiment. Most things can be included within a section—for example, text, script, graphics, and so on—or all of these can be in one contiguous block. Currently the combined limit for all alternatives of a section is 150 KB, though this can vary depending on the size and number of other sections.

If you are testing more than one section, then each section requires a unique name. Section names are case sensitive and can be up to 25 characters long. Try to use meaningful names—for example, headline 1 or product photo X—to make it easier to interpret your reports.

Tracking scripts (two) These scripts trigger Google Analytics data collection and ensure that page refreshes are counted properly. The first tracker script is part of the control that's placed on the test page. The second tracker script (also known as the conversion script) goes on the conversion page immediately after the opening <head> tag.

A generic example illustrating the positioning of the scripts is shown here:

```
<html>
 <head>

   ...
   <script><!-- Control script ---><\script>
   <script><!-- Optimizer tracking script ---><\script>
   <script><!-- Your regular GATC ---><\script>
 </head>
 <body>

   ...
   <script><!-- Page section 1 script ---><\script>
   <script><!-- Page section 2 script ---><\script>

   ...
</body>
</html>
```

Once you have installed all the tags, validate them within Website Optimizer. If errors are detected, fix them before continuing. Website Optimizer will not let you proceed to the next step without validation. There are two methods of doing this:

- Provide the URLs for your test and conversion pages. Website Optimizer will access them and validate.

- If your test pages are not externally visible—for example, if they are part of a purchase process, behind a login area, or inaccessible for some other reason—you can upload the HTML source files.

Custom Tracking Settings

If you have the following custom variables in your GATC, then you will also need to customize the control, tracking, and conversion scripts for your experiment to match:

```
_gaq.push[('_setDomainName', somevalue')]
_gaq.push[('_setCookiePath', /some/path/ofcookie')]
```

To do this, create a new script setting the customized variables to the same values set in your GATC. This new script should be in its own set of <script> tags and placed immediately above the Website Optimizer control script, in the header area of your page. Note that the control script needs the old legacy urchin.js-style customization, as follows:

```
<html>
<head>
<script>
    _udn = "somevalue";                 // from _setDomainName
    _utcp = "/some/path/ofcookie";      // from _setCookiePath
</script>

<script><!-- Control script ---><\script>
    ...
</head>
```

Step 3: Create Alternative Variations to Test

At this step, you add variations of section content within the user interface by simply pasting plaintext or HTML content into the box provided, as shown in Figure 11.37. This is required for each variation. Once you've completed this, you can preview each combination that your visitors might see.

> **Tip:** In addition to using plaintext or HTML, you can do some interesting experiments by inserting CSS and JavaScript.

Note that the content variations used for testing are hosted on Google servers; the original content remains hosted by you or your hosting provider. Each time a visitor views your test page, Google servers insert your variations randomly. Once a visitor has received a particular combination, the combination remains fixed for that visitor. For example, if the visitor returns to the same test page later during their visit or at a later visit, the same combination will be displayed to that visitor—provided, that is, they use the same device and browser when viewing your site and have not deleted or lost their cookies. If they have, they will receive another random variation.

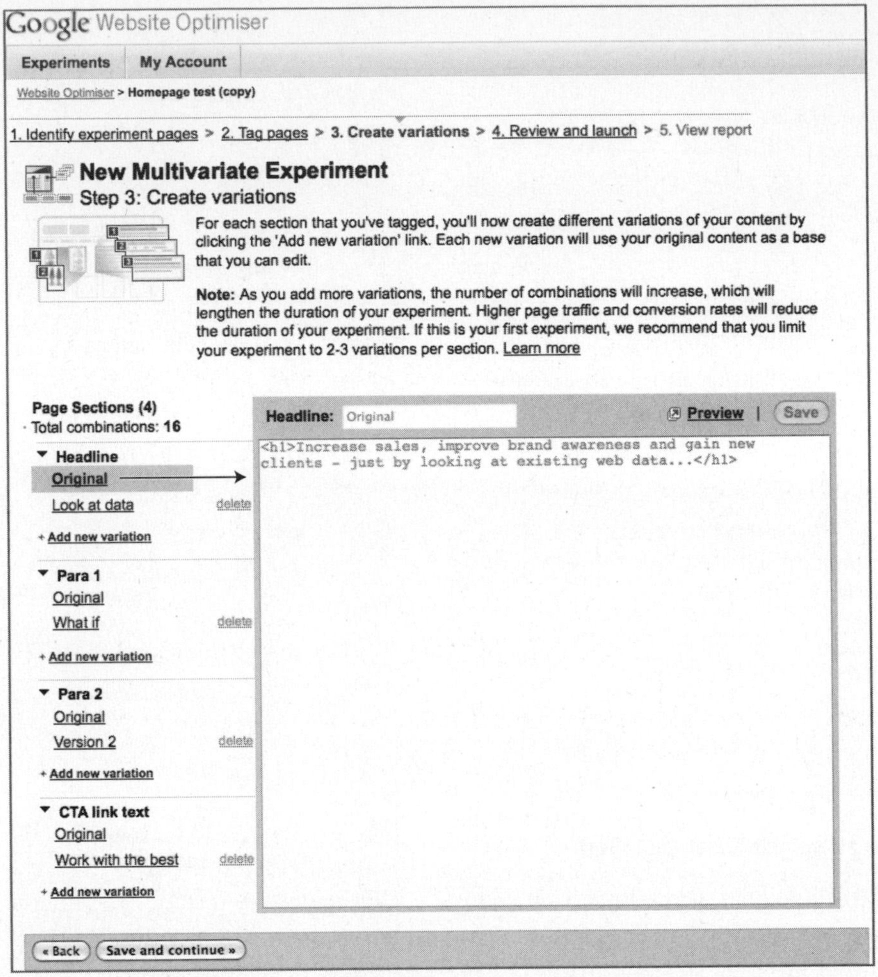

Figure 11.37 Adding variations for your test page

It is tempting to create lots of alternatives for a section under test because it is so easy to do. However, you should avoid making superfluous changes such as bold high-lighted text versus nonbold or "Click here" versus "Read more" because the number of combinations is important. When your test page is displayed during an experiment, Website Optimizer is testing the performance of not only individual variations but also the combined effect of all page sections on the page. For example, in an experiment with two page sections—headline and image with two and three variations, respectively—the following six combinations will be tested (2×3 combinations):

- Original headline + original image
- Original headline + new image
- Original headline + new image2
- New headline + original image

- New headline + new image
- New headline + new image2

Extending this to four page sections with four variations for each, you will have 256 combinations (4 × 4 × 4 × 4). As you can see, the number of combinations grows rapidly. This has obvious implications regarding the length of time the experiment needs to run in order to produce meaningful results (see the section "How Long Will an Experiment Take?").

Step 4: Review and Launch

This is where you enter the percentage of traffic to include in the experiment (1 to 100 percent); the more traffic included, the faster the experiment will run. I generally recommend you set this to 100 percent unless you have a specific reason for not doing so. Before launching the experiment, it is worthwhile to make a final check of your experiment settings. Once you start the experiment, you will not be able to change the parameters; instead, you must create a new experiment.

Once you click Start, you will return to the experiment workflow page, which has an additional section describing the progress of this experiment and the number of impressions and conversions tracked so far. Your test page will start showing different combinations immediately, but there is a delay of about an hour before reports begin displaying data. Figure 11.38 is a schematic representation of how Website Optimizer works.

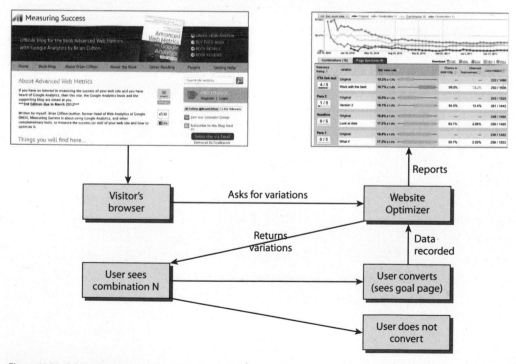

Figure 11.38 Schematic representation of how Website Optimizer works

494

How Long Will an Experiment Take?

The progress of the experiment and the estimated duration depend entirely on the amount of traffic seen on your test and conversion pages. As a guide, when selecting test pages choose pages that receive thousands of pageviews and are part of a conversion process that results in hundreds of goal conversions. The period it takes to achieve this in your Google Analytics reports is a good guide to how long it will take for your experiment to run for *each* variation.

For example, if you are testing three page sections, each with two variations, that is eight combinations to test in total ($2 \times 2 \times 2$). Each combination needs to receive approximately 100 conversions to show statistically significant test results. Assuming an average conversion rate from the test page to each goal page of 10 percent, then approximately 8,000 views of your test page are required. If that is achievable on your website within a week, then it will take approximately the same time to achieve meaningful results within Website Optimizer. If you have 256 combinations and a conversion rate of 5 percent, you require approximately 500,000 pageviews of your test page for the experiment to complete.

This highlights two important points when conducting multivariate experiments:

- Select high-traffic pages as candidates to test in order to obtain results in a reasonable time frame. As a guide, consider a multivariate test only for pages that receive in excess of 5,000 pageviews per week.

- Define a test goal as "close" as possible to the page being tested—as opposed to using your ultimate goal conversions defined in Google Analytics; for example, use "adding to the cart" or "proceeding to the next step" instead of "purchase confirmation."

Estimating Experiment Time

A handy calculator to help you estimate the potential duration of your experiment is available at

www.google.com/analytics/siteopt/siteopt/help/calculator.html

As a guide, a reasonable time frame for achieving useful experimental results is two to four weeks; otherwise, you risk losing momentum. If you estimate an experiment taking considerably longer, use A/B testing instead. Once you have narrowed the combinations in this manner, say within 64 combinations, you can return to a multivariate test.

In addition, Website Optimizer has two pruning options to improve the speed of running experiments: auto-disable and manual disable. Auto-disable allows you to automatically prune variations that underperform. Manual disable allows you to manually achieve the same thing on a per-combination basis. These features are useful in decreasing the time it takes to run an experiment to statistical significance and when you wish to prevent underperforming pages from being served to visitors, distracting them from the pages that have proven to be more effective.

Once you start seeing impressions and conversions recorded in Website Optimizer, view the preliminary results by clicking View Report. However, be careful drawing any conclusions at these early stages. At the beginning of an experiment, sample sizes will be small and results therefore highly inaccurate, that is, with large fluctuations.

For example, imagine spinning a coin 10 times. There is a possibility that all 10 spins will result in heads showing. That does not mean that heads should be favored over tails and the experiment ended—such a result can be accounted to pure chance and the *butterfly effect*. If you repeat the coin experiment 1,000 times, then overall you will observe a more even distribution, maybe 550 heads and 450 tails. Repeating the experiment a million times will give you a near-perfect prediction for the probability of receiving heads: 0.5.

The point is that patience is a virtue when it comes to testing. Allow enough data to be collected for each combination before analyzing, pruning, or selecting a winner—at least until the green or red conversion bars appear in your experiment reports.

The following case studies illustrate the abilities of Website Optimizer.

Calyx Flowers: A Retail Multivariate Case Study

This case study was produced by EpikOne (www.epikone.com) as part of its work for Calyx Flowers (www.calyxandcorolla.com) and is reproduced here with the kind permission of both parties.

As the name suggests, Calyx Flowers is a flower-distribution company, founded in 1988 and based in Vermont. Initially, Calyx Flowers had begun to invest significantly in its online marketing—particularly search engine optimization and pay-per-click advertising. However, the company felt that the increase in visitor numbers did not match the modest increase in conversions received, that is, flowers purchased. Furthermore, Google Analytics revealed significant exit rates for visitors who had viewed a product page but did not add to the cart.

In designing the Website Optimizer experiment, EpikOne chose to test whether the product page could be more effective at producing conversions. In this example, a conversion was considered successful if a visitor added a product to the shopping cart. As shown in Figure 11.36, three sections of the product page were identified for testing:

1. Change of messaging

   Would the addition of trust factors, such as customer testimonials, help?

2. Stronger call to action

   Would larger, brighter buttons for "Buy Now" help?

3. Change of brand image

   Would a different (more emotive) product image help?

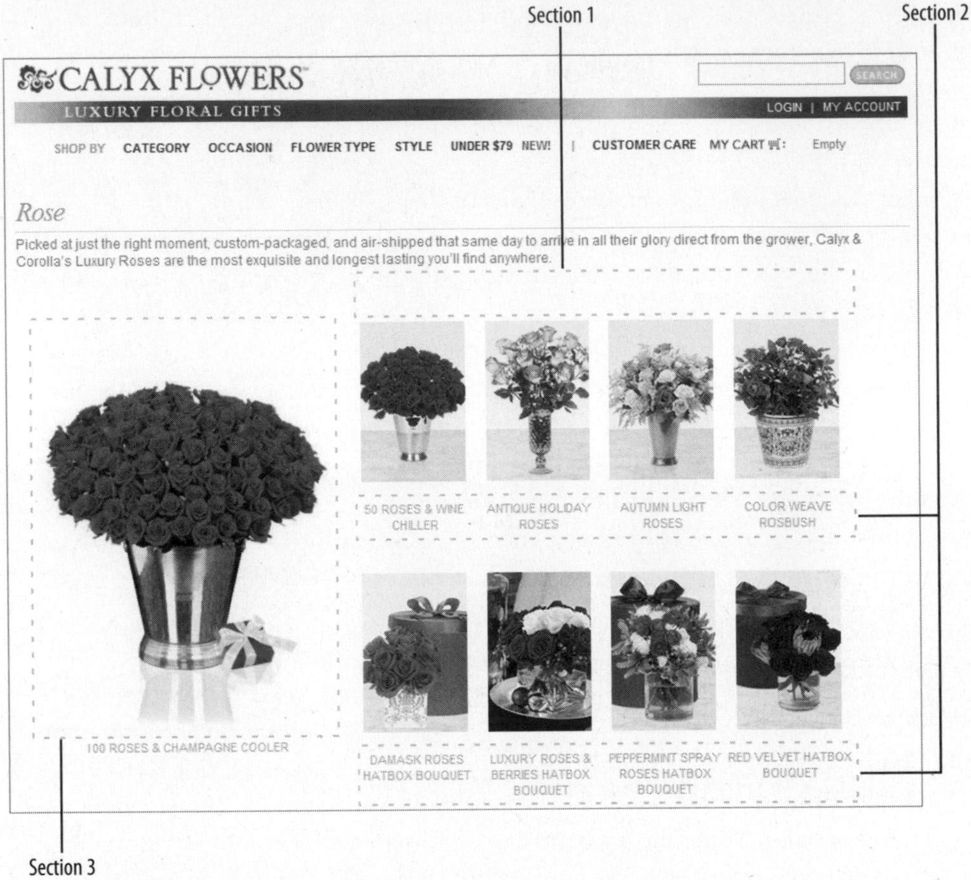

Figure 11.39 The Calyx Flowers original product page, with three test sections highlighted

For the experiment, each section had two combinations: the original and an alternative ($2 \times 2 \times 2 = 8$ combinations). Table 11.2 shows the combinations with all alternatives displayed.

▶ **Table 11.2** Multivariate test alternatives for Calyx Flowers

Section Name	Original	Alternative
Subhead	None	*Customer Favorites:* *"Calyx Flowers has mastered the art of fresh flower design! I just adore this company."* *Juliet P. Verzolini, Linda, VA*
Featured CTA	None	Order Now

Continues

► **Table 11.2** Multivariate test alternatives for Calyx Flowers *(Continued)*

Section Name	Original	Alternative
Hero shot	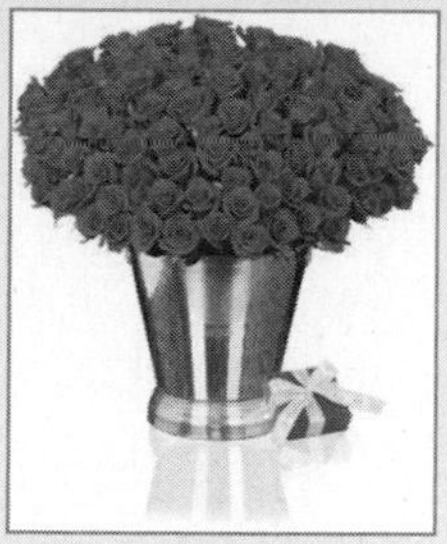	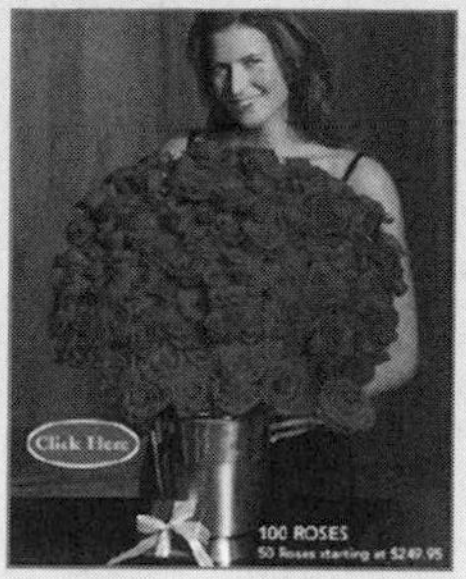

The experiment was launched to test which sections and which combinations would lead to better conversions. For this test, a conversion was defined as adding a product to the shopping cart. Enough conversions were gathered to complete the experiment within a week.

Results and Impact

When viewing results, there are two reports to consider: the Page Sections report and the Combinations report. These are shown in Figure 11.40a and Figure 11.40b, respectively.

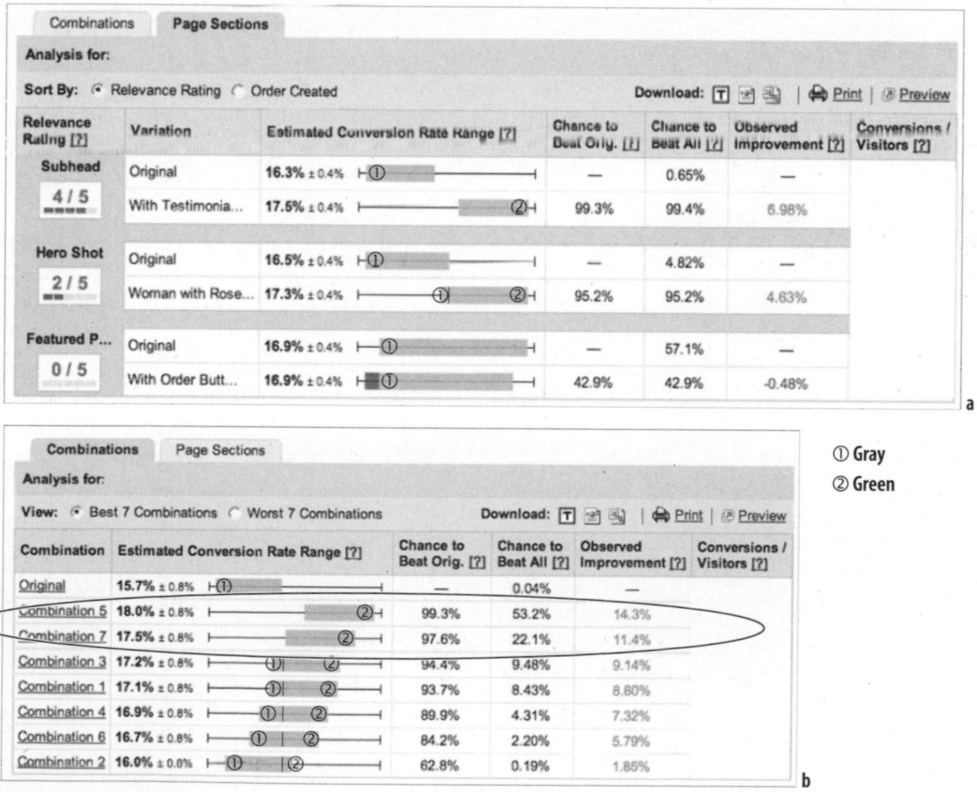

Relevance Rating [?]	Variation	Estimated Conversion Rate Range [?]	Chance to Beat Orig. [?]	Chance to Beat All [?]	Observed Improvement [?]	Conversions / Visitors [?]
Subhead 4 / 5	Original	16.3% ± 0.4%	—	0.65%	—	
	With Testimonia...	17.5% ± 0.4%	99.3%	99.4%	6.98%	
Hero Shot 2 / 5	Original	16.5% ± 0.4%	—	4.82%	—	
	Woman with Rose...	17.3% ± 0.4%	95.2%	95.2%	4.63%	
Featured P... 0 / 5	Original	16.9% ± 0.4%	—	57.1%	—	
	With Order Butt...	16.9% ± 0.4%	42.9%	42.9%	-0.48%	

Combination	Estimated Conversion Rate Range [?]	Chance to Beat Orig. [?]	Chance to Beat All [?]	Observed Improvement [?]	Conversions / Visitors [?]
Original	15.7% ± 0.8%	—	0.04%	—	
Combination 5	18.0% ± 0.8%	99.3%	53.2%	14.3%	
Combination 7	17.5% ± 0.8%	97.6%	22.1%	11.4%	
Combination 3	17.2% ± 0.8%	94.4%	9.48%	9.14%	
Combination 1	17.1% ± 0.8%	93.7%	8.43%	8.60%	
Combination 4	16.9% ± 0.8%	89.9%	4.31%	7.32%	
Combination 6	16.7% ± 0.8%	84.2%	2.20%	5.79%	
Combination 2	16.0% ± 0.8%	62.8%	0.19%	1.85%	

Figure 11.40 (a) Page Section results, (b) Combination results

The Page Sections report identifies which sections of the experiment have the greatest impact. This is indicated graphically with green and gray bar charts and numerically in the adjacent table. The Chance to Beat Orig. column is a measure of the overlap of the two (gray and green bars) conversion distributions. The smaller the overlap, the greater the separation of the distributions and therefore the higher the probability of beating the original variation. In other words, was the change in the observed conversion rate real, or did it just occur by chance (within error bars)? A clear separation of green and gray indicates it is real, with a 95 percent confidence level.

In Figure 11.40a, we can see that the addition of a testimonial has the greatest impact on conversion rate, closely followed by the change in product image. The enhanced call-to-action buttons show a negative impact (red bar)—that is, they decreased the conversion rate. However, the decrease is minimal (−0.48 percent) and the distribution overlap is large, as indicated by the Chance to Beat Orig. (42.9 percent). This means there is a 57.1 percent chance that the original section could have also had the same effect. Thus, the call-to-action section is considered to have no significant impact on conversions.

Viewing the Combinations report in Figure 11.40b, we can see that there are two superior combinations (5 and 7). Both of these contained the testimonial, with the winner also including the more emotive product image and the original call-to-action links; see Figure 11.41.

Figure 11.41 Winning combination for the Calyx Flowers product page

The best improvement of a 14.3 percent increase in conversions equates to a significant dollar improvement for the Calyx Flowers bottom line—of the order of millions of dollars per year. This has provided the evidence required that its online marketing efforts are working and provided impetus to further invest in its online channel.

YouTube: A Content-Publishing Multivariate Case Study

This case study was produced by Google in association with VKI Studios (now Cardinal Path, www.cardinalpath.com) and is reproduced here with the kind permission of both parties.

YouTube is synonymous with video sharing and has grown into one of the most highly trafficked sites on the Web. According to comScore Media Metrix, for the month of October 2011, 797 million people watched almost 88.3 billion videos.

www.comscore.com/Press_Events/Press_Releases/2011/12/More_than_200_Billion_ Online_Videos_Viewed_Globally_in_October

Because of its daily visitor volume, small changes on a website such as YouTube can make a very big difference, and it's an excellent case for a multivariate test. The goal was to increase the number of people who sign up for an account.

Three sections were tested on 100 percent of the YouTube US English home page. Figure 11.42 shows the original test page with test sections highlighted. The hypothesis was that if the prominence of the sign-up link were increased (via changes to sections 1 and 2) along with clearer highlighting of the benefits of having an account (via section 3), more people would sign up.

Figure 11.42 The YouTube home page with three test sections highlighted

For the experiment, each section had multiple possible alternatives, giving a total of 1,024 combinations ($2 \times 16 \times 32 = 1{,}024$). As shown in Figure 11.43, section 1 is a simple change of text style using all uppercase for accentuation. Section 2 is new content that in the original is empty space. Its purpose is to highlight that having a YouTube account provides additional benefits and draw attention to the call to action. There are 16 alternatives (15 plus the original blank space). Section 3 provides additional supporting information of the benefits of having an account with 32 alternatives.

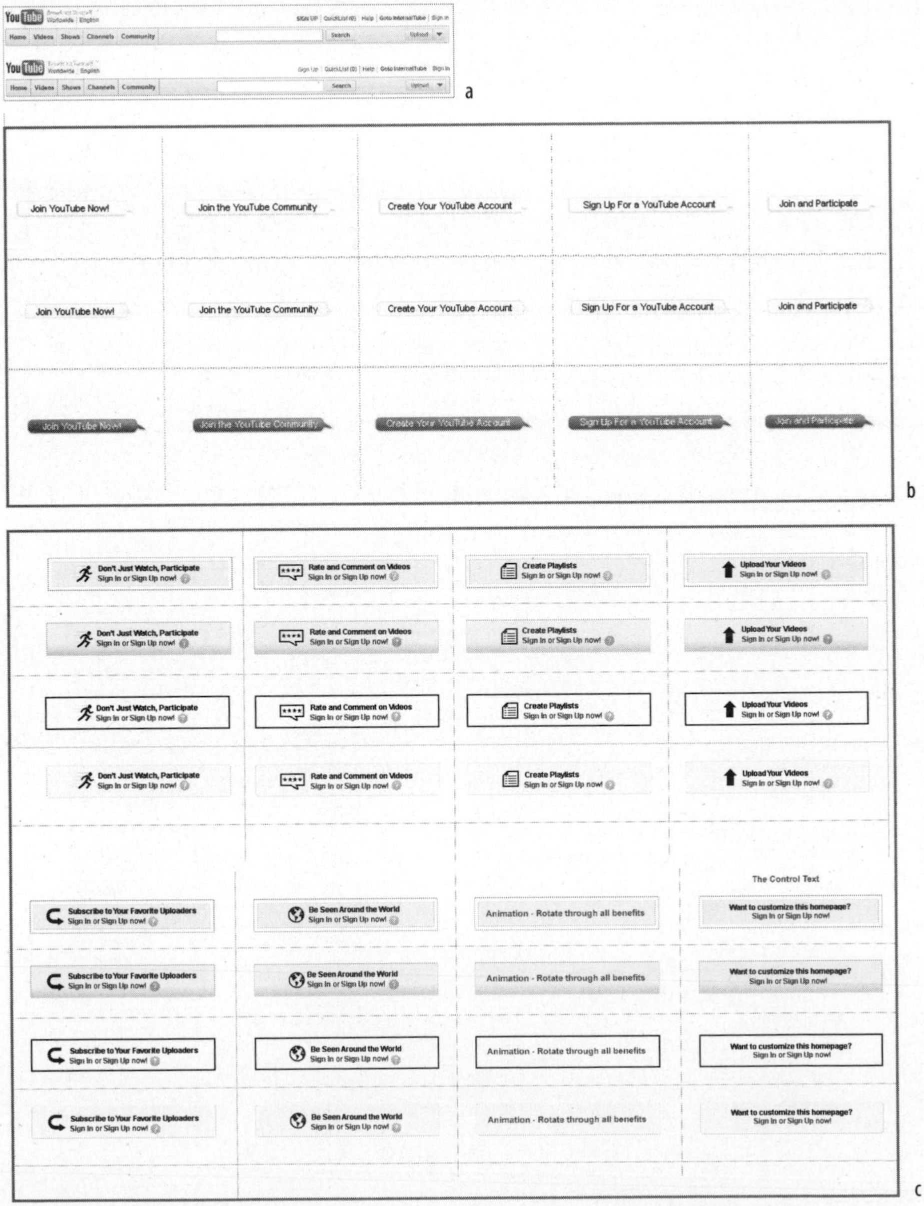

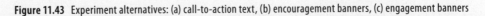

Figure 11.43 Experiment alternatives: (a) call-to-action text, (b) encouragement banners, (c) engagement banners

Results and Impact

The report of Figure 11.44 shows the presence of several winners. Although 12 are visible, the results page is paginated, so the winners stretch beyond what is shown in the screen shot. All of the top four provide a conversion uplift of greater than 15 percent and are predicted to beat the original 99.9 percent of the time, that is, almost certain. This high level of certainty is due to the very large sample size of pageviews and is therefore quite rare for most sites.

Although Combination 28, shown in Figure 11.45, is the winner with an increase in performance of 15.7 percent, all 12 combinations show overlaps in predicted conversion rates. That is, the green bars representing the spread of conversion rates at 95 percent confidence overlap. This means it is entirely possible for, say, Combination 76 to outperform Combination 28. The report shows both are better than the original, but the difference between the two could be the result of random chance. If you wanted to conclusively select a winner, further testing would be needed on the top performers.

The increased sign-up rate for YouTube of 15.7 percent represents thousands of more signups every day for YouTube. Putting this achievement into perspective, the entire experiment, including planning, execution, and result analysis, lasted less than two weeks. In addition, this large experiment with 1,024 combinations (the largest Website Optimizer test to date) shows the robustness of the technique and the promise for very-large-scale multivariate experiments.

☐ Combination	Status ⑦	Est. conv. rate ⑦	Chance to Beat Orig. ⑦	Observed Improvement ⑦	Conv./Visitors ⑦
☐ Original	Enabled	–⊢▬▬▬▬⊣+	—	—	
☆ Top high-confidence winners. **Run a follow-up experiment**					
☐ **Combination 28**	Enabled	–⊢▬▬▬▬▬▬▬⊣+	99.9%	15.7%	
☐ **Combination 52**	Enabled	–⊢▬▬▬▬▬▬▬⊣+	99.9%	15.3%	
☐ **Combination 20**	Enabled	–⊢▬▬▬▬▬▬▬⊣+	99.9%	15.2%	
☐ **Combination 68**	Enabled	–⊢▬▬▬▬▬▬▬⊣+	99.9%	15.0%	
☐ Combination 76	Enabled	–⊢▬▬▬▬▬▬⊣+	99.9%	14.9%	
☐ Combination 4	Enabled	–⊢▬▬▬▬▬▬⊣+	99.9%	14.5%	
☐ Combination 12	Enabled	–⊢▬▬▬▬▬⊣+	99.9%	13.8%	
☐ Combination 36	Enabled	–⊢▬▬▬▬⊣+	99.9%	13.0%	
☐ Combination 17	Enabled	–⊢▬▬▬▬▬⊣+	99.9%	12.9%	
☐ Combination 53	Enabled	–⊢▬▬▬▬⊣+	99.9%	12.8%	
☐ Combination 60	Enabled	–⊢▬▬▬▬⊣+	99.9%	12.6%	
☐ Combination 44	Enabled	–⊢▬▬▬▬▬⊣+	99.9%	12.4%	

Figure 11.44 Combination results: Website Optimizer highlights the top four winners, though this is arbitrary.

Figure 11.45 Winning combination for YouTube home page

Summary

In Chapter 11, you have learned the following:

To identify and optimize pages You have learned how to identify and optimize poor-performing pages using a mix of methods, including a detailed funnel analysis.

To benchmark internal site search I discussed how to measure the success of site search and put a dollar amount on its importance to your organization.

To optimize search engine marketing You have seen how to optimize your search engine marketing efforts for both paid and nonpaid search.

To monetize a non-e-commerce website You can ensure that your nontransactional site is not a pet project by monetizing it, either by assigning values to defined goals or by faking transaction calls to Google Analytics.

To track offline campaigns You have learned how to track offline marketing by using modified landing page URLs and redirection or combining with search engine marketing.

Multivariate and A/B testing We explored how to use Website Optimizer as a way to test a hypothesis or alternative design.

Integrating Google Analytics with Third-Party Applications

This book has so far focused on collecting, analyzing, and using web visitor data from within the Google Analytics user interface. You can import data from AdWords, AdSense, and Webmaster Tools and export individual reports in XML, CSV, TSV, or PDF format. This method of exporting is ideal for one-off needs or regular schedules via email. However, sometimes you require a regular pull of data, wish to integrate data into another system, or want to be creative and visualize your data in a completely different way.

In this chapter I explain the techniques used to auto-extract data, and I present case studies on how different organizations are pushing the envelope by adding extra functionality to Google Analytics.

12

In Chapter 12, you will learn:

To extract Google Analytics cookie information using JavaScript or PHP

To use the Google Analytics core reporting API

To use the Google Analytics API via case studies from third-party applications

To use Google Analytics to track phone calls

To integrate Website Optimizer with Google Analytics

Extracting Google Analytics Information

The launch of the free Google Analytics export application programming interface (API) in May 2009 was a pivotal moment in the history of Google Analytics. It paved the way for greater innovation by opening up the product so that third-party developers could build their own applications around the data. In addition, the API has provided Google with greater transparency in its data-collection methodology—you are able to query your own data as and when you wish.

If you have the necessary programming skills to develop API applications, go straight to the next section to learn which applications are already available in the wild or to start building your own. However, sometimes a simple query of the Google Analytics cookies can be sufficient for your needs. For example, a visitor subscribes or makes a purchase on your website, and you wish to pass the original referrer information, such as the search engine name and keywords used, into your customer relationship management (CRM) system. In such cases, consider using one of the approaches outlined in the following two sections: importing data using JavaScript or importing data using PHP.

Importing Data into Your CRM Using JavaScript

Campaign variables (medium, referral source, keywords, and so on) captured by Google Analytics are stored in the campaign cookie named __utmz. Using standard JavaScript methods, you can extract this information at the point when a visitor submits a form request or confirms their purchase, and you can then transmit this into your CRM, help desk, or logfile system. I'll demonstrate the method using a submit form. In summary, there are three straightforward steps:

- Add standard JavaScript functions to extract the values from the Google Analytics cookies.

- Add extra form fields in your HTML to hold the extracted cookie values.

- Call the JavaScript functions when the form is successfully submitted to extract the cookie values and place them in your hidden form fields.

The following text describes the method and necessary code. You can also download the functions from www.advanced-web-metrics.com/chapter12:

1. Copy the following two JavaScript functions into the <head> section of the HTML page containing your form:

```
<script type="text/javascript">
 function _uGC(l,n,s) {
    // used to obtain a value form a string of key=value pairs
    if (!l || l=="" || !n || n=="" || !s || s=="") return "-";
    var i,i2,i3,c="-";
```

```
        i=l.indexOf(n);
        i3=n.indexOf("=")+1;
        if (i > -1) {
            i2=l.indexOf(s,i); if (i2 < 0) { i2=l.length; }
            c=l.substring((i+i3),i2);
        }
        return c;
    }

    function setHidden(f) {
        // set values for hidden form fields
        var z = _uGC(document.cookie, "utmz=",";");
        f.web_source.value = _uGC(z,"utmcsr=","|");
        f.web_medium.value = _uGC(z,"utmcmd=","|");
        f.web_term.value = _uGC(z,"utmctr=","|");
        f.web_content.value = _uGC(z,"utmcct=","|");
        f.web_campaign.value = _uGC(z,"utmccn=","|");

        var gclid = _uGC(z,"utmgclid=","|");
        if (gclid) {                            //this is an AdWords visitor
            f.web_source.value = "google";
            f.web_medium.value = "cpc";
            //It is not possible to capture AdWords campaign details by this
            //method as GA processing is required for this. Therefore the
            //following lines are set to remove confusion should a visitor
            //use multiple referrals with the last one being AdWords.

            f.web_term.value = "";              // remove previous info if any
            f.web_content.value = "";           // remove previous info if any
            f.web_campaign.value = "";          // remove previous info if any
        }
    }
</script>
```

2. Within your HTML <form> tag of the same page, add the onSubmit event handler and hidden form fields as follows:

```
<form method="post" action="formhandler.cgi"
onSubmit="setHidden(this);">
    <input type=hidden name=web_source value="">
    <input type=hidden name=web_medium value="">
    <input type=hidden name=web_term value="">
```

```
<input type=hidden name=web_content value="">
<input type=hidden name=web_campaign value="">
...etc.
</form>
```

3. If you already have an onSubmit event handler, append the setHidden(this) call:

```
<form method="post" action="formhandler.cgi"
onSubmit="validate();setHidden(this);">
```

By this method, when a visitor submits the form to your CRM or other third-party system, a call is first made to the JavaScript function setHidden(this). This routine extracts the campaign variables from the Google Analytics __utmz cookie using the function _uGC. These are stored as hidden form fields and transmitted to your CRM system with the visitor's other form data.

Although in this example only campaign variables are extracted from the cookies and passed into your application, you can use the same method to query any of the Google Analytics __utm* cookies and include their values in your import. For example, the contents of __utma contain time-stamp information on a visitor's first and previous visit as well as how many times they have visited your site in total. An example of extracting this information is described next.

Note: Even without a CRM system, you may want to use this method. For example, most formhandler scripts allow you to log the details of a form submission. Simply append the hidden form fields to your logfile.

Importing Data into Your CRM Using PHP

Similar to using client-side JavaScript to query and extract Google Analytics cookie information, as described in the previous section, you can use server-side techniques. The following is an example using PHP, developed by João Correia and first discussed at the following location:

```
http://joaocorreia.pt/blog/2009/09/google-analytics-php-cookie-
parser/#english
```

The method defines a PHP class to parse the __utma and __umtz cookie data. This class is used to provide the integration between Google Analytics and your CRM (or other third-party) application. The code is reproduced here with permission and is also available at www.advanced-web-metrics.com/chapter12.

In summary, there are two straightforward steps:

- Add standard PHP code to the page collecting the Google Analytics cookies, such as, for example, test.php.
- Add the PHP class file to your website.
- Load test.php in your browser.

To see this example working, follow these steps:

1. Place the following PHP code on the page where you wish to view the Google Analytics cookie information (for example, test.php):

```php
<?
require("class.gaparse.php");
$aux = new GA_Parse($_COOKIE);

echo "Campaign source: ".$aux->campaign_source."<br />";
echo "Campaign name: ".$aux->campaign_name."<br />";
echo "Campaign medium: ".$aux->campaign_medium."<br />";
echo "Campaign content: ".$aux->campaign_content."<br />";
echo "Campaign term: ".$aux->campaign_term."<br />";

echo "Date of first visit: ".$aux->first_visit."<br />";
echo "Date of previous visit: ".$aux->previous_visit."<br />";
echo "Date of current visit: ".$aux->current_visit_started."<br />";
echo "Times visited: ".$aux->times_visited."<br />";
?>
```

2. Place the following code in a file named class.gaparse.php in the same directory as test.php:

```php
<?
class GA_Parse
{
  var $campaign_source;        // Campaign Source
  var $campaign_name;          // Campaign Name
  var $campaign_medium;        // Campaign Medium
  var $campaign_content;       // Campaign Content
  var $campaign_term;          // Campaign Term
  var $first_visit;            // Date of first visit
  var $previous_visit;         // Date of previous visit
  var $current_visit_started;  // Current visit started at
  var $times_visited;          // Times visited

  function __construct($_COOKIE) {
      $this->utmz = $_COOKIE["__utmz"];
      $this->utma = $_COOKIE["__utma"];
      $this->ParseCookies();
  }

  function ParseCookies(){
```

```php
    // Parse __utmz cookie
    list($domain_hash,$timestamp, $session_number, $campaign_number, ➡
    $campaign_data) = split('[\.]', $this->utmz);

    // Parse the campaign data
    $campaign_data = parse_str(strtr($campaign_data, "|", "&amp;"));
    $this->campaign_source = $utmcsr;
    $this->campaign_name = $utmccn;
    $this->campaign_medium = $utmcmd;
    $this->campaign_term = $utmctr;
    $this->campaign_content = $utmcct;

if($utmgclid) {
    $this->campaign_source = "google";
    $this->campaign_name = "";
    $this->campaign_medium = "cpc";
    $this->campaign_content = "";
    $this->campaign_term = $utmctr;
}

    // Parse the __utma Cookie
    list($domain_hash,
        $random_id,
        $time_initial_visit,
        $time_beginning_previous_visit,
        $time_beginning_current_visit,
        $session_counter) = split('[\.]', $this->utma);

    $this->first_visit = date("d M Y - H:i",$time_initial_visit);
    $this->previous_visit = date("d M Y - H:i",➡
$time_beginning_previous_visit);
    $this->current_visit_started = date("d M Y - H:i",➡
$time_beginning_current_visit);
    $this->times_visited = $session_counter;
 }
}
?>
```

3. Load test.php in your browser.

You will see something similar to Figure 12.1—simple and elegant! With the Google Analytics cookie values captured, you can then pass these into your CRM system as hidden form fields or environment variables.

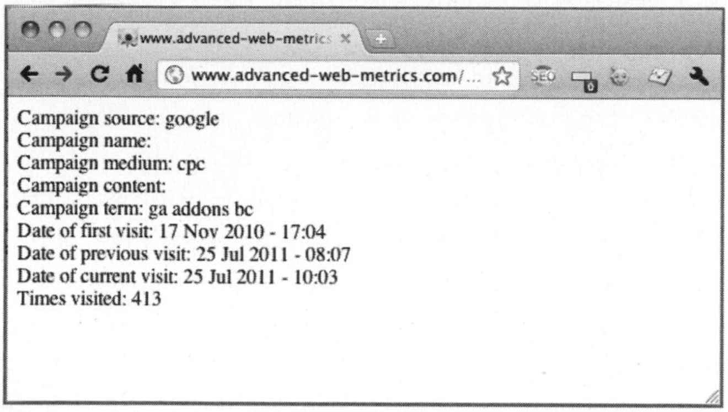

Figure 12.1 Extracting Google Analytics cookie information to import into your CRM system using PHP

Note: As per Chapter 2 and Chapter 3 (see the sections "Privacy Considerations for the Web Analytics Industry" in Chapter 2 and "Google Analytics and Privacy" in Chapter 3), you should not collect any personally identifiable information in Google Analytics—no usernames, email addresses, and such. Capturing a unique ID value at the point when a visitor is contacting you (submitting a form) is fine as long as that is transparent in your privacy statement. Using the same unique ID as your CRM system allows you to match up online submitted information from Google Analytics with your customer database.

Working with the Google Analytics Core Reporting API

The previous sections described quick and simple techniques for extracting Google Analytics cookies and importing this information into a third-party application. I will now describe how to extract *any* (and all) of your Google Analytics report data, by utilizing the Google Analytics Core Reporting application programming interface (API). The API is the basis of building your own app.

My intention is to give the reader an overview of the capabilities of the Google Analytics Core Reporting API and illustrate this with examples of what smart people around the world are doing with it. I've kept coding examples to a minimum, and I encourage you to view the online documentation at http://code.google.com/apis/analytics for detailed instructions.

The Google Analytics Core Reporting API is built on the Google Data Protocol used by many other Google services:

```
http://code.google.com/apis/gdata/docs/2.0/reference.html
```

It allows developers with the correct authorization (discussed later in this chapter) access to processed Google Analytics data. The purpose is to facilitate and propagate the use of Google Analytics data in ways the current user interface cannot provide. The Core Reporting API achieves this by allowing data to be exported without the requirement of a user interacting with the Google Analytics user interface. This provides the infrastructure for developers to build their own applications for manipulating data, whether for integrating web visitor data with other third-party systems, such as email marketing, CMS, CRM, and survey systems; providing auto-refresh functionality in Excel; producing highly customized dashboards; or creating new, innovative ways of visualizing data. The possibilities are endless. If you are trying to do something with your data that the Google Analytics interface cannot do, you can probably build an app for it—or maybe one already exists.

If you wish to see what apps are available before delving into the details of the API, skip ahead to the section "Example Apps."

Note: At present the Core Reporting API is a one-way street. That is, you can only export data from a Google Analytics account. Many users, including myself, hope that one day an import API will be made available so that third-party data can be included in the Google Analytics user interface. Possibilities include importing cost data from non-Google campaigns, allowing you to view the return on investment on all marketing activities (email, SEO, Yahoo! Search Marketing, and the like), offsite web analytics data such as social media brand mentions, and sentiment information alongside your Google Analytics onsite data.

A schematic of the Google Analytics data-querying architecture is shown in Figure 12.2. Note that this is an extension of the schematic shown in Figure 3.2 of Chapter 3, "Google Analytics Features, Benefits, and Limitations." For more information on BigTable, see `http://en.wikipedia.org/wiki/BigTable`.

To summarize the last row shown in Figure 12.2, there are currently three ways to obtain your web visitor data:

- Asking predefined questions and displaying the results in a fixed user-interface format
- Asking custom questions and displaying the results in a fixed user-interface format
- Asking custom questions that are not tied to a user interface

As you can see, whether you use the standard Google Analytics reports, custom reporting, or the Core Reporting API, all data requests go to the Google Analytics Query Engine. This lookup engine knows where to find requested information from the processed (precomputed) data tables. The secret sauce Google has created makes the query engine extremely fast and super scalable—a huge engineering achievement for a service that must handle billions of queries every day. As an aside, this is one of the key differentiators between Google Analytics and its sibling product Urchin Software. Urchin is discussed in Chapter 3.

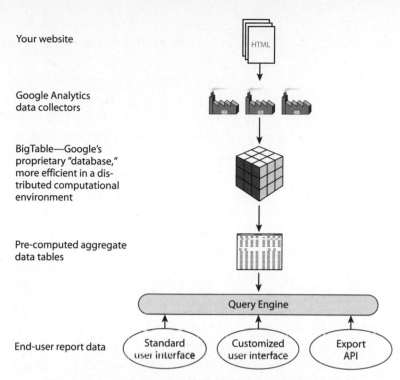

Your website

Google Analytics
data collectors

BigTable—Google's
proprietary "database,"
more efficient in a dis-
tributed computational
environment

Pre-computed aggregate
data tables

End-user report data

Figure 12.2 Schematic example of the Google Analytics Core Reporting API

At this stage it is important to realize that querying the data, by whatever method, results in a query to the processed data, that is, data that has initial computations carried out—such as time on page; whether the page is an entrance, exit, or bounce page; and whether it is a goal, part of a funnel, an event, or a transaction. The only exception to this is when building advanced segments, which results in a query to the raw (BigTable) data via the query engine.

How to Use the Core Reporting API—the Basics

The Google Analytics Core Reporting API is a REST API, meaning that its software architecture corresponds to the Representational State Transfer style. In this case, it means that you send your data request as a URL with query parameters defining the content of your "question." The Google Analytics Core Reporting API then returns an XML data feed corresponding to the "answer" of your question. See the following location for more information on the REST architecture:

    http://en.wikipedia.org/wiki/Representational_State_Transfer

The use of the REST architecture provides a straightforward, efficient process that requires knowledge of only three steps, which are discussed next:

•   Authorization

- Account query
- Report data query

Authorization

Similar to having to log in to Google Analytics, before users can view data from an application that uses the data export API, they must be granted access. The Core Reporting API requires a user to grant an application access to their data. This is achieved with a request for an authorization token from the Google Accounts API. The method prevents user credentials from being sent around the Internet for each request and is therefore more secure. Authentication takes place via the Google Accounts API only, not the Core Reporting API.

Three types of authorization services are supported:

ClientLogin username and password authentication Used for applications that run on a user's computer only, that is, not distributed to other users.

AuthSub proxy authorization Used for distributed applications. A user's username and password are never revealed to the application. Instead, the application obtains special AuthSub tokens, which it uses to act on a particular user's behalf. The end user can revoke access by the third party from their Google Account configuration page (www.google.com/accounts).

OAuth authorization Similar to AuthSub though typically used for developing an application in an environment that uses a variety of services from multiple providers.

For the purpose of simplification (more streamlined code), I consider only the ClientLogin method in this section.

To request an authorization token through ClientLogin, send a POST request to the following URL: https://www.google.com/accounts/ClientLogin. The POST body should contain a set of query parameters that appear as parameters passed by an

HTML form, using the application/x-www-form-urlencoded content type. These parameters are as follows:

- accountType: Set to GOOGLE
- Email: The full email address of the user's Google Account
- passwd: The user's Google Account password
- service: Set to analytics
- source: A string identifying your application in the form
  companyName-applicationName-versionID.

To see how straightforward communication is with the Google Analytics Core Reporting API (you do not need a degree in software programming), use the following HTML form submission to authenticate:

```
<form action="https://www.google.com/accounts/ClientLogin" Method="POST">
    <input type="hidden" name="accountType" value="GOOGLE">
    <input type="hidden" name="service" value="analytics">
    <input type="hidden" name="source" value="BClifton-testApp-1.0">
    <input type="text" name="Email" value="">
    <input type="password" name="Passwd" value="">
    <input type="submit" value="Log me in">
</form>
```

If authorization succeeds, the server returns an HTTP 200 (OK Status) code, plus three long alphanumeric codes in the body of the response: SID, LSID, and Auth. If the authorization request fails, then the server returns an HTTP 401 (Unauthorized Status) code.

While this HTML form method illustrates the simplicity of the approach, it is not very practical because you then need to cut and paste the returned token into your application! The following methods take this to the next level by handling the authentication within the script itself.

Account Query

Once your application has verified that the user has access, the next step is to find out which specific accounts the user has access to. To access the Google Analytics account feed, send an HTTP GET request to https://www.google.com/analytics/feeds/accounts/default. For this to work, you must add the authorization token to this request. Note that you cannot enter this URL via your browser address bar because the token must be inserted in the HTTP headers of the request. The following is an example of how to access the account feed through the Bourne shell using cURL (available from www.advanced-web-metrics.com/chapter12). Authorization takes place first, with the token inserted in the HTTP header of the subsequent account query.

Run the script using your preferred Linux environment—the Apple Terminal application will also suffice—and view the resulting output.

```
#!/bin/bash
USER_EMAIL="" #Insert your Google Account email here
USER_PASS="" #Insert your password here

# generate the authorization token
googleAuthToken="$(curl https://www.google.com/accounts/ClientLogin -s \
    -d Email=$USER_EMAIL \
    -d Passwd=$USER_PASS \
    -d accountType=GOOGLE \
    -d source=curl-accountFeed-v1 \
    -d service=analytics \
     | awk /Auth=.*/)"

# Feed URI
feedUri="https://www.google.com/analytics/feeds/accounts/default?➡
prettyprint=true"
# Call feedUri with the authorization token inserted into the header
curl $feedUri -s --header "Authorization: GoogleLogin $googleAuthToken"
```

Remember that users can have access to many different accounts—and within them, many different profiles. For this reason, your application cannot access any report information without first requesting the list of accounts available to the user. The resulting accounts feed returns this list. The list also contains the account profiles that the user can view. An example of the returned account and profile list is shown in Figure 12.3.

Note that the account feed request described here returns an all-or-nothing output. All account and profile information is displayed; this can be a large amount of information if the authorized user has access to many accounts and profiles. For example, Figure 12.3 is the output from a single profile, and I have access to hundreds of profiles.

To provide finer-grained control, there is a Management API. This allows you to adjust the scope of your account request—for example, only access the data from a specific profile—so that the feed response is faster and you handle data more efficiently. Further information is at the following location:

```
http://code.google.com/intl/fi-FI/apis/analytics/docs/mgmt/home.html
```

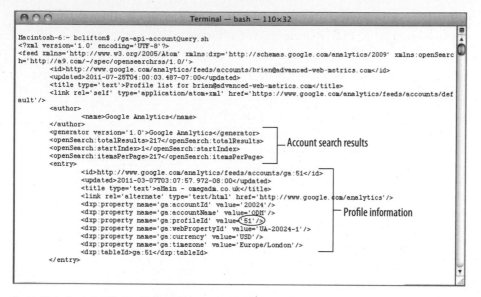

```
      ● ● ●                        Terminal — bash — 110×32
Macintosh-6:~ bclifton$ ./ga-api-accountQuery.sh
<?xml version='1.0' encoding='UTF-8'?>
<feed xmlns='http://www.w3.org/2005/Atom' xmlns:dxp='http://schemas.google.com/analytics/2009' xmlns:openSearc
h='http://a9.com/-/spec/opensearchrss/1.0/'>
        <id>http://www.google.com/analytics/feeds/accounts/brian@advanced-web-metrics.com</id>
        <updated>2011-07-25T04:00:03.487-07:00</updated>
        <title type='text'>Profile list for brian@advanced-web-metrics.com</title>
        <link rel='self' type='application/atom+xml' href='https://www.google.com/analytics/feeds/accounts/def
ault'/>
        <author>
                <name>Google Analytics</name>
        </author>
        <generator version='1.0'>Google Analytics</generator>
        <openSearch:totalResults>217</openSearch:totalResults>       ── Account search results
        <openSearch:startIndex>1</openSearch:startIndex>
        <openSearch:itemsPerPage>217</openSearch:itemsPerPage>
        <entry>
                <id>http://www.google.com/analytics/feeds/accounts/ga:51</id>
                <updated>2011-03-07T03:07:57.972-08:00</updated>
                <title type='text'>aMain - omegadm.co.uk</title>
                <link rel='alternate' type='text/html' href='http://www.google.com/analytics'/>
                <dxp:property name='ga:accountId' value='20024'/>
                <dxp:property name='ga:accountName' value='ODM'/>
                <dxp:property name='ga:profileId' value='51'/>            ── Profile information
                <dxp:property name='ga:webPropertyId' value='UA-20024-1'/>
                <dxp:property name='ga:currency' value='USD'/>
                <dxp:property name='ga:timezone' value='Europe/London'/>
                <dxp:tableId>ga:51</dxp:tableId>
        </entry>
</entry>
```

Figure 12.3 Example XML output of an API account query request

> **Note:** In the account and report query examples, JavaScript is not used because inserting the authorization token into the request HTTP header is harder to achieve. This is because JavaScript is unable to make cross-domain requests. However, a workaround for this is provided in the JavaScript client libraries available at `http://code.google.com/apis/analytics/docs/gdata/gdataLibraries.html`.

Report Query

From the list of available profiles obtained from the account query, your application can request report data. The key to this request is the profile ID for the profile obtained in the account feed (see Figure 12.3). This is the same as the profile ID number found in the user interface of the Profile Settings screen. When working with the Core Reporting API, you must specify the profile ID for each profile you require access to. You can also view a particular profile ID in the Google Analytics user interface.

The data feed provides access to all data in a selected profile. To access the Google Analytics Report Feed, send an HTTP GET request to `https://www.google.com/analytics/feeds/data`. As for the account query, you cannot achieve this using your browser address bar because the authorization token must be inserted into the HTTP headers. Authorization takes place first, with the token inserted into the HTTP header of the subsequent account query.

The following is an example of how to access the report feed through the Bourne shell using cURL (available from www.advanced-web-metrics.com/chapter12):

```bash
#!/bin/bash
USER_EMAIL="" #Insert your Google Account email address here
USER_PASS="" #Insert your password here
PROFILE_ID="" #Insert your profile ID here

# generate the authorization token
googleAuthToken="$(curl https://www.google.com/accounts/ClientLogin -s \
    -d Email=$USER_EMAIL \
    -d Passwd=$USER_PASS \
    -d accountType=GOOGLE \
    -d source=curl-accountFeed-v1 \
    -d service=analytics \
    | awk /Auth=.*/)"

# Feed URI with query parameter specifying data request
feedUri="https://www.google.com/analytics/feeds/data\
?start-date=2012-01-01\
&end-date=2012-01-31\
&dimensions=ga:source,ga:medium\
&metrics=ga:visits,ga:bounces\
&sort=-ga:visits\
&filters=ga:medium%3D%3Dreferral\
&max-results=5\
&ids=ga:$PROFILE_ID\
&prettyprint=true"

# Call feedUri with the authorization token inserted into the header
curl $feedUri -s --header "Authorization: GoogleLogin $googleAuthToken"
```

As you can see in this example, you use query parameters to indicate what analytics data you want as well as how you want it filtered and sorted. The XML output looks similar to Figure 12.3. However, rather than show this, or explain the laborious list of feed input parameters that are available, a better way to understand the usage of API report queries is via the Report Query Builder, described next.

 Note: The reference guide for dimensions and metrics can be found at http://code.google.com/apis/analytics/docs/gdata/gdataReferenceDimensionsMetrics.html.

Report Query Builder

The Google Analytics Data Feed Query Explorer lets you experiment with specifying different metrics, dimensions, filters, and so on and view the resulting query URL and corresponding data it fetches. You can try this at

http://code.google.com/apis/analytics/docs/gdata/gdataExplorer.html

The screenshot in Figure 12.4 illustrates an example of its usage. This is typically the starting point for web developers to ascertain and test their API data request calls. It enables you to understand how the query string is built and the necessary feed parameter syntax, and it is a sanity check on the results the API call returns.

Data feed URI automatically generated from your input parameters.

Data Feed URI	PermaLink		Lo

https://www.google.com/analytics/feeds/data?
ids=ga%3A2097117&dimensions=ga%3AvisitorType%2Cga%3AvisitCount%2Cga%3AdaysSinceLastVisit%2Cga%3Asource%2Cga
word%2Cga%3Amedium&metrics=ga%3Avisitors&filters=ga%3AvisitorType%3D~%5EReturn.*%3Bga%3AdaysSinceLastVisit!%3D

* ids	=	ga:2097117	aMain – AWM ▼
dimensions	=	ga:visitorType,ga:visitCount,ga:daysSinceLastVisit,ga:source,ga:keyv ▼	
* metrics	=	ga:visitors ▼	
segment	=	▼	
filters	=	ga:visitorType=~^Return.*;ga:daysSinceLastVisit!=0	
sort	=		
* start-date	=	2012–01–01	
* end-date	=	2012–01–31	
start-index	=	50	
max-results	=	25	

Select/enter your query input parameters.

Get Data Resulting data produced from the above query parameters.

ga:visitorType	ga:visitCount	ga:daysSinceLastVisit	ga:source	ga:keyword	ga:medium
Returning Visitor	11	3	diythemes.com	(not set)	referral
Returning Visitor	11	5	twitter.com	(not set)	social network
Returning Visitor	11	6	Google email signature	(not set)	Email
Returning Visitor	11	8	diythemes.com	(not set)	referral
Returning Visitor	11	8	marketmotive.com	(not set)	referral
Returning Visitor	113	1	feedburner	(not set)	social network
Returning Visitor	118	2	SES London 2011	(not set)	print
Returning Visitor	12	1	(direct)	(not set)	(none)
Returning Visitor	12	1	Google email signature	(not set)	Email
Returning Visitor	12	1	analytics.blogspot.com	(not set)	social network

Figure 12.4 Example Report Query Builder

There is a great deal more to the Google Analytics Core Reporting API, and I have covered only the foundations here. An entire book can easily be dedicated to its use. However, my intention is to whet your appetite so that you can further explore its possibilities. Once you understand the principles involved, a good reference place is the API Client Libraries & Sample Code found at

`http://code.google.com/apis/analytics/docs/gdata/gdataLibraries.html`

The API is still a beta product (referred to as "Labs" by Google), and so exact syntax is still fluid. Refer to the Google Code site as necessary: `http://code.google.com/apis/analytics`.

In summary, the Core Reporting API provides the opportunity for anyone to be innovative and creative with web visitor data. Often web measurement is considered a dry subject, which it certainly can be. Features such as motion charts, described in Chapter 5, "Reports Explained," go some way in improving the situation, but even Google cannot think of everything. The Google Analytics Core Reporting API is your chance to change that. Don't be afraid of experimenting—applying a little lateral thinking and imagination can even surprise Google!

API Quota Policy

There is currently a quota policy in place to protect the robustness of the API system. When you create and register a new project in the Google APIs Console, you are given a unique client ID to identify each application under that project. Note that all the applications under a single project share any per project limits. For unregistered applications, Google provides a very low grace quota to accommodate a small amount of testing.

General Analytics API quotas

These apply to both the Management API and Core Reporting API.

- 50,000 requests per project per day

- 10 queries per second (QPS) per IP

Quotas specific to the Core Reporting API

- 10,000 requests per profile per day

- 10 concurrent requests per profile

When an account has exceeded its quota, an authorized request for a feed results in an HTTP 503 (Service Unavailable) response, with a message in the body of the response indicating that the specific account has insufficient quota to proceed.

Example Apps

The following are example applications of cool things people are doing with the Google Analytics Core Reporting API. Most of these are freely available or operate on a *freemium* basis (free with upgrade options). The ones listed here are those that I have personally used and found to be particularly creative and innovative. A more complete list of over one hundred API apps is found at www.google.com/analytics/apps/. Those marked with an asterisk (*) are presented in the next section as case studies written in conjunction with the original developers.

Note: From a security, data privacy, and credibility viewpoint, only use third-party API applications that authenticate your Google Analytics account either with AuthSub or OAuth authorization. This ensures that your login details cannot be revealed to the application or any third party. If you are building your own app, or the app is a download that you have complete trust in and works only on your computer, the ClientLogin authorization method is fine. If in doubt, ask the developers directly. The authentication techniques used by applications listed in this book have not been verified.

Excel and Google spreadsheets

*AutomateAnalytics.com is a suite of macro functions for Microsoft Excel and Google Spreadsheets. The functions allow you to import your Google Analytics data into Excel or Google Spreadsheets via the Core Reporting API. This allows you to, for example, automatically refresh KPI tables and expand on the visualization options offered within Google Analytics. As an alternative to plug-ins, it is virtually version independent, can operate faster, and allows the end user to experiment with modifications. Further information is available at http://awm .automateanalytics.com.

Tatvic uses an alternative plug-in approach to import Google Analytics data into Excel. The tool comes with a three-step wizard to simplify the process and works on Windows XP and above with Microsoft Office 2003 onward. Further information is available at www.gaexcelplugin.tatvic.com.

Excellent Analytics is an alternative free, open-source, plug-in for Excel 2007 and later running on Windows. Designed with ordinary analysts, marketers, and salespeople in mind, it requires the minimum amount of technical knowledge to use. Further information is available at http://excellentanalytics.com.

Survey tools

*Kampyle is an online feedback analytics platform that allows website owners to create their own advanced, branded, and customized feedback forms and put them on their websites. When it's integrated with the Google Analytics Core Reporting API, visitor feedback information is combined with Google Analytics geographic, visitor-loyalty, exit-page, and landing-page information. The result provides a more holistic picture of website performance—combining the "what" with the "why." Further information is available at www.kampyle.com/page/website-feedback-google-analytics.

Custom apps

Youcalc connects to the Google Analytics Core Reporting API to provide custom analytics applications that run in iGoogle, the iPhone, intranets, and blogs—pretty much anywhere. The applications allow you to access and analyze live Google Analytics data without opening Google Analytics. You can build custom applications on live data without coding, and mesh data from AdWords or salesforce.com into one analytics application. Further information is available at www.youcalc.com/solutions/webanalytics.

ShufflePoint integrates Google Analytics with Microsoft Excel, PowerPoint, and Google Gadgets using its own powerful query language (GAQL) and a drag-and-drop query builder. Within Excel, you can associate web queries with spreadsheet ranges with refreshable GAQL queries—no add-ins or macros required. Similarly, for PowerPoint you can associate slide placeholders with GAQL queries. By using iGoogle, you can build your own Google Analytics dashboard. The ShufflePoint approach is encapsulated as "design once, refresh automatically." Further information is available at www.shufflepoint.com.

Bime is a powerful business intelligence (BI), data visualization tool provided as a software-as-a-service application. It provides a Google Analytics connector that allows you to retrieve, analyze, and visualize your analytics data using the Bime computing engine. Further information is available at www.bimeanalytics.com/solution/web-analytics.

Publishing

Google Analyticator automatically adds Google Analytics tracking to a WordPress-powered blog without the user needing to modify their website code. It comes with a customizable widget that can be used to display specific information gathered by Google Analytics. It supports all of the tracking mechanisms that Google Analytics supports, such as external link tracking, download tracking, tracking without counting administrative users, and any other advanced tracking the user wishes to add. Further information is available at http://wordpress.org/extend/plugins/google-analyticator/

pimcore is an advanced, open-source content-management system (CMS). It is used for creating and managing digital content, assets, and structured objects. With a strong online marketing focus, Google Analytics, Website Optimizer, and Webmaster Tools are integrated in to the CMS back end for centralized use. Further information is available at www.pimcore.org.

Data visualization

GAVisual is an innovative path visualization tool that allows you to understand the path people take through your site in an easy-to-follow and interactive format (for example, 21 percent of people who viewed page A went on to view page B, followed by page N, and so forth). Further information is available at http://gavisual.info.

Trendly is a monitoring and visualization tool that enables you to easily see what's changed in your Google Analytics data. Trendly uses mathematical models to take noisy data and figure out when significant changes have happened. It prepares a news feed with attractive charts that put the changes into perspective relative to everything else that's going on. Further information is available at http://trendly.com.

Email marketing

MailChimp's Analytics360 tool allows you to track the ROI of email marketing campaigns. Integration with Google Analytics gives a detailed report that shows how much revenue each campaign generates as customers click from email to website and make purchases. Email campaign reports include completed goals, value per transaction, and total ROI. Further information is available at www.mailchimp.com/features/google-analytics.

Search marketing

WordStream is a keyword-management solution that provides search marketers with integrated keyword tools for discovering, researching, analyzing, organizing, prioritizing, and acting on keyword data within their PPC and SEO campaigns. The latest version of WordStream integrates with both Google AdWords and Google Analytics. It automatically augments your existing keyword research every day with new, highly relevant keyword opportunities. WordStream also integrates your Google Analytics goal-tracking data so you can build on your initial keyword list and better understand which keyword niches are actually working (or not) on your site. Further information is available at www.wordstream.com/blog/ws/2009/11/10/future-keyword-research.

Benchmarking

SeeTheStats allows you to publish your Google Analytics data publicly—without the need for users to authenticate. Why do this? SeeTheStats is aimed at publishers wishing to be transparent to their advertisers. That is, you can view traffic levels before you purchase an ad. You can also search for other participating websites and view their traffic for comparison. Further information is available at www.seethestats.com.

Example App Case Studies

The following case studies were provided by the creators of the solutions in question—all of whom are cited—and edited by me.

Excel and Spreadsheet Integration

While Google Analytics offers a wide range of possibilities for reporting, there are many situations where additional analysis needs to be conducted elsewhere. These situations include analyzing multiple metrics and dimensions at once, merging Google Analytics metrics with data from other sources, and simultaneously analyzing a large number of accounts and profiles. For the majority of people, the most convenient platform for this kind of additional analysis is Microsoft Excel or Google Spreadsheets.

There are several ways of importing data from Google Analytics into Excel. Most obvious is the Google Analytics built-in Excel export. However, this process has to be done manually for each report set and profile. Following the introduction of the Core Reporting API, several solutions have been developed that involve installing Excel plug-ins. Mikael Thuneberg has developed an alternative approach.

Thuneberg's alternative method is to attach code containing custom functions directly to a spreadsheet. These functions use the spreadsheet's native scripting languages—Visual Basic for Applications (VBA) for Excel and Google Apps Script for Google Spreadsheets—though for both the code is hidden to the end user (in fact not required by end users). This method allows the functions to be used in the workbook just as any other of the spreadsheet's built-in functions, such as SUM, AVERAGE, and COUNT. Reports can also easily be shared with other Excel users or Google Spreadsheets users, who can refresh their data or modify queries without the need to install anything.

The Excel version of this solution works in Microsoft Office for Windows versions 2003 and later (the commercial, that is, paid-for version also supports Excel on Mac OS X). You'll need to enable macros in the application settings. While using the functions is naturally easiest and most convenient in Excel, they also work in other Microsoft Office applications. Therefore, with some programming skills, it is also possible to create PowerPoint presentations that are always up-to-date or to import Google Analytics data into an Access database.

Instructions for Working with the Functions

Basic spreadsheet skills are required to use the Thuneberg functions—no knowledge of VBA or Google Apps Script is needed. You will of course need to learn the various data feed parameters for use with the functions, as shown in the section "Report Query Builder" earlier in this chapter, and how to input array formulas in Excel—that is, formulas that fill more than one cell simultaneously, as described next.

The template file, `GA_data_fetch.xls`, has the necessary code already attached, so after enabling macros when the file opens within Excel, you can use it straight away. You can also view examples of the functions in use from within the file.

To use the functions, the first thing you need to do is to authenticate with Google Analytics. Here is how to do the authentication in Excel using the `getGAauthenticationToken` function. This function uses the ClientLogin method to authenticate with Google. Note that because you are running the template file within your own software, Excel, and not sharing it via a third-party server, the authentication method (ClientLogin) is correct for this application. To use this function, type the following into a spreadsheet cell:

```
=getGAauthenticationToken ("email","password")
```

The two parameters are your email address and password (within double quotes) to log in to your Google Analytics account. This function returns the authentication token. This has been done for you in cell D25. Note that double quotes are not required when grabbing the username and password via a cell reference, for example, D14 and D15.

For importing data, use the `getGAdata` function to generate a report query by typing the following into a cell:

```
=getGAdata(token,profile number,metrics,start date,end date,filters,➡
dimensions,sort)
```

The following list describes the fields used (left to right):

token Type the address of the cell where you have typed the authentication function. Note that in the Google Spreadsheets version, this is not used because the authentication process differs from Excel.

profile number Type the ID number of the profile from which you want data. You can obtain this from your Google Analytics admin area.

metrics Type the metrics you want to fetch, for example, **visits** or **visits&pageviews**.

start date and end date Type the start and end dates of the period from which you want data. Typing dates can be cumbersome because of the various date formats. The easiest way is to write the dates in separate cells and put references to those cells here.

filters (optional) If you want to include, for example, US visits only, type country==United States. If this field is left blank, data for all visits is fetched.

dimensions (optional) If you want to split the data by traffic source and medium, for example, type source&medium. If this field is left blank, the function fetches the site totals.

sort (optional) By default, the results are shown in alphabetical order. If you'd rather sort by the metric, type TRUE here.

The getGAdata function makes a report query through the Google Analytics Core Reporting API and returns the data to the spreadsheet. If you have included just one metric and have not included any dimensions, then you can simply write this function to a single cell and the function will return the value to that one cell—this is shown in cell Z25 of GA_data_fetch.xls. If you have used multiple metrics or included dimensions, the results will not fit into a single cell. Therefore, you need to input the function as an array formula. While Google Docs does this for you automatically, in Excel you need to follow these steps:

1. Select a range of cells.
2. Click the formula bar and write the function there.
3. Press Ctrl+Shift+Enter (simultaneously) on Windows or Cmd+Shift+Enter if using a Mac.

The function will now fill the range of cells with the query results. This is shown in the cell range AG25–AJ35 of GA_data_fetch.xls.

Usage Examples

The use cases for these functions range from ad hoc analysis to elaborate dashboards that integrate data from Google Analytics and other sources. Here are some examples of common situations where the functions can help:

Custom dashboards As discussed in Chapter 10, "Focusing on Key Performance Indicators," it is not realistic to expect senior managers or executives to log in to Google Analytics directly. Therefore, building a custom dashboard in a spreadsheet that automatically refreshes itself can be of enormous benefit. The dashboard can easily be shared throughout an organization because it does not require additional installs to be able to use it.

Merging data from multiple profiles Google Analytics currently cannot easily compare or sum metrics from different profiles—unless you open multiple browser windows or use the roll-up reporting method described in Chapter 6. These functions allow you to automate this by typing the ID numbers of the profiles into one column and getGAdata functions pointing to those profile numbers into another column.

Merging Google Analytics metrics with other data As an example, perhaps you know the cost of email marketing and would like to calculate the *cost per visit* from *email* for your site. Currently Google Analytics imports cost data only from AdWords and AdSense. However, by merging Google Analytics email visit data with data from your email marketing tool, this calculation becomes straightforward. You can calculate the return on investment for your email marketing right down to a per-campaign basis.

Innovative visualization methods By importing data into a spreadsheet, you can take advantage of its wide range of visualization features. One advanced example of using the functions is shown next.

Innovative Visualization Methods

While Google Analytics users with very basic Excel skills can get great value from using the functions to automate data importing, people with more advanced skills can use them to make advanced reporting applications. For example, Mikael Thuneberg has created an application that illustrates how different Google Analytics metrics change over time, so you can quickly get a comprehensive view of how a site's traffic, usage, and sales are developing. Figure 12.5 shows how the country breakdown of traffic to a website has varied.

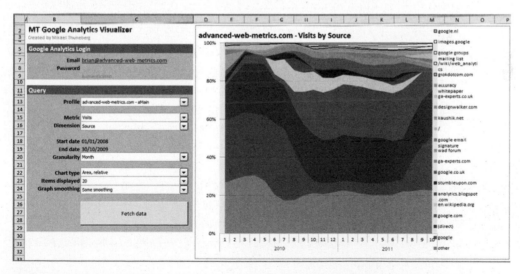

Figure 12.5 A visualization of Google Analytics data using Excel and the export API (also shown in the color insert)

The purpose of this example is to show that with some basic Excel and VBA skills, it is possible to quickly create valuable reporting applications using these spreadsheet functions. Excel includes a wide range of data illustration and analysis features that can be accessed programmatically.

Survey Tools: Voice of Customer Integration

Kampyle (www.kampyle.com) is an online feedback analytics platform that allows website owners to create their own advanced branded and customized feedback forms and put them on their sites for the benefit of their users. Website visitors can quickly and simply submit their feedback with a general grade, feedback category, subcategory, text description, and the contact details. Visitors access the feedback form through the use of a non-invasive feedback button, which can be placed in various locations on the web page.

Once visitors submit feedback, it is processed to provide a high-level management view of the data and its context. Through advanced, automated analysis, the Kampyle dashboard helps website owners get the overview and perspective needed to improve their site. The system provides the qualitative "why" visitors do what they do, to complement the "what" and "when" provided by web analytics tools such as Google Analytics. Clearly, integrating Kampyle feedback data with Google Analytics provides a more complete picture of website performance.

The Integration Approach

By using the Google Analytics Core Reporting API, a fuller, more intelligent integration of data coming from two different sources—Kampyle feedback surveys and Google Analytics visit data—is achieved. It provides the freedom to use smart business logic to supply greater insights and display combined data in the most effective way possible. Using the Core Reporting API, data can be manipulated from both sources to create intelligent reports and alerts that would let website owners know when something requires their attention.

The Kampyle system queries the client's Google Analytics information once per day. Reports on geographic distribution information, visitor loyalty, top exit pages, and top landing pages are incorporated into the Kampyle feedback data. An example of this is shown in Figure 12.6.

Top exit and landing pages hold special importance for website owners because they are where users first arrive and where they leave from. Information on these pages can be invaluable for a website owner's efforts to bring users to the website and keep them there for as long as possible (or necessary). Google Analytics is responsible for identifying the pages to which most visitors first arrive at the site (landing pages) and the pages from which most users leave a site (exit pages). For each of these pages, Kampyle can tell a website owner the average feedback grade as well as the most reported issue. A simple drill-down procedure then allows the website owner to review all the feedback received on a specific landing or exit page.

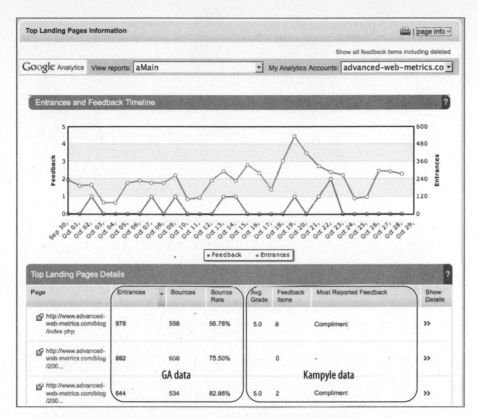

Figure 12.6 Integrated landing page data from Google Analytics and Kampyle feedback

Demographics within Google Analytics

Demographics are the characteristics of a population, in this case website visitors. Common demographics include gender, race, age, disabilities, mobility, home ownership, employment status, income level, and so forth. Having read this far into the book, you will know that Google Analytics shows visitor reports in anonymous and aggregate form. That means no personally identifiable information is collected and that data is grouped rather than presented on a per-visitor basis (see Chapter 2 and Chapter 3 for more reading on this). This is a best-practice approach for end-user privacy and is the law in many parts of the world. However, also knowing anonymous, aggregate demographic information of your visitors can be very insightful for page and campaign optimization.

For example, having demographic information can help you answer the following questions:

- What is the gender distribution of visitors to my site?
- How do different age groups convert?
- What demographic target groups are spending the most money on my site?
- How does a visitor's education level affect engagement?

Because Google Analytics doesn't have demographic information available to it, a third-party integration tool is required. UserReport is one such tool (www.userreport.com).

UserReport is a usability survey tool that allows you to augment its default set of questions with your own survey. By deploying a few lines of JavaScript code on your site, you can invite visitors to participate in a survey. If a visitor agrees, a fixed set of usability questions are asked in a pop-over window: Is this website easy to navigate? Is the information logically organized? Is the information useful and up-to-date? In addition, demographic questions are asked: Are you male or female? What is your age? Are you employed or not? What is your education level? These questions are fixed, that is, they show to every participating visitor and cannot be edited. If you wish, you can then display your own set of survey questions.

UserReport does have its own reporting suite for you to analyze participant responses. However, the clever approach that has been adopted is to integrate survey data with Google Analytics by using custom variables. The use of custom variables is the technique used to label your visitors in Google Analytics and is detailed in "Labeling Visitors, Sessions and Pages" in Chapter 9, "Google Analytics Customizations." Essentially, UserReport allows you to import your visitors' demographic information from your survey into your Google Analytics account by assigning the demographic values captured to Google Analytics custom variables. Only anonymous demographic information is transferred. The result is the ability to tie visitor demographics to your website performance. An example dashboard is shown in Figure 12.7.

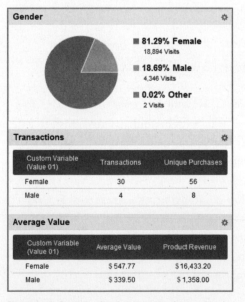

Figure 12.7 Demographic data integrated into a Google Analytics dashboard

Call Tracking with Google Analytics

Telephone calls are still an important call to action for a nontransactional commercial website. This is particularly so when an ID is required before a sale can be completed, such as, for example, within the finance industry. However, this contact point is rarely tracked, and even when it is, the data is often siloed and not part of the web analytics reports, where it can be compared against other forms of lead generation. Recently a number of vendors have started to address this issue by integrating call tracking with web analytics tools—most notably, Google Analytics.

The following system and process information was provided by Infinity Tracking Ltd., reproduced here with permission, with thanks to Paul Walsh (`www.infinity-tracking.com/awm`). The following summarizes its methodology.

The Infinity system tracks visitors who place a call after viewing your web pages. It achieves this by first capturing and then resending the original Google Analytics uniqueID (visitor ID) back to Google Analytics as a virtual pageview request when the call is made (routed through Infinity's call management servers). Each call received can then be tracked back to specific visitor activity—for example, search engine keywords from organic or paid search campaigns.

Because the same visitor ID is used for the virtual pageview call, duplicate visits are not generated, and the session appears continuous as far as Google Analytics is concerned. The virtual pageview technique is discussed in "_trackPagview: the Google Analytics Workhorse" in Chapter 7, "Advanced Implementation." The Infinity methodology is as follows:

- A JavaScript code snippet is pasted onto all pages.

- The phone number displayed on your site needs to be text (not an image), with an HTML class surrounding the number so that the Infinity code can change it dynamically—for example, `<h2 class="infinity">1-800-123-4567</h2>`.

- When a visitor lands on your site, the Infinity JavaScript waits until the Google Analytics uniqueID is available in the __utma cookie and then performs an API request to the Infinity Number Allocation Service (NAS).

- A new Infinity visitor ID number is generated and stored as a cookie along with the visitor's referral source and Google Analytics uniqueID.

- The NAS allocates a unique tracking phone number from a pool to the visitor ID, returns it to the visitor's browser for display on the page they are viewing, and logs the time of the pageview along with the phone number allocated. The unique phone number lasts the duration of the visit and for 30 minutes after (approximately 99 percent accurate at matching calls back to the visitor).

- The JavaScript code performs a find and replace in the HTML to dynamically replace the static phone number with the unique tracking phone number.
- When the phone number is called, Infinity's call servers log the call information and perform a look-back to see who was the last visitor ID to be allocated that number.
- For each phone call received, the Infinity service generates a virtual pageview request to Google Analytics using the referral source and medium of that visitor's landing page and the original Google Analytics uniqueID.

Sample results of what call tracking looks like in your Google Analytics account are shown in Figure 12.8.

Other Call Tracking Vendors

In addition to Infinity Tracking, which operates in the United States, the UK, and Canada, other Google Analytics phone-tracking solutions exist from vendors:

ClickPath (US)

http://clickpath.com

Mongoose Metrics LLC (US)

www.mongoosemetrics.com/solutions-web-analytics.php

AdCallTracker (UK)

www.adcalltracker.com

Calltracks (UK)

www.calltracks.com

AdInsight (UK)

www.adinsight.eu

ifbyphone.com (US)

http://public.ifbyphone.com/services/google-analytics-call-tracking

CallTrackID (UK)

www.freshegg.com/call-track-id.htm

As yet, no global provider exists for this approach, that is, one that can provide telephone numbers for multiple countries and integrate them with Google Analytics.

Figure 12.8 Call tracking data showing which referral sources and mediums led to a phone call

Video on Demand Tracking with Google Analytics

Video on Demand (VoD) systems allow users to select and watch video when they wish, as opposed to scheduled TV. In the United States, such systems are popular with cable TV operators because they have the necessary bandwidth to provide fast network access to their content. Given the expensive and nascent interactive cable TV capabilities, the challenge for a client using VoD, that is, the TV advertiser, is measuring the success of such *offline* campaigns.

The following case study was provided by iDimension (www.idimension.com), a US Google Analytics Certified Partner, and Liquidus (http://liquidus.net), a producer of commercial video ads for TV advertisers. With thanks to John Babb of iDimension.

> **Note:** Tracking offline marketing, including TV, is discussed in Chapter 11, "Real-World Tasks."

For this example, the TV advertiser is a global employment provider wishing to serve job opportunity videos on demand via cable TV in markets all over the United States. The cable TV operator was able to report video viewing activity but unable to track the call to action—the completion of an online job application form.

The solution was to present a unique job code at the end of each video, with a call to action to send a text message (SMS) with the unique job code to a mobile short code for more information. Sending that text message generated an automatic reply text to the candidate with a short URL to a full job description and online application form. Google Analytics allowed for the cost-effective recording and reporting of these interactions. The process is described in full next and is illustrated with a schematic flow chart in Figure 12.9.

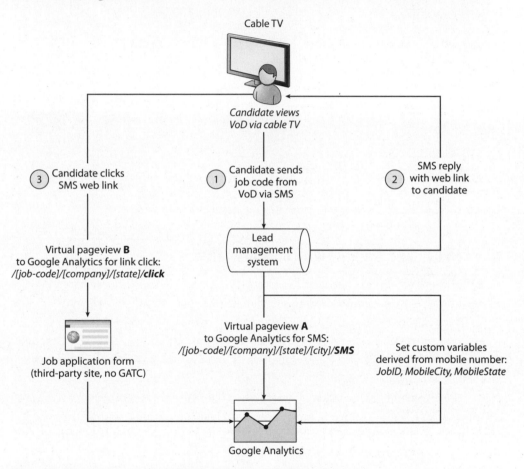

Figure 12.9 Schematic flow chart illustrating the tracking process for Video on Demand

The SMS message sent by the candidate in response to the call to action triggers sending virtual pageview A to Google Analytics. The data recorded in this virtual pageview references all of the job details for the job code in the video and confirms the delivery of the SMS message by the candidate. Additionally, the mobile number of the candidate is translated into the city and state related to the area code and recorded relative to the job code using Google Analytics custom variables. Note that the mobile number itself is not stored, per Google Analytics terms of use regarding personally identifiable information.

If the candidate clicks the short URL in the automatic reply SMS message, they browse to an intermediate web page and virtual pageview B is sent to Google Analytics before routing the visitor to the job application form hosted on a third-party site (Monster.com). The data recorded in this virtual pageview references all of the job details for the job code in the video and confirms the click of the short URL by the candidate. Figure 12.10 shows the results in Google Analytics.

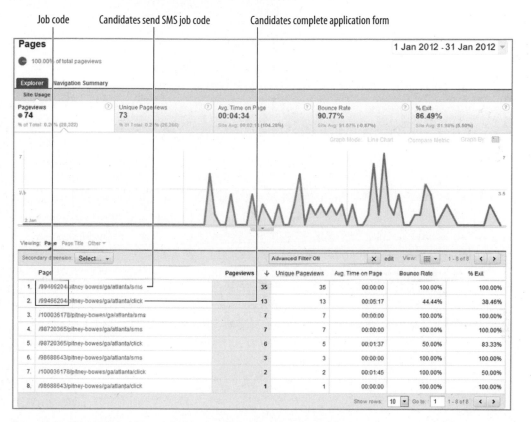

Figure 12.10 Video on Demand report showing the calls to action as virtual pageviews

The report shown in Figure 12.10 allowed the video ad producer to demonstrate to their advertising client the actual impact of VoD employment opportunities relative to the market viewing activity reported by the cable TV operators.

The Google Analytics reports show which job codes in which markets are generating text messages by candidates. In addition, they report the number of clicks to view job applications and ultimately job application submissions. The custom variable technique allows for supplemental reporting of the mobile city and state of the job candidate against the location of their job of interest. This provides an understanding of the distances candidates are prepared to travel or move for a job.

> **Note:** You may have noticed that the VoD technique described here does not create or maintain a Google Analytics uniqueID (the visitor's ID number). Hence, the two virtual pageview calls to capture data from the external sources (SMS sent and short URL clicked on) are reported as two new unique visitors in Google Analytics, which of course they are not. Compared to the challenge of tracking VoD, this is a minor point. However, for completeness, a separate profile should be used for this data.

Mobile App Tracking with Google Analytics

An app is a lightweight application tailored to a device's form factor and input-output interfaces (such as a keypad, touchpad, remote control, or display). In many cases, apps are replacing browsers as a way of connecting to the Internet and interacting with content. Initially, the growth in app usage was driven by the phenomenal success of the iPhone—some 350,000 apps were available at the iPhone App Store as of May 2011. These days, Android devices and iPads are adding to this growth—BusinessInsider.com reported that the Andriod market hit 250,000+ apps in March 2011. With so many apps available and so much usage of them (see the sidebar "How Today's Mobile Consumers Access Content"), it is becoming increasingly important to track and understand how users interact with mobile applications—beyond standard application downloads.

> ### How Today's Mobile Consumers Access Content
>
> There are two ways mobile users access online content—using a web browser or via apps. According the *comScore 2010 Mobile Year in Review*, even though apps receive more media attention, the distribution of usage is split fairly evenly. For example, 36 percent of mobile-phone-using Americans and 29 percent of Europeans browsed the mobile web in December 2010, while app access reached 34 percent and 28 percent respectively.
>
> According to the *AdMob February 2010 Survey*, Android and iPhone users spend 79 to 80 minutes per day using apps and download approximately nine new apps per month (eight for free, one paid for).
>
> According to mobile analytics provider *Flurry Analytics World Fact Book*, 33 percent (17.2 million) of the entire UK population over 13 years of age used a mobile app in May 2011.

While tracking a visitor who has come to your website via a mobile browser is no different from tracking one who has come from a regular browser, the challenge of tracking app usage is that they do not render HTML pages. You therefore cannot simply add the GATC to an app "page" and collect visitor data. Instead, virtual pageviews or events are coded into the app using one of the Google Analytics software development kits (SDKs). Two versions of the SDK are available—for Android and Apple iOS devices—and they currently support the following features:

- Pageview tracking
- Event tracking
- E-commerce tracking
- Custom variables

Note: Google Analytics SDKs are available for Android and Apple iOS from `http://code.google.com/mobile/analytics/docs/`.

The following case study was provided by Hanson Inc. (`www.hansoninc.com`), a US Google Analytics Certified Partner, and Merillat (`www.merillat.com`), a producer of kitchen cabinets. With thanks to James Bake of Hanson Inc.

Merillat, one of the largest kitchen cabinet manufacturers in the United States, positions itself as being both fun and functional. As part of its brand positioning, Merillat developed a mobile application to assist the kitchen user—the Merillat Kitchen Helper app. The purpose of the app is to help you easily find ingredient substitutions for commonly used items without leaving the kitchen! The Search by Category interface lets you find substitutions, adjust amounts, and save items you commonly use to your favorites. See Figure 12.11.

Figure 12.11 The Merillat Kitchen Helper App uses Google Analytics to track usage and engagement.

As part of the process for developing this app, a key requirement was being able to track the value of the investment in building it. For example, in addition to basic metrics such as number of visits, session length, bounce rate, and unique visitors, it was especially important to also understand user interaction—that is, users' selections of the Ingredient Substitution and Measurement Conversion tools from the main screen as well as corresponding interactions within each specific tool. The developers used the Google Analytics SDK for iOS to achieve this.

The Google Analytics SDK for iOS provides a complete solution for interacting with Google Analytics from iPhone, iPad, or iPod Touch applications. The SDK aligns to the startup to shutdown life cycle of an app. Once the initialization is complete, single method calls placed throughout the app track pageviews or events, as described next.

Initializing the Google Analytics tracker is a straightforward matter of using the sharedTracker function. This is placed in the UIApplicationDelegate, didFinishLaunchingWithOptions: method, providing your account ID and a dispatch period. The dispatch period is the time between connections to Google Analytics servers. Batching data hits together conserves battery life and connection time. Worth noting is that all tracking calls made while the user is offline are batched and released when connectivity is available. For the Merillat Kitchen Helper app, it was decided to dispatch batches every 30 seconds. An example of the initialization, written in Objective-C, is shown here:

```
#define kGANAccountId @"UA-XXXXXXXX-X"
#define kGANDispatchPeriodSec 30

- (BOOL)application:(UIApplication *)application➡
didFinishLaunchingWithOptions:(NSDictionary *)launchOptions {

// Override point for customization after application launch.

// Start the GA tracker
[[GANTracker sharedTracker] startTrackerWithAccountID:kGANAccountId➡
dispatchPeriod:kGANDispatchPeriodSec➡
delegate:nil];

//remaining code...

return YES;
}
```

For this app, all tracking was achieved using the trackEvent method.

In the proceeding example the event is triggered when a user touches a UIButton to save an ingredient substitution to their favorites list. The label parameter is the name of the ingredient, allowing Merillat to review the most popular ingredients selected in the app:

```
NSLog(@"GA: Save Ingredient to Favorites");
NSError *error;
if (![[GANTracker sharedTracker] trackEvent:@"Save Ingredient to
Favorites"➡
                                    action:@"Saved"
                                     label:ingredient.Name
                                     value:-1
                                 withError:&error]) {
    NSLog(@"GA Error: %@", error);
}
```

Most of the events tracked in the Kitchen Helper app are triggered when the
user touches a UIButton. These include converting units of measurement, conducting
searches for ingredients, and performing ingredient substitutions. For temperature
conversion, the user drags a UISlider that constantly updates values displayed on the
screen. The event for this is triggered when the view containing the slider is loaded.

A dashboard performance report for the app is shown in Figure 12.12. As a
result of the custom modifications to the Google Analytics SDK, Merillat is able to
review the number of app interactions and the level of engagement—such as tool selection (Ingredient Substitution versus Measurement Conversion) and top substitutions.
A potential future enhancement is to compare metrics with its website as a whole,
particularly geolocation information, to understand if there is a correlation between
potential customers to the store and app usage.

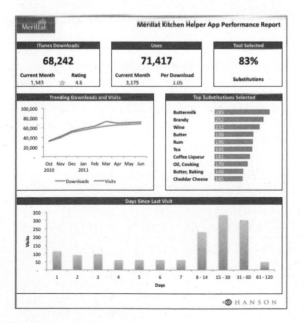

Figure 12.12 The Merillat Kitchen Helper app used
Google Analytics to track usage and engagement.

Integrating Website Optimizer with Google Analytics

An introduction to Google Website Optimizer is provided in Chapter 11, "Real-World Tasks," along with two case studies that show how, by testing alternatives, you can quickly optimize a page for better conversions—without guesswork; that is, using your visitors and customers as experiments. Ensure that you are familiar with the terminology and methods described in Chapter 11 before reading this section.

While Website Optimizer is a great page-testing tool on its own, it may not have escaped your attention that results are very black and white. That is, a conversion either happens or it doesn't—the alternative headlines, layouts, images, and so on that produce the greatest uplift in conversion are considered the winner. There is no halfway house. But what if your conversion metric is not so clear-cut? For example, maybe your test objective is to reduce a page's bounce rate, increase a visitor's time on page, or increase its $ Index value. For this, you need to integrate Website Optimizer with Google Analytics and bring in the additional metrics that Google Analytics has to offer.

Following is a summary of benefits when integrating Google Analytics with Website Optimizer:

- With Google Analytics, additional metrics become available for your test analysis, such as bounce rate, time on page, time on site, and revenue.

- You can segment data in any way available to Google Analytics, such as, for example, a breakdown of test visits and conversions based on source or medium or a breakdown based on visitor type (new or returning visitor). Website Optimizer currently has no segmenting abilities.

- You can measure additional conversion goals. Maybe the test you are running involves more than the single conversion defined in your Website Optimizer account. Google Analytics has the ability to measure up to 20 different goals.

- You are able to view the number of test visits or conversions for any time frame, such as, for example, what happened last month versus this month. On its own, Website Optimizer considers visits from when the experiment is created, with no time-frame comparison.

The listed benefits are particularly helpful when you wish to test both micro-conversions and macro-conversions. Micro-conversions are the individual funnel steps that lead to a macro-conversion. For example, a micro-conversion could be how many people add a product to their shopping cart, how many of these go on to the next funnel step—your delivery details page, for example—and so forth. The macro-conversion for this process is how many people complete the checkout process, that is, become customers. Nontransactional sites work in the same way if they have funnel steps prior to reaching a goal conversion, such as, for example, subscription sign-up or contact form completion.

If you use Website Optimizer in isolation, then you have to choose which one of these actions is defined as the test conversion and used as the benchmark for experiment success. By definition, if both micro- and macro-conversions are important, you would need to create two or more experiments. Unless you have very high traffic levels, a macro-conversion with many alternatives to test may take several months to produce statistically significant results. The advantage of combining with Google Analytics is that you can measure both the micro-conversion (add to cart) and the macro-conversion (make a purchase) simultaneously. This allows you to quickly identify alternatives that are underperforming and stop serving them—even before you have enough data on the macro-conversion for that alternative.

The Integration Method

When using Website Optimizer, you need to address two issues in order to integrate with Google Analytics:

- Generate a unique tracking URL for each test variation so alternatives can be analyzed in Google Analytics—using a separate profile.
- Tidy up Google Analytics reports so existing profile data tracks all test variations as a single page.

As you can see, the second point appears to contradict the first. However, the purpose is to first separate out the different Website Optimizer test combinations for analysis. This detail is not required in your main Google Analytics profile. Therefore, in order to maintain report simplicity, alternative test URLs are recombined in your main profile so that you receive an aggregate report for the single test page.

The approach adopted is to insert your Website Optimizer variation number into the Google Analytics tracking call. Note that you should employ this technique only when running multivariate tests. It is not required if you are running an A/B split test (or A/B/C/D ...) because each alternative already has its own unique URL.

Further Details on This Approach

This technique is discussed in *The Techie Guide to Google Website Optimizer*, coauthored by Ophir Prusak at

www.google.com/websiteoptimizer/techieguide.pdf

and as a blog post at

www.roirevolution.com/blog/2008/05/using-website-optimizer-with-google-analytics-new.php

Thanks go to Jeremy Aube of ROI Revolution for help with updating this section. Credit for coding examples goes to Eric Vasilik at

www.gwotricks.com/2009/02/poor-mans-gwoanalytics-integration.html

Generating Unique URLs for Each Multivariate Test

Website Optimizer utilizes two cookies to manage test experiments: __utmx and __utmxx. By querying the value of __utmx, you can obtain the value identifying the test combination. For example, consider a page under multivariate test with three test sections. Section 1 has three alternatives including the original, section 2 has four alternatives, and section 3 has two alternatives. That's a total of 24 combinations being tested ($3 \times 4 \times 2$). When you use the JavaScript function utmx("combination_string"), a string is returned corresponding to the combination displayed to the user, such as "0-3-1." In this example, that represents the original variation for the first section, the third test alternative in section 2, and the first test alternative in section 3. Note that the original variation of a test is always represented as combination 0.

With this knowledge, modify the Google Analytics _trackPageview call within the GATC of the test page as follows:

```
<script type="text/javascript">
var _gaq = _gaq || [];
_gaq.push(['_setAccount', 'UA-12345-1']);
(function(){try {
 var l = document.location, s = l.search;
 if (utmx('combination_string') != undefined) {
  s = s +(s.length ? '&' : '?') +'combo=' +utmx('combination_string');
  s += '&testname= button-test-3';
  // the testname variable is to allow you to easily filter out
  // a specific experiment. Change this to your experiment name
  // defined in Website Optimizer
 }
 _gaq.push(['_trackPageview', l.pathname + s]);
""}catch(err){}})();
 (function() {
    var ga = document.createElement('script'); ga.type = ➡
'text/javascript'; ga.async = true;
    ga.src = ('https:' == document.location.protocol ? ➡
'https://ssl' : 'http://www') + '.google-analytics.com/ga.js';
    var s = document.getElementsByTagName('script')[0]; s.parentNode.
insertBefore(ga, s);
  })();
</script>
```

Viewing Test Alternatives in Google Analytics

The side effect of having each test combination tracked using a unique URL is that multiple pages (each test combination) are reported in Google Analytics, such as in this example:

```
/test-page.html?combo=0-0-1&testname=button-test-3
/test-page.html?combo=0-1-2&testname=button-test-3
/test-page.html?combo=1-0-2&testname=button-test-3
```

This, of course, is visit data for a single page: test-page.html. To avoid confusion in your main Google Analytics profile, track your Website Optimizer test data in a separate Google Analytics profile and modify your main profile so all combinations are reported as a single page. To achieve this, create a new, carbon-copy profile in your Google Analytics account—see Chapter 8 for details on how to create additional profiles. When this is in place, no other change is necessary—by default each of your test page alternatives will be tracked separately for you to analyze in your new profile, as shown in Figure 12.13.

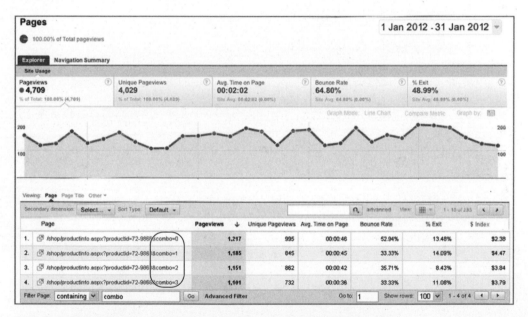

Figure 12.13 Website Optimizer test alternatives tracked in a separate Google Analytics profile

Tip: In your new profile, if you have goals, filters, or segments that use test-page.html, ensure that they don't break. For example, if your goal includes test-page.html, do not use Exact Match as the goal match type. Instead use Head Match because this will trigger a goal for test-page.html?combo=1&testname=button-test-3 as well as other combinations.

To combine all combinations and report them as a single page in your main profile, use the Google Analytics Exclude URL Query Parameters functionality. If you have used the example code presented so far, your original and test page alternatives differ only by the combo and testname parameters. Hence, add these to the list of parameters to ignore in your main profile—see Figure 12.14.

| Assets | Goals | Users | Filters | **Profile Settings** |

Edit Profile Information

General Information

Profile Name: aMain - AWM

Time zone country or territory: United Kingdom (GMT+01:00) London

Default page *optional* ?

Example: index.html

Exclude URL Query Parameters *optional*: combon,testname

Example: sid, sessionId, vid, etc ...

Currency displayed as: US Dollar (USD $)

Figure 12.14 Ignoring Website Optimizer test parameters in Google Analytics

Summary

In Chapter 12, you have learned the following:

How to extract Google Analytics cookie information You have learned to use JavaScript or PHP to query and extract information from Google Analytics cookies.

How to use the Google Analytics export API You have an overview of how to use the API and its capabilities.

What Example API solutions are available You have seen some of the clever enhancements and tools third parties are developing to augment and enhance Google Analytics data.

How to track visitors who call You know how to track visitors where the website call to action is to make a phone call.

How to integrate demographic data You learned how to combine Google Analytics with visitor demographic information from surveys.

How to track offline activity You saw an innovative way to measure the success of a TV video on demand service.

How to track apps You saw how to use the Google Analytics SDK to monitor mobile app usage and engagement.

How to integrate Website Optimizer with Google Analytics You have learned how to combine the testing capabilities of Google Website Optimizer for conversion optimization with other metrics that Google Analytics provides.

Regular Expression Overview

*Regular expressions, also referred to as* regex, *are a way for computer languages to match strings of text, such as specific characters, words, or patterns of characters. A simple everyday example of regular expressions is using wildcards for matching filenames on your computer. For example,* `*.pdf` *matches all filenames that end in* `.pdf`. *However, regex can be much more powerful (and complex) than this.*

Within Google Analytics, regular expressions are primarily used when creating profile filters (Chapter 8), advanced segments (Chapter 8), and table filters (Chapter 4).

Note: This appendix is intended as a general introduction to the fundamentals of building regular expressions within Google Analytics. In most cases this will fit your needs. However, if you need more details, there are numerous resources on the Web. For example, type "regular expression +tutorial" into Google's search bar for a list of tutorials on the topic.

Understanding the Fundamentals

A solid understanding of regex syntax is required, and the syntax remains similar across the different flavors of regex engines (POSIX, PCRE). In addition, a number of tools are available to help you troubleshoot building your regular expressions (see Appendix B).

Google Analytics uses a partial implementation of the Perl Compatible Regular Expressions (PCRE) library. I use the word *partial* because a full implementation is more powerful and flexible than a Software as a Service vendor would want it to be! If its use is unrestricted, it can be used maliciously to hack or break a website. Hence, not every feature of PCRE is included, though you would be hard-pressed to find what isn't.

Warning: Google Analytics uses only a partial implementation of PCRE, and hence advanced features may not be available. Unfortunately, the exact feature set of the regex engine is undocumented, so further guidance is difficult! However, we do know that "look ahead" and "negative look ahead" features are not available. That is, `google\.(?=com)` or `google\.(?!com)` will not work. The workaround for this particular regex when using table filters or advanced segments is to select Excluding or Does Not Match Regular Expression from the configuration drop-down menu and use `google.com` for the match.

An important point to grasp when using regular expressions is that there are two types of characters: *literals* and *metacharacters*. Most characters are treated as literals. That is, if you wanted to match a URL for *advanced*, you would type the characters as *a*, followed by *d*, followed by *v*, and so forth. The exceptions to this are metacharacters. These are characters of special meaning to the regex engine and therefore interpreted differently. The most common metacharacters are listed in Table A.1. Ensure that you understand these before proceeding.

Metacharacter	Description
.	Matches any single character.
[ ]	Matches a single character that is contained within the square brackets. Referred to as a *class*.
[^]	Matches a single character that is *not* contained within the square brackets. Referred to as a *class*.
^	Matches the beginning of the string. This is referred to as an *anchor*.
$	Matches the end of the string. This is referred to as an *anchor*.
*	Matches zero or more of the previous item.
?	Matches zero or one of the previous item.
+	Matches one or more of the previous item.
|	The OR operator. Matches either the expression before or the expression after the operator.
\	The escape character. Allows you to use one of the metacharacters for your match.
( )	Groups characters into substrings.

Regex Examples

Using only literals, you can construct simple regular expressions. However, combining literals with metacharacters provides for a more fine-grained approach to pattern matching. The best way to understand how regular expressions work is by example, and I use relevant Google Analytics matches to illustrate this.

Note: The regex engine of Google Analytics is *not* case sensitive.

First, partial matches are allowed. For example, say you wanted to view only referrals from the website www.google.com. Using a regular expression, you could use the partial keyword goog in the table filter of your Traffic Sources > Sources > All Traffic report. This will match all entries that have the letters goog in them, as shown in Figure A.1.

Although simple to implement, literals can be very powerful—as long as you can identify a unique pattern match that includes the string of interest. Taking the previous example, to be more specific, use the OR metacharacter, as in this example:

```
google\.(com|co\.uk|ca)
```

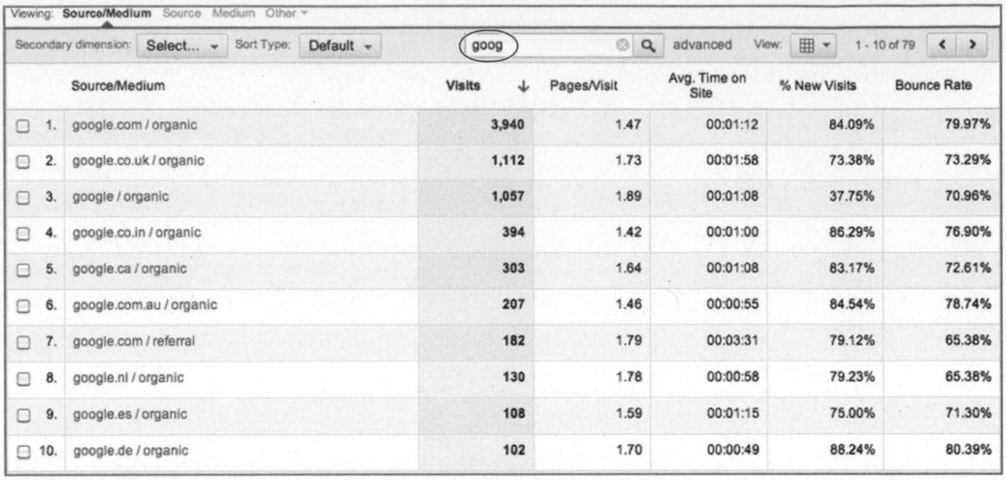

Viewing: **Source/Medium** Source Medium Other ▾						
Secondary dimension: Select... ▾ Sort Type: Default ▾			goog ⊗ 🔍 advanced View: ▦ ▾ 1 - 10 of 79 ‹ ›				

	Source/Medium	Visits ↓	Pages/Visit	Avg. Time on Site	% New Visits	Bounce Rate
☐ 1.	google.com / organic	3,940	1.47	00:01:12	84.09%	79.97%
☐ 2.	google.co.uk / organic	1,112	1.73	00:01:58	73.38%	73.29%
☐ 3.	google / organic	1,057	1.89	00:01:08	37.75%	70.96%
☐ 4.	google.co.in / organic	394	1.42	00:01:00	86.29%	76.90%
☐ 5.	google.ca / organic	303	1.64	00:01:08	83.17%	72.61%
☐ 6.	google.com.au / organic	207	1.46	00:00:55	84.54%	78.74%
☐ 7.	google.com / referral	182	1.79	00:03:31	79.12%	65.38%
☐ 8.	google.nl / organic	130	1.78	00:00:58	79.23%	65.38%
☐ 9.	google.es / organic	108	1.59	00:01:15	75.00%	71.30%
☐ 10.	google.de / organic	102	1.70	00:00:49	88.24%	80.39%

Figure A.1 Table filter using a partial match

This matches the literal google, followed by a period (this must be escaped because it is also a metacharacter), followed by com OR co.uk (period also escaped) OR ca. Because our expression now contains metacharacters, we must use the Advanced Filter area of the report table to include this—as shown in Figure A.2.

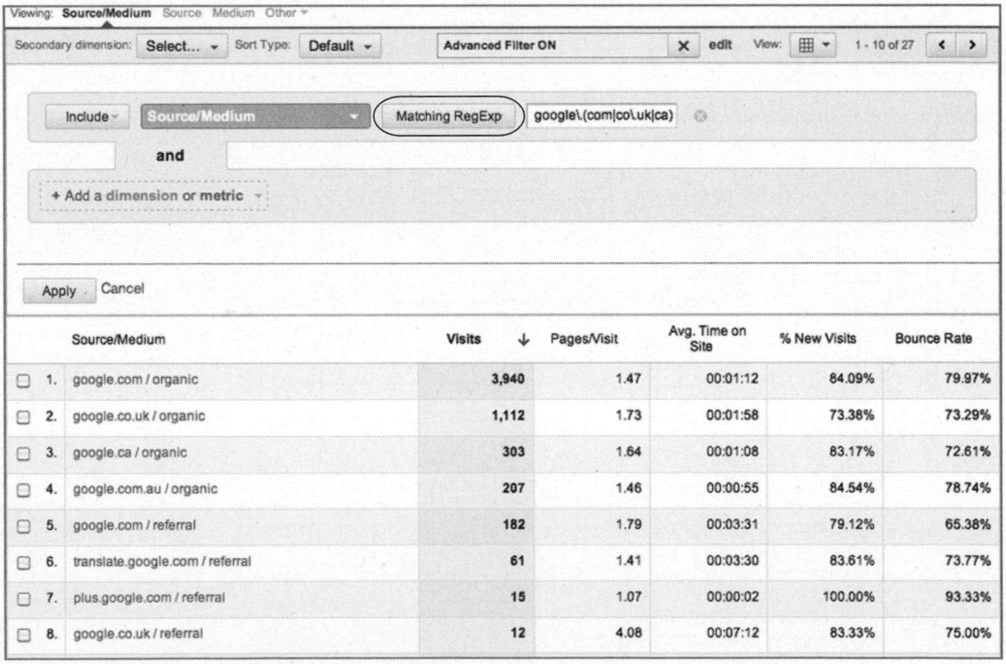

Viewing: **Source/Medium** Source Medium Other ▾						
Secondary dimension: Select... ▾ Sort Type: Default ▾		Advanced Filter ON ✕ edit View: ▦ ▾ 1 - 10 of 27 ‹ ›				

Include ▾ Source/Medium ▾ Matching RegExp google\.(com|co\.uk|ca) ⊗

and

+ Add a dimension or metric ▾

Apply   Cancel

	Source/Medium	Visits ↓	Pages/Visit	Avg. Time on Site	% New Visits	Bounce Rate
☐ 1.	google.com / organic	3,940	1.47	00:01:12	84.09%	79.97%
☐ 2.	google.co.uk / organic	1,112	1.73	00:01:58	73.38%	73.29%
☐ 3.	google.ca / organic	303	1.64	00:01:08	83.17%	72.61%
☐ 4.	google.com.au / organic	207	1.46	00:00:55	84.54%	78.74%
☐ 5.	google.com / referral	182	1.79	00:03:31	79.12%	65.38%
☐ 6.	translate.google.com / referral	61	1.41	00:03:30	83.61%	73.77%
☐ 7.	plus.google.com / referral	15	1.07	00:00:02	100.00%	93.33%
☐ 8.	google.co.uk / referral	12	4.08	00:07:12	83.33%	75.00%

Figure A.2 Table filter using the OR metacharacter

You will notice from Figure A.2 that subdomains of Google are present in the reports (rows 6 and 7). Suppose you wish to remove these from your matches. Modify the regex query as follows:

```
^google\.(com|co\.uk|ca)
```

This results in only referrers that start with the pattern google being matched. Another example to practice with includes the following syntax:

```
^go.+le\.((com[^\.])|(co\.uk[^\.])|(ca[^\.]))
```

This extends the previous example to explicitly match only Google domains that end in .com, .co.uk, and .ca. This removes referrers such as google.com.au, google.com.br, and so forth, by excluding any further ".", as shown in Figure A.3. Note that I have also been a little lazy and used go.+le to illustrate how to use the + metacharacter. That is, it is used to match one or more of the previous character—in this case, any character.

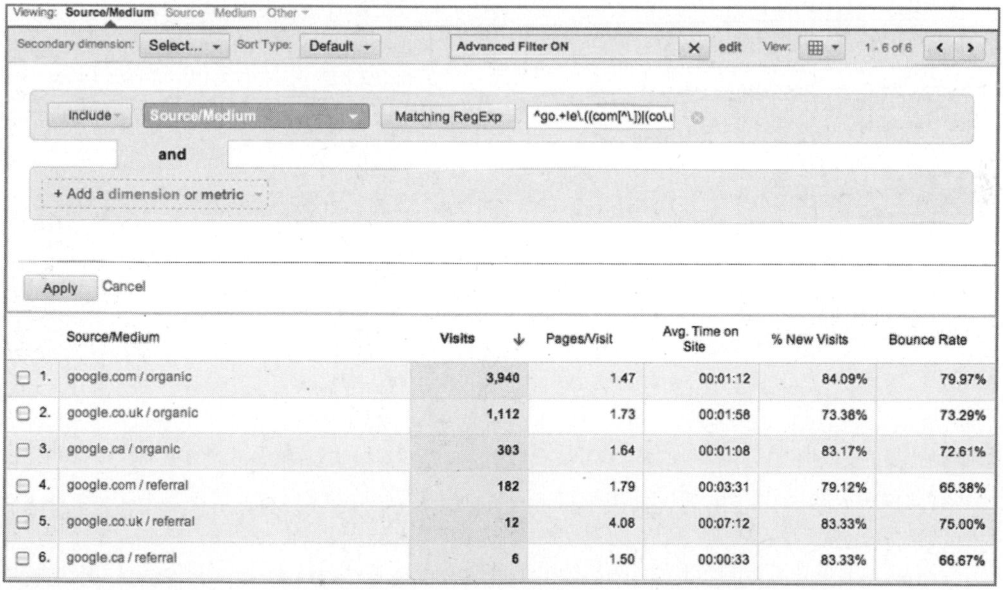

Viewing: **Source/Medium** Source Medium Other ▾

	Source/Medium	Visits ↓	Pages/Visit	Avg. Time on Site	% New Visits	Bounce Rate
☐ 1.	google.com / organic	3,940	1.47	00:01:12	84.09%	79.97%
☐ 2.	google.co.uk / organic	1,112	1.73	00:01:58	73.38%	73.29%
☐ 3.	google.ca / organic	303	1.64	00:01:08	83.17%	72.61%
☐ 4.	google.com / referral	182	1.79	00:03:31	79.12%	65.38%
☐ 5.	google.co.uk / referral	12	4.08	00:07:12	83.33%	75.00%
☐ 6.	google.ca / referral	6	1.50	00:00:33	83.33%	66.67%

Figure A.3 Table filter using multiple metacharacters

The following are examples to consider when matching URLs listed in your Content > Pages reports:

```
\?(id|pid)=[^&]*
```

This matches the filename followed by the first query parameter and its value if its name is equal to id or pid. If you have a report with URIs of the following form, this regex will match the two URIs highlighted:

```
/blog/post?pid=101
/blog/post?id=101&lang=en&cat=hacks
/blog/post?lang=en&cat=hacks&id=102
/blog/about-this-blog
```

Typically, this regex format is used when defining a goal or funnel step. Note the use of the negative class to stop the regex match. That is, this regex will match all characters after id= or pid= that do not contain &. An asterisk is used (*) to also match zero occurrences of & so that even if there is no second query parameter present, as per the first URI, the regex will still match.

An example that is useful when filtering within keyword reports (search engines and internal site search) is to consider misspellings. Perhaps you need to find all matches for "colour" and "color." The following regex will achieve this:

```
colo[u]*r
```

Here are some other misspelling examples (my name is sometimes spelled Brain!):

```
Voda(ph|f)one
Ste(ph|v)en
Br[ai][ai]n
```

Finally, although not directly relevant to Google Analytics, this is a common regex used in web development for processing forms:

```
^(.+)@([^\(\);:,<>_]+\.[a-zA-Z.]{2,6})
```

Use this to test your understanding. Broken into its constituent parts, this regex checks an email address to ascertain if it is a valid format—that is, brian@mysite.com and not brian@@my_site:com, for example. From left to right, the English interpretation is as follows:

- Match one or more of any character before the @
- Match any character after the @ but do not include any of following characters: ( ) ; ; , < > _
- Followed by a period
- Followed by between two and six characters that must include an alphabetic character (A–Z as either upper- or lowercase) or a period

I have **highlighted** the middle section of this regex to help guide your eye, that is, the part between the @ and next period.

If you have followed these examples, you are well on your way to understanding regular expressions. If not, reread this section and use one of the regex tools listed in Appendix B. Further regex examples are shown throughout this book, though none are more complicated than those shown here.

Tips for Building Regular Expressions

- Make the regular expression as simple as possible. Complex expressions take longer to process or match than simple expressions.

- Avoid the use of `.*` if possible because this expression matches everything zero or more times and may slow processing of the expression. For instance, if you need to match all of the following

  `index.html, index.htm, index.php, index.aspx, index.py, index.cgi`

  use

  `index\.(h|p|a|c)+.+`

  not

  `index.*`

- Try to group patterns together when possible. For instance, if you wish to match a file suffix of `.pdf`, `.doc`, and `.ppt`, use

  `\.(pdf|doc|ppt)`

  not

  `\.pdf|\.doc|\.ppt`

- Be sure to escape the regular expression wildcards or metacharacters if you wish to match those literal characters. Common ones are periods in filenames and parentheses in text.

- Use anchors whenever possible (`^` and `$`, which match either the beginning or end of an expression) because they speed up processing.

Useful Tools

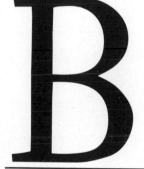

The tools I've listed here are helper applications that come in two flavors: those that help you perform a site-wide audit of your Google Analytics Tracking Code deployment and browser add-ons that help you use or manage your reports— configuration aids, segmentation help, and so forth. Often these two scenarios overlap, and marketers frequently find themselves using the same toolset as webmasters and web developers. I also list two Windows desktop applications that have helped me over the years. Regardless of your job role, all these tools are straightforward to use.

Tools to Help Audit Your GATC Deployment

The key to being able to improve your website is having good, solid, accurate data that you can rely on. A fundamental step of implementing any web analytics tool is getting the data in—there simply is no point investing in analysis if the data is flawed. After all, garbage in equals garbage out. Maintaining data integrity is key. Adding page tags, the GATC, is therefore not a one-time, "set it and forget it" process. It requires careful deployment planning and regular maintenance checks to ensure that data holes do not appear.

The following are site scan tools that can help you audit and verify the completeness of your GATC:

Web Analytics Solution Profiler (WASP) A Firefox plug-in that detects the setting of the GATC cookies plus 100 other vendor tools. Works on a page-by-page (free) and site-scanning (paid) basis:

www.webanalyticssolutionprofiler.com

ObservePoint Paid Software as a Service (SaaS) vendor. Detects the setting of the GATC cookies plus Adobe Omniture's cookies. Works as a site-scanning and monitoring/alert tool:

www.observepoint.com

How Often Should I Audit My Google Analytics Implementation?

The main factor to consider here is how often your content changes. If 10 percent of your website content changes each month, then by halfway through the year the majority of your website will have changed. The greater the change, the higher the possibility of errors. Even nonhumans such as CMS, CRM systems, and web servers can, and do, make errors. And because page tags are a hidden pieces of code, errors are not visible by simply visiting the page in your browser. The result is that page tag errors easily go unnoticed and build up rapidly on your website.

In the early stages of a GATC deployment (or redeployment), I recommend that you scan your pages weekly. Assuming there are no holes in your data collection, or they have been fixed, move to a monthly scan after eight weeks. Again, assuming data holes and anomalies have been ironed out, you should be able to move to quarterly scanning frequency by Q3. Maintain quarterly scans until your next major site redesign or a replacement CMS comes online, and then increase the frequency again.

A typical report from these tools would list the URLs scanned and show the following, for example:

- Pages scanned = 5,480 (100%)
- Pages with correctly functioning GATC = 5,220 (95.3%)
- Number of incorrect GATC = 140 (2.6%)
- Number of pages not found (error 404) = 12 (0.2%)

Browser Add-ons

Developed by third parties, add-ons are installable enhancements to your browser. They are available for the Google Chrome and Firefox browsers because historically these browsers have encouraged third-party customization. The vast majority of add-ons are free to use.

More information on Firefox add-ons is available at

`https://addons.mozilla.org/en-US/firefox.`

More information on Google Chrome add-ons (known as extensions) is available at

`http://chrome.google.com/webstore/category/extensions.`

The following add-ons work with the latest version of Google Analytics (v5) and help with your implementation and usage of it. I use all of them:

Analytics Helper (Chrome) This simple add-on displays a green icon in the browser address bar whenever a GATC is detected on a page you browse. Clicking the icon shows the account number of the tracking code, the code type (asynchronous, traditional), and a note on the positioning of code. Developed by Oliver J. Fields of Metronet, Norway. For more information see

`https://chrome.google.com/webstore/search/%22analytics%20helper%22.`

GA Copy & Paste (Chrome) An extremely powerful add-on that greatly simplifies the management and administration of goals and filters. Developed by Eduardo Cereto Carvalho of Cardinal Path. For more information see

`https://chrome.google.com/webstore/search/GA%20Copy%20and%20Paste.`

Regular Expression Checker (Chrome) Regular expressions are used throughout Google Analytics for filtering, creating advanced segments, defining goals, and configuring funnel steps. This useful add-on helps test your expressions for troubleshooting purposes. Developed by www.simon20.com. For more information see

`https://chrome.google.com/webstore/search/%22Regular%20Expression%20Checker%22.`

Google Analytics Debugger (Chrome) This official Google Analytics add-on prints useful information to the JavaScript console about any web page containing a GATC. When you enable the debug version of the GATC (`ga_debug.js`), the information shown includes error messages and warnings about your tracking code implementation and a detailed breakdown of each tracking beacon sent to Google Analytics. Developed by Google. For more information see

```
https://chrome.google.com/webstore/search/%22Google%20Analytics%20
Debugger%20%22.
```

Annotations Manager (Firefox) This Greasemonkey script allows you to copy, delete, and export your chart annotations. Developed by Vincent Giersch. For more information see

```
https://github.com/gierschv/GoogleAnalytics-AnnotationsManager.
```

Stats Calculator (All browsers) This clever bookmarklet takes a statistical approach to comparing two e-commerce conversion rates and your overall goal conversion rate. The bookmarklet performs a z-test to show the confidence interval of two selected dimensions. This shows if the differences you observe are statistically significant. Developed by Michael Wittaker. For more information see

```
http://www.michaelwhitaker.com/blog/2011/11/02/stats-calculator-google-
analytics.
```

Web Developer Toolkit (Firefox and Chrome) This add-on adds a menu bar to your browser with a whole range of useful features for anyone who has an interest in creating web pages. It has an excellent browser error console and DOM inspector as well as quick lookup tools for cookies, source code, and so forth. Developed by `chrispederick.com`. For more information see

```
https://addons.mozilla.org/en-US/firefox/addon/60.
https://chrome.google.com/webstore/search/%22web%20developer%22.
```

Firebug (Firefox) Adds debug capabilities for JavaScript, CSS, and HTML live in your browser. For more information see

```
https://addons.mozilla.org/en-US/firefox/addon/1843.
```

Live HTTP Headers (Firefox) Similar to the Chrome add-on Google Analytics Debugger, this add-on enables you to view HTTP headers of a page while you are browsing. All the communication requests sent and received by your browser can be viewed. By filtering the URLs to show only Google Analytics requests (via regexp set to `/__utm.gif.*`), you can view all the information sent to Google Analytics. For more information see

```
https://addons.mozilla.org/en-US/firefox/addon/3829.
```

GATC Plug-ins

These are scripts that make modifications to your GATC to automate tasks that can otherwise be laboriously manual.

Autotrack file downloads and outbound links Normally, to track file downloads and outbound links, you need to manually modify each link across your site—a painful process for all but the simplest of websites. This JavaScript plug-in scans all your page links for you in the background and automatically adjusts them accordingly for Google Analytics by adding an onClick event handler. There is also the option to modify the bounce rate calculation. For more information:

www.advanced-web-metrics.com/blog/auto-tracking-file-downloads-outbound-links.

Customizing the SEO list for Google Analytics For digital marketers running SEO accounts where regional differences are important. For example, Americas, Europe, Middle East, Asia, Australia. This JavaScript plug-in separates out 264 regional search engines—for example, google.co.uk, google.com, google.co.nz, and so forth—instead of just "google" as reported in Google Analytics by default. For more information:

www.advanced-web-metrics.com/blog/custom-search-engine-hack.

Desktop Helper Applications

WebBug WebBug is a Windows application that allows you to enter a URL and see exactly what is sent to the web server and what response is sent back. This is the information that your browser takes care of when rendering a page. I use this mainly to check a web server's status code response. It is very useful for tracking redirection issues—a common problem that can result in the loss of campaign variables from your landing page URLs. WebBug is free to use, Windows only, and is available for download from

http://www.cyberspyder.com/webbug.html.

The Regex Coach Regular expressions (regex) are snippets of pseudo code that match patterns within text. In Google Analytics, regular expressions are used for filtering—for both filtering within a report (table filter) and for creating separate profile reports (profile filters), for defining advanced segments, and for configuring goal conversions and funnel steps. In other words, regular expressions are important, and I refer to them throughout this book.

Going beyond the basics, things can rapidly appear complex because regular expression often appear like algebra. Therefore, before implementing your regular expression, validate it through the excellent Regex Coach application (Windows only). Regex Coach is free to use and can be downloaded from

http://weitz.de/regex-coach/.

Recommended Further Reading

This is not intended to be an exhaustive list of reading material but more a reflection of the books and resources I have read and the blogs I have participated in over the years. If you have a relevant reading resource that I am unaware of, please email me at brian@advanced-web-metrics.com *and I will endeavor to include it here and on the book's website itself (*www.advanced-web-metrics.com/blog/recommended-reading*).*

Books on Web Analytics and Related Areas

The most recently published books are listed first:

- Jim Sterne, *Social Media Metrics: How to Measure and Optimize Your Marketing Investment* (Wiley, 2010)

- Brad Geddes, *Advanced Google AdWords* (Sybex, 2010)

- Avinash Kaushik, *Web Analytics 2.0: The Art of Online Accountability and Science of Customer Centricity* (Sybex, 2009)

- Brian Halligan and Dharmesh Shah, *Inbound Marketing: Get Found Using Google, Social Media, and Blogs* (Wiley, 2009)

- Steve Jackson, *Cult of Analytics: Driving Online Marketing Strategies Using Web Analytics* (Butterworth-Heinemann, 2009)

- Steve Krug, *Rocket Surgery Made Easy: The Do-It-Yourself Guide to Finding and Fixing Usability Problems* (New Riders Press, 2009)

- Tim Ash, *Landing Page Optimization: The Definitive Guide to Testing and Tuning for Conversions* (Sybex, 2008)

- Bill Hunt and Mike Moran, *Search Engine Marketing, Inc.: Driving Search Traffic to Your Company's Web Site* (IBM Press, 2008)

- Avinash Kaushik, *Web Analytics: An Hour a Day* (Sybex, 2007)

- Jason Burby and Shane Atchison, *Actionable Web Analytics: Using Data to Make Smart Business Decisions* (Sybex, 2007)

- David Bowen, *Spinning the Web: How to Transmit the Right Messages Online* (Bowen Craggs & Co. Limited, 2006)

- Bryan Eisenberg, Jeffrey Eisenberg, and Lisa T. Davis, *Waiting for Your Cat to Bark: Persuading Customers When They Ignore Marketing* (Thomas Nelson, 2006)

- Hurol Inan, *Search Analytics: A Guide to Analyzing and Optimizing Website Search Engines* (BookSurge Publishing, 2006)

- Jakob Nielsen and Hoa Loranger, *Prioritizing Web Usability* (New Riders Press, 2006)

- Steve Krug, *Don't Make Me Think: A Common Sense Approach to Web Usability* (New Riders Press, 2005)

- Chris Sherman, *Google Power: Unleash the Full Potential of Google* (McGraw-Hill Osborne Media, 2005)

Web Resources

Reference links, listed alphabetically, to organizations that collate good material from other authors as well as produce their own content.

- CMO.com: www.cmo.com

- Econsultancy: www.econsultancy.com
- Interactive Advertising Bureau (IAB): www.iab.net
- Online Behavior: www.online-behavior.com
- Search Engine Marketing Professional Organization (SEMPO): www.sempo.org
- Web Analytics Association: www.webanalyticsassociation.org

Blog Roll for Web Analytics

Listed in alphabetical order. Most of these also have Twitter accounts so you can follow the authors you like.

Advanced Web Metrics by Brian Clifton	http://www.advanced-web-metrics.com/blog
Analytics Notes by Jacques Warren	http://www.waomarketing.com/blog
Analytics Talk by Justin Cutroni (EpikOne)	http://cutroni.com/blog/
Andy Beal's Marketing Pilgrim	http://www.marketingpilgrim.com
Blackbeaks Blog...All Things Analytics	http://www.blackbeak.com
CxFocus	http://www.cxfocus.com
Data Mining Research by Sandro Saitta	http://www.dataminingblog.com
Digital Alex by Alex Cohen	http://www.alex1cohen.com
Econsultancy	http://www.econsultancy.com/blog
FutureNow's Marketing Optimization Blog	http://www.grokdotcom.com
Gilligan on Data by Tim Wilson	http://gilliganondata.com
Engage-Digital Blog by Hugh Gage	http://www.engage-digital.com/blog
Google Analytics Blog (Google's official blog)	http://analytics.blogspot.com
Greater Returns by Aaron Gray	http://blog.greaterreturns.me
How to Change the World: A practical blog for impractical people—by Guy Kawasaki	http://blog.guykawasaki.com
Immeria :: an immersion into web analytics by Stephane Hamel	http://blog.immeria.net
Instant Cognition	http://blog.instantcognition.com
June Dershewitz on Web Analytics	http://june.typepad.com
KISSmetrics	http://blog.kissmetrics.com
Lies, Damned Lies...	http://www.liesdamnedlies.com
LunaMetrics	http://www.lunametrics.com/blog
Market Motive	http://www.marketmotive.com/blog
Marketing Productivity Blog by Jim Novo	http://blog.jimnovo.com
Michael Whitaker's web analytics blog	http://www.michaelwhitaker.com/blog
Occam's Razor by Avinash Kaushik	http://www.kaushik.net/avinash
Online Behavior	http://online-behavior.com
Rich Page Rambling by Rich Page	http://www.rich-page.com
SemAngel by Gary Angel	http://semphonic.blogs.com/semangel

ClickInsight Blog	http://blog.clickinsight.ca
Trending Upward—Web analytics for higher education	http://www.trendingupward.net
Turn Up the Silence—iPerceptions Blog	http://blog.iperceptions.com
Unofficial Google Analytics Blog	http://www.roirevolution.com/blog
Web Analysis and Online Advertising by Anil Batra	http://webanalysis.blogspot.com
Web Analysts Info by Lars Johansson	http://www.webanalysts.info/webanalytics
Web Analytics Applied by Paul Legutko (Semphonic)	http://legutko.typepad.com
Web Analytics Association Blog	http://waablog.webanalyticsassociation.org
Web Analytics Demystified	http://www.webanalyticsdemystified.com/weblog
Web Analytics Forum	http://groups.yahoo.com/group/webanalytics
Web Analytics Inside by Timo Aden (in German)	http://www.timoaden.de
Web Analytics Management by Phil Kemelor (Semphonic)	http://wam.typepad.com/wam
Web Analytics Tool Time by Jesse Gross (Semphonic)	http://tooltime.typepad.com
Web Analytics World by Manoj Jasra	http://www.webanalyticsworld.net
WebAnalyticsBook	http://www.webanalyticsbook.com
WebMetricsGuru by Marshall Sponder	http://www.webmetricsguru.com
Web Strategy by Jeremiah Owyang	http://www.web-strategist.com/blog

Index